EYEWITNESS TRAVEL GUIDES

NEW ENGLAND

LONDON, NEW YORK,
MELBOURNE, MUNICH AND DELHI
www.dk.com

Produced by St. Remy Media Inc.,
Montréal, Canada

PRESIDENT Pierre Léveillé
VICE PRESIDENT, FINANCE Natalie Watanabe
MANAGING EDITOR Carolyn Jackson
MANAGING ART DIRECTOR Diane Denoncourt
PRODUCTION MANAGER Michelle Turbide
DIRECTOR, BUSINESS DEVELOPMENT Christopher Jackson

EDITOR Neale McDevitt
ART DIRECTORS Michel Giguère, Anne-Marie Lemay
SENIOR RESEARCH EDITOR Heather Mills
RESEARCHERS Tal Ashkenazi, Jessica Braun, Genevieve Ring
PICTURE RESEARCHER Linda Castle
MAP COORDINATOR Peter Alec Fedun
SENIOR EDITOR, PRODUCTION Brian Parsons
INDEXER Linda Cardella Cournoyer
PREPRESS PRODUCTION Martin Francoeur, Jean Sirois

MAIN CONTRIBUTORS
Eleanor Berman, Patricia Brooks, Tom Bross, Patricia Harris, Pierre
Home-Douglas, Helga Loverseed, David Lyon

PHOTOGRAPHERS
Alan Briere, Ed Homonylo, David Lyons

ILLUSTRATORS
Gilles Beauchemin, Martin Gagnon, Vincent Gagnon, Stéphane Jorisch,
Patrick Jougla, Luc Normandin, Jean-François Vachon

MAPS
Dimension DPR

Filmwork by Colourscan, Singapore
Printed and bound by South China Printing Co. Ltd., China

First published in Great Britain in 2001
by Dorling Kindersley Limited
80 Strand, London WC2R 0RL

Reprinted with revisions 2003, 2004

Copyright 2001, 2004 © Dorling Kindersley Limited, London
A Penguin Company

A CIP CATALOGUE RECORD IS AVAILABLE FROM THE BRITISH LIBRARY

ISBN 0 7513 6866 0

FLOORS ARE REFERRED TO THROUGHOUT IN ACCORDANCE WITH AMERICAN
USAGE; IE THE "FIRST FLOOR" IS THE FLOOR ON STREET LEVEL

CONTENTS

HOW TO USE
THIS GUIDE 6

Sailboat off the Cape Cod coast

INTRODUCING
NEW ENGLAND

Vermont's dazzling fall foliage

West Quoddy Head Light, Maine

Mansion in Waterbury, Vermont

Costumed interpreter at
Plimoth Plantation,
Plymouth, Massachusetts

Mark Twain House
in Hartford,
Connecticut

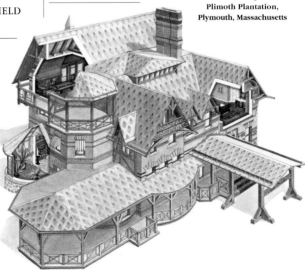

HOW TO USE THIS GUIDE

THIS GUIDE helps you to get the most from your visit to New England. *Introducing New England* maps the region and sets it in its historical and cultural context. Each of the six states, along with the city of Boston, has its own chapter describing the important sights using maps, pictures, and detailed illustrations. Suggestions on restaurants, accommodations, shopping, entertainment and outdoor activities are covered in *Travelers' Needs*. The *Survival Guide* has tips on everything from changing currency in New England to getting around in Boston.

BOSTON

Boston has been divided into five sightseeing areas, each one opening with a list of the sights described. All the sights are numbered and plotted on an *Area Map*. The detailed information for each sight is presented in numerical order, making it easy to locate within the chapter.

Sights at a Glance lists the chapter's sights by category: Historic Streets and Squares; Historic Buildings, Churches, Museums, and Theaters; Waterfront Sights; Gardens and Zoos; and Parks and Cemeteries.

1 Area Map
For easy reference, the sights are numbered and located on a map. The sights are also shown on the Boston Street Finder *on pages 122–7.*

A locator map shows where you are in relation to other areas of the city center.

2 Street-by-Street Map
This gives a bird's-eye view of the heart of each sightseeing area.

A suggested route for a walk covers the more interesting streets in the area.

All pages relating to Boston have yellow thumb tabs.

Stars indicate the sights that no visitor should miss.

3 Detailed Information on Each Sight
All the sights in Boston are described individually. Addresses, telephone numbers, opening hours, and information on admission charges and wheelchair access are also provided. The key to all the symbols used in the information block is shown on the back flap.

1 Introduction
The landscape, history, and character of each state is described here, showing how the area has developed over the centuries and what it has to offer the visitor today.

NEW ENGLAND REGION BY REGION
In this book, New England has been divided into the six states, each of which has a separate chapter. The most interesting sights to visit have been numbered on the *Pictorial Map*.

Each state of New England can be quickly identified by its color coding, which is shown on the inside front cover.

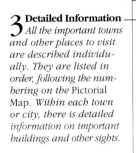

2 Pictorial Map
This shows the road network and gives an illustrated overview of the whole state. All the sights are numbered, and there are also useful tips on getting around the state.

Story boxes explore specific subjects further.

3 Detailed Information
All the important towns and other places to visit are described individually. They are listed in order, following the numbering on the Pictorial *Map. Within each town or city, there is detailed information on important buildings and other sights.*

For all the top sights, a Visitors' Checklist provides the practical information you will need to plan your visit.

4 The Top Sights
These are given two or more pages. Historic buildings are dissected to reveal their interiors; museums and galleries have color-coded floor plans; national parks have maps showing facilities and trails.

Stars indicate the best features and works of art.

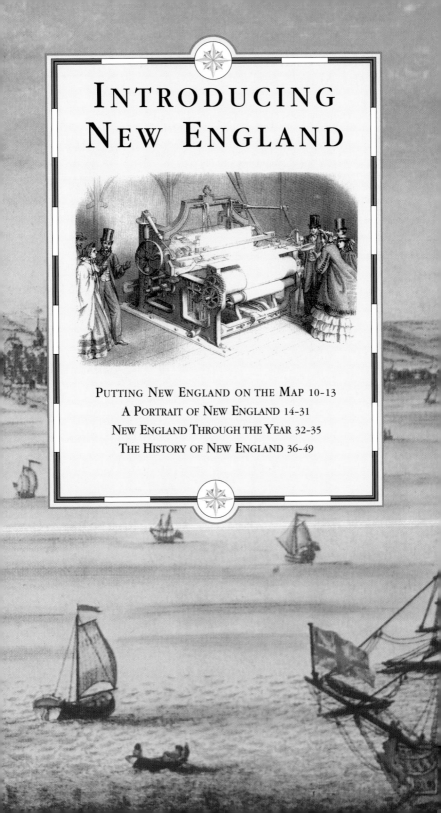

INTRODUCING
NEW ENGLAND

Putting Northern New England on the Map

COMPRISED OF VERMONT, NEW HAMPSHIRE, and Maine, this northern section is New England at its most rural and, often, wildest. Although Vermont also has its high ground in the form of the Green Mountains, it is famous for its rolling farmland. New Hampshire is known for its White Mountains and the series of spectacular passes, or notches, that nature has carved between the peaks. Massive, but sparsely populated, Maine is covered in dense forest and an intricate network of lakes, streams, and rivers. It also boasts a coastline as rugged as any found on the Eastern Seaboard.

MA

CT

RI

KEY TO COLOR CODING

Northern New England

- Vermont
- New Hampshire
- Maine

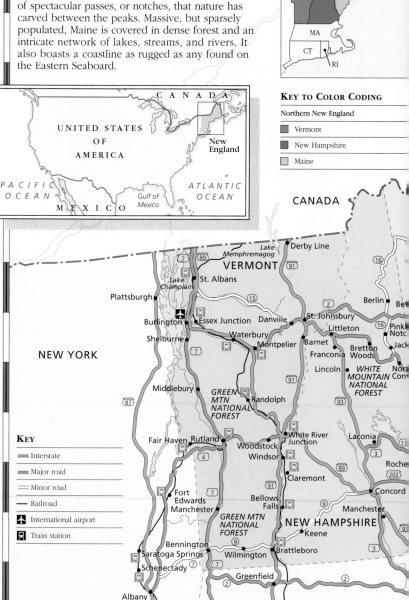

CANADA

UNITED STATES OF AMERICA

New England

PACIFIC OCEAN

MEXICO   Gulf of Mexico

ATLANTIC OCEAN

CANADA

Lake Memphremagog   Derby Line

VERMONT

Lake Champlain   St. Albans

Plattsburgh

Berlin   Be

Burlington   Essex Junction   Danville   St. Johnsbury   Littleton   Pink Notc

Shelburne   Waterbury   Montpelier   Barnet   Bretton Woods   Jack

Franconia   Nor

Lincoln   WHITE MOUNTAIN NATIONAL FOREST   Con

NEW YORK

Middlebury   GREEN MTN NATIONAL FOREST   Randolph

Fair Haven   Rutland   White River Junction   Laconia

Woodstock

Windsor   Roche

Claremont   Concord

Fort Edwards   Bellows Falls

Manchester   GREEN MTN NATIONAL FOREST   Manchester

NEW HAMPSHIRE

Bennington   Keene

Saratoga Springs   Wilmington   Brattleboro

Schenectady

Greenfield

Albany

KEY

═══ Interstate

═══ Major road

─── Minor road

─── Railroad

✈ International airport

🚉 Train station

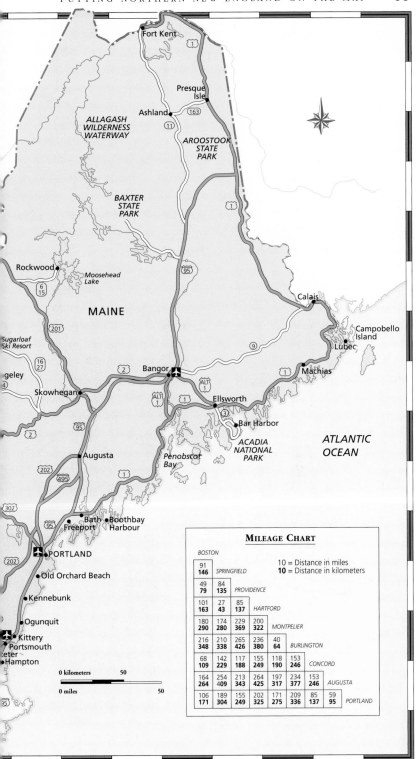

MILEAGE CHART

BOSTON

10 = Distance in miles
10 = Distance in kilometers

BOSTON									
91 **146**	SPRINGFIELD								
49 **79**	84 **135**	PROVIDENCE							
101 **163**	27 **43**	85 **137**	HARTFORD						
180 **290**	174 **280**	229 **369**	200 **322**	MONTPELIER					
216 **348**	210 **338**	265 **426**	236 **380**	40 **64**	BURLINGTON				
68 **109**	142 **229**	117 **188**	155 **249**	118 **190**	153 **246**	CONCORD			
164 **264**	254 **409**	213 **343**	264 **425**	197 **317**	234 **377**	153 **246**	AUGUSTA		
106 **171**	189 **304**	155 **249**	202 **325**	171 **275**	209 **336**	85 **137**	59 **95**	PORTLAND	

Putting Southern New England on the Map

MUCH SMALLER IN SIZE THAN the northern section, southern New England – Massachusetts, Rhode Island, and Connecticut – traditionally has been the industrial and cultural hub of the region. Massachusetts is the historical center of the New England colonies, with the first settlers disembarking at Plymouth in 1620. Ever-popular Cape Cod is a wonderful mix of beaches and understated charm. The smallest state in the country, tiny Rhode Island contains some of New England's most extravagant mansions, some found along the spectacular Cliff Walk in Newport. Connecticut's proximity to New York City to the south has graced many of its towns and cities with a cosmopolitan flavor.

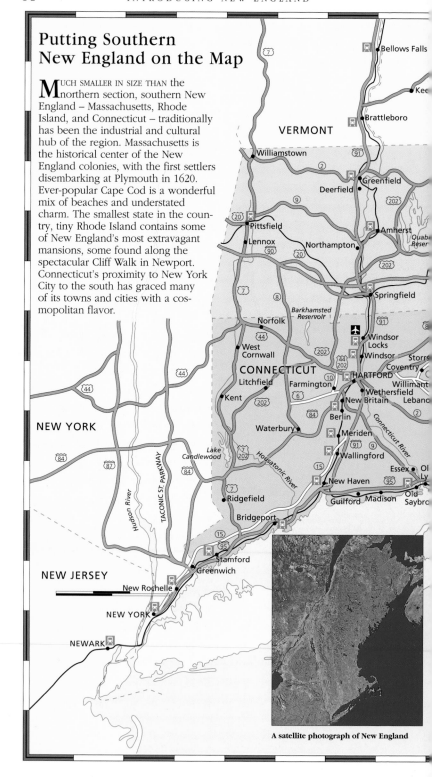

Bellows Falls

Kee

Brattleboro

VERMONT

Williamstown

Greenfield

Deerfield

Pittsfield

Lennox

Amherst

Quabi
Reser

Northampton

Springfield

Barkhamsted
Reservoir

Norfolk

Windsor
Locks

West
Cornwall

Windsor

Storrs

CONNECTICUT

Coventry

Litchfield

Farmington

HARTFORD

Willimant

Kent

Wethersfield

Lebano

New Britain

Berlin

Waterbury

Meriden

NEW YORK

Wallingford

Lake
Candlewood

Essex

Ol
Ly

New Haven

Ridgefield

Old
Saybro

Guilford

Madison

Bridgeport

Hudson River

TACONIC ST. PARKWAY

Housatonic River

Connecticut River

NEW JERSEY

Stamford

Greenwich

New Rochelle

NEW YORK

NEWARK

A satellite photograph of New England

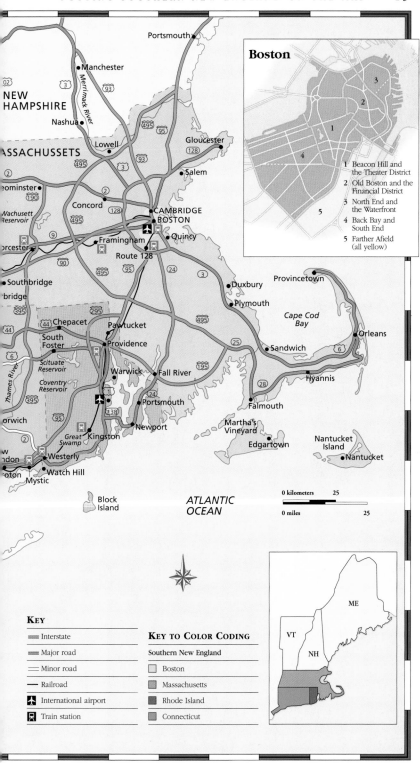

Boston

1 Beacon Hill and the Theater District
2 Old Boston and the Financial District
3 North End and the Waterfront
4 Back Bay and South End
5 Farther Afield (all yellow)

NEW HAMPSHIRE

MASSACHUSSETS

Portsmouth

Manchester

Merrimack River

Nashua

Lowell

Gloucester

Salem

eominster

Concord

CAMBRIDGE
BOSTON

Wachusett Reservoir

orcester

Framingham

Quincy

Route 128

Southbridge

bridge

Chepacet

South Foster

Pawtucket

Providence

Scituate Reservoir

Coventry Reservoir

Warwick

Fall River

Portsmouth

Duxbury

Plymouth

Cape Cod Bay

Provincetown

Orleans

Sandwich

Hyannis

Falmouth

Thames River

orwich

Great Swamp

Kingston

Newport

Martha's Vineyard

Edgartown

Nantucket Island

Nantucket

ndon

Westerly

Watch Hill

Mystic

oton

Block Island

ATLANTIC OCEAN

0 kilometers   25

0 miles   25

KEY

═══ Interstate
═══ Major road
─── Minor road
─── Railroad
✈ International airport
🚉 Train station

KEY TO COLOR CODING

Southern New England

Boston
Massachusetts
Rhode Island
Connecticut

ME

VT

NH

A PORTRAIT OF NEW ENGLAND

For many people, New England is white-steepled churches, craggy coastlines, and immaculate village greens. However, the region is also home to the opulence of Newport, Rhode Island, the beautiful suburban communities of Connecticut, and the self-assured sophistication of Boston – as well as the picture-postcard villages, covered bridges, timeless landscapes, and back-road gems.

From its beginning, the region has been shaped by both geography and climate. Early explorers charted its coastline, and communities soon sprang up by the sea, where goods and people could be ferried more easily from the Old World to the New. Much of the area's early commerce depended heavily on the ocean, from shipping and whaling to fishing and boat-building. Inland the virgin forests and hilly terrain of areas such as New Hampshire, Vermont, and Maine created communities that survived and thrived on independence. The slogan "Live free or die" on today's New Hampshire license plates is a reminder that the same spirit still lives on. New England winters are long and harsh, and spring can bring unpredictable weather. As the 19th-century author Harriet Martineau (1802–76) declared, "I believe no one attempts to praise the climate of New England." Combined with the relatively poor growing conditions of the region – glaciers during the last Ice Age scoured away much of New England's precious soil – this has meant that farming has always been a struggle against the capricious forces of nature. To survive in these northeastern states required toughness, ingenuity, and resourcefulness, all traits that became ingrained in the New England psyche. Indeed, the area today is as much a state of mind as it is a physical space.

Uncle Sam puppet

Victorian cottage in the Trinity Park district in Oak Bluffs, Massachusetts

◁ **White steeple of the Town Hall in Fitzwilliam, New Hampshire**

Former frontier outpost, Old Fort Western in Augusta, Maine – a view into New England's past

Few places in America – if any – are richer in historical connections. This is where European civilization first gained a toehold in America. And even long after the American Revolution (1776–83), New England continued to play an important role in the life of the developing nation, supplying many of its political and intellectual leaders. That spirit endures. An intellectual confidence, some may call it smugness, persists; some people would say it is with good reason since it was New England that produced the first flowering of American culture. Writers such as Henry David Thoreau (1817–62), Ralph Waldo Emerson (1803–82), Louisa May Alcott (1832–88), and Herman Melville (1819–91) became the first American writers of an international caliber. Even today, New England still figures prominently in the arts and letters, and its famous preparatory schools and the Ivy League universities and other institutions of higher learning

Statue of Samuel de Champlain

New England-born Louisa May Alcott

continue to draw some of America's best and brightest to the region.

MOUNTAINS AND SEASHORE

From the heights of the White Mountains – the highest terrain in the northeastern US – to the windswept seashore of Cape Cod, New England offers a stunning range of landscapes. And while industrialization and urbanization have left their stamp, there is plenty of the wild past still in the present. The woods of Maine, for example, look much as they did when American writer and naturalist Henry David Thoreau visited them more than 150 years ago. Vermont's Green Mountains would be instantly recognizable by the explorer Samuel de Champlain (1567–1635) who first saw them almost 400 years ago. But it is not only the countryside that has endured; there are homes scattered throughout New England that preserve an array of early American architectural styles, from Colonial to Greek Revival. Just as the terrain is varied, so, too, is New England's population. The earliest settlers to the region were mostly of English and Scottish stock. Even by the early 19th century New England was still a relatively homogenous society, but this changed dramatically during the mid-1800s as waves of Irish immigrants arrived, driven from their homeland by the potato famines.

This altered the political balance of the area. Whereas the earliest leaders tended to be of British ancestry – men such as President John Adams (1735–1826) and John Hancock (1737–93), signatories of the

Machine Shed inside the Boott Cotton Mill
Museum in Lowell, Massachusetts

their descendants directly from the Pilgrims who first came here aboard the *Mayflower*.

OUTDOOR ACTIVITIES

Despite the area's proximity to some of America's most populated areas – a mere 40-mile (64-km) commute separates Stamford, Connecticut, and New York City – it offers a wealth of outdoor activities. There is something here to keep just about any sports enthusiast satisfied. For canoeists and white-water rafters, there are the beautiful Allagash and Connecticut rivers and a captivating collection of lakes.

Rafting on the
Kennebec River

Declaration of Independence – now Irish-born politicians came to the fore. In 1884 one such man, Hugh O'Brien (1827–95), won the mayoral race in Boston. Meanwhile immigrants from Italy, Portugal, and eastern Europe also arrived, as well as an influx of French-Canadians, who flocked to the mill towns looking for employment. Still, the Irish represented a sizable part of the New England community and their impact on New England society and politics continued to grow, culminating in the election of John F. Kennedy (1917–63) in 1960 as America's first Roman Catholic president. Today some of the fourth-, fifth-, and sixth-generation Irish Americans have ascended to the top of New England's social hierarchy, although there remains a special cachet for people who can trace

For skiers, resorts such as Killington, Stowe, and Sugarloaf offer some of the best skiing in the eastern US. The region's heavy snowfalls provide a wonderful base for cross-country skiers and snowshoers as well. There's biking on the back roads of New Hampshire and excellent hiking on the Appalachian Trail and Vermont's Long Trail, considered by many as one of the best hiking trails in the world.

Of course, many popular outdoor activities center around the ocean. There's kayaking among the islands and inlets of the Maine shoreline, wind surfing off Cape Cod, and ample opportunities for sailing, fishing, swimming, and scuba diving up and down the entire New England coast.

Fisherman with a
large striped bass

The Landscape and Wildlife of New England

CONSIDERING ITS PROXIMITY to major cities, rural New England boasts a surprisingly diverse collection of wildlife, including many species of birds, moose, bears, beavers, and, rarely, bobcats. The topography of the region includes rolling hills, dense woodlands, rugged mountains, and a coastline that is jagged and rocky in some areas and sandy and serene in others. Northern Maine has the closest thing to wilderness found in the eastern United States, with hundreds of square miles of trackless land and a vast network of clear streams, rivers, and lakes. New England is also home to the White, Green, and Appalachian mountain ranges.

Bald eagles *are found around water, making Maine their favorite New England state.*

COASTLINE

From the crenelated coastline of Maine, which measures almost 3,500 miles (5,630 km) in length, to the sandy beaches of Connecticut, the New England shoreline is richly varied. Here visitors find various sea and shore birds, many attracted by the food provided by the expansive salt marshes that have been created by barrier beaches. A few miles offshore, there is excellent whale-watching.

MOUNTAIN LANDSCAPE

The western and northern parts of New England are dominated by the Appalachian Mountains, a range that extends from Georgia to Canada. The highest point is 6,288-ft (1,917-m) Mount Washington, also known for drastic weather changes at its summit. Birch and beech trees are plentiful at elevations up to 2,000 ft (610 m). At the highest elevations, pine, spruce, and fir trees are most common.

The great blue heron is the largest of the North American herons. This elegant bird is easily spotted in wetlands and on lakeshores.

White-tailed deer can be found in a range of habitats, from forest edges to open woodland. They are frequently spotted on mountainsides up to 2,000 ft (610 m).

Whales are plentiful off the coast, particularly in the Gulf of Maine from early spring to mid-October. Finbacks, minke, and right whales are most common, but humpbacks generally put on the best show, often leaping out of the water.

Coyotes were once all but extinct in the region, but in recent years their numbers have exploded. They tend to live in forested and mountainous areas, but might be seen in urban areas

NATIONAL WILDLIFE REFUGE

With 93 million acres (38 million ha) under its control, the National Wildlife Refuge (NWR) offers protection for some of the country's most ecologically rich areas. The NWR system began in 1903 when President Theodore Roosevelt (1858–1919) established Pelican Island in Florida as a refuge for birds. Twenty-eight refuges are located in New England, including ten in Massachusetts, two in Rhode Island, five in New Hampshire, seven in Maine, two in Connecticut, and two in Vermont. They offer some of the best bird-watching in the region. See www.refuges.fws/gov for more information.

Rachel Carson National Wildlife Refuge, a vast wetland stop for migratory birds

LAKES AND RIVERS

The rivers and lakes of New England provide fishermen, canoeists, and vacationers in general with a world of outdoor pleasures. The network of waterways is particularly extensive in Maine, which has more lakes than any state in the northeastern United States. Among the rivers, the Connecticut is New England's longest, at more than 400 miles (644 km) in length. It runs from the Canadian border along the Vermont-New Hampshire border through Massachusetts and Connecticut.

FORESTS

The logging industry and the switch to agricultural and grazing land – especially for sheep – decimated many of the forests of New England in the 19th and early 20th centuries, but the tide has turned. Vermont, for example, has far more forests today than it did 100 years ago. In the lower elevations, the trees are mostly deciduous, such as ash, maple, and birch, but higher up in the mountains coniferous trees such as balsam fir predominate.

The pigeon hawk, also known as the merlin, can be found throughout New England, even in urban areas.

Mallard ducks are a frequent sight throughout New England wetlands. The birds can be seen from April to October, when they migrate to warmer climes.

Chipmunks are seen virtually throughout rural New England, especially in the forests.

Moose are common in Maine, northern Vermont, and New Hampshire. Although they can be spotted in the woods, they are most often seen along the shores of lakes. Drivers should be wary of moose, especially at dawn and dusk.

Raccoons are commonly seen in wooded areas. They often pay visits to campsites, brazenly foraging for food with dexterous paws.

Fall Foliage

T HE COOL WEATHER IN THE FALL signals more than back-to-
school time in New England. It also sounds a clarion call
to hundreds of thousands of visitors to head outdoors to gaze
in wonder at one of Nature's most splendid offerings: the
annual changing of leaf colors. Planning foliage tours is an
inexact science, however. Generally, leaves start to change
earliest in more northern areas and higher up mountainsides.
On some mountains in northern New England, for example,
the leaves will begin changing color as early as August. In
general, the peak period varies from early October in the
northern part of the region to late October in the southern
section. But this can differ, depending on the weather. Cooler
temperatures than normal tend to speed up the leaf-changing
timetable and vice versa.

**Young boy during fall's
pumpkin harvest**

Blue sky
*The rich palette created by the foliage is
made even more dramatic by a backdrop
of a deep blue fall sky.*

VERMONT'S FALL COLORS
While each of the New England states
offers something for "leaf peepers," none
can top Vermont. With its rich mix of
deciduous trees, the Green Mountain
State is anything but just green in late
September and October. Inns and hotels
tend to be booked up months in
advance on the key weekends as the
Vermont countryside swells with one of
its biggest influx of out-of-state visitors.

Forest floor
*Fallen leaves are more
than just beautiful to the
eye. They will eventually
decay and replenish
the humus layer.*

Nature's paint box
One of the most remarkable features of the fall foliage season is how it transforms the scenery. Here Quechee Gorge, Vermont's Grand Canyon, has changed its verdant green cloak for one of many colors.

Maple leaf
The maple tree is one of the most common trees in New England. Its leaves change to yellow, red, or orange.

WHY LEAVES TURN

The changing of leaf colors is not just a capricious act of Nature. It is a direct response to the changing realities of the seasons. As daylight hours diminish, the leaves of deciduous trees stop producing the green pigment chlorophyll. With the disappearance of chlorophyll, other pigments that had been hidden behind the chlorophyll's color now burst into view. More pigments are produced by sugars that remain trapped in the leaves. The result is a riotous display that makes this the high point of the year for many visitors. Two of the most spectacular areas for color are Litchfield Hills, Connecticut *(see pp208–209)*, and Penobscot Bay, Maine *(see pp286–7)*. Foliage hotlines give updates and are listed on page 379.

Fall hiking
Hikers should wear bright clothing and stick to well-marked trails and paths in the fall as this is also hunting season in the area.

A single crimson leaf aglow on the forest floor

The Appalachian Trail

T HE APPALACHIAN TRAIL is one of the longest footpaths in the world at 2,168 miles (3,490 km). From its southern terminus at Springer Mountain in the state of Georgia to its northernmost point on the summit of Mount Katahdin, Maine, the trail crosses 14 states and two national

A common squirrel parks as it wends its way through forests, meadows, and mountains. The trail travels through five of the six New England states, missing only Rhode Island, and reaches its highest point in the northeast on windswept Mount Washington *(see p267)* in New Hampshire. Each year about 400 intrepid souls, called "thru hikers," complete the journey in a single trip. The vast majority of people, however, choose to walk the trail in smaller, more manageable sections. The trail is usually marked by rectangular white blazes painted on trees and rocks, and overnight hikers can take advantage of primitive shelters that are situated roughly every 10 miles (16 km).

APPALACHIAN TRAIL

☐ *New England*

--- *Appalachian Trail*

Hanover, New Hampshire
Home of Dartmouth College, Hanover is located on the Appalachian Trail. This stretch of the trail, called the Dartmouth Outing Club section, runs through a series of scenic valleys and mountain passes.

Vermont's lush *green cloak becomes a brilliant patchwork in the fall, a popular time to hike this section of the trail.*

Mount Greylock is one of the highlights of the Massachusetts section.

The Connecticut section runs through the Housatonic Highlands and the valley along the Taconic Range.

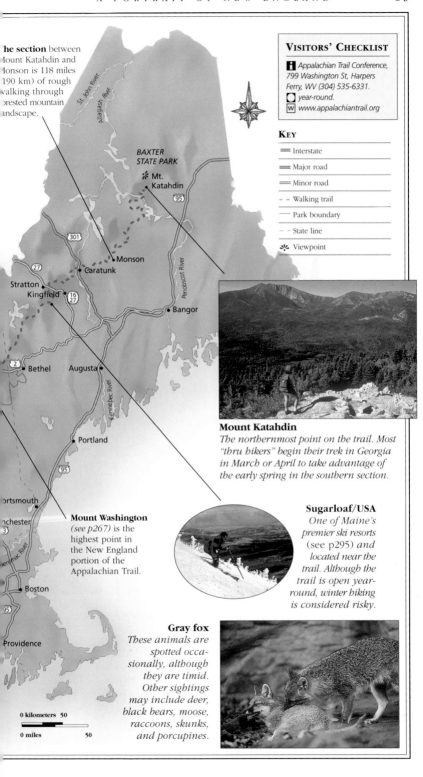

he section between
Mount Katahdin and
Monson is 118 miles
(190 km) of rough
walking through
forested mountain
landscape.

BAXTER
STATE PARK

Mt.
Katahdin

VISITORS' CHECKLIST

Appalachian Trail Conference,
799 Washington St, Harpers
Ferry, WV (304) 535-6331.
year-round.
www.appalachiantrail.org

KEY

Interstate

Major road

Minor road

- - Walking trail

Park boundary

- - State line

Viewpoint

Mount Katahdin
*The northernmost point on the trail. Most
"thru hikers" begin their trek in Georgia
in March or April to take advantage of
the early spring in the southern section.*

Mount Washington
(see p267) is the
highest point in
the New England
portion of the
Appalachian Trail.

Sugarloaf/USA
*One of Maine's
premier ski resorts
(see p295) and
located near the
trail. Although the
trail is open year-
round, winter hiking
is considered risky.*

Gray fox
*These animals are
spotted occa-
sionally, although
they are timid.
Other sightings
may include deer,
black bears, moose,
raccoons, skunks,
and porcupines.*

Maritime New England

Whaleboat figurehead

IT WAS THE SEA that helped open up the region to settlement in the 17th century. The sea also provided New Englanders with a way of life. In the early years, ships worked the fertile waters off Cape Cod for whales, fish, and lobster. Whaling reached its zenith in the 19th century, when hundreds of whaleboats fanned out to the uttermost ends of the Earth. Today the best places to explore the area's rich maritime history are the New Bedford Whaling National Historical Park and the New Bedford Whaling Museum in New Bedford, Massachusetts *(see p121)*, Mystic Seaport *(see pp214–15)*, Connecticut, and the Penobscot Marine Museum in Searsport, Maine *(see p286)*.

Ropes and pulleys
were important for hoisting sails and lowering the whaleboats.

Antique whaling harpoons
Harpoons and lances were hand-forged in New Bedford. Harpoons were thrown to attach a line to the whale. When the leviathan tired of pulling boat and men, the lance was used for the kill.

NEW ENGLAND'S WHALERS
Competition in 19th-century whaling was fierce. In 1857 some 330 whalers sailed out of New Bedford, Massachusetts, alone. The *Catalpa*, portrayed by C.S. Raleigh in his late-1800s painting, is an example of a well-outfitted whaler.

Whaleboats were lowered into the water to hunt and harpoon whales. Whale oil was used for illumination and was a valuable commodity.

Maritime art
Maritime influences still appear throughout New England. This contemporary chest by Harriet Scudder depicts an early whaling scene.

THE ICE TRADE

The cold winters of northern New England provided the source of a valuable export in the 19th century. In the days before mechanical refrigeration, ice from the region's frozen rivers, lakes, and ponds was cut up into large blocks, packed in sawdust, and shipped as far away as India. To keep the ice from melting, engineers designed ships with special airtight hulls. The ice trade finally collapsed in the late 1800s when mechanical methods for keeping perishables cool began to make ice obsolete for refrigeration in an increasing number of places in the world.

Harvesting ice

Barks were popular whaling vessels in the 19th century because they were maneuverable and could undertake long voyages.

Scrimshaw
New England sailors killed long periods of inactivity on the sea making etchings on whale teeth or jawbones. Ink and tobacco juice added color.

Whale carcasses were secured to the sides of the ship so that the blubber could be stripped and boiled onboard for its oil.

Lighthouses
Nearly 200 lighthouses dot New England's coast, testimony to the area's maritime ties.

Lobster industry
In colonial times, lobster was so common it was used as fertilizer. Today it is considered a delicacy.

New England Architecture

Scrolled door pediment

NEW ENGLAND ARCHITECTURE encompasses a variety of styles. In the early years of colonization, the influences of England predominated. But after the Revolutionary War (1775–83), the new republic wanted to distance itself from its colonial past. Drawing on French Neo-classicism, the newest European style of the late 18th century, American architects brought into being a distinctive American version known as Federal. In its efforts to define itself, New England did not reject foreign ideas, however, as evidenced by the Greek Revival style of the early 19th century and the adaptation of English and French Revival styles for the next 100 years.

First Church of Christ in West Hartford, Connecticut

COLONIAL STYLE

Colonial style, the style of the period when America was still a British colony, has two aspects: the homes of ordinary people and the more elaborate architecture of public buildings, mansions, and churches. The large wooden houses built in towns and rural areas in New England between 1607 and 1780 constitute one of the area's architectural treasures. Numerous examples survive, and the style has many regional variations. The famous Connecticut "saltbox" houses are an example. They featured distinctive close-cropped eaves and a long back roof that projected over a kitchen lean-to.

Eleazer Arnold House chimney, Providence, Rhode Island

Roof
Shingles became the main roofing material and were frequently used for walls as well.

Chimney
The large chimney provided a vital outlet for smoke.

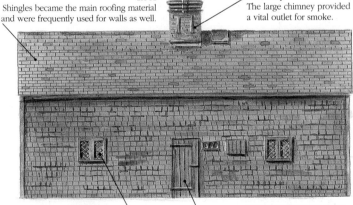

Windows
Small casement windows were fitted with diamond-shaped panes of glass imported from England.

Casement window

Jethro Coffin House was built in 1686 and is the oldest surviving structure in Nantucket, Massachusetts. A slot beside the front door allowed inhabitants to see who was standing outside.

Door
In keeping with the practical Colonial aesthetics, doors featured a simple, vertical-board design.

GEORGIAN STYLE

The term Georgian, or Palladian, refers to the mainstream classical architecture of 18th-century England, which drew on designs of 16th-century Italian architect Andrea Palladio (1508–80). In the colonies and England, these elegant buildings marked the presence of the British ruling class.

Pedimented dormers, Ladd Gilman House, in Exeter, New Hampshire

Roof
Roofs were less steeply pitched than earlier Colonial-era designs. A delicate balustrade crowns the roof.

Windows
Georgian windows were usually double-hung sash with 6 panes.

Doors
Doors featured a raised-panel design with six or more panels and classical moldings.

Vassall/Craigie/ Longfellow House in *Cambridge, Massachusetts, built in 1759. Its facade has classical columns and a triangular pediment.*

FEDERAL STYLE

American architects viewed the Federal style as a distinctive national statement. Some Federal buildings drew on both Greek and Roman architecture, representing the tenets of democracy and republicanism. Federal style is more restrained than Georgian, with less intricate woodwork.

The Colony House in Newport (see pp182–7), Rhode Island

Roof
Neoclassical roofs were often flat.

Fanlights
Fanlights, frequent in Georgian architecture, were also found in Neo-classical design.

Facade
Neoclassical facades were less decorated than Georgian. Often stories were separated by bands of stone called string courses.

Gardner-Pingree House in *Salem, Massachusetts, is known for its graceful proportions.*

GREEK REVIVAL STYLE

Popular between 1820 and 1845, this style is a more literal version of classical architecture than the Federal style. Greek Revival buildings typically borrowed the facades of ancient Greek temples, often sensitively re-creating them in wood.

Samuel Russell House in *Middletown, Connecticut, features a white exterior common in Greek Revival structures.*

Providence, Rhode Island, church door

Facade
The "temple fronts" of Greek Revival buildings were inspired by the archeological discoveries in Greece and Turkey in the 18th century.

Columns
These Corinthian columns faithfully follow conventions of ancient Greek architecture.

New England Universities

NEW ENGLAND IS NOT ONLY THE CRADLE of American civilization, it is also the birthplace of higher education in the New World. Harvard University *(see pp112–17)* was founded in 1636, only 16 years after the Pilgrims arrived at Plymouth Rock *(see pp148–9)*. Four of the country's eight renowned Ivy League colleges are located in New England: Harvard, Brown *(see p175)*, Dartmouth *(see p263)*, and Yale *(see pp222–5)*. Here higher learning goes hand in hand with tradition and culture. Many of America's most famous art collections and natural history museums are found on campus grounds. As well, many of the top-ranked liberal arts colleges are found here, including Bowdoin, Wellesley, and all-women Smith College.

1764 Rhode Island College, later Brown University, is founded in Providence, Rhode Island

1852 The Harvard crew wins inaugural Harvard-Yale Regatta – beginning one of the longest rivalries in US college sports

1778 Phillips Academy is founded by educator Samuel Phillips in Andover, Massachusetts

1781 John Phillips, uncle of Samuel, founds Phillips Exeter Academy in Exeter, New Hampshire

1801 Daniel Webster graduates from Dartmouth and goes on to an illustrious career as US statesman and orator

1636 Harvard University is founded in Cambridge, Massachusetts; 12 students enroll in the inaugural year

1701 Puritan clergymen found Collegiate School in Saybrook, Connecticut

1640	1680	1720	1760	1800	18

1640	1680	1720	1760	1800	18

1642 Physics becomes a mandatory subject at Harvard, using text by Aristotle

1777 Brown's University Hall building is used as barracks for Colonial troops during War of Independence

1817 Harvard Law School is established

1832 Yale Art Gallery is founded after US artist John Trumbull donates some 100 pieces of art from his personal collection

1717 Collegiate School is moved to New Haven, Connecticut, and is renamed Yale in 1718 in honor of benefactor Elihu Yale

1844 Yale graduate Samuel Morse sends world's first telegraphic message in Morse code

1853 Franklin Pierce, graduate of Bowdoin College in Brunswick, Maine, is elected 14th president of the United States

1861 Massachusetts Institute of Technology (MIT) is founded

1868 William Dubois is born. Dubois would go on to become the first black person to earn a Ph.D. from Harvard

1919 Philanthropist and Brown University graduate John D. Rockefeller, Jr. donates 5,000 acres (2,025 ha) of Maine's Mount Desert Island for use as a preserve. His further gifts would form almost one-third of Acadia National Park *(see pp288–9)*

1925 S.J. Perelman graduates from Brown; goes on to win Academy Award for screenplay of *Around the World in 80 Days* (1956)

1957 Theodor Geisel (Dr. Seuss), Dartmouth alumnus, publishes *The Cat in the Hat*

1992 Yale graduate Bill Clinton is elected 42nd president of the United States

2000 Academy Award-winner Elizabeth Shue *(Leaving Las Vegas)* graduates from Harvard with a degree in political science

| 1880 | 1920 | 1960 | 2000 |

| 1880 | 1920 | 1960 | 2000 |

1946 Percy Bridgman becomes first Harvard physicist to receive Nobel Prize in Physics

1969 Women are admitted to Yale's undergraduate program

2000 Yale graduate George W. Bush is elected 43rd president, following in the footsteps of his father George H.W. Bush – Yale graduate and 41st president

NEW ENGLAND BOARDING SCHOOLS

New England boasts the most prestigious collection of college preparatory, or "prep," schools in the US. The two preeminent institutions are Phillips Academy in Andover, Massachusetts, and Phillips Exeter Academy *(see p256)* in Exeter, New Hampshire. Both are private, coeducational schools and attract the sons and daughters of some of the country's wealthiest and most influential families. Other prominent prep schools include Choate Rosemary Hall in Wallingford, Connecticut, and Groton in Groton, Massachusetts.

1877 Former slave Inman Page becomes first African-American to graduate from Brown

1861 Yale awards country's first Ph.D. degrees

Campus of Phillips Exeter Academy

Literary New England

Author Nathaniel Hawthorne (1804–64)

WRITING IN HIS SEMINAL WORK *Democracy in America* (1835), French historian Alexis de Tocqueville (1805–1859) declared, "The inhabitants of the United States have, then, at present, no literature." Less than two decades later that scenario had changed radically. By then, writers such as Ralph Waldo Emerson (1803–82), Henry David Thoreau (1817–62), and Nathaniel Hawthorne (1804–64) were creating works that would take their place among the classics of 19th-century literature – and that was just in one town, Concord *(see pp144–5)*, Massachusetts. Since that first flowering, New England writers have been taking their place among the best in the world.

In 1854 he published *Walden; or, Life in the Woods,* in which he outlined how people could escape a life of "quiet desperation" by paring away the extraneous, anxiety-inducing trappings of the industrial age and living in harmony with the natural world.

Ralph Waldo Emerson, speaking to Transcendentalists in Concord

FATHER OF TRANSCENDENTALISM

Born in Boston, Ralph Waldo Emerson graduated from Harvard University in 1821 and became the pastor of the Second Church (Unitarian) in Boston in 1829. In many ways Emerson turned his back on his formal religious education in the 1830s when he founded the Transcendentalism movement. Among other things, Emerson's writings espoused a system of spiritual independence in which each individual was responsible for his or her own moral judgments. Moving to Concord in 1834, the popular essayist and lecturer soon became known as the "Sage of Concord" for his insightful teachings.

Concord was also the birthplace of Emerson's most famous disciple, Henry David Thoreau. A one-time school teacher, Thoreau worked as a pencil maker before quitting to undertake his lifelong study of nature. Deeply influenced by the Transcendentalist belief that total unity with nature was achievable, Thoreau built a small cabin at Walden Pond *(see p145)* in 1845, living as a recluse for the next two years.

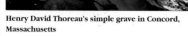

Henry David Thoreau's simple grave in Concord, Massachusetts

19TH-CENTURY LITERARY FLOWERING

It was also in Concord that Nathaniel Hawthorne penned *Mosses from an Old Manse* in 1846. Hawthorne later returned to his home-town, Salem *(see pp136–7)*, Massachusetts, where he wrote his best-known work, *The Scarlet Letter* (1850). Moving to Lenox in western Massachusetts, Hawthorne became friends with Herman Melville (1819–91), who wrote his allegorical master-piece *Moby-Dick* (1851) in

Illustration from Herman Melville's *Moby-Dick*

Visitor on the porch of the Robert Frost house in New Hampshire

neighboring Pittsfield. The book drew its inspiration from the voyage that Melville made from New Bedford, Massachusetts, to the South Seas aboard the New England whaler *Acushnet*.

Like Melville, Mark Twain (1835–1910) was not a New Englander by birth. However, it was during his long stay in Hartford *(see pp198–201)*, Connecticut, that he penned the novels that would vault him into worldwide prominence, including *The Adventures of Tom Sawyer* (1876), *The Adventures of Huckleberry Finn* (1885), and *A Connecticut Yankee in King Arthur's Court* (1889).

19TH-CENTURY WOMEN AUTHORS

Although opportunities for women were limited in 19th-century America, several New England female writers still managed to leave their mark on literature. One of the region's most famous – and mysterious – literary figures was Emily Dickinson (1830–86). Born in Amherst *(see p162–3)*, Massachusetts, she was educated at the Mount Holyoke Female Seminary *(see p162)* before withdrawing from society in her early 20s. Living the rest of her life in her family's home, Dickinson wrote more than 1,000 poems – the vast majority of which remained unpublished until after her death. Today her finely crafted poems are

Cover of sheet music for Harriet Beecher Stowe's *Uncle Tom's Cabin*

admired for their complex rhythms and intensely personal lyrics.

The greatest single indictment of the slavery that would catapult America into civil war came from the pen of Harriet Beecher Stowe (1811–96), who would later become Mark Twain's next door neighbor in Hartford. *Uncle Tom's Cabin; or, Life Among the Lowly* (1852) told the story of a slave family's desperate flight for freedom to a rapt, largely sympathetic audience worldwide. Louisa May Alcott (1832–88) – yet another Concord resident – left a lasting and loving portrait of domestic life in the United States during the Civil War in *Little Women* (1868), a perennial favorite of children.

20TH CENTURY

In the 20th century, New England continued to play a defining role in American literature, spawning native writers as diverse as "Beat" chronicler Jack Kerouac *(see p142)* and the "Chekhov of the suburbs," John Cheever (1912–82). The region has also provided a fertile base for transplanted New Englanders. The poet Robert Frost (1874–1963), a native of San Francisco, lived most of his life in Vermont and New Hampshire, and the mountains, meadows, and people of the region figure prominently in his poetry, which won the Pulitzer Prize an unprecedented four times. Poet and novelist John Updike (b.1932) has lived much of his life in Ipswich, Massachusetts, and set both *Couples* (1968) and *The Witches of Eastwick* (1984) in the northeast. Novelist John Irving was born in Exeter, New Hampshire, in 1942. Much of his later fiction is set in New England, including *The World According to Garp* (1978) and *Cider House Rules* (1985). Perhaps the area's best-known living writer is Stephen King (b.1947). The prolific master of the macabre and author of such horror stories as *The Shining* (1977) is a longtime resident of Bangor, Maine, where his Gothic-style home is one of the town's biggest tourist attractions.

Fright master and longtime Bangor resident Stephen King

NEW ENGLAND
THROUGH THE YEAR

NEW ENGLAND is really a
year-round tourist
destination – depend-
ing on what it is people are
looking to do. Generally,
spring is the shortest season.
Occurring sometime between
April and June, spring can be
short-lived but glorious, with
wildflowers bursting forth in
colorful bloom. Summer is
the busiest tourist period. With the
good weather stretching from mid-
June into early September, this part of
the year is characterized by warm

Colorful hot-
air balloon

temperatures that have people flocking to lakes and
the ocean. Fall is when
New England is at its most
beautiful, with its lush
forests changing from green
to a riot of gold, red, and
orange. The peak fall-foliage
period generally occurs
from mid-September to
late October. Winter,
which usually lasts from December
to mid-April, is often marked by
heavy snowfalls – a boon for winter
sport enthusiasts.

**Cars decorated with flowers in
Nantucket's Daffodil Festival**

SPRING

NEW ENGLAND'S shortest season is sometimes little
more than a three-week interval
between winter and summer.
As well as being the prime time
for maple syrup tapping, spring
brings with it a host of festivals.

APRIL

Boston Marathon *(third
Monday, April)*, Boston, MA.
The world's oldest and most
prestigious marathon.
Patriot's Day *(third Monday,
April)*, Lexington and
Concord, MA. Costumed reen-
actments of the pivotal battles
that were waged at the outset
of the Revolutionary War.
Daffodil Festival *(late April)*,
Nantucket, MA. The town is
decked out in millions of
yellow daffodils.

MAY

**Annual Civil War Living
History and Battles
Encampment** *(early May)*,
Hammonasset Beach State
Park, CT. Civil War reenact-
ment complete with battles.
Main Street in May *(May)*,
Plymouth, NH. Antique cars,
sidewalk musicians, and chil-
dren's activities are highlights
of this annual event.
Gaspee Days *(mid-May–mid-
June)*, Cranston and Warwick,
RI. Reenactment of the
burning of a British schooner.
Brimfield Antique Show
(May, July, and September),
Brimfield, MA. Dealers from
across the US gather at this
show to sell their wares.
Lobsterfest *(late May)*, Mystic,
CT. A lobsterbake popular
with both locals and visitors.

**Patriot Days celebration in
Lexington, Massachusetts**

**Delicious lobsters served up dur-
ing Mystic's Lobsterfest**

Waterfire *(May–Oct)*,
Providence, RI. This dazzling
art event features 100
bonfires, which are lit on
the city's three rivers.

EARLY JUNE

Taste of Hartford *(early
June)*, Hartford, CT. One of
New England's largest outdoor food festivals.
Discover Jazz Festival
(early June), Burlington, VT.
Jazz, blues, and gospel are
the highlights of this
popular festival.
Circus Smirkus *(early June–
mid-August)*. This
international youth circus
performs around New
England.

SUMMER

NEW ENGLAND summers
can be hot and humid.
This is vacation time for
students and families, making the region a very busy
place, especially the coastline and beaches.

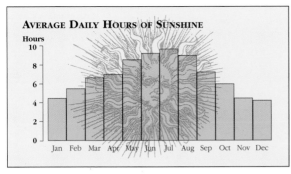

AVERAGE DAILY HOURS OF SUNSHINE

Sunshine Chart
New England's weather can vary greatly from year to year. Generally, the short spring is cloudy and wet, giving way to better weather in June. July and August are usually the sunniest months. Bright fall days out among the colorful foliage are spectacular.

LATE JUNE

Newport Music Festival *(mid-June)*, Newport, RI. Classical music concerts are held inside the city's mansions.
International Festival of Art and Ideas *(mid-June–July)*, New Haven, Hartford, Stamford, and New London, CT. A showcase of performance and visual arts.
Windjammer Days *(late June)*, Boothbay Harbor, ME. Shoreside events complement parade of graceful sailboats.
Stowe Flower Festival *(late June)*, Stowe, VT. Seminars and tours of formal gardens.
Northwest Connecticut Balloon Festival *(late June)*, Goshen, CT. Mass-ascensions, hot-air balloon rides, and fireworks highlight this festival.
Storm Trysail Club Block Island Race Week *(late June)*, Block Island, RI. This week-long event is the largest sailing event on the coast.
Williamstown Theater Festival *(late June–August)*, Williamstown, MA. Acclaimed festival of classical and new theater productions.
Jacob's Pillow Dance Festival *(late June–late August)*, Becket, MA. Ballet, jazz, and modern dance feature in the country's oldest dance festival.

JULY

Independence Day Celebrations *(July 4th)*, throughout New England. Parades, fireworks, and concerts mark the anniversary of US independence.
Tanglewood Music Festival *(early July–late August)*, Lenox, MA.

Boston Symphony and Boston Pops orchestras give concerts on beautiful estate *(see p167)*.
Riverfest *(July)*, Hartford, CT. Fireworks and free concerts along the Connecticut River.
Vermont Quilt Festival *(July)*, Northfield, VT. A premier quilting celebration.
Mozart Festival *(July, August, and October–December)*, Burlington, VT. A celebration of the music of Wolfgang Amadeus Mozart.
Revolutionary War Festival *(mid-July)*, Exeter, NH. Beer festival and fireworks bring reenactments into modern era.
Newport Regatta *(mid-July)*, Newport, RI. This huge regatta attracts some 300 boats.
Guilford Handcrafts Exposition *(mid-July)*, Guilford, CT. This event features pottery, glass, pewter, jewelry, folk art, and quilts.
Lowell Folk Festival *(late July)*, Lowell, MA. Dance troupes, musicians, and ethnic food are served up here.

AUGUST

Maine Lobster Festival *(early August)*, Rockland, ME. Lobster and live entertainment are on the menu at this popular event.

One of many festivals celebrating New England's nautical past

demonstrations, workshops, performing arts, and 200 booths selling crafts of extremely high quality.
Addison County Fair *(early August)*, New Haven, VT. This is one of the state's largest agricultural fairs.
Mystic Outdoor Arts Festival *(mid-August)*, Mystic, CT. This art show attracts 300 artists.
Newport JVC Jazz Festival *(mid-August)*, Newport, RI. International jazz stars gather to perform in this celebration of music.
Downtime Concord Fiddling Championship *(late August)*, Concord, NH. An annual fiddling tournament that attracts both the young and the old.
Brooklyn Fair *(late August)*, Brooklyn, CT. The country's oldest continuously running agricultural fair has ox pulls and livestock shows.
Champlain Valley Exhibition *(late August–early September)*, Essex Junction, VT. Horse shows and midway rides are part of this huge fair.

Ben & Jerry's Newport Folk Festival *(early August)*, Newport, RI. One of the country's top folk festivals, held at Fort Adams State Park.
League of New Hampshire Craftsmen Annual Fair *(early August)*, Newbury, NH. The oldest crafts fair in the US features craft

July 4th road markings

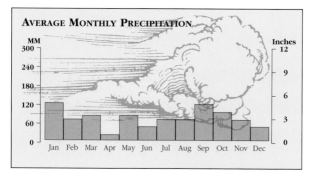

AVERAGE MONTHLY PRECIPITATION

Precipitation Chart
Spring is called "mud season" by locals, thanks to rainy skies and melting snow. Summer can be unpredictable, but is generally dry. Snow usually starts in December.

AUTUMN

MANY PEOPLE consider the fall to be New England's most beautiful season. Bright, crisp autumn days are made more glorious by the brilliant fall foliage *(see p20–21)*.

SEPTEMBER

Rhode Island Heritage Festival *(September 4th)*, Providence, RI. Thirty ethnic communities celebrate their heritage and culture with music, song, dance, arts, and food demonstrations.
Windjammer Weekend *(early September)*, Camden, ME. A celebration of Maine's fleet of classic sailing ships.
Vermont State Fair *(early September)*, Rutland, VT. One of the most popular agricultural fairs in the state.
Classic Yacht Regatta *(early September)*, Newport, RI. More than 100 vintage wooden yachts are on parade in this regatta.
Woodstock Fair *(early September)*, South Woodstock, CT. The state's second-oldest agricultural fair includes crafts, go-cart races, livestock shows, and petting zoos for children.
Mount Washington Old Car Show *(early September)*, North Conway, NH. Some 300 antique cars, trucks, and motorcycles are on display.
Norwalk Oyster Festival *(early September)*, East Norwalk, CT. This nationally acclaimed celebration includes fireworks, antique boats, and lots of oyster sampling.
The Big "E" *(last two weeks of September)*, Eastern States Exhibition Ground, West

A Harvest Festival, this one in Keene, New Hampshire

Springfield, MA. One of New England's biggest fairs, with rodeos, rides, and a circus.
Harvest Festivals *(late September)*, throughout New England. Parades, apple picking, and hay rides are just some of the festivities held around the region to celebrate the fall harvest.
Sugar Hill Antique Show *(late September)*, Sugar Hill, NH. A popular, long-running antique show attracts numerous dealers and their wares.
Northeast Kingdom Fall Foliage Festival *(late September–early October)*, throughout northern Vermont. Different towns hold foliage-

related bus tours, hiking parties, and family events.

OCTOBER

Sled Dog Derby *(October–April)*, Hanover, NH. Top dog teams and mushers compete.
Woonsocket Autumnfest *(early October)*, Woonsocket, RI. Live music, craft displays, a midway, and a Columbus Day parade top events.
New England Bach Festival *(October)*, Brattleboro, VT. A month-long musical celebration of Johann Sebastian Bach.
Haunted Happenings *(October)*, Salem, MA. A 10-day festival celebrating the city's witch-related past *(see pp136–9)* and Halloween.
PumpkinFire *(late October)*, Providence, RI. Elaborate pumpkins are created in this carving competition.
Keene Pumpkin Festival *(late Oct)*, Keene, NH. This community celebration holds the world record for most lit jack-o'-lanterns.

NOVEMBER

Holiday Craft Exhibition and Sale *(mid-November–December 31st)*, Brookfield,

Brilliant colors, heralding Northeast Kingdom Fall Foliage Festival

AVERAGE MONTHLY TEMPERATURE

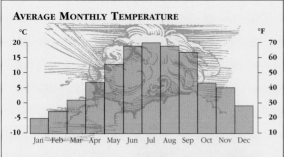

°C / °F
20 / 70
15 / 60
10 / 50
5 / 40
0 / 30
-5 / 20
-10 / 10

Jan Feb Mar Apr May Jun Jul Aug Sep Oct Nov Dec

Temperature Chart
New England temperatures vary greatly through the year. In the summer, temperatures of 90° F (32° C) are not quite frequent, while the thermometer can dip to 0° F (-18° C) or lower in winter. In general, it is warmer along the coast and in the southern section of New England.

CT. Hundreds of craft artists put unique wares up for sale.
Thanksgiving Celebration *(mid–late November)*, Plymouth, MA. Thanksgiving traditions of the past are celebrated in historic homes. Visitors can also enjoy a Victorian Thanksgiving at Plimoth Plantation *(see pp150–51)*.
Festival of Light *(late November–early January)*, Hartford, CT. Constitution Plaza is transformed into a spectacular world of more than 200,000 white lights.

WINTER

NEW ENGLAND WINTERS are often marked by heavy snowfalls, particularly in the mountainous areas farther inland. Temperatures can also plunge drastically overnight and from one day to the next. This, of course, is a boon for people who enjoy winter sports, as New England has some of the most popular ski centers in the eastern US.

DECEMBER

Christmas at Blithewold *(throughout December)*, Bristol, RI. Traditional Christmas celebrations are celebrated in this beautiful mansion.
Festival of Trees and Traditions *(early December)*, Hartford, CT. Hundreds of beautiful trees and wreaths are on display at Wadsworth Athenaeum.
Festival of Lights *(early December)*, Wickford Village, RI. This family-oriented festival includes tree- and window-decorating competitions, hayrides, and live music.

Wolfgang Amadeus Mozart, feted in Burlington, Vermont

Christmas Tree Lighting *(early December)*, Boston, MA. The huge tree in front of the Prudential Center is lit up with thousands of bright lights.
Candlelight Stroll *(mid-December)*, Portsmouth, NH. The town's historic Strawbery Banke district *(see pp254–5)* is resplendent with antique Christmas decorations.
Boston Tea Party Reenactment *(mid-December)*, Boston, MA. Costumed interpreters bring to life the famous protest that precipitated the Revolutionary War.
First Night Celebrations *(December 31st)*, throughout New England (except Maine). Family-oriented festivities that started in Boston in 1976 and are now celebrated around the world.

JANUARY

Vermont Farm Show *(late January)*, Barre, VT. Vermont's premier winter show includes a variety of agricultural displays and livestock exhibits.

Chinese New Year *(late January–early February)*, Boston, MA. The location for this colorful festival is Boston's Chinatown.

FEBRUARY

National Toboggan Championships *(February)*, Camden, ME. Daredevils of all sizes and ages come to compete in this high-speed, often hilarious, event.
Stowe Derby *(late February)*, Stowe, VT. This is one of the oldest downhill and cross-country skiing races in the country.

MARCH

New England Spring Flower Show *(March)*, Boston, MA. Meticulous landscaped gardens and thousands of new blooms announce the end of winter.
St. Patrick's Day Parades *(March 17th)*, Boston and Holyoke, MA. Two of New England's oldest and largest celebrations.
Vermont Maple Weekend *(late March)*, throughout New England. Visitors can see how maple sap is collected and made into syrup.

Musicians in Boston's St. Patrick's Day Parade

THE HISTORY OF NEW ENGLAND

T HE EARLY HISTORY *of New England is the history of the United States itself, for it is here that civilization first gained a toehold in America and where much of the drama of forming a new country was played out. But even after the rest of the country had been populated, New England continued to exert influence on the political, economic, and intellectual life of the country.*

No one can say for sure which Europeans first made landfall in New England. Some historians claim that the Vikings, after first reaching Newfoundland around AD 1000, eventually ventured as far south as Massachusetts. Others suggest that Spanish, Portuguese, or Irish explorers were the first Old World visitors. But one thing is sure: none of these peoples actually discovered the area. Native Americans already had called the region home for several thousand years. They were descendants of nomads from central Asia who had journeyed to what is now Alaska via the then-dry Bering Strait between 20,000 and 12,000 years ago. Slowly they migrated east.

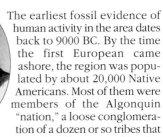

Paul Revere

The earliest fossil evidence of human activity in the area dates back to 9000 BC. By the time the first European came ashore, the region was populated by about 20,000 Native Americans. Most of them were members of the Algonquin "nation," a loose conglomeration of a dozen or so tribes that occasionally engaged in violent internecine struggles. Their inability to unite would later prove a fatal flaw when confronted by a common foe – white settlers. Unlike their Asian ancestors, the Algonquins, also known as Abenakis ("people of the dawn"), had given up nomadic life. They ate moose, deer, birds, and fish, but grew crops, too – maize, called Indian corn, beans, and pumpkins.

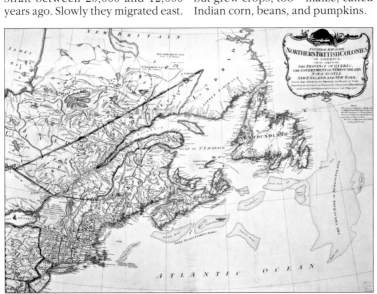

Map of the Northeast, printed in England a month after the Declaration of Independence was signed

◁ *Native American Indians Cooking and Preparing Food c.1850 by J. Fumagalli*

Embarkation and Departure of Columbus from the Port of Palos, undated painting by Ricardo Balaca

THE AGE OF DISCOVERY

The voyage of Christopher Columbus (1451–1506) to the New World in 1492 fired the imagination of maritime nations in Europe. Soon seafarers from England, France, and Spain were setting forth to explore the New World on behalf of their respective kings and queens. In 1497 the Italian explorer John Cabot (c.1425–1499) reached New England from Bristol, England, and claimed the land, along with all the territory north of Florida and east of the Rocky Mountains, for his English patron, Henry VII (1457–1509). By the end of the 16th century, helped largely by the 1588 defeat of the Spanish Armada, England was beginning to achieve mastery of the seas.

In 1606 England's King James I (1566–1625) granted a charter to two ventures to establish settlements in America. The Virginia Company was assigned an area near present-day Virginia; the Plymouth Company was granted rights to a more northern colony. This second group ran into

King James I (1566–1625)

trouble early on. One of its ships strayed off course and was captured by the Spanish near Florida. Another ship made it to New England, but had to turn back to England before winter arrived. In May 1607 two ships left Plymouth, England, with approximately 100 colonists. Three months later they made landfall at the mouth of the Kennebec River, where the settlers constructed Fort St. George. Their first winter proved to be an especially cold and snowy one, and the furs and mineral wealth fell far short of what the colonists expected. After just a year, the so-called Popham Colony was abandoned.

Despite this inauspicious beginning, the Plymouth Company hired surveyor John Smith (1580–1631) to conduct a more extensive evaluation of the territory. In 1614 Smith sailed along the Massachusetts coast, observing the region. His findings, published in *A Description of New England*, not only coined the name of the region, but also painted a glowing picture of this new land and its "greatnessse" of fish

TIMELINE

25,000-12,000 BC Central Asian nomads cross Bering Strait to become first North Americans	**7,000-1,000 BC** Warming temperatures lead to development of New England's forests

25,000 BC		10,000 BC		AD 1000	1500

10,000 BC Humans move into New England area after deglaciation

Leif Eriksson in Viking boat

AD 1000 Vikings sail to Newfoundland, Canada, and move south along the coast

and timber. Of all the places in the world, concluded Smith, this would be the best to support a new colony.

COLONIAL NEW ENGLAND

While the explorers of the early 17th century probed the shoreline of New England, events were taking place in Europe that would have a far-reaching impact on the settlement of the New World. The Reformation of the 16th century and the birth of the Protestant faith had created an upheaval in religious beliefs – particularly in England, where Henry VIII (1491–1547) had severed ties with Rome and had made sure that parliament declared him head the Church of England.

Protestant Puritans believed that the Church of England, despite its claim to represent a reformed Christianity, was still rife with Catholic practices and that their faith was being debased in England, especially after James I, who was suspected of having Catholic sympathies, succeeded Elizabeth I in 1603. Puritans were persecuted for their beliefs and found themselves facing a stark choice: stay at home to fight against overwhelming odds or start anew somewhere else.

A small, radical faction of Puritans, known as Separatists, emigrated to Holland. The lifestyle of the Dutch did not live up to the demanding standards

Puritan governor addresses Colonists in 1621

of the Separatists' stern orthodoxy. As a result, they negotiated a deal with the Plymouth Company to finance a "pilgrimage" to America. In September 1620 they set sail. After a grueling 66-day voyage, their ship, the *Mayflower*, landed at what is now Provincetown *(see p156)*, Massachusetts.

It was a short-lived stay. The barren, sandy coast seemed a forbidding place, so the ship sailed on to Plymouth Rock *(see pp148–9)*, where the fatigued Pilgrims disembarked on December 26, 1620. During the winter of 1620–21, half of the Pilgrims succumbed to scurvy and the rigors of a harsh New England winter. But with the arrival of spring, the worst seemed to be behind them. The settlers found an ally among the indigenous people in Squanto (d.1622), a member of the Pawtuxet tribe who had been taken to England in 1605. Squanto had returned to the New World in 1615, and when word reached him that the English had arrived, he soon helped them negotiate a 50-year peace treaty between the Pilgrims and the chief of the local Wampanoag tribe. Squanto also taught the newcomers how to live in their adopted home. He showed them how to shoot and trap, and told them which crops to grow. The first harvest was celebrated in the fall of 1621 with a three-day feast of thanksgiving.

Pilgrims board the *Mayflower* in 1620

1497 John Cabot explores North American coast	1607 First North American colony founded at Jamestown	1614 John Smith names territory New England	1620 Pilgrims land at Plymouth, Massachusetts, aboard the *Mayflower*	
1500	**1600**		**1615**	**1620**
1492 Christopher Columbus discovers the New World	1602 Captain Bartholomew Gosnold lands on Massachusetts coast		1616 Smallpox epidemic kills large number of New England Indians	*First feast of thanksgiving* 1621 Pilgrims celebrate feast of thanksgiving

John Smith

The Battle of Bunker Hill

George III of England

THE FIRST MAJOR BATTLE of the Revolutionary War took place in Boston on June 17, 1775, and actually was fought on Breed's Hill. The Americans had captured heavy British cannon on Breed's and Bunker hills overlooking Boston Harbor, which gave them a commanding position. Britain's first two attacks on Breed's Hill were repelled by the outnumbered defenders. The Colonial soldiers were running low on ammunition, however, which gave rise to commander Colonel William Prescott's orders, "Don't fire until you can see the whites of their eyes!" Reinforced with 400 fresh troops, British forces made a bayonet charge and seized the hill, forcing the Americans to retreat to nearby Bunker Hill. The British suffered more than 1,000 casualties to approximately 150 for the Americans. The battle reinforced the confidence of the American troops that had first been kindled by their successes at Lexington and Concord.

Bunker Hill Monument, *a granite obelisk, honors Colonial casualties.*

IN THE HEAT OF THE BATTLE

John Trumbull's 1786 painting Battle of Bunker Hill *depicts the hand-to-hand combat of the skirmish, fought mainly with bayonets and muskets. Victory came at a price. As one British soldier commented, "It was such a dear victory, another such would have ruined us."*

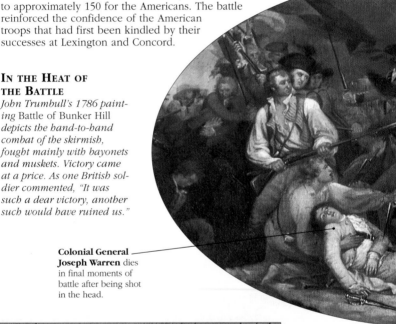

Colonial General Joseph Warren dies in final moments of battle after being shot in the head.

Declaration of Independence

Less than a year after the battle, the Second Continental Congress adopted the Declaration of Independence, which outlined the framework for democracy in the United States.

Attack on Breed's Hill
Prior to the infantry assault on the Colonial position, British men-of-war bombarded Breed's Hill with cannonade. Portions of nearby Charlestown caught fire and burned during the bombing.

A British officer prevents grenadier's *coup de grâce*.

British Firelocks
Loading a musket involved shaking gunpowder into a pan just above the trigger as well as into the barrel itself. The powder in the barrel was then tamped down with a small rod. This time-consuming process meant that soldiers stood unprotected on the battlefield as they reloaded.

British troops storm Colonial positions with renewed vigor after having suffered massive casualties on first two attempts.

British Major John Pitcairn collapses into his son's arms after being shot in chest, only to die while receiving medical treatment for his wounds.

COLONEL WILLIAM PRESCOTT

Born in Groton, Massachusetts, William Prescott (1726–95) led the Colonial forces during the battle of Bunker Hill. In the initial stages of the fight, British warships bombarded the Americans' fortified position with heavy cannon. The untested Colonial troops were taken aback, especially when a private was decapitated by a cannonball. Sensing his men were disheartened, Prescott, covered in the slain soldier's blood, leapt atop the redoubt wall and paced back and forth in defiance of the bombs bursting around him. His brave gesture galvanized the troops, who went on to make one of the most courageous stands of the Revolutionary War.

Death of Metacomet (King Philip) in 1676

COLONIAL NEW ENGLAND

From this modest beginning, the settlement began slowly to prosper and expand. Within five years the group was self-sufficient. Nine years later the Massachusetts Bay Company was founded, which sent 350 people to Salem *(see pp136–9)*.

A second, much larger group joined the newly appointed governor, John Winthrop (c.1587–1649), and established a settlement at the mouth of the Charles River. They first called their new home Trimountain, but renamed it Boston in honor of the town some of the settlers had left in England.

During the 1630s immigrants started spreading farther afield, creating settlements along the coast of Massachusetts and New Hampshire, and even venturing inland. However, the colonists' gain proved to be

England's George III (1738–1820)

the Natives' loss. Initial cooperation between both groups gave way to competition and outright hostility as land-hungry settlers moved into Indian territory. War first erupted with the Pequot tribe in 1637, which resulted in their near annihilation as a people. The hostility reached its peak at the outset of the King Philip's War (1775–6), when several hundred members of the Narragansett tribe were killed by white settlers near South Kingston, Rhode Island.

WEAKENING TIES

The sheer distance dividing England and New England and the fact that communication could move no faster than wind-borne ships meant that there was very little contact between Old World and New. The colonists were largely self-governing, and there was no representation from them in the British parliament. Efforts by London to tighten control over the colonies were sporadic and in most cases successfully resisted until the Seven Years War between Britain and France (1756–1763) assured British domination of North America.

Ironically, British success created the conditions that lessened the colonists' dependence on the mother country and also led to their growing estrangement. The colonies, especially New England, would come to feel that they no longer had to rely on British protection against the French in Canada and their Indian allies. Moreover, Britain's efforts after 1763 to derive a revenue from the colonies to help cover the debt incurred by the war and to contribute to imperial defense

TIMELINE

Harvard booster

Salem gravestone

1630		1660	1675	1690

1636 Harvard is founded, becoming America's first college

1656 Puritans of Massachusetts Bay Colony begin systematic persecution of newly arrived Quakers with imprisonment, banishment, and hanging

1676 King Philip's War ends when Wampanoag chief Metacomet is betrayed and killed

1630 Puritans led by John Winthrop found Boston

1636 Murder of two colonists, supposedly by Pequot Indians, sparks the beginning of Pequot War

1692 Salem witch trials begin, leading to the execution of 20 people

met growing resistance. The cry of "No taxation without representation" would become a rallying call to arms for the independence movement, with the most vocal protests coming from New England.

The taxation issue came to a head under the reign of King George III (1738–1820), who ascended the throne of Great Britain in 1760. The Hanoverian king believed that the

Paul Revere's 1770 engraving of the Boston Massacre

American colonists should remain under the control of Britain, and enacted a series of heavy taxes on various commodities, such as silk and sugar. In 1765 British parliament passed the Stamp Act, which placed a tax on commercial and legal documents, newspapers, agendas, and even playing cards and dice. The act had a galvanizing effect throughout New England as its incensed inhabitants banded together and refused to use the stamps. They even went so far as to hold stamp-burning ceremonies.

Parliament eventually repealed the act in 1766, but this did not end the issue. In fact, at the same time that the Stamp Act was rescinded, it was replaced by the Declaratory Act, which stated that every part of the British Empire would continue to be taxed however the parliament saw fit. To make sure that the colonists would not flout the law, the British sent two regiments to Boston to

British stamp for American colony goods

enforce its control. The troops, called Redcoats for their distinctive uniforms, proved decidedly unpopular. A series of small skirmishes between them and local sailors and workers culminated in the Boston Massacre (March 5, 1770), in which the British soldiers opened fire on an unruly crowd, killing five, including a free black man, Crispus Attucks.

REVOLUTIONARY SPIRIT

After the massacre an uneasy truce ensued. A simmering distrust remained between the two sides, and it only needed a suitable provocation to boil over again. That provocation came in the form of yet another proclamation – this one giving the East India Company the right to market tea directly in America, thus bypassing American merchants. When three ships arrived in Boston Harbor in 1773 with a shipment to unload, a group of about 60 men, including local politicians Samuel Adams (1722–1803) and John Hancock (1737–93), disguised themselves with Indian headdresses and then boarded the ships. They dumped 342 tea chests, valued at £18,000, into the harbor. The Boston Tea Party (see p89) was celebrated by the colonists as a

Protesters during the 1773 Boston Tea Party

(see p89)

1704 The *Boston News Letter*, America's first newspaper, is published

1737 John Hancock, an original signatory of the Declaration of Independence, is born

John Hancock's signature

1773 New taxes spur Boston Tea Party

1710	1725	1740	1750	1770

1713 Boatyard in Gloucester, Massachusetts, produces America's first schooner

1770 British soldiers kill five in Boston Massacre

Crowd in Philadelphia celebrating the signing of the Declaration of Independence on July 4, 1776

justifiable act of defiance against an oppressive regime. Parliament responded by passing the Intolerable Acts of 1774. These included the closing of the port of Boston by naval blockade until payment was made for the tea that had been destroyed.

On September 5, 1774, 56 representatives from the various American colonies, including New England, met in Philadelphia to establish the First Continental Congress to consider how to deal with grievances against Britain. The first concrete step toward nationhood had been taken.

Minutemen repelling the British, who were trying to march through to Concord

Although the British troops garrisoned in Boston in the mid-1770s represented a formidable force, a large part of New England lay beyond their control. In the countryside, locals stockpiled arms. In 1775 the royal governor of Massachusetts, General Thomas Gage (1721–87), learned about such a cache at Concord (see pp144–5), 20 miles (32 km) west of Boston. He ordered 700 British soldiers to travel there under cover of darkness and destroy the arms.

The Americans were tipped off by dramatic horseback rides from Boston by Paul Revere and William Dawes. By the time the troops arrived at Lexington a few miles to the east of Concord, 77 colonial soldiers had set up a defensive formation, slowing the British advance. The Redcoats pressed onward to Concord, where close to 400 American patriots, called Minutemen for their ability to muster at a moment's notice, repelled the British attack. By the end of that day, April 19, 1775, 70 British had been killed and the casualty toll was 273. American losses were 95.

TIMELINE

1774 British navy imposes blockade of Boston Harbor	**1775** Battles at Concord and Lexington mark beginning of Revolutionary War		**1783** Treaty of Paris signals end to Revolutionary War		**1789** George Washington becomes first president of the United States	
	1775	1780		1785	1790	1795
1774 First Continental Congress held in Philadelphia	**1776** Second Continental Congress ratifies the Declaration of Independence		**1781** Colonial forces win decisive battle over British at Yorktown, Virginia	**1791** First mechanical cotton mill of Samuel Slater at Pawtucket, Rhode Island		

George Washin[gton]

Slater Mill

Boston shipbuilding c.1850

The days of discussion were now clearly over. Colonial leaders signed the Declaration of Independence on July 4, 1776, and the American Revolution had begun. For the next six years the war would be waged first on New England soil, but then mostly beyond its borders at such key places as the Valley Forge encampment, Pennsylvania, and Yorktown, Virginia. Although the fighting ceased in 1781, the war officially came to an end with the signing of the 1783 Treaty of Paris.

A NEW INDUSTRIAL POWER

The fledgling United States of America was rich in natural resources, especially in New England. The region had excellent harbors that gave it access to the West Indies, Europe, and farther afield, where a developing maritime trade *(see pp24–5)* with the spices, teas, and other riches of the Far East proved increasingly lucrative. Indeed, New England ships became a familiar sight at docks from Nantucket *(see p153)* to New Guinea and from Portsmouth *(see pp252–3)* to Port-au-Prince, Haiti. New England also became a world center for the whaling

Antique harpoon

industry, as local ships plied the Seven Seas in search of the leviathans of the deep, which were killed for their oil, baleen, and blubber. The burgeoning shipbuilding industry that had sprung up along the coast also supplied a fleet of fishing boats that trolled the Grand Banks and the waters off Cape Cod, returning with their holds full of cod and halibut.

Ultimately it was an invention of the Industrial Revolution that transformed New England into an economic powerhouse. In the late 18th century, the first of Richard Arkwright's (1732–92) cotton spinning machines was imported to North America from England and installed on the Blackstone River at Pawtucket *(see pp172–3)*, Rhode Island. Previously cotton had been processed on individual looms in homes. Arkwright's device permitted cotton spinning to be carried out on factory-sized machines, which increased productivity a thousandfold. Soon mills sprang up, mainly in Massachusetts, in towns such as Lowell *(see pp142–3)*, Waltham, and Lawrence.

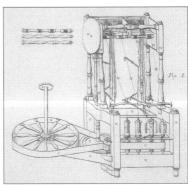
Richard Arkwright's sketch for his revolutionary cotton spinning machine

By the mid-19th century, New England held two-thirds of America's cotton mills. The region offered two main advantages: a ready supply of rivers to power the mills' machinery and an increasing flow of cheap labor. Escaping the Potato Famine in the 1840s, numerous Irish immigrants fled to Massachusetts, where the mill towns beckoned with dormitory housing for their employees. Despite their numbers, however, this group faced discrimination.

Irish peasant contemplating failed crop

In Boston many such newcomers settled in squalid tenements along the city's waterfront. Eventually the Irish would come to dominate Boston politics, but for much of the 19th century they faced a daily struggle just to survive.

The extent of industrialization was felt in a relatively small area of New England, mostly Massachusetts, Rhode Island, and Connecticut. In the hinterland of Vermont, New Hampshire, and Maine, farming and logging remained the key industries well into the 20th century. These far-flung regions provided some of the manpower for the heartland's factories, as people left the hardscrabble life of subsistence farming for new lives farther south. Northern New England also helped supply the factories with some of their raw materials. The forests of Vermont, for example, were hacked down to make grazing land for sheep, which supplied wool for the textile mills.

ABOLITIONIST NEW ENGLAND

New England's role in 19th-century America was not merely one of economic powerhouse. The region also dominated the fields of education, science, politics, and architecture, as well as serving as the cultural heart of the nation, with Boston and its environs producing some of the nation's most influential writers and thinkers. The Massachusetts capital was also the center of a prominent protest against slavery, which was firmly entrenched in the southern states and reviled in much of the North.

William Lloyd Garrison (1805–79) began publishing a newspaper called *The Liberator* in 1831. In Garrison's view, "There is only one theme which should be dwelt upon till our whole country is free from the curse – SLAVERY." His polemics in *The Liberator* drew the wrath of pro-slavery forces. The House of Representatives of the southern state of Georgia offered $5,000 for his arrest. But Garrison continued publishing his newspaper, never missing an issue until it ceased publication at the end of the Civil War (1861–65), when slavery had been expunged from American society.

Some residents of New England towns went beyond merely reading and writing about the injustices of slavery. Stirred by Garrison and the so-called abolitionist movement, some antislavery exponents offered safe houses for what came to be known as the Underground Railroad. This loosely

Abolitionist William Lloyd Garrison

TIMELINE

Colt six-shooters

	1835 Connecticut's Samuel Colt invents the six-shooter handgun	**1851–2** *Uncle Tom's Cabin* appears in serial form in *The National Era* newspaper		**1861** Civil War begins
1830		**1845**		**1860**
1831 Abolitionist William Lloyd Garrison publishes first edition of antislavery newspaper *The Liberator*		**1840** Ireland's first Potato Famine devastates country	**1851** Herman Melville publishes *Moby-Dick*, written in the southern Berkshires	**1865** Civil War ends, leaving some 620,000 Americans dead

connected network of escape routes helped slaves fleeing the South make their way to freedom in the North and in Canada, beyond the reach of slave hunters. Towns such as New Bedford *(see p121)*, Massachusetts, Portland *(see pp280–83)*, Maine, and Burlington *(see pp232–5)*, Vermont, served as key "stations" on the slaves' road to freedom. The Underground Railroad was immortalized in Harriet Beecher Stowe's novel *Uncle Tom's Cabin; or, Life Among the Lowly* (1852).

DECLINING POWER

In the latter part of the 19th century there were signs that the days of New England's industrial preeminence were over. The transcontinental railroad had opened up the West to an army of new immigrants, which flooded in after the Civil War. The New World was a far, far bigger place than it had been when the Pilgrims landed, and the opportunities were boundless. The Great Plains encompassed thousands of square miles of arable land that New England farmers could only dream about. And for those looking for a more temperate climate, many other areas of the US now beckoned.

Meanwhile, the exploitation of natural resources and the development of new technologies were changing the face of industry. The discovery of petroleum meant that whale oil lost its economic importance, while steam engines offered a way of powering mills that no longer required river water-power – one of the natural advantages upon which the region had relied.

Cover of sheet music based on Harriet Beecher Stowe's *Uncle Tom's Cabin* by artist Louisa Corbauy

Child laborer in cotton spinning plant

These problems were compounded by the fact that local labor was organizing to fight for better pay and working conditions, driving some factories to move to the South where labor costs were cheaper. Between 1880 and 1923, the South's share of the cotton-weaving industry rose from 6 percent to almost 50 percent.

The call for unionization even reached into the ranks of the police force, sparking one of America's most bitter labor confrontations. In 1919 Boston's men in blue sought to affiliate themselves with the American Federation of Labor. The city's police commissioner refused the request, and the entire force went on strike. Boston was beset by a

1884 Mark Twain publishes *The Adventures of Huckleberry Finn*, a novel he wrote at his home in Hartford, Connecticut

Modern Red Sox fan

1875	1890	1910

1882 Massachusetts-born poet/philosopher Ralph Waldo Emerson dies

1897 Country's first subway is opened in Boston

1903 Boston Red Sox win first World Series baseball championship

Ralph Waldo Emerson

wave of crime and riots, prompting the governor to send in the militia. By the time order was restored, at least five people had been killed and dozens had been wounded.

The loss of New England's economic importance was accompanied by a wave of change in the social makeup of the region. What had long been a homogeneous society – largely Protestant and of English or Scottish descent – was transformed by a rapid influx of immigrants. By the turn of the 20th century more than two-thirds of the residents of Massachusetts had at least one parent born outside the country.

The Depression of the 1930s hit the inhabitants of New England particularly hard. Unemployment in some towns topped 40 percent and wages plunged dramatically. World War II provided a temporary boost to the economy as shipyards and munition factories worked overtime to provide the military with the tools of their trade. However, with the return of peace, New England struggled to find its way in the new postwar era, and its economy continued to have its difficulties. The glory

Women making shell casings in a munitions plant during World War II

days, at least economically speaking, seemed to be irretrievable.

NEW ENGLAND REBIRTH

Even in its worse decline, as factories crumbled and residents headed for greener pastures, New England still possessed advantages that set the stage for recovery. One important factor was its concentration of higher educational institutions *(see pp28–9)*. As the Manufacturing Age gave way to the Information Age beginning in the 1960s, knowledge and adaptability became increasingly valuable commodities. With their well-endowed

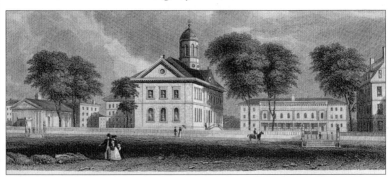

Unknown artist's depiction of Harvard University campus c.1857

TIMELINE

			1929 Stock market crash marks beginning of Great Depression			
Calvin Coolidge	1914–1918 World War I		*Depression soup kitchen*			
	1915	**1925**	**1935**	**1945**	**1955**	
	1923 Vermont's Calvin Coolidge is sworn in as country's 30th president by his father			**1939–45** World War II: US enters conflict in 1941	**1954** World's first nuclear submarine is built in Groton, Connecticut	

Falmouth Heights Beach in Cape Cod

England's stunning physical beauty: the craggy coastline of Maine, the beaches of Cape Cod *(see pp156–9)*, the picturesque Vermont villages, and the coiled-up mountains of New Hampshire. As America became more prosperous and its workers had more free time in which to spend their mounting disposable income, tourism became an even bigger business than manufacturing had once been. The skiers, fishermen, beachcombers, antique hunters, campers, and others who flocked to the Northeast year-round pumped billions of dollars into the states' economies. By the 1990s tourism ranked alongside manufacturing as one of New England's most profitable industries.

research facilities, venerable institutions such as Harvard University *(see pp112–17)* and the Massachusetts Institute of Technology *(see p111)* attracted a new generation of young entrepreneurs looking to cash in on this newest opportunity. Meanwhile a son of one of Boston's most prominent families was proving that New England's impact on the national political scene was not over yet. John F. Kennedy *(see pp104–5)*, the great-grandson of an Irish potato-famine immigrant, became American's first Catholic president in 1960.

John Fitzgerald Kennedy

Starting in the mid-1980s, companies producing computer software and biomedical technology set up shop in the Boston suburbs and southern New Hampshire. The meteoric growth of high-tech industries represented a second revolution of sorts – proving far more valuable than the Industrial Revolution of the previous century. Meanwhile certain businesses, such as the insurance trade, weathered the shifts in the economy better than traditional manufacturing ventures, with Hartford *(see pp198–201)*, Connecticut, continuing to serve as the insurance capital of the nation.

One thing that all the economic upheavals did not change was New

Somehow, it seems fitting. After all, it was the beauty of the area that had helped convince people such as John Smith, close to four centuries ago, that New England had a viable future. And now, that same natural beauty is proving to be both timeless and lucrative, helping to bring about a renaissance in the prosperity of the place where American society had begun so tenuously so many years before.

Vermont's trademark rural landscape

1961 Massachusetts-born John F. Kennedy becomes first Catholic president

1990 Thieves make off with artwork valued at $100 million from Boston's Isabella Stewart Gardner Museum

2000 Vermont becomes first state to legally recognize same-sex marriages

1960   1970   1980   1990   2000

1968 Senator Robert Kennedy is assassinated in Los Angeles

1999 John F. Kennedy, Jr. dies in plane crash off Martha's Vineyard

2004 Boston hosts Democratic National Convention

1963 President Kennedy is assassinated in Dallas

Robert F. Kennedy

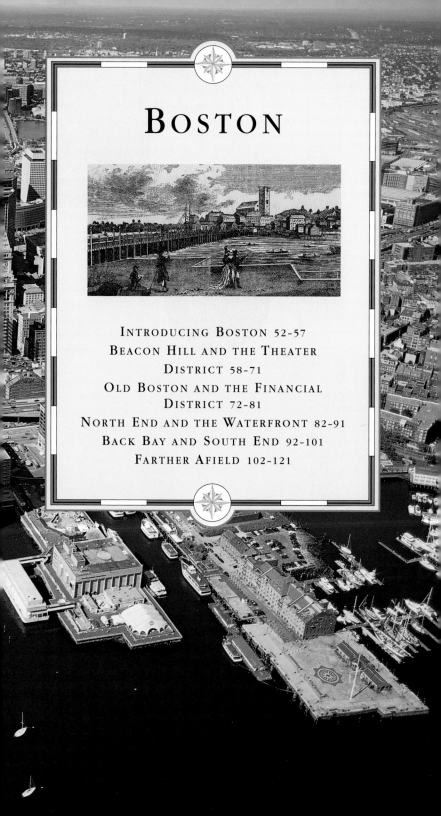

BOSTON

Boston's Best

THE CITY OF BOSTON's Athenian self-image is manifested in dozens of museums, galleries, and archives, paramount of which is the Museum of Fine Arts. The city's importance in America's history has left it with an unique legacy of old buildings, with much fine religious and civic architecture, including Trinity Church and Massachusetts State House. This strong architectural heritage continues to the present day, and includes modern structures such as the John Hancock Tower. Boston's wealth of sights, along with its many parks and gardens, make it a fascinating city to explore.

Boston Common and Public Garden
At the heart of the city, the spacious common, and smaller, more formal Public Garden, provide open space for both sport and relaxation.

Trinity Church
Perhaps Boston's finest building, this Romanesque Revival masterpiece by Henry Hobson Richardson was completed in 1877.

John Hancock Tower
Dominating the Back Bay skyline, with its mirrored façade reflecting the surroundings, the John Hancock Tower is New England's tallest building.

Museum of Fine Arts
One of the largest museums in North America, the M.F.A. is famous for its Egyptian, Greek, and Roman art, and French Impressionist paintings.

Old State House
The seat of British colonial government until independence, the building later undertook many different uses. It now houses a museum on the revolution.

Old North Church
Dating from 1723, this is Boston's oldest surviving church. Due to its role in the Revolution, it is also one of the city's most important historical sites.

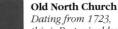

New England Aquarium
This aquarium displays a huge array of creatures from the world's oceans. Researchers here are also involved in key international fish and whale conservation programs.

0 kilometers 0.5

0 miles 0.5

Massachusetts State House
Built in the 1790s as the new center of state government, the Charles Bulfinch-designed State House sits imposingly at the top of Beacon Hill.

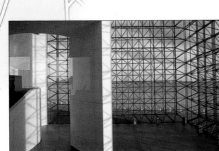

John F. Kennedy Library and Museum
The nation's 35th president is celebrated here in words and images – video clips of the first president to fully use the media make this a compelling museum.

The Freedom Trail

From Boston Common to Paul Revere House

Boston has more sites directly related to the American Revolution than any other city. The most important of these sites, as well as some relating to other freedoms gained by Bostonians, have been linked together as "The Freedom Trail." This 2.5-mile (4-km) walking route, marked in red on the sidewalks, starts at Boston Common and eventually ends at Bunker Hill in Charlestown. This first section weaves its way through the central city and Old Boston.

Elegant Georgian steeple of Park Street Church

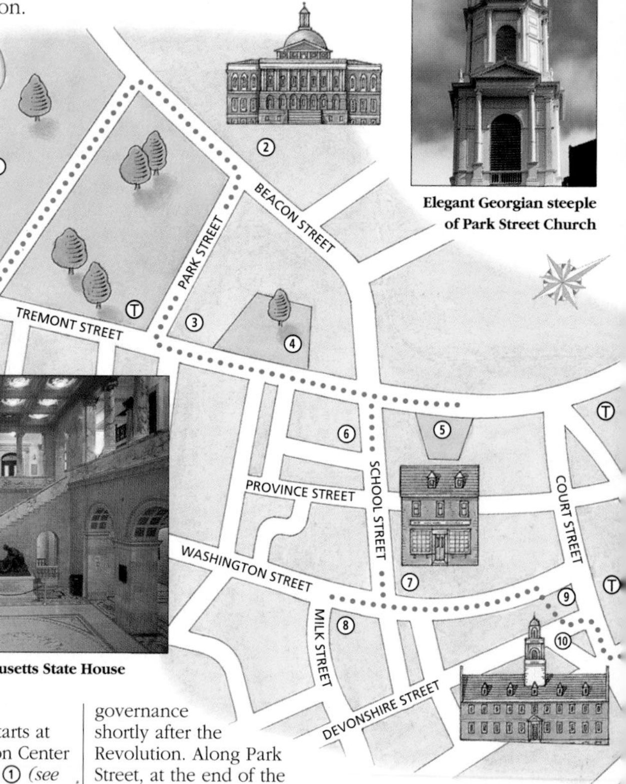

Nurses Hall in Massachusetts State House

Central City

The Freedom Trail starts at the Visitor Information Center on Boston Common ① *(see pp64–5)*. This is where angry colonials rallied against their British masters and where the British forces were encamped during the 1775–76 military occupation. Political speakers still expound from their soapboxes here, and the Common remains a center of much activity.

Walking toward the northwest corner of the Common gives a great view of the Massachusetts State House ② *(see p68–9)* on Beacon Street, designed by Charles Bulfinch as the new center of state governance shortly after the Revolution. Along Park Street, at the end of the Common, you will come to Park Street Church ③ *(see p66)*, built in 1810 and a bulwark of the antislavery movement. The church took the place of an old grain storage facility, which in turn gave its name to the adjacent Granary Burying Ground ④, one of Boston's earliest cemeteries and the final resting place of patriots John Hancock and Paul Revere *(see p120)*. Continuing along Tremont Street you will come to King's Chapel and Burying Ground ⑤ *(see p76)*. The tiny cemetery is Boston's oldest, containing, among others, the grave of city founder John Winthrop. As the name suggests, King's Chapel was the principal Anglican church in Puritan Boston, and more than half of its congregation fled to Nova Scotia at the outbreak of the Revolution. The box pew on the right just inside the front entrance was reserved for condemned prisoners to hear their last sermons before going to the gallows on Boston Common.

Heart of Old Boston

Head back along Tremont Street and turn down School Street, where a hopscotch-like mosaic embedded in the sidewalk commemorates the site of the First Public School ⑥, established in 1635. At the bottom of the street is the Boston Globe Store ⑦ *(see p77)*, a landmark more associated with Boston's literary emergence of 1845–65 than with the Revolution.

The Old South Meeting House ⑧, a short way to the south on Washington Street, is a graceful, white-spired brick church, modeled on Sir Christopher Wren's English country churches. As one of the largest meeting halls in Revolutionary Boston, "Old South's" rafters rang with many a fiery speech urging revolt against the British. A few blocks along, the Old State House ⑨ presides over the head of State Street. The colonial government building, it also served as the first state legislature, and the merchants' exchange in the basement was where Boston's colonial shipping fortunes were made. The square in front of the Old State House is the Boston Massacre Site ⑩, where British soldiers opened fire on a taunting mob in 1770, killing five and providing ideal propaganda for revolutionary agitators.

Follow State Street down to Congress Street and turn left to reach Faneuil Hall ⑪, called the "Cradle of Liberty" for the history of patriotic speeches made in its public meeting hall. Donated to the city by Huguenot merchant Peter Faneuil, the building was built primarily as Boston's first central marketplace.

The red stripe of the Freedom Trail comes in handy when negotiating the way to the North End and the Paul Revere House ⑫ on North Square. Boston's oldest house, it was home to the man known for his famous "midnight ride" *(see p120)*.

Tips for Walkers

Starting point: *Boston Common. Maps available at Boston Common Visitor Center.*
Length: *2.5 miles (4 km).*
Getting there: *Park Street Station (T Green and Red lines) to start. State (Orange and Blue lines) and Haymarket (Orange and Green lines). T stations also on route. Follow red stripe on sidewalk for the full route.*

Faneuil Hall, popularly known as "the Cradle of Liberty"

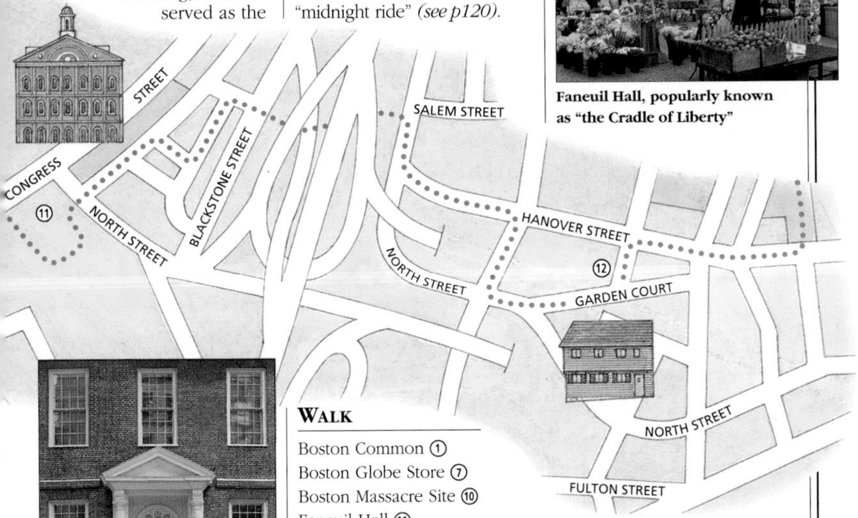
STREET
CONGRESS
⑪
NORTH STREET
BLACKSTONE STREET
SALEM STREET
HANOVER STREET
NORTH STREET
⑫
GARDEN COURT
NORTH STREET
FULTON STREET

Old State House, the seat of colonial government

Walk

Boston Common ①
Boston Globe Store ⑦
Boston Massacre Site ⑩
Faneuil Hall ⑪
First Public School Site ⑥
Granary Burying Ground ④
King's Chapel and Burying Ground ⑤
Massachusetts State House ②
Old South Meeting House ⑧
Old State House ⑨
Park Street Church ③
Paul Revere House ⑫

0 meters 250
0 yards 250

Key

••• Walk route
[T] Subway
ℹ Tourist information

The Freedom Trail

From Old North Church to Bunker Hill Monument

Dᴵꜱᴛᴀɴᴄᴇꜱ ʙᴇɢɪɴ to stretch out on the second half of the Freedom Trail as it meanders through the narrow streets of the North End, then continues over the Charles River to Charlestown, where Boston's settlers first landed. The sites here embrace two wars – the War of Independence and the War of 1812.

View from Copp's Hill terrace, at the edge of Copp's Hill Burying Ground

The North End
Following the Freedom Trail through the North End, allow time to try some of the Italian cafés and bakeries along the neighborhood's main thoroughfare, Hanover Street. Cross through the Paul Revere Mall to reach Old North Church ⑬ (see p87), whose spire

Gravestone at Copp's Hill Burying Ground

is instantly visible over the shoulder of the statue of Paul Revere on horseback. Sexton Robert Newman hung two lanterns in the belfry here, signaling the advance of British troops on Lexington and Concord in 1775. The church retains its 18th-century interior, including the traditional box pews.

The crest of Copp's Hill lies close by on Hull Street. Some of Boston's earliest gallows stood here, and Bostonians would gather in boats below to watch the hangings of heretics and pirates. Much of the hilltop is covered by Copp's Hill

Burying Ground ⑭. This was established in 1660, and the cemetery holds the remains of several generations of the Mather family – Boston's influential 17th- and 18th-century theocrats – as well as the graves of many soldiers of the Revolution. Boston's first free African American community, "New Guinea," covered the west side of Copp's Hill. A broken column marks the grave of Prince Hall, head of the Black Masons, distinguished veteran of the Revolution, and prominent political leader in the early years of the Republic. The musketball-chipped tombstone of patriot Daniel Malcolm records that he asked to be buried "in a stone grave 10 feet deep" to rest beyond the reach of British gunfire.

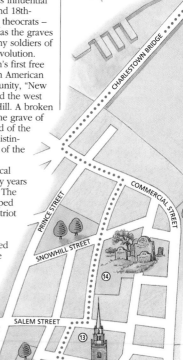

Traditional box pews inside Old North Church

Wᴀʟᴋ

Bunker Hill Monument ⑰
Bunker Hill Pavilion ⑮
Charlestown Navy Yard and
   the USS *Constitution* ⑯
Copp's Hill Burying Ground ⑭
Old North Church ⑬

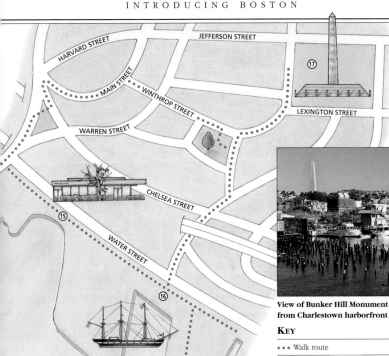

View of Bunker Hill Monument from Charlestown harborfront

KEY

● ● ● Walk route

0 meters   250

0 yards   250

Charlestown

The iron bridge over the Charles River that links the North End in Boston with City Square in Charlestown dates from 1899. Across the bridge, turn right along Constitution Road, following signs to Bunker Hill Pavilion ⑮, a privately sponsored multimedia show about the first pitched battle of the Revolution, fought here in 1775. The visitors' center for the nearby Charlestown Navy Yard ⑯ shares the building, and it is worth visiting to get an overview of the site. The colonial navy had been no match for the might of Britain's naval forces during the Revolution, and building a more formidable naval force became a priority. This was one of several shipyards that were set up around 1800. Decommissioned in 1974, the yard is now maintained by the National Park Service.

Lion carving, USS Constitution

Lying at her berth alongside Pier 1, the USS *Constitution* is probably the most famous ship in US history and still remains the flagship of the US Navy. Built at Hartt's shipyard in the North End, she was completed in 1797. In the War of 1812, she earned the nickname "Old Ironsides" for the resilience of her live oak hull against cannon fire. Fully restored for her bicentennial, the *Constitution* occasionally sails under her own power.

The granite obelisk that towers above the Charlestown waterfront is Bunker Hill Monument ⑰, commemorating the battle of June 17, 1775 that ended with a costly victory for British forces against an irregular colonial army, which finally ran out of ammunition. British losses were so heavy, however, that the battle would presage future success for the colonial forces. As a monument to the first large-scale battle of the Revolution, the obelisk, based on those of ancient Egypt, was a prototype for others across the US.

Defensive guns at Charlestown Navy Yard with view of the North End

Beacon Hill and the Theater District

By the 1790s, the south slope of Beacon Hill, facing Boston Common, had become the main seat of Boston's wealth and power. The north slope and the land up to the Charles River, known as the West End, was much poorer. Urban renewal has now cleared the slums of the West End, and the gentrification of Beacon Hill has made this one of Boston's most desirable neighborhoods. The area south of Boston Common is more down-to-earth, and home to the city's Theater District.

Sights at a Glance

Historic Streets and Squares

Bay Village [17]
Beacon Street [6]
Charles Street [1]
Chinatown [16]
Downtown Crossing [14]
Louisburg Square [2]
Mount Vernon Street [3]

Historic Buildings, Museums, and Theaters

African Meeting House [12]
Boston Athenaeum [10]
Colonial Theater [15]
Hepzibah Swan Houses [5]
Massachusetts State House pp68–9 [11]
Museum of Science and Science Park [13]
Nichols House Museum [4]
Park Street Church [8]
Shubert Theater [18]
Wang Center for the Performing Arts [19]

Parks and Cemeteries

Boston Common and Public Garden [7]
Granary Burying Ground [9]

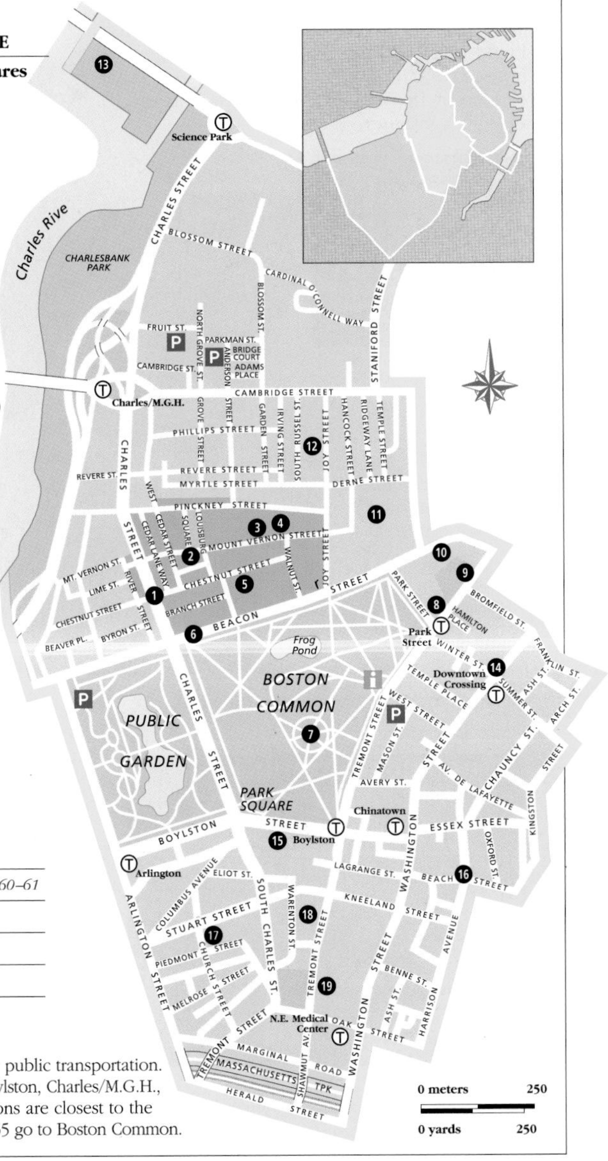

Key

Street-by-Street map *see pp60–61*
[T] "T" station
[i] Tourist information
[P] Parking

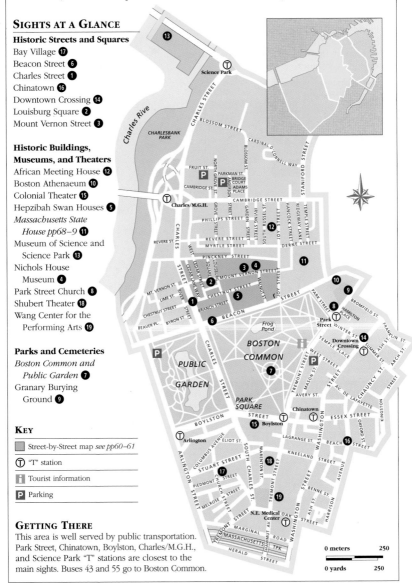

Getting There

This area is well served by public transportation. Park Street, Chinatown, Boylston, Charles/M.G.H., and Science Park "T" stations are closest to the main sights. Buses 43 and 55 go to Boston Common.

◁ **Front view of the Massachusetts State House, seen from Boston Common**

Street-by-Street: Beacon Hill

Lion door knocker, Beacon St.

FROM THE 1790s TO THE 1870s, the south slope of Beacon Hill was Boston's most sought-after neighborhood – its wealthy elite decamped only when the more exclusive Back Bay (*see pp92–101*) was built. Many of the district's houses were designed by Charles Bulfinch and his disciples, and the south slope evolved as a textbook example of Federal architecture. Elevation and view were all, and the finest homes are either on Boston Common or perched near the top of the hill. Early developers abided by a gentleman's agreement to set houses back from the street, but the economic depression of 1807–12 resulted in row houses being built right out to the street.

Cobblestone street, once typical of Beacon Hill

Louisburg Square
The crowning glory of the Beacon Hill district, this square was developed in the 1830s. Today, it is still Boston's most desirable address **2**

Charles Street Meeting House was built in the early 18th century to house a congregation of Baptists.

KEY

--- --- --- Suggested route

DE LUCA'S MARKET
"FRESHEST BY FAR SINCE 1905"

★ **Charles Street**
This elegant street is the main shopping area for Beacon Hill. Lined with upscale grocers and antique stores, it also has some fine restaurants **1**

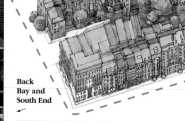

Back Bay and South End

STAR SIGHTS
★ **Charles Street**
★ **Nichols House Museum**

★ **Nichols House Museum**
This modest museum offers an insight into the life of Beacon Hill resident Rose Nichols, who lived here from 1885 to 1960 ❹

LOCATOR MAP
See Street Finder map 1

| 0 meters | 50 |
| 0 yards | 50 |

Mount Vernon Street
Described in the 19th century as the "most civilized street in America," this is where the developers of Beacon Hill (the Mount Vernon Proprietors) chose to build their own homes ❸

→ **Massachusetts State House**

Boston Common

Hepzibah Swan Houses
Elegant in their simplicity, these three Bulfinch-designed houses were wedding gifts for the daughters of a wealthy Beacon Hill proprietress ❺

Beacon Street
The finest houses on Beacon Hill were invariably built on Beacon Street. Elegant, Federal-style mansions, some with ornate reliefs, overlook the city's most beautiful green space, Boston Common ❻

Charles Street, lined with shops catering to the residents of Beacon Hill

Charles Street ❶

Map 1 B4. ⓣ *Charles/ MGH.*

THIS STREET originally ran along the bank of the Charles River, although subsequent landfill has removed it from the riverbank by several hundred feet. The main shopping and dining area of the Beacon Hill neighborhood, the curving line of Charles Street hugs the base of Beacon Hill, giving it a quaint, village-like air. Many of the houses remain residential on the upper stories, while street level and cellar levels were converted to commercial uses long ago. Though most of Charles Street dates from the 19th century, widening in the 1920s meant that some of the houses on the west side acquired new façades. The Charles Street Meeting House, designed by Asher Benjamin in 1804, was built for a Baptist congregation that practiced immersion in the then adjacent river. It is now a commercial building. Two groups of striking Greek Revival row houses are situated at the top of Charles

Street, between Revere and Cambridge Streets. Charles Street was one of the birthplaces of the antique trade in the US and now has some two dozen antique dealers.

Louisburg Square ❷

Map 1 B4. ⓣ *Charles/ MGH, Park Street.*

HOME TO millionaire politicians, best-selling authors, and corporate moguls, Louisburg Square is perhaps Boston's most prestigious address. Developed in the 1830s as a shared private preserve on Beacon Hill, the square's tiny patch of greenery surrounded by a high iron fence sends a clear signal of the square's continued exclusivity. On the last private square in the city, the narrow, Greek

Revival bow-fronted town houses sell for a premium over comparable homes elsewhere on Beacon Hill. Even the on-street parking spaces are deeded. The traditions of Christmas Eve carol singing and candlelit windows are said to have begun on Louisburg Square. A statue of Christopher Columbus, presented by a wealthy Greek merchant in 1850, stands at its center.

Mount Vernon Street ❸

Map 1 B4. ⓣ *Charles/ MGH, Park Street.*

IN THE 1890s the novelist Henry James called Mount Vernon Street "the most civilized street in America," and it still retains that air of urbane culture. Most of the developers of Beacon Hill, who called themselves the Mount Vernon Proprietors, chose to build their private homes along this street. Architect Charles Bulfinch envisioned Beacon Hill as a district of large freestanding mansions on spacious landscaped grounds, but building costs ultimately dictated much denser development. The sole remaining example of Bulfinch's vision is the Second Harrison Gray Otis House, built in 1800 at No. 85 Mount Vernon Street. The current Greek Revival row houses next door (Nos. 59–83), graciously set back from the street by 30 ft (9 m), were built to replace the single mansion belonging to Otis's chief development partner, Jonathan Mason. The original mansion was torn down after Mason's death in 1836. The three Bulfinch-designed houses at Nos. 55, 57, and 59 Mount Vernon Street were built by Mason for his daughters. No. 55 was ultimately passed on to the Nichols family *(see p63)* in 1883.

Columbus Statue, Louisburg Square

OLIVER WENDELL HOLMES AND THE BOSTON BRAHMINS

In 1860, Oliver Wendell Holmes wrote that Boston's wealthy merchant class of the time constituted a Brahmin caste, a "harmless, inoffensive, untitled aristocracy" with "their houses by Bulfinch, their monopoly on Beacon Street, their ancestral portraits and Chinese porcelains, humanitarianism, Unitarian faith in the march of the mind, Yankee shrewdness, and New England exclusiveness." So keenly did he skewer the social class that the term has persisted. In casual usage today, a Brahmin is someone with an old family name, whose finances derive largely from trust funds, and whose politics blend conservatism with *noblesse oblige* toward those less fortunate. Boston's Brahmins founded most of the hospitals, performing arts bodies, and museums of the greater metropolitan area.

Oliver Wendell Holmes (1809–94)

Drawing room of the Bulfinch-designed Nichols House Museum

Nichols House Museum ➍

55 Mount Vernon St. **Map** 1 B4.
📞 *(617) 227-6993.* Ⓣ *Park Street.*
🕐 *May–Oct: noon–4pm Tue–Sat;
Nov–Apr: noon–4pm Thu–Sat.*
⬤ *Jan.* 🖼 🚫 📷

THE NICHOLS HOUSE MUSEUM was designed by Charles Bulfinch in 1805 and offers a rare glimpse into the tradition-bound lifestyle of Beacon Hill. Modernized in 1830 by the addition of a Greek Revival portico, the house is nevertheless a superb example of Bulfinch's domestic architecture. It also offers an insight into the life of a true Beacon Hill character. Rose Standish Nichols moved into the house at 13 when her father purchased it in 1883. She left it as a museum in her 1960 will. A woman ahead of her time,

strong-willed and famously hospitable, Nichols was, among other things, a self-styled landscape designer who traveled extensively around the world to write about gardens.

Hepzibah Swan Houses ➎

13, 15 & 17 Chestnut St. **Map** 1 B4.
Ⓣ *Park Street.* ⬤ *to the public.*

THE ONLY WOMAN who was ever a member of the Mount Vernon Proprietors *(see p62)*, Mrs. Swan had these houses built by Bulfinch as wedding presents for her daughters in 1806, 1807, and 1814. Some of the most elegant and distinguished houses on Chestnut Street, they are backed by Bulfinch-designed stables that face onto Mount Vernon Street. The deeds restrict the height of the stables to 13 ft (4 m) so that her daughters would still have a view over Mount Vernon Street. In 1863–65, No. 13 was home to Dr. Samuel Gridley Howe, abolitionist and educational pioneer who, in 1833, founded the first school for the blind in the US.

Beacon Street ➏

Map 1 B4. Ⓣ *Park Street.*

BEACON STREET IS LINED with urban mansions facing Boston Common. The 1808 William Hickling Prescott House at No. 55, designed by Asher Benjamin, offers tours of rooms in Federal, Victorian, and Colonial Revival styles on Wednesdays, Thursdays, and Saturdays between April and October. The American Meteorological Society in No. 45 was built as Harrison Gray Otis's last and finest house. It had 11 bedrooms and an elliptical room behind the front parlor, where the walls and even the doors are curved.

The elite Somerset Club stands at No. 42–43 Beacon Street. Between the 1920s and. the 1940s, Irish Catholic mayor James Michael Curley would lead election night victory marches to the State House, pausing at the Somerset Club to taunt the Boston Brahmins inside.

The Parkman House at No. 33 Beacon Street is now a city-owned meeting center. It was the home of Dr. George Parkman, who was murdered by Harvard professor and fellow socialite Dr. John Webster in 1849. Boston society was torn apart when the presiding judge, a relative of Parkman, sentenced Webster to be hanged.

Elegant Federal-style houses on Beacon Street, overlooking Boston Common

Boston Common and Public Garden ❼

Acquired by Boston in 1634 from first settler William Blackstone, the 48-acre (19-ha) Boston Common served for two centuries as common pasture, military drill ground, and gallows site. British troops camped here during the 1775–76 military occupation. As Boston grew in the 19th century, the Boston Common became a center for open-air civic activity and remains so to this day. By contrast, the 24-acre (10-ha) Public Garden is more formal. When the Charles River mudflats were first filled in the 1830s, a succession of landscape plans were plotted for the Public Garden before the city chose the English-style garden scheme of George F. Meacham in 1869. The lagoon was added to the garden two years later.

The Public Garden, a popular green space in the heart of the city

Make Way for Ducklings
Based on the classic children's story by Robert McCloskey, this sculpture is of a duck and her brood of ducklings.

The Ether Monument memorializes the first use of anesthesia in 1846.

★ George Washington Statue
Cast by Thomas Ball from bronze, with a solid granite base, this is one the finest memorial statues in Boston. It was dedicated in 1869.

Lagoon Bridge
This miniature, ornamental bridge over the Public Garden lagoon was designed by William G. Preston in 1869 in a moment of whimsy. The lagoon it "spans" was constructed in 1861.

Statue of Reverend William Ellery Channing

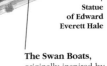

Statue of Edward Everett Hale

The Swan Boats, originally inspired by Wagner's *Löhengrin,* have been a feature of the Public Garden lake since 1877.

CHARLES STREET

★ **Shaw Memorial**
This relief immortalizes the Civil War's 54th regiment of Massachusetts Infantry, the first free black regiment in the Union Army, and their white colonel Robert Shaw.

VISITORS' CHECKLIST

Map 1 B4. Ⓣ *Park Street, Boylston Street, Arlington.*
🕐 *24 hrs.* **Visitors' Center** *146 Tremont St; (617) 426-3115.*
🕐 *8:30am–5pm Mon–Fri, 9am–5pm Sat–Sun.* **Swan Boats**
Boston Public Garden. 📞 *(617) 522-1966.* 🕐 *Jun–Aug: 10am–5pm daily; mid-May and Sep: 10am–4pm daily.* 📷
🌐 *www.bostonusa.com*

The Soldiers and Sailors Monument,
erected in 1877, features prominent
Bostonians from the time
of the Civil War.

**Blackstone
Memorial
Tablet** recalls
the purchase
of the common
in 1634 and is
cited as proof
that it belongs
to the people.

**Park
Street
subway**

Brewer Fountain was purchased at the Paris expo of 1867.

Visitors' Center

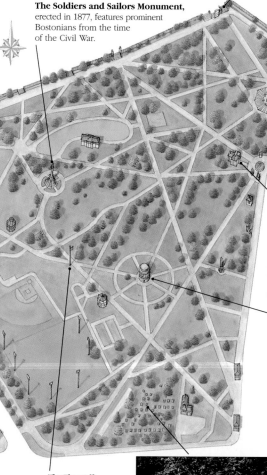

Parkman Bandstand
*This bandstand was built
in 1912 to memorialize
George F. Parkman, who
bequeathed $5 million
for the care of Boston
Common and other
parks in the city.*

**Central
Burying Ground**
*This graveyard, which
dates from 1756, holds
the remains of many
British and American
casualties from the
Battle of Bunker Hill
(1775). The portraitist
Gilbert Stuart is also
buried here.*

The Flagstaff

0 meters	100
0 yards	100

STAR FEATURES

★ **Shaw Memorial**

★ **George Washington
Statue**

Park Street Church at the corner of Tremont and Park Streets

Park Street Church ➑

1 Park St. **Map** 1 C4. (617) 523-3383. Park Street. Jul–Aug: 9am–3pm Tue–Sat; Sep–Jun: by appointment. Jul–Aug: 8:30am, 11am, 5:30pm Sun; Sep–Jun: 8:30am, 11am, 4:30pm, 5:30pm, 6:30pm Sun. www.parkstreet.org

Pᴀʀᴋ sᴛʀᴇᴇᴛ ᴄʜᴜʀᴄʜ's 217-ft (65-m) steeple has punctuated the intersection of Park and Tremont Streets since its dedication in 1810. Designed by English architect Peter Banner, who adapted a design by the earlier English architect Christopher Wren, the church was commissioned by parishioners wanting to establish a Congregational church in the heart of Boston. The church was, and still is, one of the city's most influential pulpits.

Contrary to popular belief, the sermons of Park Street ministers did not earn the intersection the nickname of "Brimstone Corner." Rather, the name came about because

during the war of 1812 the US militia, based in Boston, stored its gunpowder in the church basement as safekeeping against bombardment from the British navy.

In 1829, William Lloyd Garrison (1805–79), fervently outspoken firebrand of the movement to abolish slavery, gave his first abolition speech from the Park Street pulpit.

In 1849 a speech entitled *The War System of Nations* was addressed to the American Peace Society by Senator Charles Sumner. Much later, in 1893, the anthem *America the Beautiful* by Katharine Lee Bates debuted at a Sunday service. Today the church continues, as always, to be involved in religious, political, cultural, and humanitarian activities.

Granary Burying Ground ➒

Tremont Street. **Map** 1 C4. Park Street. 8am–4:30pm daily.

Nᴀᴍᴇᴅ ᴀꜰᴛᴇʀ the early grain storage facility that once stood on the adjacent site of Park Street Church, the Granary Burying Ground dates from 1660. Buried here were three important signatories to the Declaration of Independence – Samuel Adams, John Hancock, and Robert Treat Paine, along with Paul Revere, Benjamin Franklin's parents, merchant-philanthropist Peter Faneuil, and victims of the Boston Massacre.

The orderly array of gravestones, often featured in films and television shows set in Boston, is the result of modern groundskeeping. Few stones, if any, mark the actual burial site of the person memorialized. In fact, John Hancock may not be here at all. On the night he was buried in 1793, grave robbers cut off the hand with which he had signed his name to the Declaration of Independence, and some believe that the rest of his body was removed during 19th-century construction work.

Boston Athenaeum ➓

10½ Beacon St. **Map** 1 C4. (617) 227-0270. Park Street. 8:30am–8pm Mon, 8:30am–5:30pm Tue–Fri, 9am–4pm Sat. www.bostonathenaeum.org

Oʀɢᴀɴɪᴢᴇᴅ ɪɴ 1807, the collection of the Boston Athenaeum quickly became one of the country's leading private libraries. Sheep farmer Edward Clarke Cabot won the 1846 design competition to house the library, with plans for a gray sandstone building based on Palladio's Palazzo da Porta Festa in Vicenza, a building Cabot knew from a book in the Athenaeum's collection. The building was reopened in the fall of 2002 after having undergone extensive renovations. Among the Athenaeum's major holdings are the personal

Granary Burying Ground, final resting place for Revolutionary heroes

Stone frieze decoration on the Renaissance Revival-style Athenaeum

library that once belonged to George Washington and the theological library supplied by King William III of England to the King's Chapel *(see p76)*. In its early years the Athenaeum was Boston's chief art museum, but when the Museum of Fine Arts was proposed, it graciously donated much of its art, including unfinished portraits of George Washington purchased in 1831 from the widow of the painter Gilbert Stuart.

Massachusetts State House ⓫

See pp68–9.

African Meeting House ⓬

8 Smith Court. **Map** 1 C3.
🄲 *(617) 725-0022.*
Ⓣ *Park Street.* ☐ *Jun–Aug: 10am–4pm daily.* ⬤ *public hols.* 🈸 ✔
Ⓦ *www.afroammuseum.org*

BUILT FROM TOWN HOUSE plans by Asher Benjamin, the African Meeting House was dedicated in 1806. The oldest black church building in the US, it was the political and religious center of Boston's African American society. The interior is plain and simple but rang with the oratory of some of the 19th century's most fiery abolitionists: from Sojourner Truth and Frederick Douglass to William Lloyd Garrison, who founded the New England Anti-Slavery Society in 1832. The meeting house basement was Boston's

first school for African American children until the adjacent Abiel Smith School was built in 1831. When segregated education was barred in 1855, however, the Smith School closed. The meeting house became a Hasidic synagogue in the 1890s, as most of Boston's African American community moved to Roxbury and Dorchester. The synagogue closed in the 1960s, and in 1987 the African Meeting House reopened as the linchpin site on the Black Heritage Trail.

Museum of Science and Science Park ⓭

Science Park. **Map** 1 B2.
🄲 *(617) 723-2500.* Ⓣ *Science Park.* ☐ *Labor Day–July 3: 9am–5pm Sat–Thu, 9am–9pm Fri; July 4–Labor Day 9am–7pm Sat–Thu, 9am–9pm Fri.* ⬤ *Thanksgiving, Dec 25.* 🈸
🛗 🈸 Ⓦ *www.mos.org*

THE MUSEUM OF SCIENCE straddles the Charles River atop the flood control dam that sits at the mouth of the Charles River. The Science Park that has developed around it includes a large-format cinema and planetarium.

With more than 1,000 interactive exhibits covering natural history, medicine, astronomy, the physical sciences, and computing, the Science Museum is largely oriented to families. The Mugar Omni Theater contains a five-story domed screen with a multidimensional wrap-around sound system, and shows mostly educational films, usually with a natural science theme. The Charles Hayden Planetarium offers daily shows about stars, planets, and other celestial phenomena.

Holmes Alley, once an escape route for slaves on the run

BLACK HERITAGE TRAIL

In the first US census in 1790, Massachusetts was the only state to record no slaves. During the 19th century, Boston's substantial free African American community lived principally on the north slope of Beacon Hill and in the adjacent West End. The Black Heritage Trail links several key sites, ranging from the African Meeting House to several private homes, which are not open to visitors. Among them are the 1797 George Middleton House (Nos. 5–7 Pinckney Street), the oldest standing house built by African Americans on Beacon Hill, and the Lewis and Harriet Hayden House (No. 66 Phillips Street). Escaped slaves, the Haydens made their home a haven for runaways in the "Underground Railroad" of safe houses between the South and Canada. The walking tour also leads through mews and alleys, like Holmes Alley at the end of Smith Court, once used by fugitives to flee professional slave catchers.

Free tours of the Black Heritage Trail are led by National Park Service rangers – (617) 742-5415 – and are offered from Memorial Day weekend to Labor Day, 10am, noon, and 2pm daily, departing from the Robert Gould Shaw Memorial.

Massachusetts State House ⓫

THE CORNERSTONE OF the Massachusetts State House was laid on July 4, 1795, by Samuel Adams and Paul Revere. Completed on January 11, 1798, the Charles Bulfinch-designed center of state government served as a model for the US Capitol Building in Washington and as an inspiration for many of the state capitols around the country. Later additions were made, but the original building remains the archetype of American government buildings. Its dome, sheathed in copper and gold, serves as the zero mile marker for Massachusetts, making it, as Oliver Wendell Holmes *(see p63)* remarked, "the hub of the universe."

The State House, from Boston Common

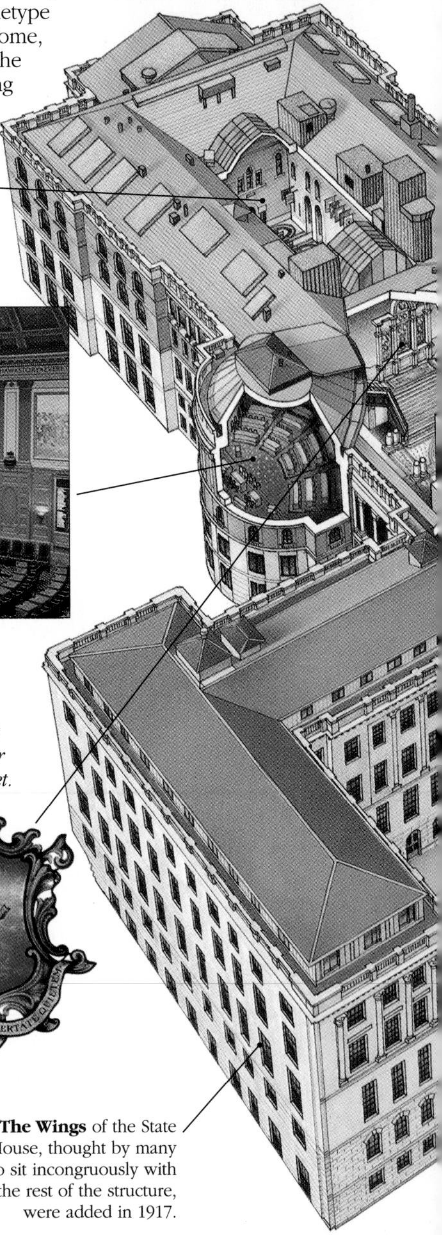

The Great Hall
is the latest addition to the State House. Built in 1990, it is lined with marble and topped by a glass dome, and is used for state functions.

★ House of Representatives
This elegant oval chamber was built for the House of Representatives in 1895. The Sacred Cod, which now hangs over the gallery, came to the State House when it first opened in 1798, and it has since hung over any place where the representatives have met.

Main Staircase
Beautiful stained-glass windows decorate the main staircase. They illustrate the varied state seals of Massachussets from its inception as a colony through to modern statehood.

STAR SIGHTS

★ Nurses Hall

★ House of Representatives

The Wings of the State House, thought by many to sit incongruously with the rest of the structure, were added in 1917.

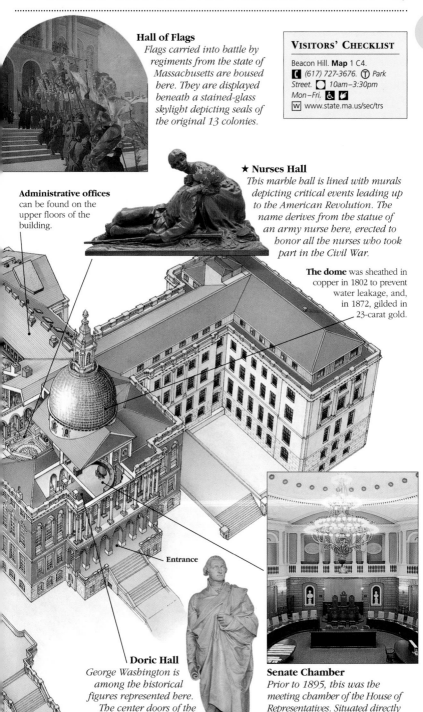

Hall of Flags
Flags carried into battle by regiments from the state of Massachusetts are housed here. They are displayed beneath a stained-glass skylight depicting seals of the original 13 colonies.

VISITORS' CHECKLIST

Beacon Hill. **Map** 1 C4.
📞 *(617) 727-3676.* Ⓣ *Park Street.* 🕐 *10am–3:30pm Mon–Fri.* ♿ 📷
Ⓦ *www.state.ma.us/sec/trs*

★ Nurses Hall
This marble hall is lined with murals depicting critical events leading up to the American Revolution. The name derives from the statue of an army nurse here, erected to honor all the nurses who took part in the Civil War.

Administrative offices
can be found on the upper floors of the building.

The dome was sheathed in copper in 1802 to prevent water leakage, and, in 1872, gilded in 23-carat gold.

Entrance

Doric Hall
George Washington is among the historical figures represented here. The center doors of the hall are opened only for a state governor at the end of his term or for a visiting head of state.

Senate Chamber
Prior to 1895, this was the meeting chamber of the House of Representatives. Situated directly beneath the State House's magnificent dome, the chamber features a beautiful sunburst ceiling, also designed by Charles Bulfinch.

Brattle Book Shop, a Boston literary landmark

Downtown Crossing ⓮

Washington, Winter & Summer Sts. **Map** 4 F1. Ⓣ *Downtown Crossing.*

A S AN ANTIDOTE to heavy traffic congestion, this shopping-district crossroads, at the intersection of Washington, Winter, and Summer Streets, was laid out as a pedestrian zone between 1975 and 1978. Downtown's department stores are the main focal points of the area, notably Macy's and Filene's, although the area also offers a range of other outlets, including bookstores, camera stores, and jewelers. Street vendors and summer lunchtime concerts create a lively scene.

The busy Macy's department store is one of a chain found throughout the US, with the most well-known store in New York. The Filene's empire has its heart in Boston, however, as it was founded here by William Filene in 1881. It is now the biggest and best-known department store in New England. The flagship store on Washington Street was completed in 1912 and is best known for its Bargain Basement, introduced in 1908. This became the store's trademark, and it is still operating, although it is no longer run by Filene's. There are remarkable bargains to be found, and you will see all kinds of Bostonians here, lured by the low prices.

Another well-known store in the area is Brattle Book Shop, just off Washington Street on West Street. Founded in 1825, this bibliophiles' treasure-house is packed with more than 250,000 used, rare, and out-of-print books, as well as back issues of magazines, maps, prints, postcards, and manuscripts. Outside the store are bins of bargain books priced between $1 and $5.

Colonial Theatre ⓯

106 Boylston St. **Map** 4 E2.
Ⓒ (617) 426-9366. Ⓣ *Boylston.*
Ⓞ *phone to check.* &
Ⓦ www.broadwayinboston.com

C LARENCE H. BLACKALL designed 14 Boston theaters during his architec-tural career, among them the Colonial, which is the city's oldest theater in continuous operation under the same name. Although plain outside, the interior is impressively opulent. Designed by H.B. Pennell, the Rococo lobby has chandeliers, gilded trim, and lofty arched ceilings. The audito-rium is decorated with figures, frescoes, and friezes.

Gilt cherub, the Colonial Theatre

The theater opened on December 20, 1900 with an extravagant performance of the melodrama *Ben Hur*. Today the theater is best remembered for premiering lavish musical productions, such as *Ziegfeld Follies*.

Chinatown ⓰

Bounded by Kingston, Kneeland, Washington & Essex Sts. **Map** 4 E2.
Ⓣ *Chinatown.*

T HIS AREA IS THE third largest Chinatown in the US after those in San Francisco and New York. Pagoda-topped telephone booths, as well as a three-story gateway guarded by four marble lions, set the neighborhood's Oriental tone.

The first 200 Chinese to settle in New England came by ship from San Francisco in 1870, recruited to break a labor strike at a shoe factory. Another wave of immigration from California in the 1880s was prompted by an economic boom that led to job openings in construction. Boston's Chinese colony was fully established by the turn of the 19th century. Political turmoil in China immediately following World War II, and more recent arrivals from Vietnam, Laos, Korea, Thailand, and Cambo-dia, have swelled Chinatown's population. Along with the area's garment and textile industries, restaurants, bakeries, food markets, and dispensers of Chinese medicine are espe-cially numerous along the main thoroughfare of Beach Street, as well as on Tyler, Oxford, and Harrison Streets.

Colorful August Moon Festival, held in Boston's Chinatown

Bay Village ⑰

Bounded by Tremont, Arlington & South Charles Sts. **Map** 4 D2. ⓣ *New England Medical Center, Boylston.*

Oﾞ RIGINALLY AN expanse of mud flats, the Bay Village area was drained in the early 1800s and initially became habitable with the construction of a dam in 1825. Many carpenters, cabinetmakers, artisans, and house painters involved in the construction of Beacon Hill's pricier town houses built their own modest but well-crafted residences here. As a result there are many similarities between the two neighborhoods.

Fayette Street was laid out in 1824 to coincide with the visit of the Marquis de Lafayette, the French general who allied himself with George Washington. Bay Street, located just off Fayette Street, features a single dwelling and is generally regarded as the city's shortest street. In 1809, poet and short-story writer Edgar Allen Poe was born in a boarding house on Carver Street, where his thespian parents were staying while in Boston on tour with a traveling theatrical company.

In the 1920s, at the height of the Prohibition era, clandestine speakeasies gave Bay Village its still-prevalent bohemian ambience. More recently, the neighborhood has become a center for Boston's gay community.

Bay Village's Piedmont Street is well known for the W. S. Haynes Company at No. 12, which has been hand-crafting flutes and piccolos since 1888, and has acquired among musicians a world-wide reputation for its instruments.

Shubert Theatre ⑱

265 Tremont St. **Map** 4 E2.
█ (617) 482-9393. ⓣ *Boylston, New England Medical Center.*
◯ *phone to check.* ♿
ⓦ www.wangcenter.org

Tﾞ HE 1,650-SEAT Shubert Theatre rivals the Colonial Theatre *(see p70)* for its long history of staging major pre-Broadway musical productions.

The vast Grand Lobby of the Wang Center for the Performing Arts

Designed by the architects Charles Bond and Thomas James, the theater features a white Neoclassical façade with a pair of Ionic columns flanking a monumental, Palladian-style window over the entrance. The theater first opened its doors in 1910, and during its heyday many stars walked the boards, including Sarah Bernhardt, W.C. Fields, Cary Grant, Mae West, Humphrey Bogart, Ingrid Bergman, Henry Ford, and Rex Harrison. Today, dance, theater, musicals, and opera are showcased here.

Wang Center for the Performing Arts ⑲

270 Tremont St. **Map** 4 E2.
█ (617) 482-9393. ⓣ *Boylston, New England Medical Center.*
◯ *phone to check.* ♿
ⓦ www.wangcenter.org

Oﾞ PENED IN 1925 as the Metropolitan Theatre and later named the Music Hall, New England's most ornate variety theater was inspired by the Paris Opera House, and was originally intended to be a movie theater. Designed by Clarence Blackall, the theater's auditorium was once one of the largest in the world. The theater was restored, transformed, and renamed as the Wang Center for the Performing Arts in 1983. The five-story Grand Lobby and seven-story auditorium are designed in Renaissance Revival style, with gold chandeliers, stained glass, ceiling murals, and jasper pillars.

Today the theater is used primarily as a venue for Broadway road shows, visiting opera productions, concerts, and motion-picture revivals. It is also the main performance venue for the prestigious Boston Ballet troupe.

THE HISTORY OF BOSTON'S THEATER DISTRICT

Boston's first theater opened in 1793 on Federal Street. Fifty years later, with patronage from the city's social elite, Boston had become a major tryout town and boasted a number of lavish theaters. The US premiere of Handel's *Messiah* opened in 1839, the US premiere of Gilbert and Sullivan's *H.M.S. Pinafore* in 1877, and the premiere of Tchaikovsky's *First Piano Concerto* in 1875. In the late 19th century theaters came under fire from the censorious Watch and Ward Society. Later, in the 20th century, dramas such as Tennessee Williams' *A Streetcar Named Desire* and Eugene O'Neill's *Long Day's Journey into Night* debuted here. Musicals included *Ziegfeld Follies*, Gershwin's *Porgy and Bess*, and works by Rodgers and Hammerstein.

A Streetcar Named Desire, starring a young Marlon Brando and Jessica Tandy

OLD BOSTON AND THE FINANCIAL DISTRICT

British Lion, Old State House

THIS IS AN AREA OF BOSTON where old and new sit one on top of the other. Some of its sights, situated in the older part of the district closest to Boston Common, predate the American Revolution. Much of what can be seen today, though, was built much more recently. The north of the district is home to Boston's late 20th-century, modernist-style City Hall and Government Center, while to the east is the city's bustling Financial District. This once formed part of Boston's harbor waterfront, a district built on mercantile wealth. Today, the wharves and warehouses have been replaced by skyscrapers belonging to banks, insurance companies, and high-tech industries.

SIGHTS AT A GLANCE

Historic Buildings and Churches

Boston Globe Store ❹
Custom House ❿
Faneuil Hall ❽
Government Center ❼
King's Chapel and Burying Ground ❷
Old City Hall ❸
Old South Meeting House ❺
Old State House pp78–9 ❻
Omni Parker House ❶
Quincy Market ❾
Verizon Building ⓫

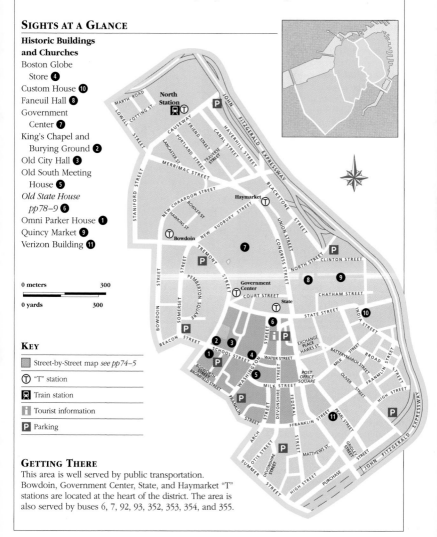

0 meters 300
0 yards 300

KEY

Street-by-Street map *see pp74–5*
Ⓣ "T" station
🚉 Train station
ℹ Tourist information
🅿 Parking

GETTING THERE

This area is well served by public transportation. Bowdoin, Government Center, State, and Haymarket "T" stations are located at the heart of the district. The area is also served by buses 6, 7, 92, 93, 352, 353, 354, and 355.

◁ **Custom House, Boston's original skyscraper and one of the most distinctive buildings on the city skyline**

Street-by-Street: Colonial Boston

AN IMPORTANT PART of Boston's Freedom Trail *(see pp54–7)* runs through this historic core of the city, the site of which predates American Independence. Naturally, the area is now dominated by more recent 19th- and 20th-century development, but glimpses of a colonial past are prevalent here and there in the Old State House, King's Chapel and its adjacent burying ground, and the Old South Meeting House. Newer buildings of interest include the Omni Parker House, as well as the towering skyscrapers of Boston's financial district, located on the northwest edges of this area.

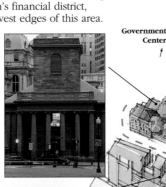

Irish Famine memorial, Washington Street

Government Center

SCHOOL STREET

PROVINCE STREET

★ King's Chapel and Burying Ground

A church has stood here since 1688, although the current building dates from 1749. The adjacent cemetery is the resting place of some of the most important figures in US history ②

Omni Parker House
This hotel (see p307) first opened its doors in 1855, then under-went many renovations. Famed for its opulence, the hotel also gained a reputation in the 19th century as a meeting place for Boston intellectuals. The current building was erected in 1927 ①

0 meters   50

0 yards   50

Old City Hall
This building served as Boston's City Hall from 1865 to 1969. Today it houses a number of offices and a trendy French restaurant ③

STAR SIGHTS

★ **Old South Meeting House**

★ **Old State House**

★ **King's Chapel and Burying Ground**

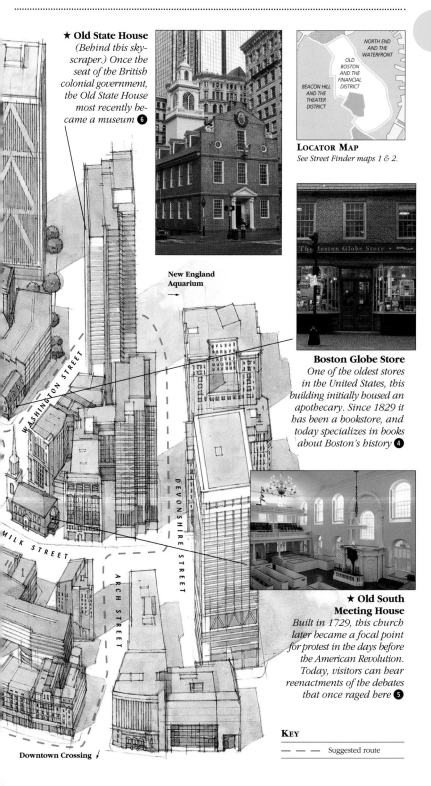

★ **Old State House**
(Behind this sky-
scraper.) Once the
seat of the British
colonial government,
the Old State House
most recently be-
came a museum **6**

LOCATOR MAP
See Street Finder maps 1 & 2.

NORTH END
AND THE
WATERFRONT

OLD
BOSTON
AND THE
FINANCIAL
DISTRICT

BEACON HILL
AND THE
THEATER
DISTRICT

New England
Aquarium →

Boston Globe Store
*One of the oldest stores
in the United States, this
building initially housed an
apothecary. Since 1829 it
has been a bookstore, and
today specializes in books
about Boston's history* **4**

WASHINGTON STREET

MILK STREET

ARCH STREET

DEVONSHIRE STREET

★ **Old South
Meeting House**
*Built in 1729, this church
later became a focal point
for protest in the days before
the American Revolution.
Today, visitors can hear
reenactments of the debates
that once raged here* **5**

KEY

– – – Suggested route

Downtown Crossing ✓

Omni Parker House ❶

60 School St. **Map** 1 C4.
☎ *(617) 227-8600.* Ⓣ *Park Street, State, Government Center.*
Ⓦ *www.omnihotels.com*

HARVEY D. PARKER, raised on a farm in Maine, became so successful as the proprietor of his Boston restaurant that he achieved his ambition of expanding the property into a first-class, grand hotel. His Parker House opened in 1855, with a façade clad in white marble, standing five stories high, and featuring the first passenger elevator ever seen in Boston. It underwent several, rapid transformations during its early years, with additions made to the main structure in the 1860s and a 10-story, French chateau-style annex completed later that century. The building saw many successive transform-ations, and its latest 14-story incarnation has stood across from King's Chapel on School Street since 1927.

This hotel attained an instant reputation for luxurious accommodations and fine, even lavish, dining, typified by 11-course menus prepared by a French chef.

Simply decorated, pure white interior of King's Chapel on Tremont Street

Among Parker House's many claims to fame are its Boston Cream Pie, which was first created here, and the word "scrod," a uniquely Bostonian term for the day's freshest seafood, still in common usage. Two former Parker House employees later became recognized for quite different careers. Vietnamese revolutionary leader Ho Chi Minh worked in the hotel's kitchens around 1915, while black activist Malcolm X was a busboy in Parker's Restau-rant in the 1940s.

King's Chapel and Burying Ground ❷

58 Tremont St. **Map** 1 C4.
☎ *(617) 523-1749.* Ⓣ *Park Street, State, Government Center.* ☐ *Jul–Aug: 9am–4pm Mon & Thu–Sat, 1–3pm Sun; Apr–Jun & Sep–Oct: 10am–3pm Mon, Fri & Sat; Nov–Mar: 10am–3pm Sat.* ✝ *11am Sun, 12:15pm Wed.* Ⓦ *www.kings-chapel.org*

BRITISH CROWN officials were among those who attend-ed Anglican services at the first chapel on this site, which was built in 1688. When New England's governor decided a larger church was needed, the present granite edifice – begun in 1749 – was constructed around the original wooden chapel, which was dismantled and heaved out the windows of its replacement. After the Revolution, the congregation's religious allegiance switched from Anglican to Unitarian. The sanctuary's raised pulpit – dating from 1717 and shaped like a wine glass – is one of the oldest in the US. High ceilings, open arches, and clear glass windows enhance the sense of spaciousness and light. The bell inside the King's Chapel is the largest ever cast by Paul Revere *(see p120)*.

Among those interred in the adjacent cemetery, Boston's oldest, are John Winthrop and Elizabeth Pain, the inspiration for adultress Hester Prynne in Nathaniel Hawthorne's moral-istic novel *The Scarlet Letter*.

PARKER HOUSE GUESTS

Boston's reputation as the "Athens of America" was widely acknowledged when members of a distinguished social club began meeting for lengthy dinners and lively intellectual exchanges in 1857. Their get-togethers took place on the last Saturday of every month at Harvey Parker's fancy new hotel. Regular participants included New England's literary elite *(see pp30–31)*: Henry Wadsworth Longfellow, Ralph Waldo Emerson, Nathaniel Hawthorne, and Henry David Thoreau, to name a few. Charles

John Wilkes Booth, infamous Parker House guest

Dickens participated while staying at the Parker House during his American speaking tours, and used his sitting-room mirror to rehearse the public readings he gave at Tremont Temple next door. The mirror now hangs on a mezzanine wall. In 1865, actor John Wilkes Booth, in town to see his brother, a fellow thespian, stayed at the hotel and took target practice at a nearby shooting gallery. Ten days later, at Ford's Theatre in Washington, he pulled a pistol and shot Abraham Lincoln.

Old City Hall ❸

45 School St. **Map** 2 D4.
📞 *Maison Robert: (617) 227-3370.*
Ⓣ *Park Street, State, Government Center.* ⭕ *Only restaurant and café open to public.*

AFINE EXAMPLE of French Second Empire architectural gaudiness, this was Boston's City Hall from 1865 to 1969 – it was superseded by the rakishly modern New City Hall structure at nearby Government Center *(see p80)*. The renovated 19th-century building now accommodates offices and an elegant French restaurant, Maison Robert *(see p329)*.

Previous occupants have included such flamboyant mayors as John "Honey Fitz" Fitzgerald and James Michael Curley. Statues here memorialize Josiah Quincy, Boston's second mayor, and Benjamin Franklin, who was born around the corner on nearby Milk Street.

19th-century French-style façade of Boston's Old City Hall

Boston Globe Store ❹

1 School St. **Map** 2 D4.
📞 *(617) 367-4000.* Ⓣ *Park Street, State, Government Center.*
⭕ *9am–6pm Mon–Fri, 9:30am–5pm Sat, 11am–4pm Sun.*
Ⓦ *www.globestore.boston.com*

ADORMERED GAMBREL roof crowns this brick landmark, which opened as Thomas Crease's apothecary shop in 1718 and was reestablished as the Old Corner Bookstore in 1829.

Moving in 16 years later, the Ticknor & Fields publishing company became a gathering place for a notable roster of authors: Emerson, Hawthorne, Longfellow, Thoreau, early feminist writer Margaret Fuller, and *Uncle Tom's Cabin* novelist, Harriet Beecher Stowe. The earliest editions of William Dean Howells' erudite *Atlantic Monthly* periodical were printed here – with Julia Ward Howe's rousing tribute to American Civil War bravado, *The Battle Hymn of the Republic*, first appearing in the February 1862 issue. Now owned and managed by the city's leading newspaper, the *Boston Globe*, the corner store specializes in books about Boston past and present.

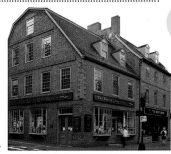

The Boston Globe Store, specializing in books about the history of Boston

Old South Meeting House ❺

310 Washington St. **Map** 2 D4.
📞 *(617) 482-6439.* Ⓣ *Park Street, State, Government Center.* ⭕ *Apr–Oct: 9:30am–5pm daily; Nov–Mar: 10am–4pm daily.* 🎦 ⭕ 🔖 🏠
Ⓦ *www.oldsouthmeetinghouse.org*

BUILT IN 1729 for Puritan religious services, this edifice, with a tall octagonal steeple, had colonial Boston's biggest capacity for town meetings – a fact capitalized upon by a group of rebellious rabble-rousers calling themselves the Sons of Liberty *(see p18)*. Their outbursts against British taxation and other royal annoyances drew increasingly large and vociferous crowds to the pews and upstairs galleries.

During a candlelit protest rally on December 16 1773, fiery speechmaker Samuel Adams flashed the signal that led to the Boston Tea Party *(see p77)* down at Griffin's Wharf several hours later. The British retaliated by turning Old South into an officers' tavern and stable for General John Burgoyne's 17th Lighthorse Regiment of Dragoons. Displays, exhibits, and a multimedia presentation entitled *Voices of Protest* relive those raucous days as well as more recent occurrences well into the 20th century. The Meeting House offers a series of lectures covering a wide range of New England topics and also holds chamber music concerts and other musical performances.

Directly across Washington Street, sculptor Robert Shure's memorial to the 1845–49 Irish Potato Famine was added to the small plaza here in 1998.

Nearby, at number one Milk Street, is Dreams of Freedom, a small, interactive museum that celebrates the city's multi-ethnicity. It also shows Boston's history as a port of entry for generations of immigrants, justifying its renown as a "Gateway to America."

Old South Meeting House, in stark contrast to the modern city

Old State House ❻

DWARFED BY THE TOWERS of the Financial District, this was the seat of British colonial government between 1713 and 1776. The royal lion and unicorn still decorate each corner of the eastern façade. After independence, the Massachusetts legislature took possession of the building, and it has had many uses since, including produce market, merchants' exchange, Masonic lodge, and Boston City Hall. Its wine cellars now function as a downtown subway station. The Old State House houses two floors of Bostonian Society memorabilia and a video presentation documenting the change from colony to republic.

Old State House amid the sky-scrapers of the Financial District

A gold sculpture of an eagle, symbol of America, can be seen on the west façade.

West Façade
A Latin inscription, relating to the first Massachusetts Bay colony, runs around the outside of this crest. The relief in the center depicts a local Native American.

Keayne Hall
This is named after Robert Keayne who, in 1658, gave £300 to the city so that the Town House, predating the Old State House, could be built. Exhibits in the room depict events from the Revolution.

Entrance

★ Central Staircase
A fine example of 18th-century workmanship, the central spiral staircase has two beautifully crafted wooden handrails. It is one of the few such staircases still in existence in the US.

SITE OF THE BOSTON MASSACRE

Cobbled circle: site of the Boston Massacre

A circle of cobblestones below the balcony on the eastern façade of the Old State House marks the site of the Boston Massacre. After the Boston Tea Party, this was one of the most inflammatory events leading up to the American Revolution. On March 5, 1770, an angry mob of colonists taunted British guardsmen with insults, rocks, and snowballs. The soldiers opened fire, killing five colonists. A number of articles relating to the Boston Massacre are exhibited inside the Old State House, including a musket found near the site and a coroner's report detailing the incident.

VISITORS' CHECKLIST

Washington and State Sts.
Map 2 D4. **C** *(617) 720-1713*
T *State.* **O** *9am–5pm daily.*
🖼 ✗ 🚶 ▯
W www.bostonhistory.org

The tower is a classic example of Colonial style. In 18th-century paintings and engravings it can be seen clearly above the Boston skyline.

British Unicorn and Lion
A royal symbol of Britain, the original lion and unicorn were torn down when news of the Declaration of Independence reached Boston in 1776.

★ **East Façade**
This façade has seen many changes. An earlier clock from the 1820s was removed in 1957 and replaced with an 18th-century replica of the sundial that once hung here. The clock has now been reinstated.

Council Chamber
Once the chambers for the royal governors, and from 1780 chambers for the first governor of Massachusetts (John Hancock), this room has seen many key events. Among them were numerous impassioned speeches made by Boston patriots.

The Declaration of Independence was read from this balcony in 1776. In the 1830s, when the building was City Hall, the balcony was enlarged to two tiers.

STAR SIGHTS

★ **East Façade**

★ **Central Staircase**

New City Hall and Government Center, a main city focal point

Government Center ❼

Cambridge, Court, New Sudbury & Congress Sts. **Map** 2 D3. Ⓣ *Government Center.*

THIS CITY CENTER development was built on the site of what was once Scollay Square, demolished as part of the trend for local urban-renewal that began in the early 1960s. This trend had already seen the building of the strikingly Modernist concrete and brick New City Hall, which stands on the eastern side of the square and houses government offices.

Some viewed the development as controversial; others did not lament what was essentially a disreputable cluster of saloons, burlesque theaters, tattoo parlors, and scruffy hotels. The overall master plan for Government Center was inspired by the outdoors vitality and spaciousness of Italian piazzas. Architects I.M. Pei & Partners re-created some of this feeling by surrounding Boston's new City Hall with a vast terraced plaza covering 56 acres (23 ha), paved with 1,800,000 bricks. Its spaciousness makes it an ideal place for events such as skateboard contests, political and sports rallies, food fairs, patriotic military marches, and concerts.

Faneuil Hall ❽

Dock Sq. **Map** 2 D3.
Ⓣ *Government Center, Haymarket, State.* **Great Hall** ◯ *9am–5pm daily.* ♿ 🏷 🎧

A GIFT TO Boston from the wealthy merchant Peter Faneuil in 1742, this Georgian, brick landmark has always functioned simultaneously as a public market and town meeting place. Master tinsmith Shem Drowne modeled the building's grasshopper weathervane after the one on top of the Royal Exchange in the City of London, England. Revolutionary gatherings packed the hall, and as early as 1763 Samuel Adams used the hall as a platform to suggest that the American colonies should unite against British oppression and fight to establish their independence; hence the building's nickname "Cradle of Liberty" and the bold posture of the statue of Sam Adams at the front of the building. Toward the end of the 18th century it became apparent that the existing Faneuil Hall could no longer house the capacity crowds that it regularly attracted. The commission to expand the building was undertaken by Charles Bulfinch, who completed the work from 1805 to 1806. The building then remained unchanged until 1898, when

Sam Adams statue, in front of Faneuil Hall

it was expanded even more according to long-standing Bulfinch stipulations. Faneuil Hall was restored in the 1970s as part of the wider redevelopment of Quincy Market.

Quincy Market ❾

Between Chatham & Clinton Sts. **Map** 2 D3. 🎔 *(617) 523-1300.* Ⓣ *Government Center, State.* ◯ *10am–9pm Mon–Sat, noon–6pm Sun.* ♿ 🅆 *www.faneuilhallmarketplace.com*

THIS IMMENSELY popular shopping and dining complex attracts nearly 14 million people every year. It was developed from the buildings of the old Quincy Market, which was the city's meat, fish, and produce market. These buildings had fallen into disrepair before they underwent a widely acclaimed restoration in the 1970s. The 535-ft (163-m) long Greek Revival-style colonnaded market hall is now filled with a selection of fast food stands and a comedy nightclub, located in the spectacular central Rotunda. Completing the ensemble are twin North and South Market buildings – these individual warehouses have also been refurbished to accommodate numerous boutiques, stores, restaurants, and pubs, as well as upstairs business offices.

Gallery of the Greek Revival main dome in Quincy Market's central hall

Custom House ❿

3 McKinley Square. **Map** 2 E3.
⌞ (617) 310-6300. Ⓣ Aquarium.
Museum ⃝ 8am–11pm daily. ⓦ
www.marriott.com/vacationclub

BEFORE LANDFILL altered
downtown topography,
early Boston's Custom House
perched at the water's edge.
A temple-like Greek Revival
structure with fluted Doric
columns, the granite building
had a skylit dome upon com-
pletion in 1847. Since 1915,
however, it has supported a
495 ft (150 m) tower with a
four-sided clock. For the best
part of the 20th century, the
Custom House was Boston's
only bona fide skyscraper.

The public has free access
to a small museum of maritime
history in the rotunda, with
objects on loan from the
Peabody Museum in Salem,
and to the observatory.

Telephone Men and Women at Work, **Verizon Building**

**Greek Revival Custom House tower,
one of Boston's most striking sights**

Verizon Building ⓫

185 Franklin St. **Map** 2 D4.
⌞ (617) 743-4747. Ⓣ State,
Aquarium. **Museum** ⃝ 24 hours
daily. ♿

DATING FROM 1947 and
overlooking the south
side of Post Office Square,
this Art Deco building is still
in use today. Dean Cornwell's
monumental 160-ft (49-m)
long *Telephone Men and
Women at Work* mural –
populated by 197 life-size
figures – has circled the lobby
since 1951 and is a truly remarkable work of art. The
small museum at street level
features an accurate restoration of Alexander Graham
Bell's Court Street laboratory,
complete with his tools,
books, workbench, and one

of his garret window-frames
overlooking a diorama of
Scollay Square. The exhibit
was constructed from parts
of Bell's original workshop,
put to one side and lovingly
preserved when the house
where he lived was demol-
ished in the 1920s. It was
opened on June 3, 1959,
coincidentally the 84th
anniversary of the invention
of the telephone. The world's
first commercial telephone
and first telephone switch-
board, both dating from May
1877, are also displayed in
the museum.

The beautifully landscaped
Post Office Square, on the
northern side of the Verizon
Building, is a small island of
green situated amid the
soaring skyscrapers of the
financial district. Vines climb
a 143-ft (44-m) long trellis
along one side of the park,
and a fountain made of green
glass cascades on the square's
Pearl Street side. A focal point
for the whole district, the
grassy square comes into its
own during the warmer
months of the year, when
office workers can be
seen sprawling across
its well-kept lawns.
The square is also
overlooked by down-
town's main post office,
housed in the John W.
McCormack courthouse
building, and Le Meridien
Hotel *(see p307)*, a classic
Renaissance Revival show-
piece completed in 1922.

ALEXANDER GRAHAM BELL (1847–1922)

A native of Edinburgh, Scotland, and son of a deaf
mother, Bell moved to Boston in 1871 to start a
career teaching speech to the deaf. Two years
later he was appointed as professor of vocal
physiology at Boston University. Bell worked
in his spare time on an apparatus for trans-
mitting sound by electrical current. History
was made on March 17, 1876, when Bell
called to his assistant in another room: "Mr.
Watson, come here. I want you." The first
demonstration of the "telephone" took place
in Boston on May 10, 1876, at the Academy
of Arts and Sciences. By 1878, he had set up
the first public telephone exchange in New
Haven, Connecticut.

NORTH END AND THE WATERFRONT

HIS WAS BOSTON's first neighborhood, and one that has been key to the city's fortunes. Fringed by numerous wharves, the area prospered initially through shipping and shipbuilding, with much of America's early trade passing through its warehouses. The more recent importance of finance and high-tech industries, however, has seen the waterfront evolve, its

Statue in Old North Church garden

old warehouses transformed into luxury apartment blocks and offices. Away from the waterfront, the narrow streets of the North End have historically been home to European immigrants, drawn by the availability of work. The area today is populated largely by those of Italian descent, whose many cafés, delis, and restaurants make it one of the city's most distinct communities.

SIGHTS AT A GLANCE

Historic Sites and Churches
Clough House ❷
Copp's Hill Burying
Ground ❶
*Old North Church
p87* ❸
Paul Revere House ❺
Paul Revere Mall ❹

Waterfront Sights
Boston Tea Party Ship ❽
Children's Museum ❾
*New England Aquarium
pp90–91* ❼
Waterfront Wharves ❻

0 meters   450

0 yards   450

KEY

▨ Street-by-Street map *see pp84–5*

Ⓣ "T" station

🚌 Bus station

🅿 Parking

GETTING THERE
This area is well served by public transportation. Aquarium "T" station is located toward the south of the area, near Long Wharf. The area is also served by buses 6, 92, 93, and 111.

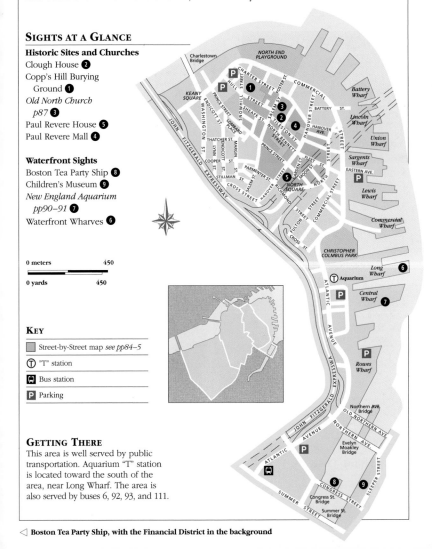

◁ **Boston Tea Party Ship, with the Financial District in the background**

Street-by-Street: North End

Old North Church clock

T HE MAIN ARTERIES of this area are Hanover and Salem Streets. Topped by the Old North Church, Salem Street is indicative of this area's historical connections – indeed the Old North Church is one of Boston's premier Revolutionary sights. In general the area consists of narrow streets and alleys, with four- and five-story tenements, many of which are now expensive condominiums. Hanover Street, like much of the area, has a distinctly Italian feel, while just south of here is North Square, site of the famous Paul Revere House *(see p88)*.

Clough House
Period furnishings can be seen in this house by Ebenezer Clough, who also helped build the Old North Church **2**

HULL STREET

SHEAFE STREET

NORTH BENNE

SALEM STREET

Charlestown

PRINCE STREET

Copp's Hill Burying Ground
During the American Revolution, the British used this low hilltop to fire cannon at American positions across Boston Harbor. Created in 1659 it is the city's second oldest graveyard **1**

★ **Old North Church**
Built in 1723 and famous for the part it played in Paul Revere's midnight ride (see p120), this is Boston's oldest religious building. On festive occasions, the North End still rings with the sound of its bells **3**

KEY

– – – Suggested route

STAR SIGHTS

★ Old North Church

★ Paul Revere House

★ Paul Revere Mall

↓
Government Center

0 meters	50
0 yards	50

★ Paul Revere Mall

Linking the Old North Church to Hanover Street, this tree-lined mall dates only from 1933. Its antique feel is enhanced by a statue of Paul Revere, which was sculpted in 1885 ❹

LOCATOR MAP
See Street Finder map 2

St. Stephen's Church
echoes the North End's Italian theme, though only by chance. Long before the first Italians arrived, Charles Bulfinch incorporated Italian Renaissance features and a bell tower into his renovation of an earlier church building.

Hanover Street is the most Italian of all Boston's streets, brought to life by restaurants and cafés, as well as the day-to-day activities of its ethnic community.

↘ **The waterfront**

★ Paul Revere House

This is the house where Paul Revere began his midnight ride (see p120). Revere's home from 1770 to 1800, it is now a museum ❺

Slate tombstones of Boston's early settlers, Copp's Hill Burying Ground

Copp's Hill Burying Ground ❶

Entrances at Charter & Hull Sts.
Map 2 D2. Ⓣ *Government Center, North Station.* ☐ *8am–5pm daily.*

Existing since 1659, this is Boston's second-oldest cemetery after the one by King's Chapel *(see p76)*. Nicknamed "Corpse Hill," the real name of the hill occupied by the cemetery derives from a local man by the name of William Copp. He owned a farm on its southeastern slope from 1643, and much of the cemetery's land was purchased from him. His children are buried here. Other more famous people

interred here include Robert Newman, the sexton who hung Paul Revere's signal lanterns in the belfry of Old North Church *(see p87)*, and Edmund Hartt, builder of the USS *Constitution (see p119)*. Increase, Cotton, and Samuel Mather, three generations of a family of highly influential colonial period Puritan ministers, are also buried here. Hundreds of Boston's Colonial-era black slaves and freedmen are also buried here, including Prince Hall, a free black man who founded the African Freemasonry Order in Massachusetts.

Decorative column, Copp's Hill

During the British occupation of Boston, the site was used by British commanders who had an artillery position here. They would later exploit the prominent hilltop location during the Revolution, when they directed cannon fire from here across Boston harbor toward American positions in Charlestown. King George III's troops were said to have used the slate headstones for target practice, and pockmarks from their musket balls are still visible on some of them.

Copp's Hill Terrace, directly across Charter Street, is a prime observation point for

Quiet, leafy street, typical of the area around Copp's Hill

views over to Charlestown and Bunker Hill. It is also the site where, in 1919, a 2.3-million-gallon molasses tank exploded, creating a huge, syrupy tidal wave that killed 21 people.

Clough House ❷

21 Unity St. **Map** 2 E2.
Ⓣ *Haymarket, Aquarium.* ☐ *Jun–Sep: 10am–2pm Wed.*

Ebenezer clough was a master mason and one of the Sons of Liberty who participated in the Boston Tea Party. One of two masons who helped to build the neighboring Old North Church *(see p87)*, he was also the head of a syndicate that laid out Unity Street in 1710 and built a series of six town houses here. The only building to survive is the one at No. 21 Unity Street, which was built in 1712 and was the house in which Ebenezer Clough himself lived. In a bad state of decay for many years and in danger of demolition, the house was saved when the Reverend P. Kellet, vicar of Christ Church, launched a fundraising campaign in 1962. A rather austere three-story building, it is typical of much of Boston's colonial architecture. Now fully restored to its former condition, the house has finely executed window and door lintels, decorated with raised brick panels over the first-floor windows and simple, carved-brick detailing over the door. The Heritage Room on the second floor features typical period furnishings and household accessories.

Clough House once stood alongside an identical brick residence, which was acquired by Benjamin Franklin in 1748. He bought the house for his two widowed sisters but never lived here himself. It was demolished in the 1930s to make way for the Paul Revere Mall *(see p88)*.

Old North Church™

CHRIST EPISCOPAL CHURCH is the official name of
Boston's oldest surviving religious edifice, which
dates from 1723. It was built of brick in the Georgian
style similar to that of St. Andrew's-by-the-Wardrobe
in Blackfriars, London, designed
by Sir Christopher Wren. The
church was made famous on April
18, 1775, when sexton Robert
Newman, aiding Paul Revere
(see p120), hung a pair of signal
lanterns in the belfry. These were
to warn the patriots in Charlestown of the westward departure
of British troops, on their way
to engage the revolutionaries.

★ **Box Pews**
*The traditional, high-sided box
pews in the church were designed
to enclose footwarmers, which were
filled with hot coals or bricks
during wintry weather.*

★ **Bell Tower
and Steeple**
*Views from the top of the
bell tower, such as this
one toward the Finan-
cial District, are well
worth the climb. Famous
as the place where
Robert Newman hung
his lanterns, the tower
contains the first set of
church bells in North
America, cast in 1745.*

Entrance

Bust of George Washington
*This marble bust of the first US
president, modeled on an earlier
one by Christian Gullager, was
presented to the church in 1815.*

Paul Revere Mall ❹

Hanover St. **Map** 2 E2.
[T] *Haymarket, Aquarium.* ♿

THIS BRICK-PAVED plaza gives the crowded neighborhood of the North End a precious stretch of open space between Hanover and Unity Streets. A well-utilized municipal resource, the Mall is always full of local people: children, teenagers, young mothers, and older residents chatting in Italian and playing cards or checkers. Laid out in 1933, and originally called the Prado, its focal point is Cyrus Dallin's equestrian statue of local hero Paul Revere, which was originally modeled in 1885. However, it was not sculpted and placed here until 1940. Bronze bas-relief plaques on the mall's side walls commemorate a number of North End residents who have played an important role in the history of Boston. Benches, a fountain, and twin rows of linden trees complete the space, which has a distinctly European feel.

At the north end of the Mall, across Unity Street, is Old North Church *(see p87)*, one of the city's most important historical sites. To the south is busy Hanover Street, which is lined with numerous Italian cafés and restaurants.

Paul Revere House kitchen, as it was in the 18th century

Paul Revere House ❺

19 North Sq. **Map** 2 E2.
☎ *(617) 523-2338.* [T] *Haymarket, Aquarium.* 🕐 *mid-Apr–Oct: 9:30am–5:15pm daily; Nov–mid-Apr: 9:30am–4:15pm daily.* ⛔ *Jan–Mar: Mon.* $ ♿ 🚫 🎧
[W] www.paulreverehouse.org

THE CITY'S oldest surviving clapboard frame house is historically significant, for it was here in 1775 that Paul Revere began his legendary horseback ride to warn his compatriots in Lexington of the impending arrival of British troops. This historic event was later immortalized in a boldly patriotic, epic poem by Henry Wadsworth Longfellow *(see p110)*. It begins "Listen, my children, and you shall hear of the midnight ride of Paul Revere."

Revere, a Huguenot descendent, was by trade a versatile gold- and silversmith, copper engraver, and maker of church bells and cannons. He and his second wife, Rachel, mother of eight of his 16 children, owned the house from 1770 to 1800. Small leaded casement windows, an overhanging upper story, and nail-studded front door all contribute to make it a fine example of 18th-century Early American architecture. In the courtyard along one side of the house is a large bronze bell, cast by Paul Revere for a church in 1804 – Revere made nearly 200 church bells. Three rooms in the house contain period artifacts, including original pieces of family furniture, items made in Revere's workshop, and colonial banknotes. The house, which by the mid-19th century had become a decrepit tenement fronted by stores, was saved from demolition by preservationists' efforts led by one of Revere's great-grandsons.

Next door, the early 18th-century Pierce-Hichborn House is the earliest brick town house remaining in New England.

View toward the Custom House and the Financial District, across Christopher Columbus Park

Rowes Wharf development, typical of Boston's waterfront regeneration

Waterfront Wharves ❻

Atlantic Avenue. **Map** 2 E4.
Ⓣ *Aquarium.*

BOSTON'S WATERFRONT is fringed by many wharves, reminders of the city's past as a key trading port. One of the largest of these is Long Wharf, established in 1710 to accommodate the boom in early maritime commerce. Once extending 2000 ft (610 m) into Boston Harbor and lined with shops and warehouses, Long wharf provided mooring for the largest ships of the time. Many sightseeing excursion boats depart from here.

Harbor Walk connects Long Wharf with other adjacent wharves, such as Union, Lewis, and Commercial wharves. Dating from the early 1800s, most are now converted to fashionable harborside appartments. Rowes Wharf, to the south of the waterfront, is a particularly fine example of such revitalization. Built of

Bostonian red brick, this modern development features a large archway that links the city to the harbor. It comprises the luxury Boston Harbor Hotel, restaurants, and a marina.

New England Aquarium ❼

See pp90–91.

Boston Tea Party Ship ❽

Congress St. Bridge. **Map** 2 E5.
🄲 *(617) 338-1773.* Ⓣ *South Station.* ☐ *Jun–Sep: 9am–6pm daily; Oct–May: 9am–5pm daily.* 🆆 www.historictours.com/boston

GRIFFIN'S WHARF, where the Boston Tea Party took place on December 16, 1773, was buried beneath landfill many years ago. Since 1973, the Danish-built sailing brig *Beaver II* has been anchored on Fort Point

Channel a short distance south of the old Griffin's Wharf site. The vessel resembles one of the three original British East India Company ships involved in the Tea Party protest. Today, modern-day patriots toss imitation bales of tea overboard, re-creating one of the acts of defiance that prompted Britain to put the Massachusetts Bay Colony under martial law.

On an adjacent pier, ship models, Tea Party memorabilia, and other educational exhibits are displayed in a museum.

Children's Museum ❾

300 Congress St. **Map** 2 E5.
🄲 *(617) 426-8855.* Ⓣ *South Station.* ☐ *mid-Jun–Aug: 10am–5pm Sat–Thu, 10am–9pm Fri; Sep–mid-Jun: 10am–5pm Tue–Sun.* 🆆 www.bostonkids.org

OVERLOOKING Fort Point Channel, a rejuvenated 19th-century wool warehouse contains one of the country's best children's museums. There are many interesting exhibits, and youngsters can participate in games and learning activities, and even climb through a two-story maze.

The recycling area provides barrels of materials for projects. A towering milk bottle stands in front of the museum and serves as a summer ice-cream stand.

Careers can be sampled as children work on a mini-construction site, or act in short stageplays. An international flavor is added by a visit to the silk merchant's house, which has been transplanted from Kyoto, and to Teen Tokyo.

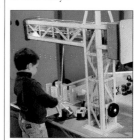

Playing on the mini-construction site at Boston's Children's Museum

New England Aquarium ❼

THE WATERFRONT's prime attraction dominates Central Wharf. Designed by a consortium of architects in 1969, the aquarium's core encloses a vast four-story ocean tank, which contains an innumerable array of marine animals. A curving walkway runs around the outside of the tank from top to bottom and provides viewpoints of the interior of the tank from different levels. Also resident at the aquarium are colonies of penguins, while the recently added west wing features changing exhibitions. The *Discovery* exhibit, a tank floating separately from the aquarium, features shows performed by sea lions.

Edge of the Sea Tidepool
A fiberglass shore recreates a world where the land meets the sea. It is home to animals such as horseshoe crabs and sea urchins.

Penguin Pool
One of the main attractions of the aquarium, the penguin pool runs around the base of the giant tank. It contains African, rockhopper, and blue penguins.

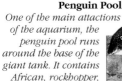

★ Boat Programs
Boat trips tour Boston Harbor where visitors explore aspects of oceanography, such as the harbor's ecosystem, or head to Stellwagen Bank, 75 minutes away, to watch whales.

Main entrance

Harbor Seals
An outdoor tank covered by a steel canopy is home to a lively colony of harbor seals.

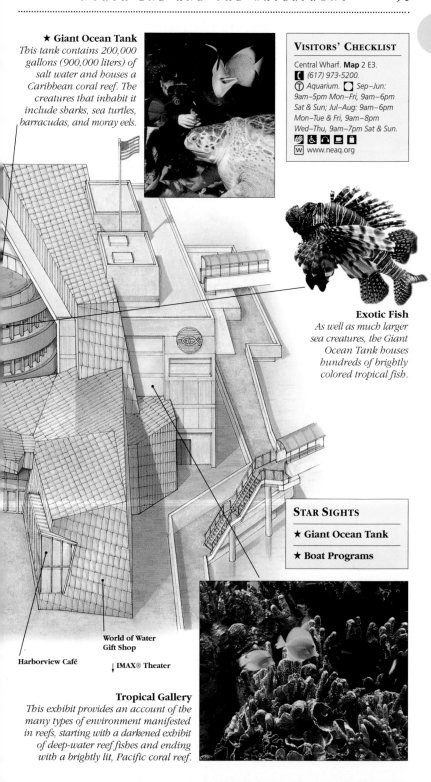

★ Giant Ocean Tank
This tank contains 200,000 gallons (900,000 liters) of salt water and houses a Caribbean coral reef. The creatures that inhabit it include sharks, sea turtles, barracudas, and moray eels.

VISITORS' CHECKLIST

Central Wharf. **Map** 2 E3.
[c] (617) 973-5200.
Ⓣ Aquarium. ☐ Sep–Jun:
9am–5pm Mon–Fri, 9am–6pm
Sat & Sun; Jul–Aug: 9am–6pm
Mon–Tue & Fri, 9am–8pm
Wed–Thu, 9am–7pm Sat & Sun.
♿ ☐ ☐ ☐ ☐
ⓦ www.neaq.org

Exotic Fish
As well as much larger sea creatures, the Giant Ocean Tank houses hundreds of brightly colored tropical fish.

STAR SIGHTS

★ Giant Ocean Tank

★ Boat Programs

**World of Water
Gift Shop**

Harborview Café

↓ **IMAX® Theater**

Tropical Gallery
This exhibit provides an account of the many types of environment manifested in reefs, starting with a darkened exhibit of deep-water reef fishes and ending with a brightly lit, Pacific coral reef.

BACK BAY AND SOUTH END

UNTIL THE 19th century Boston was situated on a narrow peninsula surrounded by tidal marshes. Projects to fill Back Bay began in the 1850s and were made possible by new inventions such as the steam shovel. The Back Bay was filled by 1880, and developers soon moved in. Planned along French lines, with elegant boulevards, Back Bay is now one of Boston's most exclusive neighborhoods. The more bohemian South End, laid out on an English model of town houses clustered around squares, is home to many artists and Boston's gay community.

Sargent mural, Boston Public Library

SIGHTS AT A GLANCE

Historic Streets and Squares
Boylston Street **8**
Commonwealth Avenue **4**
Copley Square **7**
The Esplanade **1**
Newbury Street **5**

First Baptist Church **3**
Gibson House Museum **2**
Institute of Contemporary Art **11**
John Hancock Tower **10**
Trinity Church pp98–9 **6**

Historic Buildings, Churches, and Museums
Boston Center for the Arts **12**
Boston Public Library **9**

KEY

▦	Street-by-Street map *see pp94–5*
Ⓣ	"T" station
🚆	Train station
🚌	Bus station
ℹ	Tourist information
🅿	Parking

GETTING THERE

The area has good public transportation. Arlington, Copley, and Hynes/ I.C.A. "T" stations serve the Back Bay. Back Bay/ South End and Prudential "T stations serve the South End. The area is served by buses 1, 8, 9, 10, 39, 43, 49, 55, and 302 and the Silver Line Mass Transit.

0 meters		450
0 yards		450

◁ **View of Back Bay's characteristic row houses, from the top of the Prudential Skywalk**

Street-by-Street: Back Bay

THIS FASHIONABLE DISTRICT unfolds westward from the Public Garden *(see pp64–5)* in a grid that departs radically from the twisting streets found elsewhere in Boston. Commonwealth Avenue, with its grand 19th-century mansions and parkland, and Newbury and Boylston Streets are its main arteries. Newbury Street is a magnet for all of Boston wanting to indulge in some upscale shopping, whereas the more somber Boylston Street bustles with office workers. Copley Square anchors the entire area and is the site of Henry Hobson Richardson's magnificent Trinity Church *(see pp98–9)* and the 60-story John Hancock Tower *(see p101)*, which is the tallest building in New England.

Weekly summer and fall farmers' market, Copley Square

Copley Square
This square was a marsh until 1870. It took on its present form only in the late 20th century as buildings around its edges were completed. A farmers' market, concerts, and folk-dancing feature regularly **7**

Boylston Street
The site of the Prudential Center and the Institute of Contemporary Art (see p101), Boylston Street is also the location of the fabulous New Old South Church (see p100) **8**

★ Boston Public Library
One of the first free public libraries in the world, this building was designed by Charles McKim. Inside are murals by John Singer Sargent **9**

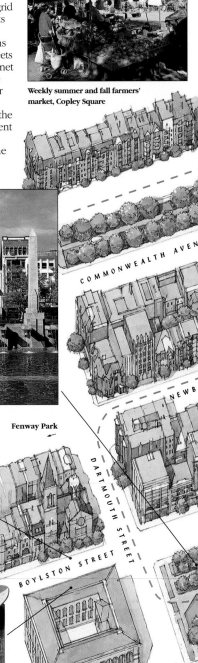

COMMONWEALTH AVEN

NEWBU

Fenway Park

DARTMOUTH STREET

BOYLSTON STREET

South End

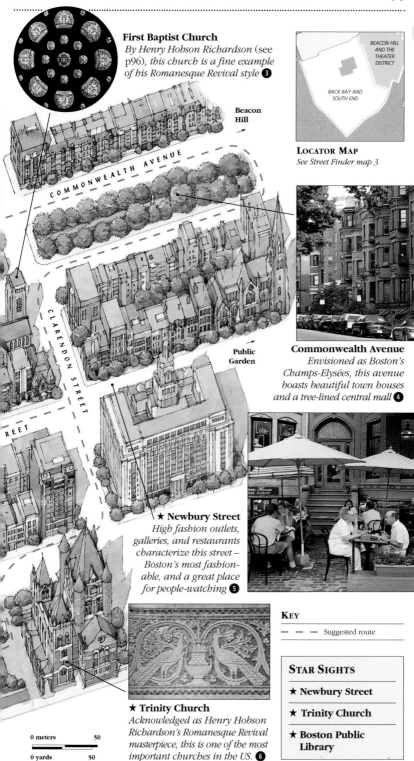

First Baptist Church
*By Henry Hobson Richardson (see
p96), this church is a fine example
of his Romanesque Revival style* ❸

Beacon
Hill

LOCATOR MAP
See Street Finder map 3

BEACON HILL
AND THE
THEATER
DISTRICT

BACK BAY AND
SOUTH END

COMMONWEALTH AVENUE

CLARENDON STREET

REET

Public
Garden

Commonwealth Avenue
*Envisioned as Boston's
Champs-Elysées, this avenue
boasts beautiful town houses
and a tree-lined central mall* ❹

★ Newbury Street
*High fashion outlets,
galleries, and restaurants
characterize this street –
Boston's most fashion-
able, and a great place
for people-watching* ❺

KEY

— — — Suggested route

★ Trinity Church
*Acknowledged as Henry Hobson
Richardson's Romanesque Revival
masterpiece, this is one of the most
important churches in the US.* ❻

| 0 meters | 50 |
| 0 yards | 50 |

STAR SIGHTS

★ Newbury Street

★ Trinity Church

★ Boston Public
Library

The Esplanade ❶

Map 1 A4. Ⓣ *Charles/ MGH.*
◯ *24 hrs daily.* ♿

Running along the Boston side of the Charles River, between Longfellow Bridge and Dartmouth Street, are the parkland, lagoons, and islands known collectively as the Esplanade. While the park is used most extensively for in-line skating, cycling, and strolling, it is also the main access point for boating on the river and the site of the city's leading outdoor concert space.

In 1929, Arthur Fiedler, then the young conductor of the Boston Pops Orchestra, chose the Esplanade for a summer concert series that became a tradition. The Hatch Memorial Shell was constructed in 1939, and its stage is widely used by musical ensembles and other groups throughout the summer. Fourth of July concerts by the Boston Pops, which are followed by fireworks, can attract upward of 500,000 spectators.

Fountains at the Esplanade, next to the Charles River

Gibson House Museum ❷

137 Beacon St. **Map** 1 A4.
◧ *(617) 267-6338.* Ⓣ *Arlington.*
◯ *Tours at 1pm, 2pm & 3pm Wed–Sun.* 📷 ✕ 📄
Ⓦ *www.gibsonhouse.org*

Among the first houses built in the Back Bay, the Gibson House preserves its original Victorian decor and furnishings throughout all six stories. The 1860 brownstone and red-brick structure was

The original Victorian-style library of the Gibson House Museum

designed in the popular Italian Renaissance Revival style for the widow Catherine Hammond Gibson, who was one of the few women to own property in this part of the city. Her grandson Charles Hammond Gibson, Jr., a noted eccentric, poet, travel writer, horticulturalist, and bon vivant, arranged for the house to become a museum after his death in 1954. As a prelude to this, Gibson began to rope off the furniture in the 1930s, thus inviting his guests to sit on the stairs to drink martinis made with his own bathtub gin.

One of the most modern houses of its day, the Gibson House boasted such technical advancements as gas lighting, indoor plumbing in the basement, and coal-fired central heating. Visitors can see a full dinner setting in the dining room or admire the whimsical Turkish pet pavilion. It is Gibson's preservation of the 1860s decor (with some modifications in 1888) that makes the museum a true time capsule of Victorian life in Boston.

Detail of Bartholdi's frieze atop the distinctive square tower of the First Baptist Church

First Baptist Church ❸

110 Commonwealth Ave. **Map** 3 C2.
◧ *(617) 267-3148.* Ⓣ *Arlington.*
◯ *for Sunday worship.* ✝ *11am Sun.* ✕ ♿

The Romanesque-style First Baptist Church on the corner of Commonwealth Avenue and Clarendon Street was Henry Hobson Richardson's first major architectural commission and became an instant landmark when it was finished in 1872. Viewed from Commonwealth Avenue, it is one of the most distinctive buildings of the city skyline.

Richardson considered the nearly freestanding bell tower, which he modeled roughly on Italian campaniles, to be the church's most innovative structure. The square tower is topped with a decorative frieze and arches protected by an overhanging roof. The frieze was modeled in Paris by Bartholdi, the sculptor who created the Statue of Liberty, and was carved in place by Italian artisans after the stones were set. The faces in the frieze, which depict the sacraments, are likenesses of prominent Bostonians of that time, among them Henry Wadsworth Longfellow and Ralph Waldo Emerson. The trumpeting angels at the corners of the tower gave the building its nickname, "Church of the Holy Bean Blowers."

Four years after the church was completed, the Unitarian congregation dissolved because it was unable to bear the expense of the building. The church stood vacant until 1881, when the First Baptist congregation from the South End took it over.

Commonwealth Avenue ❹

Map 3 B2. Ⓣ *Arlington, Copley, Hynes Convention Center/ ICA.*

BACK BAY was Boston's first fully planned neighborhood, and architect Arthur Gilman made Commonwealth Avenue, modeled on the elegant boulevards of Paris, the centerpiece of the design. At 200 ft (61 m) wide, with a 10ft (3 m) setback from the sidewalks to encourage small gardens in front of the buildings, Commonwealth became an arena for America's leading domestic architects in the second half of the 19th century. A walk from the Public Garden to Massachusetts Avenue is like flicking through a catalog of architectural styles. Few of the grand buildings on either side of the avenue are open to the public, although the Boston Center for Adult

Education at No. 5 can be toured by appointment. The mansion, which was built in 1912 in Italianate style, was a late addition to Back Bay. Textile industrialist owner Walter C. Baylies later added a ballroom modeled on the Petit Trianon in Versailles.

A statue of the fervent abolitionist William Garrison (1805–79) stands on Commonwealth Avenue's central mall.

William Garrison statue on Commonwealth Avenue

⛲ Center for Adult Education
5 Commonwealth Ave.
🌓 *(617) 267-4430.*
🕐 *9am–7pm Mon–Thu, 9am–5pm Fri.* ⬤ *Sat and Sun, May 11.*
📷 *for courses* 🚫 ♿ 🎫
🌐 www.bcae.org

Newbury Street ❺

Map 3 C2. Ⓣ *Arlington, Copley, Hynes Convention Center/ ICA.*

NEWBURY STREET is a Boston synonym for "stylish." The elegant Ritz-Carlton Hotel on the corner with Arlington Street sets an elegant tone for the street that continues with a mix of prestigious and often

well-hidden art galleries, stylish boutiques, and some of the city's most *au courant* restaurants.

Churches provide vestiges of a more decorous era. The Church of the Covenant at No. 67 Newbury contains the world's largest collection of Louis Comfort Tiffany stained-glass windows and an elaborate Tiffany lantern.

A chorus and orchestra perform a Bach cantata each Sunday at Emmanuel Church on the corner of Newbury and Berkeley Streets.

The Newbury Street Mural at the corner of Newbury and Dartmouth highlights the street's role as a place to be seen. It depicts 72 of the famous and not so famous, from Sam Adams to Tom Yawkey, who owned the Boston Red Sox for 44 years. Modern-day aspiring celebrities may be spotted at the sidewalk tables of Newbury's "hottest" restaurants, such as Sonsie (*see p331*).

⛪ Church of the Covenant
67 Newbury St. 🌓 *(617) 266-7480.*
⛪ *10am Sun.*
📷 🚫 ♿ 🎫 🎧
🌐 www.churchofthecovenant.org

Stylish Newbury Street, with its elegant shops, galleries, and restaurants, the epitome of Boston style

Trinity Church ❻

Routinely voted one of America's 10 finest buildings, this masterpiece by Henry Hobson Richardson dates from 1877. Trinity Church was founded in 1733 near Downtown Crossing, but the congregation moved the church to this site in 1871. The church is a granite and sandstone Romanesque structure standing on wooden piles driven through mud into bedrock, surmounted with granite pyramids. John LaFarge designed the interior, while some of the windows are designed by Edward Burne-Jones and executed by William Morris.

The Bell Tower
was inspired by the Renaissance cathedral at Salamanca, central Spain.

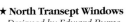

Bas-relief in Chancel
On the wall of the chancel, behind the altar, are a series of gold bas-reliefs. This one shows St. Paul before King Agrippa.

★ North Transept Windows
Designed by Edward Burne-Jones and executed by William Morris, the three stained-glass windows above the choir relate the story of Christmas.

Parish House

The Pulpit is covered with carved scenes from the life of Christ, as well as portraits of great preachers through the ages.

Chancel
Designed by Charles Maginnis, the present-day chancel was not dedicated until 1938. The seven windows by Clayton & Bell of London show the life of Christ.

David's Charge to Solomon
Located in the baptistry, to the right of the chancel, this beautiful window is also the result of a partnership between Edward Burne-Jones and William Morris. The story shown is one of the few in the church from the Old Testament.

VISITORS' CHECKLIST

Copley Sq. **Map** 3 C2. **(** (617) 536-0944. **T** Copley. **○** 8am–6pm daily. **†** 9am, 11:15am, 6pm Sun. **⊘** **&** *concerts* Sep–mid-June: noon Fri. **▯** **W** www.trinitychurchboston.org

John LaFarge's lancet windows show Christ in the act of blessing. They were designed at the request of Phillips Brooks – he wanted LaFarge to create an inspirational design for the west nave, which he could look at while preaching.

★ **West Portico**
Richardson disliked the original flat façade of Trinity Church, and so modeled the deeply sculpted west portico after St. Trophime in Arles, France. It was added after his death.

Carving of Phillips Brooks and Christ

PHILLIPS BROOKS

Born in Boston in 1835 and educated at Harvard, Brooks was a towering charismatic figure. Rector of Trinity Church from 1869, he gained a reputation for powerful sermons. From 1872 Brooks worked closely with Henry Hobson Richardson on the design of the new Trinity Church – at least five sculpted likenesses of him can be seen in and around the building.

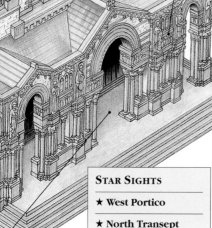

STAR SIGHTS

★ **West Portico**

★ **North Transept Windows**

Main Entrance

The New Old South Church on the corner of Copley Square

Copley Square ❼

Map 3 C2. Ⓣ *Copley.*

Named after John Singleton Copley, the great Boston painter born nearby in 1737, Copley Square is a hive of civic activity surrounded by some of Boston's most striking architecture. Summer activities include weekly farmers' markets, concerts, and even folk-dancing.

The inviting green plaza took years to develop; when Copley was born it was just a marshy riverbank, which remained unfilled until 1870. Construction of the John Hancock Tower in 1975 anchored the southeastern side of Copley Square, and the Copley Place development completed the square on the southwestern corner in 1984. Today's Copley Square, a wide open space of trees, grass, and fountains, took shape in the heart of the city in the 1990s, after various plans to utilize this hitherto wasted space were tendered.

A large plaque honoring the Boston Marathon, which ends at the Boston Public Library, was set in the sidewalk in 1996 to coincide with the 100th race. As well as pushcart vendors, the plaza has a booth for discounted theater, music, and dance tickets.

Boylston Street ❽

Map 3 C2. Ⓣ *Boylston, Arlington, Copley, Hynes Convention Center/ ICA.*

A brass teddy bear sculpture, outside F.A.O. Schwarz, is one of Boylston Street's principal landmarks. It is a reproduction of the toy company's famous New York's Fifth Avenue symbol. The French Academic-style building at the corner of Boylston and Berkeley Streets was originally built for the Museum of Natural History, which was the forerunner of the Museum of Science *(see p67)*. Its present occupant is the upscale clothier Louis. The Art Deco building at the corner of Arlington and Boylston houses Shreve, Crump & Low, Inc., Boston's finest jewelers.

Some notable office buildings stand on Boylston Street. The lobby of the New England building at No. 501 features large historical murals and dioramas depicting the process of filling Back Bay. The central tower of the Prudential Center dominates the skyline on upper Boylston Street. Adjoining the Prudential is the Hynes Convention Center. It was significantly enlarged in 1988 to accommodate the city's burgeoning convention business.

The Italian Gothic-style **New Old South Church**, which is located at the corner of Dartmouth, was built in 1874–5 by the congregation that had met previously at the Old South Meeting House *(see p77)*.

🛈 **New Old South Church**
645 Boylston St. **[** *(617) 536-1970.* **◯** *8am–7pm Mon–Fri, 9am–4pm Sat–Sun.* **🛈** *11am Sun.* 🚫 ♿ 📷 **🛖** **W** *www.oldsouth.org*

Boston Public Library ❾

Copley Square. **Map** 3 C2.
[*(617) 536-5400.* Ⓣ *Copley.* **◯** *Apr–Sep: 9am–9pm Mon–Thu, 9am–5pm Fri–Sat; Oct–May: 9am–9pm Mon–Thu, 9am–5pm Fri–Sat, 1pm–5pm Sun.* **◯** *public hols.* ♿ 📷 **🛖** **W** *www.bpl.org*

Founded in 1848, the Boston Public Library was America's first metropolitan library for the public. It quickly outgrew its original building, hence the construction of the Italian *palazzo*-style Copley Square building in 1887–95. Designed by Charles McKim, the building is a marvel of fine wood and marble detail. Bates Hall, on the second floor, is particularly noted for its soaring barrel-vaulted ceiling. Sculptor Daniel Chester French fashioned the library's huge bronze doors, Edward Abbey's murals of the Quest for the Holy Grail line the book request room, and John Singer Sargent's murals of Judaism and Christianity cover a third-floor gallery.

The library's circulating collection is housed in the 1971 Boylston Street addition, a modernist structure by architect Philip Johnson.

The vast Bates Hall in the Boston Public Library, noted for its high barrel-vaulted ceiling

John Hancock Tower ⑩

200 Clarendon St. **Map** 3 C2.
Ⓣ *Copley.*

THE TALLEST BUILDING in New England, the 740-ft (226-m) rhomboid that is the John Hancock Tower cuts into Copley Square, with its mirrored façade reflecting the surroundings, including from one angle the original Hancock building built in 1947. The innovative design has created a 60-story office building with 10,344 windows that shares the square with its 19th-century neighbors, the Romanesque Trinity Church and the Italian Renaissance Revival Copley Plaza Hotel, without dwarfing them. It was designed by Henry Cobb of the architect firm of I. M. Pei & Partners and its construction was completed in 1972. Unfortunately, the observatory on the 60th floor has been closed following the events of September 11.

View over Back Bay and the Charles River from the John Hancock Tower

Institute of Contemporary Art ⑪

955 Boylston St. **Map** 3 A3. 🄲 *(617) 266-5152.* Ⓣ *Hynes Convention Center/ ICA.* ◯ *noon–5pm Wed & Fri, noon–9pm Thu, 11am–5pm Sat & Sun.* ● *public hols.* 🈂 🄶 🄲
🅆 *www.icaboston.org*

THIS RICHARDSONIAN Romanesque brick-and-stone building was renovated in 1975 under the direction of leading Boston architect Graham Gund, and is renowned for its open design. Its new function was to house the Institute of Contemporary Art, which is one of the oldest non-collecting art organizations in the US. As there is no formal collection, the I.C.A. is able to mount cutting-edge art exhibitions that reflect the latest innovations from the contemporary art world. One of the I.C.A.'s curatorial strengths has been its broadly international vision as it has forged an identity apart from the New York art scene.

Boston Center for the Arts ⑫

539 Tremont St. **Map** 4 D3.
🄲 *(617) 426-5000.* Ⓣ *Back Bay/ South End.* **Cyclorama** ◯ *9am– 5pm Mon–Fri.* **Mills Gallery** ◯ *noon–5pm Wed, Thu, Sun; noon–10pm Fri–Sat.* ● *public hols.* 🈂 *for performances.* 🚫 🄶 🅆 *www.bcaonline.org*

THE CENTERPIECE of a resurgent South End, the B.C.A. complex includes three theaters, an art gallery, and artists' studios as well as the Boston Ballet Building, home to the company's educational programs, rehearsal space, and administrative offices.

The Tremont Estates Building at the corner of Tremont Street, an organ factory in the years after the Civil War, now houses artists' studios, rehearsal space, and an art gallery. The largest of the B.C.A. buildings is the circular, domed Cyclorama, which opened in 1884 to exhibit the 50-ft (15-m) by 400-ft (121-m) painting *The Battle of Gettysburg* by the French artist Paul Philippoteaux. The painting was removed in 1889 and is now displayed at Gettysburg National Historic Park. For many years, the Cyclorama was Boston's leading venue for indoor events such as boxing, and was also the city's wholesale flower market. Today it is a challenging performance and exhibition space.

The Mills Gallery houses exhibitions focusing on emerging contemporary artists, with a strong emphasis on multimedia installations and shows with confrontational, and often provocative, themes.

Richardsonian Romanesque-style façade of the Institute of Contemporary Art

FARTHER AFIELD

MOST OF BOSTON's historic sights are concentrated in the central colonial and Victorian city. However, the late 19th and 20th centuries saw Boston expand into the surrounding area. What were the marshlands of the Fenway now house two of Boston's most important art museums, the Museum of Fine Arts and the Isabella Stewart Gardner Museum *(see p105)*. Southeast of the city center, Columbia Point was developed in the mid-20th century and is home to the John F. Kennedy Library and Museum *(see p104)*. West of central

Statue of William Prescott, Bunker Hill Monument

Boston, across the Charles River, lies Cambridge, a city in its own right and sometimes referred to as the "Socialist Democratic Republic of Cambridge," a reference to the politics of its two major colleges, Harvard and the Massachusetts Institute of Technology. Harvard Square *(see p110)* is a lively area of bookstores, cafés, and street entertainers. Charlestown, east of Cambridge, is the site of the Bunker Hill Monument *(see p118)* and the Charlestown Navy Yard, where the US's most famous warship, the USS *Constitution*, is moored.

SIGHTS AT A GLANCE

Towns
Cambridge ❼
Charlestown ❽

Museums and Historic Sites
Isabella Stewart Gardner
    Museum ❺
John F. Kennedy Library
    and Museum ❶
John F. Kennedy National
    Historic Site ❹

Lexington ⓫
Lincoln ⓬
Museum of Fine Arts
    pp106–9 ❻
Quincy ⓭
Wellesley College ❾

Gardens and Zoos
Arnold Arboretum ❸
Franklin Park Zoo ❷
Broadmoor Sanctuary ❿

KEY

▢ Main sightseeing area
▢ Urban area
✈ Airport
🚉 Train station
━ Highway
═ Major road
═ Minor road
─ Railroad

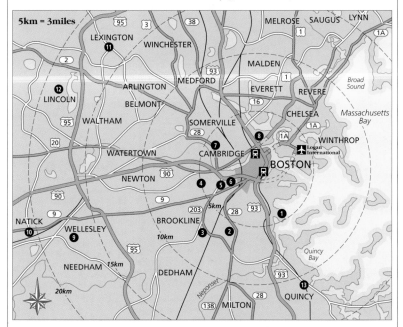

⊲ **Central courtyard of the *palazzo*-style Isabella Stewart Gardner Museum**

John F. Kennedy Library and Museum ❶

Columbia Point, Dorchester.
📞 (617) 514-1600. Ⓣ JFK/ U Mass.
🕐 9–5 daily. ● Jan 1, Thanksgiving, Dec 25. 📷 ♿ 🛍 🎧
🅦 www.jfklibrary.org

THE SOARING WHITE concrete and glass building housing the John F. Kennedy Library stands sentinel on Columbia Point near the mouth of the Boston Harbor. This striking white and black modern building by the architect I. M. Pei is equally dramatic from the interior, with a 50-ft (15-m) wall of glass looking out over the water. Exhibitions extensively chronicle the 1,000 days of the Kennedy presidency with an immediacy uncommon in many other historical museums. Kennedy was among the first politicians to grasp the power of media. The museum takes full advantage of film and video footage to use the president's own words and image to tell his story: his campaign for the Democratic Party nomination, landmark television debates with Republican opponent Richard M. Nixon (who later became infamous for the Watergate Scandal), and his many addresses to the nation.

Several rooms recreate key chambers of the White House during the Kennedy administration, including the Oval Office; gripping film clips capture the anxiety of nuclear brinksmanship during the Cuban missile crisis as well as the inspirational spirit of the space program and the founding of the Peace Corps. Recently expanded exhibits on Robert F. Kennedy's role as Attorney General touch on both his deft handling of race relations and his key advisory role to his brother. The combination of artifacts, displays, and television footage evoke both the euphoria of "Camelot" and the numb horror of the assassination.

Lowland gorilla with her baby in the simulated natural environment of Franklin Park Zoo

Franklin Park Zoo ❷

1 Franklin Park Rd. 📞 (617) 541-5466. Ⓣ Forest Hills. 🚌 16 from Forest Hills subway. 🕐 Apr–Sep: 10am–5pm Mon–Fri, 10am–6pm Sat–Sun; Oct–Mar: 10am–4pm daily. ● Jan 1, Thanksgiving, Dec 25. 📷 ♿ 🅦 www.zoonewengland.com

THE ZOO, originally planned as a small menagerie, has expanded dramatically over the past century and long ago discarded caged enclosures in favor of simulated natural environments. Lowland gorillas roam a forest edge with caves for privacy, lions lounge around a rocky kingdom, while zebras, ostriches, and giraffes are free to graze on open grassland. The Butterfly Landing is a dense garden within a large hooped enclosure where as many as 1,000 butterflies flit from flower to flower, especially on a warm afternoon. New Age and light classical music augment the sense of fantasy. In the small petting zoo youngsters can meet farm animals.

Arnold Arboretum ❸

125 Arborway, Jamaica Plain.
📞 (617) 524-1718. Ⓣ Forest Hills. 🚌 39. 🕐 sunrise–sunset daily.
Visitors Center 🕐 9am–4pm Mon–Fri, noon–4pm Sat–Sun. ● public hols, Sun (Jan, Feb only). ♿ 🅦 www.arboretum.harvard.edu

FOUNDED BY Harvard University in 1872 as a living catalog of all the indigenous and exotic trees and shrubs adaptable to New England's climate, the

Dramatic, modern structure of the John F. Kennedy Library and Museum

Arboretum is planted with more than 15,000 labeled specimens. It is the oldest arboretum in the US and a key resource for botanical and horticultural research. The Arboretum also serves as a park where people jog, stroll, read, and paint.

The park's busiest time is on the third Sunday in May – Lilac Sunday – when tens of thousands come to revel in the sight and fragrance of the lilac collection, one of the largest in the world. The range of the Arboretum's collections guarantees flowers from late March into November, beginning with cornelian cherry and forsythia. Blooms shift in late May to azalea, magnolia, and wisteria, then to mountain laurel and roses in June. Sweet autumn clematis bursts forth in September, and native witch hazel blooms in October and November. The Arboretum also has fine fall foliage in September and October.

A large scale model of the Arboretum can be seen in the Visitors' Information Center just inside the main gate.

John F. Kennedy National Historic Site ❹

83 Beals St, Brookline. ☎ (617) 566-7937. ⓣ Coolidge Corner.
◯ May–Oct: 10am–4:30pm Wed–Sun.
🖼 ∅ 👢 📷 🎧
ⓦ www.nps.gov/jofi

THE FIRST HOME of the late president's parents, this Brookline house saw the birth of four of nine Kennedy children, including J.F.K. on May 29, 1917. Although the Kennedys moved to a larger house in 1921, the Beal Street residence held special memories for the family, who repurchased the house in 1966 and furnished it with their belongings circa 1917 as a memorial to John F. Kennedy. The guided tour includes a taped interview with J.F.K.'s mother Rose. A walking tour takes in other neighborhood sites relevant to the family's early years.

Central courtyard of the *palazzo*-style Isabella Stewart Gardner Museum

Isabella Stewart Gardner Museum ❺

280 The Fenway. ☎ (617) 566-1401.
ⓣ MFA. ◯ 11am–5pm Tue–Sun.
⬤ Jan 1, Thanksgiving, Dec 25. 🖼
∅ 🎵 **Concerts** (call for schedule).
ⓦ www.gardnermuseum.org

THE ONLY THING more surprising than a Venetian *palazzo* on The Fenway is the collection of more than 2,500 works of art inside. Advised by scholar Bernard Berenson,

the strong-willed Isabella Stewart Gardner turned her wealth to collecting art in the late 19th century, acquiring a notable collection of Old Masters and Italian Renaissance pieces. Titian's *Rape of Europa*, for example, is considered his best painting in a US museum. The eccentric "Mrs. Jack" had an eye for her contemporaries as well. She purchased the first Matisse to enter an American collection and was an ardent patron of James McNeill Whistler and John Singer Sargent. The paintings, sculptures, and tapestries are displayed on three levels around a stunning skylit courtyard. Mrs. Gardner's will, which was instrumental in the setting up of the museum, stipulates the collection should remain assembled in the manner that she originally intended. Unfortunately, her intentions could not be upheld; in 1990 thieves made off with 13 of these priceless works, including a rare Rembrandt seascape, *Storm on the Sea of Galilee*, then conservatively valued in the region of $200 million.

THE EMERALD NECKLACE

Best known as designer of New York's Central Park, Frederick Law Olmsted based himself in Boston, where he created parks to solve environmental problems and provide a green refuge for inhabitants of the 19th-century industrial city. The Emerald Necklace includes the green spaces of Boston Common and the Public Garden (*see pp64–5*) and Commonwealth Avenue (*see p97*). To create a ring of parks, Olmsted added the Back Bay Fens

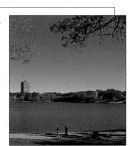

Jamaica Pond, part of Boston's fine parklands

(site of beautiful rose gardens and gateway to the Museum of Fine Arts and the Isabella Stewart Gardner Museum), the rustic Riverway, Jamaica Pond (sailing and picnicking), Arnold Arboretum, and Franklin Park (a golf course, zoo, and cross-country ski trails). The 5-mile (8-km) swath of parkland makes an excellent bicycle tour or ambitious walk.

The Museum of Fine Arts ❻

THIS MUSEUM OPENED IN 1876 on Copley Square and moved to its present location in the Fenway in 1909. It is the largest art museum in New England and one of the five largest in the United States, with a permanent collection of approximately 350,000 objects, ranging from Egyptian artifacts to paintings by John Singer Sargent. The original Classical-style building was augmented in 1981 by the addition of the West Wing, designed by I. M. Pei.

★ Japanese Temple Room
This room was created in 1909 to provide a space in which to contemplate Buddhist art. The M.F.A. has one of the finest Japanese collections outside Japan.

American Silver
The revolutionary Paul Revere (see p120) was also a noted silversmith and produced many beautiful objects, such as this ornate teapot.

First floor

Entrance

★ Egyptian Mummies
Among the museum's Egyptian and Nubian art is this tomb group of Nes-mut-aat-neru (760–660 BC) of Thebes.

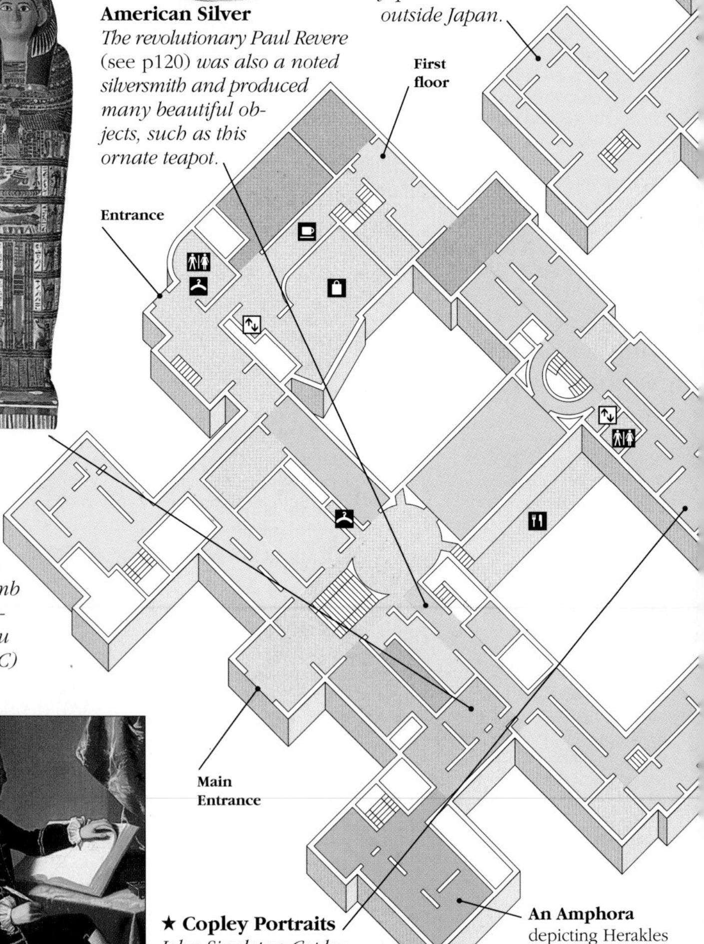

Main Entrance

★ Copley Portraits
John Singleton Copley (1738–1815) painted the celebrities of his day, hence this portrait of a dandyish John Hancock.

An Amphora
depicting Herakles and the Cretan Bull (525–520 BC) is an ancient Greek masterpiece.

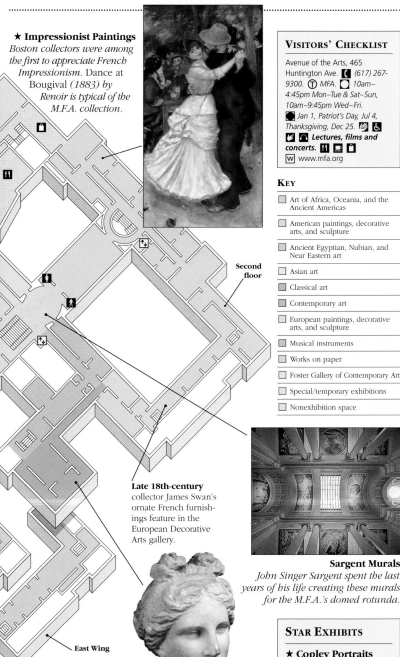

★ **Impressionist Paintings**
Boston collectors were among the first to appreciate French Impressionism. Dance at Bougival *(1883) by Renoir is typical of the M.F.A. collection.*

Second floor

VISITORS' CHECKLIST

Avenue of the Arts, 465 Huntington Ave. ⬤ *(617) 267-9300.* Ⓣ *MFA.* ⬤ *10am–4:45pm Mon–Tue & Sat–Sun, 10am–9:45pm Wed–Fri.* ⬤ *Jan 1, Patriot's Day, Jul 4, Thanksgiving, Dec 25.* ⬛ ⬛ ⬛ ⬛ **Lectures, films and concerts.** ⬛ ⬛ ⬛ ⬛ www.mfa.org

KEY

⬜	Art of Africa, Oceania, and the Ancient Americas
⬜	American paintings, decorative arts, and sculpture
⬜	Ancient Egyptian, Nubian, and Near Eastern art
⬜	Asian art
⬜	Classical art
⬜	Contemporary art
⬜	European paintings, decorative arts, and sculpture
⬜	Musical instruments
⬜	Works on paper
⬜	Foster Gallery of Contemporary Art
⬜	Special/temporary exhibitions
⬜	Nonexhibition space

Late 18th-century collector James Swan's ornate French furnishings feature in the European Decorative Arts gallery.

Sargent Murals
John Singer Sargent spent the last years of his life creating these murals for the M.F.A.'s domed rotunda.

East Wing

STAR EXHIBITS

★ **Copley Portraits**

★ **Impressionist Paintings**

★ **Egyptian Mummies**

★ **Japanese Temple Room**

GALLERY GUIDE
Classical, Far Eastern, and Egyptian artifacts can be seen on both floors of the museum. American decorative arts and painting are on the first floor, while European decorative arts and paintings are on the second.

Head of Aphrodite
This rare example of Ancient Greek sculpture dates from about 330-300 BC.

Exploring the Museum of Fine Arts

11th-century, silver Korean ewer

IN ADDITION TO THE major collections noted below, the Museum of Fine Arts has important holdings in the arts of Africa, Oceania, and the ancient Americas. The museum also houses collections of works on paper, contemporary art, and musical instruments. Several galleries, large and small, are devoted to temporary thematic exhibitions. The modern West Wing of the museum houses a seminar room, lecture hall, and well-stocked bookstore. The Classical building is undergoing a program of restoration over several years; inquire about closed galleries.

Boston Harbor by the Luminist painter Fitz Hugh Lane (1804–65)

AMERICAN PAINTINGS, DECORATIVE ARTS, AND SCULPTURE

THE AMERICAN PAINTING galleries on the first floor begin with the Colonial portrait gallery. The M.F.A. owns more than 60 portraits by John Singleton Copley, perhaps America's most talented 18th-century painter, as well as works by Gilbert Stuart and Charles Willson Peale. Another gallery houses 19th-century landscapes, including harbor scenes by Fitz Hugh Lane, an early Luminist painter. Farther on are the lush society portraits of John Singer Sargent and those of other late 19th-century artists who constituted the "Boston School." There are also notable seascapes by Winslow Homer, who often painted on the Massachusetts coast, as well as the muscular figure portraiture of Thomas Eakins. The large and airy Lane Gallery of Modern Painting

and Sculpture presents a sampling of works by 20th-century masters including Stuart Davis, Jackson Pollock, Georgia O'Keeffe, and Arthur Dove.

A corridor gallery of American silver leads from the first-floor rotunda eastward to the American decorative arts galleries. Two cases contain tea services and other pieces by Paul Revere *(see p88)*. The next gallery traces the development of the Boston style of 18th-century furniture through a definitive collection of desks, high chests, and tall clocks. The reconstructed Oak Hill dining room, parlor, and bedroom from an early 19th-century mansion evoke the well-to-do lifestyle of the Federal era. Earlier period rooms are found on the Court Level, along with a gallery of ship models and an outstanding collection of contemporary crafts.

EUROPEAN PAINTINGS, DECORATIVE ARTS, AND SCULPTURE

EUROPEAN PAINTINGS and sculpture from the 16th to the 20th centuries are on the second floor of the museum. They begin with 17th-century Dutch paintings, including a number of portraits by Rembrandt. The Koch Gallery of European Paintings from 1550 to 1700 is impressive both for the drama of the space – a great hall with travertine marble walls and high, wooden coffered ceiling – and for the range of art works, which ranges from Francisco de Zurbarán and El Greco to Paolo Veronese, Titian, and Peter Paul Rubens.

Boston's 19th-century collectors enriched the M.F.A. with wonderful French painting: the museum features several paintings by Pierre François Millet (the M.F.A. has, in fact, the largest collection of his work in the world) as well as by other well-known 19th-century French artists, such as Édouard Manet, Pierre-Auguste Renoir, and Edgar Degas. One of the museum's most popular galleries displays *Waterlilies* (1905) by Claude Monet and *Dance at Bougival* (1883) by Renoir. The M.F.A.'s Monet holdings are unsurpassed outside of Paris, and there is also a good collection of paintings by the

La Berceuse by the Dutch painter Vincent van Gogh (1853–90)

Part of the Processional Way of Ancient Babylonia (6th century BC)

Dutch artist Vincent van Gogh. Early 20th-century European art is also exhibited.

The M.F.A. is also well known for its extensive collection of European decorative arts. A series of galleries displays tableware, ceramics, and glass clustered by period from the early 17th to early 20th centuries. An impressive array of 18th-century French silver is displayed in a gallery where the walls are painted with Neoclassical Louis XVI-style motifs – these were originally installed in the town house of a New York banker. There is also a striking display of 18th-century Chinese export porcelain, which is set against the imported backdrop of a Parisian hotel's Louis XV-style interior.

ANCIENT EGYPTIAN, NUBIAN, AND NEAR EASTERN ART

THE M.F.A.'S COLLECTION of Egyptian and Nubian materials is unparalleled outside of Africa and derives primarily from M.F.A.-Harvard University excavations along the Nile, which began in 1905. The first floor houses a 1998 installation showing Egyptian Funerary Arts, which uses the M.F.A.'s superb collection of mummies from nearly three millennia to illustrate the technical and art historical aspects of Egyptian burial practices. The adjacent gallery of Ancient Near East artifacts displays Babylonian, Assyrian, and Sumerian reliefs. Another gallery is devoted to ancient Nubia, the

cultural region around the Nile stretching roughly between the modern African cities of Aswan and Khartoum.

The Egyptian and Nubian collections continue on the second floor. Highlights include two monumental sculptures of Nubian kings from the Great Temple of Amen at Napata (620–586 BC and 600–580 BC). A few of the galleries are set up to re-create Nubian burial chambers, which allows cuneiform wall carvings to be displayed in something akin to an original setting; a superb example is the offering chapel of Sekhem-ankh-Ptah from Sakkara (2450–2350 BC).

CLASSICAL ART

THE M.F.A. BOASTS one of America's top collections of Greek ceramics, particularly red- and black-figure vases, which are displayed in a large gallery on the first floor, as well as in smaller

Roman fresco, excavated from a Pompeian villa (1st century AD)

galleries on the second floor. In general, the Classical galleries of the museum are arranged thematically to highlight the influence of Greek arts on both Etruscan and Roman art. The Etruscan gallery on the first floor has several carved sarcophagi, while the Roman collection on the second floor features grave markers, portrait busts, and a series of wall panel paintings unearthed in Pompeii in an M.F.A. expedition of 1900–01.

ASIAN ART

THE ASIAN COLLECTIONS, occupying some of the most elegant galleries in the M.F.A., are said to be the most extensive under one roof in the world. The first-floor galleries are primarily devoted to Indian, Near Eastern, and Central Asian art. Among the highlights are Indian sculpture and changing exhibitions of Islamic miniature paintings and Indian narrative paintings.

A beautiful stairway adorned with carved lions and a portal of a dragon in the clouds announces the entrance to the main Chinese and Japanese galleries on the second floor. Extensive holdings and limited display space mean that specific exhibitions change often, but the M.F.A.'s exhibitions of Japanese and Chinese scroll and screen paintings is, nevertheless, unmatched in the West. The strength of the M.F.A.'s Japanese art collection is largely due to the efforts of collectors such as Ernest Fenollosa and William Bigelow Sturgis. In the 19th century they encouraged the Japanese to maintain their traditions, and salvaged Buddhist temple art when the Japanese imperial government had withdrawn subsidies from these institutions. The Buddhist Temple Room is considered to contain some of the finest examples of Asian temple art in the world.

Tang Dynasty Chinese Horse (8th century)

Cambridge ❼

PART OF THE GREATER BOSTON metropolitan area, Cambridge is, nonetheless, a town in its own right and has the mood and feel of such. Principally a college town, it is dominated by Harvard University and other college campuses. It also boasts a number of important historic sights, such as Christ Church and Cambridge Common, which have associations to the American Revolution. Harvard Square is the area's main entertainment and shopping district.

Site of the Washington Elm, on Cambridge Common

⌂ Longfellow National Historic Site

105 Brattle St. 📞 (617) 876-4491. ◯ May–Oct: 10:30am–4pm Wed–Sun. 🎫 🚫 ♿ ▣ Ⓦ www.nps.gov/long

This house on Brattle Street, like many around it, was built by Colonial-era merchants loyal to the British Crown during the Revolution. It was seized by American revolutionaries and served as George Washington's headquarters during the Siege of Boston.

The poet Henry Wadsworth Longfellow boarded here in 1837, was given the house as a wedding present in 1843, and lived here until his death in 1888. He wrote his most famous poems here, including *Tales of a Wayside Inn* and *The Song of Hiawatha*. Longfellow's status as literary dean of Boston meant that Nathaniel Hawthorne and Charles Sumner, among others, were regular visitors.

⌂ Harvard Square

🏫 (617) 491-3434. ♿ Ⓦ www.harvardsquare.com

Even Bostonians think of Harvard Square as a stand-in for Cambridge – the square was the original site of Cambridge from around 1630. Dominating the square is the Harvard Cooperative Society ("the Coop"), a Harvard institution, that sells inexpensive clothes, posters, and books. Harvard's large student population is very much in evidence here, adding color to the character of the square. Many trendy boutiques, inexpensive restaurants, and numerous cafés cater to their needs. Street performers abound, especially on the weekends, and the square has long been a place where pop trends begin. Club Passim, for example, has incubated many successful singer-songwriters since Joan Baez first debuted here in 1959.

Street musician, Harvard Square

⌂ Cambridge Common

Set aside as common pasture and military drill ground in 1631, Cambridge Common has served as a center for religious, social, and political activity ever since. George Washington took command of the Continental Army here on July 3, 1775, beneath the Washington Elm, now marked by a stone. The common served as the army's encampment from 1775 to 1776. In 1997 the first monument in the US to commemorate the victims of the Irish Famine was unveiled on the common.

⛪ Christ Church

Garden St. 📞 (617) 876-0200. ◯ 7:30am–6pm Mon–Fri & Sun, 7:30am–3pm Sat. ✝ 8am, 10am Sun; also 12:30pm & 5pm in winter. 🚫 ♿ Ⓦ www.christchurch.com

With its square bell tower and plain, gray shingled edifice, Christ Church is a restrained example of an Anglican church. Designed in 1761 by Peter Harrison, the architect of Boston's King's Chapel *(see p76)*, Christ Church came in for rough treatment as a barracks for Continental Army troops in 1775 – British loyalists had almost all fled Cambridge by this time. The army even melted down the organ pipes to cast musket balls. The church was restored for services on New Year's Eve, 1775, when George Washington and his wife, Martha, were among the worshipers. Anti-Anglican sentiment remained strong in Cambridge, and Christ Church did not have its own rector again until the 19th century.

Simple interior of Christ Church, designed prior to the Revolution in 1761

🏛 Radcliffe Institute for Advanced Studies

Brattle St. ☎ *(617) 495-1573.* ♿
[W] www.radcliffe.edu

Radcliffe College was founded in 1879 as the Collegiate Institution for Women, when 27 women began to study by private arrangement with Harvard professors. By 1943, members of Harvard's faculty no longer taught separate undergraduate courses to the women of Radcliffe, and in 1999 Radcliffe ceased its official existence as an independent college. It is now an institute for advanced study promoting scholarship of women's culture. The first Radcliffe building was the 1806 Federal-style mansion, Fay House, on the northern corner of what became Radcliffe Yard. Schlesinger Library, on the west side of the yard, is considered a significant example of Colonial Revival architecture. The library's most famous holdings are an extensive collection of cookbooks and reference works on gastronomy.

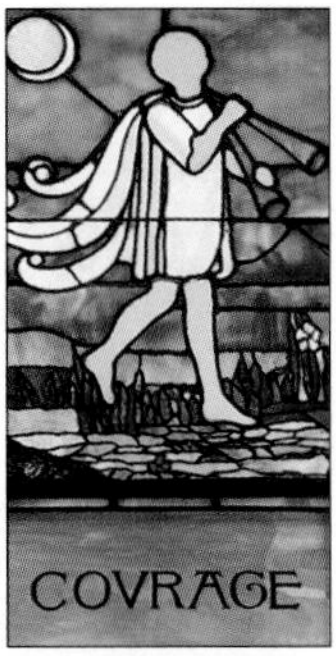
COVRAGE
Stained glass, Radcliffe Institute

🏛 M.I.T.

77 Massachusetts Ave. ☎ *(617) 253-4795.* **MIT Museum** 🕐 *10am–5pm Tue–Fri, noon–5pm Sat–Sun.* **Hart Nautical Gallery** 🕐 *9am–5pm daily.* **List Visual Arts Center** 🕐 *noon–6pm Tue–Thu & Sat–Sun, noon–8pm Fri.* 📷 🚫 ♿ 🛍 [W] www.mit.edu

Chartered in 1861 to teach students "exactly and thoroughly the fundamental principles of positive science with application to the industrial arts," the Massachusetts Institute of Technology has evolved into one of the world's leading universities in engineering and the sciences. Several architectural masterpieces dot M.I.T.'s 135-acre (55-ha) campus along the Charles River, including Eero Saarinen's Kresge Auditorium and Kresge Chapel, built in 1955. The Wiesner Building is a major collaboration between architect I. M. Pei and several artists, including Kenneth Noland, whose relief mural dominates the atrium. The building houses the **List Visual Arts Center**, noted for its avant-garde art.

The **Hart Nautical Gallery** in the Rogers Building focuses on marine engineering, with exhibits ranging from models of ships to exhibits of the latest advances in underwater research. The **M.I.T. Museum** blends art and science with exhibits such as Harold Edgerton's groundbreaking stroboscopic flash photographs, and the latest holographic art.

Visitors' Checklist

[T] *Harvard.* 🚌 *1, 69.*
ℹ **Harvard Square Information Booth** *(617) 497-1630 or (800) 862-5678,* **Cambridge Office of Tourism** *(617) 441-2884.*
⛔ *Sun.* 🎉 *late June.*
[W] www.harvard.edu **or** www.cambridge.usa.org

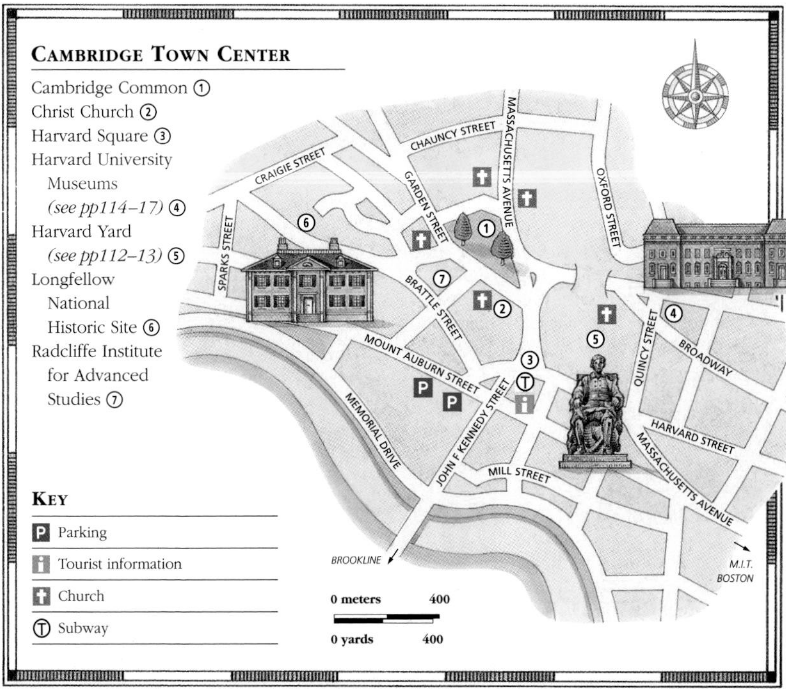
CAMBRIDGE TOWN CENTER
Cambridge Common 1
Christ Church 2
Harvard Square 3
Harvard University Museums (see pp114–17) 4
Harvard Yard (see pp112–13) 5
Longfellow National Historic Site 6
Radcliffe Institute for Advanced Studies 7
KEY
P Parking
Tourist information
Church
T Subway
CHAUNCY STREET
CRAIGIE STREET
GARDEN STREET
MASSACHUSETTS AVENUE
OXFORD STREET
SPARKS STREET
BRATTLE STREET
MOUNT AUBURN STREET
QUINCY STREET
BROADWAY
HARVARD STREET
MEMORIAL DRIVE
JOHN F KENNEDY STREET
MILL STREET
BROOKLINE
M.I.T.
BOSTON
0 meters 400
0 yards 400

Harvard Yard

IN 1636 Boston's well-educated Puritan leaders founded a college in Newtowne. Two years later cleric John Harvard died and bequeathed half his estate and all his books to the fledgling college. The colony's leaders bestowed his name on the school and rechristened the surrounding community Cambridge after the English city where they had been educated. The oldest university in the US, Harvard is now one of the world's most prestigious centers of learning. The university has expanded to encompass more than 400 buildings, but Harvard Yard is still at its heart.

Holden Chapel
Built in 1742, the chapel was the scene of revolutionary speeches and was later used as a demonstration hall for human dissections.

Hollis Hall was used as barracks by George Washington's troops during the American Revolution.

Massachusetts Hall, built in 1720, is Harvard's oldest building.

★ Old Harvard Yard
This leafy yard dates from the founding of the college in 1636. Freshman dormitories dot the yard, and throughout the year it is a focal point for students.

Harvard University Information Center ↙

★ John Harvard Statue
This statue celebrates Harvard's most famous benefactor. Almost a place of pilgrimage, graduates and visitors invariably pose for photographs here.

University Hall, designed by Charles Bulfinch, was built in 1816.

★ Widener Library
This library memorializes Harry Elkins Widener, who died on the Titanic *in 1912. With more than 3 million volumes, it is the third largest library in the US.*

★ Memorial Church
This church was built in 1931 and copies earlier styles. For example, the steeple is modeled on that of the Old North Church (see p87) in Boston's North End.

Memorial Hall, a Ruskin Gothic building, memorializes Harvard's Union casualties from the Civil War.

✦ **Sackler and Peabody Museums, and Harvard Museum of Natural History** *(see pp116–17)*

Sever Hall
One of the most distinctive of Harvard's Halls, this Romanesque style-building was designed by Henry Hobson Richardson.

Fogg Art and Busch-Reisinger Museums *(see pp114–15)*

Tercentenary Theater

STAR SIGHTS

★ **Old Harvard Yard**

★ **John Harvard Statue**

★ **Widener Library**

★ **Memorial Church**

0 meters   50

0 yards   50

Carpenter Center for Visual Arts
Opened in 1963, the Carpenter Center is the only building in the US designed by the avant-garde French architect Le Corbusier.

The Harvard University Museums

HARVARD'S MUSEUMS were originally conceived to revolutionize the process of education; students were to be taught by allowing them access to artifacts from around the world. Today, this tradition continues, with the museums housing some of the world's finest university collections: art from Europe and America in the Fogg Art and Busch-Reisinger Museums; archaeological finds in the Peabody Museum; Asian, Islamic and Indian art in the Sackler Museum, and a vast collection of artifacts in the Harvard Museum of Natural History.

Main entrance to the Fogg Art and Busch-Reisinger Museums

Fogg Art and Busch-Reisinger Museums

32 Quincy St. (617) 495-9400.
10am–5pm Mon–Sat, 1–5pm Sun. Dec 24, public hols.
 W www.artmuseums.harvard.edu

Until the Fogg Art Museum was created by a surprise bequest in 1891, Harvard, like most universities, used prints of famous paintings and casts of sculptures to teach art history. Both the Fogg and the Busch-Reisinger, which was grafted onto the Fogg in 1991, have select collections of art from Europe and America.

The Fogg building was completed in 1927, and is a red-brick Georgian building similar to other buildings at Harvard. The collections, which focus on Western art from the late Middle Ages to the present, are organized around a central courtyard modeled on a 16th-century church in Montepulciano, Italy. The ground-floor corridors surrounding the courtyard feature 12th-century capitals from Moutiers St-Jean in Burgundy, France.

Two small galleries near the entrance, and the two-story Warburg Hall, display the Fogg's collections that prefigure the Italian

Renaissance. The massive altarpieces and suspended crucifix in the Warburg are particularly impressive.

The ground floor galleries on the left side of the entrance are devoted to 17th-century Dutch, Flemish, French, and Italian paintings, including four studies by Francesco *Trevisiani's Massacre of the Innocents*, a masterpiece destroyed in Dresden during World War II. Another room details Gian Lorenzo Bernini's use of clay models for his large-scale marbles and bronzes.

The museum's second level features the emergence of landscape as a subject in French 19th-century painting. Galleries along the front of the building change exhibitions frequently, often focusing on drawings and graphic arts. The highlight of the second level is the Maurice Wertheim collection of Impressionist and Post-Impressionist art, most of it collected in the late 1930s. With a number of important paintings by Renoir, Manet, and Degas, the Wertheim gallery is the Fogg's most popular.

Surprises lurk in an adjacent gallery of art made in France 1885-1960, often by expatriate artists. Edvard Munch's 1891 painting of *Rue de Rivoli*, for example, is both bright and impressionistic, in contrast with his collection of bleak Expressionist paintings.

The museum also houses rotating displays from its collection of 19th- and 20th-century African art.

Werner Otto Hall, which contains the Busch-Reisinger Museum, is entered through the second level of the Fogg. The museum's collections focus on Germanic art and design from after 1880, with

Bernini Model (1674-75) *Gian Lorenzo Bernini crafted this clay model of a kneeling angel to guide the artisans casting his larger bronze.*

First floor

Main entrance

GUIDE TO THE FOGG ART AND BUSCH-REISINGER MUSEUMS

Art from the Middle Ages to the 18th century is on the first floor of the Fogg Art Museum. French and American art from the 19th and 20th centuries and 20th-century American art are on the second floor. The Busch-Reisinger Museum focuses on Germanic art.

Light-Space Modulator (1923–30) by the Hungarian Moholy-Nagy

an emphasis on German Expressionism. Harvard was a safe haven for many Bauhaus artists, architects, and designers who fled Nazi Germany, and both Walter Gropius and Lyonel Feininger chose the Busch-Reisinger as the depository of their personal papers and drawings.

Periodic exhibitions explore aspects of the work and philosophy of the Bauhaus movement. Although small, the museum owns major paintings and sculptures by 20th-century masters such as Max Beckmann, Lyonel Feininger, Wassily Kandinsky, Moholy-Nagy, Paul Klee, Oskar Kokoschka, Emil Nolde, and Franz Marc.

Calderwood Courtyard of the Fogg Art Museum

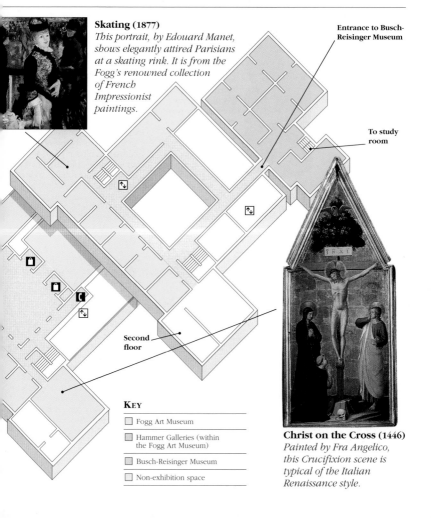

Skating (1877)
This portrait, by Edouard Manet, shows elegantly attired Parisians at a skating rink. It is from the Fogg's renowned collection of French Impressionist paintings.

Entrance to Busch-Reisinger Museum

To study room

Second floor

Christ on the Cross (1446)
Painted by Fra Angelico, this Crucifixion scene is typical of the Italian Renaissance style.

KEY

☐ Fogg Art Museum

☐ Hammer Galleries (within the Fogg Art Museum)

☐ Busch-Reisinger Museum

☐ Non-exhibition space

Peabody Museum of Archaeology and Ethnology

11 Divinity St. 📞 *(617) 496-1027.*
🕐 *9am–5pm daily.*
⚫ *Jan 1, Jul 4, Thanksgiving, Dec 25.*
📷 ♿ 🎁
🌐 www.peabody.harvard.edu

The Peabody Museum of Archaeology and Ethnology was founded in 1866 as the first museum in the Americas devoted solely to anthropology. The many collections, which include several million artifacts and more than 500,000 photographic images, come from all around the world. Initially, in the 19th century, the museum's pioneering archaeological and ethnological research began relatively close to home with excavations of Mayan sites in Central America. The Peabody also conducted some of the first and most important research on the precontact Anasazi people of the American Southwest and on the cultural history of the later Pueblo tribes of the same region. Joint expeditions sponsored by the Peabody Museum and the Museum of Fine Arts *(see pp106–9)* also uncovered some of the richest finds of dynastic and predynastic Egypt. Research continued in all these areas well into the 20th century and later

Native American totem pole, Peabody Museum

broadened to embrace the cultures of the islands of the South Pacific.

The Hall of the North American Indian on the ground level was completely overhauled in the 1990s. Most of the artifacts are displayed in a way that puts them in the context of the time when they were gathered, when European and Native cultures first came into contact. For example, the Native American tribes of the Northern Plains are interpreted largely through an exhibition detailing the Lewis and Clark expedition of 1804–06; these two explorers undertook to find a route, by water, from East to West Coast, and on their way collected innumerable artifacts. Other outstanding exhibits include totem carvings by Pacific Northwest tribes and a wide range of historic and contemporary Navajo weavings. The third floor is devoted to Central American anthropology, with casts of some of the ruins uncovered at Copán in Honduras and Chichen Itza in Mexico. The fourth floor concentrates on Polynesia, Micronesia, and other islands of the Pacific.

A gift shop sells outstanding folk art, music, and decorative items made by the modern-day descendants of the peoples detailed in the museum.

Triceratops skull in the Harvard Museum of Natural History

Harvard Museum of Natural History

26 Oxford St. 📞 *(617) 495-3045.*
🕐 *9am–5pm daily.*
⚫ *Jan 1, Jul 4, Thanksgiving, Dec 25.*
📷 ♿ 🎁
🌐 www.hmnh.harvard.edu

The Harvard Museum of Natural History is actually three museums rolled into one, all displayed on a single floor of a turn-of-the-century classroom building. It includes the collections of the Mineralogical and Geological Museum, the Museum of Comparative Zoology, and the Botanical Museum. The straightforward presentation of labeled objects exudes an infectious, old-fashioned charm, yet their initial appearance belies the fact that these are some of the most complete collections of their kind.

The mineralogical galleries include some of Harvard University's oldest specimen collections, the oldest of which dates from 1783. Virtually every New England mineral, rock, and gem type is represented here, including rough and cut gemstones and one of the world's premier meteorite collections.

The zoological galleries owe their inception to the great 19th-century biologist Louis Agassiz and include his personal arachnid collection. The collection of taxidermied bird, mammal, and reptile specimens is comprehensive, and there is also a collection of dinosaur skeletons. Children are most fascinated by the giant kronosaurus (a type of prehistoric sea serpent) and the skeleton of the first triceratops ever described in

Frog mask fom Easter Island in the South Pacific, Peabody Museum

scientific literature. There are also fossil exhibits of the earliest invertebrates and reptiles, as well as skeletons of still-living species, including a collection of whale skeletons.

The collections in the botanical galleries include the Ware Collection of Blaschka Glass Models of Plants, popularly known as the "glass flowers." Between 1887 and 1936, father and son artisans Leopold and Rudolph Blaschka created these 3,000 exacting models of 850 plant species. Each species is illustrated with a scientifically accurate lifesize model and magnified parts. While the handblown models were created as teaching aids, they are a unique accomplishment in the glassblowers' art and are as prized for their aesthetic qualities as their scientific utility.

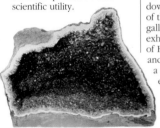

Amethyst specimen in the Harvard Museum of Natural History

Sackler Museum

485 Broadway, Cambridge.
📞 (617) 495-9400. ⬛ 10am–5pm Mon–Sat, 1–5pm Sun. ⬤ public holidays. 🖼 ♿ 🛍
W www.artmuseums.harvard.edu

Named after a famous philanthropist, physician, and art collector, the Arthur M. Sackler Museum is home to Harvard's collection of ancient, Asian, Islamic and late Indian art. Opened in 1985, it is housed in a modern building designed by James Stirling and his firm of architects based in London, England, and is itself a bold artistic statement. Aware that Harvard University had long embarked on a tradition of erecting many unique buildings in the area just north and east of Harvard Yard, Stirling was prompted to introduce the innovatively

designed building to the world as "the newest animal in Harvard's architectural zoo." The exterior borrows details and decorative devices from several surrounding buildings, while the starkly modern interior galleries provide optimal display space. The 30-ft (10-m) entrance lobby features a 1997 wall-painting by the Conceptual artist Sol Lewitt, whose trademark is colorful geometric shapes, which appear to float in space.

The Sackler is best toured by ascending to the permanent collections on the fourth floor and working back down to the lobby. The head of the stairwell terminates at gallery 10, where changing exhibitions highlight aspects of Harvard's collections of ancient Greek art, including a coin collection from the empire of Alexander the Great and unusually extensive selections of red and black pottery with decorative friezes. A small adjacent gallery displays Egyptian, ancient Near Eastern, Etruscan, and Bronze Age art. Most of Harvard's early Egyptian acquisitions were transferred to the Museum of Fine Arts *(see pp106–9)*, the

Southeast Asian Buddha head, Sackler Museum

Sackler's partner in a number of archaeological expeditions. The fourth floor galleries continue to flow, one to another, without a corridor, passing through a large gallery devoted to ancient Roman art, and then continuing eastward through Indian and Southeast Asian collections, much of which consists of Buddhist sculptures and figures from Hindu mythology. The fourth floor ends in three galleries of Chinese art situated at the front of the building: the first houses Chinese sculpture; the next Chinese Buddhist stone sculpture; the last room archaic Chinese bronzes, jades, and ceramics, many of which were the gifts of Harvard-affiliated diplomats. These collections are thought to be among the finest of Chinese art in the West.

The second-floor galleries host changing, thematic exhibitions of the Sackler's extensive collections of Islamic art from the Near East and central Asia. The first-floor gallery, behind the ticket booth, hosts ambitious and thought-provoking special exhibitions.

Buddhist sculptures, part of the Sackler's Asian and Indian collections

Charlestown

S ITUATED ON THE NORTH BANK of the Charles River, directly opposite the North End, Charlestown exudes history. The site of the infamous Battle of Bunker Hill, when American troops suffered huge losses in their fight for independence, today the district forms a major part of Boston's Freedom Trail (see pp54–57). As well as sights from the American Revolution, visitors can see USS *Constitution*, pride of the post-revolutionary American Navy, which took part in the 1812 war with Britain. Also of interest is the Charlestown Navy Yard.

Granite obelisk of the Bunker Hill Monument, erected in 1843

🏛 Bunker Hill Monument
Monument Square. 📞 (617) 242-5641. ◯ 9am–5pm daily (until 6pm in summer). ● Jan 1, Thanksgiving, Dec 25. ⓦ www.charlestown.ma.us

In the Revolution's first pitched battle between British and colonial troops, the British won but failed to escape from Boston. Following the June 17, 1775 battle, American irregulars were joined by other militia to keep British forces penned up until George Washington forced their evacuation by sea the following March. A Tuscan-style pillar was erected in 1794 in honor of Dr. Joseph Warren, a Boston revolutionary leader who died in the battle, but Charlestown citizens felt something grander was in order. They began raising funds in 1823, laid the cornerstone in 1825 and dedicated the 221-ft (67-m) granite obelisk in 1843. It was the tallest monument in the US until the Washington Monument was erected in 1885. There is no elevator, but 294 steps lead to the top and spectacular views.

🏛 Bunker Hill Pavilion
Water St. 📞 (617) 241-7575. ◯ Apr–Nov: 9am–5pm daily. ● Thanksgiving. 🍴 🚫 ♿

Next to Charlestown Navy Yard, Bunker Hill Pavilion shows a multimedia presentation *The Whites of Their Eyes*. The title comes from the purported order that American troops not fire until they could see the whites of the Redcoats' eyes. The show consists of a series of color slides projected on 14 screens, audio effects, and lifesized costumed figures.

🍴 City Square
When John Winthrop arrived with three shiploads of Puritan refugees in 1630, they settled first in the marshes at the base of Town Hill, now City Square. A small public park now marks the site of Winthrop's Town House, the very first seat of Boston government. Today, one of Boston's most famous restaurants, Olives (see p333), faces onto the square.

Municipal art in City Square

🍴 John Harvard Mall
Ten families founded Charlestown in 1629, a year before the rest of Boston was settled. They built their homes and a palisaded fort on Town Hill, a spot now marked by John Harvard Mall. Several bronze plaques within the small enclosed park commemorate events in the early history of the Massachusetts Bay Colony (see p42), one plaque proclaiming "this low mound of earth the memorial of a mighty nation." A small monument pays homage to John Harvard, the young cleric who ministered to the Charlestown settlers and who left his name, half his estate, and all his books to the fledgling college at Newtowne when he died in 1638 (see pp112–13).

🍴 Warren Tavern
2 Pleasant St. 📞 (617) 241-8142. ◯ lunch (Mon–Fri), dinner daily, brunch Sat–Sun. ⓦ www.warrentavern.com

Dating from 1780, Warren Tavern was one of the first buildings erected after the British burned Charlestown. It was named after Joseph Warren, president of the Provincial Congress in 1774 and a general in the Massachusetts Army. He enlisted as a private with the Continental Army for the Battle of Bunker Hill, where he was killed. The tavern, once derelict, has been restored to its 18th-century style. By contrast, the food is modern fare.

Old-fashioned clapboard houses on Warren Street

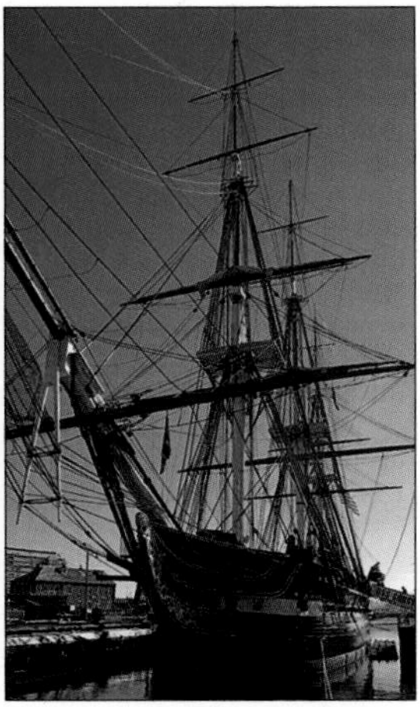

USS *Constitution*, built in 1797, moored in Charlestown Navy Yard

🏛 Charlestown Navy Yard

☎ *(617) 242-5601.* 🕐 *Sep–Jun: 9am–5pm; Jun–Labor Day: 9am–6pm.* ● *Jan 1, Thanksgiving, Dec 25.* ♿ ☕ [W] www.nps.gov/bost/cnyintro.htm

Boston's deep harbor and long tides made Charlestown a logical site for one of the US Navy's first shipyards, established in 1800. For 174 years, as the Navy moved from wooden sailing ships to steel giants, Charlestown Navy Yard played a key role in supporting the US Atlantic fleet. On decommissioning, the facility was transferred to the National Park Service to interpret the art and history of naval shipbuilding. The yard was designed by Alexander Parris, architect of Quincy Market *(see p80)*, and was one of the first examples of industrial architecture in Boston.

Drydock No. 1, built in 1802, was the one of the first docks that could be drained of water – its first occupant was USS *Constitution*. Rangers also give tours of the World War II destroyer USS *Cassin Young*.

🏛 USS *Constitution*

Charlestown Navy Yard. ☎ *(617) 242-5670.* 🕐 *May–Oct: 10am–4pm daily, Nov–Apr: 10am–4pm Thu–Sun.* ♿ ☕ **Museum:** 🕐 *May–Oct: 9am–6pm daily; Nov– Apr: 10am–5pm daily.* ● *Jan 1, Thanksgiving, Dec 25.* 🚫📷 ♿ [W] www.ussconstitutionmuseum.org

The oldest commissioned warship afloat, the USS *Constitution* was built in the North End and christened in 1797. She saw immediate action in the Mediterranean protecting American shipping from the Barbary pirates. In the War of 1812, she won fame and her nickname of "Old Ironsides" when cannonballs bounced off her in a battle with the British ship *Guerriere*. She won 42 battles, lost none, captured 20 vessels, and was never boarded by an enemy. She was nearly scuttled several times, and at one time was reduced to serving as a floating barracks. In 1830, Oliver Wendell Holmes penned the poem *Old Ironsides* that rallied public support to save the ship, while on another occasion, in the 1920s, schoolchildren sent in their pennies and nickels to salvage her. She underwent her most thorough overhaul in time for her 1997 bicentennial, able to carry her own canvas into the wind for the first time in a century. On July 4 each year, she is taken out into the harbor for an annual turnaround that reverses her position at the Navy Yard pier to insure equal weathering on both sides. A small museum documents her history.

> **VISITORS' CHECKLIST**
>
> [T] *Community College.*
> 🚌 *93.* ⛴ *from Long Wharf.*
> 🛒 *Wed.* 🎉 *June 24.*

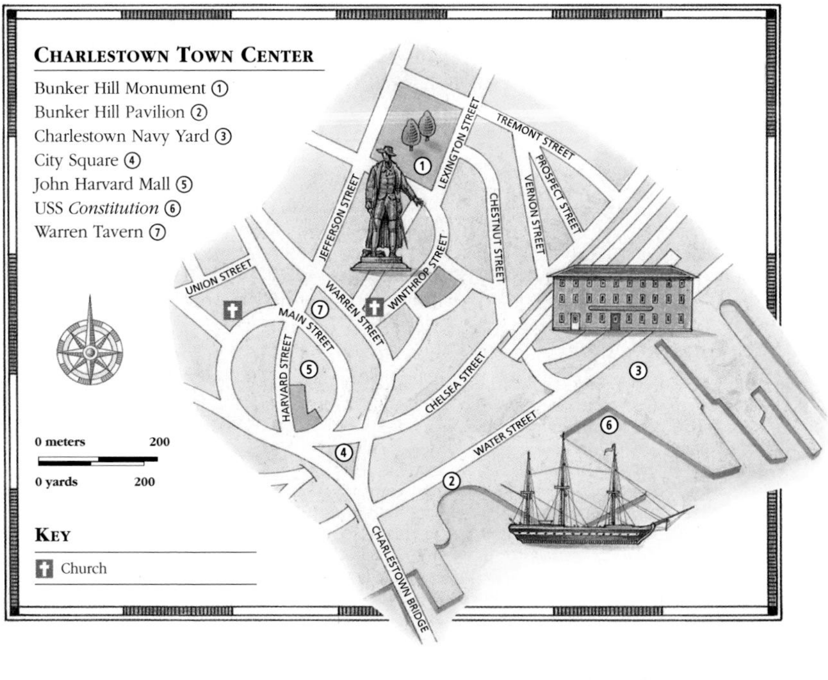
CHARLESTOWN TOWN CENTER
Bunker Hill Monument ①
Bunker Hill Pavilion ②
Charlestown Navy Yard ③
City Square ④
John Harvard Mall ⑤
USS Constitution ⑥
Warren Tavern ⑦
0 meters 200
0 yards 200
KEY
Church
TREMONT STREET
LEXINGTON STREET
PROSPECT STREET
VERNON STREET
CHESTNUT STREET
JEFFERSON STREET
WINTHROP STREET
UNION STREET
WARREN STREET
MAIN STREET
HARVARD STREET
CHELSEA STREET
WATER STREET
CHARLESTOWN BRIDGE

Wellesley College

106 Central St, Wellesley. ☎ *(781) 283-1000.* **Museum** *(781) 283-2051.* ◯ *year-round: call for hours.*

FOUNDED IN 1875, this top college for women has former First Lady Hillary Rodham Clinton (b.1947), now Senator (D) from New York, among its graduates. The grounds of the hilly Gothic campus overlooking Lake Waban are a virtual arboretum, with trees tagged for easy identification.

The main attraction is the **Davis Museum and Cultural Center**, with its collection of 5,000 paintings, prints, photos, drawings, and sculptures spanning the ages from classical to contemporary. The dramatic building was the first US project for noted Spanish architect Jose Rafael Moneo (b.1937).

Broadmoor Wildlife Sanctuary ❿

280 Eliot St, S Natick. ℹ *(508) 655-2296 .*

NINE MILES (14.5 KM) of walking trails go through field, woodland, and wetland habitats. A boardwalk skirts the bank of Indian Brook before crossing a marsh. The 110-ft (33.5-m) bridge spanning the brook is an ideal lookout from which to photograph beavers, otters, and wood ducks. In winter the sanctuary is popular with snowshoe enthusiasts.

Nature Center ◯ *9am–5pm Tue–Fri, 10am–5pm Sat, Sun & public hols.* ♿
Trails ◯ *dawn to dusk.* ♿ ♿

Former First Lady Hillary Rodham Clinton, a Wellesley College grad

Lexington ⓫

🏛 *31,500.* ℹ *1875 Massachusetts Ave (781) 862-1450.*
Ⓦ *www.lexingtonchamber.org*

LEXINGTON AND NEIGHBORING Concord are forever linked in history as the settings for two bloody skirmishes that acted as catalysts for the Revolutionary War *(see p144)*. It was here on April 19, 1775, that armed colonists, called minutemen, clashed with British troops on their way to Concord in search of rebel weaponry. The *Minute Man* statue stands on the town common, now known as **Lexington Battle Green**. The battle is reenacted each year in mid-April. The local Historical Society maintains three buildings linked to the battle that now display artifacts from that era. **Buckman Tavern** served as both the meeting place for the minutemen before the confrontation and as a makeshift hospital for their wounded. Paul Revere alerted the colonists of the advancing British troops and is said to have stopped here following his historic ride *(see box below)*. Revere also stopped at the **Hancock-Clarke House** to warn Samuel Adams (1722–1803) and John Hancock (1737–93), two of the eventual signatories to the Declaration of Independence. **Munroe Tavern** served as headquarters for British forces.

🏛 **Historical Society Houses**
Hancock-Clarke House 36 Hancock St. **Buckman Tavern** 1 Bedford St. **Munroe Tavern** 1332 Massachusetts Ave. ☎ *(781) 862-1703.* ♿

Lincoln ⓬

🏛 *7,700.*

LOCATED JUST 13 MILES (21 km) from Boston at the midway point between Concord and Lexington, Lincoln was once called "Niptown" because it was comprised of parcels of land that were "nipped" from neighboring towns. Today this wealthy rural community is noted for its interesting array of sightseeing attractions.

Buckman Tavern at Lexington, meeting place of the minutemen

PAUL REVERE'S RIDE

Under the cover of night on April 18, 1775, Boston silversmith Paul Revere (1734–1818) took on a daring mission. Rowing silently past British ships in the harbor, he reached Charlestown, borrowed a horse, and rode to Lexington to spread the alarm: the British were approaching to arrest patriots John Hancock and Samuel Adams in Lexington and seize rebel arms in Concord. Detained by British troops on the way to Concord, he was released just in time to see the first shots fired on Lexington Green. Nearly 100 years later, his heroics were immortalized in the 1860 poem "Paul Revere's Ride" by New Englander Henry Wadsworth Longfellow.

Outdoor sculptures at DeCordova Sculpture Park

The **DeCordova Sculpture Park,** the largest park of its kind in New England, displays some 70 contemporary large-scale American sculptures as part of its changing outdoor exhibition. The estate was bequeathed to the town by wealthy entrepreneur and patron of the arts Julian DeCordova (1850–1945). The museum is famous for its collection of contemporary New England artworks.

Walter Gropius (1883–1969), the founder of the original Bauhaus school of design in Germany – and one of the 20th century's most influential architects – fled Adolf Hitler's regime in 1934 to become a professor at Harvard in 1937. By 1935 Gropius had built his unique home by combining traditional New England elements, such as clapboard and fieldstone, with modern flourishes of chrome banisters and acoustical plaster. **Gropius House** stands as a prime example of Bauhaus design.

Art and architecture are also celebrated at the **Codman House,** built in 1730 and expanded in the 1790s by merchant John Codman. Home to five generations of the Codman family, the structure was expanded again in 1860, adding 18th-century architectural details to the interior and exterior. The three-story house is set on a 16-acre (6.5-ha) estate and contains wonderful neoclassical furnishings.

At **Drumlin Farm,** which is a Massachusetts Audubon Society property, visitors have an opportunity to see a working New England farm in action as well as to enjoy bird-watching and nature walks.

The farm has hands-on learning activities for children.

🏛 DeCordova Museum and Sculpture Park
51 Sandy Point Rd. 📞 *(781) 259-8355.* **Museum** ⦿ *11am–5pm Tue–Sun.* 📷 ♿ 🛍 **Sculpture park** ⦿ *8am–10pm daily.*

🏚 Gropius House
68 Baker Bridge Rd. 📞 *(781) 259-8098.* ⦿ *Jun–mid-Oct: 11am–4pm Wed–Sun; mid-Oct–Jun: 11am–4pm Sat–Sun.* 📷 🎫 *hourly.* ♿ *first floor only.* 📷 🚫

🏚 Codman House
Codman Rd. 📞 *(781) 259-8843.* ⦿ *Jun–mid-Oct: 11am–4pm Wed–Sun.* 📷 🎫 *hourly.*

🦌 Drumlin Farm Education Center and Wildlife Sanctuary
Rte 117. 📞 *(781) 259-9807.* ⦿ *Mar–Oct: 9am–5pm Tue–Sun; Nov–Feb: 9am–4pm Tue–Sun.* 📷 ♿ 📷

Quincy ⓭

🚗 *84,985.* ℹ️ *(617) 847-1454.*

NOW A SUBURB south of Boston, Quincy was once home to five generations of the Adams family, among them the second and sixth presidents of the US. The 12.5-acre (5-ha) **Adams National Historical Park** has 12 buildings, including the John Adams Birthplace, where the second president was born in 1735. His son, John Quincy Adams (1767–1848), was born just steps away at what is now called The John Quincy Adams Birthplace. Other structures include the Old House, home to four generations of the family, and a church, where both presidents and their wives are buried. A trolley provides transportation between sites and the visitor center.

🏚 Adams National Historical Park
1250 Hancock St. 📞 *(617) 770-1175.* **Visitor Center** ⦿ *mid-Apr–mid-Nov: 9am–5pm daily.* 📷 🎫 ♿ *partial.*

Environs: New Bedford, 49 miles (79 km) south on the coast, was once one of the world's major whaling ports. This working-class town lends its name to the **New Bedford Whaling National Historical Park.** The 13-block site was established to commemorate whaling history and heritage. An introductory video, walking maps, and guided tours with rangers are available at the visitor center. Among the town's main attractions is the excellent **New Bedford Whaling Museum.** The museum has assembled one of the finest and most comprehensive collections of whaling artifacts in the world, as well as model ships and carved figureheads. Whenever it is in port, the twin-masted wooden schooner *Ernestina*, which is an 1894 floating National Historic Landmark, offers tours of the deck and day cruises in warm weather.

🏚 New Bedford Whaling National Historical Park
33 William St. 📞 *(508) 996-4095.* ⦿ *9am–5pm daily.* ♿ 📷
🏛 New Bedford Whaling Museum
18 Johnny Cake Hill. 📞 *(508) 997-0046.* ⦿ *9am–5pm daily.* 📷 🎫 ♿ 📷
🏚 Schooner *Ernestina*
State Pier. 📞 *(508) 992-4900.* 📷 *dock tours and day sails May–Oct; call for schedules and reservations.*

Model ships on display at the New Bedford Whaling Museum

BOSTON STREET FINDER

THE KEY MAP BELOW shows the area of Boston covered by the *Street Finder* maps, which can be found on the following pages. Map references, given throughout this guide, for sights, restaurants, hotels, shops, and entertainment venues refer to the grid on the maps. The first figure in the map reference indicates which *Street Finder* map to turn to (1 to 4), and the letter and number that follow refer to the grid reference on that map.

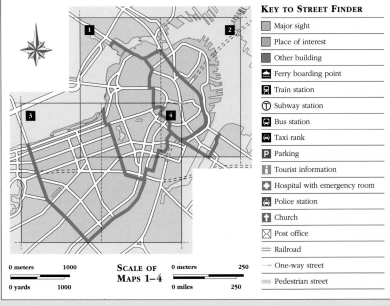

KEY TO STREET FINDER

▨	Major sight
▨	Place of interest
▢	Other building
⛴	Ferry boarding point
🚆	Train station
Ⓣ	Subway station
🚌	Bus station
🚕	Taxi rank
P	Parking
ℹ	Tourist information
✚	Hospital with emergency room
👮	Police station
✝	Church
⊠	Post office
═	Railroad
→	One-way street
▬	Pedestrian street

0 meters	1000
0 yards	1000

SCALE OF MAPS 1–4

0 meters	250
0 miles	250

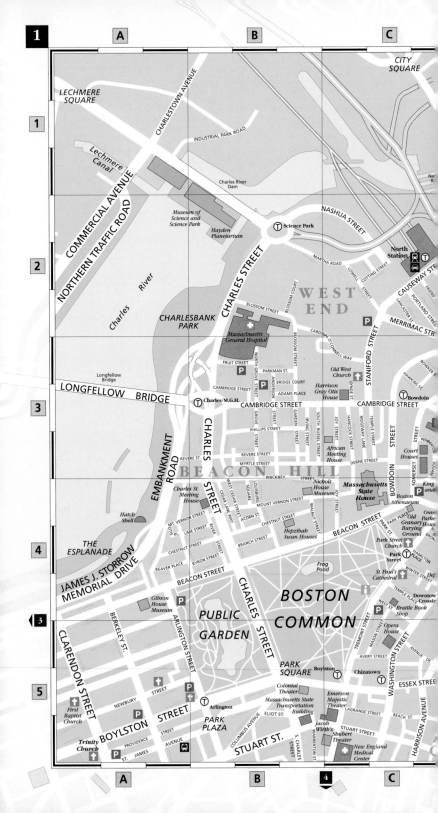

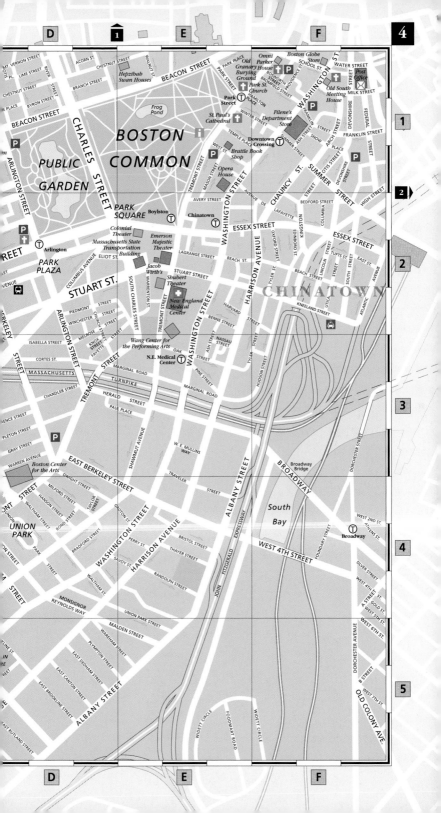

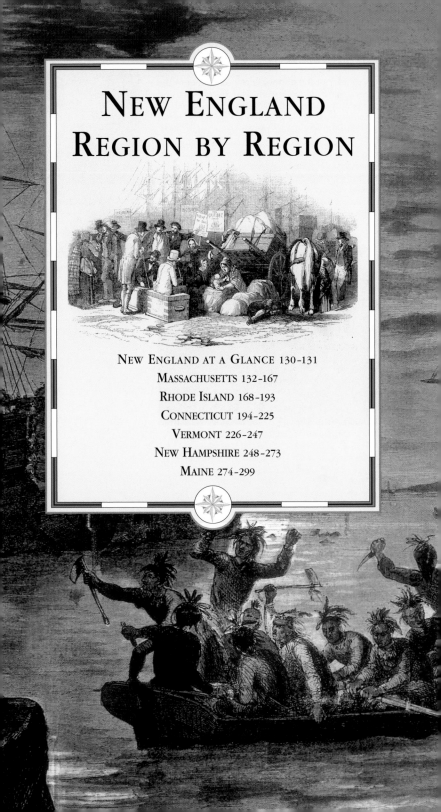

NEW ENGLAND REGION BY REGION

New England at a Glance

Tucked away in the northeasternmost corner of the United States, New England is rich in history and natural beauty. Many of the country's earliest settlements were established within these six states, with the seeds of the Revolutionary War taking root most firmly in Massachusetts. Interspersed along large tracts of rural countryside, heavy forests, and sweeping coastlines, Ivy League universities and college towns bring an influx of modernity to this historically significant region.

Vermont's fall foliage usually peaks in mid-October.

The Towne House in Old Sturbridge Village was built in 1796. Located in Sturbridge, Massachusetts, the village is one of the New England's most popular living-history museums (see p160).

Mark Twain House in Hartford, Connecticut, is where the famous US author penned many of his most beloved works. The house was commissioned in 1873 for the then hefty sum of $45,000 (see pp200–201).

0 kilometers   100

0 miles   50

Sugarloaf/USA *is one of Maine's premier ski centers. The mountain has the second-largest vertical drop of all New England ski slopes (see p362–3).*

Lobster boats *dot the waters near Isle au Haut at Ferry Landing.*

The Chase House *is featured in the Strawbery Banke restoration project in Portsmouth, New Hampshire (see pp254–5).*

The Breakers *is one of Newport, Rhode Island's most opulent mansions. Designed after 16th-century palaces in Italy, the 70-room masterpiece was used as the summer "cottage" for the wealthy Vanderbilt family (see pp186–7).*

MASSACHUSETTS

O F ALL THE NEW ENGLAND STATES, *Massachusetts may have the most diverse mix of natural and man-made attractions. Miles of wide sandy beaches beckon along the eastern seaboard; green mountains and rich culture characterize the Berkshire Hills in the west. America's early architecture has been well protected, from the lanes of Boston to villages dotting coast and countryside.*

Many of America's pivotal events have been played out against the backdrop of Massachusetts. In 1620 a group of 102 British Pilgrims sailing to the Virginia Colony were blown off course and forced to land farther north. Their colony at Plymouth *(see pp150–51)* was the first permanent English settlement in North America. More than 100 years later the seeds of the American Revolution took strongest root in Boston, blossoming into the nation of the United States and forever altering the course of world history.

Massachusetts has always been New England 's industrial and intellectual hub. The machinery of the American Industrial Revolution chugged to life in the early 19th century in Lowell *(see p142)* and other mill towns. Later the high-tech labs in Cambridge *(see pp110–11)* would help lead the nation into the computer age. In 1944 scientists at Harvard University *(see pp112–17),* the oldest and most prestigious college in the nation, developed the world's first digital computer. Today the venerable university attracts visitors from around the world wanting to tour its beautiful campus and explore the multitude of treasures in its magnificent museums.

Travelers can also tread the same ground as some of the country's most influential leaders. Quincy *(see p121)* honors the father and son team of John Adams (1735–1826) and John Quincy Adams (1767–1848), the nation's second and sixth presidents. Fashionable Hyannis Port on Cape Cod *(see pp154–9)* is home to the Kennedy clan *(see p159)* compound. Of course, the Cape is best known for its expanse of sand dunes and beaches along the Cape Cod National Seashore *(see pp154–5).*

Part of the stunning sculpture collection at Chesterwood in Stockbridge

◁ **Sunset on Duxbury Beach**

Exploring Massachusetts

MASSACHUSETTS IS A WONDERFUL DESTINATION for travelers in that such a diverse array of attractions is squeezed into a relatively small area. Art, music, theater, and dance can be found in abundance in many of the state's larger urban areas and busy college towns. Scenic seascapes, historic villages, and whale-watching junkets await along the coast and Cape Cod *(see pp154–9)*. Understandably, the coastal beaches are popular spots in summer. Venturing inland, visitors will come upon centuries-old towns, verdant forests and meadows, and countless opportunities for antiquing. As is the case with all the New England states, fall is one of the most beautiful times of year to visit.

Blooming wildflowers beside the Deerfield River

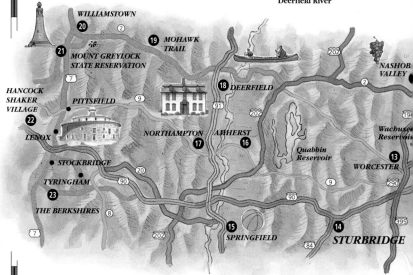

GETTING AROUND

Interstate 93 and Interstate 95 are the two largest and most popular north-south routes leading into Boston. Interstate 495 loops outside Boston, thereby bypassing much of the heavy traffic. Highway 2 and Interstate 90 are the two biggest east-west routes. Boston's Logan International Airport is New England's largest airport. Amtrak has rail links between Boston and New York City and Boston and Portland, Maine with stops in between. Bus lines such as American Eagle, Bonanza Bus, Concord Trailways, Greyhound, and Peter Pan service most of Massachusetts. Passenger and car ferries sail year-round from Cape Cod (leaving from Woods Hole) to Martha's Vineyard and from Hyannis to Nantucket. Advance reservations are essential for cars.

Brant Point, at the entrance to Nantucket Harbor

Sights at a Glance

Amherst **16**
The Berkshires **23**
Cape Cod **12**
Cape Cod National Seashore pp154–5 **11**
Concord **6**
Deerfield **18**
Duxbury **8**
Hancock Shaker Village **22**

Lowell **3**
Martha's Vineyard **9**
Mount Greylock State Reservation **21**
Nantucket Island **10**
Nashoba Valley **5**
Northampton **17**
Plymouth **7**
Salem **1**

Springfield **15**
Sturbridge **14**
Sudbury **4**
Williamstown **20**
Worcester **13**

Tours
Mohawk Trail *pp164–5* **19**
North Shore *pp140–41* **2**

See Also

The impressive Minute Man Visitor Center in Lexington

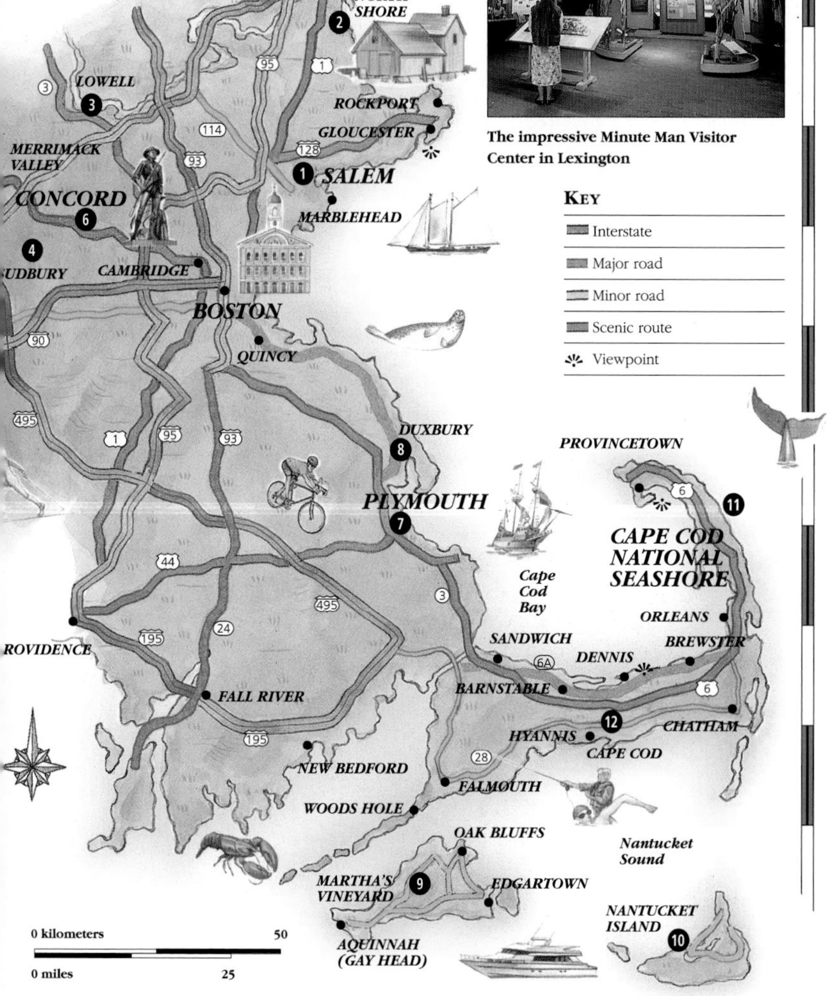

Key

Interstate
Major road
Minor road
Scenic route
Viewpoint

Salem [1]

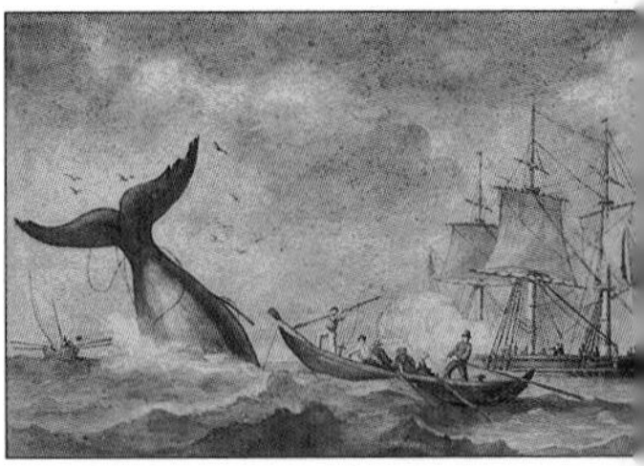

An 1842 whaling scene from the Peabody Essex Museum

ALTHOUGH IT IS BEST KNOWN for the infamous witch trials of 1692, which resulted in the execution of 20 innocent people, this coastal town has other, less sensational claims to fame. Founded in 1626 by Roger Conant (1592–1679), Salem grew to become one of New England's busiest 18th- and 19th-century ports, its harbor filled with clipper ships carrying treasures from around the globe. Present-day Salem is a bustling, good-natured town that has the ability to celebrate its rich artistic and architectural heritage, all the while playing up its popular image as the witchcraft capital of America.

Exploring Salem

Salem's main attractions are situated in clusters in the harbor and downtown areas. The historic waterfront can be explored on foot, as can the busy area along Essex and Liberty streets *(see pp138–9).*

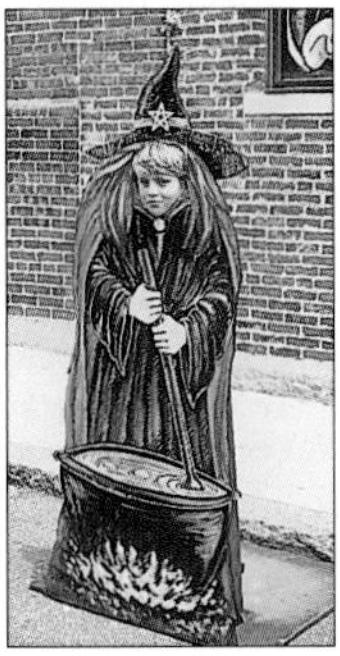

Photo opportunities for Salem visitors

🏛 Peabody Essex Museum

East India Sq. ☎ *(800) 745-4054.* ○ *Nov–Mar: 10am–5pm Tue–Sat, noon–5pm Sun; Apr–Oct: 10am–5pm Mon– Sat, noon–5pm Sun.*

🎧 ☕ ♿ 🛍

The dramatic Moshe Safdie building, opened in 2003, gave the Peabody Essex soaring galleries to display its collection of more than 2.4 million objects, including some of the worlds largest holdings of Asian art and artifacts. Among the exhibits are treasures brought back from the Orient, the Pacific, and Africa by Salem's sea captains. Highlights include jewelry, porcelain figures, ritual costumes, scrimshaw, figureheads, and navigational instruments. The buildings on Essex Street trace more than 300 years of New England history with art, furniture, china, silver, and military memorabilia.

🏛 Salem Maritime National Historic Site

Orientation Center 193 Derby St. ☎ *(978) 740-1660.* ○ *9am–5pm daily.* ● *Jan 1, Thanksgiving, & Dec 25.* ♿

Salem's heyday as a maritime center has been preserved here. At its peak, the town's harbor was serviced by some 50 wharves. Today this waterfront complex maintains three restored wharves that date back to the 1700s, including the 2,100-ft (640-m) Derby Wharf. The *Friendship,* a

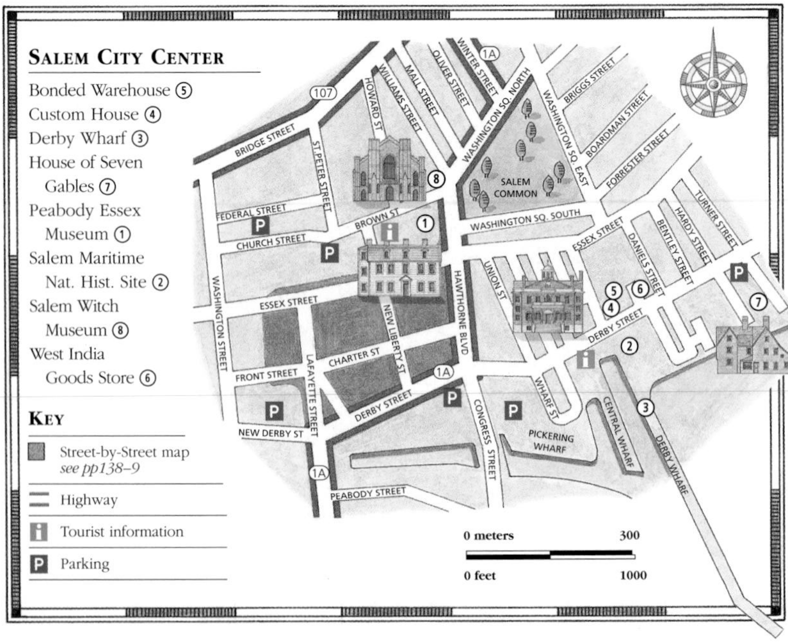
SALEM CITY CENTER
Bonded Warehouse 5
Custom House 4
Derby Wharf 3
House of Seven Gables 7
Peabody Essex Museum 1
Salem Maritime Nat. Hist. Site 2
Salem Witch Museum 8
West India Goods Store 6
KEY
Street-by-Street map see pp138–9
Highway
Tourist information
Parking
BRIDGE STREET
FEDERAL STREET
CHURCH STREET
ESSEX STREET
FRONT STREET
NEW DERBY ST
CHARTER ST
DERBY STREET
PEABODY STREET
WASHINGTON STREET
LAFAYETTE STREET
NEW LIBERTY ST
HAWTHORNE BLVD
CONGRESS STREET
ST. PETER STREET
BROWN ST
HOWARD ST
WILLIAMS STREET
MALL STREET
OLIVER STREET
WINTER STREET
WASHINGTON SQ. NORTH
WASHINGTON SQ. EAST
WASHINGTON SQ. SOUTH
SALEM COMMON
BRIGGS STREET
BOARDMAN STREET
FORRESTER STREET
TURNER STREET
HARDY STREET
BENTLEY STREET
DANIELS STREET
UNION ST
WHARF ST
CENTRAL WHARF
DERBY WHARF
PICKERING WHARF
107
1A
0 meters 300
0 feet 1000

Blacksmith at the Salem 1630 Pioneer Village

VISITORS' CHECKLIST

38,000. 🚢 From Boston's Long Wharf. ✈ 14 miles (22 km) S in Boston. 🛈 2 New Liberty St (978) 740-1650. 📷 Maritime Festival (Jul), Haunted Halloween (Oct). 🌐 www.salem.org

reconstruction of an East Indiaman sailing ship built in 1797, is moored at the dock.

Buildings at the site include the 1819 Custom House where author Nathaniel Hawthorne (1804–64) worked as a surveyor in the late 1840s. The redbrick structure, described in Hawthorne's novel *The Scarlet Letter* (1850), contains his office and desk.

🏚 House of Seven Gables Historic Site
54 Turner St. 📞 *(978) 744-0991.* ⭕ *Nov–Jun 10am–5pm daily; Jul–Oct: 10am–7pm daily.* ⚫ *first 3 weeks Jan, Thanksgiving, Dec 25.* 📷 🎟 *obligatory.* ♿ *partial.* 📷 🌐 *www.7gables.org*
Fans of author Nathaniel Hawthorne should make a pilgrimage to this 1668 house. The Salem-born writer was so taken with the Colonial-style home that he used it as the setting in his novel *House of Seven Gables* (1851). As well as its famous seven steeply pitched gables, the house also has a secret staircase. The site contains some other early homes, including Hawthorne's birthplace, a gambrel-roofed 18th-century residence moved from Union Street in 1958.

🏛 Salem Witch Museum
19 1/2 Washington Sq N. 📞 *(978) 744-1692 or (800) 544-1692.* ⭕ *Jul–Aug: 10am–7pm daily; Sep–Jun: 10am–5pm daily.* ⚫ *Jan 1, Thanksgiving, Dec 24, & 25.* ♿ 📷 🌐 *www.salemwitchmuseum.com*
Salem's most visited sight commemorates the town's darkest hour. In 1692 150 people were jailed and 20

executed after being charged with practicing witchcraft. According to some, Nathaniel Hawthorne – who was profoundly disturbed by reports of the events – added a "w" to his last name to distance himself from descendants of Judge Hathorne, the man who presided over the witch trials. A 30-minute multimedia reenactment of the witch-hunt and subsequent trials gives visitors a chilling look at the frenzy that once gripped Salem. The town capitalizes on its association with witches each year in October with one of the nation's largest and most colorful celebrations of Halloween.

🏛 Salem 1630 Pioneer Village
Forest River Pk. 📞 *(978) 745-0525.* ⭕ *mid-Apr–Nov: 10am–5pm Mon–Sat, 12pm–5pm Sun.* 📷 ♿ *partial.* 📷
Salem's earliest settlement is re-created at this museum, complete with thatched cottages, workshops, gardens, and animals. Costumed guides demonstrate daily chores and activities common to 17th-century settlers.

ENVIRONS: Just four miles (6 km) from town lies the region's most picturesque

spot: Marblehead. When President George Washington (1732–99) visited the town, he said it had "the look of antiquity." This still holds true today.

Settled in 1629 and perched on a rocky peninsula, this village displays its heritage as a fisherman's enclave and a thriving port. Crisscrossed by hilly, twisting lanes, the historic district is graced with a wonderful mix of merchants' homes, shipbuilders' mansions, and fishermen's cottages. With more than 200 houses built before the Revolutionary War and nearly 800 built during the 1800s, the district is a catalog of American architecture. Included among the historic buildings is the spired **Abbot Hall**, the seat of local government built in 1876, where the famous *The*

Clock Tower at Abbot Hall in Marblehead

Spirit of '76 painting (1875) by Archibald Willard (1836–1918) is hanging. Built in 1768 for a wealthy businessman, **The 1768 Jeremiah Lee Mansion** has a sweeping entrance hall, mahogany woodwork, and superb hand-painted wallpaper. A drive along the shoreline will reveal the lighthouse at Point O'Neck that has guided ships since 1835.

🏚 Abbot Hall
Washington Sq. 📞 *(781) 631-0000.* ⭕ *call for hours.* ♿
🏚 The 1768 Jeremiah Lee Mansion
161 Washington St. 📞 *(781) 631-1768.* ⭕ *Jun–mid-Oct: 10am–4pm Tue–Sat.* 📷 🎟

Street-by-Street: Historic Salem

L IKE MANY NEW ENGLAND TOWNS, Salem has enjoyed
a rebirth in recent years. Downtown renewal
programs have revitalized the city core, particularly
around Essex Street. Specialty shops, cobblestone
walkways, restaurants, and a pedestrian mall offer
visitors an array of diversions, including stores specializing in the occult. Travelers are best served by
stopping by the Visitor Center operated by the
National Park Service, where they can watch a
27-minute film on the region's history and pick
up maps to guide their tour.

Peabody Essex Museum
*houses the 1765 portrait of
Sarah Erving by John S. Copley.*

Old Town Hall
*The red-brick building
is now a popular
venue for concerts.*

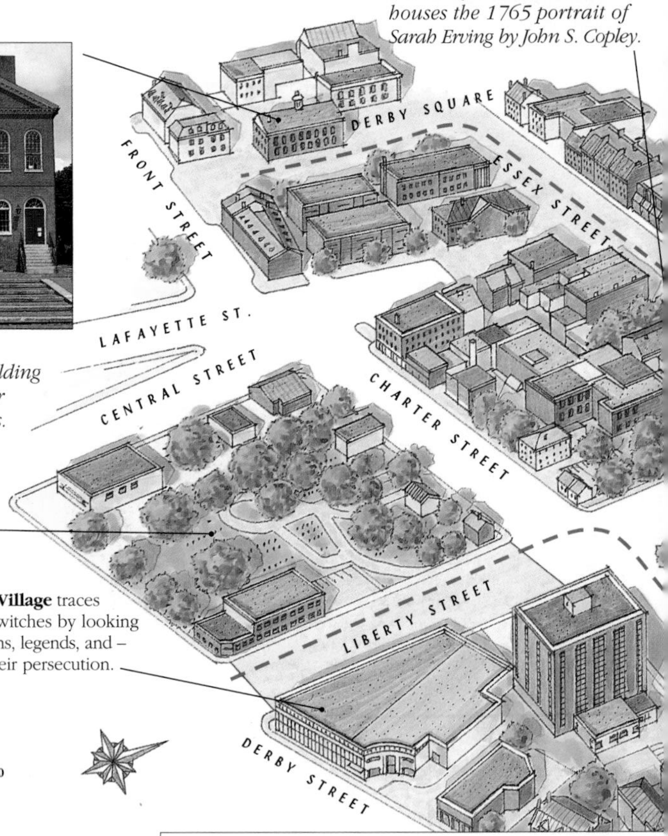

FRONT STREET

DERBY SQUARE

ESSEX STREET

LAFAYETTE ST.

CENTRAL STREET

CHARTER STREET

**Old Burying
Point Cemetery**

Salem Witch Village traces
the history of witches by looking
at their traditions, legends, and –
ultimately – their persecution.

LIBERTY STREET

DERBY STREET

0 yards   50

0 meters   50

KEY

☐   Pedestrian mall

– –   Suggested route

STAR SIGHTS

★ **Gardiner-Pingree
House**

★ **Essex Street
Pedestrian Mall**

SALEM WITCH TRIALS

In 1692 Salem was swept by a wave of
hysteria in which 200 citizens were
accused of practicing witchcraft. In all
150 people were jailed and 19 were
hung as witches, while another man
was crushed to death with stones. No
one was safe: two dogs were executed
on the gallows for being witches. Not
surprisingly, when the governor's wife
became a suspect, the trials came to an
abrupt and officially sanctioned end.

**Early accused:
Rebecca Nurse**

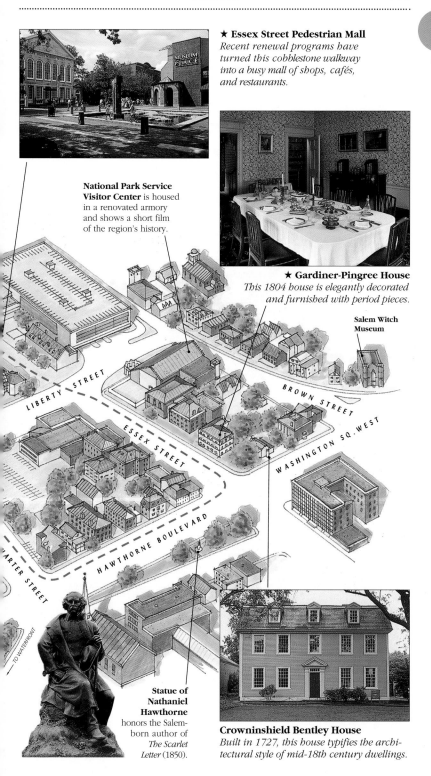

★ **Essex Street Pedestrian Mall**
Recent renewal programs have turned this cobblestone walkway into a busy mall of shops, cafés, and restaurants.

National Park Service Visitor Center is housed in a renovated armory and shows a short film of the region's history.

★ **Gardiner-Pingree House**
This 1804 house is elegantly decorated and furnished with period pieces.

Salem Witch Museum

LIBERTY STREET

ESSEX STREET

BROWN STREET

WASHINGTON SQ. WEST

HAWTHORNE BOULEVARD

CHARTER STREET

TO WATERFRONT

Statue of Nathaniel Hawthorne honors the Salem-born author of *The Scarlet Letter* (1850).

Crowninshield Bentley House
Built in 1727, this house typifies the architectural style of mid-18th century dwellings.

Tour of the North Shore ❷

THE SCENIC TIP of the North Shore is a favorite escape for harried Bostonians and vacationers who come for the quaint towns, sandy beaches, and whale-watching excursions that are found here in abundance. Ipswich, founded in 1633, still has more than 40 houses built before 1725. It is also known for its sandy beaches, marshes, dunes and seafood, especially clams. The rocky shores of Cape Ann hold diverse pleasures, including artists' colonies, mansions, and opportunities for swimming and boating.

Fisherman's Memorial statue

Fishermen casting into the surf on a North Shore beach

Ipswich ⑧
A wealth of 17th century architecture makes this a fine town to explore.

Antiquing
Antique stores can be found throughout the North Shore region, particularly in Essex along Main Street.

Manchester-by-the-Sea ①
A scenic harbor, luxurious mansions, and a wide beach are town highlights.

Magnolia ②
This Gloucester village is known for magnificent summer homes and the Medieval-style Hammond Castle Museum.

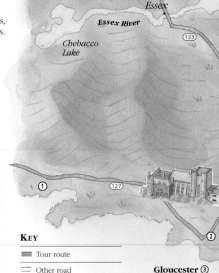

Gloucester ③
Famous for its *Fisherman's Memorial* statue, this is a lively town with a busy harbor

KEY

▬ Tour route

═ Other road

☀ Viewpoint

0 kilometers   3

0 miles   3

The World's First Fried Clam

The town of Essex has a proud culinary distinction: it was here that the clams were first fried. In 1916 Lawrence "Chubby" Woodman and his wife were selling raw clams by the road. Following a friend's suggestion, they tried deep-frying a clam. The popularity of the new-dish snack helped Woodman open his own restaurant – still one of the region's most popular today.

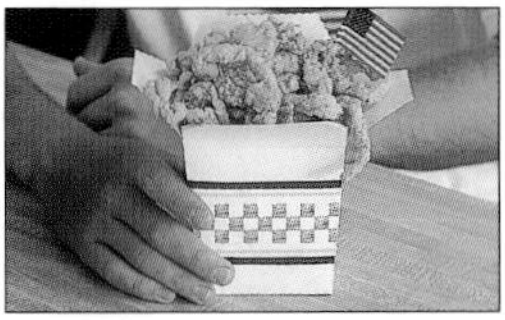
Fried clams to go from Woodman's restaurant in Essex

Tips for Drivers

Tour length: *31 miles (50 km) with detour to Wingaersheek Beach.*
Starting point: *Rte 127 in Manchester-by-the-Sea.*
Stopping-off points: *Seafood abounds in places such as Gloucester, Rockport, Essex, and Newburyport. Lodgings are plentiful, but reservations are advised during the peak period of June to October.*

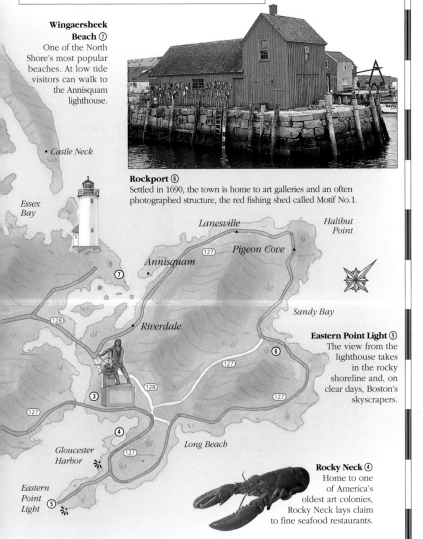

Wingaersheek Beach 7
One of the North Shore's most popular beaches. At low tide visitors can walk to the Annisquam lighthouse.

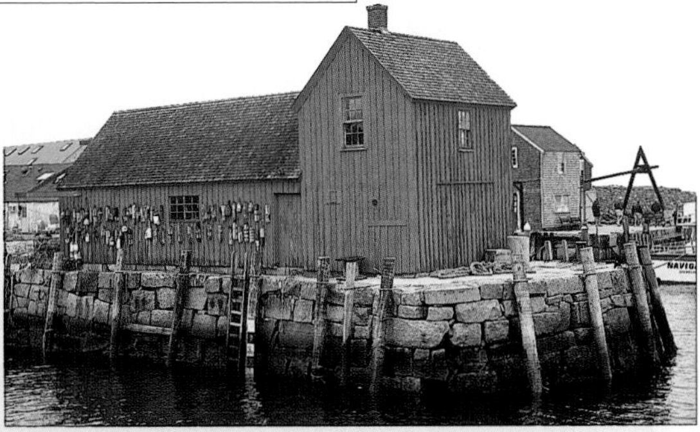

Rockport 6
Settled in 1690, the town is home to art galleries and an often photographed structure, the red fishing shed called Motif No.1.

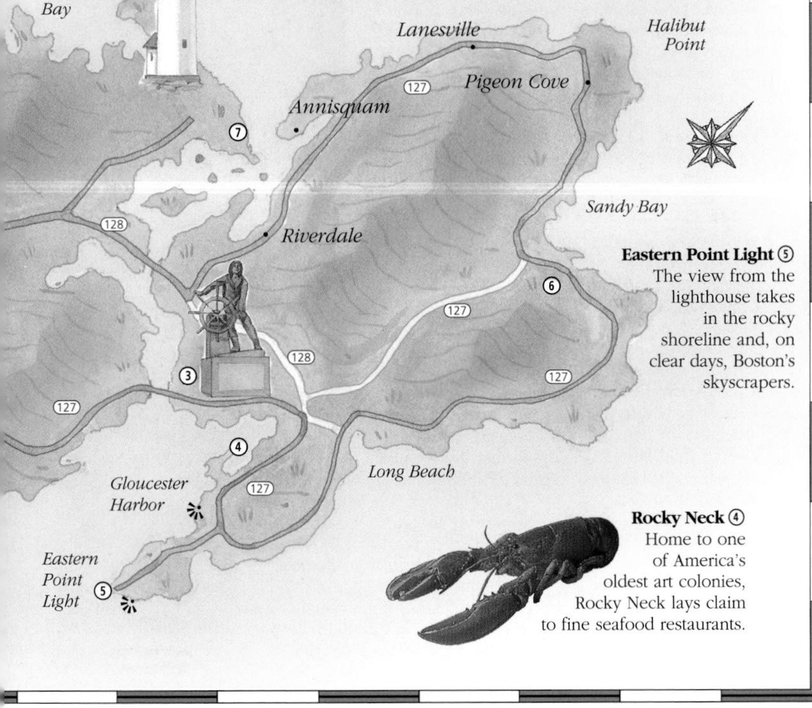
Castle Neck
Essex Bay
Lanesville
Halibut Point
Pigeon Cove
Annisquam
127
7
Sandy Bay
128
Riverdale
6
127
3
128
127
127
4
Long Beach
Gloucester Harbor
127
Eastern Point Light
5

Eastern Point Light 5
The view from the lighthouse takes in the rocky shoreline and, on clear days, Boston's skyscrapers.

Rocky Neck 4
Home to one of America's oldest art colonies, Rocky Neck lays claim to fine seafood restaurants.

Power looms on display in the Boott Cotton Mills Museum

Lowell ❸

🏃 103,000. ✈ 30 miles (48 km) S in Boston. 🚌 ℹ 9 Central St, Ste 201 (978) 459-6150.

L OWELL HAS THE distinction of being the country's first industrial city, paving the way for the American Industrial Revolution. In the early 19th century, Boston merchant Francis Cabot Lowell (1775–1817) opened a cloth mill in nearby Waltham and equipped it with his new power loom – a vast improvement over the old manual methods. The increase in production was so great that the mill quickly outgrew its quarters and was moved to the town of East Chelmsford (later renamed for Lowell). Set on 400 acres (162 ha) and using power provided by a steep drop in the Merrimack River, the business expanded to include 10 giant mill complexes, which employed more than 10,000 workers.

While the town prospered, it was at the expense of its workers, many of whom were unskilled immigrants exploited by the greedy mill owners. Eventually laborers organized and there were many strikes. The most successful was the 1912 Bread and Roses Strike, which began in neighboring Lawrence and spread to Lowell. While that confrontation helped improve conditions for workers, the relief was temporary. In the 1920s companies began to move south in search of cheaper labor. The death knell came in 1929. The country was rocked by the Great Depression and the mills closed, leaving Lowell a ghost town.

In 1978 the **Lowell National Historical Park** was established to rehabilitate more than 100 downtown buildings and preserve the town's unique history. The Market Mills Visitor Center on Market Street offers a free introductory video show, walking tour maps, guided walks with rangers, and tickets for canal boat tours of the city's waterways. From March to November, antique trolleys take visitors to the **Boott Cotton Mills Museum**, the centerpiece of the park, where 88 vintage power looms produce a deafening clatter. Interactive exhibits trace the Industrial Revolution and the growth of the labor movement. Also in Lowell, the **American Textile History Museum** traces the history of 300 years of American textiles, from early spinning and weaving to mass production.

Lowell has non-industrial attractions as well. The **New England Quilt Museum** displays both antique and contemporary examples of the quilt-maker's art, and the **Sports Museum of New England** has interactive exhibits on sports in the state. Painter James McNeill Whistler (1834–1903), most famous for his portrait of his mother, was born in Lowell while his father was in charge of the railroad works for the city's mills. Whistler's birthplace is now a museum that displays prints of some of his work, but focuses more on 19th- and 20th-century American art, especially regional artists.

♿ **Lowell National Historical Park**
246 Market St. 📞 (978) 970-5000.
🕐 year-round: 9am–5pm daily. ♿ tours & exhibits. 📷 call for hours. ♿

🏛 **Boott Cotton Mills Museum**
400 John St. 📞 (978) 970-5000.
🕐 year-round: 9:30am–5pm daily. 📷♿

🏛 **American Textile History Museum**
491 Dutton St. 📞 (978) 441-0400.
🕐 year-round: 9am–4pm Tue, Wed, Fri, 9am–8pm Thu, 10am–5pm Sat–Sun. ● public hols. 📷 📷 ♿

🏛 **New England Quilt Museum**
18 Shattuck St. 📞 (978) 452-4207.
🕐 year-round: 10am–4pm Tue–Sat; May–Dec: 12pm–4pm Sun. ● public hols. 📷♿

Bedroom display at the New England Quilt Museum in Lowell

LOWELL'S JACK KEROUAC

Lowell native Jack Kerouac was the leading chronicler of the "beat generation," a term that he coined to describe members of the disaffected Bohemian movement of the 1950s. Although he lived elsewhere for most of his adult life, his remains are buried in the town's Edson Cemetery. Excerpts from Kerouac's most famous novel, *On the Road* (1957), and other of his writings are inscribed on granite pillars in the Kerouac Commemorative Park on Bridge Street.

Jack Kerouac (1922–69)

Part of the Fruitlands Museums' Shaker collection

🏛 **Sports Museum
of New England**
25 Shattuck St. 🔲 *(978) 452-6775.*
⭕ *summer: 10am–5pm Tue–Sat,
12pm–5pm Sun; winter: 10am–5pm
Thu–Sat.* 🈁 ♿
🏛 **Whistler House
Museum of Art**
243 Worthen St. 🔲 *(978) 452-7641.*
⭕ *year-round: 11am–4pm Wed–Sat.*
🈁 ♿

Sudbury ❹

🏯 *16,500.* ✈ *24 miles (39 km)
E in Boston.*

THE PICTURESQUE TOWN
of Sudbury is home
to a number of historic sites,
including the 1797 First Parish
Church and the 1723 Loring
Parsonage. Longfellow's
Wayside Inn, one of the
nation's oldest inns, was built
c.1700 and was immortalized
in Henry Wadsworth
Longfellow's poetry collection
entitled *Tales of a Wayside
Inn* (1863). In the 1920s the
building was purchased
by industrialist Henry Ford
(1863–1947), who restored
it, filled it with antiques,
and surrounded it with other
relocated structures, such as a
rustic gristmill, a schoolhouse,
and a general store.

Nashoba Valley ❺

ℹ️ *43 Buena Vista St, Devens (978)
772-6976.*

FED BY THE NASHOBA RIVER,
Nashoba Valley is an
appealing world of meadows
and orchards and colonial
towns built around village
greens. The region is particularly popular in May when
the apple trees are in bloom,
and again in fall when the
apples are ripe for picking
and the surrounding hills are
ablaze in autumn colors.
The **Fruitlands Museums**,
the valley's major
attraction, com-
prises four
museums, two
outdoor sites,
and a tearoom on
beautiful hilltop
grounds that include
nature trails and pic-
nic areas with valley views.
Founder Clara Endicott Sears
(1863–1960), a philosopher,
writer, collector, and early
preservationist, built her home
here in 1910 and began gathering properties of historical
significance. Her first acquisi-
tion was Fruitlands, the "New
Eden" commune based partly
on vegetarianism and self-
sufficiency initiated by
Bronson Alcott (1799–1888)

**Fruitlands Museums'
rocking horse**

and fellow Transcendentalists.
Alcott was the father of author
Louisa May Alcott (1832–88)
and was the model for the
character of Mr. March in her
book *Little Women* (1868). The
restored farmhouse now serves
as a museum and includes
memorabilia of Alcott, Ralph
Waldo Emerson (1803–82), and
other Transcendentalist leaders.
Five years later, Sears
acquired a building in nearby
Shaker Village. The 1790
structure, the first office building in the village, now houses
a collection of traditional
Shaker furniture, clothing, and
artifacts. The American Indian
Museum opened its doors in
1928 to display Sears' personal collection of Native
American artifacts.
Another of the region's
attractions is the **Nashoba
Valley Winery**, a beautiful
55-acre (22-ha) orchard that
produces wines
from fruits such
as apples, pears,
peaches,
plums, blue-
berries, straw-
berries, and
elderberries. More
than 10 varieties
of apples are
grown here. On weekends
the winery offers tours.

🍴 **Fruitlands Museums**
102 Prospect Hill Rd, Harvard. 🔲
(978) 456-3924. ⭕ *mid-May–Oct:
11am–4pm Mon–Fri, 11am–5pm
Sat–Sun.* 🈁 ♿ *partial.*
🍇 **Nashoba Valley Winery**
100 Wattaquodoc Hill Rd, Bolton.
🔲 *(978) 779-5521.* ⭕ *year-round:
10am–5pm daily.* **Winery tours**: *year-
round: 11:30am–4pm Sat–Sun.* 🈁

Henry Wadsworth Longfellow's Wayside Inn, one of the nation's oldest

Concord

T HE PEACEFUL, PROSPEROUS suburban look of modern-
day Concord masks an eventful past. This small
town was at the heart of two important chapters in US
history. The first was marked by a single dramatic
event, the Battle of Concord on April 19, 1775, which
signaled the beginning of the Revolutionary War. The
second spanned several generations, as 19th-century
Concord blossomed into the literary heart and soul of
the US, with many of the nation's great writers establishing homes here. The influence of both important
periods is in full evidence today.

North Bridge in Minute Man National Historical Park

Exploring Concord
At Concord's center lies
Monument Square. It was
also at the center of the battle
fought between British troops
and Colonists more than 200
years ago. Having seized the
gun cache and other supplies
of rebel forces, the British
soldiers began burning them.
Nearby Colonist forces spotted the smoke and, believing
the town was being torched,
rushed to its defense, precipi-
tating the Revolutionary War.

🚩 Minute Man National Historical Park
174 Liberty St. 🛈 (978) 369-6993
ext 22. ◗ Apr–Oct: 9am–5pm daily;
Nov–Mar: 9am–4pm daily. ● Jan 1,
Thanksgiving, & Dec 25. ♿
🅦 www.nps.gov/mima

On April 19, 1775,
a group of militia,
ordinary citizens, and
Colonist farmers
known as minutemen
confronted British
troops who were
patrolling the North
Bridge. The minute-
men fought valiantly,
driving three British
companies of troops
from the bridge and
chasing them back to Boston.
    This 990-acre (400-ha) park
preserves the site and tells the
story of the American victory.
The Minute Man Visitor Center
also features a massive battle
mural and a 22-minute
multimedia show called "Road
to Revolution." The Battle
Road Trail traces the five-mile

(8-km) path followed by the
British as they advanced from
Lexington to Concord – the
same route they took in their
retreat back to Boston.
    The park's North Bridge Unit
is the place where the first
major engagement was fought.
This so-called "shot heard
around the world" set off the
war. Across the bridge is the
famous *Minute Man* statue by
Concord native Daniel Chester
French (1850–31). A short trail
leads from the bridge to the
North Bridge Visitor Center. A
reenactment of the battle takes
place every year in April in
Concord and Lexington.

🏛 Concord Museum
Jct of Lexington Rd & Cambridge Tpk.
🛈 (978) 369-9763. ◗ Jan–Mar:
11am–4pm Mon–Sat, 1pm–4pm Sun;
Apr–Dec: 9am–5pm Mon–Sat,
12pm–5pm Sun. 🅧 ♿ 🅦 www.
concordmuseum.org
The museum's
eclectic holdings
include decorative
arts from the 17th,
18th, and 19th cen-
turies, such as clocks,
textiles, and metal-
ware. History buffs
will want to see the
lantern that Paul
Revere ordered hung
in the steeple of Old
North Church to warn
Colonists of the British
advance *(see pp120–21)*.

*Minute Man
statue in Concord*

🚩 The Old Manse
269 Monument St. 🛈 (978) 369-3909.
◗ mid-April–Oct: 10am–5pm
Mon–Sat, 12pm–5pm Sun. 🅧
The parsonage by the North
Bridge was built in 1770 by
the grandfather of writer Ralph

Along the Battle Road, **by John Rush, a representation of what a battle of the time might have been like**

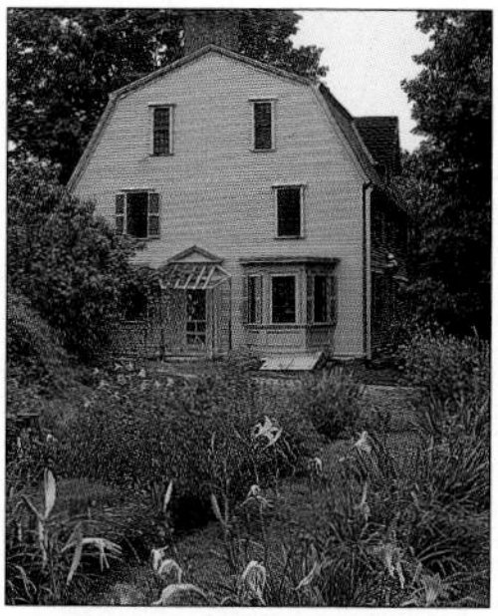

Concord's Old Manse: home to 19th-century literary giants

Waldo Emerson (1803–82), who lived here briefly. Author Nathaniel Hawthorne (1804–-64) and his wife rented the house during the first three years of their marriage (loving inscriptions are scratched into the windows). The house got its name from Hawthorne's *Mosses from an Old Manse* (1846), the collection of short stories he wrote here. On display are family possessions and period furniture.

Emerson House

Cambridge Tpk. ☎ *(978) 369-2236.* 🕒 *mid-Apr–late Oct: 10am–4:30pm Thu–Sat, noon–4:30pm Sun & public hols.* $

Ralph Waldo Emerson lived in this house from 1835 until his death in 1882, writing essays, organizing lecture tours, and entertaining friends and admirers. Much of Emerson's furniture, writings, books, and family memorabilia are on display.

Walden Pond State Reservation

915 Walden St. ☎ *(978) 369-3254.* 🕒 *call for hours.* $ 🍴 ♿

Essayist Henry David Thoreau (1817–62) lived in relative isolation at Walden Pond from July 1845 to September 1847. During his stay, he compiled the material for his seminal work *Walden; or, Life in the Woods* (1854). In the book, he called for a return to simplicity in everyday life and a respect for nature. Because of Thoreau's deep influence on future generations of environmentalists, Walden Pond is widely considered to be the birthplace of the conservationist movement.

The pond itself is surrounded by 333 acres (135 ha) of mostly undeveloped woodlands. The area is popular for walking, fishing, and swimming, and today is far from the solitary spot that Thoreau described, even though the reservation limits the number of visitors to no more than 1,000 people at one time.

Visitors' Checklist

👥 *17,750.* ✈ *21 miles (34 km) W in Boston.* [i] *58 Main St (978) 369-3120.* 📅 *Battle of Concord Reenactment (Apr).* [W] *www.concordmachamber.org*

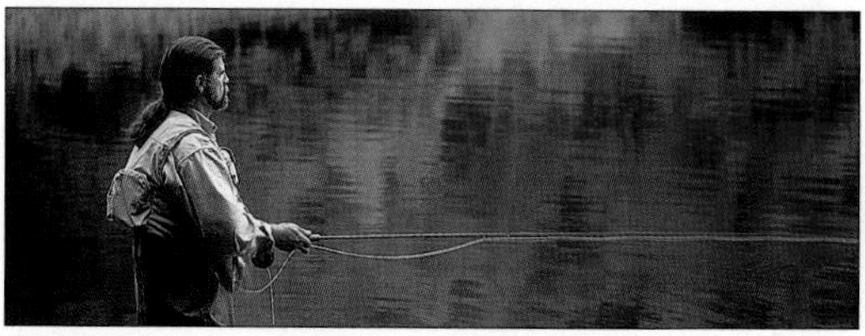

Fisherman on the tranquil waters of Walden Pond

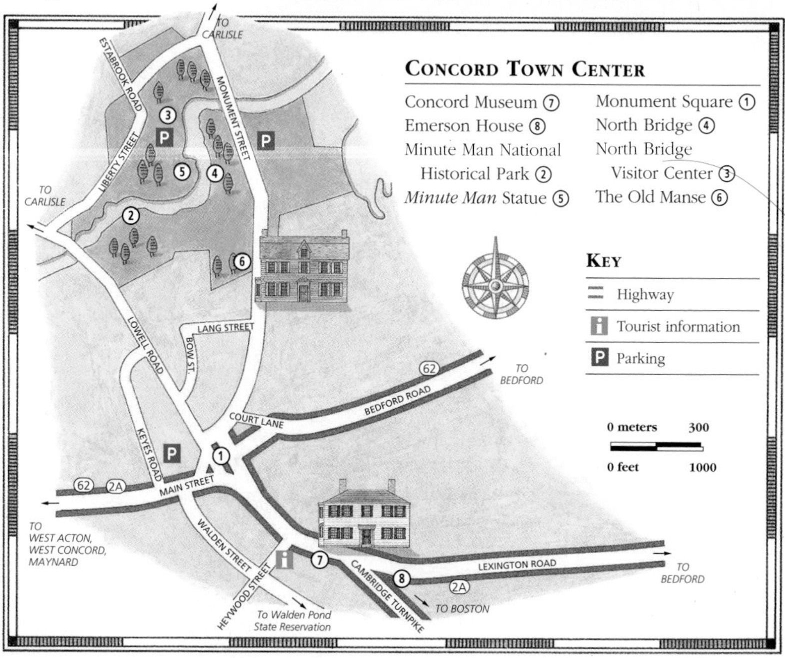
CONCORD TOWN CENTER
Concord Museum 7
Emerson House 8
Minute Man National Historical Park 2
Minute Man Statue 5
Monument Square 1
North Bridge 4
North Bridge Visitor Center 3
The Old Manse 6
KEY
Highway
Tourist information
Parking
0 meters 300
0 feet 1000
TO CARLISLE
ESTABROOK ROAD
MONUMENT STREET
LIBERTY STREET
TO CARLISLE
LOWELL ROAD
LANG STREET
BOW ST.
KEYES ROAD
COURT LANE
BEDFORD ROAD
TO BEDFORD
MAIN STREET
TO WEST ACTON, WEST CONCORD, MAYNARD
WALDEN STREET
HEYWOOD STREET
To Walden Pond State Reservation
CAMBRIDGE TURNPIKE
TO BOSTON
LEXINGTON ROAD
TO BEDFORD

Mayflower II, replica of the original Pilgrim sailing ship

Plymouth ⓿

🚶 52,000. ✈ 40 miles (64 km) NW in Boston. 🚢 to Provincetown (seasonal). 🚏 130 Water St (508) 747-7533 or (800) USA-1620. W www.visit-plymouth.com

I N 1620, 102 PILGRIMS aboard the ship *Mayflower* sailed into Plymouth harbor and established what is considered to be the first permanent English settlement in the New World. Today the town bustles with tourists exploring the sites of America's earliest days, including **Plimoth Plantation** *(see pp150–51)*, 2.5 miles (4 km) from town. The plantation is a realistic reconstruction and living-history museum of the Pilgrim village. Plymouth itself is a popular seaside resort, complete with a 3.5-mile- (6-km-) long beach, harbor cruises, and fishing excursions. In the fall, the surrounding bogs turn ruby red as the annual cranberry harvest gets underway. Plymouth is popular for its "Progress," which takes place each

Friday in August at 6pm and on Thanksgiving Day at 10am.Visitors come to witness the solemn re-enactment of the Pilgrims' slow procession to Burial Hill, where a short service is held.

Most of the historic sights can be accessed on foot by the Pilgrim Path that stretches along the waterfront and downtown areas. A sightseeing trolley connects points of interest and features a 40-minute history of the town. Ensconced in a monument at the harbor is the country's most famous boulder, Plymouth Rock, marking the spot where the Pilgrims are said to have first stepped ashore. The ***Mayflower II***, a replica of the 17th-century sailing ship that carried the Pilgrims over from England, is moored by Plymouth Rock. At just 106 ft (32 m) in length, the vessel seems far too small to have made a transatlantic voyage, especially considering the horrific weather it encountered. Walking along the cramped deck, visitors will marvel at the Pilgrims' courage.

Even after surviving the brutal crossing, many Pilgrims succumbed to illness and malnutrition during their first winter in Plymouth. Their remains are buried

across the street on Coles Hill, which is fronted by a statue of Massasoit, the Wampanoag Indian chief who allied himself with the new-comers and aided the sur-vivors by teaching them the growing and use of native corn. It was with Massasoit and his people that the Pilgrims celebrated their famous first Thanksgiving. Coles Hill offers a panoramic view of the harbor.

Burial Hill at the head of the Town Square was the site of an early fort and the final resting place of many mem-bers of the original colony, including Governor William Bradford (1590–1656). Each Friday in August, citizens dressed in Pilgrim garb walk from Plymouth Rock to the hill to reenact the church ser-vice attended by the 51 sur-vivors of the first winter.

Perched on a hilltop over-looking town, the 81-ft (25-m) National Monument to the Forefathers is dedicated to the Pilgrims who made the dangerous voyage to the New World. The Pilgrim Mother Fountain was erected in honor of the women who made the original voyage. Twenty-five set sail from England, but only four of them survived.

Opened in 1824, the **Pilgrim Hall Museum** is one of America's old-est public museums, housing the largest existing collection of Pilgrim-era furniture, decorative arts, and even armor. Some of the personal possessions on display include bibles, cradles, and the sword of one of the most colorful Pilgrims, Myles Standish (c.1584–1656), a former soldier of fortune who went on to found nearby Duxbury *(see p149)*. The museum also contains the only portrait of a *Mayflower* passenger and the hull of the *Sparrow Hawk*, a 1626 sailing ship. For a treatment of the Pilgrims' saga that particularly appeals

Statue of Massasoit

Signing the Mayflower Compact, one of 26 scenes at the Plymouth National Wax Museum

◁ **Cape Cod National Seashore, Head of the Meadow Beach**

Pilgrim Hall exhibits furniture, armor, and art

to children, take in the **Plymouth National Wax Museum**. Some 180 life-size wax figures in 26 settings help trace the Pilgrims' journey from their native England to Holland and then across the Atlantic to the New World. Among the scenes re-created are the landing at Plymouth Rock and the first Thanksgiving. Sound and light effects heighten the drama.

Plymouth has six historic homes of special interest. Among them is the **1677 Harlow Old Fort House**, constructed of timbers that were originally part of the Pilgrim fortification. The house is furnished with period pieces and is the setting for demonstrations of early pioneer skills such as carding, spinning, weaving, and candle dipping. Pottery is made on the premises at the town's oldest home, the **Richard Sparrow House**, c.1640. The original site of the **Mayflower Society House** was built in 1754 and extensively renovated in 1898. What was the old kitchen is now the office for the General Society of Mayflower Descendants. Its research library has one of the finest genealogical collections in the country.

Travelers will find many cranberry bogs on the roads outside Plymouth. Nearby, in South Carver is the **Ocean Spray Cranberry World**.

This one-of-a-kind attraction is the place to go to learn everything there is to know about cranberries. Exhibits outline the evolution of cranberry harvesting through the ages and a variety of cranberry-based dishes are prepared in a demonstration kitchen. Visitors also have the opportunity to sample some of the delicious cranberry products.

🏛 *Mayflower II*
State Pier. ☎ (508) 746-1622.
◯ Apr–Nov: 9am–5pm daily. 🌐
🏛 **Pilgrim Hall Museum**
75 Court St. ☎ (508) 746-1620.
◯ year round: 9:30am–4:30pm daily. ● Jan. 🌐
🏛 **Plymouth National Wax Museum**
16 Carver St. ☎ (508) 746-6468.
◯ 9am–5pm daily (extended summer hours). ● Dec–Feb. 🌐
♿ **1677 Harlow Old Fort House**
119 Sandwich St. ☎ (508) 746-0012. ◯ Jul & Aug: 11am–2pm Tue–Fri. 🌐 🚻
♿ **Richard Sparrow House**
42 Summer St. ☎ (508) 747-1240.
◯ Apr–late Dec: 10am–5pm Mon–Tue, Thu–Sun; late Dec–Apr: 10am–5pm Sat.
🌐 ♿ call first. 🚻
♿ **Mayflower Society House**
4 Winslow St. ☎ (508) 746-2590.
◯ call for hours. 🌐
🏛 **Ocean Spray Cranberry World**
Edaville RR, South Carver. ☎ (508) 866-8190. ◯ Jul–Oct: 11am–5pm Sat–Sun. ☑ ♿ 🚻

Duxbury ❽

🏃 15,350. 🛫 34 miles (54 km) N in Boston. 🛈 32 Court St, Plymouth (508) 747-0100.

Duxbury was settled in 1628 by a group of Pilgrims who found that the Plymouth colony was getting too crowded. Two who made the move, John Alden (c.1598–1687) and Myles Standish (c.1584–1656), were on the *Mayflower* crossing. Today the town is best known for its nine-mile- (14-km-) long beach.

The last home of Alden and his wife was the 1653 **Alden House**. The structure has several features of note, including gunstock beams and a ceiling plastered with crushed clam and oyster shells.

King Caesar House, the home of another prominent resident, is one of the town's grandest structures. Ezra Weston II, an 18th-century shipping magnate, had a fortune large enough to earn him the nickname "King Caesar." It also allowed him the luxury of building this stately Federal mansion in 1808. Today the house is furnished with period pieces, French wallpaper, and a small museum celebrating the region's maritime history.

The **Art Complex Museum** has everything from Asian and European art to Shaker furniture and contemporary New England art. A traditional Japanese tea ceremony is held on the last Sunday of the month, June through August.

Shaker piece at Art Complex Museum

♿ **Alden House**
105 Alden St. ☎ (781) 934-9092.
◯ mid-May–mid-Oct: noon–4pm Mon–Sat. 🌐 ♿
♿ **King Caesar House**
King Caesar Rd. ☎ (781) 934-6106.
◯ mid-Jun–Labor Day: 1pm–4pm Wed–Sun; day after Labor Day–Sep: 1pm–4pm Sat–Sun. 🌐 🚻
🏛 **Art Complex Museum**
189 Alden St. ☎ (781) 934-6634.
◯ year-round: 1pm–4pm Wed–Sun.

Plimoth Plantation

PLIMOTH PLANTATION is a painstakingly accurate re-creation of the Pilgrim's 1627 village. Encircled by a palisade, the settlement's rudimentary thatched dwellings are furnished with reproductions of 17th-century pieces. Throughout the site, costumed interpreters portraying historically accurate personages from the original colony go about their daily tasks of salting fish, gardening, and musket drills. Even the plantation's livestock have been bred to represent the types of cattle, goats, and chickens common in the 17th century.

Colony Governor William Bradford

Plimoth Plantation
Costumed interpreters mingle with visitors on the village's busy central street.

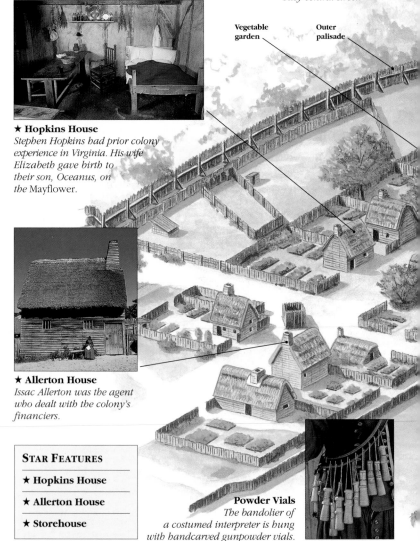

★ Hopkins House
Stephen Hopkins had prior colony experience in Virginia. His wife Elizabeth gave birth to their son, Oceanus, on the Mayflower.

Vegetable garden

Outer palisade

★ Allerton House
Issac Allerton was the agent who dealt with the colony's financiers.

Powder Vials
The bandolier of a costumed interpreter is hung with handcarved gunpowder vials.

STAR FEATURES

★ Hopkins House

★ Allerton House

★ Storehouse

KEY

☐ Illustrated
☐ Not illustrated

1 Fort/Meetinghouse
2 Standish and Alden Houses
3 Winslow and Cooke Houses
4 Bradford House
5 Allerton House
6 Cow Shed
7 Hopkins House
8 Brewster and Browne Houses
9 Dutch Barn
10 Fuller House
11 Forge
12 Storehouse

VISITORS' CHECKLIST

Rte 3A. 🏠 137 Warren Ave
(508) 746-1622. ◯ Apr–Nov:
9am–5pm daily. 🖼 ♿ limited
access to certain parts of site;
wheelchairs available upon
request. 📷
Ⓦ www.plimoth.org

Palmer
House

★ Storehouse
*Everyday provisions were
stored here, along with furs
and other goods to be
shipped to England.*

0 meters 10
0 yards 10

Local Reeds
*Used for thatching,
reeds were long-
lasting, easily
repaired, and vir-
tually waterproof.*

Dutch Barn

The Cow Shed
*Cows and other
livestock were
housed in what
was often called
the "beasthouse."
It opens into an
enclosed paddock.*

Martha's Vineyard scene: fishing boat outside fishing shack

Martha's Vineyard **9**

🏃 13,900. ✈ West Tisbury.
⛴ Woods Hole; Hyannis; Falmouth;
New Bedford. 🚌 Beach Rd, Vineyard
Haven (508) 693-0085.
🅆 www.mvy.com

T HE VINEYARD, as the locals call it, is the largest of all New England's vacation islands at 108 sq miles (280 sq km). Just a 45-minute boat ride from shore, it is blessed with a mesmerizing mix of scenic beauty and the understated charm of a beach resort. Bicycle trails abound here and opportunities for hiking, surf fishing, and some of the best sailing in the region add to the Vineyard's lure. Each town has its own distinctive mood and architectural style, making for interesting exploring.

Vineyard Haven
Most visitors arrive on Martha's Vineyard aboard ferries that sail into this waterfront town,

which was largely destroyed by fire in the 1800s. Vineyard Haven is sheltered between two points of land known as East and West Chop, each with its own landmark lighthouse.

Edgartown
As the center of the island's whaling industry in the early 1800s, Edgartown was once home to wealthy sea captains and merchants. The streets are lined with their homes.
    The main building of the **Martha's Vineyard**

Victorian home with gingerbread ornamentation in Oak Bluffs

Historical Society complex is the c.1730 Thomas Cooke House. The beautiful 12-room structure is filled with antique furniture, ship models, scrimshaw, and gear used by whalers.
    At the eastern end of the waterfront, visitors can catch the ferry to Chappaquiddick Island, a rural outpost that is popular for its beaches and opportunities for bird-watching, surf fishing, canoeing, and hiking. This quiet enclave was made famous by a fatal accident in 1969, when a car driven by Senator Edward Kennedy (b.1932) went off the bridge, killing a young woman passenger.

🏛 **Martha's Vineyard Historical Society**
59 School St. 🚇 (508) 627-4441.
◯ mid-Jun–Sep: 10am–5pm
Tue–Sat; Oct–mid-June: 1pm–4pm
Wed–Fri, 10am–4pm Sat; Jan–Feb:
10am–4pm Sat. ● Sun. 🈂 ♿ 🚻

Oak Bluffs
Tourism began on Martha's Vineyard in 1835 when local Methodists began using the undeveloped area to pitch their tents during their summer revival meetings. The setting proved popular and more people came every year in search of sunshine and salvation. Gradually the tent village gave way to a town of colorful gingerbread cottages, boardinghouses, and stores, and was named Cottage City. In 1907 it was renamed Oak Bluffs. The town is home to the **Flying Horses Carousel**, the oldest continuously operating carousel in the country. Today's children delight in riding on it as much as those of the 1870s.

🎠 **Flying Horses Carousel**
Oak Bluffs Ave. 🚇 (508) 693-9481.
◯ Memorial Day–Labor Day: daily,
call for hours. 🈂 🚻

Western Shoreline
Unlike the Vineyard's busier eastern section, the western shoreline is tranquil and rural. The area, which includes the towns of North and West Tisbury, Menemsha, and Aquinnah (the recently renamed Gay Head), is

---

WHALE-WATCHING

Whale off the coast of Martha's Vineyard

From April to mid-October the waters off Nantucket Island and Cape Cod come to life with the antics of finback, right, minke, and humpback whales. These gentle behemoths bang their massive tails, blow clouds of bubbles, and sometimes fling their entire bodies into the air only to come crashing down in mammoth back or belly flops. Whales are most numerous during July and August, and cruises are offered from many ports, including Provincetown and Barnstable on the Cape, Vineyard Haven on Martha's Vineyard, and the Straight Wharf in the town of Nantucket.

Colored cliffs of Aquinnah on western shore of Martha's Vineyard

graced by a number of private homes and pristine beaches, many of them strictly private.

Tiny West Tisbury remains a rural village of picket fences, a white-spired church, and a general store. In Menemsha, a working fishing fleet fills the harbor, and the weathered fishermen's shacks, fish nets, and lobster traps look much as they did a century ago. Windswept Aquinnah at the western edge of the island is famous for its steep multi-hued clay cliffs – a favorite subject of photographers.

Nantucket Island ⑩

🏯 *9,000 (year-round).*
✈ *West Tisbury.* ⛴ *Hyannis & Oak Bluffs.* ❚ *48 Main St (508) 228-1700.* Ⓦ *www.nantucketchamber.org*

L YING OFF THE southern tip of Cape Cod *(see pp156–9),* Nantucket Island is a 14-mile-(22-km-) long enclave of tranquility. With only one town to speak of, the island remains an untamed world of kettle ponds, cranberry bogs, and lush stands of wild grapes and blueberries, punctuated by the occasional lighthouse.

In the early 1800s the town of Nantucket was the envy of the whaling industry, with a

Brant Point Light on Nantucket Island

fleet of about 100 vessels. The town's architecture reflects those glory days, with the magnificent mansions of sea captains and merchants – made rich from their whaling profits – lining Main Street. Today the town has the nation's largest concentration of pre-1850s houses.

The **Nantucket Historical Association** (NHA) operates 11 historical buildings in town. One of the most important sites is the Whaling Museum on Broad Street (closed for renovation in 2004, reopening in 2005). It sheds light on the whaling industry through exhibits of ship models, tools, ship's logs, portraits, scrim-shaw, and a huge whale skeleton. Also located on Broad Street, the Peter Foulger Museum hosts changing exhibitions that high-light the NHA collection of furniture, baskets, portraits, and other artifacts. The Fair Street Museum, which is attached to the Quaker Meeting House, is a reminder that the island was once a refuge for many Quakers seeking freedom to practice their religion. It now houses the NHA Research Library. The library has a huge collection of diaries and letters, manuscripts, business documents, ships' logs, maps and charts, and genealogical materials, as well as more than 45,000 photographs.

🏛 **Nantucket Historical Association (NHA)**
15 Broad St. ❚ *(508) 228-1894.* **Historic buildings** ⬜ *call for hours.* 🖼 🚻 ♿ *Whaling Museum only.* ⬛

ENVIRONS: Just eight miles (13 km) from the town of Nantucket lies the tiny village of **Siasconset**. The village, which is called "Sconset" by locals, is located on the eastern shore of the island and easily lives up to the description offered by one 18th-century visitor: "Perfectly unconnected with the real world and far removed from its perturbations." Set between cranberry bogs and rose-covered bluffs overlooking the Atlantic Ocean, the village's narrow lanes are lined with miniature cottages that are among the oldest of the island. These are fishermen's shanties, many of them constructed out of wood rescued from shipwrecks, accounting for Sconset's old nickname, "Patchwork Village."

Once Sconset was a summer colony for actors, attracting such luminaries of the American stage as Lillian Russell (1861–1922) and Joseph Jefferson (1829–1905), who made the 35-minute ride from the town of Nantucket via an island railroad. Today there are only a few inns remaining. The majority of Sconset's summer visitors own or rent homes, a fact that serves to keep the beaches uncrowded and the village peaceful.

Cape Cod National Seashore ⑪

National Park sign

S TRETCHING MORE THAN 40 miles (64 km) from Chatham in the south to Provincetown in the north, Cape Cod National Seashore is one of the Eastern Seaboard's true gems. With the backing of President John Kennedy (1917–63) the seashore was established in 1961 to protect the fragile sand dunes and beaches, salt marshes, glacial cliffs, and wood-lands. While the delicate landscape has been under federal protection since then, certain features have been added, including bike trails, hiking paths, and specially designated dune trails for off-road vehi-cles. Historical structures are interspersed among the seashore's softly beautiful natural features.

★ Old Harbor Life-Saving Station
This 1897 station houses a museum containing turn-of-the-century rescue equipment and shipwreck paraphernalia. During the summer months, traditional rescue methods are sometimes demonstrated.

★ Province Lands Area
The barren, windswept landscape of the Province Lands Area has long been an inspiration for writers and artists. Here beech forests give way to horseshoe-shaped dunes and white sand beaches.

Overview
Visitors get an overview of the area in the park's visitor centers.

KEY

▬▬	Major road
▬▬	Minor road
- -	Walking trail
—	Park boundary
ℹ	Tourist information
P	Parking
⛴	Ferry (seasonal)
🏕	Picnic area
☼	Viewpoint

0 kilometers   2

0 miles   2

Long Point Light

Race Point Beach
Race Point Light
Race Point Road
Provincetown
Provincetown Harbor
Herring Cove Beach
To Glouchester
Long Point
To Boston
To Plymouth

VISITORS' CHECKLIST

Rte 6, Cape Cod. 🚹 *Salt Pond Visitor Center, Rte 6, Eastham (508) 255-3421.* 🕐 *year-round.* 🔲 *www.nps.gov/caco*

★ **Atwood Higgins House**
This 1730s Colonial-style home typifies the houses of early settlers to the region.

Wildflowers *bloom throughout the seasons at the National Seashore.*

★ **Atlantic White Cedar Swamp Trail**
A nature trail, part of which is a boardwalk over swamp, leads through forested swampland and stands of scrub oak and pitch pine to Marconi Station.

Marconi Beach, *a broad and sandy expanse near South Wellfleet, is named after Guglielmo Marconi (1874–1937), who transmitted the world's first wireless message from this area in 1903.*

STAR FEATURES

★ **Old Harbor Life-Saving Station**

★ **Province Lands Area**

★ **Atlantic White Cedar Swamp Trail**

★ **Atwood Higgins House**

Cape Cod

MORE THAN 13 MILLION PEOPLE arrive each summer to enjoy the boundless beaches, natural beauty, and quaint colonial villages of Cape Cod. Extending some 70 miles (113 km) into the sea, the Cape is shaped like an upraised arm, bent at the elbow with the Atlantic Ocean and the Cape Cod National Seashore (see pp154–5) and ending with the fist at Provincetown. Crowds are heaviest along Route 28, where beaches edge the warmer waters of Nantucket Sound and Buzzard's Bay. Towns along Route 6A, the old Kings Highway, retain their colonial charm, with many of the old homes now serving as antique shops and inns.

Exploring the Lower Cape

First-time visitors to Cape Cod are almost always confused when they are given directions by locals. This is because residents have divided the Cape into three districts with names that do not make much sense. The Mid- and Upper Cape is actually the southernmost portion closest to the mainland, while the Lower Cape is the northernmost section.

The Lower Cape takes in the long elbow of the peninsula that curls northward and forms Cape Cod Bay. The towns of Chatham, Brewster, Orleans, Eastham, Wellfleet, Truro, and Provincetown are all located in this section of Cape Cod.

Provincetown

This picturesque town at the northern tip of the Cape has a colorful history. The Pilgrims first landed here in 1620 and stayed for five weeks before pushing on to the mainland. During that time they drew up the Mayflower Compact, a forerunner of the American Constitution. "P-Town," as it is called, later grew into a major 18th-century fishing center. By the beginning of the 20th century, P-Town had become a bustling artists' colony. Today this popular and eccentric town is one of New England's most vibrant destinations. Visitors should be warned, however, that in the summer months the

Pilgrim Monument

town's population can swell from 3,500 to more than 80,000.

The place where the Pilgrims first landed is marked by a bronze plaque on Commercial Street and commemorated by the tallest granite structure in the US, the 252-ft (77-m) **Pilgrim Monument**. On a clear day, the view from the top extends all the way to Boston. Eclectic displays in the adjacent museum include exhibits of Pilgrim history as well as marine and Arctic artifacts.

The **Whydah Pirate Museum** is named for a ship that sank in a storm off Cape Cod after being captured by pirates. It exhibits artifacts such as gold dubloons, weapons, clothing, and West African gold jewelry. The region's rich cultural history is celebrated in the galleries of the **Provincetown Art Association and Museum**, where works by local artists

Fishermen on their boat in Provincetown harbor

are displayed. One of the town's busiest locales is MacMillan Wharf, the center of nautical activity, including the jumping-off point for whale-watching cruises (see p152).

Pilgrim Monument and Provincetown Museum

High Pole Hill Rd. (508) 487-1310. Apr–Jun & Sep–Nov: 9am–5pm daily; Jul–Aug: 9am–7pm daily.

Whydah Pirate Museum

16 MacMillan Wharf. (508) 487-8899. May & Sep–Oct: 10am–5pm daily; June–Aug: 10am–7pm daily; Nov–Dec: 10am–5pm Sat–Sun.

Provincetown Art Association and Museum

460 Commercial St. (508) 487-1750. call for hours.

ENVIRONS: Just 17 miles (27 km) south of Provincetown lies Wellfleet, an early whaling center that possesses one of the Cape's largest concentrations of art galleries.

Busy streets of Cape Cod's Provincetown in the summertime

Farther down the Cape is Eastham, home to the **Old Schoolhouse Museum**, a one-room school built in 1869. Neighboring Orleans is a commercial center with access to the very beautiful Nauset Beach and its much-photographed lighthouse.

⛪ Old Schoolhouse Museum

Nauset Rd, Eastham. ☎ *(508) 255-0788.* ◯ *Jul–Aug: 1pm–4pm Mon–Fri; Sep: 1pm–4pm Sat.*

Chatham

Chatham rests on the very point of the Cape's "elbow," the place where Nantucket Sound meets the Atlantic Ocean. An attractive, upscale community, it offers fine inns, a Main Street filled with attractive shops, and a popular summer playhouse. Housed in an 1887 Victorian train station, the **Railroad Museum** contains models, photos, memorabilia, and vintage trains that can be boarded. Fishing boats unload their catch at the pier every afternoon, and the surrounding waters offer good opportunities for amateur anglers to fish for bluefish and bass.

Chatham is also the best place to plan a trip to the **Monomoy National Wildlife Refuge**. Encompassing two islands, this huge reserve attracts migrating birds and is a nesting habitat for such endangered birds as the piping plover and the roseate tern. Deer are spotted here, as are the numerous gray and harbor seals that bask on the rocks.

⛪ Railroad Museum

Depot Rd. ☎ *(508) 945-5199.* ◯ *mid-Jun–mid-Sep: 10am–4pm Tue–Sat.* ♿

✹ Monomoy National Wildlife Refuge

Wikis Way, Morris Island. ☎ *(508) 945-0594.* ◯ *call for information about boat service to refuge.*

Brewster

Named for Elder William Brewster (1567–1644), who was a passenger on the *Mayflower*, Brewster is another town graced with lovely 19th-century houses of wealthy sea captains. It is also home to a particularly handsome church, the 1834 First Parish Brewster Unitarian Universalist Church. Some pews are marked with names of prominent captains.

Children will love the interactive exhibits found at the **Cape Cod Museum of Natural History**. An observation area looking out on the salt-marsh habitat of birds allows visitors close-up views of the natural world. The 82-acre (33-ha) grounds are laced with three walking trails with boardwalks that cross salt marshes. The museum also offers interesting guided "eco-treks" and cruises to nearby Nauset Marsh and Monomoy Islands.

The five-building **New England Fire and History Museum** houses a helmet collection, 30 antique fire

engines, and firefighter gear dating back to the 1700s. Elsewhere visitors can tour a blacksmith shop and a Victorian apothecary or view the diorama of the 1871 fire that devastated Chicago.

⛪ Cape Cod Museum of Natural History

869 Rte 6A. ☎ *(508) 896-3867.* ◯ *year-round: 9:30am–4:30pm Mon–Sat, 11am–4:30pm Sun.* 🅿 ♿ ☕

⛪ New England Fire and History Museum

1439 Main St/Rte 6A. ☎ *(508) 896-5711.* ◯ *Memorial Day–mid-Sep: 10am–4pm Mon–Fri; mid-Sep–Columbus Day: 12pm–4pm Sat–Sun.* ☕

Red and white Nauset Light on the Lower Cape

Exploring the Mid- and Upper Cape

STRETCHING FROM BOURNE AND SANDWICH in the west to Yarmouth and Harwich in the east, Cape Cod's Mid- and Upper sections offer travelers a broad range of vacation experiences. Be it sunbathing on the tranquil beaches of Nantucket Sound by day or partaking in the fashionable nightlife of Hyannis once the sun has set over Cape Cod Bay, this section of the Cape has a little something for every taste.

Hyannis boatbuilder and his remodeled Russian torpedo boat

Dennis

This gracious village has developed into a vibrant artistic center and is home to the 1927 **Cape Playhouse**, America's oldest professional summer theater, as well as some of the Cape's finest public golf courses. The list of stage luminaries who started their career here is impressive. Playhouse grads include eventual Academy Award-winners Humphrey Bogart, Bette Davis, and Henry Fonda. The Playhouse complex also includes the **Cape Museum of Fine Arts**, displaying the works of Cape Cod artists. A short drive to the east, the Scargo Hill Tower is open to the public and offers brilliant views of the surrounding landscape.

Cape Playhouse
820 Rte 6A. *(508) 385-3911.* call for show times.

Cape Museum of Fine Arts
Cape Playhouse grounds. *(508) 385-4477.* year-round: 10am–5pm Mon–Sat, 1pm–5pm Sun. Oct–May: Mon & public hols.

Hyannis

The Cape's largest village is also a busy shopping center and the transportation hub for regional train, bus, and air service. The harbor is full of yachts and sightseeing boats. Surprisingly, one of Hyannis' most popular forms of transportation does not float. The **Cape Cod Central Railroad** takes travelers for a scenic two-hour round-trip to the Cape Cod canal. Hyannis

was one of the Cape's earliest summer resorts, attracting vacationers as far back as the mid-1800s. In 1874 President Ulysses S. Grant (1822–85) vacationed here, followed by President Grover Cleveland (1837–1908) years later. The most famous estate is the Kennedy compound, summer playground of one of America's most famous political dynasties. The heavily screened compound is best seen from the water aboard a sightseeing cruise.

After John Kennedy's assassination in 1963, a simple monument was erected in his honor: a pool and fountain and a circular wall bearing Kennedy's profile. The **John F. Kennedy Hyannis Museum** on the ground floor of the Old Town Hall covers the years he spent vacationing here, beginning in the 1930s, and is brought to life with photos, oral histories, and Kennedy family videos.

Cape Cod Central Railroad
252 Main St. *(508) 771-3800 or (888) 797-7245.* late May–late Oct: Tue–Sun; call for trip times.

John F. Kennedy Hyannis Museum
397 Main St. *(508) 790-3077.* call for hours.

Barnstable

This attractive harbor town is the hub of Barnstable County, a widespread region extending to both sides of the Cape. The **Donald Trayser Museum** contains a potpourri of exhibits, including ship models, nautical equipment, Native American artifacts, carpentry

Popular sightseeing mode of transportation: Cape Cod Central Railroad

THE KENNEDY CLAN

The center of the Kennedy compound in Hyannis Port is the "cottage" that multi-millionaire Joseph Kennedy (1888–1969) and his wife Rose (1890–1995) bought in 1926. The much-expanded structure was a vacation retreat for the Kennedys and their nine children. John Fitzgerald Kennedy (1917–63), the country's 35th president, and his brothers and sisters continued to summer here long after they had started families of their own. In 1999, JFK's son, John Jr, was flying to the compound for a family wedding when his plane crashed off Martha's Vineyard.

John and Jacqueline Kennedy at their cottage in Hyannis Port

tools, and an old wooden jail. The bustling harbor offers whale-watching cruises, and several conservation properties make for fine hiking.

🏛 Donald Trayser Museum
Rte 6A, Cobb's Hill. 📞 *(508) 362-2092.* ⭘ *mid-Jun–mid-Oct: 1:30pm–4:30pm Tue–Sun.*

Falmouth
Falmouth, settled by Quakers in 1661, grew into a resort town in the late 1800s. The picturesque village green and historic Main Street reflect a Victorian heritage.

Falmouth's coastline is ideal for boating, windsurfing, and sea kayaking. As well, the town is graced with 12 miles (19 km) of beaches. Old Silver is the most popular beach, but Grand Avenue has the most dramatic views of Vineyard Sound. Nature lovers will find walking and hiking trails, salt marshes, tidal pools, and opportunities for beach-combing and bird-watching. The 3.3-mile (5 km) Shining Sea Bike Path offers vistas of beach, harbor, and woodland on the way to Woods Hole.

Woods Hole
This is home to the world's largest independent marine science research center, the Woods Hole Oceanographic Institution (WHOI).

Visitors to the **WHOI Exhibit Center** can explore two floors of displays and videos explaining coastal ecology and highlighting some of the organization's findings. Exhibits include a replica of the interior of the *Alvin*, one of the pioneer vessels developed for deep-sea exploration.

🏛 WHOI Exhibit Center
15 School St. 📞 *(508) 289-2663.* ⭘ *call for hours.* 💰 *donation.* 🕐 *Jul–Aug by appt.* ♿

Sandwich
The oldest town on the Cape is straight off a postcard: the First Church of Christ overlooks a picturesque pond fed by the brook that powers the water-wheel of a colonial-era gristmill. The church has what is said to be the oldest church bell in the US, dating to 1675. The **Dexter Grist Mill**, built in 1654, has been restored and is grinding again, producing cornmeal that is available at the gift shop.

Antique bottle in Glass Museum

Another industry is celebrated at the **Sandwich Glass Museum**. Between 1825 and 1888, local entrepreneurs invented a way to press glass that was prized for its colors. Nearly 5,000 pieces of Sandwich glass are handsomely displayed here.

The most unique attraction in Sandwich is **Heritage Museums and Gardens**, a 75-acre (30-ha) garden and museum built around the collection of pharmaceutical

magnate and inveterate collector Josiah Kirby Lilly, Jr (1893–1966). The artifacts fill three buildings. The Military Museum includes military miniatures, antique firearms, and a wing devoted to Native American relics. A collection of 37 antique cars is displayed in a reproduction of a Shaker barn. The Art Museum contains everything from folk art and a collection of Currier and Ives prints to changing exhibits and a working 1912 carousel – a favorite with visitors. Outside, the grounds are planted with more than 1,000 varieties of trees, shrubs, and flowers, including superb rhododendrons.

🏭 Dexter Grist Mill
Maine & Water Sts. 📞 *(508) 833-1632.* ⭘ *call for hours.* 💰

🏛 Sandwich Glass Museum
129 Main St. 📞 *(508) 888-0251.* ⭘ *Feb–Mar: 9:30am–4pm Wed–Sun; Apr–Dec: 9:30am–5pm daily.* 💰 🕐 ♿

🏭 Heritage Museums and Gardens
67 Grove St. 📞 *(508) 888-3300.* ⭘ *mid-May–mid-Oct: 9am–6pm Sat–Wed, 9am–8pm Thu–Fri; Nov–mid-May: call for hours.* 💰 ♿

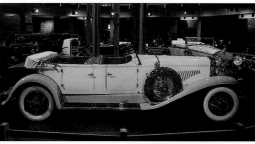
Film star Gary Cooper's 1930 Duesenberg at Heritage Plantation

Old Sturbridge Village

AT THE HEART OF THIS OPEN-AIR MUSEUM are about 40 vintage buildings that have been restored and relocated from all over New England. Laid out like an early 19th-century village, Old Sturbridge is peopled by costumed interpreters who go about their daily activities. The village common is ringed by the meetinghouse, a tin shop, a shoe shop, and homes. Elsewhere a blacksmith works the forge, farmers tend crops, and millers work the gristmill. Inside buildings visitors will find re-created period settings, early American antiques, and demonstrations of such crafts as spinning and weaving.

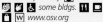

VISITORS' CHECKLIST

Rte 20, Sturbridge.
📞 (508) 347- 3362. –
🕐 Jan–mid-Feb: 9:30am–4pm
Sat–Sun; mid-Feb–Mar:
9:30am–4pm Tue–Sun; Apr–Oct:
9:30am–5pm daily. ● Dec 25.
🦽 ✍ ♿ some bldgs. 🍴 🖭
🅿 🔤 www.osv.org

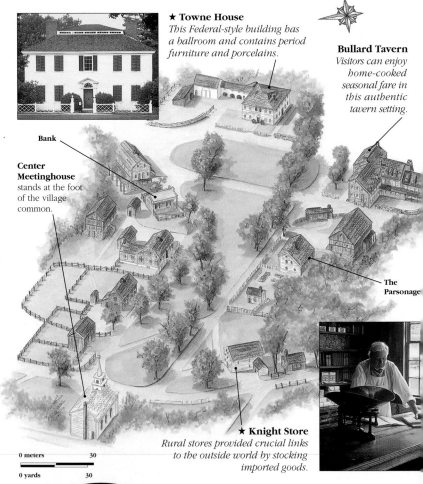

★ Towne House
This Federal-style building has a ballroom and contains period furniture and porcelains.

Bullard Tavern
Visitors can enjoy home-cooked seasonal fare in this authentic tavern setting.

Bank

Center Meetinghouse stands at the foot of the village common.

The Parsonage

★ Knight Store
Rural stores provided crucial links to the outside world by stocking imported goods.

0 meters   30
0 yards   30

Home-baked goods
Visitors can watch as costumed interpreters go about such daily activities as preparing food.

STAR SIGHTS

★ Towne House

★ Knight Store

Worcester ⑬

🏙 170,000. ✈ Worcester Airport.
🚏 🚉 ℹ️ 30 Worcester Center Blvd
(508) 753-2920 or (800) 231-7557.

WORCESTER HAS always been on the cutting edge. During the American Industrial Revolution, local designers developed the nation's first mechanized carpet weavers and envelope folders. This spirit of invention reached its pinnacle in 1926, when Worcester native Dr. Robert Goddard (1882–1945) launched the world's first liquid-fuel rocket.

Higgins Armory Museum display

Not all of Worcester's forward thinking has been reserved for the development of new machines, however. Over time this city, which is built on seven hills, became home to 10 colleges and universities plus a center for biological research that in the 1950s developed the first birth-control pill.

Worcester's most unusual attraction is the **Higgins Armory Museum**, a showcase for more than 70 suits of armor and a multitude of ancient weapons. The artifacts date back to medieval and Renaissance Europe, ancient Greece and Rome, and feudal Japan, and are displayed in a hall adorned with stained glass and tapestries. Young museumgoers are allowed to actually don ancient garb from the try-on costume collection.

Housed in a handsome late 19th-century stone building, the **Worcester Art Museum** has distinguished itself as an important repository. Its impressive collection contains some 35,000 objects spanning 5,000 years, including a 12th-century chapter house that was rebuilt stone by stone on the premises. The museum's holdings of East and West Asian art and Japanese woodblock prints are balanced wonderfully by a good number of works by such Western masters as Claude Monet (1840–1926), Thomas

Gainsborough (1728–88), and Pablo Picasso (1881–1973).

Just two miles (3 km) from downtown, the **Ecotarium** promotes a better understanding of the region's environment and its wildlife. Interactive exhibits invite hands-on learning experiences. The surrounding grounds contain a wildlife center for injured and endangered animals, aquarium exhibits, and a 14-inch (35-cm) sky-watching telescope. A three-story museum, also located on the 60-acre (24-ha) grounds, houses a planetarium.

🏛 **Higgins Armory Museum**
100 Barber Ave. 📞 (508) 853-6015.
⏰ year-round: 10am–4pm Tue–Sat,
noon–4pm Sun. 🅿️ &

🏛 **Worcester Art Museum**
55 Salisbury St. 📞 (508) 799-4406.
⏰ year-round: 11am–5pm Wed, Fri,
Sun, 11am–8pm Thu, 10am–5pm
Sat. 🅿️ &

✳️ **Ecotarium**
222 Harrington Way. 📞 (508) 929-2700. ⏰ year-round: 10am–5pm
Tue–Sat, noon–5pm Sun. 🅿️ &

ENVIRONS: North Grafton, 10 miles (16 km) southeast, has a long history of clockmaking. In the early 1800s brothers Benjamin, Simon, Ephraim, and Aaron Willard were regarded as the some of New England's best craftsmen, designing new styles for timepieces. The timepieces were given such names as Eddystone Lighthouse, Skeleton, and Act of

Parliament. Today more than 70 Willard timepieces and elegant tall clocks are on display in the family's original 18th-century homestead.

🏛 **Willard House and Clock Museum**
11 Willard St, North Grafton.
📞 (508) 839-3500. ⏰ year-round:
10am–4pm Tue–Sat, 1pm–4pm Sun.
🅿️ 🎥 obligatory. & partial.

Sturbridge ⑭

STURBRIDGE'S ROOTS are literally in the land. Soon after its founding in 1729, residents planted apple orchards, some of which are still in operation. The town's main attraction is its living-history museum: Old Sturbridge Village (see p160).

The 1748 Parsonage in Old Sturbridge Village

ENVIRONS: Located nine miles (14 km) west, the village of Brimfield blossoms three times each year as America's flea market capital. The Brimfield Antique Show attracts hundreds of dealers, filling every field, sidewalk, and front porch in town. Treasure hunters descend to the village by the thousands to shop for wares ranging from valuable antiques to the truly kitsch.

Scraping recent layers of paint off an antique carousel horse at the Brimfield flea market

Springfield ⓯

🏃 *153,000.* ✈ *15 miles (24 km) SW in Windsor Locks, CT.* 🚌 🚋 ℹ *1441 Main St (413) 787-1548 or (800) 723-1548.* W *www.valleyvisitor.com*

NOW A CENTER FOR banking and insurance, Springfield owes much of its early success to guns. The **Springfield Armory** – the first armory in the US – was commissioned by George Washington (1732–99) to manufacture arms for the Colonial forces fighting in the Revolutionary War. Today the historic armory is part of the National Park Service and maintains one of the most extensive and unique firearms collections in the world.

In 1891 Dr. James Naismith (1861–1939), an instructor at the International YMCA Training Center, now Springfield College, invented the game of basketball. **Basketball Hall of Fame** traces the development of the game from its humble beginnings, in which peach baskets

Emblem of the Basketball Hall of Fame in Springfield

were used as nets, to its evolution as one of the world's most popular team sports.

Along with its collection of basketball memorabilia, the state-of-the-art museum features interactive displays. Children and adults can play against former stars in virtual reality games or test their own shooting skills.

Court Square on Main Street is the revitalized center of the city, lined with 19th-century churches, civic and commercial buildings, and a 300-ft- (91-m-) high tower

housing carillon bells. Nearby is **The Quadrangle**, a collection of four museums of art, science, and history. The George Walter Vincent Smith Art Museum displays a noted collection of Oriental decorative arts and Islamic rugs. Galleries at the Museum of Fine Arts contain European and American paintings, sculpture, and decorative arts. Children love the Springfield Science Museum, with its live animal Solutia Eco-Center, hands-on exhibits, Phelon African Hall, planetarium, and Dinosaur Hall, with its life-sized model of *Tyrannosaurus rex*. The Connecticut Valley Historical Museum tells Springfield's story through changing exhibits. The Dr. Seuss National Memorial, commemorating Springfield-native Theodor Geisel (1904–91), better known as popular children's author Dr. Seuss, was opened in June 2002.

🏛 **Springfield Armory National Historic Site**
One Armory Sq. ℂ *(413) 734-8551.* ◯ *year-round: 10am–4:30pm Tue–Sun.* ● *Jan 1, Thanksgiving, & Dec 25.* 🎟 ♿
🏛 **Basketball Hall of Fame**
1150 W Columbus Ave. ℂ *(413) 781-6500.* ◯ *10am–6pm Sun–Thu, 10am–8pm Fri–Sat.* ● *Jan 1, Thanksgiving, & Dec 25.* 🎟 🎟 ♿
🏛 **The Quadrangle**
State & Chestnut Sts. ℂ *(413) 263-6800.* **Four museums** ◯ *year-round: 12pm–5pm Wed–Fri, 11am–4pm Sat–Sun.* 🎟 ♿ *partial.*

ENVIRONS: Some 11 miles (18 km) north, the hamlet of South Hadley is home to **Mount Holyoke College** (1837), the nation's oldest women's college. Poet Emily Dickinson (1830–86) was one of Mount Holyoke's most famous graduates. The 800-acre (320-ha) campus encompasses two lakes and a series of nature trails. College sites worth a visit include the **Art Museum** and the **Talcott Greenhouse**, which is located in a Victorian-style greenhouse.

Farther north in Hadley, the summit of 954-ft (291-m) Mount Holyoke in **Skinner**

Dinosaur model dwarfing visitor in Springfield's Science Museum

State Park offers a panorama of the oxbow bend in the Connecticut River. The park is well known for massive laurel displays in June and flaming foliage in autumn.

🏛 **Mount Holyoke College Art Museum**
Mount Holyoke College. ℂ *(413) 538-2245.* ◯ *11am–5pm Tue–Fri, 1pm–5pm Sat–Sun.* ♿
🌿 **Talcott Greenhouse**
Mount Holyoke College. ℂ *(413) 538-2116.* ◯ *year-round: 9am–4pm Mon–Fri, 1pm–4pm Sat–Sun.* ♿
🎿 **Skinner State Park**
Rte 47. ℂ *(413) 586-0350.* ◯ *May–Oct: dawn–dusk.* 🚗 *on weekends.*

Amherst ⓰

🏃 *23,000.* ✈ *41 miles (66 km) S in Windsor Locks, CT.* 🚌 🚋 ℹ *409 Main St (413) 253-0700.*

THIS IDYLLIC COLLEGE town is home to three different institutes of higher learning. The most popular with visitors is Amherst College, with its central green and traditional ivy-covered buildings. Founded in 1821 for under-privileged youths hoping to enter the ministry, the school has grown into one of the most selective small colleges in the US. The college's excellent **Mead Art Museum** includes the Rotherwas Room, an ornately paneled English hall c.1600. The varied collection of the **Pratt Museum of Natural History** includes dinosaur and woolly mammoth skeletons and assorted mineral displays.

Poet Emily Dickinson was one of Amherst's most famous citizens. In her late 30s, Dickinson withdrew from society and spent the rest of her life in the family home, where she died in 1886. The second-floor bedroom of the **Emily Dickinson Homestead** has been restored to the way it was during the years 1855–86, when the reclusive poet wrote her most important verse. Her work remained unpublished until after her death. Over time critics proclaimed it to be the work of a poetic genius. The **Jones Library** has displays on Dickinson's life and works, as well as collections on poet Robert Frost, who taught at Amherst College in the 1940s.

 Mead Art Museum
Amherst College. (413) 542-2335. ○ Sep–May: 10am–4:30pm Tue–Sun, 10am–9pm Thu; call for summer hours.

Pratt Museum of Natural History
Amherst College. (413) 542-2165. ○ year-round: 9am–3:30pm Mon–Fri, 10am–4pm Sat, noon–5pm Sun.

Emily Dickinson Homestead
280 Main St. (413) 542-8161. ○ call for hours. obligatory.

Jones Library
43 Amity St. (413) 256-4090. ○ 9am–5:30pm Mon–Wed, Fri, Sat, 9am–8:30pm Tue & Thu, 1pm–5pm Sun. Jun–Aug: Sun. **Special collections** ○ year-round: 10am–1pm & 2pm–5pm Mon & Sat, 10am–5pm Tue–Fri.

Northampton **❶**

30,000. ✈ 36 miles (58 km) S in Windsor Locks, CT. 99 Pleasant St (413) 584-1900.

A LIVELY CENTER for the arts and known for its fine dining, Northampton has a well preserved Victorian-style Main Street lined with craft galleries and shops. The town is also home to the 1871 **Smith College**, the largest privately endowed women's college in the nation. The handsome campus has a notable **Museum of Art** and the **Lyman Plant House and Conservatory**, known for its flower shows and the

Beautiful bloom at Smith College's Lyman Plant House

arboretum and gardens. South of Northampton in Holyoke, visitors can explore the trails in the 1800-acre (728-ha) **Mount Tom State Reservation**. Nearby is the Norwottuck Rail Trail, a popular walking and biking path that runs along an old railroad bed connecting Northampton to neighboring Amherst.

Smith College Museum of Art
Elm St, Northampton. (413) 585-2760. for renovation until 2003; call for new hours.

Lyman Plant House and Conservatory
College Lane, Northampton. (413) 585-2740. ○ year-round: 8:30am–4pm daily. Thanksgiving & Dec 25.

Mount Tom State Reservation
125 Reservation Rd, Holyoke. (413) 534-1186. ○ year-round: 8am–dusk daily. **Visitors center** ○ Memorial Day–Labor Day: Wed–Sun. Call for hours. partial.

Deerfield **❶**

5,300. ✈ 52 miles (84 km) S in Windsor Locks, CT. 18 Miner St, Greenfield (413) 773-9393.

A ONE-TIME FRONTIER outpost that was almost annihilated by Indian raids in the late 1600s, Deerfield survived and its farmers prospered, building gracious clapboard homes along the mile-long (1.6-km) center avenue known simply as "The Street."

Sixty of these remain within **Historic Deerfield** and are carefully preserved. Some of the buildings now serve as museums, exhibiting a broad range of period furniture and decorative arts, including silverware, ceramics, and textiles. The Flynt Center of Early New England Life schedules changing exhibitions on early life in western Massachusetts. Visitors seeking a photo opportunity can drive to the summit of **Mount Sugarloaf State Reservation** in South Deerfield for views of the Connecticut River Valley.

Historic Deerfield
The Street, Old Deerfield. (413) 774-5581. ○ year-round: 9:30am–4:30pm daily. Thanksgiving, Dec 24 & 25. www.historic-deerfield.org

Mount Sugarloaf State Reservation
US 116, South Deerfield. (413) 586-8706. ○ May–Dec: 8am–dusk daily.

White clapboard house and picket fence in historic Deerfield

Tour of the Mohawk Trail ⓲

Oᴿɪɢɪɴᴀʟʟʏ ᴀɴ ɪɴᴅɪᴀɴ ᴛʀᴀᴅᴇ ʀᴏᴜᴛᴇ, this trail was a popular artery for early pioneers. In 1914 the trail, which stretches for 63 miles (100 km) from Orange to North Adams along Route 2, became a paved road. The choicest section of the route, from Greenfield to North Adams, was the first officially designated scenic drive in New England. This twisting road offers magnificent mountain views, particularly in the sharp hairpin curves leading into North Adams, and is one of the most popular fall foliage routes.

Charlemont ②
The town is dominated by the massive statue *Hail to the Sunrise.*

Hairpin Turn ③
This sharp bend in the road offers soaring views of Mount Greylock.

Key

🟥 Tour route

〰 Other road

🏵 Viewpoint

North Adams ④
North Adams is near America's only naturally formed marble bridge.

Williamstown ⓴

🏠 8,000. ✈ 47 miles (75 km) W in Albany, NY. 🚌 ℹ Jct Rtes 2 & 7 (413) 458-9077 or (800) 214-3799.

Aʀᴛ ʟᴏᴠᴇʀꜱ ᴍᴀᴋᴇ pilgrimages to Williamstown for **The Sterling and Francine Clark Art Institute** to see its private collection, which features Old Masters and French Impressionists, including more than 30 Renoirs. The **Williams College Museum of Art** is also notable, with holdings of everything from ancient Assyrian stone reliefs to the last self-portrait by Andy Warhol (1927–87). A four-story skylight now complements the original 1846 octagonal structure. Fine art is not the only show in town, however. In summer fans flock to the Williamstown Theater Festival. Founded in 1954, the festival is known for its high quality productions and for attracting

Degas statue at Clark Institute

A 19th-century Steinway at The Sterling and Francine Clark Art Institute

big-name Broadway and Hollywood stars.

🏛 **The Sterling and Francine Clark Art Institute**
225 South St. 📞 (413) 458-2303. 🅾 Jul–Aug: 10am–5pm daily; rest of year: 10am–5pm Tue–Sun. 📷 (Jun–Oct only). 🎫 ♿

🏛 **Williams College Museum of Art**
Main St. 📞 (413) 597-2429. 🅾 year-round: 10am–5pm Tue–Sat, 1pm–5pm Sun. ♿

Eɴᴠɪʀᴏɴꜱ: More art can be found 7 miles (11 km) east in North Adams at the new **Massachusetts Museum of Contemporary Art** (MASS MoCA). Seven interconnected buildings, part of a 19th-century factory, with enormous indoor spaces, elevated walkways, and outdoor courtyards display cutting-edge art. The complex is able to house sculptures and paintings that are too large for most conventional museums.

🏛 **Massachusetts Museum of Contemporary Art**
87 Marshall St. 📞 (413) 664-4481. 🅾 11am–5pm Wed–Mon. 📷 ♿ 🚻

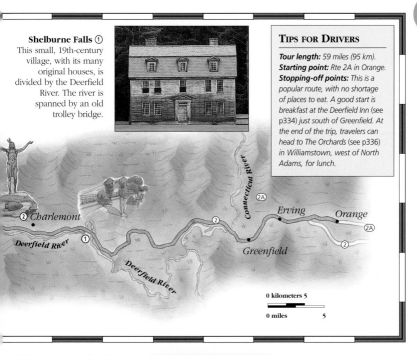

Shelburne Falls ①
This small, 19th-century village, with its many original houses, is divided by the Deerfield River. The river is spanned by an old trolley bridge.

② Charlemont

Deerfield River ①

Connecticut River

Erving Orange (2A)

(2A)

Greenfield

Deerfield River

0 kilometers 5

0 miles 5

Mount Greylock State Reservation ㉑

Off Rte 7, Lanesborough.
🛈 *(413) 499-4262.*

A ROAD LEADS drivers to the top of Mount Greylock, the highest peak in the state at 3,491 ft (1,064 m). Once at the top, visitors can climb the 92-ft (28-m) Summit Veteran's Memorial Tower, commemorating the state's war dead, for a panoramic view of five states. Also at the summit is Bascom Lodge, a 1930s stone and timber structure offering maps, guides, and rustic lodging. The Appalachian Trail *(see pp22–3)*, the popular 2,000-mile (3,200-km) hiking path running from Georgia to Maine, crosses Mount Greylock's summit.

Authentic Shaker door latch at Hancock Shaker Village

Summit Veteran's Memorial Tower atop Mount Greylock

Hancock Shaker Village ㉒

Rte 20, outside Pittsfield. 📞 *(413) 443-0188.* ⃝ *late May–mid-Oct: 9:30am–5pm daily; guided tours only mid-Oct–late May: 10am–3pm daily.* ● *Jan 1, Thanksgiving, Dec 25.* 🎫 📷 ⛔ 🍽
Ⓦ *www.hancockshakervillage.org*

F OUNDED IN 1783, this was the third in a series of 19 Shaker settlements established in the Northeast and Midwest as utopian communities. The Shakers, so-called because they often trembled and shook during moments of worship and prayer, believed in celibacy and equality of the sexes, with men and women living separately but sharing authority and responsibilities. At its peak in the 1830s, there were 300 residents living in the village. Now the community has no resident Shakers.

Twenty of the 100 original buildings have been restored, including the tri-level round stone barn, cleverly designed so that as many as 52 head of cattle could be fed by a single farmhand from a central core. The Brick Dwelling can house up to 100 people, and has a meeting room used for week-day worship and a communal dining room, where traditional Shaker fare is served on select Saturday evenings.

Presentations on the Shaker way of life are offered, including demonstrations of chair-, broom-, and oval box-making. In the Discovery Room visitors may try on reproduction Shaker clothing and also try their hand at crafts such as weaving. An orientation exhibit and videos in several buildings provide historical background.

Picturesque Bash Bish Falls in
Mount Washington State Forest

The Berkshires ㉓

🔼 37 miles (60 km) NE in Albany,
NY. 🚉 Pittsfield. ℹ️ Berkshire
Common Plaza, Pittsfield
(413) 443-9186 or (800) 237-5747.

Visitors have long been
attracted to the peaceful
wooded hills, green valleys,
rippling rivers, and waterfalls
of this western corner of
Massachusetts. Among the
first tourists were writers
such as Henry Wadsworth
Longfellow (1807–82),
Herman Melville (1819–91),
and Nathaniel Hawthorne
(1804–64). When the three
wrote about the natural
beauty of the area, the location caught the attention of
many of the region's wealthy
people, who began to spend
their summers here. Now
the region is a year-round
playground, popular for
its culture as well as for the

ample opportunities it provides for outdoor recreation.
The area is speckled with
small towns and country
villages. Great Barrington
to the south and Pittsfield to
the north are the com-
mercial centers of the
region, while Lenox
and Stockbridge are
cultural meccas. The
old cotton and woolen
mills in Housatonic are
finding new life as art
galleries, and Main
Street of Sheffield is
lined with interesting
little antique shops.
Among the most pop-
ular walking and hik-
ing trails in the Berkshires are
Bartholemew's Cobble in
Sheffield and Bash Bish Falls
in the **Mount Washington
State Forest**. A trail leads to
the summit of Monument
Mountain and affords beautiful views. Reputedly, it was
on a hike up the mountain
that Herman Melville first
met Nathaniel Hawthorne,
forming a friendship that
resulted in Melville's dedicat-
ing his novel *Moby-Dick* to
his fellow author.

🦌 Mount Washington
State Forest
Rte 41 S. 📞 (413) 528-0330.
🅾️ Memorial Day–Columbus Day. 🏕️

Pittsfield
Although primarily a commercial hub, Pittsfield is central to
several interesting sites, most
notably Hancock Shaker
Village *(see p165)*. The town's
literary shrine is **Arrowhead**,
an 18th-century home in the
shadow of Mount Greylock,

where Herman Melville
lived from 1850 to 1863
and where he wrote his
masterpiece *Moby-Dick*.
Some say the mountain's
shape resembles the great

Life-sized model of Stegosaurus at
Berkshire Museum in Pittsfield

white whale in Melville's
classic tale.
The **Berkshire Museum**
has a large collection of
items covering a variety
of disciplines, including
history, natural science,
and fine art. The museum's
aquarium is stocked with
more than 100 fish and
sea creatures. The galleries
are notable for their works
by such 19th-century
American masters as
George Inness (1825–94)
and Frederic Church
(1826–1900).

🏛️ Arrowhead
780 Holmes Rd. 📞 (413) 442-
1793. 🅾️ May–Oct: 9:30am–5pm
daily; rest of year by appt. 🏕️
🎫 ♿ first floor only. 🚻 🚫
🏛️ Berkshire Museum
39 South St. 📞 (413) 443-7171.
🅾️ year-round: 10am–5pm
Mon–Sat, 12pm–5pm Sun.
🏕️ ♿ 🚻 🚫

Lenox
In the late 1800s the
gracious village of Lenox
became known as the
"inland Newport" for the
lavish summer "cottages"
built by prominent families
such as the Carnegies and
the Vanderbilts. Before the
1929 Great Depression,
there were more than 70
grand estates gracing the
area. While some of the
millionaires have since
moved away, many of
their lavish homes remain
in service as schools, cultural institutions, resorts,
and posh inns. One of the

Gathering hay by oxcart at Hancock Shaker Village

Typical townhouse in the village of Lenox

more prominent mansions is **The Mount**, built in 1902 by Pulitzer Prize-winning author Edith Wharton (1862–1937).

Lenox gained new status as a center of culture in 1937 when the 500-acre (202-ha) Tanglewood estate became the summer home of the Boston Symphony Orchestra. Music lovers flock for concerts to the 1,200-seat Seiji Ozawa Hall or the open

Figures of *Andromeda* and *Memory* at Chesterwood

Music Shed, where many enjoy picnicking and listening to the music on the surrounding lawn. Jazz and popular concerts are interspersed with the classical program. Tanglewood's name is credited to Nathaniel Hawthorne, who lived in a house on the estate at one time and wrote some of his short stories here.

The Mount
2 Plunkett St. ((413) 637-1899.
○ May–Oct: 9am–5pm daily.
▨ ☑ ♿ ▯ ◪

Stockbridge
Stockbridge was founded in 1734 by missionaries seeking to educate and convert the local Mohegan Indians. The

simple **Mission House** (c.1739) was built by Reverend John Sergeant for his bride. Today the house contains period pieces and Indian artifacts.

The town's quaint main street, dominated by the 1897 Red Lion Inn, has been immortalized in the popular paintings of Norman Rockwell (1894–1978), one of America's most beloved illustrators. The painter lived in Stockbridge for 25 years, and the country's largest collection of Rockwell originals can be seen at the **Norman Rockwell Museum**.

Stockbridge has been home to its share of prominent residents, including sculptor Daniel Chester French (1850–1931), who summered at his **Chesterwood** estate. It was here that French created the working models for his famous *Seated Lincoln* (1922) for the Lincoln Memorial in Washington, DC. The models remain in the studio along with other plaster casts. During the summer months the grounds are used to exhibit sculpture.

Naumkeag Museum and Gardens is a graceful 1885 mansion built for Joseph H. Choate, US ambassador to Britain and one of the era's leading attorneys. The 26-room house is appointed with its original furnishings and an art collection that spans three centuries. Of note is the exhibit of Chinese porcelains. The grounds are a work of art also, with manicured paths and formal gardens.

⊞ Mission House
19 Main St. ((413) 298-3239. ○
Memorial Day–Columbus Day:
10am–5pm daily. ▨ ◪

⊞ Norman Rockwell Museum
Rte 183. ((413) 298-4100 ext.
220. ○ May–Oct: 10am–5pm daily;
Nov–Apr: 10am–4pm Mon–Fri, 10
am–5pm Sat–Sun. ● Thanksgiving,
Dec 25, Jan 1. ▨ ☑ ♿ ▯

⊞ Chesterwood
4 Williamsville Rd.((413) 298-
3579. ○ May–Oct: 10am–5pm daily.
▨ ☑ ♿ partial. ◪

⊞ Naumkeag Museum and Gardens
Prospect Hill. ((413) 298-3239. ○
Memorial Day–Labor Day: 10am–5pm
daily. ▨ ◪

THE ARTS IN THE BERKSHIRES

The Berkshires region has one of America's richest summer menus of performing arts. As well as Boston Symphony Orchestra concerts at Tanglewood, Aston Magna presents baroque concerts at St. James Church in Great Barrington, the Berkshire Opera performs at the Mahaiwe Theater in Great Barrington, and the Berkshire Choral Festival is held in Sheffield. The Jacob's Pillow Dance Festival in Becket, the oldest such event in the nation, presents leading international companies. Shakespeare & Company, the Berkshire Theater Festival, the Williamstown Theater Festival, and the Great Barrington Theater Company are among the oldest and most respected summer theaters in the nation.

Relaxed setting for the Tanglewood summer concert series

RHODE ISLAND

W ITH AN AREA OF JUST OVER *1,200 sq miles (3,100 sq km),* *Rhode Island is the smallest of the 50 states. However, its* *historic towns, unspoiled wilderness areas, and a pris-* *tine shoreline dotted with inlets and tranquil harbors make the place* *a lively and easily explored holiday destination.*

For such a small state, "Little Rhody" was founded on big ideals. Driven from the Massachusetts Bay colony in 1636 for his outspoken beliefs on religious freedom, clergyman Roger Williams (1604–83) established a set-tlement on the banks of Narragansett Bay. He called the town Providence and founded it upon the tenets of freedom of speech and religious tolerance – principles that would be formally introduced in the First Amendment to the US Constitution in 1781. This forward-thinking spirit made Rhode Island the site of America's first synagogue and Baptist church and some of the nation's earliest libraries, public schools, and colleges. In May 1776 Rhode Island followed the lead of New Hampshire and formally declared its independence from British rule.

Although its 400-mile (645-km) shoreline is con-sidered small in com-parison to those of neighboring states, Rhode Island has earned its nickname, the Ocean State. In the 17th century, its port towns were primary players in the bur-geoning maritime trade with the West Indies. Today some 120 public beaches provide opportuni-ties for swimming, scuba diving, boating, windsurfing, and fishing. Pleasure craft can be seen skimming the waters of Narragansett Bay. Home to the America's Cup yacht races between 1930–85, Newport is well known as one of the world's great yachting centers. But not all of Rhode Island's allure is found on the water-front. More than 50 percent of the state is covered in woodland. The 11 state parks are ideal for nature walks; three of them allow camping.

Fishing at dusk on beautiful Narragansett Bay

◁ **Linden Place, Bristol, Rhode Island**

Exploring Rhode Island

NOT AN ISLAND AT ALL, the state of Rhode Island does, however, contain dozens of islets and peninsulas along the Atlantic coastline. They dot Narragansett Bay, which takes a huge bite out of the eastern portion of the state. Craggy cliffs, grass-covered bluffs, and golden sand beaches mark the shoreline of the Ocean State, which offers an abundance of opportunities for fishing, swimming, boating, surfing, and other aquatic activities. Inland numerous lakes, reservoirs, and swamps (in South County) maintain the maritime atmosphere. Most activity in Rhode Island centers around its two major cities, Providence *(see pp174–7)* and Newport *(see pp182–7)*, but the smaller roads across the western part of the state are perfect for tranquil country drives.

Vacationers in front of the visitor's pavilion at Point Judith

KEY

▬▬▬	Interstate
▬▬▬	Major road
▭▭▭	Minor road
▬▬▬	Scenic route
☆	Viewpoint

0 kilometers   8

0 miles   8

SIGHTS AT A GLANCE

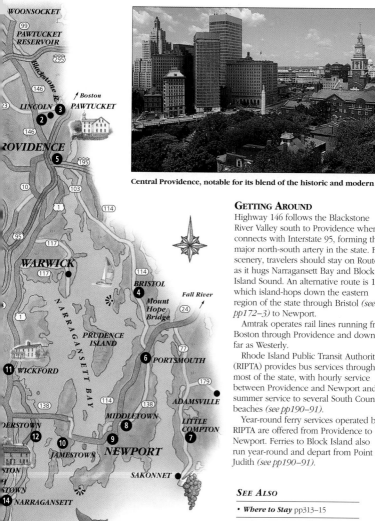

Central Providence, notable for its blend of the historic and modern

GETTING AROUND

Highway 146 follows the Blackstone River Valley south to Providence where it connects with Interstate 95, forming the major north-south artery in the state. For scenery, travelers should stay on Route 1 as it hugs Narragansett Bay and Block Island Sound. An alternative route is 114, which island-hops down the eastern region of the state through Bristol *(see pp172–3)* to Newport.

Amtrak operates rail lines running from Boston through Providence and down as far as Westerly.

Rhode Island Public Transit Authority (RIPTA) provides bus services throughout most of the state, with hourly service between Providence and Newport and a summer service to several South County beaches *(see pp190–91)*.

Year-round ferry services operated by RIPTA are offered from Providence to Newport. Ferries to Block Island also run year-round and depart from Point Judith *(see pp190–91)*.

SEE ALSO

- **Where to Stay** pp313–15

- **Where to Eat** pp336–9

Yachts by the score in the harbor at Newport

Classroom display at the Museum of Work and Culture, Woonsocket

Woonsocket ❶

🚶 44,000. 🚹 42 S Main St (401) 724-2200.

A MAJOR MANUFACTURING center located on the busy Blackstone River, Woonsocket was transformed from a relatively small village to a booming mill town by the development of the local textile industry in the 19th and early 20th centuries. Although the textile industry declined after World War II, the city remains one of the major manufacturing hubs.

The **Museum of Work and Culture** focuses on the impact of the Industrial Revolution on the region. The day-to-day lives of the factory owners, managers, and immigrant workers are examined and explained with the help of a re-created 1934 union hall, hands-on displays, models, and multimedia exhibits.

🏛 **Museum of Work and Culture**
42 S Main St. 📞 (401) 769-9675. ◯ 9:30am–4pm Mon–Fri, 10am–5pm Sat, 1pm–5pm Sun. 🚫 ♿

The Great Road ❷

🚹 (401) 762-0250.

A N OFTEN overlooked gem, the stretch of Great Road (Route 123) between Saylesville and Lime Rock follows the course of the Moshassuck River for 0.6 mile

Eleazer Arnold House near Lincoln on the Great Road

(1 km) and yields eight historically significant buildings. Four of these buildings are open by appointment and include the 1680 **Eleazer Arnold House** and the 1704 **Friends Meetinghouse**, New England's oldest Quaker meeting house in continuous

use. Constructed in 1807 as a toll station and later serving as a hotel, **North Gate,** just off the Great Road, now contains a small museum room decked out with early 18th-century furniture. Farther along the road, **Hannaway Blacksmith Shop** is a one-story, 19th-century structure recently restored for blacksmith demonstrations and special events.

🏚 **Eleazer Arnold House**
487 Great Rd. 📞 (617) 227-3956. ◯ 1pm–5pm Sun. 🚫 obligatory; call for appt.
🏚 **Friends Meetinghouse**
374 Great Rd. 📞 (401) 723-2515. 🚫 obligatory; call for appt.
🏚 **North Gate**
Rte 246. 📞 (401) 725-2847. 🚫 obligatory; call for appt.
🏚 **Hannaway Blacksmith Shop**
671 Great Rd. 📞 (401) 333-1100 ext 249. 🚫 obligatory; call for appt.

Pawtucket ❸

🚶 73,000. 🚹 175 Main St (401) 724-2200.

T HIS BUSTLING INDUSTRIAL CITY, built on hills sliced by the Blackstone, Moshassuck, and Ten Mile rivers is generally acknowledged to be the birthplace of America's Industrial Revolution. It was here in 1793 that mechanical engineer Samuel Slater (1768–1835) built the country's first water-powered cotton-spinning mill.

A major historic landmark, the **Slater Mill Historic Site** includes the restored Slater Mill and the 1810 Wilkinson Mill, complete with an authentic 19th-century machine shop and the only 8-ton (7-tonne) waterwheel in the US.

Pawtucket's Slater Mill Historic Site, home of the first water-powered cotton-spinning mill in the US

McCoy Stadium, playing field of the Pawtucket Red Sox baseball team

Also on the site, the 1758 Sylvanus Brown House is furnished with the machinery and personal effects of Sylvanus Brown, a millwright and pattern-maker.

At the 200-acre (81-ha) **Slater Memorial Park** on the Ten Mile River, there are hiking trails, paddleboats, tennis courts, picnic areas, sunken gardens, and a functional 1895 Looff carousel. The park is also home to the city's oldest dwelling, the 1685 **Daggett House**, which contains exhibits of 17th-century furnishings and antiques.

The **Pawtucket Red Sox** baseball team plays games at McCoy Stadium. This minor league team has players who, once they have honed their skills, may move on to play in baseball's major league for the Boston Red Sox.

Pawtucket Red Sox logo

🏟 **Slater Mill Historic Site**
Roosevelt & Slater Aves. 🄲 (401) 725-8638. ⭕ Jun–Oct: 10am–5pm Tue–Sat, 1pm–5pm Sun; Nov–May: 10am–5pm Sat, 1pm–5pm Sun. ⬤ Jan 1, Thanksgiving, & Dec 25. 🈵 🄲 ♿

🌿 **Slater Memorial Park**
Newport Ave. 🄲 (401) 728-0500 ext 252. ⭕ year-round: 8:30am–9pm daily. ♿

🏛 **Daggett House**
Slater Park off Rte 1A. 🄲 (401) 724-5748. 🈵 obligatory; call for appt. 🈵

Pawtucket Red Sox
McCoy Stadium, Columbus Ave.
🄲 (401) 724-7300. ⭕ Apr–early Sep; call for schedule. 🈵 ♿

Bristol ❹

🏙 21, 650. 🚂 Thames St (401) 245-0750. ⭕ www.onlinebristol.com

BRISTOL BLOSSOMED in the late 18th century when its status as a major commercial, fishing, whaling, and ship-building center made it the nation's fourth-busiest port.

The many elegant Federal and Victorian mansions lining Hope, High, and Thames streets attest to those prosperous days. One such fine home is the 1810 **Linden Place**, where scenes from *The Great Gatsby* (1974) were filmed. The Federal-style mansion was built by General George DeWolf (1772–1844) with money he had made from his sugar plantations in Cuba and the slave trade. Regular concerts and tours are offered.

The tasteful trappings of wealth are also in evidence at **Blithewold Mansion and Gardens**. Built in 1894 for Pennsylvania coal baron Augustus Van Wickle (1856–98), the mansion was rebuilt in 1907. It has many gardens and trees from the Far East. The grounds offer spectacular views of Narragansett Bay (*see p169*).

Boating has always been popular with the rich and famous, and Bristol's history as the producer of America's greatest yachts is traced at the **Herreshoff Marine Museum/America's Cup Hall of Fame**.

Photos, models, and a variety of restored ships are displayed in the large warehouse.

A branch of Brown University (*see p175*), the **Haffenreffer Museum of Anthropology** has exhibits of artifacts from indigenous peoples around the world. The museum's North American Indian collection is of particular interest to visitors.

Colt State Park, a 460-acre (186-ha) shoreline park features a three-mile (5-km) shoreline drive along Narragansett Bay, a bicycle trail, many picnic areas, and playing fields. Also on the park grounds is the **Coggeshall Farm Museum**, a replica of a 1790s coastal farm with barn, weaver shed, blacksmith shop, and domesticated animals. Cyclists and inline skaters can tour the picturesque East Bay Bike Path, leading some 14.5 miles (23 km) from Bristol to Providence along the coast-hugging route of an old railroad line.

Art from the Haffenreffer

🏛 **Linden Place**
500 Hope St. 🄲 (401) 253-0390.
⭕ May–Columbus Day: 10am–4pm Thu–Sat, 12pm–4pm Sun. 🈵 🄲 ♿

🏛 **Blithewold Mansion**
101 Ferry Rd. 🄲 (401) 253-2707.
Mansion ⭕ mid-Apr–mid-Oct: 10am–4pm Wed–Sun; call for winter hours. ⬤ public hols. **Grounds**
⭕ 10am–5pm daily. 🈵 ♿

🏛 **Herreshoff Marine Museum/America's Cup Hall of Fame**
1 Burnside St. 🄲 (401) 253-5000. ⭕ May–Oct: 10am–5pm daily. 🈵 🄲 ♿

🏛 **Haffenreffer Museum of Anthropology**
300 Tower St. 🄲 (401) 253-8388.
⭕ Jun–Aug: 11am–5pm Tue–Sun; Sep–May: 11am–5pm Sat & Sun. 🈵

🌿 **Colt State Park**
Rte 114. 🄲 (401) 253-7482.
⭕ daily. ♿

🏛 **Coggeshall Farm Museum**
Poppasquash Rd off Rte 114.
🄲 (401) 253-9062. ⭕ Mar–Sep: 10am–6pm daily; Oct–Feb: 10am–5pm daily. 🈵 ♿

Providence ●

First Unitarian Church bell

Sandwiched between Boston and New York on busy I-95, Providence is often overlooked by hurried travelers. This is a pity, since the city is blessed with a rich history well worth exploring. Perched on seven hills, Providence started life as a farming community before taking advantage of its location on the Seekonk River to develop into a flourishing seaport in the 17th century. The city then evolved into a hub of industry in the 19th century, with immigrants from Europe pouring in to work in the burgeoning textile mills.

Stately buildings along Benefit Street's Mile of History

Interior courtyard at Rhode Island School of Design's Museum of Art

🏛 **RISD Museum of Art**
224 Benefit St. 📞 *(401) 454-6500.* ⏺ *year-round: 10am–5pm Tue–Sun, 10am–9pm 3rd Thu of month.* ⬤ *public hols.* 📷 ♿

🏛 **Providence Athenaeum**
251 Benefit St. 📞 *(401) 421-6970.* ⏺ *year-round: 10am–7pm Mon–Thu, 9am–5pm Fri–Sat, 1pm–5pm Sun.* ⬤ *weekends during summer.*

🕍 **First Unitarian Church**
310 Benefit St. 📞 *(401) 421-7970.* ⏺ *daily.* ♿

🕍 **First Baptist Church in America**
75 N Main St. 📞 *(401) 454-3418.* ⏺ *year-round: call for hours.* 📷 *call.* ♿

Exploring Providence

Providence is bisected by the Providence River, with the Downtown district *(see pp176–7)* on the west bank and College Hill to the east. Walking through College Hill, visitors will pass a large number of 18th-century buildings, including the redbrick colonial Market House, built along the waterway in the 1770s and now part of Rhode Island School of Design (RISD).

🕍 Benefit Street's Mile of History

Benefit St. 📞 *(401) 274-1636.*
Along Benefit Street's Mile of History there are more than 100 houses ranging in style from Colonial and Federal to Greek Revival and Victorian. This lovely, tree-lined street passes RISD's **Museum of Art**, which houses a small but comprehensive collection of artworks from Ancient Egyptian to contemporary American. Also on Benefit Street is the 1838 Greek Revival **Providence Athenaeum**. This is where author Edgar Allen Poe (1809–49) courted Sarah Whitman, the woman who was the inspiration for his poem *Annabel Lee* (1849). The library, one of the oldest in America, has a collection dating back to 1753. Other architectural gems include the **First Unitarian Church**, which possesses a 2,500-lb (1,350-kg) bell, the largest ever cast by silversmith and Revolutionary War hero Paul Revere *(see p120).*

Key

═	Interstate
═	Highway
🚉	Train station
▬	Railroad
ℹ	Tourist information
P	Parking

Founded in 1638 by Roger Williams and built in 1774–5, the First Baptist Church in America is noted for its Ionic columns, intricately carved wood interior, and large Waterford crystal chandelier.

🏛 Governor Stephen Hopkins House

15 Hopkins St. 🅲 (401) 331-2134.
⬤ Apr–Dec: 1pm–4pm Wed & Sat.
🖼 obligatory.

The 1707 **Governor Stephen Hopkins House** belonged to one of Rhode Island's two signatories to the Declaration of Independence, and contains fine 18th-century furnishings.

🏛 Brown University

45 Prospect St. 🅲 (401) 863-1000. ⬤ call for hours.
🖼🅰🏠🖼

Founded in 1764, Brown is the seventh-oldest college in the US and one of the prestigious Ivy League schools (see pp28–9). The campus, a rich

Statue on Brown University campus

blend of Gothic and Beaux Arts styles, is a National Historic Landmark. The John Hay Library has an eclectic collection that includes artifacts and memorabilia relating to President Abraham Lincoln (1809–65), 5,000 toy soldiers and miniatures, and vintage sheet music. Other buildings of note include University Hall, where French and colonial troops were quartered during the American Revolution; Manning Hall, which houses the University Chapel; the John Carter Brown Library, with its fascinating collection of Americana; and the List Art Center, a striking building designed by Philip Johnson (b.1906) and featuring classical and contemporary art.

🏛 John Brown House

52 Power St. 🅲 (401) 331-8575.
⬤ Jan–Feb: 10am–5pm Fri & Sat, 12pm–4pm Sun; Mar–Dec: 10am–5pm Tue–Sat, 12pm–4pm Sun. ⬤ Mon & public hols. 🖼🖼🏠

This Georgian mansion was built in 1786 for John Brown (1736–1803) and designed by his brother Joseph (1733–85). A successful merchant

and shipowner, John played a lead role in the burning of the British customs ship *Gaspee* in a pre-Revolutionary War raid in 1772. The John Brown House was the most lavish of its era, introducing Providence to many new architectural elements, including the projecting entrance, Doric portico, and the Palladian window above it. There are Neoclassical pediments over paired doorways, a grand staircase with twisted balusters, ornate plaster ornamented ceilings, and intricate detailing inside arches over windows and mantels.

Sparing no expense, Brown ordered wallpapers from France and furniture from famed cabinetmakers Townsend and Goddard. The 12-room house has been impeccably restored and is a repository for some of the finest furniture and antiques of that period.

The 1786 John Brown House, an excellent example of Georgian architecture

0 meters 250
0 yards 250

To Roger Williams Park and Zoo

Downtown Providence

DOWNTOWN PROVIDENCE, to the west of the Providence River, has undergone several recent renewal phases. In all, $1 billion has been pumped into the rejuvenation project since 1983. Keeping a balance with the old and the new, Providence municipal officials have managed to clean out previously blighted areas by restoring historic buildings, installing more green spaces, and building pedestrian malls and markets. The reclaimed waterfront and developing arts and entertainment district have helped inject new vitality into the city's core. Visitors are best served by exploring on foot so they are free to poke into the numerous shops, cafés, and restaurants.

Exploring Downtown Providence

Providence's rebirth is more than just physical; it is also cultural. The Trinity Repertory Company on Washington Street is home to one of the best theater groups in the country and has performances year-round. Just a block away, the Providence Performing Arts Center, a 1928 movie palace, features Broadway shows, concerts, entertainment for children, and big-screen films, with free organ recitals in the fall.

The Trinity Repertory Company, housed in a 1917 historic theater

♣ Waterplace Park and Riverwalk

Memorial Blvd. 🄲 *(401) 751-1177.*
🄾 *9am–4:30pm daily.* ● *Jan 1, Thanksgiving, & Dec 25.*
One of the newest and brightest additions to the downtown area is this 4-acre (1.6-ha) walkway at the junction of the Moshassuck, Providence, and Woonasquatucket rivers. Visitors can stroll the park's cobblestone paths, float under footbridges in rented kayaks,

canoes, or gondolas, or enjoy the free concerts and the Waterfire extravaganza during the summer months.

🏛 The Arcade

65 Weybosset St. 🄲 *(401) 598-1199.*
🄾 *year-round: 10am–5pm Mon–Fri, 11am–4pm Sat.* ● *Sun & public hols.* 🄶 🄿 🄷 🄳
Known as the "Temple of Trade," this 1828 Greek Revival building has the distinction of being the first indoor shopping mall in the US. The massive, three-story stone complex covers an entire block in Providence's old financial district and has been acclaimed as "one of the three finest commercial buildings in 19th-century America" by New York's Metropolitan Museum of Art. Similar columns on the Westminster entrance match the six 22-ft- (6.7-m-) high Ionic granite columns on Weybosset. Inside a skylight extends the entire length of the building, providing light even on rainy days. Restored in 1980, this lively marketplace contains specialty shops, clothing boutiques, and several restaurants.

♨ Federal Hill

Visitors will know they are in Little Italy once they pass through Federal Street's impressive arched gateway, decorated with a traditional bronze pine nut. A stripe down the center of the street – in the colors of the Italian flag – confirms that this lively neighborhood in the Federal Hill district is truly Italian in spirit. Bordered by Federal and Broadway streets and

Atwells Avenue, the area is marked by Italian groceries, restaurants, bakeries, import shops, and a pleasant old-world plaza.

The 1828 three-story Arcade, lined with boutiques and restaurants

♨ Rhode Island State House

82 Smith St. 🄲 *(401) 222-2357.*
🄾 *8:30am–4:30pm Mon–Fri.* ● *public hols.* 🄶 *self-guided, others by appt.* 🄶 🄿 🄳
Dominating the city landscape, this imposing building was constructed in 1904 by the prominent New York firm McKim, Mead, & White. The white Georgian marble dome is one of the largest self-supported domes in the world. A bronze statue called *Independent Man*, a longtime symbol of Rhode Island's free spirit, tops the magnificent dome. Among the displays in the statehouse are a full-length portrait of President George Washington (1732–99) by Gilbert Stuart (1755–1828),

Rhode Island State House, with its white marble dome

Roger Williams (1603–1683)

More than an exponent of religious freedom, Roger Williams was also a friend and champion of the area's indigenous inhabitants. He defied the strict restraints of the Massachusetts Bay Colony, believing that all people should be free to worship as they liked without state interference. Banished from Massachusetts for his outspoken views, he established his own colony of Rhode Island and Providence Plantations, obtaining the land from the Narragansett Indians so that "no man should be molested for his conscience sake." It became the country's first experiment in religious liberty.

a portrait of Providence resident and Civil War General Ambrose Burnside (1824–81) by Emanuel Leutze (1816–68), and the original state charter of 1663.

☒ Roger Williams Park and Zoo

1000 Elmwood Ave. ☎ (401) 785-3510. 🚌 Kennedy Plaza. **Park** 🕐 dawn to dusk daily. **Zoo** 🕐 mid-Apr–mid-Oct: 9am–5pm Mon–Fri, 9am–6pm Sat–Sun; mid-Oct–mid-Apr: 9am–4pm daily. ● Dec 25. 🐾 zoo. 🎫 ♿ 🎁 🍴

In 1871 Betsey Williams, a direct descendant of Roger Williams, donated 102 acres (41 ha) of prime real estate to the city for use as parkland. Since that time, another 320 acres (130 ha) of property have been added to the site. Once farmland, the park now

Historic cookbooks from the Culinary Archives and Museum

holds gardens and greenhouses, ponds, a lake with paddleboats and rowboats for rent, jogging and cycling paths, and a tennis center. Children especially love the carousel and train, the planetarium, and the Museum of Natural History.

Without a doubt, the highlight of the park is the zoo, which has more than 900

animals and 156 species. Dating back to 1872, the zoo is one of the oldest in the nation, but this has not stopped it from keeping up to date. Exhibits include the Plains of Africa, with elephants, zebras, giraffes, and cheetahs; a Madagascar exhibit of endangered lemurs; the Australasia area, with open-air aviary; and an underwater window for viewing penguins and polar bears as they cavort in the water.

🏛 Culinary Archives and Museum at Johnson & Wales University

315 Harborside Blvd. ☎ (401) 598-2805. 🕐 10am–4pm Tue–Sat. ● public hols. 🎫 W www.culinary.org

This one-of-a-kind museum contains half a million items relating to the culinary arts – hardly surprising since Johnson & Wales University is devoted to training chefs. The museum was created in 1979, when Chicago chef Louis Szathmary donated his vast collection of culinary oddities, including a cannibal eating bowl from Fiji and rings worn by bakers that had been excavated at Pompeii. Exhibits include diners that used to be towed from place to place and stoves and ranges.

Roger Williams Park and Zoo, a highlight of downtown Providence

Boats moored at the Sakonnet Wharf near Little Compton

Portsmouth ❻

🏃 16,850. 🛈 23 America's Cup Ave, Newport (401) 845-9123 or (800) 976-5122.

Portsmouth figures greatly in Rhode Island history. It was the second settlement in the old colony, founded in 1638 just two years after Providence. The town was also the site of the 1778 Battle of Rhode Island, the only major land battle fought in the state during the American Revolution. Bad weather and fierce British resistance forced the US troops to retreat. With the British in hot pursuit, only the courage of the American rear guard enabled most of

Delightful denizens of the Green Animals Topiary Garden

the soldiers to escape to the sanctuary of Butts Hill Fort. Today some of the fort's redoubts are still visible from Sprague Street, where plaques recount the battle.

The **Green Animals Topiary Garden** is a more whimsical attraction. Located on a Victorian estate, this lighthearted garden is inhabited by a wild array of topiary creations. In all, some 80 animal shapes – including elephants, camels, giraffes, bears, birds, even a dinosaur – have been trimmed and sculpted from a selection of yew, English boxwood, and California privet. Elsewhere on the grounds, formal flower gardens, a rose arbor, and a museum with an extensive collection of Victorian-era toys delight even the very youngest visitors.

🍁 **Green Animals Topiary Garden**
Cory's Lane. 📞 (401) 847-1000. ⬤ May–Oct: 10am–6pm daily. ⓖ

Little Compton ❼

🏃 3,350. 🛈 23 America's Cup Ave, Newport (401) 845-9123 or (800) 976-5122.

Residents of Little Compton relish their isolated nook at the end of a peninsula that borders Massachusetts with good reason: Little Compton is one of the most charming villages in the entire state, protected from the outside world by the surrounding farmlands and woods.

The white-steepled United Congregational Church stands over Little Compton Commons. Beside the church lies the old Commons Burial Ground,

with the gravesite of Elizabeth Padobie (c.1623–1717). The daughter of *Mayflower* Pilgrims Priscilla and John Alden, Padobie was the first white woman born in New England. The 1680 **Wilbor House** was home to eight generations of the Wilbor family. The house is furnished with period pieces and antique household items. Elsewhere on the grounds visitors can explore a one-room schoolhouse and artist's studio. An 1860 barn displays old farm tools, sleighs, a one-horse shay, oxcart, and buggies.

Nearby **Sakonnet Vineyards** is the largest winery in New England. There are free daily wine tastings and guided tours. Beyond the vineyard on Route 77 is Sakonnet Wharf, where the curious can watch fishermen arrive with their catches.

Sakonnet Vineyards in Little Compton

◁ Old Harbor, Block Island

🏛 **Wilbor House**
548 W Main Rd. ☎ (401) 635-4035.
🔵 Jun–Oct: 1pm–5pm Thu–Sun.
📷

🏛 **Sakonnet Vineyards**
162 W Main Rd. ☎ (401) 635-8486.
🔵 year-round: 11am–5pm daily.
📷 on the hour, last tour at 4pm. ♿

ENVIRONS: Four miles (6 km)
northeast is Adamsville.
Gray's Store dates back to
1788, which gives it the
distinction of being the oldest
general store in the country. It
contains the first post office
(1804) in the area and still has
its original soda fountain,
candy and tobacco cases, and
ice chest.

Middletown's popular Third Beach

Gray's Store, built in 1788, on
Main Street in Adamsville

🏛 **Gray's Store**
4 Main St. ☎ (401) 635-4566.
🔵 9am–5pm Mon–Sat, 12pm–4pm
Sun & public hols.

Middletown ❽

🏘 19,950. ℹ 23 America's Cup
Ave, Newport (401) 845-9123 or
(800) 976-5122.

NESTLED BETWEEN Newport
(see pp182–7) and
Portsmouth on Aquidneck
Island, Middletown is known
primarily for its two popular
beaches. **Third Beach** is
located on the Sakonnet River
and is outfitted with a boat
ramp. A steady wind and relatively calm water make the
beach a favorite among wind-
surfers and families with
young children.

Third Beach runs into the
largest and most beautiful
beach on the island.
Sachuest, or
Second Beach,
is widely con-
sidered one of
the best places
to surf in south-
ern New England.
This spacious strand is
rippled with sand dunes
and equipped with
campgrounds. Purgatory
Chasm, a narrow cleft in the
rock ledges on the east side
of Easton Point, provides a
scenic outlook over both the
beach and 50-ft- (15-m-) high
Hanging Rock.

Second Beach has yet
another advantage; it is adjacent to the **Norman Bird
Sanctuary**, a 450-acre
(182-ha) wildlife area with
seven miles (11 km) of walking trails that are ideal for
birding. Some 250 species
have been sighted at this
sanctuary, including herons,
egrets, woodcocks, thrashers,
ducks, and swans. The
refuge is home to numerous
four-legged animals, such as
rabbits and red foxes. A
small natural history
museum is also
located on the
site, and during
the winter
months the
sanctuary trails
are used by cross-
country skiers.
Amateur entomolo-
gists will enjoy pay-
ing a visit to the
Newport Butterfly Farm.
Colorful species from all
around the world can be
found in a giant, specially
designed, screened-in greenhouse. Visitors are free to
walk among the flowers and
observe the beautiful insects
as they feed on nectar and
lay eggs.

Inhabitant of
Newport
Butterfly Farm

🏖 **Third Beach**
Third Beach Rd. ☎ (401) 849-2822.
🔵 Memorial Day–Labor Day: life-
guards on duty 8am–6pm daily. 📷
🏖 **Second Beach**
Third Beach Rd. ☎ (401) 849-2822.
🔵 Memorial Day–Labor Day: life-
guards on duty 8am–6pm daily. 📷
🦋 **Norman Bird
Sanctuary**
583 Third Beach Rd. ☎ (401) 846-
2577. 🔵 year-round: 9am–5pm
daily. ⚫ Thanksgiving & Dec 25.
📷 📷
🦋 **Newport Butterfly Farm**
594 Aquidneck Ave. ☎ (401) 849-
9519. 🔵 May–Sep: 11am–4pm daily.

Waterfowl in Middletown's Norman Bird Sanctuary

Newport ❾

A CENTER OF TRADE, culture, wealth, and military activity for more than 300 years, Newport is a true sightseeing mecca. Historical firsts abound in this small city. America's first naval college and synagogue are here, as are the oldest library in the country and one of the oldest continuously operating taverns. Any visit to the city should include a tour of the mansions from the Gilded Age of the late 1800s, when the rich and famous flocked here each summer to beat New York's heat. These summer "cottage" retreats of the country's wealthiest families, the Vanderbilts and Astors among them, are some of America's grandest private homes.

Exploring Newport
Like Italy, Newport has a distinctly boot-shaped outline. The city's famous mansions are located on the southeastern side, or the heel of the boot. Newport's harborfront is to the west, where the laces would be. The city's most interesting streets, America's Cup Avenue and Thames Street, are found here. Pedestrians will find restaurants, shops, and colonial buildings, including the 1726 Trinity Church.

🏛 Museum of Newport History
127 Thames St. 📞 (401) 846-0813. ◷ Apr–Oct: 10am–5pm Mon & Wed–Sat, 1pm–5pm Sun; Nov–Mar: 10am–4pm Fri–Sat, 1pm–4pm Sun. ● Tue. 🌐 🚫
The Brick Market, a commercial hub during the 18th century, is now a museum that provides an excellent introduction to the city's history and architecture. Self-guided tours include an audiovisual exploration of the downtown in a 19th-century omnibus.

✡ Touro Synagogue
85 Touro St. 📞 (401) 847-4794. ◷ call for times. 📷 every half hour. ✡ Shabbat and all Jewish hols. 📱 🚫
America's oldest synagogue, Touro was erected in 1763 by Sephardic Jews who had fled Spain and Portugal in search of religious tolerance. Designed by architect Peter Harrison (1716–75), it is considered one of the country's finest examples of 18th-century architecture. Services still follow the Sephardic rituals of its founders.

⚓ Fort Adams State Park
Harrison Ave. 📞 (401) 847-2400. ◷ sunrise to sunset daily. 🚩 **Museum of Yachting** 📞 (401) 847-1018. ◷ mid-May–Oct: 10am–4pm daily; Nov–mid-May: by appt. 🌐 🍴 🚻

Fort Adams, centerpiece of Fort Adams State Park

Fort Adams is one of the largest military forts in the country. Completed in 1857 at a cost of $3 million, it was designed to house 2,400 troops. The property surrounding the fort is equipped with facilities for swimming, soccer, rugby, and picnicking. Each year Newport's world-famous music festivals (see p33) are held here.
The park also is home to the Museum of Yachting, which chronicles Newport's famed yachting history. One

Public grass courts at the International Tennis Hall of Fame

of the museum's highlights is its collection of classic luxury boats in its outdoor basin.

🏛 International Tennis Hall of Fame
194 Bellevue Ave. 📞 (401) 849-3990. ◷ 9:30am–5pm daily. ● Thanksgiving & Dec 25. 🎾 courts available to public. 🌐 ♿ 🚫
The hall is housed in the Newport Casino, once a private club for Newport's elite. Founded in 1880, the club installed grass tennis courts to introduce its members to the latest sports rage. The first US National Lawn Tennis Championship, later known as the US Open, was held here in 1881. Today the hall displays everything from antique rackets to the "comeback" outfit worn by Monica Seles (b.1972). The grass courts are the only ones in the US open to the public.

🚶 Cliff Walk
Begins at Memorial Blvd. 📞 (401) 845-9123. ◷ year-round: dawn–dusk daily. 🌐
This 3.5-mile (5.5-km) walk along Newport's rugged cliffs offers some of the best views of the Gilded-Age mansions. Local fishermen preserved public access to the trail by going to court when wealthy mansion-owners tried to have it closed. The walk was designated a National Recreation Trail in 1975. The Forty Steps, each step named for someone lost at sea, lead to the ocean.

The breathtaking Cliff Walk, popular with residents as well as visitors

International Yacht Restoration School

449 Thames St. (401) 848-5777.
10am–5pm Mon–Sat.

Students at work at International Yacht Restoration School

Founded in 1993, this small school provides a fascinating look at yacht restoration. Visitors can observe students from the mezzanine, and tour the waterfront campus to see the *Coronet*, built in 1885. The world's oldest grand yacht is currently undergoing restoration by the school.

Redwood Library and Athenaeum

50 Bellevue Ave. (401) 847-0292.
9:30am–5:30pm Mon & Fri–Sat,
9:30am–8pm Tue & Wed–Thu,
1pm–5pm Sun. public hols.

Completed in 1750, the Redwood is the oldest continuously operating library in America and is one of the country's earliest examples of temple-form buildings. Apart from books, the library also contains a fine colonial portrait collection.

Newport Mansions

Preservation Society of Newport County, 424 Bellevue Ave. (401) 847-1000. May–Oct: 10am–5pm daily; winter: call for hours. Dec 24 & 25. obligatory. partial.

Redwood Library and Athenaeum's stately interior

Built between 1748 and 1902, 12 of these summer "cottages," most of them along Bellevue Avenue, are open

for guided tours. Modeled on European palaces and decorated with the finest artworks, the mansions were used for only 10 weeks of the year. The Breakers *(see pp186–7)* is one of the finest examples.

Naval War College Museum

686 Cushing Rd. (401) 841-4052.
10am–4pm Mon–Fri. There are strict security measures. Oct–Jun: Sat–Sun.

This site preserves the history, art, and science of naval warfare and the heritage of Narragansett Bay. Founded in 1885, the college is the oldest naval institute of higher learning in the world. The museum houses ship models and maritime art.

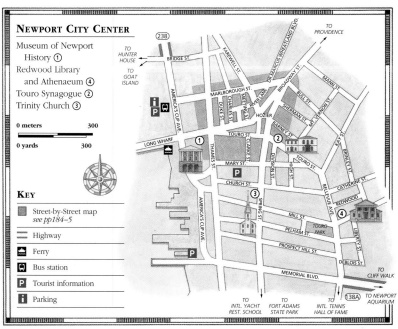

NEWPORT CITY CENTER

Museum of Newport History ①
Redwood Library and Athenaeum ④
Touro Synagogue ②
Trinity Church ③

0 meters 300
0 yards 300

KEY

Street-by-Street map *see pp184–5*

Highway

Ferry

Bus station

Tourist information

Parking

Around Washington Square

N EWPORT'S FIRST SETTLERS were religious moderates fleeing persecution at the hands of Puritans in the Massachusetts Bay colony. With its accessible harbor, the town quickly developed into a thriving seaport. However, its location also made it vulnerable. When Rhode Island declared independence from colonial rule in 1776, British forces occupied the city. Before they were driven out in 1780, the occupying army destroyed much of the town. Thanks to preservation efforts, a number of colonial buildings survive. Several of them can be seen on this tour around historic Washington Square, the center of Newport's political and economic life during colonial times.

Historic marker

Architectural detail *is typical of the Washington Square district.*

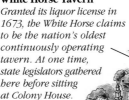

White Horse Tavern
Granted its liquor license in 1673, the White Horse claims to be the nation's oldest continuously operating tavern. At one time, state legislators gathered here before sitting at Colony House.

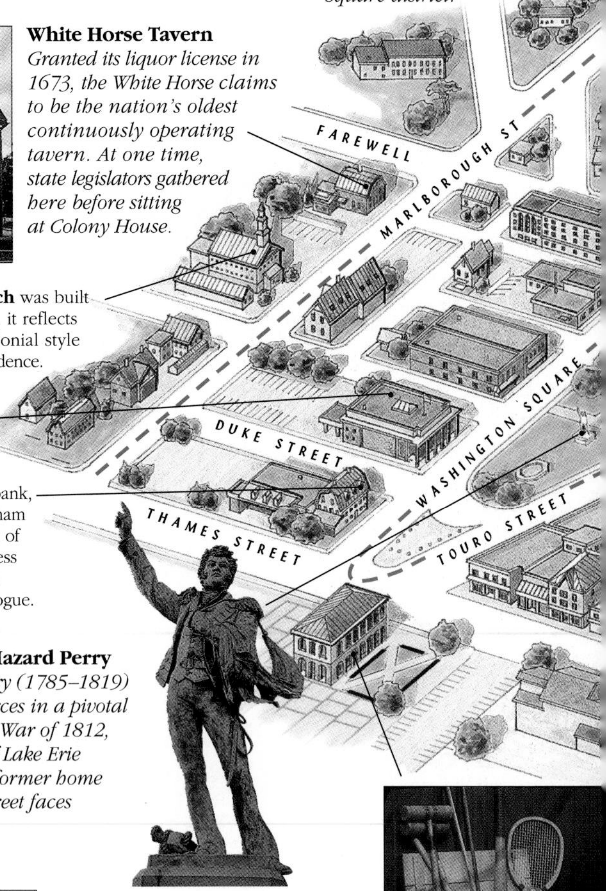

St. Paul's Methodist Church was built in 1805. A simple structure, it reflects the continuation of the Colonial style in the decades after independence.

Bank of Newport

Rivera House, currently a bank, was once the home of Abraham Rivera, a prominent member of Newport's Jewish and business communities. Rivera laid the cornerstone of Touro Synagogue.

FAREWELL

MARLBOROUGH ST

DUKE STREET

THAMES STREET

WASHINGTON SQUARE

TOURO STREET

Statue of Oliver Hazard Perry
Oliver Hazard Perry (1785–1819) defeated British forces in a pivotal naval battle in the War of 1812, securing control of Lake Erie for the US. Perry's former home at No. 29 Touro Street faces the statue.

STAR SIGHTS

★ **Museum of Newport History**

★ **Touro Synagogue**

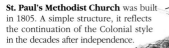

★ **Museum of Newport History**
The Brick Market, once the center of commerce, has been renovated to house this museum (see p182) that brings to life Newport's economic, social, and sporting past.

Colony House
This grand structure from 1739 was the state's main seat of government until 1900. Rhode Island's declaration of independence was read from the balcony in May 1776, two months before the July 4th proclamation in Philadelphia.

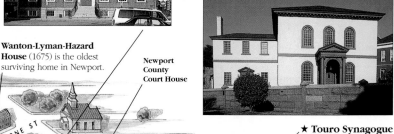

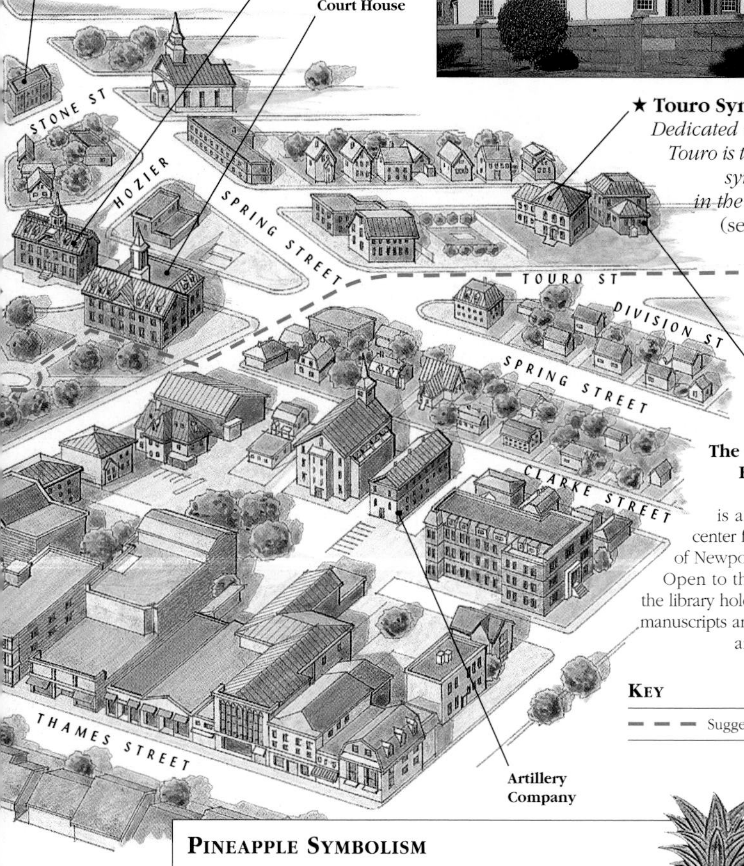

Wanton-Lyman-Hazard House (1675) is the oldest surviving home in Newport.

Newport County Court House

★ **Touro Synagogue**
Dedicated in 1763, Touro is the oldest synagogue in the country (see p182).

STONE ST

HOZIER

SPRING STREET

TOURO ST

DIVISION ST

SPRING STREET

CLARKE STREET

The Newport Historical Society
is a resource center for studies of Newport history. Open to the public, the library holds historic manuscripts and a small art gallery.

THAMES STREET

Artillery Company

KEY

– – – Suggested route

PINEAPPLE SYMBOLISM

While on trade missions to Africa and the West Indies, Newport's sailors ate fresh fruit to ward off scurvy. What they did not eat, they brought home to their families. It became tradition in Newport to place a pineapple on the gatepost when the seagoing man of the house had returned safely. In time, the fruit became a local symbol of hospitality and was often incorporated into the front door's transom or applied directly to the door itself. Pineapples appear on many old Newport homes.

0 meters   25

0 yards   25

The Breakers

THE ARCHITECTURE and ostentation of the Gilded Age of the late 1800s reached its pinnacle with the Breakers, the summer home of railroad magnate Cornelius Vanderbilt II (1843–99). Completed in 1895, the four-story, 70-room limestone structure surpassed all other Newport mansions in extravagance. US architect Richard Morris Hunt (1827–95) modeled the building after the 16th-century palaces in Turin and Genoa. Its interior is adorned with marble, alabaster, stained glass, gilt, and crystal.

The Structure
Built in the Italian Renaissance style, the Breakers is alleged to have cost more than $10 million – a huge sum of money in 1895.

Visitors' entrance, west side

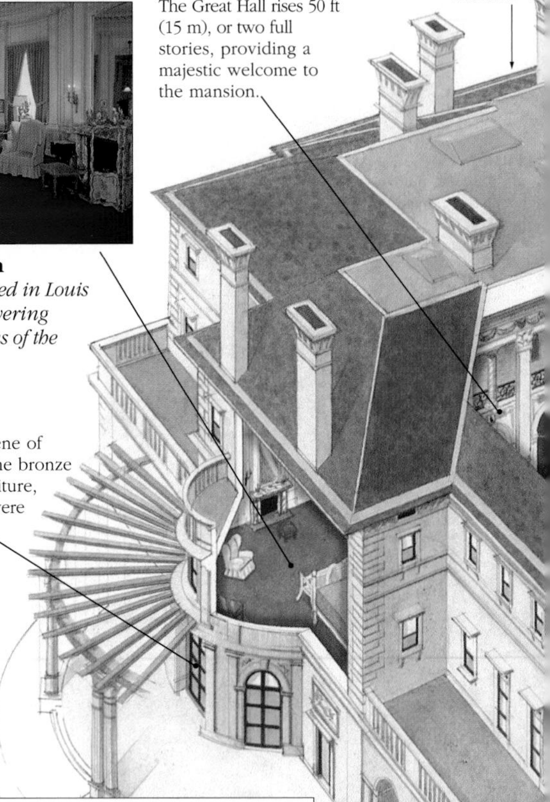

The Great Hall
The Great Hall rises 50 ft (15 m), or two full stories, providing a majestic welcome to the mansion.

★ Mrs. Vanderbilt's Bedroom
This sumptuous room is decorated in Louis XVI style. Its flowered wall covering and upholstery are reproductions of the original silk and cotton fabrics.

The Music Room
This grand room was the scene of many dances and recitals. The bronze and crystal chandeliers, furniture, and gilt decorative touches were modeled on Italian designs.

STAR FEATURES

★ **Mrs. Vanderbilt's Bedroom**

★ **The Dining Room**

★ **The Morning Room**

A MAGNATE'S LIFE

Cornelius Vanderbilt II inherited the mantle as head of the Vanderbilt empire in 1885. He directed the family businesses, mainly railroads, with his brother William for 11 years before suffering a paralyzing stroke. He convalesced at the Breakers, but died in 1899 at the age of 56. At the time of his death, the local gossip held that he had more money than the US Mint.

Cornelius Vanderbilt II

Covered walkway

★ The Dining Room
The most richly adorned room in the mansion, the two-story, 2,400-sq-ft (220-sq-m) dining room has two huge crystal chandeliers and a stunning arched ceiling.

VISITORS' CHECKLIST

Ochre Point Ave. 📞 *(401) 847-1000.* 🚌 *67.* ⏱ *mid-Apr–Oct: 10am–5pm daily; call for winter hours.* ⬤ *Thanksgiving, Dec 24, Dec 25.* 🎫 *every 15 minutes.* ♿ 🚫
🌐 *www.NewportMansions.org*

Upper Loggia
The upper loggia offers a view of the sunrise over the Atlantic Ocean. Its ceiling is painted to look like canopies against a clouded sky.

Sculpted Archways
Ornately carved archways are inspired by Italian Renaissance-style palazzos.

The Billiard Room
The Billiard Room features several costly wall marbles; the arches and mantel are decorated with yellow alabaster. The mahogany billiard table was built by Baumgarten of New York. Steel beams were needed to support the huge chandeliers.

★ The Morning Room
The ceiling of this east-facing room is adorned with paintings of the Four Seasons, the mahogany doors with the Four Elements. All cornices, pilasters, and panels were made in France and shipped to Newport.

Sunbathing on the rocks at Beavertail Lighthouse and State Park

Jamestown ⑩

🏃 5,000. 🚹 23 America's Cup
Ave, Newport (401) 845-9123 or
(800) 976-5122.

NAMED FOR England's King
James II (1633–1701),
Jamestown is located on
Conanicut Island and linked
to Newport (see pp182–7)
and the mainland by a pair
of bridges. During the
Revolutionary War, British
troops torched much of the
town, sparing very few of the
houses from that era.

The town is best known for
the **Beavertail Lighthouse
and State Park**, perched at
the southernmost tip of the
island. The first lighthouse
here was built in 1749 and
was subsequently replaced by
the present structure in 1856.
As with many New England
lighthouses, the coastal vistas
from Beavertail are beautiful.
The winds, currents, and surf
can be heavy at times, but on
calm days hiking, climbing,
and sunbathing on the rocks
are favorite pastimes.

Situated on the site of an
early fort and artillery battery,
Fort Wetherill State Park
offers great scenic outlooks,
picnic tables, and a boat
ramp. The park is a popular
place for saltwater fishing,
boating, and scuba diving.
Legend has it that notorious
privateer Captain Kidd
(1645–1701) stashed some of
his plundered loot in the
park's Pirate Cave.

🌿 **Beavertail Lighthouse
and State Park**
Beavertail Pt. 🅒 (401) 423-9941.
Park ◯ dawn to dusk daily.
Lighthouse ◯ call for hours. 🅿 ♿
🌿 **Fort Wetherill State Park**
Fort Wetherill Rd. 🅒 (401) 423-
1771. ◯ dawn to dusk daily. 🅿 ♿

Wickford ⑪

🏃 25,000. 🚹 4808 Tower Hill Rd,
Wakefield (401) 789-4422 or (800)
548-4662. 🅦 www.wickford.com

CONSIDERED a part of North
Kingston, the quaint
village of Wickford lies in
the northernmost point of
Washington County, also
known as South County.
Wickford's many 18th- and
19th-century houses are a
magnet for artists and
craftsmen. John Updike (see
pp30–31), author of Rabbit
Run (1960), has family roots
here. The 1745 Updike House
on Pleasant Street is just one
of some 60 buildings con-
structed before 1804.

Daytrippers hailing from
Providence and Connecticut
are apt to jam Wickford's
picturesque harbor and busy
streets. Among the many
shops along Brown and Main
streets, the Shaker Shop is
a favorite for its replicas of
old Shaker furniture, quilts,
and boxes.

Old Narragansett Church
(more commonly called Old
St. Paul's) is one of the oldest
Episcopal churches in the US,
dating back to 1707, with box
pews, an organ from 1660,
and an upstairs gallery to
which plantation slaves were

Wickford's tranquil harbor

relegated. Artist Gilbert Stuart (1755–1828) was baptized here in a silver baptismal font given to the church as a gift by England's Queen Anne (1665–1714).

ENVIRONS: One mile north of town is **Smith's Castle**, one of America's oldest plantation houses. In 1678 settler Richard Smith built a dwelling on the site. Hardly a castle, the structure served as a garrison for

Smith's Castle, just outside of Wickford

the soldiers who had participated in the 1675 Great Swamp Fight against the Narragansett Indians. The battle resulted in a mass slaughter of Indians, which set off a chain of tragic events culminating in the retaliatory destruction of the garrison and the death of 40 soldiers. Later the structure was rebuilt and acquired by the Updike family in 1692. Subsequent additions and renovations transformed the structure into one of the most handsome plantation houses on the Rhode Island shore. The house contains fine paneling, 17th- and 18th-century furnishings, china, and a chair once owned by Roger Williams (*see pp169, 177*).

🏛 **Smith's Castle**
55 Richard Smith Dr. 🄲 *(401) 294-3521.* ⏰ *call for hours.* ♿ ▣

Saunderstown 🕑

🏚 *27,000.* ℹ *8045 Post Rd, North Kingston (401) 295-5566.*

L OCATED BETWEEN Wickford and Narragansett, this town has two main attractions. The gambrel-roofed **Gilbert Stuart Birthplace** was built in 1751 along

the Mattatuxet River. Stuart (1755–1828), whose portraits of US presidents were to bring him lasting fame, was born here. His best-known portrait, that of George Washington, graces the US one-dollar bill.

On the first floor of the house, Stuart's father built a large kitchen and snuff mill, the first in America, powered by a wooden water-wheel. The upstairs living quarters are furnished with authentic period pieces.

Also in town is the 18th-century **Silas Casey Farm**. Still in operation, the farm has been occupied by the same family for 200 years. The 360-acre (146-ha) property is ringed by almost 30 miles (48 km) of stone walls. The house contains original furniture, paintings, and prints, and visitors can tour the family cemetery.

Plaque at Stuart Birthplace

🏛 **Gilbert Stuart Birthplace**
815 Gilbert Stuart Rd. 🄲 *(401) 294-3001.* ⏰ *Apr–Oct: 11am–4pm Thu–Mon.* ● *Nov–Mar.* ♿ ▣

🏛 **Silas Casey Farm**
2325 Boston Neck Rd. 🄲 *(401) 295-1030.* ⏰ *Jun–mid-Oct: 1–5pm Tue, Thu, Sat.* ● *Nov–May.*
♿ ▣ ♿

South Kingstown 🕤

🏚 *26,700.* ℹ *322 Main St (401) 783-2801.*

S OUTH KINGSTOWN is a 55-sq-mile (142-sq-km) town that encompasses 15 villages,

including Kingston, Green Hill, Wakefield, and Snug Harbor. The town is home to the **Museum of Primitive Art and Culture**. Located in an 1856 post office, the museum displays weapons, tools, and implements of aboriginal cultures around the world, including a range of artifacts from prehistoric New England.

After visiting the museum, travelers can enjoy some of the region's outdoor charms. Sightseers, particularly those with cameras, will want to make the trek to the top of the observation post at Hannah Robinson Rock and Tower, where they are greeted with expansive views of the Atlantic Ocean and the Rhode Island seashore.

The South County Bike Path is a 3.7-mile (6-km) paved trail, starting at the Kingston train station, which takes cyclists through Great Swamp, the scene of the 1675 slaughter of 2,000 Narragansett Indians at the hands of soldiers and settlers – one of the bloodiest battles ever fought in New England. The swamp is now a pristine 3,300-acre (1,335-ha) wildlife refuge called the **Great Swamp Management Area** and is home to creatures such as coyotes, mink, wild turkeys, and ring-necked pheasants. Nature trails lead visitors through dense woodland, past a dike to a boardwalk into a marsh. Birders should pack binoculars and visit the refuge in the spring, when songbirds are spotted during their annual migration.

🏛 **Museum of Primitive Art and Culture**
1058 Kingston Rd. 🄲 *(401) 783-5711.* ⏰ *year-round: 10am–2pm Tue–Thu.* ♿

⚔ **Great Swamp Management Area**
Liberty Lane off Great Neck Rd.
🄲 *(401) 789-0281.*
⏰ *dawn to dusk daily.*

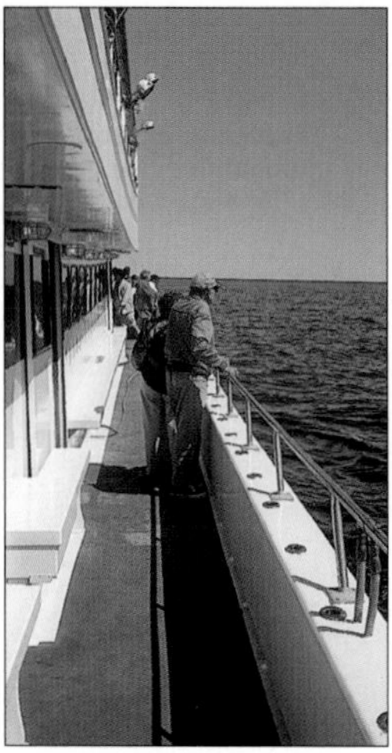

Whale-watching off Point Judith, a popular summer activity

Narragansett [14]

👥 *18,000.* ✈ *TF Green Airport.* ℹ *36 Ocean Rd. (401) 783-7121.*

In the late 19th century this town's waterfront area gained national fame as a fashionable resort, complete with a large casino. In 1900 a devastating fire razed the 1884 casino and many of the lavish hotels. All that remains of the ornate 1884 casino are **The Towers**, two stone towers linked by a Romanesque Revival-style arch.

Today rolling dice have given way to rolling waves, as the town beach offers some of the best surfing on the East Coast. Nearby the **South County Museum** depicts early Rhode Island life with displays of children's toys, farm tools, weapons, a cobbler's shop, a general store, and a working print shop.

🏰 The Towers
35 Ocean Rd. ☎ *(401) 782-2597.* ○ *Jul–Aug: 12pm–4pm Sat–Sun, 7pm–10pm Thu.* ● *Sep–Jun.* 👉 *call for hours.* ♿

🏛 South County Museum
Strathmore St. off Rte 1.
☎ *(401) 783-5400.* ○ *May–Oct: 11am–4pm Wed–Mon.* 🚫

Environs: Located at the south end of the Narragansett peninsula, **Point Judith** and **Galilee** are departure points for numerous whale-watching cruises, sightseeing boat tours, ferries to Block Island (*see pp192–3*), and charters for deep-sea fishing. Toward the end of World War II, a German U-boat was sunk just two miles (3 km) off the Point Judith Lighthouse. Today the lighthouse affords beautiful views of the ocean. Galilee is famous for its Blessing of the Fleet festival in late July *(see p33)*. The Galilee Salt Marsh is popular for birding.

Charlestown [16]

👥 *6,000.* ✈ 🚌 ℹ *4945 Old Post Rd (401) 364-3878.*

This small town stretches along four miles (6.4 km) of lovely beaches, encompassing the largest saltwater marsh in the state and several parks. It is also a convenient base for nature lovers. The 2,000-acre (810-ha) **Burlingame State Park** on Watchaug Pond is equipped with campgrounds, nature trails, swimming and picnic

South County Beaches [15]

Driving along Highway 1 between Narragansett and Watch Hill, travelers will pass some 100 miles (161 km) of pristine white sand beaches. These thin strands of sand are all that separate Block Island Sound from a series of tidal salt ponds, some of which have been designated national wildlife refuges. The ponds are big lures for bird-watchers hoping to study the egrets, sandpipers, and herons that swim and wade in the salty marshes. Many of the beaches are free to the public, except for parking fees.

Key

- Major road
- Other road
- Ferry
- ✈ Airport
- Viewpoint

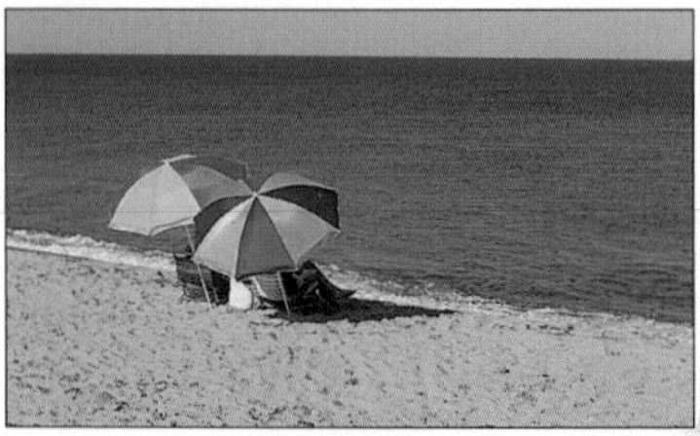

Misquamicut State Beach [5]
The state's largest beach has gentle surf and a nearby old-time amusement park with rides and diversions for children.

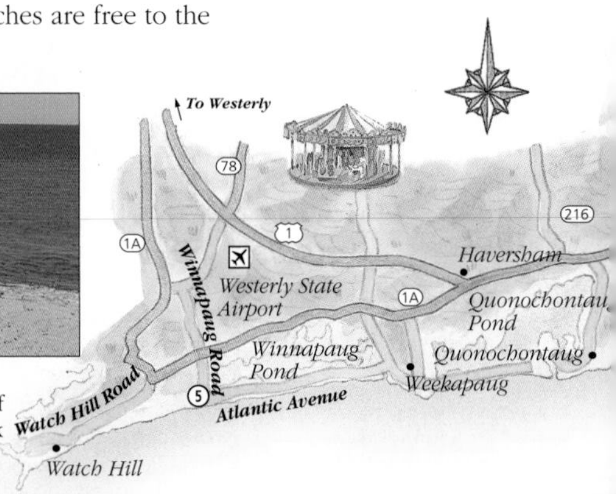
To Westerly
78
216
1
1A
Winnapaug Road
Westerly State Airport
Haversham
Quonochontau
Pond
Winnapaug Pond
Quonochontaug
Weekapaug
Watch Hill Road
5
Atlantic Avenue
Watch Hill

areas, trails for road and mountain bikes, as well as fishing and boating. Birders will enjoy the Audubon Society's **Kimball Wildlife Refuge**, located on the south side of the park. The refuge is a habitat for many kinds of waterfowl and migrating birds, and has a network of easy footpaths.

More outdoor enjoyment can be found at the 172-acre (70-ha) **Ninigret Park**. Maintained trails lead cyclists and hikers through the

grounds, which are graced with a spring-fed swimming pond, tennis courts, and baseball fields. During the winter months, the trails are used by cross-country skiers.

Burlingame State Park
Rte 1A. ☎ (401) 322-7994.
⬤ Apr–Oct: dawn–dusk daily.
🚫 for camping facilities.

Kimball Wildlife Refuge
Prosser Trail. ☎ (401) 949-5454.
⬤ dawn–dusk daily.

Ninigret Park
Rte 1A. ☎ (401) 364-1222.
⬤ dawn–dusk daily. 🚫 ♿

Nature trails through the Kimball Wildlife Refuge

Watch Hill ⑰

ℹ️ *1 Chamber Way, Westerly (401) 596-7761.*

A VILLAGE within the town of Westerly, Watch Hill has been an upscale resort and beach haven for the rich and famous since the 19th century. Strolls along Bay Street yield beautiful views of the many gingerbread-trimmed Victorian houses perched on rocky hills above the beach. Visitors to Watch Hill can enjoy the village's relaxed atmosphere, with a little window shopping or sunbathing down at the beach. Believed to be the oldest carousel in the US, the 1867 **Flying Horse Carousel** on the beach is a favorite of children. The vantage point of the Watch Hill Lighthouse offers views of neighboring Connecticut's Fishers Island.

🎠 **Flying Horse Carousel**
Bay St. ☎ (401) 596-7761. ⬤ Memorial Day–Labor Day: 11am–9pm Mon–Fri, 10am–9pm Sat–Sun. 🚫 🖥️ 🍴

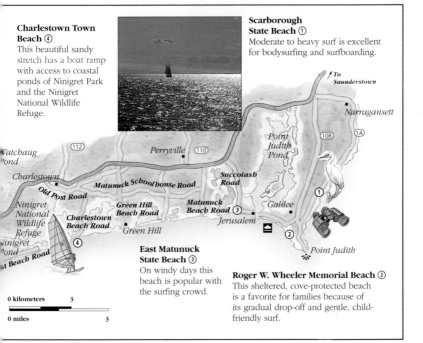

Charlestown Town Beach ④
This beautiful sandy stretch has a boat ramp with access to coastal ponds of Ninigret Park and the Ninigret National Wildlife Refuge.

Scarborough State Beach ①
Moderate to heavy surf is excellent for bodysurfing and surfboarding.

East Matunuck State Beach ③
On windy days this beach is popular with the surfing crowd.

Roger W. Wheeler Memorial Beach ②
This sheltered, cove-protected beach is a favorite for families because of its gradual drop-off and gentle, child-friendly surf.

0 kilometers   3
0 miles   3

Tour of Block Island ⑱

Southeast Light

LYING 13 miles (21 km) off the coast, the haven of Block Island has long been a favorite getaway spot for New Englanders. With 25 percent of its wild landscape under protection, Block Island is a wonderful destination for outdoor enthusiasts who enjoy such activities as swimming, fishing, sailing, bird-watching, kayaking, canoeing, and horseback riding. Some 30 miles of natural trails entice hikers and cyclists alike to experience the island's natural beauty firsthand.

Colorful lobster buoys ashore on Block Island

Great Salt Pond ④
Completely protected from the ocean, Great Salt Pond has three marinas and is an excellent spot for kayaking and fishing. New Harbor is Block Island's prime marina and boating center.

Rodman's Hollow ③
Nature trails lead hikers through the glacial depression of Rodman's Hollow Natural Area. The wildlife refuge is home to hawks and white-tailed deer. One path takes visitors to the beach at Black Rock Point at the southern extremity of the island.

Great Salt Pond

Dead Man's Cove

Cormorant Point

Champlin Road

Grace Cove Road

Beacon Hill

West Side Road

Beacon Hill Road

Center Road

Cooneymus Swamp

Dickens Road

Cooneymus Road

Black Rock Road

Lakeside Drive

Black Rock Point

KEY

▬▬	Tour route
═	Other road
☆	Viewpoint
⛴	Ferry
✕	Airport

0 meters   500

0 yards   500

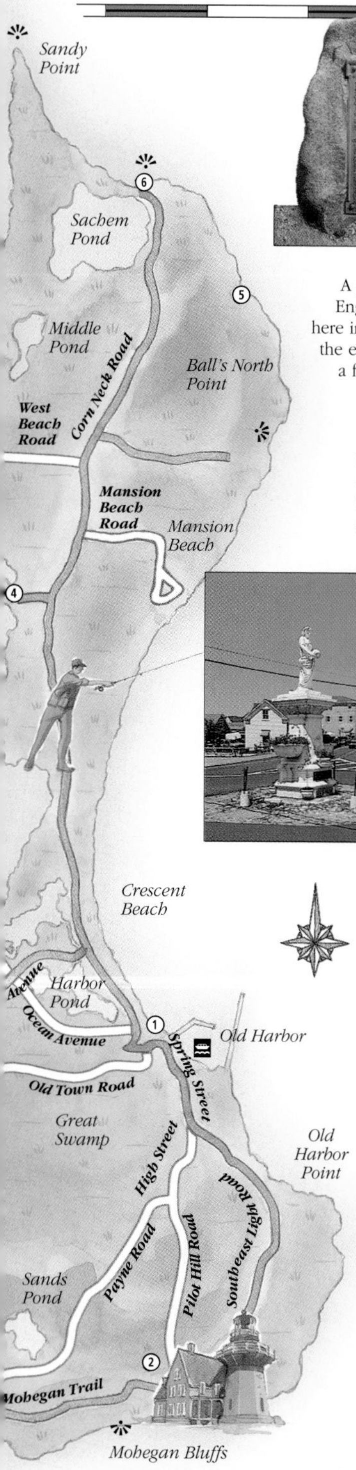

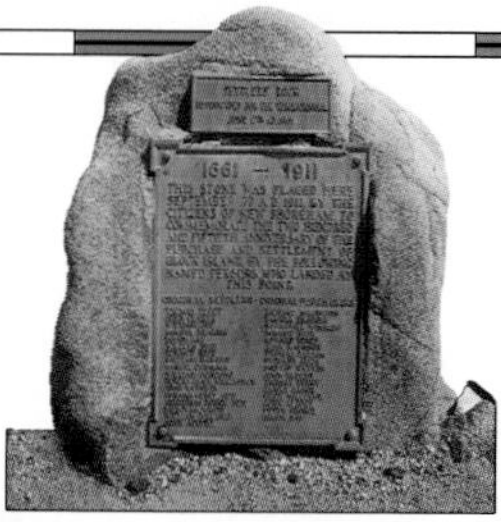

Settlers Rock 6
A plaque honors the 16 Englishmen who landed here in 1661. The rock is at the edge of Sachem Pond, a favorite for swimming and kayaking.

Tips for Drivers

Tour length: *18 miles (29 km).*
Getting there: *Regularly scheduled flights from Westerly, RI, and chartered flights from other mainland airports. Year-round ferry service from Point Judith, RI. Ferries carry cars by advance reservations only, (401) 783-4613.*
Stopping-off point: *Old Harbor, the island's only village, has inns and several quaint restaurants overlooking the ocean* *(see pp335–7)**.*

Clayhead 5
Offers wonderful views of the Atlantic Ocean and is the starting point for a popular nature trail that goes all the way to Settlers Rock.

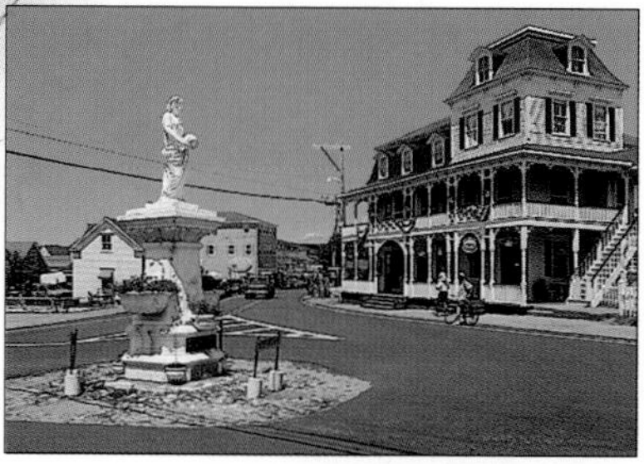

Old Harbor 1
This village is the main hub of activity on the island. Victorian houses, hotels, and shops line the streets, and anglers can charter boats to fish for striped bass, bluefish, flounder, and cod.

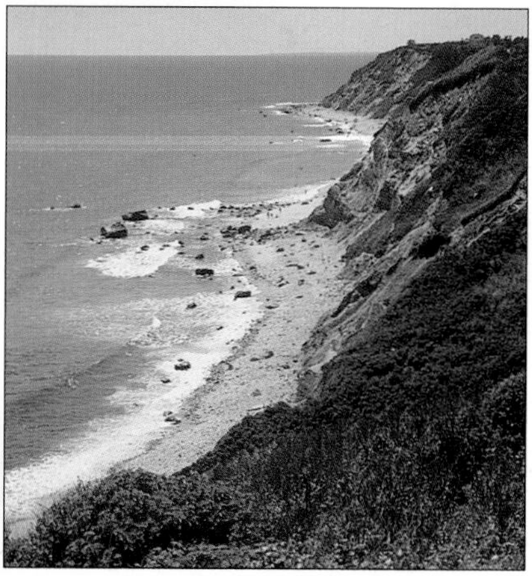

Mohegan Bluffs 2
The name of the bluffs goes back to 1590, when local Manisses Indians tossed 50 Mohegan invaders off these dramatic 200-ft- (61-m-) high red clay cliffs into the waters below. Built in 1875, the Southeast Light was once the most powerful in New England.

CONNECTICUT

CONNECTICUT IS QUINTESSENTIAL NEW ENGLAND. *Its quiet charm is evident everywhere, in scenic villages replete with white steepled churches, immaculate village greens, covered bridges, and old-fashioned clapboard houses ringed by stone walls. Even the state's most bustling cosmopolitan centers contain enclaves of picturesque serenity that invite visitors to poke about at their leisure.*

The third-smallest state in the US, Connecticut is brimming with history. One of the country's original 13 colonies, Connecticut has always been a trendsetter, beginning with its adoption in 1639 of the Fundamental Orders of Connecticut – the New World's first constitution. It was on Connecticut soil that the nation's first public library, law school, and amusement park were built. Scholars and soldiers can thank the fertile minds of state residents for giving them the first dictionary and pistol, gourmands for the hamburger and corkscrew, and children for the three-ring circus, lollipop, and Frisbee.

Water has played an important role in shaping the state. The Housatonic, Naugatuck, Connecticut, and Thames rivers have been feeding the interior woodlands for thousands of years and acted as the main transportation arteries for early inhabitants. Fueled by waterpower, mill towns sprang up along the rivers, eventually giving way to larger commercial centers. Today these waterways are the arenas of canoeists looking for their next adventure. Houseboats and tour boats offer road-weary passengers unique views of the picturesque towns that hug the banks.

Autumn's annual explosion of color makes it the favorite time of year for visitors to meander along Connecticut's byways, hike the Berkshires, wander the Appalachian Trail (*see pp22–3*), and indulge in the seasonal bounty of country inns. In addition, the state calendar bulges with eclectic events. Old-fashioned county fairs are held concurrently with cutting-edge performing arts showcases and regattas. When people have had their fill of ballooning and antiquing, they can sample the wares in one of the state's late-summer oyster festivals.

Mystic Seaport's calm harbor

◁ **First Church of Christ Congregational, Farmington, built in 1652**

Exploring Connecticut

COMPACT ENOUGH TO CROSS in a few hours, Connecticut has treasures that entice travelers to stay for days. The magnificent shoreline, stretching 105 miles (170 km) from Greenwich near the New York State line northeast to Rhode Island, is scalloped by coves, inlets, and harbors, and dotted with state parks, beaches, and marinas. The coast is punctuated by historically significant houses, culminating in Mystic Seaport *(pp214–15)*, a recreated 18th- and 19th-century seafaring village. The area also attracted America's Impressionist artists. Their works are shown in the state's many museums *(pp202–203)*. Inland hills and valleys are dotted with tiny postcard-perfect villages.

Hartford's Bushnell Park

Beach at Mount Tom State Park

GETTING AROUND

Hugging the coast, Interstate 95 serves as the primary east-west link. Interstate 84 follows a similar route from Danbury through Hartford and beyond. The major north-south artery is Interstate 91. Metro North runs trains from New York City to New Haven. Amtrak's New York-Boston line makes stops along Connecticut's shoreline. Several major bus companies, including Peter Pan Trailways, Bonanza, and Greyhound, offer interstate services. Seasonal ferries operate New London-Block Island, Rhode Island, and year-round services run New London-Orient Point, New York, as well as Bridgeport–Port Jefferson.

0 kilometers   10

0 miles   10

SEE ALSO

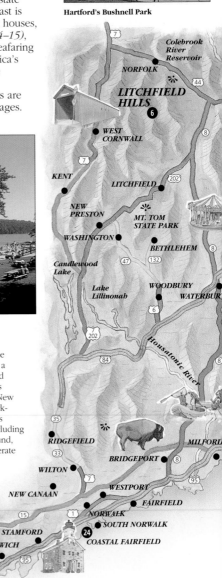

Colebrook River Reservoir

NORFOLK

LITCHFIELD HILLS **6**

WEST CORNWALL

KENT

LITCHFIELD

NEW PRESTON

MT. TOM STATE PARK

WASHINGTON

BETHLEHEM

Candlewood Lake

Lake Lillinonah

WOODBURY

WATERBUR

Housatonic River

RIDGEFIELD

MILFORD

WILTON

BRIDGEPORT

NEW CANAAN

WESTPORT

FAIRFIELD

NORWALK

SOUTH NORWALK

STAMFORD

24 COASTAL FAIRFIELD

GREENWICH

SIGHTS AT A GLANCE

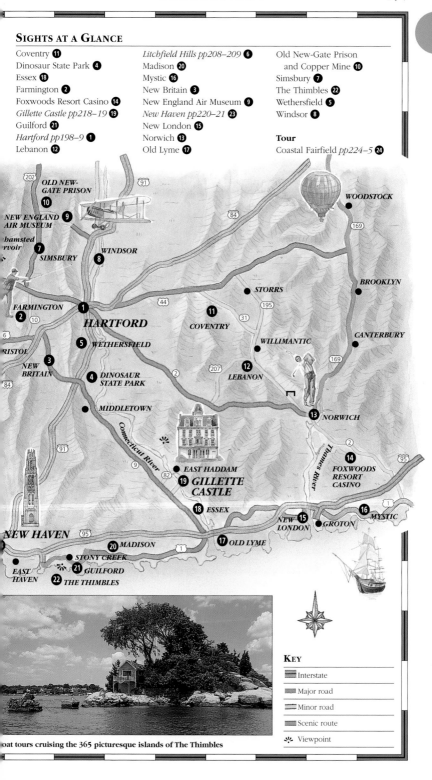

KEY

Interstate

Major road

Minor road

Scenic route

Viewpoint

oat tours cruising the 365 picturesque islands of The Thimbles

Hartford ❶

Elizabeth Park sign

Serving first as an ancient Saukiog Indian settlement and later as a Dutch trading post, Connecticut's capital was founded in 1636 by the Reverend Thomas Hooker (1586–1647) and a group of 100 Englishmen from the Massachusetts Bay Colony. By the late 19th century, Hartford was basking in its Golden Age, thanks to both an economic boom in the insurance industry and a cultural flowering typified by resident authors Mark Twain *(see pp200–201)* and Harriet Beecher Stowe *(see pp30–31)*. In recent decades, an ambitious revitalization program has helped breathe new life into the downtown core.

Exploring Hartford

Approaching the city by car, travelers are greeted by sunlight gleaming off the gold-leaf dome of the hilltop **State Capitol**. Many of Hartford's most popular attractions are easily accessed on foot from the Capitol building, which has an information office for tourists.

🏛 Old State House

800 Main St. **[** (860) 522-6766. **◯** *year-round: 10am–4pm Mon–Fri, 11am–4pm Sat.* **●** *last two weeks Aug & public hols.* **🔲 ♿ 🏠**
The 1796 State House, designed by Charles Bulfinch (1763–1844), is the country's oldest Capitol building. Its graceful center hall, grand staircase, and ornate cupola make the Old State House one of the nation's finest examples of Federal architecture. Of interest are the Great Senate Room and the courtroom where the slave ship *Amistad* trial of 1839 was held. Actors stage reenactments of the trial, which eventually absolved a group of Africans accused of mutiny.

⛪ Center Church and Ancient Burying Ground

675 Main St. **Church [** (860) 249-5631. **◯** *by appt.* **🔲** *by appt.* **Burying Ground [** (860) 561-2585. **◯** *10am–4pm daily.*
Five stained-glass windows designed by US artist Louis Comfort Tiffany (1848–1933) grace the 1807 Center Church (First Church of Christ in Hartford). The church's Ancient Burying Ground contains some 415 headstones dating back to 1648, including that of Hartford's founding father Thomas Hooker. Across Main Street is the 527-ft- (160-m-) high Travelers Tower office building, the tallest man-made observation post in the state.

🏛 Wadsworth Atheneum

600 Main St. **[** (860) 278-2670. **◯** *11am–5pm Tue–Fri, 10am–5pm Sat–Sun, 11am–8pm first Thu of each month.* **●** *Mon & public hols.* **🏷** *free Thu & before 12pm Sat.* **🔲 ♿ 🖥 🏠**
Established in 1842, this

The imposing facade of the Wadsworth Athenaeum

museum has the distinction of being the oldest continuously operating public art museum in the country. Its extensive collection has 45,000 pieces and spans five centuries. It is particularly strong in Renaissance, Baroque, and Impressionist works, as well as in European decorative arts. The museum is especially noted for its extensive collection of American paintings, including works by Thomas Cole (1801–48) and Frederic Church (1826–1900). Outside in the Burr Mall is the monumental red steel sculpture called *Stegosaurus* (1973) by Connecticut resident Alexander Calder (1898–1976).

Alexander Calder's *Stegosaurus*

🏛 Harriet Beecher Stowe House

77 Forest St. **[** (860) 522-9258. **◯** *year-round: 9:30am–4:30pm Tue–Sat, 12pm–4:30pm Sun.* **●** *Oct–May: Mon & public hols.* **🏷** *obligatory.* **♿** *first floor.* **🏠 ⊘**
Located next to the Mark Twain House *(see pp200–201)*, this home is adorned with gingerbread ornamentation typical of late 19th-century Victorian design. Stowe's fame as the author of the anti-slavery novel *Uncle Tom's Cabin* (1852) overshadowed her skill as an interior decorator, demonstrated by the elegance of her 1871 home. The Stowes lived here until Harriet's death in 1896.

East Senate Chambers of Hartford's Old State House

🌲 Bushnell Park

Trinity and Elm Sts. ☎ (860) 232-6710. ○ *year-round.* 🚩 *May–Sep.* ♿ **Carousel** ○ *May–Aug: 11am–5pm Tue–Sun.* 🎫

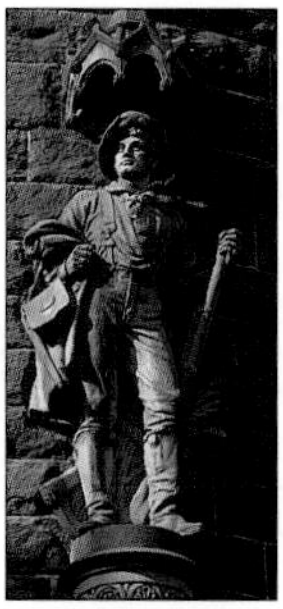

Soldiers and Sailors Memorial

Shaded by 100 tree varieties, the 40-acre (16-ha) park is the lush creation of noted landscape architect and Hartford native Frederick Law Olmsted (1822–1903). Children adore the park's 1914 Bushnell Carousel, with its 48 hand-carved horses, ornate "lovers' chariots," and refurbished Wurlitzer band organ. The 115-ft- (35-m-) tall Soldiers and Sailors Memorial Arch honors those who saw duty in the American Civil War (1861–65).

🌲 Elizabeth Park Rose Gardens

Prospect Ave. ☎ (860) 242-0017. **Gardens** ○ *dawn to dusk daily.* **Greenhouses** ○ *10am–4pm daily.*

Ninety-acre (28-ha) Elizabeth Park was the first city-owned rose garden in the United States. Each year more than 900 varieties of rose bloom on approximately 15,000 bushes. The park also has delightful herb, perennial, and rock gardens as well.

🏛 State Capitol

210 Capitol Ave. ☎ *(860) 240-0222.* ○ *tours every hour 9:15am–1:15pm Mon–Fri, plus Apr–Oct: 10:15am–2:15pm Sat.* ♿ ☕

The State Capitol was designed by Richard Upjohn (1828–1903) in the high Victorian-Gothic style. It is constructed primarily of marble and granite and has a golden dome. Highlights of the grand interior are the oak woodwork and the ornate oak charter chair.

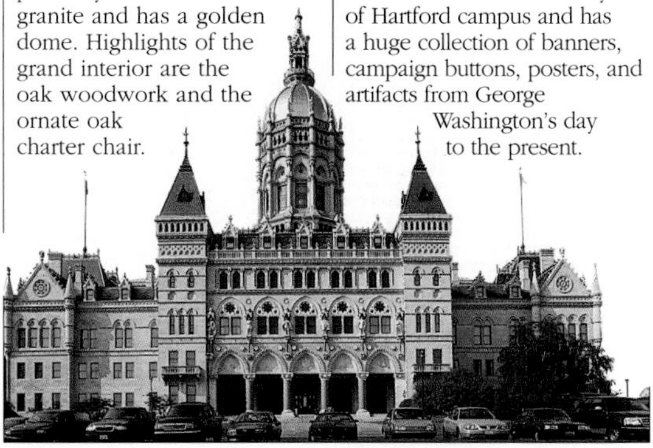

The Connecticut State Capitol, overlooking Bushnell Park

Visitors' Checklist

👥 *139,000.* ✈ *Bradley International Airport.* 🚌 🚆 *1 Union Place.* ℹ *31 Pratt St (860) 244-8181 or (800) 793-4480.* 🎉 *Mark Twain Days (summer).* [W] *www.enjoyhartford.com*

🏛 Museum of American Political Life

200 Bloomfield Ave. ☎ *(860) 768-4090.* ○ *year-round: 11am–4pm Tue–Fri.* ● *public hols.* 🎫

West Hartford, 5 miles (8 km) from Hartford, hosts the Museum of American Political Life. It sits on the University of Hartford campus and has a huge collection of banners, campaign buttons, posters, and artifacts from George Washington's day to the present.

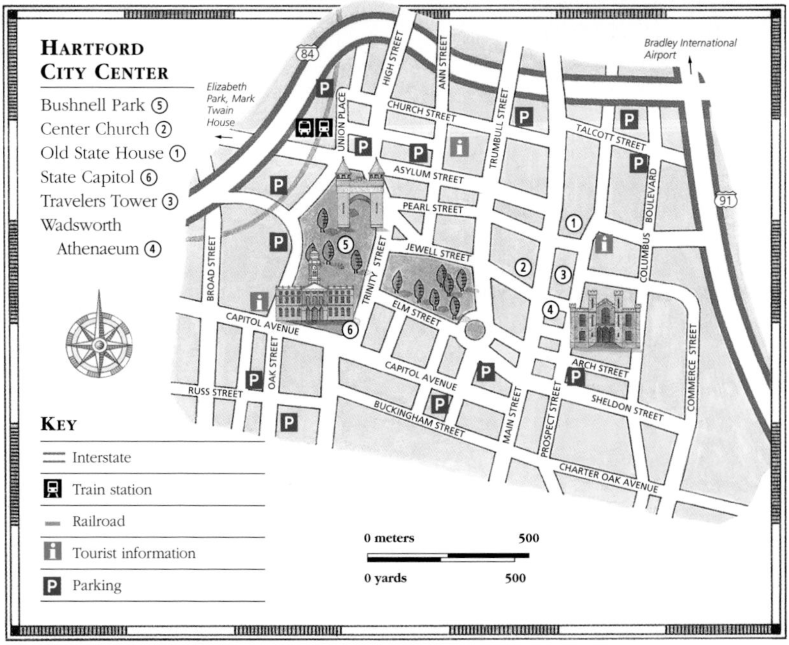
Hartford City Center
Bushnell Park 5
Center Church 2
Old State House 1
State Capitol 6
Travelers Tower 3
Wadsworth Athenaeum 4
Key
Interstate
Train station
Railroad
Tourist information
Parking
Elizabeth Park, Mark Twain House
Bradley International Airport
84
91
High Street
Ann Street
Church Street
Union Place
Trumbull Street
Talcott Street
Asylum Street
Pearl Street
Jewell Street
Trinity Street
Elm Street
Broad Street
Capitol Avenue
Oak Street
Russ Street
Buckingham Street
Main Street
Prospect Street
Arch Street
Sheldon Street
Charter Oak Avenue
Columbus Boulevard
Commerce Street
0 meters 500
0 yards 500

Mark Twain House

Brickwork

MARK TWAIN (1835–1910) lived here from 1874 to 1891 and penned six novels. Based in part on a floor plan sketched out by Twain's wife, Olivia, the 19-room home is a masterpiece of the Picturesque-Gothic style – combining both the sense of high style and playfulness personified by its owners. Legend has it that Twain, a former riverboat pilot, had his architect design the home with expansive upper balconies, peaked gables, and towering turrets in order to give the house the appearance of one of his beloved Mississippi steamboats. A new visitor center illuminates Twain's life and work.

North face of Mark Twain House, showing peaked gable and turret

★ **Billiard Room**
Twain wrote some of his best-known works, including The Adventures of Tom Sawyer *(1876), in the tranquility of the Billiard Room.*

★ **Library**
The ornate fireplace mantel was carved in Scotland in 1869 for a castle that burned down before it was installed.

STAR FEATURES

★ **Billiard Room**

★ **Library**

★ **Master Bedroom**

Turret-style bay windows

The Conservatory
houses a statue of Eve by Karl Gerhardt (1853–1940). Twain had helped finance Gerhardt's studies in Europe.

VISITORS' CHECKLIST

351 Farmington Ave. ☎ (860) 247-0998 ext 26. 🚌 all buses marked E Farmington Ave. 🕐 May–Oct & Dec: 9:30am–5pm Mon–Sat, 12pm–5pm Sun; Jan–Apr & Nov: 9:30am–4pm Mon & Wed–Sat, 12pm–4pm Sun. ● Jan 1, Easter Sunday, Thanksgiving, Dec 24 & 25. 📷 🎫 obligatory, last tour 4pm. ♿ first floor only. W www.marktwain.org

★ Master Bedroom

Twain rhapsodized about the Master Bedroom, claiming it possessed "the most comfortable bedstead that ever was [and one that brings] peace to the sleepers."

The decorative treatment of the railings is indicative of the "Stick" style of the 1870s.

Entrance

The massive wooden door leads into the neo-Tudor-style Entrance Hall, famous for its ornamental carvings.

MARK TWAIN

Raised in the frontier town of Hannibal, Missouri, on the banks of the Mississippi River, young Samuel Langhorne Clemens (better known as Mark Twain) was exposed to a strange cast of characters. Steamboat captains, gamblers, circus performers, actors, and minstrel showmen were just some of the people who passed through the town. As an adult, Twain worked as a typesetter, printer, miner, journalist, soldier, lecturer, editor, and even steamboat captain before finally trying his hand at writing full-time in 1870.

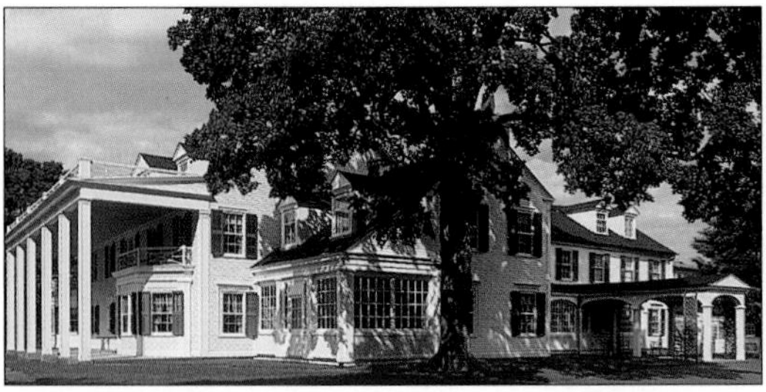

Graceful exterior of the Hill-Stead Museum in Farmington

Farmington ❷

👥 *21,050.* ℹ *31 Pratt St, Hartford (860) 244-8181 or (800) 793-4480.*

Perched on the banks of the surging Farmington River, this quiet enclave has long been the starting point for canoeists, fishermen, and bird-watchers. The skies above the Farmington River Valley are also a busy place, popular with hang gliders and hot-air balloonists taking in the spectacular vistas from on high. Several companies offer champagne flights over the scenic valley, while others offer candlelit tours of the town's historic homes.

The interior of the **Hill-Stead Museum** has remained unchanged since the 1946 death of its original owner Theodate Pope Riddle (1867–1946). Pope, one of the country's first female architects, designed the Colonial–Revival mansion, which was completed in 1901. Her will stipulated that upon her death nothing in the house could be changed, altered, or moved. The result is a fascinating home frozen in the Edwardian period. On display is the Riddle family's fine collection of French and American Impressionist paintings, including works by Edgar Degas (1834–1917), Édouard Manet (1832–83), Mary Cassatt (1845–1926), and James Whistler (1834–1903). The museum also contains splendid examples of American and European furniture and decorative arts. Particularly noteworthy on the grounds of the 150-acre (61-ha) estate is the sunken garden. The **Stanley-Whitman House** is a well-preserved example of the framed overhang style of early 18th-century architecture of New England. The house, furnished with Colonial pieces, is often used as a venue for craft demonstrations and exhibits. Elsewhere in Farmington, admirers of old cemeteries will find many markers of interest in the Ancient Burying Ground, with gravestones dating back to 1661. In the Riverside Cemetery, one tombstone marks the grave of Foone, an African slave who drowned in the town's canal after being freed in the *Amistad* trial *(see p198)*.

🏛 **Hill-Stead Museum**
35 Mountain Rd. ☎ *(860) 677-4787.* ○ *May–Oct: 10am–5pm Tue–Sun; Nov–Apr: 11am–4pm Tue–Sun.* ● *Mon & public hols.* 💳 🚶 *obligatory.* ♿ *partial.* [W] www.hillstead.org

🏛 **Stanley-Whitman House**
37 High St. ☎ *(860) 677-9222.* ○ *May–Oct: 12pm–4pm Wed–Sun; Nov–Apr: 12pm–4pm Sat–Sun.* 💳 🚶 ♿ *partial.*

Environs: Twenty miles (32 km) south of Farmington lies the blue-collar town of Waterbury. The town is

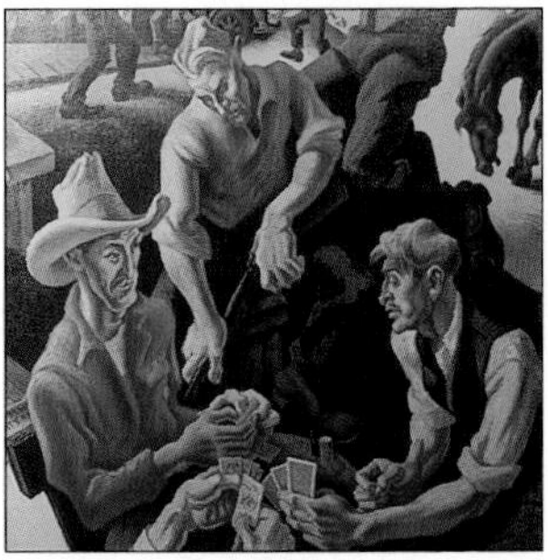

Arts of the West **by Thomas Hart Benton at the New Britain Museum of American Art**

Impressionist Art Trail

Between 1885 and 1930 Connecticut was a magnet for many American artists. Childe Hassam (1859–1935), J. Alden Weir (1852–1919), Willard Metcalf (1858–1925), and others depicted marshes, seascapes, harbors, and farms in a style called American Impressionism. Their works are in ten museums on a self-guided trail that winds from Greenwich to New London.

Sights at a Glance

Bruce Museum, Greenwich ①
Bush-Holley Historic Site, Cos Cob ②
Florence Griswold Museum, Old Lyme ⑨
Hartford Steam Boiler Company, Hartford ⑧
Hill-Stead Museum, Farmington ⑥
Lyman Allyn Art Museum, New London ⑩
New Britain Museum of American Art, New Britain ⑤
Wadsworth Athenaeum, Hartford ⑦
Weir Farm, Ridgefield and Wilton ③
Yale University Art Gallery, New Haven ④

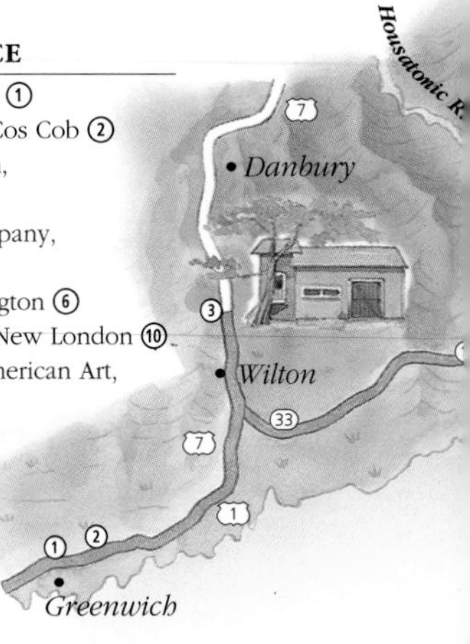

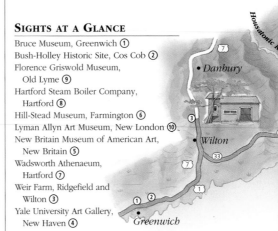

proud of its ethnic roots, as evidenced by its 240-ft- (73-m-) tall Clock Tower, modeled on the city hall in Siena, Italy. Tools, decorative arts, and reconstructed workers' quarters in the **Mattatuck Museum** help trace Waterbury's rise to fame as the "Brass City" during the 19th and early 20th century.

🏛 **Mattatuck Museum**
144 W Main St, Waterbury. 📞 (203) 753-0381. ◯ year-round: 10am–5pm Tue–Sat, 12pm–5pm Sun. ● Mon, Sun in Jul & Aug, & public hols. 📷 ✔ ♿ 🖥

New Britain ❸

🏔 70,000. 🛈 1 Grove Place, Suite 301 (860) 225-3901.

L YING AT THE GEOGRAPHIC center of the state, New Britain is also the midpoint between Boston to the north and New York to the south. Travelers to either city should stop to visit the **New Britain Museum of American Art**. The repository's 19 galleries house a distinguished collection of art from the Colonial period to the present. Almost every well-known US artist is represented here, including Georgia O'Keeffe (1887–1986), Andrew Wyeth (b.1917), Alexander Calder (1898–1976), and Isamu Noguchi (1904–88). The American Impressionist collection is also important.

🏛 **New Britain Museum of American Art**
56 Lexington St, New Britain. 📞 (860) 229-0257. ◯ year-round: 12pm–5pm Tue, Thu, Fri & Sun, noon–7pm Wed, 10am–5pm Sat. 📷

Dinosaur State Park ❹

400 West St, Rocky Hill. 📞 (860) 529-8423. **Park** ◯ 9am–4:30pm daily. **Exhibit center** ◯ 9am–4:30pm Tue–Sun. ● public hols. 📷

D URING THE LOWER JURASSIC period some 200 million years ago, the dinosaurs that roamed this region literally left their mark on the land. Today some 500 prehistoric tracks are preserved beneath this park's huge geodesic dome. Also on display is a life-size model of an eight-

One of 500 ancient tracks at Dinosaur State Park

ft- (2-m-) tall *Dilophosaurus*, the creature that most likely left the prints. Two large dioramas tell the story of the Connecticut Valley during the Triassic and Jurassic periods. A highlight of this exhibit is a replica of *Coelophysis*, the bones of which were found in the area. A thrill for children and amateur paleontologists is the chance to make plaster casts of the tracks as part of the interpretive programs. (Call ahead to find out what to bring.) The park also has a picnic area and miles of nature trails that double as cross-country skiing runs.

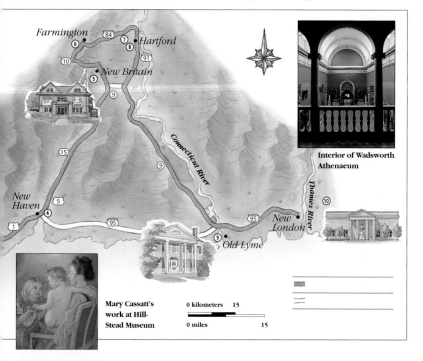

Interior of Wadsworth Athenaeum

Mary Cassatt's work at Hill-Stead Museum

0 kilometers   15

0 miles   15

Street-by-Street: Wethersfield [5]

Now an affluent Hartford suburb, Wethersfield began as the state's first settlement in 1634. In 1640 its citizens held an illegal public election – America's first act of defiance against British rule. The town also hosted the 1781 Revolutionary War conference between George Washington (1732–99) and his French allies, during which they finalized strategies for the decisive American victory in Yorktown. Preserved within a 12-block area, Old Wethersfield stands as a primer of American architecture, with numerous houses from the 18th to 20th centuries. The centerpiece is the Webb-Deane-Stevens Museum, a trio of dwellings depicting the differing lifestyles of three 18th-century Americans: a wealthy merchant, a diplomat, and a leather tanner.

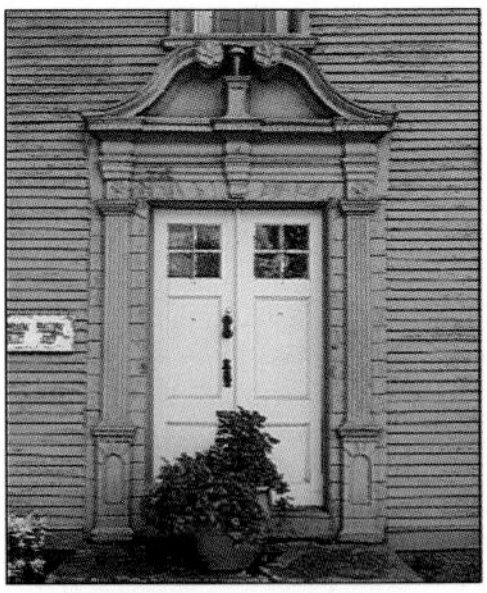

A Connecticut River-style entrance built in 1767

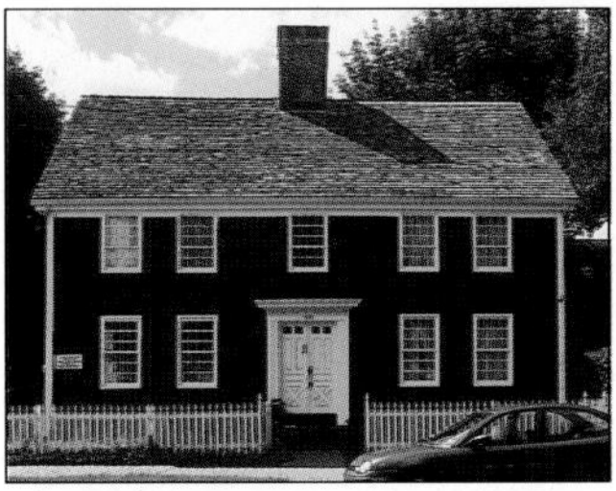

133 Main Street
This 1787 house was the home of Reverend Joseph Emerson, who ran the Female Seminary at the Old Academy at 150 Main.

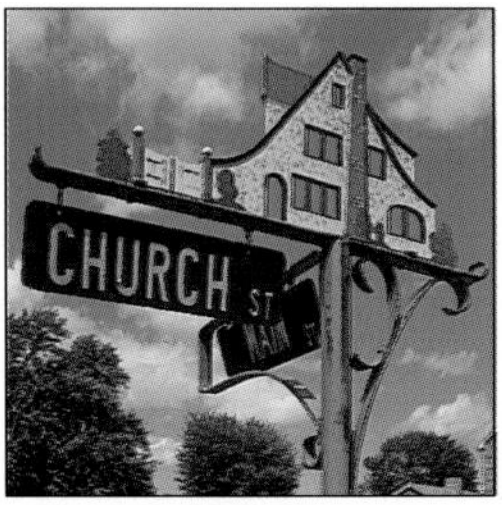

Church and Main
The house atop the street sign marks the area of one of Connecticut's first suburban communities.

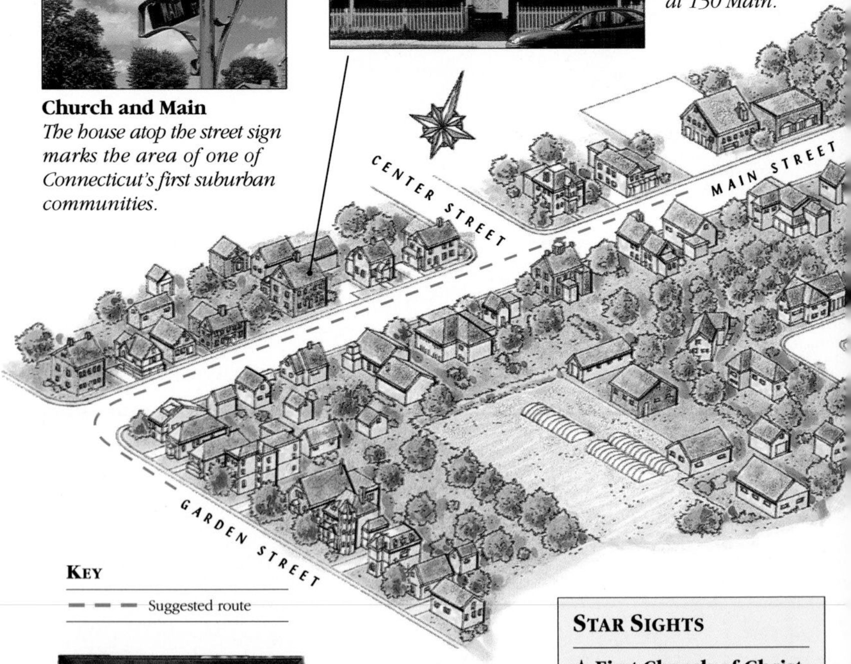

Key

— — — Suggested route

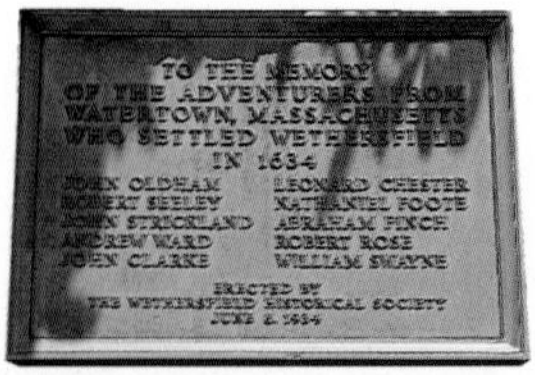

Memorial Plaque
This simple plaque pays tribute to the Massachusetts adventurers who settled here in 1634.

Star Sights

- ★ **First Church of Christ**
- ★ **Webb-Deane-Stevens Museum**
- ★ **Buttolph Williams House**

◁ **Cruising through The Thimbles, a collection of 365 islands and islets**

★ First Church of Christ

One of only three Colonial meeting houses left in the state, the 1761 church included presidents George Washington (1732–99) and John Adams (1735–1826) among its worshipers.

VISITORS' CHECKLIST

🚶 26,000. ✈ Bradley International Airport, 17 miles (27 km) N in Windsor Locks. 🚌 from Hartford. ℹ Greater Hartford Tourism District, 31 Pratt Street, Hartford. (860) 244-8181 or (800) 793-4480. 🅦 www.enjoyhartford.com

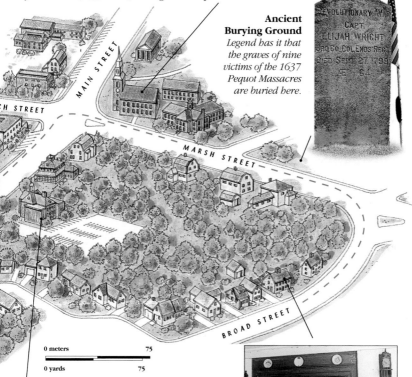

Ancient Burying Ground
Legend has it that the graves of nine victims of the 1637 Pequot Massacres are buried here.

MAIN STREET

CH STREET

MARSH STREET

BROAD STREET

| 0 meters | 75 |
| 0 yards | 75 |

Wethersfield Museum & Visitors' Center

★ Buttolph Williams House

Built c.1720, this house exemplifies the era's austere architecture. The parlor is shown at right.

Webb-Deane-Stevens Museum

The Joseph Webb House, built in 1751, is part of the Webb-Deane-Stevens Museum. Shown at right is wallpaper from one of the upstairs bed chambers.

Litchfield Hills ❻

American Clock and Watch Museum

Nestled in the folds and foothills of the Berkshire Hills and Taconic Mountains in the northwesternmost section of Connecticut, the Litchfield Hills region covers some 1,000 sq miles (2,590 sq km), or one-quarter of the state. Many people consider this to be the most scenic part of Connecticut. Anchored by the Housatonic River, the bucolic landscape of woods, valleys, lakes, and wildlife offers unparalleled opportunities for canoeing, kayaking, white-water rafting, tubing, fly-fishing, and hiking. In autumn, traffic along the winding roads can slow as the brilliant fall foliage entrances sightseers. A steady influx of the wealthy into the area has resulted in the gentrification of Litchfield's 26 towns and villages, with boutiques and bistros popping up beside traditional craft shops and historic homes and gardens.

Fishing at Mount Tom State Park outside Litchfield

Bristol

🏚 62,000. ℹ 10 Main St (860) 584-4718.

Bristol's past as a premier clock manufacturing center is celebrated at the American Clock and Watch Museum on Maple Street. Housed in an 1801 mansion, this vast collection includes 5,000 clocks and watches.

Bristol is also home to the Lake Compounce Theme Park, the nation's oldest amusement park. Complete with the fastest and longest wooden roller coaster on the East Coast, a haunted house, and a white-water raft ride, the park on Lake Avenue has been entertaining families since 1846. More family fun can be found on Riverside Avenue in the form of the Carousel Museum of New England. Its collection of antique carousels is one of the finest in the world.

Woodbury

🏚 9,400. ℹ Litchfield.

With its 45 shops and dealers, this is a popular haunt for antique lovers. Antique furnishings from the late 18th century can also be found at the Glebe House on Hollow Road. This minister's farmhouse is surrounded by the Gertrude Jekyll Garden, the noted English landscaper's only garden on US soil. The town is also blessed with five churches from various eras that have been wonderfully preserved.

New Preston

ℹ Litchfield.

New Preston offers access to 95-acre (38-ha) Lake Waramaug State Park. The lake is especially beautiful in the autumn, when the glorious colors are reflected on its mirrorlike surface. Visitors can rent canoes for peaceful paddles around the shoreline, and some 80 campsites cater to enthusiasts who want to linger and enjoy the great outdoors. The Hopkins Vineyard, perched above the lake, offers wine tastings along with tours of its facilities.

Litchfield

🏚 8,850. ℹ Litchfield Hills Visitors' Bureau, PO Box 968, Litchfield (860) 567-4506.

Picturesque Litchfield has many noteworthy historic buildings, such as South Street's 1784 Tapping Reeve House and Law School, the country's first law school.

Just on the outskirts of town on Route 202, Mount Tom State Park has trails leading to the 1,325-ft (404-m) summit. The lake is ideal for scuba diving, swimming, boating, and fishing.

Elegant Bellamy-Ferriday House and Garden in Bethlehem

Bethlehem

🚶 *3,700.* 🛈 *Litchfield.*
One of the town's highlights
is the Bellamy-Ferriday House
and Garden, the 18th-century
home of Reverend Joseph
Bellamy (1719–90), founder
of the first theological
seminary in America. Located
on Main Street, this 13-room
house displays Ferriday family
delftware, furniture, antiques,
and Oriental art.

West Cornwall

🛈 *Litchfield.*
Tiny West Cornwall is best
known for its covered bridge.
The 1841 bridge, which spans
the Housatonic River, is only
one of two such spans in the
state open to car traffic.

Norfolk

🚶 *2,000.* 🛈 *Litchfield.*
Founded in 1758, this small
village is located in the northwest corner of the state. Its
village green is known for
two key reasons: a monument
that was designed by architect
Stanford White (1853–1906)
and US sculptor Augustus
Saint-Gaudens *(see pp262–3)*;
and the Music Shed. The
latter is an auditorium on the
Ellen Batell Stoeckel Estate
that hosts the highly
acclaimed annual Norfolk
Music Festival.

Re-created Algonkian village at the Institute for American Indian Studies

Washington

🚶 *3,950.* 🛈 *Litchfield.*
At the Institute for American
Indian Studies, situated on
Curtis Road, those with a
bent for history can examine
a pre-contact Algonkian
village, artifacts from 10,000
years ago, and exhibits of
northwest Connecticut's
Woodland Indians. The
grounds contain a re-created
archaeological dig.

Kent

🚶 *2,900.* 🛈 *Litchfield.*
Art lovers should go out of
their way to visit this small

community. It is well known
for having the highest concentration of galleries in the
region. The Bachelier-
Cardonsky Gallery on Main
Street and the Paris-New
York-Kent Gallery on Kent
Station Square are two of the
most popular. North of town
travelers indulge in outdoor
fun at Kent Falls State Park. A
short hike into the 295-acre
(119-ha) park will reward visitors with stunning views of
what many people consider
the most impressive waterfall
in Connecticut. Picnic facilities
overlook the idyllic scene.

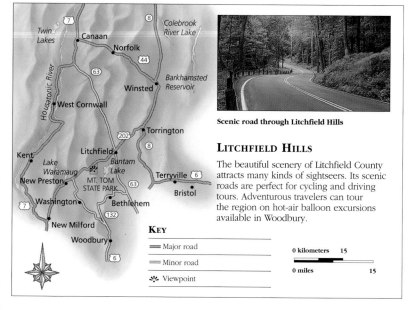
Scenic road through Litchfield Hills

LITCHFIELD HILLS

The beautiful scenery of Litchfield County
attracts many kinds of sightseers. Its scenic
roads are perfect for cycling and driving
tours. Adventurous travelers can tour
the region on hot-air balloon excursions
available in Woodbury.

KEY

━━ Major road

━━ Minor road

🌿 Viewpoint

0 kilometers   15

0 miles   15

Picturesque bridge over the Connecticut River outside the town of Windsor

Simsbury ❼

🏃 22,000. ℹ️ 800 Hopmeadow St (860) 658-2500.

ORIGINALLY A QUIET COLONIAL farming community, Simsbury grew into something of a boomtown in the early 1700s with the discovery of copper in the region. The wheels of US industry started turning here with the opening of the nation's first steel mill in 1728. Three centuries of local history are squeezed into the **Phelps Tavern Museum and Homestead**. Among the six historic buildings located on the site are a one-room 1740 schoolhouse, a Victorian carriage house, a colonial-era barn, and the fully furnished home of an 18th-century sea captain. Exhibits outlining 300 years of agriculture in the region stand next to displays of industrial tools and antique farm implements.

🏛 **Phelps Tavern Museum and Homestead**
800 Hopmeadow St. 【 (860) 658-2500. ◯ mid-May–Columbus Day: noon–4pm Tue–Sat; rest of year: call for hours. ● public hols. 🌀 🖼 summer: 1pm–4pm.

Windsor ❽

🏃 27,800. ℹ️ 96 Palisado Ave (800) 248-8283.

WINDSOR WAS SETTLED in the early 1630s by Pilgrims from Plymouth (see pp148–9), making it the oldest permanent English settlement in the state – a claim disputed by the residents of nearby Wethersfield (see pp206–207). A drive along Palisado Avenue passes several historic houses.
The 1758 **John & Sarah Strong House** is an old surviving frame structure named after the newlyweds who built it and lived in it for four years before heading west to settle. It has an excellent collection of furnishings reflecting the history of Windsor. Next door is the **Dr. Hezekiah Chaffee House**, a three-story brick Georgian-Colonial built in the mid-1700s. The home is appointed with period furniture and features changing exhibits. Visitors may also tour the adjoining Palisado Green. Here nervous settlers built a walled stockade during the 1637 war with the Pequot Indians. Further down the road stands the 1780

Sea captain's home, Phelps Homestead Museum Complex

Georgian home of the state's first senator, Oliver Ellsworth (1745–1807). Today the **Oliver Ellsworth Homestead** contains interior design details from the era, including the original wallpaper.

🏛 **John & Sarah Strong House**
96 Palisado Ave. 【 (860) 688-3813. ◯ year-round: 10am–4pm Tue–Sat. ● Sun–Mon & public hols. 🌀 includes admission to Dr. Hezekiah Chaffee House. 🖼

🏛 **Dr. Hezekiah Chaffee House**
96 Palisado Ave. 【 (860) 688-3813. ◯ year-round: 10am–4pm Tue–Sat. ● Sun–Mon & public hols. 🌀 includes admission to John & Sarah Strong House. 🖼

🏛 **Oliver Ellsworth Homestead**
778 Palisado Ave. 【 (860) 688-8717. ◯ mid-May–mid-Oct: 12pm–4:30pm Tue–Wed & Sat. 🌀

ENVIRONS: Fifteen miles (24 km) north of Windsor, the **Connecticut Trolley Museum** takes visitors on a nostalgic journey. A round-trip through the grounds on an antique trolley highlights permanent displays of classic trolley cars dating from 1894 to 1949. The Connecticut Fire Museum is annexed to the museum and tells the colorful history of state firefighting.

🏛 **Connecticut Trolley Museum**
58 North Rd, East Windsor. 【 (860) 627-6540. ◯ Apr–Memorial Day: 10am–5pm Sat, 12pm–5pm Sun; Memorial Day–Labor Day: 10am–5pm Wed–Sat, 12pm–5pm Sun; Sep–Dec: 10am–4pm Sat, noon–4pm Sun. 🌀 access to both museums.

New England Air Museum 9

Bradley International Airport, Windsor Locks. ((860) 623-3305. ☐ 10am–5pm daily. ● Jan 1, Thanksgiving, & Dec 25. 🖼 🔧 & 🚻
W www.neam.org

AVIATION FANS can indulge their flights of fancy at the largest aviation museum in the Northeast. The impressive collection of 80 aircraft spans the complete history of aviation beginning with pre-Wright Brothers flying machines right up to present-day jets and rescue helicopters. Located near Bradley International Airport, the museum is housed in and around two cavernous hangars. Highlights include a Bunce-Curtiss Pusher, a vintage 1909 Blériot and a Sikorsky VS-44 Flying Boat, the last of the four-engined flying boats.

To experience the thrill of flying, visitors can strap themselves into a simulator of the Grumman Tracer.

One of the planes on display at the New England Air Museum

Old New-Gate Prison and Copper Mine insignia

Old New-Gate Prison and Copper Mine 10

i 115 Newgate Rd, East Granby. ((860) 653-3563. ☐ mid-May–Oct: 10am–4:30pm Wed–Sun. 🖼 🔧 & 🚻

WHEN FINANCIAL WOES forced the sale of this less than prosperous 18th-century copper mine, its new proprietors found a novel but grim use for the dark hole in the ground. In 1773 the local government transformed the nation's first chartered copper mine into the state's first colonial prison. Over the course of

its infamous career, the jail held everyone from horse thieves to captured British soldiers. New-Gate represented a particularly brutal form of punishment, with prisoners living and sleeping in damp, sunless tunnels. Mercifully, the prison was abandoned in 1827, although tours of its lower chamber still inspire shivers.

Coventry 11

🏠 11,350. ℹ 1195 Main St (860) 742-1085.

COVENTRY IS THE BIRTHPLACE of Nathan Hale (1755–76), one of the inspirational heroes of the American Revolution (1775–83). Just minutes before he was to be hanged by the British for being a spy, the 21-year-old Coventry schoolteacher uttered his now famous last words, "I only regret that I have but one life to lose for my country."

The **Nathan Hale Homestead** is an anomaly in that its namesake never actually lived in the house. The existing structure, located on the site where Hale was born, was built by Hale's brothers and father in 1776, the same year he was executed.

Some of Hale's belongings are on display, including his Bible, army trunk, silver shoe buckles, and boyhood "fowling piece," which is hung above the fireplace in the dining room.

Coventry is also home to the **Caprilands Herb Farm**, a 20-acre (8-ha) operational farm with more than 30 herb gardens. The greenhouse and grounds are open to the public, as is the restored 18th-century barn. At the end of a visit, some of the more than 300 types of herbs grown here can be purchased.

🚏 **Nathan Hale Homestead**
2299 South St. ((860) 742-6917. ☐ mid-May–mid-Oct: 1pm–4pm Wed–Sun & by appt. 🖼 🔧 & partial.
🚏 **Caprilands Herb Farm**
534 Silver St. ((860) 742-7244. ☐ year-round:10am–5pm daily. ● public hols.

The 10-room Nathan Hale Homestead in Coventry

Lebanon ⓬

🏠 6,500. ✈ Hartford. 🚗🚆 New London. 🅿 856 Trumbull Hwy (860) 642-6579.

THIS EASTERN Connecticut community is steeped in American Revolution history. It was here on the 160-acre (65-ha) common that French hussars trained before joining their American allies in Yorktown for the climactic battle of the conflict. Lebanon native and artist John Trumbull (1756–1843), whose paintings can be seen in Hartford's Wadsworth Atheneum (see p198) and New Haven's Yale University Art Gallery, put down his paintbrush long enough to design the town's 1807 Congregational Church.

Also overlooking the green is the **Governor Jonathan Trumbull's House**. Father to John and governer of the colony and the state of Connecticut from 1769 to 1784, Trumbull was the only governer of the 13 colonies to remain in office before, during and after the Revolutionary War. Behind the house is the **Doctor William Beaumont Homestead**, birthplace of one of the world's pioneers of gastric medicine.

🏛 **Governor Jonathan Trumbull's House**
169 W Town St. 📞 (860) 642-7558. ◻ mid-May–mid-Oct: 1pm–5pm Tue–Sat. 🎫

🏛 **Doctor William Beaumont Homestead**
169 W Town St. 📞 (860) 642-6579. ◻ mid-May–mid-Oct: 1pm–4pm Sat. 🎫

ENVIRONS: Twelve miles (19 km) to the east, Canterbury is home to the

Prudence Crandall House. Crandall (1803–90) raised the ire of citizens when, in 1832, she admitted a young black student to her private school for girls. Undaunted by threats of boycotts, Crandall kept the school open and attracted students, many of whom were black, from other states. Public outcry was such that the local government pushed through a law forbidding private schools to admit black children from out of state. Crandall was subsequently jailed and brought to trial. It was only after an angry mob attacked the school in 1834 that the heroic Quaker woman reluctantly closed its doors forever. Today the museum commemorates Crandall's struggle and traces local black history.

🏛 **Prudence Crandall House**
Canterbury Green. 📞 (860) 546-9916. ◻ 10am–4:30pm Wed–Sun. ● mid-Dec–Jan. 🎫

Norwich ⓭

🏠 35,000. 🅿 69 Main St (860) 886-4683.

NORWICH HAS the dubious distinction of being the birthplace of Benedict Arnold (1741–1801), forever synonymous with traitor for betraying Colonial forces during the American Revolution. In contrast, the Colonial Cemetery contains graves of soldiers, both American and French, who died fighting for the American cause during the war.

A two-story colonial structure consisting of a pair of annexed saltboxes, the **Christopher Leffingwell House**, is named after a financier of the Colonial side in the

American Revolution. During the war, Leffingwell's house and tavern were used for secret meetings. The interior, full of late 17th- and 18th-century furniture, has never been remodeled, making it of special interest.

🏛 **Christopher Leffingwell House**
348 Washington St. 📞 (860) 889-9440. ◻ Apr–mid-Oct: 1pm–4pm Tue–Sun & by appt. ● public hols. 🎫

ENVIRONS: Located five miles (8 km) south of Norwich is the **Shantok Village of Uncas**, final resting place of Native American leader Uncas (d.1683). Inspiration for James Fenimore Cooper's novel *Last of the Mohicans* (1826), Uncas provided early colonists with the plot of land for the original Norwich settlement and sided with them during the Pequot War of the 1630s. An obelisk memorializing Uncas was erected here in 1840.

A Leffingwell sculpture

🏛 **Shantok Village of Uncas**
Rte 32 S of Norwich. ◻ dawn to dusk daily. 🎫

Foxwoods Resort Casino ⓮

Rte 2. 📞 (800) PLAYBIG. **Casino** ◻ 24 hrs daily. ♿ 🏨 🍴 ◻ 🚫 🎫 📷

FIRST OF THE NATIVE American-operated casinos in New England, this gaming facility has hundreds of games tables, more than 5,800 slot machines, and high-stakes bingo and poker. In addition, the 1,500-seat Fox Theater attracts international stars.

Also on casino grounds is the **Mashantucket Pequot Museum**, a state-of-the-art research and exhibition center of Native American history. Multimedia displays and touch-screen computers provide a detailed study of the natural history of the area

The War Office in Lebanon, once Jonathan Trumbull's store

Life-size Native American figures at the Mashantucket Pequot Museum

and its earliest inhabitants. Walking through a replica Pequot Village c.1500, visitors come upon life-size figures depicting aspects of local Native American life.

🏛 Mashantucket Pequot Museum
110 Pequot Trail. **[** (860) 396-6800 or (800) 411-9671. **○** *Memorial Day–Labor Day: 9am–5pm; rest of year: 9am–5pm Wed–Mon.* **●** *Jan 1, Thanksgiving, & Dec 25.*

New London ⑮

🏃 26,000. 🚉 🛈 *470 Bank St (860) 444-2206 or (800) 863-6569.*

BRITISH FORCES LED by traitor Benedict Arnold razed New London during the American Revolution. Rebounding from the attack, the town enjoyed new-found prosperity during the whaling industry during the 19th century. The four colonnaded Greek Revival mansions along Whale Oil Row attest to the affluence of that era.

Remarkably, many homes survived Arnold's torching, including the **Joshua Hempsted House**. Built in 1678, the dwelling is insulated with seaweed and represents one of the few 17th-century homes left in the state. Connecticut College houses

the **Lyman Allyn Art Museum**, a repository of decorative arts and a dollhouse collection. Also on campus, the 750-acre (303-ha) college Arboretum encompasses a variety of ecosystems, native trees and shrubs, trails, and ponds. At the edge of town is **Monte Cristo Cottage**, boyhood home of Nobel Prize-winning playwright Eugene O'Neill (1888–1953). The two-story cottage, which served as the setting for his Pulitzer Prize-winning play *Long Day's Journey into Night* (1957), is now a research library, with some of O'Neill's belongings on display.

🏚 Joshua Hempsted House
Jct of Hempstead, Jay, & Truman Sts. **[** (860) 443-7949. **○** *mid-May–mid-Oct: noon–4pm Thu–Sun.* 📷 ✍ *obligatory.*

🏛 Lyman Allyn Art Museum
625 Williams St. **[** (860) 443-2545. **○** *year-round: 10am–5pm Tue–Sat, 1–5pm Sun.* **●** *public hols.* 📷 ✍ *by appt.* ♿

🏚 Monte Cristo Cottage
325 Pequot Ave. **[** (860) 443-0051. **○** *Memorial Day–Labor Day: 10am–5pm Tue–Sat, 1–5pm Sun; mid-Sep–Oct: 1–5pm Sat & Sun.* **●** *public hols.* 📷

ENVIRONS: Directly across the river from New London is Groton. The USS *Nautilus*, the world's first nuclear-powered

submarine is berthed at the **Submarine Force Museum** on the Naval Submarine Base. **Fort Griswold Battlefield State Park** is where British troops under Benedict Arnold killed surrendered American soldiers in 1781. A 134-ft (41-m) obelisk memorial and a battle diorama mark the event.

🏛 Submarine Force Museum
Crystal Lake Rd. **[** (860) 694-3174. **○** *mid-May–mid-Oct: 9am–5pm Wed–Mon, 1–5pm Tue; rest of year: 9am–4pm Wed–Mon.* ♿

🏃 Fort Griswold Battlefield State Park
Monument & Park Aves. **[** (860) 445-1729. **Museum ○** *May–Labor Day: 10am–5pm daily.* **Park ○** *year-round: 8am–sunset daily.*

Sea lion sculpture on the rocks at Mystic Aquarium

Mystic ⑯

🏃 2,600. 🛈 *28 Cottrell St (860) 572-9578.*

WHEN SHIPBUILDING waned, Mystic turned to tourism. Today Mystic Seaport (*see pp214–15*) and **Mystic Aquarium**, a world-class venue, make the town bustle. Seals and sea lions cavort in the outdoor Seal Island; indoors is a colony of African black-footed penguins and 3,500 sea creatures. They have the world's largest outdoor beluga tank and the 14,000-seat theater has daily shows.

🏛 Mystic Aquarium
55 Coogan Blvd. **[** (860) 572-5955. **○** *Jul–Labor Day: 9am–6pm daily; Labor Day–Nov: 9am–5pm daily; Dec–mid-Mar: 10am–4pm Mon–Fri, 9am–5pm Sat & Sun; mid-Mar–Jun: 9am–5pm daily.* **●** *Jan 1, Thanksgiving, & Dec 25.* 📷 ♿ 🍴

World's first nuclear-powered sub, USS *Nautilus*, berthed at Groton

Mystic Seaport

Town welcome

WHAT BEGAN AS A MODEST collection of nautical odds and ends housed in an old mill in 1929 has grown into the world's largest maritime museum. The 17-acre (7-ha) working replica of a 19th-century port is a complex of more than 40 buildings open to the public, including a bank, chapel, tavern, rope-making shops, and one-room schoolhouse from the 1800s. Despite its fascinating exhibits of ship models and authentic scrimshaw, Mystic Seaport's main attraction remains its preservation shipyard and its fleet of antique ships, including the *Charles W. Morgan*, the last remaining vessel in the nation's fleet of 19th-century whalers.

Seagoing Connection
Almost every building in town sports a nautical motif.

Whaleboat Exhibit
A fully equipped whaleboat contains all the gear carried in such vessels in the late 1800s. It is housed in a shed on Chubb's Wharf.

Burrows House
The early 1800s home of a shopkeeper and his milliner wife re-creates coastal domestic life.

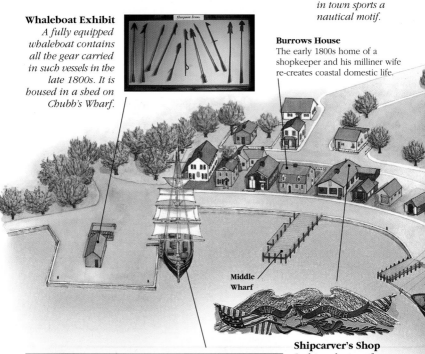

Middle
Wharf

Shipcarver's Shop
Independent craftsmen carved figureheads and other decorations, such as this American eagle, for shipbuilders.

★ **The *Charles W. Morgan***
The last wooden whaling ship in the world was built for a Quaker merchant in 1841. Visitors can tour the quarters of officers and crew.

STAR FEATURES

★ **Mystic River Scale Model**

★ **The *Charles W. Morgan***

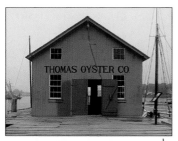

Thomas Oyster House

Initially used as a culling shop to sort oysters by size, the 1874 building was later used to shuck oysters before shipping them on ice.

VISITORS' CHECKLIST

75 Greenmanville Ave (Rte 7).
(888) 9-SEAPORT or (860) 572-5315. **Ships & exhibits** 9am–5pm daily. **Grounds** 9am–6pm daily. Dec 25.
W www.visitmysticseaport.com

Village Green Bandstand

Sometimes used as a concert venue, especially for July 4th celebrations.

The *L.A. Dunton*

This 1921 schooner is the last existing example of the once-popular New England round-bow fishing vessels.

The *Sabino*

Built in 1908 in East Boothbay, Maine, the coal-fueled steamship Sabino *takes passengers on cruises along the Connecticut coast.*

The *Joseph Conrad*

Built in Denmark in 1882, this is one of the museum's three largest ships. It serves as a training vessel.

★ Mystic River Scale Model

Inside is a 50-ft- (17-m-) long model giving a bird's-eye view of Mystic in 1870. It has more than 250 detailed buildings.

Lighthouse

This structure is a copy of the 1746 Brant Point Lighthouse on Nantucket, the second lighthouse to be built in New England.

The Harpist by Alphonse Jongers at the Florence Griswold Museum

Old Lyme ⑰

🏛 6,800. 🛈 470 Bank St, New London (860) 444-2206.

ONCE A SHIPBUILDING center, Old Lyme is home to numerous 18th- and 19th-century houses. Originally built for merchants and sea captains, many became residences of the artists who established a colony here in the early 1900s.

The **Florence Griswold Museum** is intimately linked to the arts. Not only are the walls of this 1817 mansion adorned with some of the country's great paintings, but some of the walls are works of art themselves.

The mansion became the home of Captain Robert Griswold and his daughter Florence. An art patron, Florence began letting rooms in the 1890s to New York artists looking for a summer by the sea. She hosted Henry Ward Ranger (1858–1916), Childe Hassam (1859–1935), and Clark Voorhees (1871–1933), spawning the Old Lyme Art Colony.

Now a featured stop on the American Impressionist Art Trail (*see pp202–203*), the museum has more than 900 works by artists who at one time lived in the house or nearby. Many of Griswold's guests painted on the wall panels of the dining room as thanks for her generosity.

🏛 Florence Griswold Museum

96 Lyme St, Old Lyme. 📞 (860) 434-5542. 🕐 Jan–Apr: 1–5pm Wed–Sun; May–Dec: 10am–5pm Tue–Sat, 1pm–5pm Sun. 🎨 📷 ♿

Essex ⑱

🏛 2,500. 🛈 393 Main St, Middletown (860) 347-0028.

IN A RECENT SURVEY naming America's top small towns, Essex was at the head of the list. Sited on the Connecticut River, the village is surrounded by a series of sheltered coves and has a bustling marina and tree-lined, virtually crime-free streets.

The **Connecticut River Museum**, a restored 1878 warehouse, is perched on a dock overlooking the water. Its collection and exhibits of maritime art and artifacts tell the story of this once-prominent shipbuilding town, where the *Oliver Cromwell* – the first warship built for the American Revolution (1775–83) – was constructed. The museum's conversation piece is a replica of the world's first submersible craft, the *Turtle*, a squat, single-seat vehicle built in 1775. Transportation is also the focus at the **Essex Steam Train & Riverboat Ride**, where guests take an authentic, coal-belching steam engine for a 12-mile (19-km) scenic tour. At the midpoint, passengers can take a 90-minute cruise down the river aboard a riverboat.

🏛 Connecticut River Museum

67 Main St. 📞 (860) 767-8269. 🕐 year-round: 10am–5pm Tue–Sun. ● Labor Day, Thanksgiving, Dec 24–25, Jan 1. 🎨 📷 ♿

🚂 Essex Steam Train & Riverboat Ride

Exit 3 off Rte 9. 📞 (860) 767-0103 or (800) 377-3987. 🕐 call for ride times. 🎨 📷 🍴

ENVIRONS: Five miles (8 km) north of Essex is Chester, home to **Goodspeed-at-Chester**, a theater that presents new musicals. Across the Connecticut River the town of East Haddam offers spectacular views of river traffic from the **Goodspeed Opera House**. This late-Victorian "wedding cake" gem is the setting for new musicals and revivals, which are staged from April to December.

🎭 Goodspeed-at-Chester

N Main St / Rte 82, Chester. 📞 (860) 873-8668. 🕐 call for show times. 🎨 ♿

🎭 Goodspeed Opera House

Rte 82, East Haddam. 📞 (860) 873-8668. 🕐 call for show times. 🎨 ♿

Replica of the first submersible at Connecticut River Museum

Gillette Castle ⑲

See pp218–19.

Madison ⑳

🏛 16,000. 🛈 22 Scotland Ave (203) 245-7394.

MADISON IS A RESORT TOWN full of antique stores and boutiques, including a specialty store that stocks British kippers, bangers, and pork pies. Several historic homes are open for viewing, including the 1685 **Deacon John Grave House**. The structure has served as tavern, armory, courthouse, and infirmary, but has always belonged to the Graves. One of the oldest artifacts on display is the family's bookkeeping ledger, with entries from 1678 to 1895.

Madison is also home to **Hammonasset Beach State Park**, the largest shoreline park in the state. Poking into Long Island Sound, the peninsula has a two-mile- (3-km-) long beach that attracts swimmers, sailors, scuba divers, and sunbathers. The park has baseball diamonds, picnic areas, and a 541-site campground.

🏛 Deacon John Grave House

581 Boston Post Rd. 📞 *(203) 245-4798.* ◻ *May–Sep: 1pm–4pm Wed–Sat.* 🎫

🏖 Hammonasset Beach State Park

I-95, exit 62. **Park** 📞 *(203) 245-2785.* **Campground reservations** 📞 *(877) 668-2267.* **Park** ◻ *8am–dusk daily.* 🎫 ☑ ♿

The boardwalk at Hammonasset Beach State Park in Madison

Guilford ㉑

🏘 *20,000.* 🚉 *393 Main St, Middletown (860) 347-0028 or (800) 486-3346.*

Iᴺ 1639 ʀᴇᴠᴇʀᴇɴᴅ Henry Whitfield (1597–1657) led a group of Puritans from Surrey, England, to a wild parcel of land near the West River. There they established the town of Guilford. A year later, fearing an attack by local Mennuncatuk Indians, the colonists built a three-story stronghold out of local granite. The Tudor Gothic-style fort, the oldest stone dwelling of its type in New England, now serves as the **Henry Whitfield Historical Museum**. The austere interior has a 33-ft- (10-m-) long great hall and 17th-century furnishings.

Guilford is graced by dozens of historic 18th-century homes. Both the **Hyland House**, a classic early saltbox (*see p26*), and the 1774 **Thomas Griswold House** are open to view. **Dudley Farm**, a 19th-century working farm and living history museum, demonstrates agricultural techniques of the era. In mid-July craftsmen gather on Guilford Green for the Guilford Handcraft Exposition (*see p33*).

🏛 Henry Whitfield State Historical Museum

248 Old Whitfield St. 📞 *(203) 453-2457.* ◻ *Feb–mid-Dec: 10am–5pm Wed–Sun; mid-Dec–Jan: by appt only.* 🎫

🏛 Hyland House

84 Boston St. 📞 *(203) 453-9477.* ◻ *Jun–Labor Day: 10am–4pm Tue–Sun; mid-Sep–mid-Oct: 10am–4pm Sat–Sun.* ⬤ *Columbus Day.* 🎫 🔲 *obligatory.*

🏛 Thomas Griswold House

171 Boston St. 📞 *(203) 453-3176.* ◻ *Jun–Labor Day: 11am–4pm Tue–Sun; mid-Sep–Oct: 11am–4pm Sat–Sun.* 🎫 🔲 *obligatory.* ♿

🏛 Dudley Farm

2351 Durham Rd. 📞 *(203) 457-0770.* ◻ *year-round: 10am–2pm Mon–Sat.* ⬤ *Sun.*

The Thimbles ㉒

🚤 *from Stony Creek Dock.* 🚉 *(203) 488-9878.*

Fʀᴏᴍ sᴛᴏɴʏ ᴄʀᴇᴇᴋ, travelers can cruise to the Thimble islands aboard one of several tour boats that operate in the area. Many of the 365 islands are little more than large boulders visible only at low tide. Some of the privately owned islands sport small communities. One colorful legend about this clutch of islands centers on circus midget General Tom Thumb (1838–83) courting a woman on Cut-In-Two Island. Another has the privateer Captain Kidd (1645–1701) hiding plundered treasure on Money Island while being pursued by the British fleet. Today cruisers watch seals or take in glorious fall colors.

The Thimbles, home to seals, whales, and colorful legends

Gillette Castle ⑲

Entrance sign

OSTENTATIOUS AND BIZARRE, Gillette Castle is the antithesis of New England architectural grace. However, visitors to the 24-room granite mansion always leave with a smile. Actor William Gillette (1853–1937) based the design of his 1919 dream home on medieval castles, complete with battlements and turrets. The castle is rife with such oddities as Gillette's homemade trick locks, furniture set on wheels and tracks, a cavernous 1,500-sq-ft (139-sq-m) living room, and a series of mirrors starting in his bedroom that permitted him to see who was arriving downstairs in case he wished to be "indisposed" or make a grand entrance.

Park and goldfish pond, a pleasing vista

221 Baker Street Secret Room

Servants' quarters

The View
The castle has a view of the Connecticut River and its traffic. Gillette lived on a houseboat for five years while the castle was constructed.

The Study
Gillette spent much of his time in the Study. The chair at his desk is on a set of small tracks so it can be easily moved back and forth.

Castle Grounds
Following Gillette's death, the castle and its 117 acres (47 ha) became a state park. His railroad with its two locomotives used to carry guests on a three-mile (5-km) tour through the property. Now visitors walk the trails.

STAR FEATURES

★ **The Great Hall**

★ **Library Museum**

Main Entrance
The huge oak door through which visitors must pass is equipped with an elaborate homemade lock.

WILLIAM GILLETTE

An eccentric playwright and actor who reputedly made $3 million playing Sherlock Holmes on the stage, William Gillette paid homage to his literary meal ticket by re-creating the fictional sleuth's London sitting room as described in Sir Arthur Conan Doyle's books. Gillette spent $1 million to build his folly and in his will stipulated that it never fall into the hands of "any blithering saphead."

★ Library Museum
Gillette's gallery of pastoral artwork and seascapes is housed here.

— Mezzanine

Castle Exterior
Constructed on a steel framework, the castle is built of fieldstone bought from local farmers and lifted up the hill on an aerial tram designed by Gillette.

Outdoor terrace

Outdoor terrace

★ The Great Hall
Exposed stone walls are five feet (1.5 m) thick in some places, and heavy oak covers steel beams. Gillette had a generator installed to provide power, but the castle is still dark and baronial.

New Haven ㉓

THE LAND ON WHICH CONNECTICUT'S third most populous city stands was purchased from the Quinnipiac Indians in 1638 for a few knives, coats, and hatchets. The city's location on the coast where the West, Mill, and Quinnipiac rivers flow into Long Island Sound has helped make it one of the state's major manufacturing centers. Over the centuries, items ranging from clocks and corsets to musical instruments, carriages, and Revolutionary War cannonballs have been made here. In 1716 Yale University *(see pp222–5)* moved from Saybrook to New Haven, establishing the city as a center for education, technology, and research. Today New Haven also offers opportunities for attending theater, opera, dance performances, and concerts.

Amistad Memorial

Exploring Downtown New Haven

The 16-acre (6-ha) New Haven Green is the central section of the original nine symmetrical town squares the Puritans laid out in New Haven, the first planned city in America. The Green has been the focal point of local life ever since, serving as the setting for many of New Haven's activities and festivals. Three churches, all built between 1812 and 1815, sit on the Green on Temple Street. United Church on the Green (often called North Church for its northern location) is in the style of London's St. Martin-in-the-Fields. Graced by a beautiful Tiffany stained-glass window, the First Church of Christ (Center Church) is considered an architectural masterpiece of the American Georgian style. The crypt beneath the church holds the remains of some of the city's original

colonists. Among the notables buried here are Benedict Arnold's first wife, Margaret, and James Pierpont (1659–1714), one of the founders of Yale University. Trinity Church on the Green was one of the first Gothic-style churches in America.

Looming on the corner of Court and Church streets is the monumental Greek

Tiffany stained-glass window at First Church of Christ

Revival post office, now the Federal District Court, designed in 1913 by James Gamble Rogers (1867–1947), architect of many of Yale University's Gothic Revival buildings. City Hall faces the Green on Church Street and epitomizes high Victorian style, with its polychrome limestone-and-sandstone facade. In front of City Hall, the 14-ft- (4-m-) tall bronze Amistad Memorial, which honors Senghe Pieh (also known as Joseph Cinque), leader of the *Amistad* revolt *(see p198)*, is on the exact site of the jail where the mutinous slaves were held.

In late April the Green becomes the stage for Powder House Day, a reenactment of one of Benedict Arnold's few celebrated moments. At the start of the American Revolution, Arnold, then a captain in the militia, seized control of a municipal arsenal and led his troops to Boston to help bolster the sagging Colonial forces.

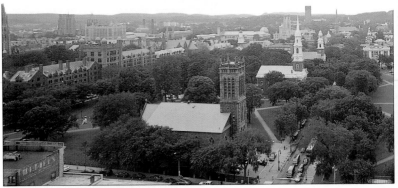

Church spires around New Haven Green

⚜ New Haven Colony Historical Society
114 Whitney Ave. **(** *(203) 562-4183.* ⬜ *year-round: 10am–5pm Tue–Fri.* ⬤ *public hols.* 📷 🔲

This handsome Colonial Revival house traces the city's cultural and industrial growth from 1638 to the present. Exhibits include such items as Eli Whitney's cotton gin, the sign that hung over Benedict Arnold's George Street shop, a fine collection of colonial pewter and china, and permanent galleries on the *Amistad* and the city's maritime history.

⛩ Grove Street Cemetery
227 Grove St, gate at N end of High St. **(** *(203) 787-1443.* ⬜ *year-round: 8am–4pm daily.* 📷 ♿

Established in 1797 and covering 18 acres (7 ha), this was the first cemetery in the US to be divided into family plots. Walking through its 1848 Egyptian Revival gate, visitors will find a veritable who's who of New Haven. Eli Whitney (1765–1825), Noah Webster (1758–1843), Charles Goodyear (1800–1860), and Samuel F.B. Morse (1791–1872) are just some of the distinguished citizens buried in this cemetery.

The colorful 1916 carousel at Lighthouse Point Park

New Haven Parks
Among New Haven's many attractive parks, the 84-acre (34-ha) **Lighthouse Point Park** on Long Island Sound is a standout. The park has nature trails, a picnic grove, a bird sanctuary, swimming facilities, a 1916 Coney Island-style carousel, and an 1840 lighthouse. **East Rock Park**

offers a spectacular view of Long Island Sound, New Haven, and the harbor and is crisscrossed by 10 miles (16 km) of nature trails. The 123-acre (50-ha) **Edgewood Park** has a duck pond, nature trail, in-line skating rink, and playground. Black Rock Fort, from the Revolutionary War period, and Fort Nathan Hale, vintage Civil War era, offer splendid views of New Haven Harbor.

✖ Lighthouse Point Park
2 Lighthouse Rd. **(** *(203) 946-8790.* **Park** ⬜ *year-round: dawn–dusk daily.* **Beach** ⬜ *Memorial Day–Labor Day: dawn–dusk daily.* 📷 ♿

✖ East Rock Park
E Rock Park. **(** *(203) 946-6086.* ⬜ *year-round: 8am–dusk daily.*

✖ Edgewood Park
Edgewood Ave. **(** *(203) 946-8028.* ⬜ *year-round: dawn–dusk daily.* ♿

🏛 Eli Whitney Museum
915 Whitney Ave, Hamden. **(** *(203) 777-1833.* ⬜ *late May–Labor Day: 11am–4pm daily; Labor Day–late May: noon–5pm Fri & Sun, 10am–3pm Sat.* ⬤ *public hols.* 📷 ♿

On the northern outskirts of New Haven in the suburb of Hamden is the Eli Whitney Museum. One of the nation's earliest inventors, Whitney (1765–1825) was best known for developing the cotton gin, thereby automating the labor-intensive task of separating cotton from its seeds. Another of Whitney's inventions, a musket with inter-changeable parts, revolutionized manu-facturing and helped fuel the Industrial Revolution. The museum contains examples of Whitney's innovations and expla-nations of how they changed the way people work.

✖ Connecticut Audubon Coastal Center
1 Milford Point Rd, Milford. **(** *(203) 878-7440.* **Center** ⬜ *year-round: 10am–4pm Tue–Sat, 12pm–4pm Sun.* ⬤ *gate closed at dusk.* 📷 🔲 ♿ 🔲 **w** www.ctaudubon.org

Just 15 miles (16 km) south-west of New Haven, travelers come upon the Connecticut Audubon Coastal Center, one of the state's best birding sites. This 8.4-acre (3-ha) bird and wildlife sanctuary and nature center is situated on Long Island Sound at the mouth of the Housatonic River. Visitors can take nature walks along the beach or around the salt marsh and climb a 70-ft (21-m) tower overlooking Long Island Sound.

Eli Whitney Museum in Hamden, just north of New Haven

🏛 Shore Line Trolley Museum
17 River St, East Haven. **(** *(203) 467-6927.* ⬜ *call for hours.* 📷 ♿ *partial.* 🔲

Five miles (8 km) to the east of New Haven in East Haven is the Shore Line Trolley Museum. The oldest rapid-transit car and first electric freight locomotive are among 100 vintage trolleys from 1878 onward on display. The museum also offers a three-mile (5-km) trolley ride through salt marshes and woods on the oldest suburban trolley line in the country.

The 1840 lighthouse at Lighthouse Point Park

Yale University

FOUNDED IN 1701, THIS IVY LEAGUE SCHOOL is one of the most prestigious institutions of higher learning in the world. The list of Yale's distinguished alumni includes Noah Webster (1758–1843), who compiled the nation's first dictionary, Samuel Morse (1791–1872), inventor of Morse code, and five US presidents, including George W. Bush (b.1946). While its law and medical schools attract much of the attention, Yale's other graduate programs (ranging from divinity to drama) are no less demanding. In some ways avant-garde, in others staunchly traditional, Yale admitted its first female Ph.D. student before the turn of the 20th century, but didn't become fully co-educational until 1969.

Wrexham Tower, Branford College, on the Yale campus

Exploring Yale Campus

Yale's campus comprises much of New Haven's downtown core, with the main section located on the western flank of the New Haven Green. Campus buildings reflect the architectural eclecticism that runs through the university. Connecticut Hall is Yale's oldest building and the only one left of a row of Georgian buildings on the Old Campus, Yale's original quadrangle. Nathan Hale *(see p211)* and US President William Howard Taft (1857–1930) had rooms here when they were students.

Yale's oldest building, Connecticut Hall, constructed in 1717

After World War I, James Gamble Rogers (1867–1947) designed the Memorial Quadrangle, a beautiful Gothic complex that is now the heart of the campus. Another Rogers design, Harkness Tower, completed in 1921, was modeled on St. Botolph's Tower in Boston, England, and has a facade covered with sculptures celebrating Yale's history and traditions. Each day at noon and again at 6pm the beautiful sounds of the bell tower's carillon can be heard throughout New Haven. On the Memorial Gate near the tower, the school's motto is inscribed: "For God, for country, and for Yale."

Post-World War II architects have left their mark on campus, too. The Yale School of Art and Architecture is as controversial today as when it was built in the 1960s. From the outside this 36-level building seems to stand only seven stories tall. The collection of buildings that makes up Ezra Stiles and Morse Colleges at Broadway and Tower is by architect Eero Saarinen (1910–61), who based the design on an Italian mountain village. Philip Johnson's Kline Biology Tower, Yale's skyscraper, was completed in 1965.

🏛 Yale Center for British Art

1080 Chapel St. **C** *(203) 432-2800.*
🕐 *year-round: 10am–5pm Tue–Sat, 12pm–5pm Sun.* ● *public hols.* 🎦
🚻 🛗

In 1966 philanthropist Paul Mellon (1907–99) donated his collection of British art to the university. This was no small gift, considering it consisted of more than 50,000

KEY

i Tourist information

P Parking

Library Court in the Yale Center for British Art

paintings, prints, drawings, watercolors, and rare books and documents. Needing the right space to display its artistic windfall, the university hired American architect Louis Kahn (1901–74) to design an elegant new center. Thus was born this important collection covering the major art schools and masters from Tudor times to the present.

The museum has the largest collection of British art outside the UK. Included among the paintings are works by William Hogarth (1697–1764), Thomas Gainsborough (1727–88), and Joseph Turner (1775–1851). The fourth floor of the museum is arranged chronologically so that visitors are given an overview.

Sterling Memorial Library

128 Wall St. [(203) 432-2798.
○ year-round: 8:30am–12am Mon–Thu, 8:30am–5pm Fri, 10am–5pm Sat, 1pm–12am Sun. ● Sat in Aug.
This striking library with stained-glass windows and Gothic arches is the largest on campus. It contains some 4 million items, including rare Babylonian tablets.

Gothic entrance to the Sterling Memorial Library

Beinecke Rare Book and Manuscript Libraries

121 Wall St. [(203) 432-2977.
○ year-round: 8:30am–5pm Mon–Fri, 10am–5pm Sat. ● Sat in Aug & public hols.
American architect Gordon Bunshaft (1909–90) built the walls of this library out of translucent marble. This unique design helps filter the sunlight, which could harm the library's illuminated medieval manuscripts and 7,000 books. The library owns a host of rare books and manuscripts, but its prized possession is one of the world's few remaining Gutenberg Bibles.

Statue of Elihu Yale (1649–1721)

HISTORIC NEW HAVEN GREEN

0 meters 200
0 yards 200

YALE UNIVERSITY CAMPUS

Yale University Art Gallery
1111 Chapel St. ☎ *(203) 432-0600.* ◯ *year-round: 10am–5pm Tue–Sat (until 8pm Thu), 1–6pm Sun.* ● *public hols.* 💳 ♿ 🛍
This top collection of Asian, African, European, American, and pre-Columbian art reflects the generosity and taste of Yale alumni and benefactors. The museum, founded in 1832, has approximately 100,000 objects in its huge collection, including many in the sculpture garden.

Housed in two units and divided over four floors, the gallery's vast collection highlights art as far back as ancient Egypt. The gallery is one of the finest medium-size museums in the US and is famous for its collection of American paintings, furniture, and decorative arts. Among its prized American pieces is John Trumbull's *The Battle of Bunker's Hill* (1786). Visitors can view more contemporary works, including paintings by Pablo Picasso, Vincent Van Gogh, Édouard Manet, Claude Monet, and Jackson Pollock.

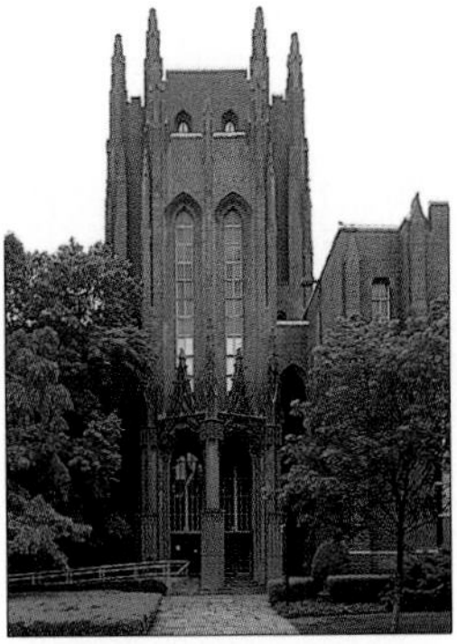
Entrance to the Peabody Museum of Natural History

Peabody Museum of Natural History
170 Whitney Ave. ☎ *(203) 432-5050.* ◯ *year-round: 10am–5pm Mon–Sat, noon–5pm Sun.* ● *public hols.* 📷 💳 ♿ 🛍 [W] www.peabodyyale.edu
Visitors entering the museum are dwarfed by the imposing skeleton of a 67-ft- (20-m-) high *Brontosaurus* – an apt introduction to this outstanding museum, famous for its collection of dinosaurs.

Children migrate to the Great Hall of Dinosaurs, where they can mingle with the mastodon and socialize with the *Stegosaurus*. Included among the many fossils and realistic dioramas is a 75-million-year-old turtle.

Tour of Coastal Fairfield County [24]

P.T. Barnum

TRAVELERS FOLLOWING Interstate 95 are bound to strike it rich along the "Gold Coast," so nicknamed because of the luxurious estates, marinas, and mansions concentrated between Greenwich and Southport. This, the southernmost corner of the state, has attractions sure to meet everyone's taste. The shoreline is dusted with numerous beaches offering a variety of summer recreation opportunities. Nature preserves, arboretums, planetariums, and the state's only zoo will appeal to naturalists of all ages. People of a more artistic bent can visit the area's numerous small galleries or visit some of its larger, well-established museums.

New Canaan Historical Society building

Stamford's First Presbyterian Church has the largest mechanical-action organ in the state.

Greenwich ⑥
Blessed with a stunning coastline, this town is home to the Bush-Holley Historic Site, the state's first Impressionist art colony.

Stamford ⑤
This major urban area has a lively downtown and the First Presbyterian Church, which is shaped like a fish.

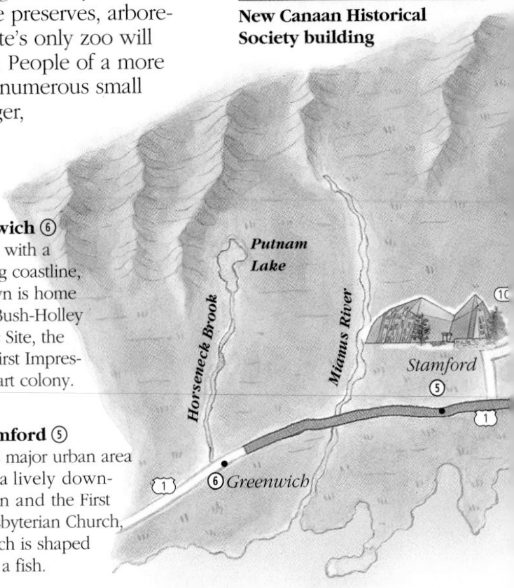
Putnam Lake
Horseneck Brook
Mianus River
Stamford
5
1
1
6 Greenwich

Archelon, at 10 ft (3 m), ranks as the largest turtle that ever roamed the planet.

The Peabody's third floor has a slightly more contemporary feel, with displays of mounted animals that range from the very large – bison, bears, and musk oxen – to the very small – snakes, birds, and mice. Elsewhere visitors can examine the Peabody's exhibits on the cultures of ancient Egypt, Mesoamerica, Polynesia, and the Plains Indian.

🏛 Yale Collection of Musical Instruments
15 Hillhouse Ave. 【 *(203) 432-0822.*
⬤ *Sep–Jun: 1pm–4pm Tue–Thu. Call for concert times.* ⬤ *Jul–Aug.* 🈲 ✔
by appt. ♿ *partial.*
A must stop for the musically inclined, this stunning

collection of instruments, considered among the top ten of its kind, has 800 objects, including historic woodwind and stringed instruments. The collection was started by New Haven piano manufacturer Morris Steinert (1831–1912). Steinert's love of music (he also founded the New Haven Symphony) saw him travel to Europe to

collect and restore antique instruments, especially claviers and harpsichords, forerunners to his beloved piano. Some of the collection's violins and harpsichords date back centuries. The museum holds a series of concerts from September to April. Many of the concerts are performed using the historic instruments.

Angelic detail on Yale's graceful High Street Bridge

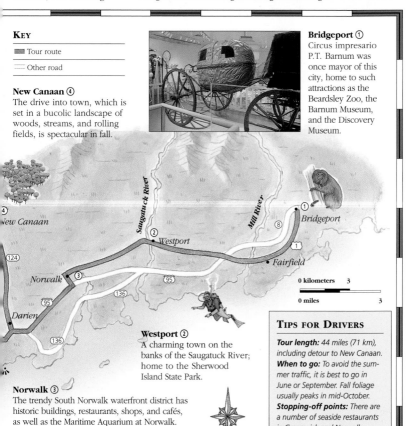

KEY

▬▬ Tour route

══ Other road

New Canaan ④
The drive into town, which is set in a bucolic landscape of woods, streams, and rolling fields, is spectacular in fall.

Bridgeport ①
Circus impresario P.T. Barnum was once mayor of this city, home to such attractions as the Beardsley Zoo, the Barnum Museum, and the Discovery Museum.

Saugatuck River
Mill River

④ New Canaan
② Westport
124
Norwalk ③
136
95
Darien
136

8
① Bridgeport
1
Fairfield

0 kilometers   3
0 miles   3

Westport ②
A charming town on the banks of the Saugatuck River; home to the Sherwood Island State Park.

Norwalk ③
The trendy South Norwalk waterfront district has historic buildings, restaurants, shops, and cafés, as well as the Maritime Aquarium at Norwalk.

TIPS FOR DRIVERS

Tour length: *44 miles (71 km), including detour to New Canaan.*
When to go: *To avoid the summer traffic, it is best to go in June or September. Fall foliage usually peaks in mid-October.*
Stopping-off points: *There are a number of seaside restaurants in Greenwich and Norwalk.*

VERMONT

VERMONT WAS GIVEN ITS NAME BY EXPLORER *Samuel de Champlain in 1609. The word means "Green Mountain" in French, and must have seemed most suitable when he gazed upon the fertile landscape. Almost 400 years later, Vermont is still very much an enclave of unspoiled wilderness, with thick forests blanketing the rolling hills and the valley lowlands.*

In all there are just over a half a million people living in Vermont, one of the most rural states in the Union. The countryside is replete with manicured farms where the state's trademark black and white Holstein cattle graze against a backdrop of natural beauty. The pastoral landscape, dotted with pristine villages and covered bridges, evokes the idealized images found in paintings by longtime resident Norman Rockwell *(see p241)*. An anti-billboard law ensures that the countryside is not blighted by obtrusive advertisements.

Vermonters may be small in number, but they are nationalistic and often have led the country's conscience on social and political issues. The Stars and Stripes are a familiar sight in Vermont; the American flag, "Old Glory" as is it known, decorates many a front porch.

It is hardly surprising that people from around the world are attracted to this green corner of the US. Each season brings new opportunities to enjoy nature. When the countryside is covered in a blanket of snow, picturesque towns are transformed into bustling ski centers. Outdoor enthusiasts have long known that Vermont possesses some of the best boating, hiking, camping, and fishing in the country. Vermont is also a magnet for painters, writers, musicians, and poets who enrich the cultural life of the state. Regional theaters, museums, and art galleries are prominent attractions. But Vermont is at its scenic best in the fall, when thousands of "leaf peepers" come to see the natural phenomenon of leaves changing color *(see pp20–21)*. What makes the season so special here is the variety of colors that the trees manifest, from the palest mustard to flaming scarlet.

Grazing Holstein cows, a favorite breed in Vermont, in a typical state setting

◁ Vermont's trademark rural landscape

Exploring Vermont

Unlike New England's coastal states, with attractions most often found along the water's edge, Vermont's highlights are sprinkled liberally throughout the state. The northeastern region boasts mountains, forests, and the fjordlike Lake Willoughby *(see pp230–31)*. Snaking down the western border, Lake Champlain and its islands *(see p236)* provide the backdrop for the collegial spirit of Burlington *(see pp232–5)* and the one-of-a-kind Shelburne Museum *(see pp238–9)*. Pre–Revolutionary War villages grace the south and provide good base camps for hikers looking to trek the Appalachian Trail *(see pp22–3)* or enjoy the natural splendor of the Green Mountain National Forest *(see p244)*.

Burlington's waterfront, well used by sailors and boaters

See Also

- ***Where to Stay*** pp317–19
- ***Where to Eat*** pp342–3

Key

- Interstate
- Major road
- Minor road
- Scenic route
- Viewpoint

Sights at a Glance

Ben & Jerry's Ice Cream Factory 8
Bennington 15
Brattleboro 17
Bread and Puppet Museum 3
Burlington pp232–5 5
Grafton 18
Green Mountain National Forest 14
Killington 12
Lake Champlain 6
Lake Willoughby 2
Mad River Valley 10
Manchester 13
Middlebury 11
Montpelier 9
St. Johnsbury 1
Shelburne Museum pp238–9 7
Stowe 4
Wilmington 16
Woodstock 19

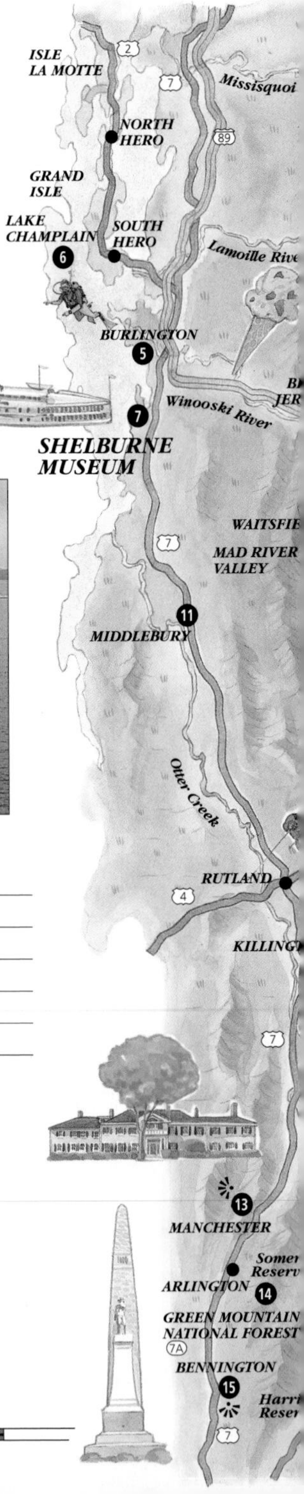

ISLE LA MOTTE
2
7
Missisquoi
NORTH HERO
89
GRAND ISLE
LAKE CHAMPLAIN
6
SOUTH HERO
Lamoille Rive
BURLINGTON
5
Winooski River
7
SHELBURNE MUSEUM
WAITSFIE
MAD RIVER VALLEY
7
11
MIDDLEBURY
Otter Creek
RUTLAND
4
KILLING
7
13
MANCHESTER
ARLINGTON
14
GREEN MOUNTAIN NATIONAL FOREST
7A
BENNINGTON
15
7

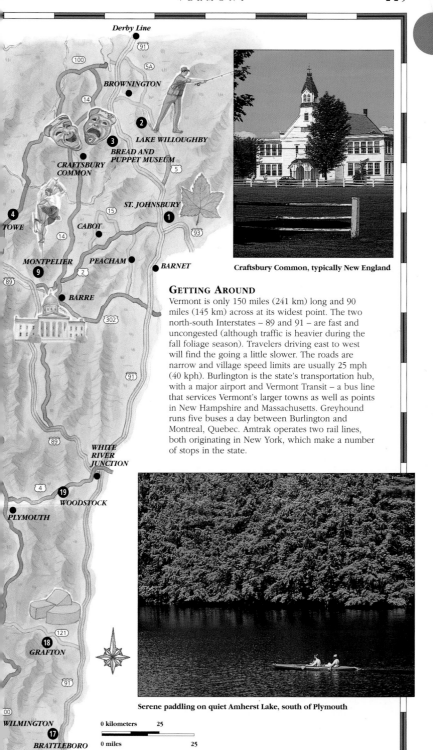

Derby Line

BROWNINGTON

LAKE WILLOUGHBY

BREAD AND
PUPPET MUSEUM

CRAFTSBURY
COMMON

ST. JOHNSBURY

TOWE

CABOT

MONTPELIER

PEACHAM

BARNET

BARRE

WHITE
RIVER
JUNCTION

WOODSTOCK

PLYMOUTH

GRAFTON

WILMINGTON

BRATTLEBORO

Craftsbury Common, typically New England

GETTING AROUND

Vermont is only 150 miles (241 km) long and 90
miles (145 km) across at its widest point. The two
north-south Interstates – 89 and 91 – are fast and
uncongested (although traffic is heavier during the
fall foliage season). Travelers driving east to west
will find the going a little slower. The roads are
narrow and village speed limits are usually 25 mph
(40 kph). Burlington is the state's transportation hub,
with a major airport and Vermont Transit – a bus line
that services Vermont's larger towns as well as points
in New Hampshire and Massachusetts. Greyhound
runs five buses a day between Burlington and
Montreal, Quebec. Amtrak operates two rail lines,
both originating in New York, which make a number
of stops in the state.

Serene paddling on quiet Amherst Lake, south of Plymouth

0 kilometers   25

0 miles   25

St. Johnsbury ❶

🏘 7,800. ✈ 77 miles (125 km)
W in Burlington. 🚌 ℹ 357 Western
Ave (802) 748-3678 or (800) 639-
6379.

Tranquil waters of Lake Willoughby

THIS SMALL industrial town, which is the unofficial capital of Vermont's northeast region – also called the "Northeast Kingdom" – sits atop a promontory at the convergence of the Moose, Sleeper, and Passumpsic rivers. The town is named for Saint Jean de Crèvecour, who was a friend of Revolutionary War hero Ethan Allen. It was the Frenchman who suggested that "bury" be added to the name because there were too many towns called St. John.

It was here in 1830 that Thaddeus Fairbanks (1796–1886), a mechanic, invented the platform scale, an easier and more accurate method of weighing than the balances of the time. The Fairbanks scale, as it came to be known, put St. Johnsbury on the map and boosted the growth of other pioneer industries, notably the manufacturing of maple products.

The Fairbanks family collected art and antiques, which now are housed in the **Fairbanks Museum and Planetarium** – one of the area's finest natural history museums. This Romanesque-style brick Victorian building, now on the National Historic Register, contains over 150,000 artifacts, including 4,500 stuffed birds and animals, and tools, dolls, and toys.

Also on Main Street is the **St. Johnsbury Athenaeum Art Gallery**, a Victorian gem with gleaming woodwork, paneled walls, and circular staircase. The gallery highlights the landscapes of the Hudson River School of painting. Popular in the 1800s, the movement was the first native school of American art, and focuses on the beauty of the natural world. Albert Bierstadt (1830–1902), whose massive canvas *Domes of Yosemite* (1867) hangs here, was one of its leaders.

🏛 **Fairbanks Museum and Planetarium**
1302 Main St. 📞 (802) 748-2372.
Museum ⏰ year-round: 9am–5pm
Mon–Sat; Apr–Dec: 1pm–5pm Sun.
⬤ Jan–Mar: Sun. **Planetarium**
⏰ call for show times. 🏷 ♿ 🎁
🌐 www.fairbanksmuseum.org
🏛 **St. Johnsbury Athenaeum Art Gallery**
1171 Main St. 📞 (802) 748-8291.
⏰ year-round: 10am–8pm Mon &
Wed, 10am–5:30pm Tue & Thu–Fri,
9:30am–4pm Sat. 🏷 ♿ 🎁

ENVIRONS: Nineteen miles (30 km) to the west is Cabot, where one of the state's best-known agricultural products – cheddar cheese – is made. The **Cabot Creamery**, a farmers' cooperative, was started in 1919 and now produces a mind-boggling 100 million lbs (45.5 million kg) of cheese a year. The creamery offers tours and free tastings.

🏭 **Cabot Creamery**
Main St., Cabot, Rte 215. 📞 (802)
563-3393 or (800) 837-4261. ⏰
Jun–Oct: 9am–5pm daily; Nov–May:
9am–4pm Mon–Sat. ⬤ Jan 1, Sun in
Jan, Thanksgiving, & Dec 25. 🏷 ♿

Lake Willoughby ❷

Rte 5A near Barton. 📞 (802) 525-
1137.

TRAVELERS HEADING east from Barton climb a crest on the road only to be met with the breathtaking view of this beautiful body of water. The narrow glacial lake, which plunges 300 ft (90 m) in certain areas, is flanked by two soaring cliffs: Mount Pisgah at 2,750 ft (840 m) and Mount Hor at 2,650 ft (810 m). Jutting straight out of the water, the mountains give the lake the appearance of a rugged Norwegian fjord or a resort in Switzerland, garnering it the nickname the "Lucerne of America."

With trails leading around both promontories, this is a haven for hikers and swimmers looking for a secluded spot. There are wonderful picnic and camping areas along the beaches at either end of the five-mile (8-km) lake. Several resorts and bed and breakfast establishments ring the shores. The lake itself offers plenty of recreational opportunities – fishing, boating, scuba diving – and there are three nearby golf courses.

ENVIRONS: Because of its isolated location 11 miles (18 km) northwest of Lake Willoughby, Brownington has retained the look of an 18th-century village, with few modern touches. The **Old Stone House** museum documents the history of the region. Twenty-two miles (35 km) to the north of the lake lies Derby Line – really two communities in one. The northern half, which is in Quebec, Canada, is called

Art on walnut wall panels at St.
Johnsbury Athenaeum Art Gallery

Rock Island. The border between Canada and the US runs through the middle of the **Haskell Free Library and Opera House**, a stately granite and brick building constructed in 1904.

Part of the audience sits in the US, but the stage is in Canada. The building's wealthy benefactor, Mrs. Martha Stewart Haskell (1831–1906), wanted both communities to enjoy her gift.

⊞ Old Stone House
28 Old Stone House Rd. 📞 (802) 754-2022. ⭘ call for hours. ⌦ ✿ obligatory. ♿ 🅿
▦ Haskell Free Library and Opera House
93 Caswell Ave. 📞 (802) 873-3022. **Library** ⭘ year-round: 10am–5pm Tue–Wed & Fri–Sat, 10am–8pm Thu. **Opera House** ⭘ May–Oct: call for hours. ⬤ Sun–Mon. ⌦

Bread and Puppet Museum ❸

Exit 25 Rte 122 near Glover. 📞 (802) 525-3031 or (802) 525-6972. ⭘ May–Oct: 10am–6pm daily; call for show times. 🅿

Aɴ ᴇxᴛʀᴀᴏʀᴅɪɴᴀʀʏ place down a quiet rural road, this museum is a century-old, two-story building, which once served as a barn to shelter dairy cattle. The cattle

A selection of fanciful creatures at the Bread and Puppet Museum

The Austrian-style Trapp Family Lodge

have gone, but every inch of space is taken up by paintings, masks, and other theatrical knickknacks, most notably puppets of all shapes and sizes, dressed in outlandish costumes in every style. The props belong to the internationally famous Bread and Puppet Theater company, founded in 1962. The troupe members live communally on the surrounding farm. Their productions are notable for the masterful use of giant puppets and are made even more fun by enlisting the help of the local population.

Typical Vermont church in Craftsbury Common

Eɴvɪʀᴏɴs: Small and graceful Craftsbury Common, just 14 miles (22 km) southwest, is pure Americana. Gnarled old trees, planted in 1799 to commemorate the death of George Washington (1732–99), the first president of the US, line the main street. The village green is flanked by handsome clapboard homes with black shutters, and is anchored at one corner by a typical New England church with a white wooden steeple. In winter the area is popular with cross-country skiers.

Stowe ❹

🏙 3,500. ✈ 40 miles (64 km) W in Burlington. 🚌 51 Main St (802) 253-7321, (877) 467-8693 or (800) 247-8693. 🖥 www.gostowe.com

Iᴛ ɪs ʜᴀʀᴅʟʏ sᴜʀᴘʀɪsɪɴɢ that the Von Trapp family, whose daring escape from Austria during World War II was the inspiration behind the 1965 movie *The Sound of Music*, chose Stowe as their new home. The pretty village is ringed by mountains, which reminded them of the Alpine region they had left behind. Their Trapp Family Lodge *(see p319)* is part of the 2,700-acre (1,092-ha) estate. The giant wooden chalet is one of the area's most popular hotels.

The village has been a major ski and outdoor activity center since the 1930s. In winter it draws hordes of skiers looking to enjoy the region's best slopes *(see pp362–3)*. Mountain Road begins in the village and is lined with chalets, motels, restaurants, and pubs; it leads to the area's highest peak, 4,393-ft (1,339-m) Mount Mansfield. Many local spas and resorts offer gourmet meals, and massages and other health treatments.

In summer there are still opportunities to enjoy the outdoors. Visitors can hike, rock-climb, fish, and canoe, or walk, cycle, or inline skate along the paved, meandering 5.5 mile (8.5 km) Stowe Recreational Path. It winds from Stowe's village church across the West Branch River, then through woodlands.

Burlington ❺

BURLINGTON IS ONE OF VERMONT'S most popular tourist destinations. It is a lively university town with almost half of its population of just over 40,000 made up of students or people associated with the University of Vermont (UVM) and the city's four colleges. One of the oldest universities in the country, UVM was founded in 1791, the same year that Vermont officially joined the United States. Burlington's strategic location on the eastern shore of Lake Champlain *(see p236)* helped it prosper in pioneer times, and today it is Vermont's center of commerce and industry. The town is also rich in grand old mansions, historic landmarks, interesting shops, and restaurants and has an attractive waterfront. The famed American Revolution patriot Ethan Allen (1738–89), omnipresent throughout the state, has his final resting place here in Greenmount Cemetery.

FLYNN
RATDOG 23
FLYNN GARDEN TOUR 23

The restored Flynn Theater, close to City Hall Place

Exploring Burlington

The center of Burlington is compact and easy to explore on foot. Battery Street, near the waterfront, is the oldest, most historic part of the city and a jumping-off point for ferries to New York State and sightseeing trips around Lake Champlain. More than 200 buildings in the downtown core have been renovated in recent years, and visitors will find many architectural landmarks, including the First Unitarian Church *(see pp234–5)*.

Battery Park, at the north end of Battery Street where it meets Pearl Street, was the site of a battle between US soldiers and the British Royal Navy. Burlington saw several skirmishes during the War of 1812, and scuba divers have found military artifacts at the bottom of the lake. Five shipwrecks, three lying close to Burlington, can be explored by divers who register with the Waterfront Diving Center on Battery Street.

These days Battery Park is a much more peaceful place. Lake Champlain is at its widest point here, and visitors who stroll through the park are rewarded with lovely views of Burlington Bay and the backdrop of the Adirondack Mountains on the other side of the lake. Entertainment is presented in the park on Thursday and Sunday evenings in summer.

Burlington's cultural life comes to the fore during its annual jazz festival in June. Venues for this popular concert series include City Hall Place, Waterfront Park, the Church Street Marketplace *(see pp234–5)*, and the Flynn Theater. A former vaudeville theater and movie palace, the Flynn has had its Art Deco interior carefully restored, and now stages a variety of cultural events throughout the

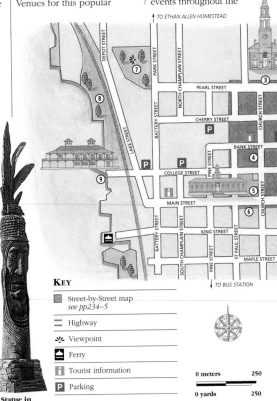

Statue in Battery Park

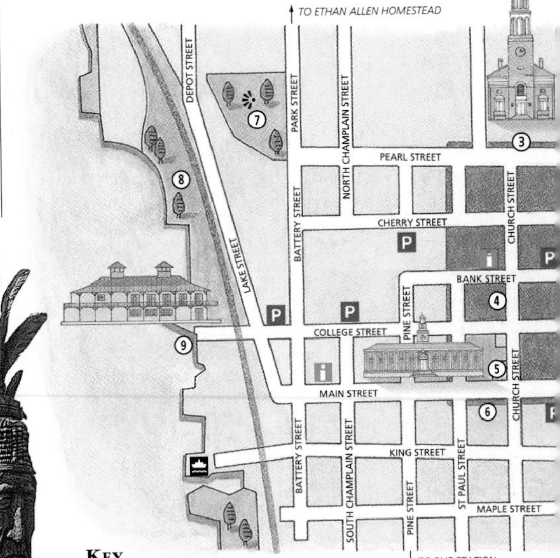
TO ETHAN ALLEN HOMESTEAD
DEPOT STREET
PARK STREET
NORTH CHAMPLAIN STREET
PEARL STREET
BATTERY STREET
CHERRY STREET
CHURCH STREET
LAKE STREET
BANK STREET
PINE STREET
COLLEGE STREET
MAIN STREET
KING STREET
ST PAUL STREET
SOUTH CHAMPLAIN STREET
MAPLE STREET
TO BUS STATION
0 meters 250
0 yards 250

KEY

- Street-by-Street map *see pp234–5*
- Highway
- Viewpoint
- Ferry
- [i] Tourist information
- [P] Parking

Lake steamer with a full complement of sightseers

year. A Mozart festival, which started here at the University of Vermont, runs for three weeks in the summer and has spread to other communities. Concerts are held in St. Paul's Cathedral, UVM's Recital Hall, City Hall Park, and Shelburne Farms south of the city.

Spirit of Ethan Allen III

Burlington Boat House, College St. (802) 862-8300. May–Oct: 9am–7pm daytime and sunset dinner cruises (reservations necessary).

Tall-stack steamers used to ply the waters of Lake Champlain. Today visitors can board the three-decker cruise ship, *Spirit of Ethan Allen III*, which holds 500 passengers. Its 90-minute trip gives a good historical overview as the captain narrates entertaining tales of the Revolutionary War.

Robert Hull Fleming Museum

61 Colchester Ave. (802) 656-0750. May–mid-Sep: 12pm–4pm Tue–Fri; mid-Sep–May: 9am–4pm Tue–Fri; year-round: 1pm–5pm Sat–Sun. public hols.

The museum is located on the campus of the University of Vermont, up on a hillside overlooking the city. Built in 1931, the elegant Colonial Revival building houses a huge collection of artifacts – more than 19,000 items – ranging from ancient Mesopotamia to modern times. Some of the items on display include European and American paintings and sculptures, Native Indian crafts, costumes, textiles, glassware, and numerous archeological remains.

Statue of Penelope in the Fleming Museum

Shelburne Farms

1611 Harbor Rd. (802) 985-8686. May–mid-Oct: 9am–5pm daily. partial.
Seven miles (11 km) south of town are Shelburne Museum (*see pp238–9*) and Shelburne Farms, a historic 1,400-acre (566-ha) estate. The parklike grounds of the latter include rolling pastures, woodlands, and a working farm. Tours are given of the dairy. Children can pet the animals in designated areas.

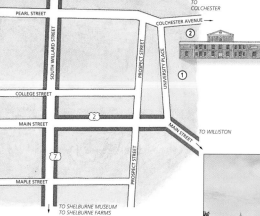

BURLINGTON TOWN CENTER

Part of the stately University of Vermont campus

Street-by-Street: Historic District

THE FOUR-BLOCK SECTION known as the Church Street Marketplace is located at the center of the city's historic district. The neighborhood has been converted into a pedestrian mall complete with trendy boutiques, patio restaurants, specialty stores, factory outlets, craft shops, and, naturally, a Ben & Jerry's *(see p236)*. The marketplace, thronged with shoppers and sightseers at the best of times, is at its most vibrant in the summer months, with numerous street performers and musicians adding color and action. The district also has its share of historical attractions, including the 1816 First Unitarian Church.

Richardson Building
This 1895 chateau-style building was a 19th-century department store.

The Masonic Temple is Church Street's tallest structure.

★ First Unitarian Church
Standing at the head of Church Street, the First Unitarian Church was built in 1816 and stands as the oldest house of worship in Burlington.

The Burlington Montgomery Ward Building, built in 1929, is on the National Register of Historic Places. Its graceful lines and colorful facade typify pre-Depression architecture.

Central-Union Blocks
This was the first major development on upper Church Street. It now houses restaurants and pubs.

STAR SIGHTS

★ City Hall

★ First Unitarian Church

Pedestrian Mall
This section of the mall – particularly lively on weekends – is popular among students and tourists for its many shops and terraces. Cafés, pubs, and restaurants are housed in Queen Anne-style buildings from the late 1800s.

Second Merchants Bank
was built in 1895 by Burlington architect Sydney Greene.

★ City Hall
This 1928 building marks the southern boundary of the marketplace and is made of local brick, marble, and granite.

KEY

☐	Pedestrian mall
– –	Suggested route

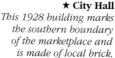

0 meters 25

0 yards 25

Abraham Block was once considered the most striking commercial block in the state.

City Hall Park
The park is a popular outdoor concert venue. It features a poured concrete fountain and two granite monuments. One honors those who died in the Civil War; the other, soldiers who died in World War II.

Sailing and boating, popular on beautiful Lake Champlain

Lake Champlain ❻

Vermont-New York border from Whitehall to Alburg. ⛴ *Burlington.* 🚌 ℹ️ *60 Main St, Burlington (802) 863-3489 or (877) 686-5253.*

Said to be the home of "Champ," a water serpent that could be a distant cousin of Scotland's Loch Ness Monster, Lake Champlain was named for French explorer Samuel de Champlain (1567–1635). He discovered and explored much of the surrounding region. Some 120 miles (190 km) long and 12 miles (19 km) wide, the lake has its western shore in New York State, while the eastern sector is in Vermont. Scenic hour-long ferry rides run regularly between Burlington and Port Kent, New York.

Sometimes called the sixth Great Lake because of its size, Champlain has 500 miles (800 km) of shoreline and is sprinkled with about 70 islands. At the lake's northern end, the Alburg Peninsula and a group of thin islands (North Hero, Isle La Motte, and Grand Isle) give glimpses of the region's colorful past.

At Ste. Anne's Shrine on Isle La Motte is a statue of Champlain. Grand Isle is home to America's oldest log cabin (1783). The villages of North and South Hero were named in honor of brothers Ethan and Ira Allen. Their volunteers, the Green Mountain Boys, helped secure Vermont's status as a separate state.

Some of Lake Champlain's treasures are underwater, preserved in a marine park where scuba divers can explore shipwrecks resting on sandbars and at the bottom of the lake.

The **Lake Champlain Maritime Museum** at Basin Harbor gives an overview of the region's marine history. On display are ship models, old divers' suits, and photographs of Lake Champlain steamers, the most famous of which was the SS *Ticonderoga*, built in 1906 and now part of the collection of Americana at the nearby Shelburne Museum *(see pp238–9).*

🏛 **Lake Champlain Maritime Museum**
4472 Basin Harbor Rd, Vergennes. ☎ *(802) 475-2022.* ⏰ *May–mid-Oct: 10am–5pm daily.* ♿ ⛔

Shelburne Museum ❼

See pp238–9

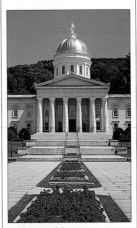

Gold dome of the Vermont State House in Montpelier

Ben & Jerry's Ice Cream Factory ❽

Rte 100, Waterbury. ☎ *(802) 244-5641 or (866) BJTOURS.* ⏰ *Jun: 9am–5pm daily; Jul–Aug: 9am–8pm daily; Sep–Oct: 9am–6pm daily; Nov–May: 10am–5pm daily.* ♿ ⛔ 🍴 🏪 🌐 www.benjerry.com

Although Ben Cohen and Jerry Greenfield hail from Long Island, New York, they have done more than any other "flatlanders" to put Vermont's dairy industry on the map. In 1977 these childhood friends paid $5 for a correspondence course on making ice cream and parlayed their knowledge into a hugely successful franchise.

Ben and Jerry use the richest cream and milk from local farms to produce their ice cream and frozen

Ben & Jerry's bus, gaily decorated with dairy cows

yogurt. The Ben & Jerry trademark is the black and white Holstein cow, embellishing everything in the gift shop.

Tours of the factory start every 15 minutes and run for 30 minutes. Visitors learn all there is to know about making ice cream. They are given a bird's-eye view of the factory floor, and at the end of the tour a chance to sample the products and sometimes test new flavors.

Montpelier ❾

👥 *8,400.* ✈ *40 miles (64 km) NW in Burlington.* 🚌 🚉 ℹ️ *134 State St (802) 828-0587 or (800) VERMONT.*

Montpelier is the smallest state capital in the US, but its diminutive stature is advantageous: The city is impeccably clean, friendly, and easily seen on foot. Despite its size, Montpelier has a grand, imposing building to house its state politicians and legislators. The **Vermont State House,** which dates back to 1859, replaced an earlier building that was destroyed by fire. It is now a formidable Greek Revival structure, complete with a gilt cupola and giant fluted pillars of granite that were hewn from one of the quarries at neighboring Barre.

The **Vermont Historical Society Museum**, run by the local historical society, is housed in a replica of a 19th-century hotel. The museum, which was recently fully renovated, has also opened an additional center in Barre.

⊞ Vermont State House
115 State St. ☎ (802) 828-2228. ○ year-round: 8am–4pm Mon–Fri. ☑ late Jun–mid-Oct: 10am–3:30pm Mon–Fri, 11am–2:30pm Sat. ● public hols. ▨ ♿ ▥

🏛 Vermont Historical Society Museum
109 State St. ☎ (802) 828-2291. ○ 9am–4:30pm Tue–Fri, 9am–4pm Sat. ▨ ☑ ♿

Environs: Seven miles (11 km) to the south, Barre (pronounced "berry") is the self-proclaimed granite capital of the world. In the 19th century, Italian and Scottish stonemasons came here to work the pale, white and blue-gray rock.

The region still is a hive of granite-related activity, with several large plants producing stone for tombstones (many have ended up in Barre's Hope Cemetery on Merchant Street), statues, and monuments. In nearby Graniteville, the **Rock of Ages Quarry** is the biggest such operation. Visitors can watch – from the safety of an observation deck – as the stone is being

hewn from the huge 475-ft (134-m) pit. Shuttle buses run regularly, taking visitors between the quarry and the Graniteville visitor center.

⛏ Rock of Ages Quarry
773 Main St, Graniteville. ☎ (802) 476-3119. ○ May–Oct: 8:30am–5pm Mon–Sat, 12pm–5pm Sun. ▨ ☑ ♿

Mad River Valley ⑩

Central VT along Rte 100. 🅸 Rte 100, Waitsfield (802) 496-3409. 🅰 Waitsfield, mid-May–Columbus Day: 9:30am–1pm Sat. ⓦ www.madrivervalley.com

Located in central Vermont, Mad River Valley is most famous for outdoor activities that include hiking, cycling, hunting, and especially skiing.

One popular stop is the Mad River Glen ski area *(see p362),* which attracts die-hard traditionalists who enjoy their sport the old-fashioned way – without fancy high-speed gondolas (though there are four chairlifts) and snow-making equipment. With only a couple of dozen trails, Mad River Glen caters to the country's most skilled skiers – in fact, its motto is "Ski it if you can."

Sugarbush, on the other hand, has more than 100 trails and a vertical drop of 2,650 ft (800 m). It is the polar opposite of Mad River Glen. This trendy resort, which caters to beginners and intermediate skiers as well as those who are more

Moss Glenn Falls near Warren in Mad River Valley

advanced, has the most modern snowmaking facilities and lifts. It was very popular with the 1960s "jet set," but now a more "retro" crowd who own time-share condos frequents the slopes. A state-of-the-art express "people mover" connects what used to be two separate ski areas: Lincoln Peak and Mount Ellen.

Activities in and around Waitsfield, the small, fashionable, and wealthy community that is the center of this tourist region, include hiking, hunting, and – of all things – polo. The local landmark is a round barn, which is one of only a dozen remaining in the state. It is a venue for cultural functions and art exhibits. It sits next to an elegant inn and restaurant that has been converted from an 1806 farmhouse.

Bucolic scenery outside of Waitsfield, a popular summer destination

Shelburne Museum ❼

★ **Circus Building**
The horseshoe-shaped building houses a 500-ft- (152-m-) long miniature circus parade. The west entrance foyer features this 3,000-piece miniature circus.

MORE THAN JUST an eclectic repository, the Shelburne Museum celebrates three centuries of American ingenuity, creativity, and diversity. Here folk art, antique tools, duck decoys, and circus memorabilia are displayed on the same grounds as scrimshaw, Native American artifacts, and paintings by such US artists as Winslow Homer (1836–1910) and Grandma Moses (1860–1961). Established in 1947 by collector Electra Webb (1888–1960), the museum's 37 historic structures and their contents constitute one of the nation's finest museums.

Big Chief statue

Vintage 1920s carousel

Museum Store
Handicrafts by New England artisans are sold here.

McClure Visitor Center and Round Barn
The first two floors of this 1901 barn feature changing exhibits. The visitor center is located on the top floor.

KEY

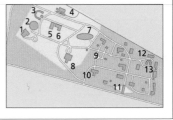

☐ **Illustrated**
☐ **Not Illustrated**

1 Museum Store and Entrance
2 McClure Visitor Center and Round Barn
3 Circus Building and Carousel
4 Railroad Station

5 Beach Gallery
6 Beach Lodge
7 SS *Ticonderoga*
8 Electra Havemeyer Webb Memorial Building
9 Lighthouse
10 Webb Gallery
11 Covered Bridge
12 Meeting House
13 Horseshoe Barn

★ **Railroad Station**
The station was built in 1890 in Shelburne, Vermont, and relocated here. It houses a variety of railroad memorabilia, including telegraphy systems, vintage railroad maps, a restored stationmaster's office, and men's and women's waiting rooms.

VISITORS' CHECKLIST

Rte 7, 7 miles (11 km) S of
Burlington. ☎ *(802) 985-3346.*
🕐 *Apr–mid-May: 1pm–4pm daily
(selected buildings only); mid-
May–mid-Oct: 10am–5pm daily.*
● *mid-Oct–Mar, Thanksgiving, &
Dec 25.* 📷 ♿ 🚻 🍴 ◻ ◻ 📷
*flash photography restricted in
some buildings.*
🔲 *www.shelburnemuseum.org.*

Locomotive 220, a 1915
10-wheel steam locomotive,
hauled freight and passenger
trains. Engine 220 could pull
12.5 tons (11 tonnes) of
dead weight.

Beach Lodge contains a variety
of big-game trophies and Native
American artifacts.

**1871 Lake
Champlain Lighthouse**
*Built to warn ships off
reefs in the lake, the
building now
tells of the life
led by lighthouse
keepers.*

★ **SS *Ticonderoga***
*A National Historic
Landmark, the SS
Ticonderoga was res-
cued from the scrap
heap by Webb in
1950. Today the for-
mer Lake Champlain
steamship is open for
visitors to explore.*

STAR FEATURES

★ **Railroad Station**

★ **Circus Building**

★ **SS *Ticonderoga***

Middlebury ⓫

🏛 8,500. 🛬 36 miles (58 km)
N in Burlington. 🚉 ℹ 2 Court St
(802) 388-7951 or (800) 733-8376.

Mᴵᴰᴰᴸᴱᴮᵁᴿʸ, founded in
1761, is the archetypal
New England town. It has
not one, but two village
greens, or "commons," tall-
spired churches, a prestigious
college, and a collection of
Colonial-era homes. In all
Middlebury lays claim to more
than 300 buildings that were
constructed during the 18th
and early 19th centuries.
Chief among them are the
Congregational Church,
the Battell and Beckwith
commercial blocks, and the
Middlebury Inn, a classic brick
Georgian-style hostelry with
shuttered windows that dates
back to 1827.

The town, which sits
on Otter Creek, gets
its name from the
days of stage
coaches when
Middlebury
served as the
transit point on
Vermont's main
north-south and
east-west routes.
Morgan horses,
one of the first
US native breeds,
were often seen
on this route. Today visitors
can tour the **UVM Morgan
Horse Farm** for a look at this
versatile and historic breed.

At one time Otter Creek
powered the machinery for
a thriving wool and grain
industry. The restored Frog
Hollow Mill is now the home
of the **Vermont State Craft
Center**, which exhibits the
work of more than 250 local
artists and craftspeople.
History buffs will enjoy the
**Henry Sheldon Museum of
Vermont History**, an 1829
house that documents the
early 19th century through its
collection of furniture, textiles
and clothing, and portraits.

Folk art and folk ways are
the themes running through
the exhibits at the **Vermont
Folklife Center**, a former
Masonic Hall. Until recently,
the Folklife Center was
housed in a home dating back

Peaceful campus of Middlebury College

Morgan Horse Farm

to the early 1800s in which
Gamaliel Painter (1743–1819),
the founder of **Middlebury
College**, once lived. The college's 500-acre (200-ha) campus is a delightful place to
explore, with
graceful archi-
tecture, an art
gallery, and
green spaces.

The college's
Bread Loaf cam-
pus in nearby
Ripton is nestled
in the Green
Mountain
National Forest
(see p244) near
the scenic
Robert Frost
Interpretive
Trail. Named for
the famous American poet
who spent summers here
from 1938 to 1962, the path is
flanked with quotations from
Frost's poems set on plaques.

🔘 **UVM Morgan
Horse Farm**
Rte 23 NW of Middlebury in
Weybridge. 🄲 (802) 388-2011. ⬤
May–Oct: 9am–4pm daily. 🈳 🄲 🄳
🄳 **Vermont State Craft
Center at Frog Hollow**
Main & Mill Sts. 🄲 (802) 388-3177.
⬤ call for hours. 🄳
🏛 **Henry Sheldon Museum
of Vermont History**
1 Park St. 🄲 (802) 388-2117.
⬤ year- round: 10am–5pm
Mon–Sat. 🈳
🏛 **Vermont Folklife Center**
3 Court St. 🄲 (802) 388-4964.
⬤ Jun–Dec: 11am–4pm Tue–Sat;
Jan–May: 11am–4pm Thu–Sat. 🄳
🎓 **Middlebury College**
College St. 🄲 (802) 443-5000. ⬤
year-round: Mon–Fri. 🄲 🄳

Killington ⓬

🏛 1,000. ✈ 5 miles (8 km) W in
Rutland. ℹ Rte 4, West Killington
(802) 422-3333 or (800) 621-6867.

Sᴾᴼᴿᵀʸ ᵀʸᴾᴱs who like
outdoor adventure and a
lively social life head for this
year-round resort. Killington
has a highly developed
tourism infrastructure, with
hundreds of condominiums,
vacation homes, ski lodges
and B&Bs, golf courses, hiking
and bike trails, and an
adventure center with water
slides and a climbing wall. It
operates the largest ski center
(see p362) in the eastern
United States, with 200 runs
for alpine skiing and
snowboarding spread across
seven peaks including nearby
Pico Mountain. Killington
itself is the second-highest peak in
Vermont at 4,240 ft (1,295 m).
Two of the best cross-country
ski centers in the eastern US –
Mountain Top Inn *(see p317)*
and Mountain Meadows *(see*

**One of the numerous trails at
Killington, Vermont**

p318) – are also situated in the Killington area.

The ski season here usually lasts eight months, longer than anywhere else in Vermont, and one of the gondolas that ferry skiers to the peaks runs during the summer and fall as well. It is worth taking a ride to the top for the spectacular views. On a clear day, visitors can glimpse parts of five states and distant Canada. Killington also keeps busy throughout the summer with arts and crafts shows, barbecues, and music festivals.

Manchester ⓭

🏠 3,860. ✈ 33 miles (53 km) N in Rutland. 🚌 🛈 Suite 1, 5046 Main St (802) 362-2100.

M ANCHESTER is actually made up of three separate communities: Manchester Depot and Manchester Center, the outlet centers of New England, and Manchester Village. The sum of these parts is a picturesque destination surrounded by mountains, typical of scenic southern Vermont. There are two major ski areas: Stratton, a recently enlarged complex with more than 90 trails and a hillside ski village with shops and restaurants; and Bromley, a busy, family-oriented ski area.

Manchester has been a popular vacation resort since the 19th century, when wealthy urbanites used to head to the mountains to escape the summer heat. The town's marble sidewalks fringed by old shade trees, the restored Equinox hotel *(see p318)*, and several stately homes evoke that era. Today's tourists take pleasure in following the Equinox Skyline Drive, with its panoramic view of the countryside from the crest of Mount Equinox. Many visitors enjoy spending their time hunting for brand-name bargains in the designer outlets and factory stores.

One of Manchester's largest and most elegant houses is **Hildene**, a 24-room Georgian Revival manor house built by Robert Lincoln (1843–1926), a lawyer, diplomat, and the son of President Abraham Lincoln (1809–65). Among the mansion's most notable features are its 1,000-pipe Aeolian organ and Lincoln family memorabilia. The grounds are graced with an impeccable formal garden, based largely on a pattern taken from a stained-glass window.

Also housed in a stately Georgian mansion, the **Southern Vermont Arts Center** rotates its permanent collection of 700 paintings and photographs. The hilly 400 acres (160 ha) also contain a striking sculpture garden. Elsewhere the **American Museum of Fly Fishing** claims to house the largest collection of fly-fishing paraphernalia in the world.

Antique kitchenware on display at elegant Hildene

The collection, which often travels to other museums, includes hundreds of rods, reels, and flies used by famous people such as singer Bing Crosby, literary giant Ernest Hemingway, and former president Jimmy Carter.

♨ Hildene
Rte 7A. 📞 (802) 362-1788. ⏰ mid-May–Oct: 9:30am–4pm daily. 📷 🎫 every 30 mins. ♿
🏛 Southern Vermont Arts Center
West Rd. 📞 (802) 362-1405. ⏰ May–Oct: 10am–5pm Tue–Sat, 12pm–5pm Sun; Nov–Apr: 10am–5pm Mon–Sat. 📷 ♿ 🛈
🏛 American Museum of Fly Fishing
Seminary Ave. 📞 (802) 362-3300. ⏰ year-round: 10am–4pm daily. ● public hols. 📷 ♿

ENVIRONS: Nine miles southwest lies little Arlington, with two major claims to fame: angling and art. Nearby Batten Kill River is considered by experienced fishermen to be one of the best trout rivers in the state, if not the whole of New England. Local anglers may have served as subjects for artist Norman Rockwell (1894–1978) during the years that he lived here. The **Norman Rockwell Exhibition** houses a collection of his work and photographs of some of the townsfolk he used as models.

🏛 Norman Rockwell Exhibition
Rte 7A. 📞 (802) 375-6423. ⏰ May–Oct: 9am–5pm daily; Nov–Apr: 10am–4pm daily. ● Thanksgiving, & Dec 25. 📷 ♿

NORMAN ROCKWELL IN VERMONT

Painter and illustrator Norman Rockwell, famous for idealized depictions of small-town America, lived in Arlington at the height of his career, from 1939 to 1954. His paintings were so detailed they looked almost like photographs, and the magazine covers that he designed for publications such as *Saturday Evening Post*, the *Ladies' Home Journal*, and *Look*, have become collectors' items. Admirers of his work should be sure to visit the Norman Rockwell Museum in Stockbridge, Massachusetts *(see pp166–7)*, and Arlington *(see right)*.

Norman Rockwell surveys his work surrounded by friends and his son c.1944

Green Mountain National Forest

i *Forest Supervisor, Green Mountain National Forest, 231 N Main St, Rutland.* **C** *(802) 747-6700.* **Hapgood Campground** **C** *(877) 444-6777 for reservations (all other campgrounds on first-come, first-served basis).* ◻ *year-round.* ▨ *to campgrounds.*

THIS HUGE SPINE of greenery and mountains runs for 350,000 acres (142,850 ha) – almost the entire length of the state – along two-thirds of the Green Mountain range. The mountains, many more than 4,000 ft (1,200 m) high, have some of the best ski centers in the eastern United States, including Sugarbush *(see p237)* and Mount Snow *(see p246)*. A large network of snowmobile and cross-country ski trails are also maintained throughout the winter months.

The National Forest is divided into northern and southern sectors, and encompasses six wilderness areas; sections of the forest have remained entirely undeveloped – no roads, no electricity, and even paths may be poorly marked or non-existent. While hard-core backcountry hikers and campers may enjoy this

Woodward Reservoir in the Green Mountain National Forest

challenge, the majority of travelers will prefer to roam the less primitive areas of the forest. Picnic sites and camp-grounds are found through-out, along with more than 500 miles (805 km) of hiking paths, including the challenging Long and Appalachian trails *(see pp22–3)*.

Many lakes, rivers, and, reservoirs offer excellent boating and fishing opportunities. On land, bike paths (both mountain and road) are numerous and specially designated paths are open to horseback riders. Regardless of their mode of transportation, visitors are encouraged to stay on the paths in order to preserve the delicate ecosystem. Markers indicate designated lookout points and covered bridges. The

town of Stratton in the southern portion of the Green Mountain range offers recreational activities such as golf, horseback riding, sailing, and fly fishing, as well as alpine and cross-country skiing. The Stratton Arts Festival is held in the fall. Nearby Bromley Mountain Ski Center has been a popular family resort since the 1930s.

Bennington ⓯

🏛 *16,800.* ✈ 🚌 **i** *100 Veterans Memorial Dr (802) 447-3311 or (800) 229-0252.* 📅 *Wed & Fri.* 🖳 *www.bennington.com*

ALTHOUGH IT IS TUCKED away in the southwest corner of the Green Mountain National Forest bordering Massachusetts and New York

Dense woodlands of the Green Mountain National Forest

◁ Paper Mill Village Bridge, originally built in 1889, near Bennington

State, Bennington is no backwoods community. The third-largest city in the state, Bennington is an important manufacturing center and home to Bennington College, the faculty of which once included cutting-edge engineer Buckminster Fuller (1895–1983).

Three covered bridges (just off Route 67) herald the approach to town. These 19th-century wooden structures, built with roofs to protect them against the harsh Vermont winter, are nicknamed "kissing bridges" because in the days of horses and buggies they provided a discreet shelter for courting couples to embrace.

Bennington was established in 1749 and a few decades later Ethan Allen arrived on the scene to lead the Green Mountain Boys, a citizen's militia originally created to protect Vermont from the expansionist advances of neighboring New York. Allen would later make his name as a patriot during the Revolutionary War by leading his men into battle and scoring several decisive victories against British forces.

The revolutionary era comes alive during a walking tour of the **Old Bennington Historic District** just west of the downtown core, where a typical New England village green is ringed by pillared Greek Revival structures and Federal-style brick buildings. The 1806 **First Congregational Church**, with its vaulted plaster and wood ceilings, is a striking and much-photographed local landmark. Next to it is the Old Burying Ground, resting place of five Vermont governors

The pulpit of Bennington's First Congregational Church

and the beloved poet Robert Frost *(see pp30–31)*.

Looming over the Historic District is the 306-ft- (93-m-) high **Bennington Battle Monument**, a massive stone obelisk that, when it was built in 1891, was the tallest war monument in the world. It commemorates a 1777 battle in nearby Willoomsac Heights, when the colonial forces defeated the British army and their allies, leading to the surrender of their commander, General John Burgoyne (1722–92). An elevator takes visitors to an observation area that affords panoramic views of Vermont and the neighboring states of New York and Massachusetts.

The turbulent times of the Revolutionary and Civil wars are also recalled at the **Bennington Museum and Grandma Moses Gallery**. The museum houses several dozen paintings by famed folk artist Anna Mary "Grandma" Moses (1860–1961), who lived in the Bennington area. A farmer's wife with no formal training in art, Moses started

The 1891 Bennington Battle Monument

painting landscapes as a hobby when she was in her mid-70s. She was "discovered" by the critics in 1940, when a collection of her art was shown at a private exhibition in the Museum of Modern Art in New York City. At that time the 79-year-old primitive artist was being hailed as an important new talent. By the time she died in 1961 at the age of 101, Grandma Moses had produced some 1,600 works of art, including a series of tiny country scenes painted on mushrooms. The collection in Bennington includes her only known self-portrait.

The Museum's comprehensive collection of Americana also includes uniforms, furniture, and examples of pottery from Bennington's ceramics industry, which reached its peak in the mid-1800s. The display of American glassware includes examples of the decorative Art Nouveau style that was popularized by Louis Comfort Tiffany (1848–1933).

Portrait of Governor Paul Brigham

🏛 **Old Bennington Historic District**
📞 (802) 447-3311 or (800) 229-0252.
⛪ **First Congregational Church**
Monument Ave. 📞 (802) 447-1223.
🕐 11am Sun. ♿
🏛 **Bennington Battle Monument**
15 Monument Circle. 📞 (802) 447-0550. ◯ mid-April–late Oct: 9am–5pm daily. 📷 ♿
🏛 **Bennington Museum and Grandma Moses Gallery**
W Main St. 📞 (802) 447-1571. ◯ Jun–Oct: 9am–6pm daily; Nov–May: 9am–5pm daily. ● Thanksgiving, Dec 25, Jan 1. 📷 ♿ 🚻

Wilmington ⑯

🏠 *1,950.* ✈ *8 miles (13 km) NW in West Dover.* ℹ *21 W Main St (802) 464-8092 or (877) 887-6884.*

Wilmington is the largest village in the Mount Snow Valley, with several dozen restaurants and stores catering to the tourists who come to enjoy outdoor sports at the nearby mountain. Like so many of Vermont's small towns, its Main Street is lined with restored 18th- and 19th-century buildings, many listed on the National Register of Historic Places.

Standing 3,600 ft (1,100m) tall, **Mount Snow** is named after the original owner of the land, farmer Reuben Snow, although most visitors believe the name refers to the abundance of white stuff that during winter is the resort's *raison d'être*.

In the late 1990s, more than $35 million was spent on upgrading the ski center, which now has 134 trails, many of them wooded, spread over 765 acres (310 ha). Mount Snow was one of the first ski resorts in the US to provide facilities for snowboarders, with dedicated learning areas for beginners and facilities for advanced surfers. The center also opened the first mountain-bike school in the country. Outdoor summer attractions include 45 miles (72 km) of challenging bike trails (some are also ski runs), hiking

Verdant farmlands around the town of Wilmington

routes, an inline skate and skateboard park, and a climbing wall. The 18-hole **Mount Snow Golf Course** awaits those looking for a more sedate diversion.

🎿 **Mount Snow**
Rte 100. 📞 *(802) 464-3333 or (800) 245-7669.* 🕐 *year-round.* 🎿 ♿

⛳ **Mount Snow Golf Course**
Rte 100. 📞 *(802) 464-4254; call for tee times.* 🕐 *7am–dusk Mon–Fri, 6am–dusk Sat–Sun & public hols.* 🎿

Brattleboro ⑰

🏠 *12,500.* ✈ *20 miles (32 km) NE in Keene, NH.* 🚌 🚂 ℹ *180 Main St (802) 254-4565.* 🛍 *May–Oct: Wed & Sat.*

Perched on the banks of the Connecticut River on the New Hampshire border, Brattleboro is the first major town that northbound travelers encounter as they enter the state. Fort Dummer was originally established here in 1724, making it the state's first European settlement. For that reason, Brattleboro has adopted the slogan "Where Vermont Begins."

A bustling center of commerce and industry, the town is also a hub of tourism. As is the case with so many other Vermont towns, there is a historic district with many Colonial-era buildings of architectural interest. In the 1840s, after the Vermont Valley Railroad was laid to provide a vital link to the outside world, natural springs were discovered in the area and Brattleboro took on a new personality as a spa town where people came for "cures" and health treatments.

The former railroad station is now home to the **Brattleboro Museum and Art Center**, which contains a collection of organs manufactured by the entrepreneurial Estey family, whose instruments were exported around the world. The Brattleboro

Antique organ in the Brattleboro Museum and Art Center

Music Center, which is located on Walnut Street, stages an annual Bach Festival and a summer Jazz Festival.

🏛 **Brattleboro Museum and Art Center**
Main & Vernon Sts. 📞 *(802) 257-0124.* 🕐 *mid-May–mid-Dec: 12pm–6pm Tue–Sun.* 🎿 ♿

Grafton ⑱

🏠 *600.* ✈ *47 miles (76 km) N in Rutland.* ℹ *56 Townshend Rd (802) 843-2255.*

A thriving industrial center 200 years ago, Grafton suffered a steady decline until by the 1960s it was almost a ghost town. But in 1963 David Mathey (1890–1972), a wealthy investment banker, established a foundation with the mandate to restore historic structures and revitalize commercial life. Today the village is an architectural treasure trove of 19th-century buildings.

Two tourist attractions are also thriving commercial enterprises: the **Grafton Village Cheese Company**, with its hearty cheddars, and the Old Tavern at Grafton *(see p318)*, a hostelry since 1801. Over the years, the inn has hosted author Rudyard Kipling (1865–1936), and President Theodore Roosevelt (1858–1919).

Grafton mailbox

⬛ Grafton Village Cheese Company
533 Townshend Rd. **(** *(802) 843-2221 or (800) 472-3866.* ⬭ *year-round: 8am–4pm Mon–Fri, 10am–4pm Sat–Sun.* ⬛ ⬛

ENVIRONS: Eighteen miles (29 km) to the north lies the hamlet of Plymouth Notch. The tiny community was the birthplace of Calvin Coolidge (1872–1933), the 30th president of the US. The **Calvin Coolidge State Historic Site** encompasses an 1850s general store and post office once run by Coolidge's father, a cheese factory, a schoolhouse, and the Coolidge family home.

In Weston, 21 miles (34 km) west of Plymouth Notch, visitors will find the **Vermont Country Store**. The store is famous for its enormous and eclectic array of merchandise, personally selected by its owner, Lyman Orton. Not only are these items highly original – be they badger-hair shaving brushes or hand-blown glasses that sea captains once used to forecast the weather – they are also always of the highest quality.

▥ Calvin Coolidge State Historic Site
Rte 100A. **(** *(802) 672-3773.* ⬭ *late May–mid-Oct: 9:30am–5pm daily.* ▨ ⬛ ⬛

One of the many beautiful homes in the village of Woodstock

⬛ Vermont Country Store
Rte 100, Weston. **(** *(802) 824-3184.* ⬭ *year-round: 9am–5pm Mon–Sat.*

Woodstock ⓭

▨ *1,000.* ✈ *31 miles (50 km) W in Rutland.* ⬛ ⬛ *18 Central St (802) 457-3555, (888) 496-6378.*

EVEN IN VERMONT, a state where historic, picturesque villages are commonplace, Woodstock stands out. Founded in 1761, the town is an enclave of renovated brick and clapboard Georgian houses. The restoration of the town came about as a result of the generosity of philanthropists such as the Rockefeller family and railroad magnate Frederick Billings (1823–90). An early proponent of reforestation, Billings personally financed the planting of 10,000 trees throughout the village.

Billings Farm & Museum is still a working entity. The 1890 farmhouse has been restored and there are seasonal events open to the public, such as plowing competitions in the spring and apple-cider pressing in the fall. The museum also traces Vermont's agricultural past with old photographs and exhibits of harvesting implements, butter churns, and ice cutters.

The **Vermont Raptor Center** is a reserve where injured birds of prey are cared for until they can be returned to the wild. As well as operating conservation programs and summer day camps for children, the naturalists here give frequent presentations about the owls, falcons, and eagles that have come under their care.

▥ Billings Farm & Museum
River Rd. **(** *(802) 457-2355.* ⬭ *May–Oct: 10am–5pm daily; call for winter hours.* ▨ ⬛ ⬛
▧ Vermont Raptor Center
27023 Church Hill Rd. **(** *(802) 457-2779.* ⬭ *year-round: 10am–4pm daily.* ⬤ *Sun.* ▨ ⬛ ⬛

ENVIRONS: Six miles (10 km) east of town is the stunning Quechee Gorge. The best view of the chasm is on Route 4, which crosses the gorge via a steel bridge. A short hiking trail leads from the parking lot on the east side down to the Ottauquechee River below.

THE RISE OF CALVIN COOLIDGE

Calvin Coolidge was born in tiny Plymouth to parents who ran a general store. His humble upbringing endowed him with traits that would carry him to the presidency in the 1920s: honesty, frugality, and industry. Known as "Silent Cal," because he wasted little time on small talk, Coolidge guided the US to a period of economic prosperity before the onset of the Great Depression of 1929.

Boyhood home of Calvin Coolidge

NEW HAMPSHIRE

N EW HAMPSHIRITES ARE KNOWN *for their fiercely independent nature, born of necessity in the early 1600s when European settlers established outposts in this mountainous and heavily forested region. This natural beauty is still in evidence, in the soaring peaks of the White Mountains, the pristine water of Lake Winnipesaukee, and the small, but scenic coastline.*

There can be no better expression of New Hampshire's individualistic spirit than the state motto, "Live Free or Die," which is stamped on every state license plate. Six months before the July 4, 1776 signing of the Declaration of Independence, New Hampshire became the very first state to formally declare its separation from Great Britain. Ever cautious of centralized government, modern New Hampshirites proudly point out that they pay no personal income tax, nor is sales tax levied on most consumer goods in the state – a boon for tourists looking for bargains.

The landscape that helped forge the determined mindset of early settlers has changed little in the ensuing centuries. It is estimated that more than 90 percent of the state is undeveloped, with dense forest covering more than three-quarters of its land.

The northern part of the state is wild country, its woodlands bisected by the mighty Connecticut River and rippled by the tall peaks of the White Mountains *(see p265)*. Campers, climbers, and canoeists reign here. The hundreds of lakes and ponds that quilt central New Hampshire attract vacationers year-round looking to boat, fish, cross-country ski, and snowmobile. In the southwest, sightseers drive across rolling farmland that is punctuated by scenic villages and covered bridges. Even the industrial heartland of the Merrimack Valley is predominantly rural. A mere 15-minute drive from the downtown cores of the state's major commercial centers of Concord *(see pp258–9)* and Manchester *(see p258)* will transport travelers to the tranquility of dairy farms or quiet country roads.

Early October view of the Presidential Range in the White Mountains

◁ Canterbury Shaker Village, founded in 1792

Exploring New Hampshire

N EW HAMPSHIRE'S COMPACT BORDERS make it ideal
for sightseeing. Some attractions can be
enjoyed on foot, as with the spectacular board-
walked chasm of Franconia Notch *(see pp272–3)*,
or by car, as with a breathtaking fall-foliage tour
along the Kancamagus Highway *(see p270)*. The
remains of colonial battlements, the Shaker villages
at Enfield *(see p262)* and Canterbury *(see pp260–
61)*, and the historic homes of poets, politicians,
and presidents are sprinkled throughout the state.
Called the Granite State for its extensive granite
formations and quarries, New Hampshire's rough
edges are softened somewhat in its many fine museums. The Currier Gallery of Art *(see p258)* is one
such establishment, giving visitors the chance to
view work by some of the world's great masters.

Bridge over the Flume Gorge in
Franconia Notch State Park

GETTING AROUND

Interstates 93 and 89 are the largest and most
popular north-south routes in the state, with
numerous smaller roads branching off to more
remote areas. Drivers should be aware of two New
Hampshire realities: heavier traffic during peak
fall-foliage season, especially on the weekends;
and moose crossings. While moose sightings are
thrilling, collisions with the huge animals can be
extremely dangerous. Travelers should drive with
caution at all times. The Amtrak "Northeastern"
service stops in Exeter, Durham, and Dover.
Travelers may also take Amtrak to White River
Junction, Vermont, or to Boston and link up with a
bus line from there. Commercial bus lines servicing
the area include C&J Transport, Concord
Trailways, and Greyhound bus lines *(see p375)*.
The state's largest airport is found in the south in
Manchester *(see p258)*, although Maine's Portland
International Airport is a good jumping-off point
for northeastern New Hampshire.

KEY

━━ Interstate

━━ Major road

━━ Minor road

━━ Scenic route

☆ Viewpoint

*WHITE
MOUNTAIN
NATIONAL
FOREST*

15 HANOVER   *Newfou
Lo*

13

*ENFIELD
SHAKER
MUSEUM*

*SAINT-GAUDENS
NAT. HISTORIC SITE*

14

112

120

4

12 *NE
LONDO*

103

*LAKE SUNAPEE
REGION* **10**

☆

HENNIK

Connecticut River

9

KEENE
7

202

*MONADNOCK
STATE PARK* ☆ **5**

119 *RHODODENDRON*
6 *STATE PARK*

101

Lengthy Cornish-Windsor Bridge outside Cornish

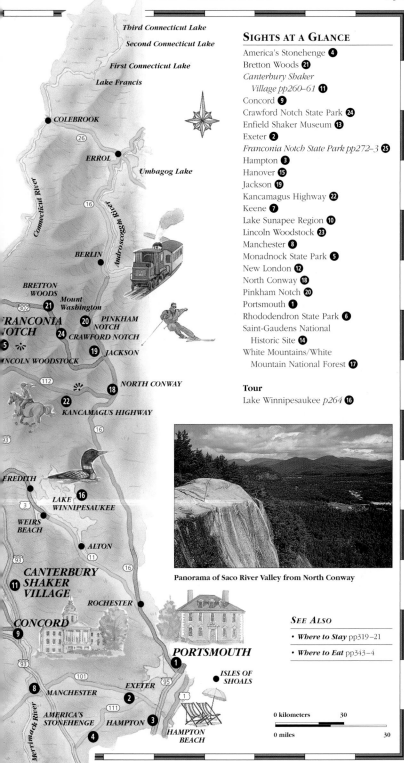

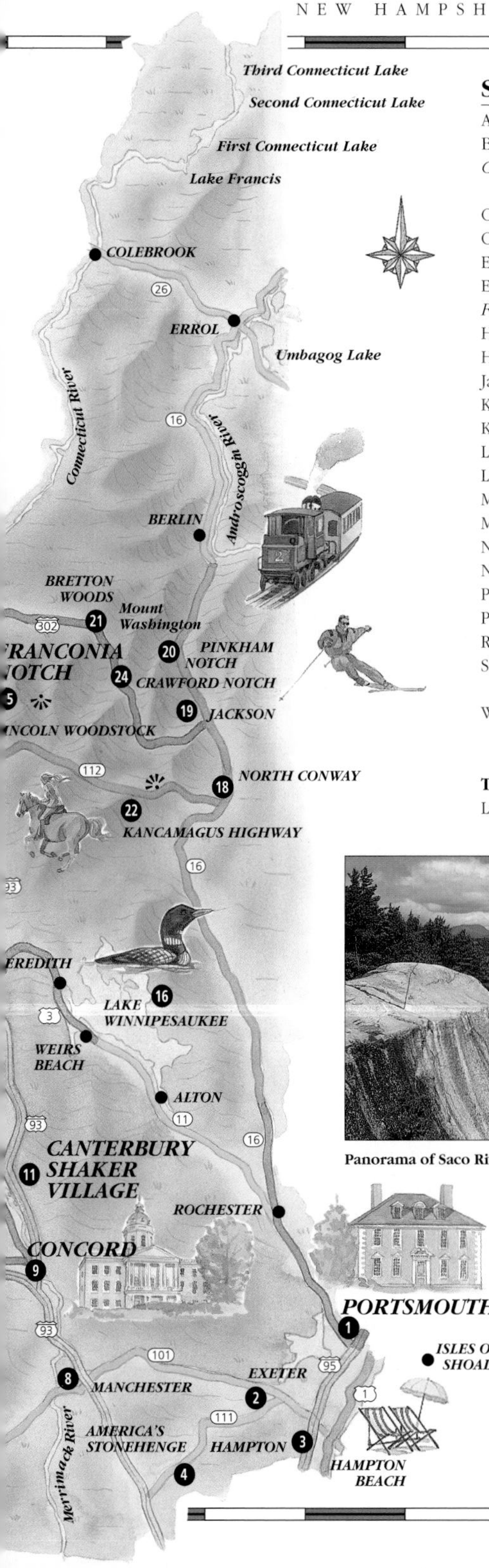
Third Connecticut Lake
Second Connecticut Lake
First Connecticut Lake
Lake Francis
COLEBROOK
26
ERROL
Umbagog Lake
Connecticut River
16
Androscoggin River
BERLIN
BRETTON WOODS
302
21
Mount Washington
FRANCONIA NOTCH
20
PINKHAM NOTCH
24
CRAWFORD NOTCH
5
19
JACKSON
LINCOLN WOODSTOCK
112
18
NORTH CONWAY
22
KANCAMAGUS HIGHWAY
16
93
MEREDITH
16
LAKE WINNIPESAUKEE
3
WEIRS BEACH
ALTON
11
93
16
11
CANTERBURY SHAKER VILLAGE
ROCHESTER
CONCORD
9
PORTSMOUTH
1
93
101
ISLES OF SHOALS
95
EXETER
8
MANCHESTER
2
1
111
Merrimack River
AMERICA'S STONEHENGE
HAMPTON
3
4
HAMPTON BEACH

Sights at a Glance

America's Stonehenge 4
Bretton Woods 21
Canterbury Shaker Village pp260–61 11
Concord 9
Crawford Notch State Park 24
Enfield Shaker Museum 13
Exeter 2
Franconia Notch State Park pp272–3 25
Hampton 3
Hanover 15
Jackson 19
Kancamagus Highway 22
Keene 7
Lake Sunapee Region 10
Lincoln Woodstock 23
Manchester 8
Monadnock State Park 5
New London 12
North Conway 18
Pinkham Notch 20
Portsmouth 1
Rhododendron State Park 6
Saint-Gaudens National Historic Site 14
White Mountains/White Mountain National Forest 17

Tour

Lake Winnipesaukee *p264* 16

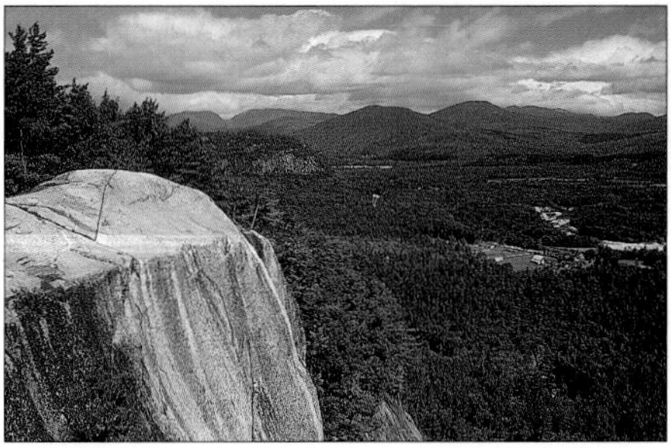

Panorama of Saco River Valley from North Conway

See Also

• ***Where to Stay*** pp319–21

• ***Where to Eat*** pp343–4

0 kilometers 30

0 miles 30

Portsmouth ❶

WHEN SETTLERS ESTABLISHED a colony here in 1623, they called it Strawbery Banke *(see pp254–5)* in honor of the berries blanketing the banks of the Piscataqua River. In 1653 the name was changed to Portsmouth, a reflection of the town's reputation as a hub of maritime commerce. First a fishing port, the town enjoyed prosperity in the 18th century as a link in the trade route between Great Britain and the West Indies. During the years leading up to the American Revolution, the town was a hotbed of revolutionary fervor and the place where colonial naval hero John Paul Jones (1747–92) built his warship, the *Ranger.*

Favorite with tourists: Portsmouth's Market Street

Exploring Portsmouth

Girded by the Piscataqua River and the North and South Mill ponds, compact Portsmouth is easily explored on foot. The town's past permeates the downtown core, especially along busy Market Street. Historic buildings, some constructed in the 19th-century by wealthy sea captains, have been restored and turned into museums, boutiques, and restaurants. The city also has a number of brew pubs and microbreweries that produce local ales. More than 70 historic sites, including houses and gardens, can be found along the Portsmouth Harbour Trail, a walking tour of the Historic District.

Beautiful exterior of Moffat-Ladd House in Portsmouth

🏠 Governor John Langdon House

143 Pleasant St. [(603)-436-3205.
◯ Jun–mid-Oct: 11am–5pm Fri–Sun. ● Labor Day. 🖾 🗹 ♿
The son of a farmer of modest means, John Langdon (1741–1819) became one of Portsmouth's most prominent citizens. Langdon enjoyed great prosperity as a ship captain, merchant, and shipbuilder before becoming the governor of New Hampshire and a US senator. In 1784 he built this imposing Georgian mansion. The house is known for its ornate Rococo embellishments. The grounds feature a grape arbor and a large rose garden.

🏠 Moffatt-Ladd House

154 Market St. [(603) 436-8221.
◯ mid-Jun–mid-Oct: 11am–4pm Mon–Sat, 1–5pm Sun. 🖾 🗹 ♿
One of Portsmouth's first three-story homes, this elegant 1763 mansion was built for wealthy maritime trader and sea captain John Moffatt. The house's boxy design was a precursor to the Federal style of architecture that would later become popular

throughout the country. The house, located on the Portsmouth Harbour Trail, is graced by a grand entrance hall, a series of family portraits, and period furnishings.

🏠 Wentworth-Gardner House

50 Mechanic St. [(603) 436-4406.
◯ mid-Jun–mid-Oct: 1pm–4pm Tue–Sun. ● public hols. 🖾 ♿
Also located on the Portsmouth Harbour Trail, this 1760 house is considered to be one of the best examples of Georgian architecture in the country. The house's beautiful exterior has rows of multi-paned windows, symmetrical chimneys, and a pillared entrance. The interior has 11 fireplaces, hand-painted wallpaper, and graceful carvings that took artisans a year to complete.

TO CHAMBER OF COMMERCE
USS ALBACORE
ISLES OF SHOALS
STEAMSHIP CO.

Piscataqua River

John Paul Jones

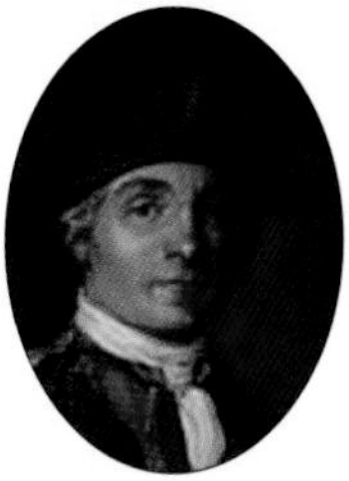

Born in Scotland, John Paul Jones (1747–92) went to sea as a cabin boy when he was only 12 years old. He worked his way up to being the first mate on a slave ship, then later the commander of a merchant vessel in Tobago. A hard taskmaster, Jones escaped to America before he was to go on trial for the deaths of several sailors he had punished. Regarded as an outlaw by the British, Jones went on to become an illustrious naval commander for the US. During the American Revolution, Jones led a series of daring raids up and down the British coast for which he was awarded a gold medal by Congress.

USS *Albacore*

Albacore Park, 600 Market St. ☎ *(603) 436-3680.* 🕐 *May–Oct: 9:30am–5:30pm daily; Nov–Apr: 9:30am–4pm Thu–Mon.* 🎟

This sleek submarine was the fastest underwater vessel of its type when it was launched from the Portsmouth Naval Shipyard in 1953. It gives visitors access to the cramped quarters of submariners and an idea of what life was like for the submarine's 55 crew members. Exhibits in the visitor center trace the vessel's history.

🏛 Children's Museum of Portsmouth

280 Marcy St. ☎ *(603) 436-3853.* 🕐 *mid-Jun–Sep: 10am–5pm Mon–Sat, 1–5pm Sun; Oct–mid-Jun: 10am–5pm Tue–Sat, 1–5pm Sun.* 🎟 ♿

This museum features a series of interactive exhibits where kids can command a submarine or fly in the replica of a space shuttle. Elsewhere aspiring paleontologists are invited to don lab coats and help with the excavation of dinosaur fossils, while budding musicians can play instruments from around the world.

Visitors' Checklist

👥 *26,000.* 🚌 *10 Ladd St.* ✈ *36 Airline Ave.* ℹ *500 Market St or Market Sq (603) 436-1118.* 🚍 *mid-May–Oct: 8:30am–1pm.* 🎉 *Market Square Day (Jun), Prescott Park Arts Festival (Jul–Aug daily).* [W] *www.portsmouthchamber.org*

Water Country

Rte 1 S of Portsmouth. ☎ *(603) 427-1111.* 🕐 *Jun–Labor Day: call for hours.* 🎟 🍴

Eighteen water rides, a huge wave pool, a pirate ship, and a man-made lagoon await visitors to New England's largest water park. Smaller children can enjoy the slides and fountains in designated areas, while the more adventurous thrill-seekers can careen down looping water slides.

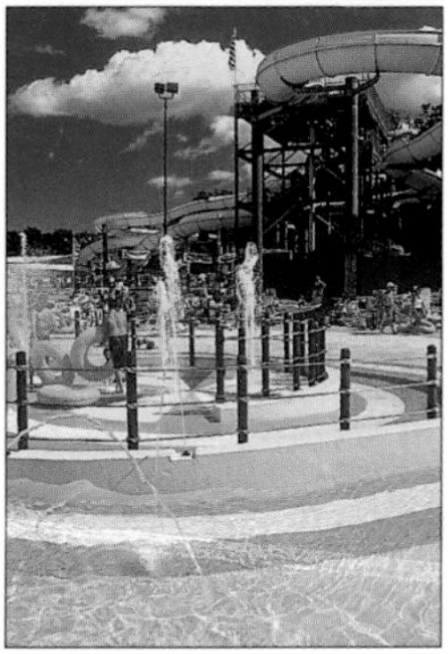

Popular destination on summer days: Water Country

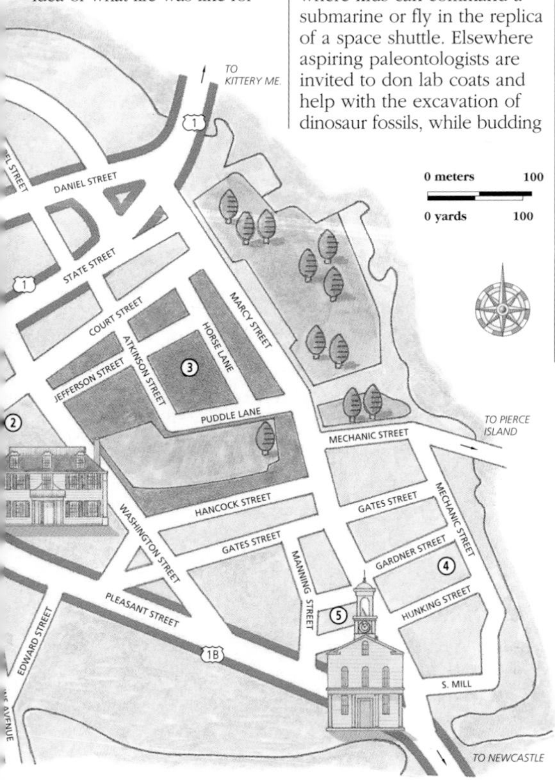

TO KITTERY ME.
1
DANIEL STREET
STATE STREET
1
COURT STREET
ATKINSON STREET
HORSE LANE
MARCY STREET
JEFFERSON STREET
3
2
PUDDLE LANE
MECHANIC STREET
TO PIERCE ISLAND
HANCOCK STREET
WASHINGTON STREET
GATES STREET
GATES STREET
MECHANIC STREET
GARDNER STREET
4
MANNING STREET
5
HUNKING STREET
PLEASANT STREET
EDWARD STREET
1B
S. MILL
TO NEWCASTLE
0 meters 100
0 yards 100

Portsmouth City Center

Children's Museum of Portsmouth (5)
Gov. John Langdon House (2)
Moffat-Ladd House (1)
Strawbery Banke Museum (3)
Wentworth-Gardner House (4)

Key

▒	Street-by-Street map *see pp254–5*
═	Highway
ℹ	Tourist information
[P]	Parking

Street-by-Street: Strawbery Banke

Aldrich Garden bloom

THIS OUTDOOR MUSEUM near the waterfront is located on the very spot on which Portsmouth was founded. Tracing the history of the town, this 10-acre (4-ha) site contains more than 40 buildings that depict life from 1695 to 1955. Those houses open to the public are furnished in period style and contain interesting collections of decorative arts, ceramics, and assorted artifacts. Many of the buildings are set amid gardens cultivated according to their eras, from early pioneer herb gardens to formal Victorian flower beds.

Traditional transport
Visitors can tour Strawbery Banke on authentic horse-drawn carriages.

Family Activity Center is housed in an 1821 building and is now used for youth and family programs.

Aldrich Garden
This Colonial Revival garden is planted with flowers mentioned in the poetry of Portsmouth native Thomas Bailey Aldrich (1836–1907).

COURT STREET

ATKINSON STREET

JEFFERSON STREET

COURT STREET

WHIDDEN PLACE

WASHINGTON STREET

0 meters 50

0 yards 50

STAR SIGHTS
★ Chase House
★ Jones House
★ Sherburne House

★ **Chase House**
Built c.1762, this elegant home is furnished with sumptuous pieces from several periods.

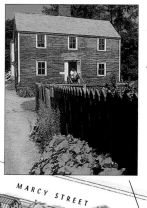

Jackson House
Displays in this mid-18th-century home feature the various trends of interior decor that have come and gone over the last 160 years.

Visitors' Checklist

Marcy St. (603) 433-1100.
May–Oct: 10am–5pm Mon–Sat, noon–5pm Sun; Nov–Apr: 10am–2pm Thu–Sat, noon–2pm Sun. *limited.*
www.strawberybanke.org

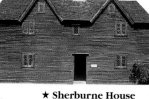

★ Sherburne House
Built in 1695, the home now serves as an exhibit on 17th-century house design and construction.

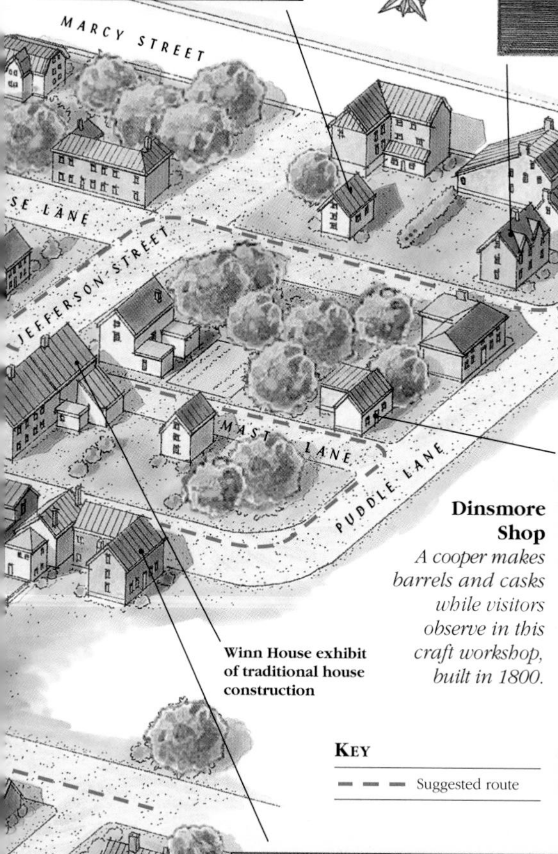

MARCY STREET
SE LANE
JEFFERSON STREET
MAST LANE
PUDDLE LANE
WASHINGTON STREET

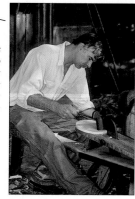

Dinsmore Shop
A cooper makes barrels and casks while visitors observe in this craft workshop, built in 1800.

Winn House exhibit of traditional house construction

Key

– – – Suggested route

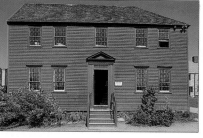

★ Jones House
Housed in a 1790 structure, the Exhibit and Archaeology Center displays a variety of artifacts excavated on the site.

Exeter ❷

🏃 14,500. ✈ 15 miles (24 km)
E in Portsmouth. ℹ 120 Water St
(603) 772-2411.

THE QUIET LITTLE town of
Exeter southwest of
Portsmouth was much less
tranquil during the century
and a half leading up to
the American Revolution
(1775–83). The community
sprang up around the falls
linking the freshwater Exeter
River and the salty Squamscott
River. It was founded in 1638
by the Reverend John
Wheelwright (1592–1679),
an outspoken cleric who
was thrown out of the
Massachusetts colony for
his radical views.

During the turbulent years
leading up to American
Independence, outraged
townspeople openly defied
the British government. They
drove off officials who had
been dispatched to cut down
trees for the British Navy,
burned their leaders in effigy,
and finally declared independence from Britain, setting a
precedent for the
rest of the colonies.

Dominating the
center of town,
Phillips Exeter
Academy stands as
one of the country's
most prestigious
preparatory schools.
The complex of
more than 100 ivy-
clad brick buildings
fronted by manicured lawns
was founded in 1781.

Other points of interest
include the **Gilman Garrison**

**Exeter farmers
market sign**

House, a fortified log
building dating back to the
late-17th century, and the
**American Independence
Museum,** which houses
an original copy of the
Declaration of Independence
as well as a draft of the
American Constitution.

🎏 **Gilman Garrison House**
12 Water St. 📞 (603) 436-3205.
🕐 Jun–mid-Oct: 11am–5pm
Sat–Sun. 🎟 🗹 obligatory. ♿
🏛 **American Independence
Museum**
1 Governors Lane. 📞 (603) 772-2622.
🕐 May–Oct: 10am–4pm Wed–Sat,
11–4pm Sun. 🎟 🗹 obligatory. 🅿 🚫

Hampton ❸

🏃 15,000. ✈ 12 miles (19 km)
N in Portsmouth. ℹ 1 Park Ave
(603) 926-8718.

ONE OF NEW HAMPSHIRE'S
oldest towns, Hampton
is situated at the geographic
center of the many state
parks and public beaches
that line Highway 1A, the
coast road. Public recreation
areas stretch from
Seabrook Beach, a
sandy shore dotted
with dunes, to the
rugged shoreline of
**Odiorne Point State
Park** in Rye to the
north. The park has
biking trails, tidal
pools, and a board-
walk spanning a salt-
water marsh. The
park's Science Center also
runs interpretive nature programs that are especially
appealing to young visitors.

**Exterior of the American
Independence Museum in Exeter**

Ten miles (6 km) to the south
of the factory outlet shopping
mecca of North Hampton,
travelers will come upon the
popular **Hampton Beach**.
This miniature version of
Atlantic City (without the
gambling) comes complete
with a venue that hosts big-
name entertainers and an old-
fashioned boardwalk lined
with video arcades, ice-cream
shops, and stalls selling
T-shirts and tacky souvenirs.
Open year-round, Hampton
Beach is busiest during hot
summer months, when
vacationers come to enjoy
the miles of clean, golden
beaches, including a separate
area designated for surfers.
Swimmers and jet skiers test
the waters, para-sailers soar
overhead, and deep-sea
fishing and whale-watching
charter boats are available
from Hampton Harbor.
Hampton Beach is not the
place for people looking for
quiet, but it is geared toward
family fun, with game
arcades, water slides, magic
shows, and a series of free
concerts and fireworks.

Away from the casino and busy boardwalk, the blue skies and tranquil surf of Hampton Beach

**⚔ Odiorne Point
State Park**
Rte 1A, Rye Beach. ☎ *(603) 436-
7406.* **Science Center** ◯ *year-
round: 10am–5pm daily.* ● *Jan 1,
Thanksgiving, & Dec 25.* 📷 ♿
Park ◯ *year-round: 8am–dusk.* 📷
🚇 Hampton Beach
☎ *(800) 438-2826 or
(603) 926-8718.*

America's
Stonehenge ❹

Haverhill Rd, North Salem. ☎ *(603)
893-8300.* ◯ *Feb–mid-Jun:
9am–5pm daily; mid-Jun–Aug: 9am–
6pm daily; Sep–Oct: 9am–5pm daily;
Nov–Jan: 9am–4pm daily.* 📷

Aᴌᴛʜᴏᴜɢʜ ɴᴏᴛ ɴᴇᴀʀʟʏ as
imposing as its British
namesake, this is an intrigu-
ing place nonetheless.
Believed to be one of the
oldest man-made complexes
this side of the Atlantic, the
30-acre (12-ha) grounds of
America's Stonehenge are
scattered with standing
stones, walls, and stone
chambers. Archeologists,
historians, and astronomers
have argued for decades
about the origins of the site,
with credit going to everyone
from ancient Greeks to way-
ward aliens. Today one of the
most popular theories has
Native American tribes constructing this megalithic complex as a giant calendar to
measure the movements of
the sun and the moon.
Excavations have turned up a
wealth of ancient remains,
including stone pottery, tools,
and petroglyphs that have
been carbon-dated to
between 3,000 and 4,000
years old. One of the more
gruesome parts of the site is
the five-ton (4.5-
tonne) Sacrificial
Table, carved
with grooves that
researchers believe
may have been
troughs for collect-
ing the blood of
victims. Special
events are held at
the site during the
spring and fall
equinox and at
the winter and
summer solstice.

Mount Monadnock, popular with climbers and hikers

Monadnock
State Park ❺

Off Rte 124, W of Jaffrey. ☎ *(603)
532-8862.* ◯ *year-round.* 📷 ⬛ ✖

Sᴛᴀɴᴅɪɴɢ sᴏᴍᴇ 3,165 ft
(965 m) high, Mount
Monadnock has two claims to
fame. It is said to be one of
the most climbed mountains
in the world (it is not unusual
to find several hundred hikers
milling around its peak) and it
has spawned a term used in
geology. A "monadnock" is an
isolated hill or mountain of
resistant rock rising above a
plain that has been created
by glacial activity.
The mountain's popularity
has a lot to do with its campsites, scenic picnic areas, and
numerous hiking trails. Within
the 5,000-acre (2,000-ha) park,
there are 40 miles (64 km) of
trails, many of which lead to
the summit. The climb to the
peak of the metamorphic
schist pinnacle takes more
than three hours, but on clear
days intrepid hikers are
rewarded with gorgeous
views of all six New England
states. Markers along the trails
have been erected in memory
of such men of letters as
Ralph Waldo Emerson

(1803–82) and Henry David
Thoreau (1817–62), both of
whom climbed to the peak.
The visitor's center gives an
overview of the hiking trails,
the history of the mountain,
and information about the
local flora and fauna. The
campsites are open year-
round and in the winter
months the trails are popular
with cross-country skiers.

Rhododendron
State Park ❻

Off Rte 119, W of Fitzwilliam. ☎
(603) 239-8153. ◯ *year-round:
dawn–dusk daily.* 📷 ♿ *partial.*

Nᴇᴡ ᴇɴɢʟᴀɴᴅ's ʟᴀʀɢᴇsᴛ
grove of wild rhododen-
drons bursts into a celebration
of pink and white in June
through mid-July. The 450-
acre (180-ha) park has more
than 16 acres (6 ha) of giant
rhododendron bushes.
Walking through the rhododendrons, some of which
grow to more than 20 ft (6 m)
high, is a feast for the senses
in summer, but there are flo-
ral highlights in other seasons
as well. In the spring the
woodland park is carpeted
with trilliums. By May the
apple trees are heavy with
blossoms. During
summer, visitors
will find flowering
mountain laurel and
wildflowers such as
jack-in-the-pulpit
and delicate pink
lady slippers. The
park is equipped
with picnic areas
and hiking trails that
offer spectacular
views of Mount
Monadnock and the
surrounding peaks.

Ancient ruins of America's Stonehenge

Keene ❼

🏚 *25,350.* ✈ *58 miles (93 km) E in Manchester.* 🚌 🛈 *48 Central Sq (603) 352-1303.*

KEENE IS THE LARGEST town in southern New Hampshire's Monadnock region. The nation's first glass-blowing factory was founded in nearby Temple in 1780, and soon after Keene became one of the region's hotbeds of arts and crafts. By the 19th century the town was famous for the production of high-quality glass and pottery and for its thriving wool mill. The **Horatio Colony Museum** is the former home of a descendant of the mill-owning family. Its period furnishings give a good idea of upper-class life in the mid-1800s. Today the focus of Keene's thriving cultural life is Keene State College, located on what is reputed to be the widest Main Street in the world. The college has several theaters and art studios where events are staged throughout the year.

🏛 **Horatio Colony Museum**
199 Main St. 📞 *(603) 352-0460.* ⭘ *May–mid-Oct: 11am–4pm Wed–Sun.* 📷 *obligatory.*

ENVIRONS: Half a dozen covered bridges *(see p263)* lie within a 10-mile (16-km) radius of Keene, giving the region the nickname "Currier and Ives country." Road markers direct drivers to each span. These "kissing bridges," where young couples would steal secret embraces as they rode their buggy through them, have long been favorite subjects of photographers.

W. Swanzey Thompson Covered Bridge near Keene

Manchester ❽

🏚 *105,250.* ✈ *1 Airport Rd.* 🚌 🛈 *889 Elm St (603) 666-6600.* 💈 *(603) 622-7531.*

IN 1805 A MODEST MILL was built on the east bank of the Merrimack River. Fueled by waterpower, the Amoskeag Mill continued to expand until by the beginning of the 20th century it claimed the title as the largest textile mill in the world. At its peak, the operation employed some 17,000 people and its complex of brick buildings stretched for more than one mile (1.5 km). Today the structures that once held workers and heavy machinery are used for restaurants, college classrooms, and even residential housing.

This former industrial center is now known for the **Currier Gallery of Art**, New Hampshire's premier art museum. The museum's diverse collection of over 12,000 items includes works by such European masters as John Constable (1776–1837), Claude Monet (1840–1926), and Henri Matisse (1869–1954).

The museum's west wing houses an extensive collection of the works of 20th-century American painters such as Andrew Wyeth (b.1917) and Georgia O'Keeffe (1887–1986), famous for her surrealistic renditions of New Mexico's landscapes. The decorative arts section displays a large selection of period furniture, silverware, and 18th- and 19th-century glassware, including a collection of rare glass paperweights from France.

The museum's largest piece is the nearby Zimmerman House. The single-story home was built in 1950 by pioneering American architect Frank Lloyd Wright (1867–1959). The simple, elegant lines of its exterior are typical of Wright's Usonian style of utilitarian design. Shuttles take visitors from the museum to the house, and guided tours (by advance reservation) of its interior highlight textiles and furniture designed by Wright.

🏛 **Currier Gallery of Art**
201 Myrtle Way. 📞 *(603) 669-6144.* ⭘ *year-round: 11am–5pm Mon, Wed, Fri, Sun, 11am–8pm Thu, 10am–5pm Sat.* 🎫 🚫 ♿ 🏪 🖥 🚫

Concord ❾

🏚 *37,500.* ✈ *25 miles (49 km) S in Manchester.* 🚌 🛈 *40 Commercial St (603) 224-2508.*

NEW HAMPSHIRE'S CAPITAL is a quiet little town, but thanks to its prominent political position, it has been associated with a number of important historical figures. Mary Baker Eddy (1821–1910),

Painting in the Currier Gallery of Art in Manchester

CONCORD COACHES

In 1827 Concord-based wheelwright Lewis Downing and coach builder J. Stephens Abbot built the first Concord Coach, designed to withstand the unforgiving trails of the undeveloped West. The 1-ton (1-tonne) stagecoaches were, in their own way, as revolutionary as the Internet is today because they helped facilitate communications across the vast emerging hinterland. Wells Fargo, the famous transportation company, relied heavily on the coaches during the California Gold Rush (1848–55) to carry mail and passengers on parts of the route between New York City and San Francisco.

founder of the Christian Science Church, spent much of her life here. The **Pierce Manse** was the one-time home of Franklin Pierce (1804–69), the 14th president of the US.

The 1819 **State House**, built from New Hampshire granite and Vermont marble, is one of the oldest in America. Inside the building are several hundred paintings of the state's better known residents and political figures. In its heyday, the Eagle Hotel on Main Street, now an office building, hosted the likes of presidents Andrew Jackson and Benjamin Harrison, aviator Charles Lindbergh, and former first lady Eleanor Roosevelt.

Concord schoolteacher Christa McAuliffe (1948–86) unfortunately gained her fame through tragedy. On January 28, 1986, McAuliffe boarded the *Challenger* space shuttle as the first civilian to be launched into space by NASA. Seventy-three seconds after the lift-off, with her husband and children watching from the ground, the shuttle exploded

into a fireball and crashed, killing McAuliffe and her six fellow astronauts.

McAuliffe's memory lives on in the form of **The Christa McAuliffe Planetarium**. Capped by a giant glass pyramid, this futuristic museum was opened on June 21, 1991, to teach people about astronomy and the exploration of space. Visitors can enjoy such rotating multimedia shows as "Through the Eyes of Hubble" – the universe as seen through the powerful telescope used by NASA – and "Destination Mars."

THE CHRISTA McAULIFFE PLANETARIUM

Entrance to Christa McAuliffe Planetarium

🚌 **Pierce Manse**
14 Horseshoe Lane. 📞 *(603) 225-4555.* ☐ *mid-Jun–mid-Sep: 11am–3pm Mon–Fri.* 🖼 🅿 ♿

🚌 **State House**
107 N Main St. 📞 *(603) 271-2154.*
Visitor center ☐ *year-round: 8am–4:30pm Mon–Fri.* ♿ ☐

🏛 **The Christa McAuliffe Planetarium**
3 Institute Dr. 📞 *(603) 271-7827.*
☐ *year-round: 10am–2pm Mon–Wed, 10am–5pm Thu–Sat, 12pm–5pm Sun. Call for show times.* 🖼 ♿ ☐ ⬤ *week after Labor Day.*

Lake Sunapee Region ❿

ℹ *143 Main St, New London (603) 526-6575 or (877) 526-6575.*

THIS SCENIC REGION, dominated by 2,743-ft-(835-m-) high Mount Sunapee and the 10-mile-(16-km-) long lake at its feet, is a major drawing card for outdoor enthusiasts, particularly boaters and skiers. Many locals have vacation and weekend homes here, and an increasing number of retirees are also moving to the region, attracted not only by the scenery but also by the activity-oriented lifestyle.

Lake Sunapee (its name is said to be derived from the Penacook Indian words for "wild goose water") has been attracting visitors for well over a century. In the mid-1800s, trains and steamships used to transport tourists to hotels that rimmed the lake. The steamships have long since gone, but vacationers can rent canoes, picnic on the beach, or take a narrated trip on a sightseeing boat. **Mount Sunapee State Park**'s namesake peak attracts hikers and climbers during the summer months and skiers during the winter. The Mount Sunapee ski area in the park is the largest ski area between Boston and the White Mountains.

🎿 **Mount Sunapee State Park**
Rte 103. 📞 *(603) 763-2356.*
☐ *year-round.* ♿

Sightseeing boat on Lake Sunapee

Canterbury Shaker Village ⑪

FOUNDED IN 1792, THIS VILLAGE was occupied for 200 years, making it one of the longest-lasting communities of the religious group in the country. Shakers also lived in nearby Enfield *(see pp262)*. Their belief in strict separation from the rest of the world and in celibacy eventually led to their demise. The last member of this colony died in 1992, and now 25 of the original buildings are open to the public. Millponds, nature trails, and traditional gardens punctuate the 690-acre (280-ha) site. Skilled artisans re-create Shaker crafts, known for their workmanship.

Canterbury Shaker Village
The village is dominated by the central Dwelling House (below).

The belfry
is a distinctive shape and contains a bell made by Revolutionary War hero Paul Revere.

Shaker Brooms
The common flat broom was invented in 1798 by Shaker Brother Theodore Bates. Shakers believed that cleanliness mirrored spiritual purity.

THE CREAMERY RESTAURANT

Creamery Restaurant
This 1905 creamery serves traditional Shaker fare for lunch and weekend candlelit dinners.

Brethren's Retiring Room

STAR FEATURES

★ **Dining Room**

★ **Old Library and Museum**

★ **Sisters' Retiring Room**

★ **Dining Room**
This area once held as many as 60 Shakers per sitting.

KEY

☐ **Illustrated building**

1 Trustees' Office
2 The Infirmary
3 Meeting House
4 Dwelling House
5 Sisters' Shop
6 Carriage House
7 The Creamery
8 Carpenter Shop
9 Fire House/Power House
10 Laundry
11 Horse Barn
12 School House
13 Syrup Shop

VISITORS' CHECKLIST

288 Shaker Rd, Canterbury. **C**
*(603) 783-9511 or (866) 783-
9511.* ☐ *May–Oct: 10am–5pm
daily; Apr, Nov–Dec: 10am–4pm
Sat & Sun.* 🖼 ✓ 🍴 🛒 ♿
W *www.shakers.org.*

Dormer rooms were used
for summer sleeping and as
clothes cupboards.

Popular Stop
*Historic buildings, a
restaurant, and a gift
shop make Canterbury a
favorite tourist destination.*

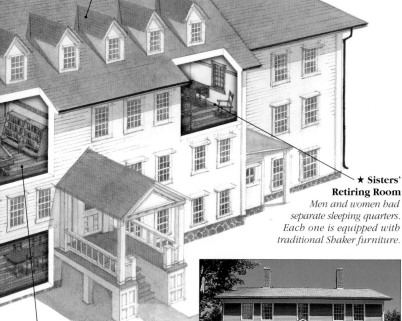

★ **Sisters'
Retiring Room**
*Men and women had
separate sleeping quarters.
Each one is equipped with
traditional Shaker furniture.*

★ **Old Library and Museum**
*The library contains 1,500
Shaker books and documents
and a museum.*

The Infirmary
*Built in 1811, this building served as the
hospital, pharmacy, dental office, and morgue.*

New London ⑫

🏃 3,700. ✈ 28 miles (45 km) NW in Lebanon. 🚌 🚉 *Main St (603) 526-6575 or (877) 526-6575.*

NEW LONDON'S PERCH atop a crest gives it an enviable view of the surrounding forests during the fall foliage season. The bucolic setting also serves as a wonderful backdrop for the town's rich collection of colonial and early 19th-century buildings. Of these, the architectural centerpiece is **Colby-Sawyer College**, an undergraduate liberal arts school founded in 1837. The college organizes numerous cultural programs, including plays, lectures, films, concerts, and art exhibitions. More cultural fun can be had farther down the street at the **New London Barn Playhouse**. Housed in a refurbished 1820s barn, the theater stages popular plays and musicals during the summer months.

🏛 **Colby-Sawyer College**
Main St. 📞 *(603) 526-2010.* ○ *year-round: 9am–5pm Mon–Fri.*
🚻 🅿 🚹
🎭 **New London Barn Playhouse**
290 Main St. 📞 *(603) 526-4631 or (603) 526-6710.* ○ *mid-Jun–Sep: call for hours.* 🅿

Enfield Shaker Museum ⑬

Rte 4A, Enfield. 📞 *(603) 632-4346.* ○ *late May–Oct: 10am–5pm daily; Nov–late Dec: 4pm–7pm Fri, 10am–4pm Sat, noon–4pm Sun; Jan–late May: 10am–4pm Sat, noon–4pm Sun.* 🅿
🚻 🅿 🚹

FACING RELIGIOUS persecution in Britain in the mid-18th century, several groups of Shakers, a sect that broke away from the Quakers, fled to North America under the spiritual guidance of Mother Ann Lee (1736–84). The Shaker village at Enfield was founded in 1793, one of 18 such communities in the US.
Between the founding of Enfield and the 1920s, the Shakers constructed more than 200 buildings, of which

Colby-Sawyer College in New London

13 remain. And while they farmed more than 3,000 acres (1,200 ha) of land, property was under the ownership of the community, not individuals. Members were celibate and they were strict pacifists, devoting their "hands to work and hearts to God." At one time the Enfield Shakers numbered over 300, but, as in similar communities, their numbers gradually dwindled. In 1923 the last 10 members moved to the Canterbury Shaker Village (*see pp260–61*) north of Concord. The last Canterbury Shaker died as recently as 1992 at the age of 96.
The exhibits at the museum illustrate how the Shakers lived and worked. Visitors will come across fine examples of Shaker ingenuity, including one of their many inventions: sulfur matches. The buildings are filled with the simple but practical wooden furniture for which the Shakers, who were consummate craftspeople, were famous. The 160-year-

old Great Stone Dwelling, the largest such structure ever built by these industrious people, has been turned into a 24-room inn.

Saint-Gaudens National Historic Site ⑭

Rte 12A N of Cornish-Windsor Bridge. 📞 *(603) 675-2175.* ○ *late May–Oct: 9am–4:30pm daily.* 🅿 🅿 🚹

THIS NATIONAL HISTORIC SITE celebrates the life of Augustus Saint-Gaudens (1848–1907), the preeminent US sculptor of his time. When Saint-Gaudens moved to Cornish in 1885, it marked the beginning of the town's evolution into an art colony. Artists, writers, and musicians alike were attracted to the town by the talent of Saint-Gaudens, whose family had emigrated to the US from Ireland when he was just a baby. Something of a world traveler, Saint-Gaudens became an apprentice cameo cutter in New York and later studied at the École des Beaux-Arts in Paris. He also won several commissions in Rome. By the time that he returned to New York, his reputation as a brilliant sculptor had been well established. His work, usually of heroic

Saint-Gaudens' angel

Great Stone Dwelling in the Enfield Shaker Museum

subject matter, can be found throughout the country. New England is home to many Saint-Gaudens masterpieces, including Boston's Shaw Memorial (1897).

Eventually Saint-Gaudens grew tired of the big-city pace, buying an old tavern near the Connecticut River and turning it into a home and studio. Many of his greatest works were created here, including the famous statue of Abraham Lincoln (1809–65) in Lincoln Park, Chicago. Today this historic 1805 structure is filled with the sculptor's furniture and samples of his small, detailed sketches for large bronzes. A number of his sculptures are scattered around the 150-acre (61-ha) property, which is laid out with formal gardens and pleasing walking trails flanked by tall pines and hemlocks.

ENVIRONS: Just two miles (3 km) south of the Saint-Gaudens site, visitors will come upon the Cornish-Windsor Bridge. Spanning the Connecticut River

Model for Boston's Shaw Memorial

between New Hampshire and Vermont, the structure is the longest covered bridge in New England at 460 ft (140 m). Three other covered bridges can be found in the vicinity of Cornish.

Hanover ⑮

🏃 9,200. ✕ 6 miles (10 km) SE in Lebanon. 🚍 ℹ️ 216 Nugget Arcade Building (603) 643-3115.

Hanover, with a traditional village green ringed by historic brick buildings, is the archetypal New England college town. Situated in the upper valley region of the Connecticut River, it is a pleasant stop for visitors following the Appalachian Trail, which goes right

through the center of town. Hanover is the home of **Dartmouth College**, the northernmost of the country's Ivy League schools. The college was originally known as Moor's Indian Charity School, and was founded in 1769 to educate and convert Abenaki Natives. Today some 4,500 students participate in programs that include one of the oldest medical schools in America, the Thayer School of Civil Engineering (1867), and the Amos Tuck School of Business Administration (1900). The school's famous graduates include statesman Daniel Webster (1782–1852) and former vice president Nelson Rockefeller (1908–79).

The college has a number of noteworthy sights. The **Baker/Berry Memorial Library** is decorated by a series of thought-provoking murals tracing the history of the Americas painted by Mexican artist José Clemente Orozco (1883–1949) in the early 1930s. The **Hood Museum of Art** has a diverse collection that includes Native American and African art, early American and European paintings, and works by such noted modern artists as Pablo Picasso (1881–1973).

🎭 **Dartmouth College**
🎫 (603) 646-1110. ♿ &
🎭 **Baker/Berry Memorial Library**
Dartmouth College. 🎫 (603) 646-2560. ⭘ year-round: call for hours. &
🏛️ **Hood Museum of Art**
Dartmouth College. 🎫 (603) 646-2808. ⭘ year-round: 10am–5pm Tue & Thu–Sat, 10am–9pm Wed, 12pm–5pm Sun. ♿ & ⦸ 🅿️

Gallery in Dartmouth's Hood Museum of Art in Hanover

COVERED BRIDGES

American bridge builders began covering their wooden spans in the early 19th-century to protect the truss work and planking from the harsh weather. Originally the bridges were built by locals, meaning that each one had design elements specific to its region. Covered bridges built in farming communities were wide enough and tall enough to accommodate a wagon loaded with hay. Bridges leading into town had the added luxury of pedestrian walkways. The bridges, though, were more than just river crossings. Fishermen cast their lines beneath the spans, children used them as platforms from which to dive into the water below, birds nested among the rafters, and social dances were sometimes held beneath their roofs.

One of New Hampshire's covered bridges outside Cornish

Tour of Lake Winnipesaukee ⑯

Flashy sign at Weirs Beach

THIS STUNNING LAKE has a shoreline that meanders for 240 miles (386 km), making it the biggest stretch of waterfront in New Hampshire. Ringed by mountains, Winnipesaukee is scattered with 274 islands. Around its shores are sheltered bays and harbors, with half a dozen resort towns where visitors can enjoy activities ranging from canoeing to shopping for crafts and antiques.

TIPS FOR DRIVERS

Tour length: 70 miles (113 km).
Starting point: Alton, at junction of Hwys 11 & 28.
Stopping-off points: Popular Weirs Beach eateries include Paradise Beach Club and Patio Garden Restaurant. Center Sandwich's Chequers Harbor and Corner House Inn are popular. Wolfeboro has many places to eat, including Loves Quay Restaurant, Rumors Café, and West Lake Asian Cuisine.

Squam Lake ④
This pristine body of water was where the movie *On Golden Pond* (1981) was filmed. The lake is ideal for boating and fishing.

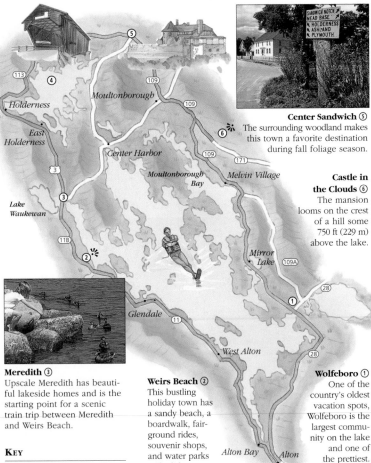

Center Sandwich ⑤
The surrounding woodland makes this town a favorite destination during fall foliage season.

Castle in the Clouds ⑥
The mansion looms on the crest of a hill some 750 ft (229 m) above the lake.

Holderness

East Holderness

Moultonborough

Center Harbor

Moultonborough Bay

Melvin Village

Lake Waukewan

Mirror Lake

Glendale

West Alton

Alton Bay

Alton

Meredith ③
Upscale Meredith has beautiful lakeside homes and is the starting point for a scenic train trip between Meredith and Weirs Beach.

Weirs Beach ②
This bustling holiday town has a sandy beach, a boardwalk, fairground rides, souvenir shops, and water parks with slides.

Wolfeboro ①
One of the country's oldest vacation spots, Wolfeboro is the largest community on the lake and one of the prettiest.

KEY

▬▬ Tour route

── Other road

☀ Viewpoint

0 kilometers　5

0 miles　　　　5

White Mountains/ White Mountain National Forest ⑰

ℹ️ *719 Main St, Laconia (603) 528-8721.* **Camping** 🅲 *(877) 444-6777 or in Canada (518) 885-3639. Call for availability and reservations.* ♿ ▨

NEW HAMPSHIRE'S heavily forested northland is an outdoor paradise, encompassing a national forest, several state parks, more than 1,200 miles (1,900 km) of hiking trails, several dozen lakes, ponds and rivers, and 23 campgrounds. The White Mountain National Forest, a small portion of which lies in neighboring Maine, sprawls over 770,000 acres (311,600 ha).

The most beautiful wilderness area in the state, the National Forest is home to an abundance of wildlife, including a large population of moose. These giant members of the deer family are very shy, but they can be seen from the road at dawn or dusk, lumbering back and forth from their feeding grounds or standing in a swampy pond.

This region offers all manner of outdoor activities – from bird-watching and skiing to rock climbing and kayaking – but even less sporty travelers will revel in the spectacular scenery visible from their car. More than 20 summits soar to over 4,000 ft (1,200 m). Driving through the White Mountains,

Ranger station marker

visitors encounter one scenic vista after another: valleys flanked by forests of pine, waterfalls tumbling over rocky outcrops, and trout rivers hissing alongside the meandering roads.

In 1998 a stretch of road, the 100-mile- (161-km-) long White Mountains Trail, was designated as a National Scenic and Cultural Byway. The trail loops across the Mount Washington Valley, through Crawford Notch (*see p271*), North Conway, and Franconia Notch (*see pp272–3*).

Brilliant fall foliage colors, interspersed with evergreens, transform the rugged countryside into a living palette. The leaves of different trees manifest a rich variety of shades – flaming red maples, golden birch, and maroon northern red oaks. Driving during the fall can be a beautiful but slow-moving experience since thousands of "leaf peepers" are on the

Brightly colored engine of the Conway Scenic Railroad

roads. Accommodations can also be difficult to find unless they are booked well in advance.

North Conway ⑱

🚶 *2,500.* ✈ *70 miles (112 km) SE in Portland, ME.* ℹ️ *Main St (603) 356-3171 or (800) 367-3364.*

THE GATEWAY TO the sublime beauty of the White Mountains, North Conway is, surprisingly, also a bustling shopping center. This mountain village now has more than 200 factory outlets and specialty shops lining its Main Street. Prices are low in the first place, even for designer names such as Calvin Klein, Ralph Lauren, and L.L. Bean, but because there is no sales tax in New Hampshire, all purchases become even better bargains.

Locals are quick to point out that there are many other attractions in and around North Conway, including canoe trips on the Saco River and a ride into the mountains in an old-fashioned train aboard the **Conway Scenic Railroad**. At the **Story Land** theme park children can ride on an antique German carousel, a pirate ship, or Cinderella's coach.

🚂 **Conway Scenic Railroad**
Rte 16 in North Conway. 🅲 *(603) 356-5251 or (800) 232-5251.* 🕐 *call for schedule.* ▨ 🅲 ♿
🎡 **Story Land**
Rte 16 in Glen. 🅲 *(603) 383-4186.* 🕐 *mid-Jun–Labor Day: 9am–6pm daily; late May–mid-Jun & Labor Day–Columbus Day: 10am–5pm Sat–Sun.* ▨ ♿

Breathtaking view from Cathedral Ledge just outside North Conway

Red and white covered bridge leading into Jackson

Jackson ⑲

🚶 750. ✈ 77 miles (125 km) SE in Portland, ME. 🛈 Rte 16B (603) 383-9356 or (800) 866-3334.

THIS MOUNTAIN VILLAGE is tucked away on a back road off Route 16B, but drivers will not miss it because the entrance is marked by its distinctive red and white covered bridge. The picturesque 200-year-old community is, along with the nearby villages of Intervale, Bartlett, and Glen, the main center for accommodation in the Mount Washington area.

Jackson was at one time a favorite getaway spot for big-city Easterners, but the hard times of the Great Depression of the 1930s saw the town slip into disrepair. Developers rediscovered this quiet corner of New Hampshire in the 1980s and began restoring several of the town's best hotels.

Jackson is a popular base camp for winter sports enthusiasts because the region is blessed with more than 110 downhill ski runs and a network of more than 200 miles (320 km) of cross-country trails. The main ski centers are Black Mountain, the Wildcat Ski Area, and the recently enlarged Attitash Bear Peak *(see p363)*. With 273 acres (113 ha) of skiable terrain served by 12 lifts, Attitash is the state's biggest ski center.

Summer sports abound here as well. The region's numerous peaks and valleys make this prime hiking and mountain-biking country, and a restored 18-hole course gives golfers the chance to play a round against one of the most scenic backdrops in New England. After having worked up a sweat, bikers and hikers can cool off under the waterfalls of the Wildcat River in Jackson Village.

Pinkham Notch ⑳

🛈 Rte 16 N of North Conway (603) 466-2721. ◷ 6:30am–10pm daily.

NAMED AFTER Joseph Pinkham, who according to local lore explored the area in 1790 with a sled drawn by pigs, this rocky ravine runs between Gorham and Jackson. The lofty Presidential Range girds the western flank of Pinkham Notch, while the 4,415-ft (1,346-m) Wildcat Mountain looms to the east.

Backcountry adventurers love this part of the state because of its great variety of activities. Skiing at the Wildcat Ski Area is among the best in the state, and its high elevation makes for a long season, running from November to April. In the summer, visitors can ride to the summit aboard the aerial gondola. Picnic areas at the top offer great views of Mount Washington and the Presidential Range.

Hiking trails lace Pinkham Notch, including a section of the fabled Appalachian Trail *(see pp22–3)*. These well-maintained paths range from less demanding nature walks suitable for whole families to lung-testing climbs best attacked by serious hikers. Along the way, visitors are led past some of the region's most captivating sights, including waterfalls, rivers, scenic overlooks, and pristine ponds tucked away

Sublime beauty of the Presidential Range from Pinkham Notch

Striking exterior of the Mount Washington Hotel and Resort

in thick woodland. Lucky travelers may spot raccoons, beaver, deer, and even the occasional moose.

Bretton Woods ㉑

550. 96 miles (155 km) SE in Portland, ME. (603) 745-8720 or (800) 346-3687.

THIS TINY ENCLAVE situated on a glacial plain at the base of the Presidential Range has an unusual claim to fame: it hosted the United Nations Monetary and Financial Conference in 1944. The meetings established the International Monetary Fund and laid the groundwork for the World Bank, a response to the need for currency stability after the economic upheavals of World War II. The delegates also set the gold standard at $35 an ounce and chose the American dollar as the international standard for monetary exchange.

The setting for this vital meeting was the **Mount Washington Hotel and Resort** (see p319). It is easy to imagine the reaction of delegates when they first caught sight of this grand Spanish Renaissance-style hotel from a sweeping curve in the road. Opened in 1902, the hotel's sparkling white exterior and crimson roof stand out in stark contrast to Mount Washington, looming 6,288 ft (1,917 m) skyward behind the edifice.

The hotel has entertained a host of distinguished guests, including British Prime Minister Sir Winston Churchill (1874–1965), inventor Thomas Edison (1847–1931), baseball star Babe Ruth (1895–1948), and three presidents.

Apart from its sublime setting, what makes the hotel so impressive is its sheer size. Designated a National Historic Landmark, the 200-room structure was built by 250 skilled craftsmen from Italy. Today the hotel is surrounded by more than 17,300 acres (7,000 ha) of parkland, and its numerous facilities include a 27-hole golf course laid out by the famous Scottish designer Donald Ross (1872–1948). Nearby Bretton Woods ski area (see p362) offers alpine skiing along with 62 miles (100 km) of cross-country trails.

Sir Winston Churchill, a Mount Washington visitor

Mount Washington Hotel and Resort
Rte 302, Bretton Woods. (603) 278-1000 or (800) 258-0330.

ENVIRONS: The Mount Washington Valley, in which Bretton Woods is located, is dominated by the 6,288-ft (1,917-m) peak of Mount Washington, the highest in the northeastern United States. Other imposing peaks belonging to the Presidential Range – Adam, Jefferson, Madison, Monroe, and Eisenhower – surround Mount Washington, which has the dubious distinction of having the worst weather of any mountain in the world. Unpredictable snowstorms are not unusual, even during the summer months; the highest wind ever recorded on Earth was clocked here in April 1934: 230 mph (370 kph). During the last century, the mountain has claimed the lives of almost 100 people caught unaware by Mount Washington's temperamental climate.

On clear days, however, when the mountain is in a good mood, nothing compares to the panoramic view from the top. Brave souls hike to the summit by one of the many trails, drive their own cars up the winding Mount Washington Auto Road, or puff their way slowly to the top in the deservedly famous **Mount Washington Cog Railroad**. Billed as "America's oldest tourist attraction," the railroad started operating in 1869.

The train, powered by steam locomotives, chugs its way up the cog track to the top of the mountain belching steam. The 3.5-mile (5.6-km) route to the top is one of the steepest tracks in the world, climbing at a heart-stopping 37 percent grade at some points. At the top, passengers can visit the Sherman Adams Summit Building, with the Summit Museum, and Mount Washington Observatory, one of the world's leading mountain weather stations.

Mount Washington Cog Railroad
Off Rte 302, Marshfield Base Station. (603) 278-5404 or (800) 922-8825. May–Oct: call for hours. W www.thecog.com

Mount Washington Cog Railroad

Perfect spot on Chocorua Lake for the view of Mount Chocorua

Kancamagus Highway ②

Rte 112 between Lincoln & Conway.
🛈 *Saco District Ranger Station, 33 Kancamagus Hwy (603) 447-5448.*

Touted by many as the most scenic fall-foliage road in New England, this stretch of highway runs through the White Mountain National Forest *(see p265)* between Lincoln and Conway. The road covers about 34 miles (55 km) of Route 112 and offers exceptional vistas from the Pemi Overlook as it

Sabbaday Falls, a highlight of the Kancamagus Highway

climbs 3,000 ft (914 m) through the Kancamagus Pass. Descending into the Saco Valley, the well-traveled road joins up with the Swift River, following the aptly named waterway into Conway. The highway provides fishermen with easy access to the river, home to brook and rainbow trout.

Campgrounds and picnic areas along the entire length of highway give travelers ample opportunity to relax and eat lunch on the banks of cool mountain streams. Maintained by the US Forest Service, the campgrounds are equipped with toilets and one has shower facilities; all are operated on a first-come, first-served basis. Well-marked trails also allow drivers to stretch their legs in the midst of some of the most beautiful scenery in the state. One of the most popular trails is the short loop that leads travelers to the oft-photographed Sabbaday Falls. Closer to Conway, road signs guide drivers to several scenic areas that afford views of cascades, rapids, and rivers.

The area is home to a wide variety of wildlife, including resident birds such as woodpeckers and chickadees, as well as migratory songbirds who breed here in the summer. Larger inhabitants include deer, moose, and the occasional black bear.

Clark's Trading Post in North Woodstock

Lincoln Woodstock ②

🏠 *1,300.* ✈ *66 miles (106 km) SW in Lebanon.* 🛈 *Rte 112 & Connector Rd, Lincoln (603) 745-6621 or (800) 227-4191.* Ⓦ *www.lincolnwoodstock.com*

Not including its convenient location near the White Mountains *(see p265),* the region's main attraction is **Clark's Trading Post,** a strange combination of circus acts, amusement park rides, and museums. Children especially love the trained bears and the over-the-top performers. A session at Clark's "bumper boat" marina, in which participants try to ram each other's boat, is where the younger set can blow off the steam that may have built up on a leaf-peeping drive.

🏛 **Clark's Trading Post**
Rte 3, Lincoln. ☎ *(603) 745-8913.*
Call for hours & show times. 🏛

◁ **Silver Cascades, Crawford Notch State Park, in the autumn**

ENVIRONS: Tiny Lincoln is located just three miles (5 km) northwest of North Woodstock. The town's location at the western end of the Kancamagus Highway and at the southern entrance to Franconia Notch State Park *(see pp272–3)* have turned it into a base camp for both backwoods adventurers and stick-to-the-road sightseers. Nearby **Loon Mountain** is one of the state's premier ski resorts. However, in the summer it offers a number of activities, from guided nature walks and tours of caves to horseback riding, mountain biking, and a gondola ride to the summit.

Loon Mountain
E of I-93, near Lincoln. *(603) 745-6281or (800) 229-5666.*

View from the Willey House in Crawford Notch State Park

Challenging climbing wall at Loon Mountain outside of Lincoln

Crawford Notch State Park ㉔

Rte 302 between Twin Mountains & Bartlett. *(603) 374-2272.*
Camping *(603) 271-3628 for reservations.* year-round.

THIS NARROW PASS, which squeezes through the sheer rock walls of Webster and Willey mountains, gained notoriety in 1826. One night a severe rain sent tons of mud and stone careening into the valley below, heading straight for the home of innkeeper Samuel Willey and his family. Alerted by the sounds of the avalanche, the family fled outdoors, where all seven were killed beneath falling debris. Ironically the lethal avalanche bypassed the house, leaving it unscathed. Several writers, including New Englander Nathaniel Hawthorne *(see p30)*, have immortalized the tragedy in literature. The house still stands today and is now in service as a visitors center.

Once the notch was threatened by over-logging. However, the establishment of the state park in 1911 has ensured protection of this rugged wilderness. Today white-water boaters come here to test their mettle on the powerful Saco River, which carves its way through the valley. Fishermen ply the park's more tranquil ponds and streams in search of sport and a tasty dinner of trout or salmon.

People who prefer to keep their feet dry can still enjoy the water on a short hiking trail leading to the Arethusa Falls. Towering more than 200 ft (61 m) in the air, this magnificent cascade is New Hampshire's tallest waterfall. Elsewhere drivers will get wonderful views of the Silver Cascades and Flume Cascades waterfalls without leaving the comfort of their car.

ROBERT FROST AND NEW HAMPSHIRE

The natural beauty of New Hampshire was an inspiration to one of America's best-loved poets: Robert Frost (1874–1963). Born in San Francisco, California, the four-time winner of the Pulitzer Prize moved to Massachusetts with his family when he was 11. After working as a teacher, a reporter, and a mill hand, Frost moved to England in 1912. Upon his return to the US in 1915, Frost settled in the Franconia Notch area *(see pp272–3)*. The majestic setting inspired him to pen many of his greatest works, including his famous poem *Stopping by Woods on a Snowy Evening* (1923).

Robert Frost farm in Derry, New Hampshire

Franconia Notch State Park ㉕

Canoeing on Profile Lake

THIS SPECTACULAR mountain pass carved between the Kinsman and Franconia ranges is graced with some of the state's most spectacular natural wonders. Foremost among them was the Old Man of the Mountain, a rocky outcropping on the side of a cliff that resembled a man's profile, until the nose and forehead came crashing down in May 2003. Other attractions compensate for the loss including a boardwalk and stairways which lead visitors through the Flume Gorge, a narrow, granite chasm slashed in two by the Flume Brook, while an aerial tramway carries passengers to the summit of Cannon Mountain in eight minutes. Also within the park is Boise Rock, a picnic area by a mountain spring that offers views of the Cannon Cliffs and Echo Lake.

Glacial Boulder
This glacial boulder is one of the sights on the Flume Trail.

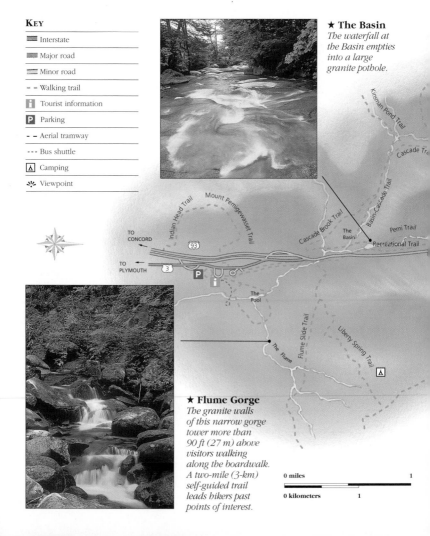

KEY

- Interstate
- Major road
- Minor road
- - - Walking trail
- **i** Tourist information
- **P** Parking
- - - Aerial tramway
- --- Bus shuttle
- **A** Camping
- ☀ Viewpoint

★ The Basin
The waterfall at the Basin empties into a large granite pothole.

★ Flume Gorge
The granite walls of this narrow gorge tower more than 90 ft (27 m) above visitors walking along the boardwalk. A two-mile (3-km) self-guided trail leads hikers past points of interest.

TO CONCORD — 93

TO PLYMOUTH — 3

0 miles   1
0 kilometers   1

Scenic Views
Hikers are rewarded with many beautiful panoramas along the park's trails.

Wild Bunchberrys
This fruit can be found throughout the lush Franconia Notch region.

Echo Lake
The 28-acre lake is great for picnicking, boating, and swimming.

★ Profile Lake
A favorite among fly-fisherman looking for brook trout, Profile Lake reflects the brilliant colors of fall foliage on the rounded slopes of Cannon Mountain.

STAR FEATURES

★ **The Basin**

★ **Flume Gorge**

★ **Profile Lake**

MAINE

....

MAINE TRULY IS THE GREAT OUTDOORS. *More than 5,500 miles (8,850 km) of inlets, bays, and harbors make up its spectacular coastline. Inland deep forests and jutting mountain peaks complement 32,000 miles (51,500 km) of rivers and 6,000 glacial lakes. However, for all its wild mystique, Maine also includes quaint villages, appealing cities, and discount shopping meccas.*

Maine has a long and rich history. While some historians maintain that the Vikings probed the rocky coast as early as the 11th century, European settlement began in earnest 500 years later, beginning with the Popham Beach colony of 1607. Although this original colony was short-lived, it spawned a succession of similar settlements at Monhegan (1622), Saco (1623), and Georgeana (1624). The last – renamed York *(see p278)* in 1652 – became the English America's first chartered city in 1642.

While Maine has always been one of the more sparsely populated states in the Union, it has been at the center of numerous territorial disputes, beginning with its abrupt seizure by Massachusetts in 1652 (an unhappy forced marriage, which ended in 1820 when Maine was granted statehood). Between 1675 and 1748 a series of four bloody wars was fought between British colonials and their French counterparts in Quebec. At the outset of the Revolutionary War (1775–83), Portland *(see pp280–83)* was bombarded and burned by the British as an example to other colonies harboring similar anti-Loyalist sentiments.

Traveling through Maine it is easy to see what all the fuss was about. The state's trove of unspoiled wilderness is interspersed with wonderfully preserved relics of its past. Beautiful Colonial homes can be found throughout the state. The importance of seafaring in the region's history is evident in the lighthouses *(see p279)*, maritime museums, and the sea captains' mansions found up and down the coast. And although tourism is now Maine's number one industry, the state has remained remarkably undeveloped, retaining much of the natural splendor that first attracted settlers so many centuries ago.

Hot summer shoreline along Old Orchard Beach

◁ **Cape Neddick Lighthouse at York Beach**

Exploring Maine

Maine's most popular attractions are found dotted along its coast, beginning in the southeast with the beach playgrounds of Ogunquit *(see pp278–9)*, Old Orchard *(see p279)*, and the resort towns of the Kennebunks *(see p279)*. The scenery gets more dramatic as travelers move north through Boothbay Harbor *(see p285)*, Pemaquid Point *(see p285)*, and Muscongus Bay. The tiny villages are perfect starting points for sailing and kayaking excursions. Yachts and windjammers ply the waters of the Penobscot Bay region *(see pp286–7)*, while Acadia National Park *(see pp288–9)* stands as Maine's coastal jewel. Farther north, the rising sun first strikes the US at Cobscook Bay. World-class hiking, boating, and mountain-biking opportunities are found inland among the state's many mountains, lakes, and rivers.

Stone fortifications at Fort William Adams Park in Portland

Getting Around

Interstate 95 is the only major artery in the state. As a result, the smaller scenic routes along the coastline are often congested with summer traffic. Many coastal towns can be reached from Boston by Concord Trailways bus lines. Amtrak runs a service from Boston to Portland with stops en route. Maine State Ferry Service has numerous routes to and from various seashore destinations. Both Portland and Bangor have international airports. The scarcity of public roads in northern Maine means that occasionally logging roads are used, which are operated much like toll roads and are best tackled with four-wheel drive vehicles.

0 kilometers   30

0 miles   30

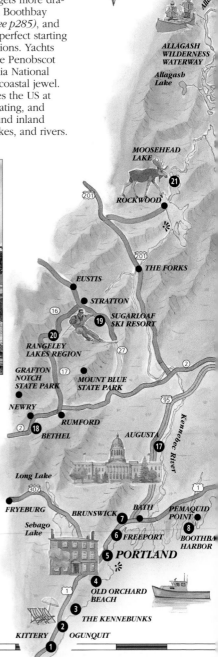

ALLAGASH WILDERNESS WATERWAY

Allagash Lake

MOOSEHEAD LAKE

(21)

ROCKWOOD

THE FORKS

EUSTIS

STRATTON

SUGARLOAF SKI RESORT

(19)

(16)

(20)

RANGELEY LAKES REGION

(27)

GRAFTON NOTCH STATE PARK

(17)

MOUNT BLUE STATE PARK

NEWRY

(18)

RUMFORD

BETHEL

AUGUSTA

(17)

Kennebec River

Long Lake

FRYEBURG

BRUNSWICK

(7)

BATH

PEMAQUID POINT

(8)

Sebago Lake

(6)

FREEPORT

BOOTHBAY HARBOR

(5)

PORTLAND

(4)

OLD ORCHARD BEACH

(3)

THE KENNEBUNKS

(2)

KITTERY   OGUNQUIT

(1)

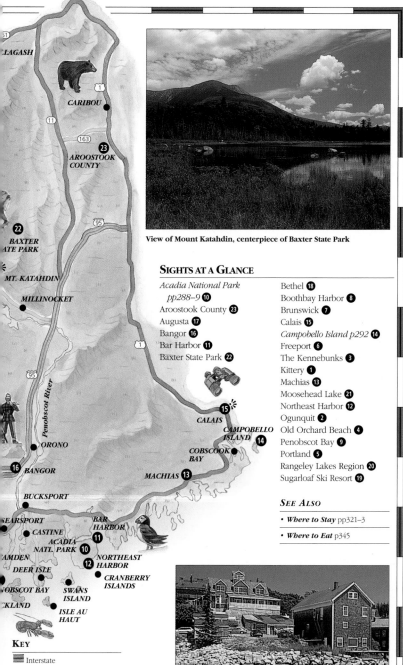

View of Mount Katahdin, centerpiece of Baxter State Park

SIGHTS AT A GLANCE

SEE ALSO

• *Where to Stay* pp321–3

• *Where to Eat* p345

KEY

▬ Interstate

▬ Major road

▬ Minor road

▬ Scenic route

☼ Viewpoint

Picturesque Stonington village on Deer Isle

Kittery ❶

🏠 9,500. ✈ 49 miles (78 km)
NE in Portland. 🛈 1 Stonewall Lane,
York, (207) 439-7545.

THE SOUTHERN COAST of
Maine begins at the
Piscataqua River and Kittery,
a town with a split personality. Founded in 1647, Kittery
boasts the oldest church in
the state, the 1730 **First
Congregational Church**.
Many fine old mansions line
the streets, including the John
Bray House, one of the oldest
dwellings in Maine. **Fort
McClary**, now a state historic
site, has fortifications dating
to the early 1800s and a
hexagonal blockhouse, and
the **Kittery Historical and
Naval Museum** is filled with
ship models and exhibits
explaining maritime history.
Despite its wealth of historical
attractions, Kittery is best
known for a more contem-
porary lure – the more than
100 factory outlet stores
promising bargains along
Route 1, where shoppers can
buy name brands at a discount.

🏠 **First Congregational
Church**
23 Pepperrell Rd. 📞 (207) 439-0650.
🕐 8am & 10am Sun.
🏛 **Fort McClary State
Historic Site**
Rte 103 E of Kittery. 📞 (207) 384-
5160. 🕐 late May–Sep: 9am–dusk
daily. 🎫
🏛 **Kittery Historical and
Naval Museum**
Rogers Rd. 📞 (207) 439-3080.
🕐 Jun–mid-Oct: 10am–4pm Tue–
Sat; mid-Oct–early Dec: 10am–4pm
Wed & Sat. 🎫 ♿ partial.

**Hexagonal Fort McClary block-
house in Kittery**

ENVIRONS: Four miles (6 km)
from Kittery, visitors will come
upon York Village. Settled in
the 1630s, the village later grew
into an important trading center, its wharves and warehouses
filled with treasures from the
lucrative West Indies trade.
A collection of seven historic
buildings maintained by the
Old York Historical
Society, **Old York**
traces town history
over three centuries.
A repository for his-
torical items, Old York
has a superb collec-
tion of regional deco-
rative arts housed in
more than 30 period
rooms and galleries.
Tours begin at
Jefferds' Tavern, a
colonial hostelry, and
include two historic
homes, a 1745 one-
room schoolhouse, and the
John Hancock Warehouse,
named after its owner, an
original signatory of the
Declaration of Independence.
Down the street, the 1719 Old
Gaol (jail) stands as one of the
country's oldest public buildings. Dark, foreboding dun-
geons tell of harsh conditions

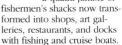

**Lobster trap
buoys**

faced by the felons who served
their sentences within the jail's
three-ft- (1-m-) thick walls.

🏛 **Old York**
Lindsay Rd. 📞 (207) 363-4974.
🕐 Jun–mid-Oct: 10am–5pm Tue–Sat,
1pm–5pm Sun. 🎫 🚫 last tour at
4pm. 🏠 🚫 indoors.

Ogunquit ❷

🏠 900. ✈ 36 miles (58 km)
NE in Portland. 🛈 36 Rte 1 S
(207) 646-2939.

IT IS EASY TO SEE why the
Abenaki Indians called
this enclave Ogunquit, or
"Beautiful Place by the Sea."
Maine beaches do not come
any better. From mid-May to
Columbus Day, trolleys shuttle
visitors to this powdery three-
mile (5-km) stretch
of sand and dunes
that curves around
a backdrop of
rugged cliffs. Atop
the cliffs is the
1.25-mile (2-km)
Marginal Way, a
footpath that offers
walkers dramatic
vistas of the ocean.
Perkins Cove,
home of the only
pedestrian draw-
bridge in the US, is
a quaint jumble of
fishermen's shacks now transformed into shops, art galleries, restaurants, and docks
with fishing and cruise boats.
This picturesque outpost
attracted an artist's colony as
early as 1890, establishing it
as a haven for the arts. The
handsome **Ogunquit Museum
of American Art** was built in

Scenic ocean vista at Marginal Way in Ogunquit

1952 by the eccentric but wealthy Henry Strater, who served as its director for more than 30 years. Constructed of wood and local stone, the museum has wide windows to allow views of the rocky cove and meadows. A three-acre (1-ha) sculpture garden and lawns also make the most of the breathtaking setting. The permanent collection includes art by many notable American painters.

🏛 **Ogunquit Museum of American Art**
183 Shore Rd. ☏ (207) 646-4909.
◷ Jul–mid-Oct: 10:30am–5pm Mon–Sat, 2pm–5pm Sun.
⬤ Labor Day.

The Kennebunks ❸

🚗 30 miles (48 km) NE in Portland.
ℹ 17 Western Ave, Kennebunk (207) 967-0857.

FIRST A THRIVING PORT and busy shipbuilding center, then a summer retreat for the wealthy, the Kennebunks are made up of two villages, Kennebunkport and Kennebunk.

The profusion of fine Federal and Greek Revival structures in Kennebunkport's historic village is evidence of the fortunes made in shipbuilding and trading from 1810 to the 1870s. With its 100-ft- (30-m-) tall white steeple and belfry, the 1824 South Congregational Church is a favorite subject for photographers. History of a different sort can be found at the **Seashore Trolley Museum**, where some 200 antique streetcars are housed, including one vehicle from New Orleans named "Desire." Visitors can embark on a tour of the countryside aboard one of the restored trolleys.

The scenic drive along Route 9 offers views of surf along rocky Cape Arundel. At Cape Porpoise hungry travelers can sample lobster pulled fresh from

Kennebunkport signpost

the Atlantic. Kennebunk is famous for its beaches, most notably Kennebunk Beach, which is actually three connected strands. One of the town's most romantic historic homes is the 1826 Wedding Cake House. According to the local lore, George Bourne was unexpectedly called to sea before his marriage. Although a very hastily arranged wedding took place, there was no time to bake the traditional wedding cake. Instead, the shipbuilder vowed to his bride that upon his return he would remodel their home to look like a wedding cake. Today the Gothic spires, ornate latticework, and gingerbread trim offer proof that Bourne was a man of his word. Housed in four restored 19th-century buildings, **The Brick Store Museum** offers glimpses into the past with displays of decorative arts. It also offers interesting architectural walking tours of the town's historic area.

🏛 **Seashore Trolley Museum**
195 Log Cabin Rd, Kennebunkport. ☏ (207) 967-2800. ◷ mid-May–mid-Oct: 10am–5pm daily; early May & late Oct: 10am–5pm Sat–Sun. 🅿 ♿
🏛 **The Brick Store Museum**
117 Main St, Kennebunk. ☏ (207) 985-4802. ◷ May–Dec: 10am–4:30pm Tue–Fri, 10am–1pm Sat. ⬤ public hols. 🅿

Old Orchard Beach ❹

🏙 9,000. 🚗 13 miles (21 km) NE in Portland. 🚉 ℹ First St (207) 934-2500 or (800) 365-9386.

ONE OF MAINE'S OLDEST seashore resorts, Old Orchard Beach's seven miles (11 km) of sandy shoreline and low surf make it a favorite spot for swimming. Kids love the pier lined with game booths, food stands, a roller coaster, a 60-ft (18-m) water slide, and a 36-hole miniature golf course complete with pools and waterfalls. A new floating marina caters to water sports.

Fresh lobster from the Cape Porpoise area in southern Maine

Portland 5

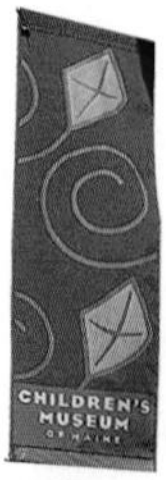

Children's Museum banner

POET AND PORTLAND NATIVE Henry Wadsworth Longfellow (1807–82) described Maine's largest city as "the beautiful town that is seated by the sea." Longfellow was inspired by Portland's fortunate location on the crest of a peninsula with expansive views of Casco Bay and the Calendar Islands on three sides. Once a prosperous port and an early state capital, Portland has been devastated by no less than four major fires, resulting in a preponderance of sturdy stone Victorian buildings that line many of its streets today.

Exploring Portland

A thriving arts community and a downtown with interesting shopping and dining are all part of a stroll along Congress Street and through the restored Old Port Exchange area *(see pp282–3)*. The West End has fine homes and a splendid Western Promenade overlooking the water. The working waterfront and nearby beaches add to the city's charm.

Portland Museum of Art

7 Congress Sq. ☎ *(207) 775-6148.*
○ *year-round: 10am–5pm Tue, Wed, Thu, Sat, Sun, 10am–9pm Fri; late May–mid-Oct: 10am–5pm Mon.*
$ ♿

After an expansion in 2002, Portland's premier fine art collection now fills three distinctive buildings, spanning Federal, Beaux-Arts, and post-modern design. One gallery showcases 19 paintings and extensive graphic art by the Portland area's most famous artist, Winslow Homer (1836–1910). Other highlights include works by Andrew Wyeth (b.1917), Paul Gauguin (1848–1903), and Pablo Picasso (1881–1973).

Children's Museum of Maine

142 Free St. ☎ *(207) 828-1234.*
○ *year-round: 10am–5pm Tue–Sat, 12pm–5pm Sun; May–Sep: 10am–5pm Mon.* ● *public hols.* $ 🛍

This historic brick building houses three floors of interactive exhibits designed for youngsters. Displays include Toddler Park, Ship Ahoy!, Climbing Wall, Star Lab, and Camera Obscura.

Wadsworth-Longfellow House

489 Congress St. ☎ *(207) 879-0427.*
○ *May–Oct: 10am–4pm daily.* $ 🗣
♿ *first floor.* 🛍

Poet Henry Wadsworth Longfellow grew up in this 1785 house. The materials for the Georgian home were transported from Philadelphia on a barge. The house contains family mementos, portraits, and furnishings.

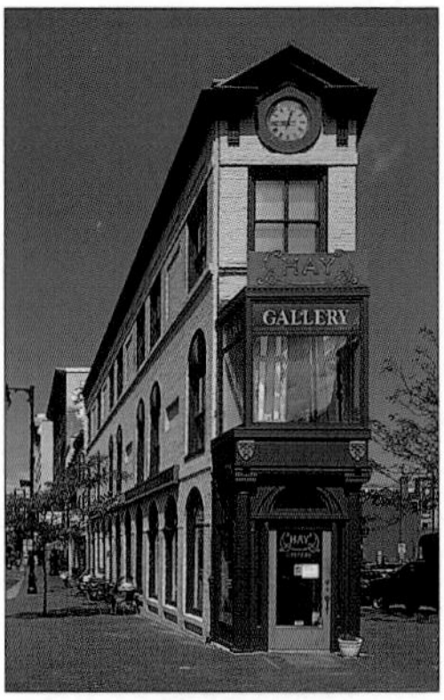

The distinctive Hay Gallery in Portland's downtown arts district

Victoria Mansion

109 Danforth St. ☎ *(207) 772-4841.*
○ *May–Oct: 10am–4pm Tue– Sat, 1pm–5pm Sun; late Nov & Dec: 11am–5pm Wed–Sun.* ● *Jan–May, Nov, Jul 4, & Dec 25.* $ 🗣 *every half hour.* 🛍

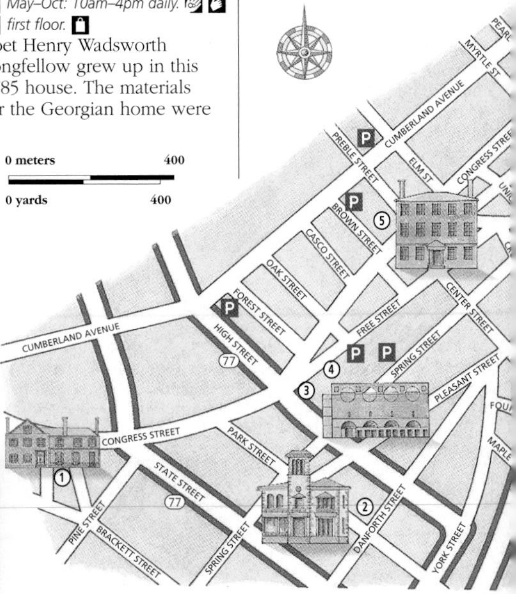

PORTLAND CITY CENTER

Children's Museum of Maine 4
Neal Dow Memorial 1
Old Port 6 *(see pp282–3)*
Portland Museum of Art 3
Victoria Mansion 2
Wadsworth-Longfellow House 5

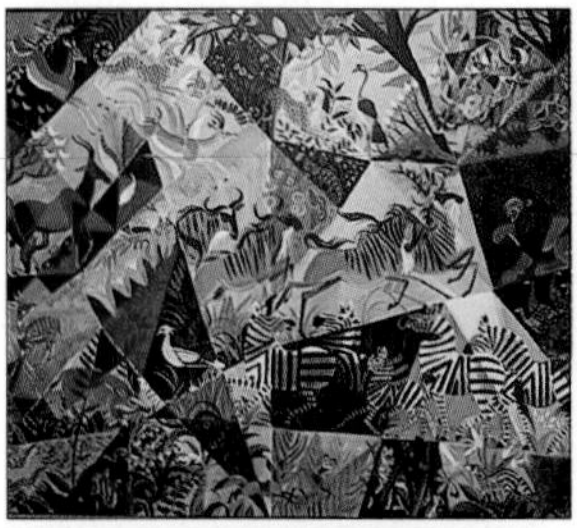
Dahlov Ipcar's *Blue Savannah* in the Portland Museum of Art

Coastal fishing on the outskirts of Portland

This sumptuous brownstone villa was completed in 1860 to serve as the summer home of Ruggles hotelier Sylvester Morse (c.1816–93). The interior has extraordinary interior detail, such as painted *trompe l'oeil* walls and ceilings, wood paneling, marble mantels, and a flying staircase.

🏠 George Tate House

1270 Westbrook St. 🕻 *(207) 774-6177.* ◯ *Jun–Oct: 10am–4pm Tue–Sat, 1pm–4pm Sun.* ● *Nov–May, Jul 4, & Labor Day.* 📷 🚻 🏛
In 1755 George Tate, an agent of the British Royal

Navy, constructed an elegant gambrel-roofed home with rich wood paneling, patterned floors, a dogleg staircase, and eight fireplaces. Now a National Historic Landmark, the house has fine period furnishings and an 18th-century garden where tea is served on summer Wednesdays.

🏠 Neal Dow Memorial

714 Congress St. 🕻 *(207) 773-7773.* ◯ *11am–4pm Mon–Fri.* ● *Jan, Feb.*
Neal Dow (1804–97), one of Portland's prominent citizens, built this Federal-style mansion in 1829. Twice serving as the city's mayor, Dow was an abolitionist and prohibitionist who also championed the causes of women's rights and prison reform. The Dow family's original furnishings, paintings, china, and silver are displayed along with memorabilia of Dow's career.

🏛 Maine Narrow Gauge Railroad Co. & Museum

58 Fore St. 🕻 *(207) 828-0814.* ◯ *year-round: 10am–4pm daily.* 🚻 **Train ride** ◯ *mid-May–mid-Oct on the hour; call for other times.* 📷
Scenic trips along a three-mile (5-km) stretch of the waterfront are the highlight of this museum dedicated to the railroad that served much of Maine from the 1870s to the 1940s. Exhibits include vintage locomotives and a restored caboose.

🏠 Portland Observatory

138 Congress St. 🕻 *(207) 774-5561.* ◯ *late May–mid-Oct: 10am–5pm daily.* 📷 🚻 🏛

Constructed in 1807, this octagonal landmark is the last surviving 19th-century signal tower on the Atlantic. The 102-step climb to the upper deck is worth the effort.

🏛 Museum at Portland Head Light at Fort Williams Park

12 Captain Strout Circle. 🕻 *(207) 799-2661.* ◯ *Jun–Oct: 10am–4pm daily; Apr, May, Nov, Dec: 10am–4pm Sat & Sun.* 📷 🚻
First illuminated in 1791 by order of President George Washington (1732–99), the lighthouse has been the subject of poetry, postage stamps, and photographs. The keeper's house is now a museum with exhibits on the history of the world's beacons. The large surrounding park, just four miles (6.5 km) from downtown, features a beach and picnic areas.

Portland Observatory atop Munjoy Hill

KEY

🟦	Street-by-Street map *see pp282–3*
═	Highway
ℹ	Tourist information
🅿	Parking

Freeport ❻

🏠 *7,000.* ✈ *17 miles (31 km) SW in Portland.* ℹ *23 Depot St (207) 865-1212 or (800) 865-1994.*

ALTHOUGH FREEPORT dates back to 1789, shoppers would argue that it did not arrive on the scene until 1917, when the first L.L. Bean clothing store opened its doors. Today this retail giant is open 24 hours a day, 365 days a year, and, with more than 3.5 million customers annually, L.L. Bean is easily Maine's biggest man-made attraction. Since the 1980s more than 150 other brand-name outlets have opened here.

Travelers who make it past the shops will discover a working harbor in South Freeport, where seal-watching tours and sailing cruises depart. The shoreline includes **Wolfe's Neck Woods State Park**, 233 acres (94 ha) of tranquility wrapped along Casco Bay.

Freeport's most unusual sight is the **Desert of Maine**. Originally a late-1700s farm, the area was severely over-tilled and over-logged. The topsoil eventually disappeared altogether, giving way to glacial sand deposits and creating a 40-acre (16-ha) desert of sand dunes. Visitors can walk the nature trails with a guide who narrates the history of the area, or ride on an open cart. The farm museum is housed in a 1783 barn.

🌿 **Wolfe's Neck Woods State Park**
Wolfe's Neck Rd. 📞 *(207) 865-4465.* ⏰ *year-round: May–Sep: 9am–dusk daily; Sep–May: 9am–6pm daily.* 🎫 ⬛ ♿
🏜 **Desert of Maine**
95 Desert Rd. 📞 *(207) 865-6962.* ⏰ *May–mid-Oct: 8:30am–6pm daily.* 🎫 ♿

Brunswick ❼

🏠 *21,000.* ✈ *33 miles (53 km) SW in Portland.* 🚌 ℹ *59 Pleasant St (207) 725-8797.*

BRUNSWICK is best known as the home of Bowdoin College and as the land entry for the scenic panoramas of the town of Harpswell – a peninsula and three islands jutting out into Casco Bay.

Founded in 1794, the college claims a number of distinguished alumni, including explorers Robert Peary (1856–1920) and Donald MacMillan (1874–1970). The **Peary-MacMillan Arctic**

Peary-MacMillan Arctic Museum on Bowdoin College campus

Museum honors the two, who in 1909 became the first to reach the North Pole. Exhibits trace the history of polar exploration and display the journals of both men.

The **Pejepscot Historical Society** offers displays of Brunswick history in its three museums and offers tours of both Skolfield-Whittier House, a 17-room Italianate mansion built in 1858 by a shipyard

Seemingly endless acres of sand in Desert of Maine, Freeport

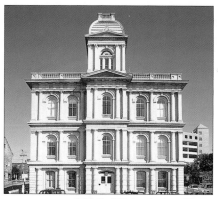

★ **United States Custom House**
Built following the Civil War (1861–5), this regal building contains gilded ceilings, marble staircases, and chandeliers.

State of Maine Armory
was designed to resemble a fortress and once was home to several units of the reserve militia known as the National Guard.

Antique shops *can be found throughout the Old Port district.*

| 0 meters | 50 |
| 0 yards | 50 |

KEY

– – – Suggested route

PEARL STREET

SILVER STREET

FORE STREET

COMMERCIAL STREET

★ **Mariner's Church**
Built in 1828, the building is an eclectic mix of Greek Revival and Federal styles, and is now used to house a variety of shops and businesses.

Freeport ❻

🏃 7,000. ✈ 17 miles (31 km)
SW in Portland. 🚏 23 Depot St
(207) 865-1212 or (800) 865-1994.

ALTHOUGH FREEPORT dates
back to 1789, shoppers
would argue that it did not
arrive on the scene until
1917, when the first L.L.
Bean clothing store opened
its doors. Today this retail
giant is open 24 hours a day,
365 days a year, and, with
more than 3.5 million customers annually, L.L. Bean
is easily Maine's biggest
man-made attraction. Since
the 1980s more than 150
other brand-name outlets
have opened here.

Travelers who make it
past the shops will discover
a working harbor in South
Freeport, where seal-watching
tours and sailing cruises
depart. The shoreline includes
**Wolfe's Neck Woods State
Park**, 233 acres (94 ha) of
tranquility wrapped along
Casco Bay.

Freeport's most unusual
sight is the **Desert of Maine**.
Originally a late-1700s farm,
the area was severely over-
tilled and over-logged. The
topsoil eventually disappeared
altogether, giving way to
glacial sand deposits and creating a 40-acre (16-ha) desert
of sand dunes. Visitors can
walk the nature trails with a
guide who narrates the history
of the area, or ride on an open
cart. The farm museum is
housed in a 1783 barn.

L.L. BEAN AND OUTLET SHOPPING

Leon Leonwood Bean (1872–1967) likely
would be amazed if he could see the result
of his dislike for cold, wet feet. The hunting shoe he developed in 1912 with leather
uppers on rubber overshoe bottoms began
a company that now claims more than a
billion dollars in sales worldwide and
carries anything needed for outdoor
excursions. Bean's showroom has
grown into a mammoth flagship store
that includes a 785-sq-ft (73-sq-m-)
pond stocked with trout.

Bust of L.L. Bean

🌿 **Wolfe's Neck Woods
State Park**
Wolfe's Neck Rd. 📞 (207) 865-
4465. 🕐 year-round: May–Sep:
9am–dusk daily; Sep–May: 9am–
6pm daily. 🎫 🅿 ♿
🏜 **Desert of Maine**
95 Desert Rd. 📞 (207) 865-6962.
🕐 May–mid-Oct: 8:30am–6pm
daily. 🎫 ♿

Brunswick ❼

🏃 21,000. ✈ 33 miles (53 km) SW
in Portland. 🚉 🚏 59 Pleasant St
(207) 725-8797.

BRUNSWICK IS best known as
the home of Bowdoin
College and as the land entry
for the scenic panoramas of
the town of Harpswell – a
peninsula and three islands
jutting out into Casco Bay.

Founded in 1794, the col-
lege claims a number of
distinguished alumni, including explorers Robert Peary
(1856–1920) and Donald
MacMillan (1874–1970). The
Peary-MacMillan Arctic

**Peary-MacMillan Arctic Museum
on Bowdoin College campus**

Museum honors the two,
who in 1909 became the first
to reach the North Pole.
Exhibits trace the history of
polar exploration and display
the journals of both men.

The **Pejepscot Historical
Society** offers displays of
Brunswick history in its three
museums and offers tours of
both Skolfield-Whittier House,
a 17-room Italianate mansion
built in 1858 by a shipyard

Seemingly endless acres of sand in Desert of Maine, Freeport

Coastal fishing on the outskirts of Portland

This sumptuous brownstone villa was completed in 1860 to serve as the summer home of Ruggles hotelier Sylvester Morse (c.1816–93). The interior has extraordinary interior detail, such as painted *trompe l'oeil* walls and ceilings, wood paneling, marble mantels, and a flying staircase.

🏛 George Tate House

1270 Westbrook St. 📞 (207) 774-6177. ◐ Jun–Oct: 10am–4pm Tue–Sat, 1pm–4pm Sun. ● Nov–May, Jul 4, & Labor Day. 🚫 🅿 ♿

In 1755 George Tate, an agent of the British Royal Navy, constructed an elegant gambrel-roofed home with rich wood paneling, patterned floors, a dogleg staircase, and eight fireplaces. Now a National Historic Landmark, the house has fine period furnishings and an 18th-century garden where tea is served on summer Wednesdays.

🏛 Neal Dow Memorial

714 Congress St. 📞 (207) 773-7773. ◐ 11am–4pm Mon–Fri. ● Jan, Feb.

Neal Dow (1804–97), one of Portland's prominent citizens, built this Federal-style mansion in 1829. Twice serving as the city's mayor, Dow was an abolitionist and prohibitionist who also championed the causes of women's rights and prison reform. The Dow family's original furnishings, paintings, china, and silver are displayed along with memorabilia of Dow's career.

🏛 Maine Narrow Gauge Railroad Co. & Museum

58 Fore St. 📞 (207) 828-0814. ◐ year-round: 10am–4pm daily. ♿ Train ride ◐ mid-May–mid-Oct on the hour; call for other times. 🚫

Scenic trips along a three-mile (5-km) stretch of the waterfront are the highlight of this museum dedicated to the railroad that served much of Maine from the 1870s to the 1940s. Exhibits include vintage locomotives and a restored caboose.

🏛 Portland Observatory

138 Congress St. 📞 (207) 774-5561. ◐ late May–mid-Oct: 10am–5pm daily. 🚫 🅿 ♿ ℹ

Constructed in 1807, this octagonal landmark is the last surviving 19th-century signal tower on the Atlantic. The 102-step climb to the upper deck is worth the effort.

🏛 Museum at Portland Head Light at Fort Williams Park

12 Captain Strout Circle. 📞 (207) 799-2661. ◐ Jun–Oct: 10am–4pm daily; Apr, May, Nov, Dec: 10am–4pm Sat & Sun. 🚫 ♿

First illuminated in 1791 by order of President George Washington (1732–99), the lighthouse has been the subject of poetry, postage stamps, and photographs. The keeper's house is now a museum with exhibits on the history of the world's beacons. The large surrounding park, just four miles (6.5 km) from downtown, features a beach and picnic areas.

Portland Observatory atop Munjoy Hill

KEY

🟦 Street-by-Street map see pp282–3

━ Highway

ℹ Tourist information

🅿 Parking

(map of Portland with labeled streets: Franklin Street, Pearl Street, Middle Street, Silver Street, Market Street, Commercial Street, Maine State Pier, Portland Pier, Central Wharf, Union Wharf, Portland Fish Pier)

Street-by-Street: Old Port

THIS ONCE-DECAYING NEIGHBORHOOD near the harbor has been restored and is now the city's liveliest area, filled with shops, art galleries, restaurants, and bars. The Old Port's narrow streets are lined with classic examples of Victorian-era commercial architecture. From the docks, ships take passengers out for deep-sea fishing excursions and harbor tours; ferries to Nova Scotia, Canada, save travelers some 850 miles (1,370 km) of driving. Cruises include mailboat rides and excursions to the Calendar Islands, where visitors can enjoy everything from cycling to sea kayaking.

Lively District
The Old Port has numerous pubs and outdoor terraces.

Centennial Block
has a facade made of Maine granite.

Charles Q. Clapp Block
This distinctive building was designed by self-taught architect Charles Quincy Clapp in 1866.

First National Bank
is a typical example of Queen Anne commercial style. Its sandstone and brick exterior features a corner tower and tall chimneys.

Dolphins Statue
The statue is situated in the small cobblestone area in the middle of the Old Port district.

Mary L. Deering Block,
built for the prominent Deering family, is a mix of Italian and Colonial Revival styles.

Seaman's Club
Built after the devastating fire of 1866, the building is known for its striking Gothic windows.

owner, and the Joshua L. Chamberlain House, a Civil War museum.

🏛 Peary-MacMillan Arctic Museum

Hubbard Hall, Bowdoin College. **(** *(207) 725-3416.* **○** *year-round: 10am–5pm Tue–Sat; 2pm–5pm Sun.* **●** *public hols.* **&**

🏛 Pejepscot Historical Society

159 Park Row. **(** *(207) 729-6606.* **○** *call for opening hours and tour times for each museum.*

ENVIRONS: Nine miles (14 km) east lies Bath, long a ship-building center. Its stately homes were built with the profits from this lucrative industry. In 1608 colonists constructed the *Virginia*, the first British boat produced in the New World. Since then, some 4,000 ships have been constructed here. The **Maine Maritime Museum** operates the country's only surviving wooden shipbuilding yard. The modern Maritime History Building annex is a repository of nautical models, paintings, and memorabilia.

Nautical art from the Maine Maritime Museum in Bath

🏛 Maine Maritime Museum

243 Washington St. **(** *(207) 443-1316.* **○** *9:30am–5pm daily.* **●** *Jan 1, Thanksgiving, & Dec 25.* **📷** *call for times.* **&** *partial.* **📷**

Boothbay Harbor ❽

👥 *2,500.* **✈** *38 miles (61 km) N in Augusta.* **🚌** *192 Townsend Ave (207) 633-2353 or (800) 266-8422.*

T HE BOATING CAPITAL of the mid-coast, Boothbay Harbor bustles with the influx of summer tourists. Dozens of boating excursions cast off from the dock. Visitors might choose to take an hour's sail along the coast aboard a majestic windjammer, a 41-mile (66-km) cruise up the

Boothbay Harbor's busy boardwalk area

Kennebec River, or the popular day trip to the artists' retreat on Monhegan Island (*see p287*). Sightseers can participate in a wide range of activities, including puffin and whale-watching expeditions. The harbor is at its best in late June, when majestic tall ships parade in under full sail for the annual Windjammer Days festival.

Boothbay Harbor whale watch sign

The town itself is chock-a-block with shops and galleries. **Marine Resources Aquarium**, a haven for parents of restless children on rainy days, is equipped with a large touch tank filled with sea creatures, which can be touched – including a dogfish head shark.

✘ Marine Resources Aquarium

194 McKown Point Rd. **(** *(207) 633-9559.* **○** *late May–Sep: 10am–5pm daily.* **📷** **📷** **&**

ENVIRONS: A scenic 30-mile (48-km) drive up the coast brings travelers to Pemaquid Point, complete with shelves of granite cliffs that jut from the sea. Rising dramatically above a bluff and offering panoramic views of the coastline, the 1827 **Pemaquid Point Light** houses the **Fisherman's Museum** in the old light-keeper's home. The **Pemaquid Art Gallery** is on the grounds and shows the work of local artists. There is a bonus for history buffs at the 8-acre (3-ha) **Colonial Pemaquid State History Site**, which

includes a 1695 graveyard and a replica of **Fort William Henry**. English colonists fought French invaders at this spot in several forts that date from the early 17th century onward. A small museum contains a diorama of the original 1620s settlement and displays a collection of tools, pottery shards, and household items that reflect the rustic lives of the early settlers.

🚨 Pemaquid Point Light

Rte 130. **(** *(207) 677-2494.* **○** *mid-May–mid-Oct: 10am–5pm Mon–Sat, 11am–5pm Sun.* **📷** **&** **Fisherman's Museum ○** *May–Oct: call for hours.* **& Pemaquid Art Gallery ○** *May–Oct: call for hours.*

🚨 Colonial Pemaquid State History Site/ Fort William Henry

Off Rte 130. **(** *(207) 677-2423.* **○** *late May–early Sep: dawn to dusk.* **🍴**

Pemaquid Point Light and the Fisherman's Museum

Penobscot Bay ❾

PENOBSCOT BAY IS PICTURE-BOOK MAINE, with high hills seemingly rolling straight into the ocean, wave-pounded cliffs, sheltered harbors bobbing with fishing boats, and lobster traps piled high on the docks. Windjammer sailboats, ferries, and numerous cruise ships carry passengers to offshore islands, setting sail from ports such as Rockland, Camden, and Lincolnville, popular stops on the bay's western shore. The former shipbuilding centers of Searsport and Bucksport lie beyond. The more remote eastern shore leads to serene, perfectly preserved villages such as Castine and Blue Hill.

Sailboats moored in the safe confines of Camden Harbor

Secluded cliff-top view of Penobscot Bay

Exploring Penobscot Bay

To sail across Penobscot Bay covers a mere 35 miles (56 km) from its southernmost outpost of Port Clyde to its northern tip at Stonington. However, typical of Maine's ribboned coast, the same voyage takes almost 100 miles (160 km) by car. Either mode of transportation will offer stunning views of one of Maine's coastal highlights.

Rockland

🛈 *1 Harbor Pk (207) 596-0376 or (800) 562-2529.*

Long a fishing town and commercial center, Rockland is now evolving into a tourist destination. These days lobster boats share the harbors with excursion boats, state ferries, and the schooners of Maine's windjammer fleet. However, the Lobster Festival, on the first full weekend of August, remains the town's biggest event.

On land the Farnsworth Art Museum on Main Street showcases some of the giants of US art, including

Rockwell Kent (1882–1971), and Edward Hopper (1882–1967). The new $10-million Wyeth Center is devoted to the works of N.C. (1882–1945), Andrew (b.1917), and Jamie (b.1946) Wyeth, three generations of talented artists who painted in Maine for many years. Two miles (3.2 km) south of Rockland on Route 73, the Owls Head Transportation Museum makes an interesting stop. It houses aircraft, cars, bicycles, and carriages and occasionally hosts air shows.

Camden

🛈 *Commercial St, Public Landing (207) 236-4404 or (800) 223-5459.*

The compact village is ideal for exploring on foot. Shady streets are lined with elegant homes and spired churches, and a host of shops border the waterfront. Among the fine inns on High Street is the Whitehall, with a room dedicated to Pulitzer Prize-winning poet Edna St. Vincent Millay (1892–1950), who went to school in Camden.

Fans of Millay might also want to visit Camden Hills State Park on Route 1, where a short road leads to the top

of 796-ft (242-m) Mount Battie. Standing on this point overlooking Penobscot Bay, Millay was inspired to write her first volume of poetry.

Searsport

🛈 *Main & Steamboat (207) 548-0173.*

Searsport was once a major shipbuilding port. Now a handful of restored sea captains' homes on Church Street house the collection of the Penobscot Marine Museum. An extensive collection of maritime art, ship models, navigational instruments and imported goods and displays of shipbuilding tools help tell the story of those glory days.

Considered to be the antiques capital of Maine, the town is chock-a-block with shops and has large and busy flea markets on weekends in the summer.

Bucksport

🛈 *263 Main St (207) 469-6818.* ⬛

Bucksport looks across the Penobscot River to New England's biggest stronghold, the 125-acre (51-ha) Fort Knox State Park. Built in

Vintage aircraft at Owls Head Transportation Museum

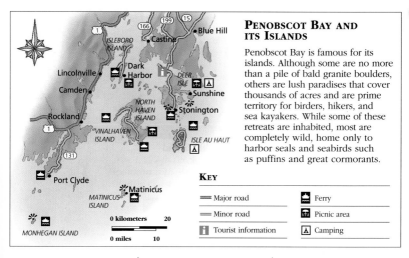

PENOBSCOT BAY AND ITS ISLANDS

Penobscot Bay is famous for its islands. Although some are no more than a pile of bald granite boulders, others are lush paradises that cover thousands of acres and are prime territory for birders, hikers, and sea kayakers. While some of these retreats are inhabited, most are completely wild, home only to harbor seals and seabirds such as puffins and great cormorants.

KEY

▬▬ Major road	⛴ Ferry
▬ Minor road	⛩ Picnic area
ℹ Tourist information	⛺ Camping

---

the mid-1800s, the huge octagonal structure is found on Route 174. It was used as a training facility for troops during the Civil War (1861–5). Visitors can explore barracks, storehouses, and even some underground passages.

Castine
ℹ *Emerson Hall, Court St* *(207) 326-4502.*
Founded in the early 17th century and coveted for its strategic location overlooking the bay, Castine has flown the flags of France, Britain, Holland, and the US.

Relics of Castine's turbulent past can still be seen at Fort George on Wadsworth Cove Road, the highest point in town. Fort George was built by the British in 1779 and witnessed the American Navy's worst defeat during the Revolutionary War, a battle in which more than 40 colonial ships were either captured or destroyed. The fort is always open. Across from Fort George on Battle Avenue is the Maine Maritime Academy.

On Perkins Street, the two-story Wilson Museum houses a collection that includes everything from Balinese masks and pre-Inca pottery to minerals and farm tools. It is closed during the fall and winter months.

Blue Hill
ℹ *Blue Hill Town Hall* *(207) 374-3242.*
Surrounded by fields of blueberries and with many of its white clapboard buildings listed on the National Historic Register, Blue Hill is a living postcard. Visitors will get a great view if they climb up Blue Hill Mountain.

Deer Isle
ℹ *Rte 15 at Eggemoggin Rd* *(207) 348-6124.* ⛴
Deer Isle, reached from the mainland via a graceful suspension bridge, is actually a series of small islands linked by causeways. Island highlights include the towns of Deer Isle and Stonington, and the famous Haystack Mountain School of Crafts.

Isle au Haut
ℹ *Rte 15 at Eggemoggin Rd* *(207) 348-6124.* ⛴
A mail boat from Stonington covers the eight miles (13 km) to Isle au Haut. Almost half the island, some 2,800

White-tailed deer, a common sight throughout the Penobscot Bay area

wooded acres (1,133 ha), belongs to Acadia National Park *(see pp288–9)* and offers 20 miles (32 km) of hiking.

Monhegan Island
ℹ *(207) 596-0376 or (800) LOBCLAW.*
This unspoiled enclave has no cars, no commotion, and until recently no electricity. Only a half mile (0.8 km) wide and 1.7 miles (2.7 km) long, this island is smaller than New York City's Central Park, and is a favored retreat for birders and hikers who enjoy rough trails along rocky cliffs and through deep forest. Painter Jamie Wyeth is one of the prominent current residents of a summer artists' colony. Cruise companies operate round-trip excursions from Port Clyde, Boothbay Harbor, and New Harbor.

North Haven Island
ℹ *(207) 867-4433.* ⛴
Eight miles (13 km) long and 3 miles (5 km) wide, North Haven is a refined summer colony and home to 350 hardy year-round residents. Much of the island remains open fields and meadows filled with wildflowers.

Vinalhaven
ℹ *(207) 863-4826.* ⛴
Tiny Vinalhaven is a perfect place for a swim or a hike. Inland moors and green spaces are balanced by a granite shoreline and a harbor bustling with lobster boats.

Rolling hills near Eagle Lake on the outskirts of Bar Harbor

Bar Harbor ⓫

🏛 5,000 ✈ 11 miles (17 km) NW in Trenton. 🚌 Island Explorer (free)
ℹ 93 Cottage St (207) 288-5103.

WITH A COMMANDING location on Frenchman Bay, Bar Harbor is Mount Desert Island's lively tourist center. Artists Thomas Cole (1801–48) and Frederic Church (1862–1900) discovered the area's beauty in the 1840s and their brilliant work attracted the wealthy. In the 19th century, the town was a summer haven for some of America's richest people, including the Astors and the Vanderbilts.

Today Bar Harbor is a thriving waterside resort that attracts 5,000,000 visitors each year. From here people can explore Acadia National Park *(see pp288–9)* or the mid-Maine coastline, or grab a ferry to Nova Scotia, Canada.

🏛 Bar Harbor Historical Society Museum
33 Ledgelawn Ave. 📞 (207) 288-0000.
◯ Jun–Oct: 1pm–4pm Mon–Sat.
In 1947 a fire destroyed 17,000 acres (6,880 ha) of wilderness and a third of Bar Harbor's

lavish summer homes, all but ending the village's reign as a high-society enclave. A display of early photographs shows the grand old days and the devastating effects of the fire. Happily for visitors, several of the remaining summer showplaces have been turned into gracious inns *(see pp321–2)*.

🎭 Criterion Theater
35 Cottage St. 📞 (207) 288-3441. 🗃
A perennial favorite, this is an Art Deco gem that is listed on the National Register of Historic Places. The theater offers films, live music, and theater performances.

🏛 Abbe Museum
26 Mount Desert St. 📞 (207) 288-3519. ◯ late May–mid-Oct: 10am–5pm daily (Jul–Sep until 9pm Thu–Sat); mid-Oct–late May: 10am–5pm Thu–Sun. ◐ Jan. 🗃 🛗
This museum celebrates Maine's Native American heritage with exhibits, hands-on programs and workshops taught by Native artists. There is a seasonal branch next to the Wild Gardens of Acadia, which has some 300 species of local plants.

🦞 Bar Harbor Oceanarium & Lobster Hatchery
Rte 3. 📞 (207) 288-5005. ◯ mid-May–Oct: 9am–5pm Mon–Sat.
🗃 🛗 🛗 🛗
Bar Harbor Oceanarium, 8.5 miles (14 km) northwest of town, is where to see harbor seals, explore a salt marsh on Thomas Bay Marsh Walk, or visit the Maine Lobster Museum, which has demonstrations of lobstering by real fishermen. The hatching and raising process is explained at the separate Lobster Hatchery.

🦌 Acadia Zoo
Rte 3 in Trenton. 📞 (207) 667-3244.
◯ May–Jun & Sep: 10am–4pm daily; Jul–Aug: 9:30am–8pm daily. 🗃 🛗
A popular family attraction, the Acadia Zoo is located in Trenton across the bridge from Mount Desert Island, where pastures, streams, and woods shelter some 45 species of animals, including reindeer, wolves, monkeys, and moose. A barn has been converted into a rain-forest habitat for monkeys, birds, reptiles, and other denizens of the Amazon.

Northeast Harbor ⓬

✈ 12 miles (19 km) N in Trenton.
ℹ Sea St (207) 276-5040.

NORTHEAST HARBOR IS the center of Mount Desert Island's social scene. The village has a handful of upscale shops, a few dining places, many handsome but rambling summer mansions, and a scenic harbor where boats set sail for nearby Cranberry Islands.

Chartered cruise boat in Bar Harbor

★ **Cadillac Mountain**
The 1,527-ft- (465-m-) tall Cadillac Mountain is the highest point on the Atlantic Coast. Hiking trails and an auto road lead to spectacular panoramas at the summit.

Jordan Pond
Many visitors stop at beautiful Jordan Pond, where a restaurant serves lunch, afternoon tea, and dinner from late May to late October.

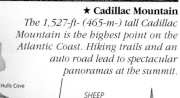

★ **Sand Beach**
Sand Beach is one of only two lifeguarded beaches in the park, but the ocean water, which rarely exceeds 55° F (15° C), discourages many swimmers.

★ **Thunder Hole**
The ocean's relentless pounding on the island's cliffs has created the natural phenomenon known as the Thunder Hole. When the tide rises during heavy winds, air trapped in this crevice is compressed and expelled with a resounding boom.

Rolling hills near Eagle Lake on the outskirts of Bar Harbor

Bar Harbor ⓫

🏃 5,000 ✈ 11 miles (17 km) NW in Trenton. 🚌 Island Explorer (free) ℹ 93 Cottage St (207) 288-5103.

WITH A COMMANDING location on Frenchman Bay, Bar Harbor is Mount Desert Island's lively tourist center. Artists Thomas Cole (1801– 48) and Frederic Church (1862– 1900) discovered the area's beauty in the 1840s and their brilliant work attracted the wealthy. In the 19th century, the town was a summer haven for some of America's richest people, including the Astors and the Vanderbilts.

Today Bar Harbor is a thriving waterside resort that attracts 5,000,000 visitors each year. From here people can explore Acadia National Park (see pp288–9) or the mid-Maine coastline, or grab a ferry to Nova Scotia, Canada.

🏛 **Bar Harbor Historical Society Museum**
33 Ledgelawn Ave. 📞 (207) 288-0000. ⬭ Jun–Oct: 1pm–4pm Mon–Sat.
In 1947 a fire destroyed 17,000 acres (6,880 ha) of wilderness and a third of Bar Harbor's

lavish summer homes, all but ending the village's reign as a high-society enclave. A display of early photographs shows the grand old days and the devastating effects of the fire. Happily for visitors, several of the remaining summer showplaces have been turned into gracious inns (see pp321–2).

🎭 **Criterion Theater**
35 Cottage St. 📞 (207) 288-3441. ⬭
A perennial favorite, this is an Art Deco gem that is listed on the National Register of Historic Places. The theater offers films, live music, and theater performances.

🏛 **Abbe Museum**
26 Mount Desert St. 📞 (207) 288-3519. ⬭ late May–mid-Oct: 10am–5pm daily (Jul–Sep until 9pm Thu–Sat); mid-Oct–late May: 10am–5pm Thu–Sun. ● Jan. 🖉 ♿
This museum celebrates Maine's Native American heritage with exhibits, hands-on programs and workshops taught by Native artists. There is a seasonal branch next to the Wild Gardens of Acadia, which has some 300 species of local plants.

🦭 **Bar Harbor Oceanarium & Lobster Hatchery**
Rte 3. 📞 (207) 288-5005. ⬭ mid-May–Oct: 9am–5pm Mon–Sat.
🖉 🖉 ♿ 🚻
Bar Harbor Oceanarium, 8.5 miles (14 km) northwest of town, is where to see harbor seals, explore a salt marsh on Thomas Bay Marsh Walk, or visit the Maine Lobster Museum, which has demonstrations of lobstering by real fishermen. The hatching and raising process is explained at the separate Lobster Hatchery.

🦌 **Acadia Zoo**
Rte 3 in Trenton. 📞 (207) 667-3244. ⬭ May–Jun & Sep: 10am–4pm daily; Jul–Aug: 9:30am–8pm daily. 🖉 ♿
A popular family attraction, the Acadia Zoo is located in Trenton across the bridge from Mount Desert Island, where pastures, streams, and woods shelter some 45 species of animals, including reindeer, wolves, monkeys, and moose. A barn has been converted into a rain-forest habitat for monkeys, birds, reptiles, and other denizens of the Amazon.

Northeast Harbor ⓬

✈ 12 miles (19 km) N in Trenton. ℹ Sea St (207) 276-5040.

NORTHEAST HARBOR is the center of Mount Desert Island's social scene. The village has a handful of upscale shops, a few dining places, many handsome but rambling summer mansions, and a scenic harbor where boats set sail for nearby Cranberry Islands.

Chartered cruise boat in Bar Harbor

PENOBSCOT BAY AND ITS ISLANDS

Penobscot Bay is famous for its islands. Although some are no more than a pile of bald granite boulders, others are lush paradises that cover thousands of acres and are prime territory for birders, hikers, and sea kayakers. While some of these retreats are inhabited, most are completely wild, home only to harbor seals and seabirds such as puffins and great cormorants.

KEY

▬ Major road	⛴ Ferry
▬ Minor road	⊞ Picnic area
ℹ Tourist information	Ⓐ Camping

---

the mid-1800s, the huge octagonal structure is found on Route 174. It was used as a training facility for troops during the Civil War (1861–5). Visitors can explore barracks, storehouses, and even some underground passages.

Castine

ℹ *Emerson Hall, Court St (207) 326-4502.*

Founded in the early 17th century and coveted for its strategic location overlooking the bay, Castine has flown the flags of France, Britain, Holland, and the US.

Relics of Castine's turbulent past can still be seen at Fort George on Wadsworth Cove Road, the highest point in town. Fort George was built by the British in 1779 and witnessed the American Navy's worst defeat during the Revolutionary War, a battle in which more than 40 colonial ships were either captured or destroyed. The fort is always open. Across from Fort George on Battle Avenue is the Maine Maritime Academy.

On Perkins Street, the two-story Wilson Museum houses a collection that includes everything from Balinese masks and pre-Inca pottery to minerals and farm tools. It is closed during the fall and winter months.

Blue Hill

ℹ *Blue Hill Town Hall (207) 374-3242.*

Surrounded by fields of blueberries and with many of its white clapboard buildings listed on the National Historic Register, Blue Hill is a living postcard. Visitors will get a great view if they climb up Blue Hill Mountain.

Deer Isle

ℹ *Rte 15 at Eggemoggin Rd (207) 348-6124.* ⛴

Deer Isle, reached from the mainland via a graceful suspension bridge, is actually a series of small islands linked by causeways. Island highlights include the towns of Deer Isle and Stonington, and the famous Haystack Mountain School of Crafts.

Isle au Haut

ℹ *Rte 15 at Eggemoggin Rd (207) 348-6124.* ⛴

A mail boat from Stonington covers the eight miles (13 km) to Isle au Haut. Almost half the island, some 2,800

White-tailed deer, a common sight throughout the Penobscot Bay area

wooded acres (1,133 ha), belongs to Acadia National Park *(see pp288–9)* and offers 20 miles (32 km) of hiking.

Monhegan Island

ℹ *(207) 596-0376 or (800) LOBCLAW.*

This unspoiled enclave has no cars, no commotion, and until recently no electricity. Only a half mile (0.8 km) wide and 1.7 miles (2.7 km) long, this island is smaller than New York City's Central Park, and is a favored retreat for birders and hikers who enjoy rough trails along rocky cliffs and through deep forest. Painter Jamie Wyeth is one of the prominent current residents of a summer artists' colony. Cruise companies operate round-trip excursions from Port Clyde, Boothbay Harbor, and New Harbor.

North Haven Island

ℹ *(207) 867-4433.* ⛴

Eight miles (13 km) long and 3 miles (5 km) wide, North Haven is a refined summer colony and home to 350 hardy year-round residents. Much of the island remains open fields and meadows filled with wildflowers.

Vinalhaven

ℹ *(207) 863-4826.* ⛴

Tiny Vinalhaven is a perfect place for a swim or a hike. Inland moors and green spaces are balanced by a granite shoreline and a harbor bustling with lobster boats.

Acadia National Park ⑩

L OCATED PRIMARILY ON Mount Desert Island,
the 35,000-acre (14,164-ha) Acadia National
Park, a wild, unspoiled paradise, is heavily visited
in summer. Wave-beaten inland forests await
travelers. The park's main attraction is the Loop
Road, a 27-mile (43-km) drive that climbs and dips
with the pink granite mountains of the east coast
of the island before swinging inland past Jordan
Pond, Bubble Pond, and Eagle Lake. Visitors who
want a closer, more intimate look at the flora and
fauna can do so on foot, bike, or horseback.

Vintage Carriage Roads
*Forty-five miles (72 km) of old
broken-stone carriage roads can
be used for hiking and cycling.*

**Acadia's
Wildlife**
*The park is home
to numerous
animals includ-
ing woodchucks,
white-tailed deer,
red foxes, and
the occasional
black bear.*

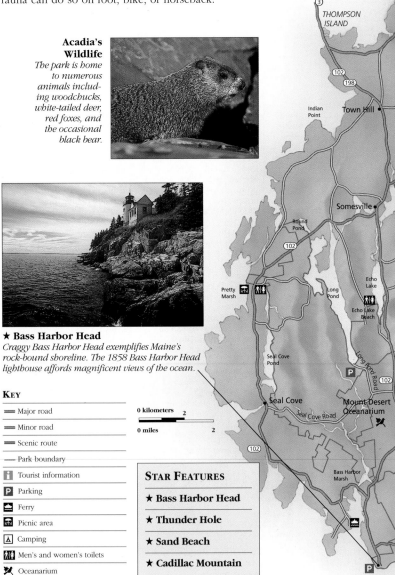

★ **Bass Harbor Head**
*Craggy Bass Harbor Head exemplifies Maine's
rock-bound shoreline. The 1858 Bass Harbor Head
lighthouse affords magnificent views of the ocean.*

THOMPSON
ISLAND

Indian
Point

Town Hill

Somesville

Round
Pond

Pretty
Marsh

Long
Pond

Echo
Lake

Echo Lake
Beach

Seal Cove
Pond

Seal Cove

Mount Desert
Oceanarium

Bass Harbor
Marsh

Bass Harbor Head

KEY

▬	Major road
▬	Minor road
▬	Scenic route
- -	Park boundary
🛈	Tourist information
P	Parking
⛴	Ferry
🔲	Picnic area
Δ	Camping
🚻	Men's and women's toilets
✘	Oceanarium

0 kilometers   2
0 miles   2

STAR FEATURES

★ **Bass Harbor Head**

★ **Thunder Hole**

★ **Sand Beach**

★ **Cadillac Mountain**

♣ Asticou Terrace and Thuya Lodge and Gardens

Rte 3 S of Rte 198 jct. 📞 *(207) 276-5130.* ⏰ *Jul–Sep: 7am–7pm.* 💳 *for gardens.*

The harbor can best be admired from the stunning Asticou Terraces. A granite path snakes along the hillside, yielding ever-wider vistas as it ascends, with benches and a gazebo placed at strategic viewpoints. At the top of the hill are Thuya Lodge, with collections of paintings and books, and Thuya Gardens, with flowers beds and a reflecting pool that descends to the harbor's edge.

ENVIRONS: Somes Sound, a finger-shaped natural fjord that juts five miles (8 km) into Mount Desert Island, separates Northeast Harbor from quiet Southwest Harbor.

Whimsical sculpture in Asticou Gardens

The village's close ties to the sea are celebrated in the **Mount Desert Oceanarium**. Located in a former ship's chandlery, the oceanarium features 20 tanks teeming with live coastal sea animals and exhibits on scallops, whales, lobsters, tides, fishing gear, and the weather. Children enjoy getting acquainted with the horseshoe crabs, sea snails, starfish, and other inhabitants of the touch tank. A drive or bike ride beyond Southwest Harbor leads to unspoiled villages, including Bass Harbor, where tourists are few and visitors can explore the 1858 Bass Harbor Head Light.

✠ Mount Desert Oceanarium

172 Clark Point Rd. 📞 *(207) 244-7330.* ⏰ *mid-May–mid-Oct: 9am–5pm Mon–Sat.* 💳 ♿ 🅿

Machias ⑬

🏠 *2,900.* ✈ *91 miles (146 km) W in Bangor.* ℹ *112 Dublin St (207) 255-4402 or (800) 377-9748.*

SITUATED AT THE MOUTH of the river of the same name, Machias retains many of the handsome old homes that sprang up during its days as a prosperous 19th-century lumber center. The town's name comes from the Micmac Indians and means "bad little falls," a reference to the waterfall that cascades in the center of town. There is a good view of the falls from the footbridge in Bad Little Falls Park, a mid-town oasis.

Machias proclaims itself as the wild blueberry capital of Maine. It also lays claim to the region's oldest building, the 1770 **Burnham Tavern**, now a museum with period furnishings, paintings, and historic photographs. It was here that plans were made for the first naval battle of the Revolutionary War in 1775 (*see pp43–45*). Following that heated meeting, local men sailed out into Machias Bay on the small sloop *Unity* and captured the British man-of-war HMS *Margaretta*. Models of the two ships can be seen at

THE LOBSTER INDUSTRY

Harbors filled with lobstering boats and piers piled high with traps are familiar sights in the state that is America's undisputed lobster capital. Maine harvests over 40 million lbs (18 million kg) of this tasty crustacean each year. No visit is complete without a trip to a lobster pound, where patrons pick a live lobster from the tank, wait for it to be steamed, and savor the sweet meat at a picnic table overlooking the ocean.

Lobster fishermen

the **Gates House**, a restored 1807 Federal-style home in nearby Michiasport.

The town is set on the Machias River, a demanding canoeing route. **Roque Bluffs State Park** to the southwest of town offers swimming in a 60-acre (24-ha) freshwater pond and a one-mile- (1.6-km-) long sweep of beach. The park has a launching ramp for sea kayaks, which are popular in Machias Bay. Birders go to nearby Cutler for boat trips to Machias Seal Island, home to puffins, Arctic terns, and razorbill auks.

🏛 Burnham Tavern

Main St. 📞 *(207) 255-4432.* ⏰ *mid-Jun–Sep: 9am–5pm Mon–Fri.* 💳 🅿

⌂ Gates House

Rte 92, Michiasport. 📞 *(207) 255-8461.* ⏰ *mid-Jun–mid-Sep: 12:30pm–4:30pm Tue–Sat.* 💳

♣ Roque Bluffs State Park

Rogue Bluffs Rd, Rogue Bluffs. 📞 *(207) 255-3475.* ⏰ *mid-May–Oct: 9am–dusk.* 💳 ♿

Footbridge in Bad Little Falls Park in Machias

Campobello Island ⑭

IN 1964 2,800 ACRES (1,133 ha) of Campobello Island were designated as a memorial to President Franklin Delano Roosevelt (1882–1945). The main settlement of Welshpool was where the future president spent most of his summers, until 1921 when he contracted polio. Undaunted, Roosevelt went on to lead the US through the Great Depression and World War II. The highlight of the park – which actually lies in Canada and is the only international park in the world – is Roosevelt Cottage, a 34-room summer home that displays Roosevelt's personal mementos.

VISITORS' CHECKLIST

ℹ️ Rte 774. **📞** (506) 752-2922.
Roosevelt Cottage ◯ mid-May
–mid-Oct: 9am–5pm daily (EST).
♿ & W www.fdr.net.

KEY

━━ Major road

══ Minor road

▬▬ Scenic route

— Park boundary

- - Walking trail

ℹ️ Tourist information

P Parking

🏕 Picnic area

△ Camping

🌿 Viewpoint

★ Roosevelt Cottage
Built in 1897, the sprawling wood-frame structure is one of a cluster of cottages that once belonged to wealthy families.

Mulholland Point
has an 1885 lighthouse and a waterfront picnic site that offers good views of the FDR Memorial Bridge and Lubec.

Lower Duck Pond Bog is a prime habitat for such birds as killdeer, American black duck, and great blue heron.

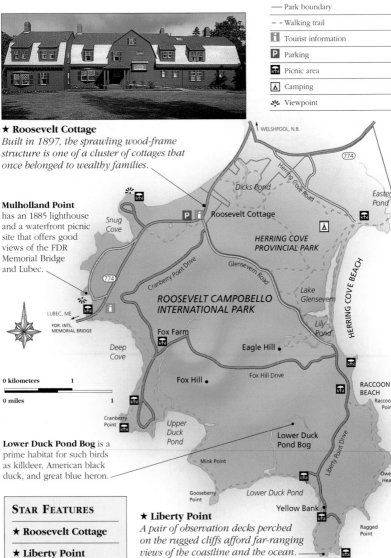

WELSHPOOL, N.B.

774

Dicks Pond

Eastern Pond

Herring Cove Road

Roosevelt Cottage

HERRING COVE
PROVINCIAL PARK

Snug Cove

Glensevern Road

Cranberry Point Drive

774

ROOSEVELT CAMPOBELLO
INTERNATIONAL PARK

Lake Glensevern

Lily Pond

HERRING COVE BEACH

LUBEC, ME

FDR. INTL.
MEMORIAL BRIDGE

Fox Farm

Eagle Hill

Deep Cove

Fox Hill Drive

RACCOON BEACH

Fox Hill

Raccoon Point

0 kilometers 1

0 miles 1

Cranberry Point

Upper Duck Pond

Lower Duck Pond Bog

Liberty Point Drive

Mink Point

Owen Head

Gooseberry Point

Lower Duck Pond

Yellow Bank

Ragged Point

Liberty Point

STAR FEATURES

★ Roosevelt Cottage

★ Liberty Point

★ Liberty Point
A pair of observation decks perched on the rugged cliffs afford far-ranging views of the coastline and the ocean.

Privately owned Hamilton's Folly mansion in Calais

Calais ⑮

🧍 *4,000.* ✈ *229 miles (424 km) W in Bangor.* ℹ *7 Union St (207) 454-2211.*

PERCHED ON the west bank of the St. Croix River opposite St. Stephen, New Brunswick, Calais is Maine's busiest border crossing to Canada. The two countries share jurisdiction over nearby St. Croix Island, where in 1604 explorers Samuel de Champlain (1567–1635) and the Sieur de Monts (c.1560–1630) established the first white settlement in North America north of Florida. The island is accessible only by boat, a difficult trip due to strong currents and tides that can run as high as 28 ft (8.5 m).

Calais was devastated by a gigantic fire in 1870. One of the few buildings that survived the conflagration is Hamilton's Folly mansion at No. 78 South Street. The Victorian house was so dubbed by locals because of its ostentatious design – a tribute to excess that bankrupted its owner.

Outdoor activities abound here. The St. Croix River is a challenging waterway for canoeists and a prime spot for salmon fishing. Three miles (5 km) southwest of Calais is the Baring Unit of the **Moosehorn National Wildlife Refuge**, 12,000 acres (4,856 ha) of wilderness that beckons hikers, bird-watchers, and naturalists. Man-made eagle nesting platforms have been erected

along Route 1 north of town. Visitors should watch for the 400-sq-ft (120-sq-m) observation deck on this road for the best views. Also, there are a number of commercial farms that allow visitors to pick their own blueberries.

🦌 **Moosehorn National Wildlife Refuge**
Charlotte Rd S of Calais. 🛈 *(207) 454-7161.* **Park** ◯ *year-round: 9am–sunset.* **Office** ◯ *year-round: 7:30am–4pm Mon–Fri.* ♿

Bangor ⑯

🧍 *33,200.* ✈ *287 Godfrey Blvd.* ◻ ℹ *519 Main St (207) 947-0307.*

THE WORLD'S LEADING lumber port in the 1850s, Bangor remains the commercial center of northern Maine. The town's Penobscot River harbor was once loaded with ships carrying pine logs from nearby sawmills. This past is saluted with a 31-ft (9.5-m), 3,200-lbs (1,450-kg) statue of the mythical lumberjack Paul Bunyan on Main Street. Industrial might aside, Maine's second-largest city also draws visitors because of its ideal location as a base camp for treks to Acadia National Park *(see pp288–9)* and the forestlands that stretch to the north.

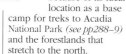

Ripe blueberries in Calais

The city has a number of noteworthy residences from both the past and the

present. The stately homes spared by a 1911 fire still line the West Market Square Historic District and the Broadway area. Maine-born horror author Stephen King lives in a mansion at No. 47 West Broadway, complete with a wrought-iron fence festooned with iron bats and cobwebs. The Greek Revival 1836 Thomas Hill House is headquarters for the **Bangor Museum and Center for History**. The State Street facility holds changing exhibits.

One of Bangor's most pleasant green spaces is the **Mount Hope Cemetery**. Established in 1834, the cemetery is gardenlike and beautifully landscaped with ponds, bridges, and paved paths that attract strollers and inline skaters. This spirit of movement is also celebrated at the **Cole Land Transportation Museum**. The museum's collection contains more than 200 vehicles dating from the 19th century, ranging from fire engines and horse-drawn logging sleds to antique baby carriages.

🏛 **Bangor Museum and Center for History**
159 Union St. 🛈 *(207) 942-5766; also at 6 State St.* 🛈 *(207) 942-1900.* ◯ *Apr–Dec: noon–4pm Tue–Fri.* 📷 ✔

⚰ **Mount Hope Cemetery**
State St. ◯ *7:30am–dusk Mon–Fri.* ✔ ♿

🏛 **Cole Land Transportation Museum**
405 Perry Rd. 🛈 *(207) 990-3600.* ◯ *May–early Nov: 9am–5pm daily.* 📷

Bangor's West Market Historic District

Augusta ⓱

🏛 *20,0300.* ✈ *75 Airport Rd.*
ℹ *21 University Dr (207) 623-4559.*

Maine's state capital is a relatively quiet city of 20,000. The 1832 **Maine State House**, the centerpiece of the government complex on the Kennebec River, was built of granite quarried from neighboring Hallowell. Major expansions have left only the center block from the original design by Boston architect Charles Bulfinch (1763–1844). Exhibits include political portraits and battle flags. Across the street, the **Blaine House** has been serving as the governor's mansion since 1919. The 28-room Colonial-style home was built in 1832 for a local sea captain.

Costumed interpreter at Old Fort Western in Augusta

The **Maine State Museum** has exhibits spanning "12,000 years of Maine history." One highlight is the "Made in Maine" exhibit, which re-creates a water-powered woodworking mill. The **Old Fort Western** is a restoration of one of New England's oldest surviving wooden forts, dating from 1754. The fort was built on the site where the Plymouth Pilgrims *(see pp150–51)* had established their trading post the previous century.

🚩 **Maine State House**
State & Capitol Sts. ☎ *(207) 287-1400.* ◯ *year-round: 8am–5pm Mon–Fri.* 🗓 *9am–1pm Sat.* ♿

Imposing facade of the Maine State House in Augusta

🚩 **Blaine House**
192 State St. ☎ *(207) 287-2121.* ◯ *year-round: 2pm–4pm Tue–Thu & by appt.* 🗓 *call to arrange.* ♿

🏛 **Maine State Museum**
State Capitol Complex, State St. ☎ *(207) 287-2301.* ◯ *year-round: 9am–5pm Mon–Fri, 10am–4pm Sat.* ◯ *public hols.* 🗓 🗓 ♿

🏛 **Old Fort Western**
16 Cony St. ☎ *(207) 626-2385.* ◯ *call for hours.* 🗓 ♿

ENVIRONS: Heading southwest from Augusta, travelers will get a rare look at the last active Shaker community in the US. Established in the 18th century, the Sabbathday Lake Shaker Community is home to a mere handful of residents who still adhere to their traditional beliefs of simplicity, celibacy, and communal harmony. Tours of the 17-building village include a stop at the **Shaker Village Museum** to see the beautiful furniture and ingenious inventions that became Shaker trademarks.

Nestled at the feet of Maine's western mountain ranges, Poland Springs is famous for the water taken from its spring. Continuing west, travelers will come upon Sebago Lake, a favorite among fishermen because of its delicious salmon.

Lifeguard's chair on the shore of tranquil Sebago Lake

🏛 **Sabbathday Shaker Village Museum**
707 Shaker Rd, New Gloucester.
☎ *(207) 926-4597.* ◯ *late May–mid-Oct: 10am–4:30pm Mon–Sat.*
🗓 🗓 ♿

Bethel ⓲

🏛 *2,500.* 🛫 *70 miles (113 km) S in Portland.* ℹ *30 Cross St (207) 824-2282 or (800) 442-5826.*

A picturesque historic district, a major New England ski resort, and proximity to the White Mountains give Bethel year-round appeal. First settled in 1796, the town grew into a farming and lumbering center, and with the coming of the railroad in 1851 quickly became a popular resort. The line-up of classic clapboard mansions on the town green includes the Federal-style **Moses Mason House** (c.1813), which has period pieces and Rufus Porter murals on two floors.

Scenic drives are found in all directions, taking in tiny, unspoiled colonial hamlets such as Waterford to the south and beautiful mountain terrain to the north. **Sunday River Ski Resort** *(see p362)*, six miles (10 km) north of town in Newry, has eight mountains and more than 100 ski trails. Evans Notch, a natural pass through the White Mountain peaks, offers many memorable views, including the Roost, a suspension bridge high above the Wild River and a favorite with photographers. **Grafton Notch State Park** has even more spectacular scenery along its drives and hiking trails. The park's special spots include waterfalls bearing such fanciful names as Screw Auger and Mother Walker, and sweeping views from Table Rock and the top of Old Speck Mountain.

♈ Moses Mason House
10–14 Broad St. *(207) 824-2908.* ○ *Jul–early Sep: 1pm–4pm Tue–Sun.*

☸ Sunday River Ski Resort
Off Rte 2 in Newry. *(207) 824-3000 or (800) 5432-SKI.* ○ *9am–4pm Mon–Fri, 8am–4pm Sat–Sun.*
♣ Grafton Notch State Park
Rte 26 NW of Newry. *(207) 824-2912.* ○ *mid-May–mid-Oct.*

Sugarloaf ⑲

ℹ *(207) 237-2000 or (800) 843-5623.*

Maine's highest ski mountain, Sugarloaf is the centerpiece of this touristic village packed with hotels, restaurants, and hundreds of condominiums. Downhill skiers have been flocking to the **Sugarloaf/USA** ski center *(see p362)* for years, attracted by the more than 100 trails and a vertical drop of 2,800 ft (870 m). The center also offers cross-country skiing, snowshoeing, and ice skating.

In summer, the emphasis shifts to the resort's 18-hole golf course, boating on the lakes and rivers, and hiking in the surrounding Carrabassett Valley. The resort is also famous for a network of more than 50 miles (80 km) of mountain-biking trails through terrain ranging from flat trails to challenging circuits full of steep climbs and descents.

Screw Auger Falls in Grafton Notch State Park

☸ Sugarloaf/USA
Carrabassett Valley. *(207) 237-2000 or (800) 843-5623.* ○ *8:30am–3:50pm daily.* ⌂ *in lodge.*

Rangeley Lakes Region ⑳

ℹ *6 Park Rd (207) 864-5364 or (800) 685-2537.*

Set against a backdrop of mountains, this rustic area encompasses a series of pristine lakes that have long been a magnet for any kind of outdoor enthusiast. In summer fishermen ply the waterways for trout and salmon, while canoeists frequently spot a moose or two lumbering along the shoreline. While the area has become

Moose crossing sign

popular with mountain bikers recently, the beauty of the place is no secret. Hikers have been enjoying the vistas from the summit of **Bald Mountain** and tramping the section of the Appalachian Trail running along **Saddleback Mountain** for decades.

Elsewhere, the popular **Rangeley Lake State Park** provides vacationers with facilities for swimming, fishing, birding, boating, and camping, and 1.2 miles (2 km) of lakefront. Toward the southeast, **Mount Blue State Park** is home to Lake Webb, a favorite haunt of fishermen because of its plentiful population of black bass, trout, and salmon. The park is dominated by the towering 3,187-ft (971-m) Mount Blue.

☸ Bald Mountain
(207) 864-7311.
☸ Saddleback Mountain
(207) 864-5671. ○ *9am–4pm Mon–Fri; daily during the ski season.*
♣ Rangeley Lake State Park
South Shore Dr, Rangeley.
(207) 864-3858. ○ *mid-May–Sep: 9am–dusk.*
♣ Mount Blue State Park
West Rd, Weld. *(207) 585-2347.* ○ *mid-May–Sep: daylight hours.* **Camping** *(800) 332-1501 or (207) 287-3824.*

Challenging snowboarding on Sugarloaf, Maine's second-highest mountain at 4,237 ft (1,290 m)

The dramatic 1,800-ft- (550-m-) high cliffs of Mount Kineo on Moosehead Lake

Moosehead Lake ㉑

ℹ *Rte 15, Greenville (207) 695-2702, (207) 695-2702 or (888) 876-2778.*
w *www.mooseheadlake.org*

Forty miles (64 km) long and blessed with 320 miles (515 km) of mountain-rimmed shoreline, Moosehead Lake is one of the largest bodies of freshwater within any state in the Northeast. A popular destination for hunters, fishermen, hikers, and canoeists since the 1880s, the region is attracting a whole new breed of outdoor enthusiasts: mountain bikers, skiers, and snowmobilers.

Greenville, the region's largest town, is the starting point for excursions into the deep boreal forests known as the Great North Woods, including seaplane services that fly visitors to remote fishing camps. **Big Squaw Mountain Resort** *(see p322)* in Greenville offers affordable skiing and its chairlift provides panoramic views of the countryside all year.

The **Moosehead Marine Museum** tells of the history of the steamboat in Greenville, beginning in 1836 when the town was a logging center. One of the museum's prized possessions is the *Katahdin*, a restored 1914 steamboat and the last of a fleet of 50 such boats that plied the lake during the peak lumbering years. The *Katahdin* offers lake cruises and excursions to Mount Kineo, the sheer cliff face of which is the most prominent landmark on the lake. Local Native Americans considered the mountain sacred. The tiny settlement of Rockwood, the closest town to Mount Kineo, provides views of the mountain from rustic lakeside lodgings *(see p323).*

🎿 Big Squaw Mountain Resort

Rte 15 between Greenville & Rockwood. **ℂ** *(207) 695-1000.*
Chairlift ○ *ski season: 9am–4pm; weekends in summer and fall.* ♿ ♿

🏛 Moosehead Marine Museum

12 Lily Bay Rd, Greenville.
ℂ *(207) 695-2716.* **Museum** ○ *Jun–mid-Oct: 10am–2pm daily.*
Cruises ○ *call for times and reservations.* ♿

Baxter State Park ㉒

ℹ *64 Balsam Dr, Millinocket (207) 723-5140.* **Office** ○ *8am–4pm Mon–Fri.* **Park** ○ *mid-May–mid-Oct.* ♿ **w** *www. baxterstateparkauthority.com*

This park was named for Governor Percival Proctor Baxter (1876–1969). Baxter was instrumental in the effort to preserve this magnificent land, purchasing more than 200,000 acres (81,000 ha) and donating it to the state over 30-odd years with the stipulation that it was never to be developed. The park encompasses 46 mountain peaks, 18 of them over 3,000 ft (900 m), including Katahdin, Maine's tallest.

The park's 200 miles (320 km) of hiking trails are unsurpassed, and range from demanding climbs to easy family walks. Henry David Thoreau *(see p30)* tried the trek in 1846, but never made it to the 5,267-ft (1,605-m) summit of Katahdin. However, thousands of hikers are successful each year, and the trails are crowded with climbers in summer and fall. Some hardy souls can be seen completing the last steps of the famous Appalachian Trail *(see pp22–3)*, which runs from Springer Mountain, Georgia, to its terminus atop Katahdin.

Deer, bear, raccoons, and other wildlife are abundant in this park, and ponds such as Grassy, Sandy Stream, and Russell are favorite watering spots for Maine's official state animal: the moose.

Majestic Mount Katahdin, a popular hiking destination

◁ **Monhegan Harbor, with Manana Island in the distance**

Autumn colors in Aroostook State Park

Aroostook County ㉓

🛈 *Main St, Caribou (207) 498-8736 or (888) 216-2463.*

M AINE'S LARGEST and most northern county, Aroostook covers an area greater than the combined size of Connecticut and Rhode Island. The region is best known for agriculture, with some one million acres (405,000 ha) producing nearly two billion lbs (907 million kg) of potatoes each year, plus lush crops of clover, oats, barley, and broccoli. In summer endless acres of potato fields are covered with blossoms, a vision in pink and white. Another four million acres (1,620,000 ha) of land is forested, mostly owned by paper companies that process the lumber in 50 local pulp and paper mills.

In summer hikers trek the trails in **Aroostook State Park**, fly fishermen plumb the streams for salmon and trout, and canoeists and kayakers paddle the Allagash River. When the heavy winter snows come, snowmobilers arrive in large numbers to explore the entire 1,600 miles (2,500 km) of the Interstate Trail System.

Aroostook County begins in the south in Houlton, a quiet town with a Market Square Historic District of 28 19th-century buildings. A French dialect can be heard in the northern St. John Valley, the legacy of Acadians who settled here in 1785. The **Acadian Village** consists of 16 original and reconstructed buildings from the early days. **The New Sweden Historical Museum** remembers a Swedish colony that settled not far from Caribou in the late 19th century.

🌼 **Aroostook State Park**
87 State Park Rd, S of Presque Isle. 📞 *(207) 768-8341.* ⏰ *year-round: for camping; mid-May–mid-Oct: daylight hours; accessible for cross-country skiing and snow-mobiling in winter.* 🅿 ♿ ♿

🏛 **Acadian Village**
Rte 1, Van Buren. 📞 *(207) 868-5042.* ⏰ *mid-Jun–mid-Sep: 12pm–5pm.* 🎫

🏛 **The New Sweden Historical Museum**
Capitol Hill & Station Rds., New Sweden. 📞 *(207) 896-3018.* ⏰ *Jun–mid-Sep: 12pm–4pm Tue–Sat, 2pm–5pm Sun.*

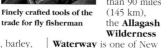
Finely crafted tools of the trade for fly fisherman

ENVIRONS:
Starting at Lake Chamberlain and extending north for more than 90 miles (145 km), the **Allagash Wilderness Waterway** is one of New England's most stunning natural areas. The waterway and its many lakes and streams have been protected since 1966. The Allagash has also been designated a National Wild and Scenic Rivers System.

The state owns the land flanking the waterway for 500 ft (150 m) on each side, assuring a protected habitat for dozens of animals and more than 120 bird species. Anglers will find numerous brook trout and whitefish.

A trek up or down the Allagash system is the ultimate canoe trip in the state, and one that generally takes between five and ten days. Especially beautiful spots are Allagash Lake, a tranquil side trip where no motors are allowed, and Allagash Falls, a dramatic 40-ft (12-m) drop that necessitates carrying the canoe (called "portaging") for about a third of a mile (0.5 km). The canoeing season runs from late May to early October.

🛶 **Allagash Wilderness Waterway**
🛈 *Maine Bureau of Parks and Lands, 106 Hogan Rd, Bangor (207) 941-4014.* ⏰ *year-round.* 🎫

Frog in the protected habitat of the Allagash Wilderness Waterway

---

MAINE'S GREAT RAFTING RIVERS

Maine is famous for three whitewater rivers, the Kennebec, the Dead, and the west branch of the Penobscot. The first two rivers meet near the town called The Forks, southwest of Moosehead Lake, where more than a dozen rafting companies offer equipment and guided trips (*see p357*). The Millinocket area services paddlers bound for the Penobscot, famed among rafters for its challenging drop through a vertical walled canyon below the Ripogenus Dam.

Kennebec River rafters in the challenging whitewater

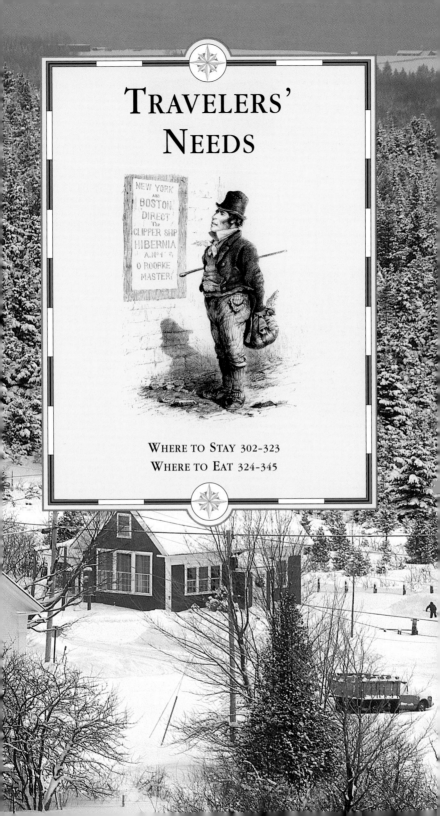

Travelers' Needs

WHERE TO STAY

THE INCREDIBLY varied accommodations of the New England states are tailored to suit virtually all tastes and budgets. If you are looking to commune with nature and save a few dollars at the same time, you can take your pick of campsites *(see pp356–9)* sprinkled liberally throughout the six states. Rustic country inns and bed and breakfasts (B&Bs) are plentiful, offering travelers quaint facilities and a more personal

Sign for rustic inn in Cape Cod

touch. Hotels and motels are also popular choices, conveniently located in or around busy tourist destinations. From the most posh hotel in Boston to a historic Vermont B&B or a rugged backcountry camping experience in Maine, New England has a place for everyone. During the summer vacation season, lodgings can sometimes be hard to come by, so it is always best to book in advance. This is also true during the fall-foliage season.

Luxurious Foxwoods Resort Casino near Mystic, Connecticut

HOTELS

NEW ENGLAND HAS NO shortage of hotel chains. The majority of the large chains, such as Holiday Inn, Hilton, Hyatt, Marriott, and Ramada, offer standard amenities that include such things as a bar, dining room, and exercise facilities. Although one hotel room is generally indistinguishable from the next, they are all impeccably clean and come equipped with a television, room service, and a private bathroom – comforts not always found in B&Bs.

The luxury hotels, usually found in city centers, can be very lavish. Lush decor, fine dining, and valet services are the earmarks of such establishments. The area's large casinos and resorts are also known for their lavishness.

It is always best to notify the reservation clerk should you be arriving late. Most hotels will hold your reservation only until 6pm, especially during the tourist season.

MOTELS

IF YOU ARE ON a budget, motels offer you the best and most flexible value for your money. Often found on the outskirts of cities and towns, motels also dot the New England roads most frequented by travelers. While you will not find the same amenities as in the big hotels, motels will offer you convenience and comfort at significantly lower prices. The standard motel room is equipped with a private bathroom, color TV, and heat and air

Antiques and antique furnishings, a typical feature of New England B&Bs

conditioning. The more modern places usually have two double beds, making it easier to accommodate your whole family in a single room.

BED AND BREAKFASTS AND INNS

AMERICAN B&BS can differ greatly from their European counterparts. Very often they are not the cozy one- or two-room guest lodgings located in the owner's personal residence like those you would come across in Europe. Increasingly, New England B&Bs are professionally operated businesses in which guests live in separate accommodations from the owner or caretaker. This style of B&B tends to be larger in size and have more rooms than its more traditional counterpart. The loss of intimacy usually comes with the added bonus of private bathrooms and added services. Of course, traditionalists can still find small, cozy B&Bs throughout New England. Regardless of the size, all B&Bs offer distinctive lodgings and a breakfast, which may vary in size and style from one establishment to another.

Like B&Bs, inns come in all shapes and sizes, from the very rustic to the large resort-style lodging. Not only do inns serve breakfast and

Mount Washington Hotel and Resort in Bretton Woods, New Hampshire

dinner, the larger ones can come with such "extras" as swimming pools, gardens, and taverns. Depending on their location, many inns are affiliated with local tennis or golf clubs.

Because some B&Bs and inns are historic homes appointed with beautiful antique furniture, they usually prohibit smoking and often do not allow children. The **New England Innkeepers Association**, or one of its state branches, is a good lodging resource.

Vine-covered exterior of Daggett House in Edgartown, Massachusetts

PRICES AND RESERVATIONS

RATES AND AVAILABILITY can fluctuate from season to season. Prices are generally highest in the peak tourist periods (July–August and mid-September–late October) and in the cities, coastal areas, and other prime vacation destinations. The reverse is true with ski resorts, when winter months are the most expensive. Booking your accommodations well in advance is always the safest way to avoid complications. This is especially true if you are looking forward to staying at a B&B or inn in which rooms are limited.

To save money you should try booking in cities on the weekend and in the country during the week. Many hotels in urban areas such as Boston cater to business travelers and may offer reduced rates from Friday to Sunday. Conversely, many of the rural lodgings, popular with the weekend crowd, slash their prices substantially during the week.

Always inquire about package deals offered by motels and hotels. Discounted meals and free passes to local attractions are sometimes thrown in as added incentive for you to stay with them. Some inns and B&Bs also work in conjunction with each other to promote inn-to-inn tours for cyclists and cross-country skiers, offering special rates for accommodations along the tour route.

To avoid unpleasant surprises, it is always prudent to ask about any restrictions, including those on children, pets, and smoking.

HOW TO BOOK

MOST OF THE MAJOR hotels have toll-free reservation numbers, and it is fairly common practice now to take reservations by fax or via the Internet. Room rates are usually quoted for two people sharing a room, including tax or breakfast; all B&Bs, of course, provide a morning meal. Local tourist offices are also excellent sources of information regarding accommodations.

Beautiful room at the Inn by the Sea in Cape Elizabeth, Maine

HIDDEN EXTRAS

YOU SHOULD BE aware that the prices quoted for many accommodations are not entirely accurate in terms of what you will be greeted with on your final bill. Often the quoted rates do not include taxes, which can increase the bill significantly – even in the haven of New Hampshire, which has no sales tax, but does have lodging and restaurant taxes. Hotels in large urban areas often charge for their parking facilities, sometimes substantially. If you are staying in Boston, for example, parking costs could amount to $20–$25 per day.

BUSINESS TRAVELERS

OUTSIDE OF the major hotels, most New England accommodations are ill-equipped for the modern business traveler. The big chains, however, have the technology to send and receive faxes and provide Internet access. Some of Boston's newly refurbished properties offer multi-line phones, in-room fax machines, and private voice mail. If you are planning on booking into an older property, you should always make sure that it has been upgraded with the facilities you might require.

DISABLED TRAVELERS

ALTHOUGH FEDERAL law requires that all businesses provide access and facilities for the disabled, the practical reality is that this is not always the case. The vast majority of large private and chain hotels are modern enough to be equipped with the necessary facilities, including visual notification of the fire alarm, incoming phone calls, and the doorbell. Many also have some suites designated specifically for the disabled. However, many of New England's older buildings and B&Bs have narrow hallways that can obstruct wheelchairs and have no ramps. As always, it is best to check in advance.

WHERE TO STAY IN BOSTON

THE CENTRALLY LOCATED Back Bay has the greatest concentration of hotels, convenient for tourists as well as

B&B bedroom at Arlington, Vermont's Inn on Covered Bridge Green

for business travelers. In the gentrifying South End, an increasing number of restored Victorian townhouses have been converted into B&Bs. Accommodations in the downtown financial district near the waterfront cater to business people during the week, but often offer good value to vacationers on the weekends. Across the Charles River, Cambridge has a large number of hotels, particularly around Harvard Square and among the Kendall Square office towers. In more suburban Brookline along the Green Line Trolley routes west of the Back Bay, several guesthouses as well as more upscale B&Bs offer additional alternatives. One plus for travelers: Boston hotels now house many of the city's top restaurants, including Clio in the Eliot Hotel, the Federalist at Fifteen Beacon, Julien at the Hotel Meridien, and Aujourd'hui at the Four Seasons Hotel.

Boston hotels are particularly busy in May and June for college graduations, July

and August for summer vacations, and September and October for the fall-foliage season. Throughout the course of a year, many Boston hotels cater to business travelers, including the hotels downtown around the Hynes Convention Center, and in Cambridge's Kendall Square. This means that the rates are often lowest on weekends.

The city does have a good selection of smaller hotels and B&Bs, often offering more personal service and charm than the big convention hotels. If you are looking for a classic B&B – a room or two in the owner's home – you should contact one of the B&B booking agencies, such as the **Bed & Breakfast Agency of Boston**, **Host Homes of Boston**, or the **Bed and Breakfast Associates Bay Colony, Ltd.** A recent trend is the "boutique" hotel, a small, elegantly appointed accommodation with solicitous service. Be warned: these luxury boutiques are among the most expensive lodging options.

Like most American cities, Boston has its share of chain hotels in all price categories. There are few budget chain properties within the city itself, although visitors will find lower-priced chains, such as **Fairfield Inn**, in

Boston's Seaport Hotel, busy during the summer

surrounding communities. In fact, this chain is popular throughout the New England region. While short on charm, these accommodations offer functional budget lodgings. Good-value B&B accommodations near Boston can be found in the North Shore towns of Rockport *(see p141)* and Salem *(see pp138–9)*. Both of these attractive seaside towns have good selections of mid-priced B&Bs, and are easily accessible by the MBTA commuter rail. Contact the **North of Boston Convention and Visitors Bureau** for more detailed information.

The stylish Hotel Pemaquid in New Harbor, Maine

Middlebury Inn in Vermont

HOSTELS

H OSTELS HAVE LONG been a way for people – especially students – to slash their traveling budget. However, unlike the more extensive European model, New England's hostel network is somewhat underdeveloped. Rhode Island, for example, has no facilities at all. The good news is that some of the region's prime locations (including Boston and Cape Cod) do have hostels. A list of member hostels and their locations is available from **Hostelling International– American Youth Hostels (HI/AYH)**. **HI/AYH Eastern New England Council** provides information on hostels in New Hampshire, Maine, and Massachusetts. Connecticut and Vermont are covered by the **HY/AYH Yankee Council**. A short walk from the Hynes Convention Center, the **Boston International Youth Hostel** offers a variety of rooms, including some very affordable six-bed dormitories and several private doubles.

DIRECTORY

BED AND BREAKFAST AND INN AGENCIES

Bed & Breakfast Agency of Boston
47 Commercial Wharf #3
Boston, MA 02110.
((800) 248-9262 or
(617) 720-3540.
W www.boston-bnbagency.com

Bed and Breakfast Associates Bay Colony, Ltd.
PO Box 57166,
Babson Park Branch,
Boston, MA 02457-0166.
((888) 384-7203 or
(617) 720-0522.
W www.bnbboston.com

Host Homes of Boston
PO Box 117,
Waban Branch,
Boston, MA 02468-0001.
((800) 600-1308 or
(617) 244-1308.
W www.hosthomesofboston.com

New England Innkeepers Association
PO Box 1089,
North Hampton,
NH 03862-1089.
((603) 964-6689.
W www.newenglandinns.com

HOSTELS AND BUDGET ACCOMMODATIONS

Best Western International
((800) 528-1234.
W www.bestwestern.com

Boston International Youth Hostel
12 Hemenway St,
Boston, MA 02115.
((617) 536-9455.
W www.bostonhostel.org

Days Inn
((800) 329-7466.
W www.daysinn.com

Fairfield Inn
((800) 228-2800.
W www.marriott.com

Hostelling International
8401 Colesville Rd, Suite 600,
Silver Spring, MD, 20910.
((301) 495-1240.
(membership information).
((800) 909-4776.
(reservation service).
W www.hiayh.org

Hostelling International Eastern New England Council
1105 Commonwealth Ave,
Boston, MA 02215.
((617) 779-0900.
W www.usahostels.org

Hostelling International Yankee Council
PO Box 87
Windsor, CT 06095.
((860) 683-2847.

North of Boston Convention and Visitors Bureau
17 Peabody Sq, Peabody, MA
01960. ((978) 977-7760 or
(800) 742-5306.
W www.northofboston.org

Choosing a Hotel

THESE HOTELS have been selected across a wide price range for their excellent facilities, good location, character, and value. They are listed by area and then by price category, with symbols highlighting some of the amenities that may influence your choice of where to stay. Map references for Boston hotels help you locate the hotels on the Street Finder (pp122–7).

	CREDIT CARDS	NUMBER OF ROOMS	RECOMMENDED RESTAURANT	CHILDREN'S FACILITIES	GARDEN OR TERRACE
BOSTON					
BEACON HILL AND THE THEATER DISTRICT					
JOHN JEFFRIES HOUSE $$ 14 David G. Mugar Way. **Map** 1 B3. [(617) 367-1866. **FAX** (617) 742-0313. Redbrick inn at the foot of Beacon Hill overlooking the Charles River. Rooms are Victorian in style, and while some are tiny, the two-room suites are good value. Most of the rooms have kitchenettes. Breakfast is not included. 🚭 ♨ ⬆ 🔒 ♿	AE DC MC V D	46 (19)			▪
MILNER HOTEL $$ 78 Charles St S. **Map** 4 E2. [(800) 453-1731 or (617) 426-6220. **FAX** (617) 350-0360. [w] www.milner-hotels.com Modest European-style budget hotel with basic rooms. Avoid the tiny standard rooms. Close to the heart of the Theater District. 🚭 ♨ ⬆ 🍴	AE DC MC V D	67 (5)			
HOLIDAY INN SELECT GOVERNMENT CENTER $$$ 5 Blossom St. **Map** 1 B3. [(800) 465-4329 or (617) 742-7630. **FAX** (617) 742-4192. [w] www.sixcontinentshotels.com A modern, 15-story, business-class chain hotel. On the north side of Beacon Hill near Massachusetts General Hospital, a short walk from Government Center. 🚭 ⬆ 🍸 ♒ 🍴 🔒 P ♿	AE DC MC V	303 (3)	●		
BEACON HILL HOTEL & BISTRO $$$$ 19 Charles St. **Map** 1 B4. [(888) 959-2444 or (617) 723-7575. **FAX** (617) 723-7525. [w] www.beaconhillhotel.com Uniquely designed, air-conditioned rooms in small, sophisticated hotel on Beacon Hill, close to Newbury Street. Private roof deck. 🚭 ♨ 🔒 P ♿	AE DC MC V D	13 (1)	▪		▪
BOSTON PARK PLAZA HOTEL $$$$ 64 Arlington St. **Map** 4 D2. [(800) 225-2008 or (617) 426-2000. **FAX** (617) 457-7456. [w] www.bostonparkplaza.com Opened in 1927, this grand luxury hotel is classically Bostonian. Elegantly appointed, the spacious rooms also boast many modern amenities, such as voice mail and dataports. 🕐 🚭 ♨ ⬆ 🍸 ♒ 🍴 🔒 P ♿	AE MC V D	950 (22)	▪	●	
CHARLES STREET INN $$$$ 94 Charles St. **Map** 1 B4. [(877) 772-8900 or (617) 314-8900. **FAX** (617) 371-0009. [w] www.charlesstreetinn.com Deluxe boutique hotel in an 1860s townhouse. All the sumptuous antique-filled rooms have working fireplaces, as well as whirlpool tubs, two-line telephones, internet connections, and CD players. 🚭 ♨ ⬆ 🔒 ♿	AE DC MC V D	9			
RADISSON HOTEL BOSTON $$$$ 200 Stuart St. **Map** 4 D2. [(800) 333-3333 or (617) 482-1800. **FAX** (617) 451-2750. [w] www.radisson.com Comfortable hotel with lots of amenities, near theaters and Back Bay. Convenient for tourists and business travelers. 🚭 ♨ ⬆ 🍸 ♒ 🍴 🔒 P ♿	AE DC MC V D	356 (30)	●		
SWISSÔTEL BOSTON $$$$ One Ave de Lafayette. **Map** 4 D2. [(888) 73-SWISS or (617) 451-2600. **FAX** (617) 451-0054. [w] www.swissotel.com A tower houses this modern, well-appointed hotel that caters to business travelers but also offers good-value weekend specials. The area is a bit seedy but close to Downtown Crossing. 🕐 🚭 ♨ ⬆ 🍸 ♒ 🍴 🔒 P ♿	AE DC MC V D	471 (30)	●	▪	
TREMONT BOSTON A GRAND HISTORIC WYNDHAM HOTEL $$$$ 275 Tremont St. **Map** 4 E2. [(877) 999-3223 or (617) 426-1400. **FAX** (617) 482-6730. [w] www.wyndham.com The refurbished lobby of this imposing 1925 brick and stone building is decorated with pillars and carved granite. Rooms are more simple but have greater flair than those in a standard chain hotel. 🚭 ♨ ⬆ 🍸 🍴 🔒 P ♿	AE DC MC V D	322	▪	●	

<table>
<tr><td colspan="2"></td><td>CREDIT CARDS</td><td>NUMBER OF ROOMS</td><td>RECOMMENDED RESTAURANT</td><td>CHILDREN'S FACILITIES</td><td>GARDEN OR TERRACE</td></tr>
</table>

Price categories for a standard double room per night, inclusive of breakfast, service charges, and any additional taxes:

$ under $100
$$ $100–$150
$$$ $150–$200
$$$$ $200–$250
$$$$$ over $250

CREDIT CARDS
Major credit cards accepted: *AE* American Express; *DC* Diners Club; *MC* MasterCard/Access; *V* Visa, *D* Discover Card.

NUMBER OF ROOMS
Number of rooms in the hotel (suites shown in parentheses).

RECOMMENDED RESTAURANT
Good restaurant within the hotel.

CHILDREN'S FACILITIES
Hotel has various facilities for young children.

GARDEN OR TERRACE
Hotel has a garden, courtyard, or terrace.

	Credit Cards	Number of Rooms	Recommended Restaurant	Children's Facilities	Garden or Terrace
FOUR SEASONS $$$$$ 200 Boylston St. **Map** 4 D2. ☎ *(800) 332-3442 or (617) 338-4400.* **FAX** *(617) 423-0154.* W *www.fourseasons.com* The ultimate in service and luxury, and consistently ranked among the top hotels in the city. It has grand reception rooms and sumptuous bedrooms, many overlooking the Public Garden. 24 🖕 🎿 🔌 🍴 🏊 🍽 🛏 P ♿	AE DC MC V D	274 (72)	■	●	

OLD BOSTON AND THE FINANCIAL DISTRICT

	Credit Cards	Number of Rooms	Recommended Restaurant	Children's Facilities	Garden or Terrace
HARBORSIDE INN OF BOSTON $$ 185 State St. **Map** 2 E3. ☎ *(888) 723-7565 or (617) 723-7500.* **FAX** *(617) 670-6015.* W *www.hagopianhotels.com* The small guest rooms in this old mercantile warehouse have exposed brick walls, period furniture, and wooden floors with Oriental rugs. Near Faneuil Hall but surrounded by the "Big Dig." 🎿 🔌 🍴 🛏 ♿	AE DC MC V D	54 (2)			
SHAWMUT INN $$ 280 Friend St. **Map** 1 C2. ☎ *(800) 350-7784 or (617) 720-5544.* **FAX** *(617) 723-7784.* W *www. shawmutinn.com* Simply furnished rooms, all with kitchenettes, in a former state office building across the street from North Station. A fine budget choice; suites are good value for families. 🖕 🎿 🔌 🛏 ♿	AE MC V D	65 (11)	■	●	
BOSTON WYNDHAM DOWNTOWN $$$$ 89 Broad St. **Map** 2 E4. ☎ *(800) 996-3426 or (617) 556-0006.* **FAX** *(617) 556-0053.* W *www.wyndham.com/boston* This Art Deco former office building was converted to a hotel in 1999. The classy lobby and the bathrooms retain original marble floors; rooms are traditionally furnished with modern facilities. 🎿 🎿 🔌 🍴 🍽 🛏 P ♿	AE DC MC V D	362 (66)	■		
OMNI PARKER HOUSE $$$$ 60 School St. **Map** 2 D4. ☎ *(800) 843-6664 or (617) 227-8600.* **FAX** *(617) 742-5729.* W *www.omnihotels.com* Home of the Parker House Roll and Boston Cream Pie, this traditional and comfortable hotel has been open since 1855. 24 🎿 🎿 🔌 🍴 🍽 🛏 ♿	AE DC MC V D	551 (21)	■	●	
FIFTEEN BEACON $$$$$ 15 Beacon St. **Map** 1 C4. ☎ *(877) 982-3226 or (617) 670-1500.* **FAX** *(617) 670-2525.* W *www.xvbeacon.com* Coolly opulent boutique hotel in a former office building. Chic rooms all have a high-style mix of traditional and contemporary furnishings, with facilities including CD players and fax machines. 24 🎿 🔌 🍴 🍽 🛏 ♿	AE DC MC V D	61 (2)	■		
LE MERIDIEN $$$$$ 250 Franklin St. **Map** 2 E4. ☎ *(800) 543-4300 or (617) 451-1900.* **FAX** *(617) 423-2844.* W *www.lemeridienboston.com* In a former Federal Reserve Bank building, this deluxe hotel in the heart of the Financial District pampers business travelers and often offers affordable weekend getaway packages. 24 🎿 🎿 🔌 🍴 🏊 🍽 🛏 P ♿	AE DC MC V D	326 (26)	■	●	
MILLENNIUM BOSTONIAN HOTEL $$$$$ Faneuil Hall Marketplace. **Map** 2 D3. ☎ *(800) 343-0922 or (617) 523-3600.* **FAX** *(617) 523-2454.* W *www.millenniumhotels.com* Three mazelike redbrick former warehouse buildings opposite Faneuil Hall are home to this upscale traditional hotel. Rooms have small balconies. Complimentary airport limousine service. 24 🎿 🎿 🔌 🍴 🍽 🛏 P ♿	AE DC MC V D	201 (17)	■		■
NINE ZERO $$$$$ 90 Tremont St. **Map** 4 F1. ☎ *(617) 772-5800.* **FAX** *(617) 772-5810.* W *www.ninezero.com* Located in the heart of downtown, one block from Boston Common, this deluxe hotel pampers business travelers with a full complement of high-tech facilities, including broadband internet access. 24 🎿 🎿 🔌 🍴 🍽 🛏 P ♿	AE DC MC V D	190 (1)	■	●	

For key to symbols see back flap

	CREDIT CARDS				

Price categories for a standard double room per night, inclusive of breakfast, service charges, and any additional taxes:

$ under $100
$$ $100–$150
$$$ $150–$200
$$$$ $200–$250
$$$$$ over $250

CREDIT CARDS
Major credit cards accepted: *AE* American Express; *DC* Diners Club; *MC* MasterCard/Access; *V* VISA, *D* Discover Card.

NUMBER OF ROOMS
Number of rooms in the hotel (suites shown in parentheses).

RECOMMENDED RESTAURANT
Good restaurant within the hotel.

CHILDREN'S FACILITIES
Hotel has various facilities for young children.

GARDEN OR TERRACE
Hotel has a garden, courtyard, or terrace.

		CREDIT CARDS	NUMBER OF ROOMS	RECOMMENDED RESTAURANT	CHILDREN'S FACILITIES	GARDEN OR TERRACE
NORTH END AND THE WATERFRONT						
SEAPORT HOTEL $$$$ One Seaport Lane. **Map 2 F5.** (877) 732-7678 or (617) 385-4000. FAX (617) 385-4001. W www.seaporthotel.com A modern, towering business hotel next to the World Trade Center, every room has an internet hookup, plus in-room conferencing facilities. Weekend specials are attractive.		AE DC MC V D	426 (24)	■	●	
BOSTON HARBOR HOTEL $$$$$ 70 Rowes Wharf. **Map 2 E4.** (800) 752-7077 or (617) 439-7000. FAX (617) 330-9450. W www.bhh.com This opulent hotel with classically elegant furnishings overlooks the harbor. Although the "Big Dig" construction rumbles nearby, the hotel and its fine contemporary restaurant are oases of calm.		AE DC MC V D	230 (15)	■	●	
MARRIOTT LONG WHARF $$$$$ 296 State St. **Map 2 E3.** (800) 228-9290 or (617) 227-0800. FAX (617) 227-2867. W www.marriott.com An upscale, modern chain hotel in a great harborfront location which has been given a $11.5 million renovation.		AE DC MC V D	400 (11)		●	
BACK BAY AND SOUTH END						
463 BEACON STREET GUEST-HOUSE $ 463 Beacon St. **Map 3 A2.** (617) 536-1302. FAX (617) 247-8876. W www.463beacon.com This stately five-story guest house is good value. Rooms vary, but some have fireplaces and other original features, plus microwaves and fridges; most have a private bath. Breakfast not included. Weekly maid service.		MC DC V D	20			
CHANDLER INN HOTEL $$ 26 Chandler St. **Map 4 D3.** (800) 842-3450 or (617) 482-3450. FAX (617) 542-3428. W www.chandlerinn.com A simple but friendly inn in a former Coast Guard station, two blocks from most of the South End's restaurants. The small rooms with simple motel-style furnishings sleep up to two people.		AE DC MC V D	56			
THE COLLEGE CLUB $$ 44 Commonwealth Ave. **Map 3 C2.** (617) 536-9510. FAX (617) 247-8537. W www.thecollegeclubofboston.com A hidden gem and excellent value, this ornate Victorian town house near the Public Garden is home to a private club. It rents six lovely double rooms, and five more austere singles that share bathrooms.		MC V	12			
82 CHANDLER STREET B&B $$$ 82 Chandler St. **Map 4 D3.** (617) 482-0408. FAX (617) 482-0659. W www.channel1.com/82chandler Located on a residential South End street, this long-established B&B has three guest rooms, plus two studio apartments. All units are well furnished; four have kitchenettes, only two have TVs.			5			
CLARENDON SQUARE INN $$$ 198 West Brookline St. **Map 3 C4.** (617) 536-2229. FAX (617) 266-2993. W www.clarendonsquare.com A stylish B&B in an elegantly restored 1860s South End townhouse. Rooms all have fireplaces. There is a roof deck with hot tub.		AE MC V	3		●	■
COPLEY HOUSE APARTMENTS $$$ 239 West Newton St. **Map 3 B3.** (800) 331-1318 or (617) 236-8300. FAX (617) 424-1815. W www.copleyhouse.com Studio and one-bedroom apartments. Ask for details, as apartments vary significantly in style and quality. Breakfast not included.		AE DC MC V D	65			

MIDTOWN HOTEL $$$ 220 Huntington Ave. **Map** 3 B4. ☎ *(800) 343-1177 or (617) 262-1000.* [FAX] *(617) 262-8739.* [W] *www.midtownhotel.com* Family-friendly 1960s hotel near Symphony Hall. Simple, clean rooms. Front and side rooms are more spacious than those in rear. 🚭 📺 ⇅ 🏊 🛎 [P] ♿	AE DC MC V D	159 (2)		●	
NEWBURY GUESTHOUSE $$$ 261 Newbury St. **Map** 3 B2. ☎ *(800) 437-7668 or (617) 437-7666.* [FAX] *(617) 262-4243.* [W] *www.hagopianhotels.com* In Boston's chic shopping neighborhood, this brownstone guest house caters to business people and fashionable vacationers. Tasteful rooms are furnished with Victorian-style reproductions. Book well in advance. 🚭 ⇅ [P] ♿	AE DC MC V D	32			■
BACK BAY HILTON $$$$ 40 Dalton St. **Map** 3 A3. ☎ *(800) 874-0063 or (617) 236-1100.* [FAX] *(617) 867-6104.* [W] *www.hilton.com* Modern 26-story boutique hotel behind the Hynes Convention Center with well-equipped rooms. Prices are often lower than at comparable Back Bay hotels, especially on weekends. 🚭 📺 ⇅ 🍸 🏊 🏋 🛎 [P] ♿	AE DC MC V D	384 (6)		●	■
HOTEL COLONNADE $$$$ 120 Huntington Ave. **Map** 3 B3. ☎ *(800) 962-3030 or (617) 424-7000.* [FAX] *(617) 424-1717.* [W] *www.colonnadehotel.com* This 1970's hotel has been renovated inside to provide large and comfortable rooms. The swimming pool is a singles hotspot. 🚭 📺 ⇅ 🍸 🏊 🏋 [P] ♿	AE DC MC V D	284	■	●	
COPLEY SQUARE HOTEL $$$$$ 47 Huntington Ave. **Map** 3 C3. ☎ *(800) 225-7062 or (617) 536-9000.* [FAX] *(617) 267-3547.* [W] *www.copleysquarehotel.com* The rooms in this comfortably appointed older hotel have traditional reproduction furnishings and more character than many nearby high-rise hotels. 🚭 📺 ⇅ 🍸 🛎 [P] ♿	AE DC MC V D	143 (11)	■	●	
ELIOT SUITE HOTEL $$$$$ 370 Commonwealth Ave. **Map** 3 A2. ☎ *(800) 443-5468 or (617) 267-1607.* [FAX] *(617) 536-9114.* [W] *www.eliothotel.com* Graciously furnished, all-suite hotel, built in 1925. Rooms have separate sitting rooms, plus business amenities including fax machines and dataports. Home of fine French-American restaurant Clio. [24] 🚭 📺 ⇅ 🍸 🛎 [P] ♿	AE DC MC V	95 (95)	■	●	
CHARLESMARK HOTEL $$$$$ 655 Boylston St. **Map** 3 C2. ☎ *(617) 247-1212.* [FAX] *(617) 247-1224.* [W] *www.charlesmarkhotel.com* This boutique hotel, situated in a 1892 townhouse building, is perfectly located for shopping and sightseeing. Small rooms feature custom-made furniture and modernist decór. 🚭 ⇅ 🛎 [P] ♿	AE MC V D	33			
FAIRMONT COPLEY PLAZA BOSTON $$$$$ 138 St. James Ave. **Map** 3 C2. ☎ *(800) 527-4727 or (617) 267-5300.* [FAX] *(617) 247-6681.* [W] *www.fairmont.com* The gold lions guarding the hotel entrance are a city landmark. Known as the "grande dame" of Boston, this ornately appointed, palatial hotel is the epitome of luxury. [24] 🚭 📺 ⇅ 🍸 🏋 🛎 [P] ♿	AE DC MC V D	379 (60)	■	●	
THE LENOX $$$$$ 710 Boylston St. **Map** 3 B2. ☎ *(800) 225-7676 or (617) 536-5300.* [FAX] *(617) 267-1237.* [W] *www.lenoxhotel.com* This highly regarded and recently refurbished 100-year-old hotel has sumptuously appointed rooms with all manner of luxuries. It is also home to the excellent Azure restaurant *(see p332)*. 🚭 📺 ⇅ 🍸 🏋 🛎 [P] ♿	AE DC MC V D	212 (12)	■	●	
THE RITZ-CARLTON BOSTON $$$$$ 15 Arlington St. **Map** 4 D2. ☎ *(800) 241-3333 or (617) 536-5700.* [FAX] *(617) 536-9340.* [W] *www.ritzcarlton.com* Large luxury hotel, built in 1927, overlooking the Public Garden. It has undergone extensive renovation work, which was completed in 2002. [24] 🚭 📺 ⇅ 🍸 🏋 🛎 [P] ♿	AE DC MC V D	275 (42)	■	●	
THE RITZ-CARLTON BOSTON COMMON $$$$$ 10 Avery St. **Map** 4 E2. ☎ *(800) 241-3333 or (617) 574-7100.* [FAX] *(617) 574-7200.* [W] *www.ritzcarlton.com* Opened in 2001, this ultra-contemporary and glamorous hotel offers a range of facilities, such as a business center, access to a sports club and a multiplex cinema in a superb location. [24] 🚭 📺 ⇅ 🍸 🏋 🛎 [P] ♿	AE DC MC V D	193 (43)	■		■

For key to symbols see back flap

Price categories for a standard double room per night, inclusive of breakfast, service charges, and any additional taxes:

$ under $100
$$ $100–$150
$$$ $150–$200
$$$$ $200–$250
$$$$$ over $250

CREDIT CARDS
Major credit cards accepted: *AE* American Express; *DC* Diners Club; *MC* MasterCard/Access; *V* VISA, *D* Discover Card.

NUMBER OF ROOMS
Number of rooms in the hotel (suites shown in parentheses).

RECOMMENDED RESTAURANT
Good restaurant within the hotel.

CHILDREN'S FACILITIES
Hotel has various facilities for young children.

GARDEN OR TERRACE
Hotel has a garden, courtyard, or terrace.

Hotel	Credit Cards	Number of Rooms	Recommended Restaurant	Children's Facilities	Garden or Terrace
WESTIN COPLEY PLACE $$$$$ 10 Huntington Ave. Map 3 C3. ☎ *(800) 228-3000 or (617) 262-9600.* [FAX] *(617) 424-7483.* [W] *www.westin.com* This 36-story hotel buzzes with business traffic. Comfortable and upscale, it has excellent facilities and great views. [24] 🚭 ❄ ⇅ 🍸 🏊 💼 📺 [P] ♿	*AE DC MC V D*	*803 (44)*	■	●	
FARTHER AFIELD					
INN AT LONGWOOD $ 123 Longwood Ave, Brookline. ☎ *(617) 566-8615.* [FAX] *(617) 738-1070.* [@] *lwdin@tiac.net* [W] *www.go.boston.com/longwoodinn* Victorian-style mansion, now a budget inn. It retains an air of faded elegance, although the rooms are basic. Breakfast not included. ❄ [P] ♿		*22*		●	
CONSTITUTION INN $$ 150 Second Ave, Charlestown. ☎ *(617) 241-8400.* [FAX] *(617) 241-2856.* Run by the armed services, most of the basic rooms have two twin beds, but several have queen-sized ones. Breakfast not included. 🚭 ❄ ⇅ 🏊 💼 ♿	*AE MC V*	*150 (3)*			
IRVING HOUSE $$ 24 Irving St, Cambridge. ☎ *(877) 547-4600 or (617) 547-4600.* [FAX] *(617) 576-2814.* [W] *www.irvinghouse.com* This wooden-framed Victorian house inn has simple rooms (some are quite small) and an attractive terrace. Some rooms share baths. 🚭 ❄ [P] ♿	*AE DC MC V*	*44*		●	■
BERTRAM INN $$$ 92 Sewall Ave, Brookline. ☎ *(800) 295-3822 or (617) 566-2234.* [FAX] *(617) 277-1887.* [W] *www.bertraminn.com* A restored 1907 Arts and Crafts-style home, with a parlor, sunporch, and cozy, antique-filled rooms. Children over 10 welcome. 🚭 ❄ 📺 [P]	*AE DC MC V D*	*14 (4)*			■
HARVARD SQUARE HOTEL $$$ 110 Mt. Auburn St, Cambridge. ☎ *(800) 458-5886 or (617) 864-5200.* [FAX] *(617) 864-2409.* [W] *www.doubletreehotels.com* Location is the best feature of this refurbished hotel in the heart of Harvard Square. The rooms are basic but comfortable. Ask for a room at the front, as the rear rooms have no view. 🚭 ❄ ⇅ 📺 [P] ♿	*AE DC MC V D*	*73*		●	
HOTEL @ MIT – UNIVERSITY PARK $$$ 20 Sidney St, Cambridge. ☎ *(800) 222-8733 or (617) 577-0200.* [FAX] *(617) 494-8366.* [W] *www.hotel@mit.com* This contemporary hotel, owned by Massachusetts Institute of Technology, is filled with technology such as ergonomically designed furniture, in-room internet access, and phones with voice mail. 🚭 ❄ ⇅ 🍸 💼 📺 [P] ♿	*AE DC MC V D*	*210 (28)*		●	■
INN AT HARVARD $$$ 1201 Massachusetts Ave, Cambridge. ☎ *(800) 458-5886 or (617) 491-2222.* [FAX] *(617) 520-3711.* [W] *www.theinnatharvard.com* Modern four-story hotel, built around a sunny atrium. The rooms are comfortable and filled with period furniture. [24] 🚭 ❄ ⇅ 🍸 📺 [P] ♿	*AE DC MC V D*	*113 (1)*	■	●	
MARY PRENTISS INN $$$ 6 Prentiss St, Cambridge. ☎ *(617) 661-2929.* [FAX] *(617) 661-5989.* [W] *www.maryprentissinn.com* An antique-filled B&B in a Greek Revival-style house. There is a spacious sundeck and modern amenities include dataports. 🚭 📺 [P]	*AE MC V*	*20 (5)*			■
A CAMBRIDGE HOUSE BED AND BREAKFAST INN $$$$ 2218 Massachusetts Ave, Cambridge. ☎ *(800) 232-9989 or (617) 491-6300.* [FAX] *(617) 868-2848.* [W] *www.acambridgehouse.com* This 1892 house is now an exquisitely restored Victorian fantasy, with four-poster beds and working fireplaces. Children over six welcome. 🚭 ❄ [P]	*AE DC MC V D*	*15*			

GRYPHON HOUSE — $$$$
9 Bay State Rd, Boston. (877) 375-9003 or (617) 375-9003.
FAX (617) 425-0716. W www.gryphonhouseboston.com
This five-story bowfronted 1895 boutique hotel has gracious antiques-filled public rooms and large suites furnished in a variety of styles. Bathrooms have deep tubs, and some rooms have river views.
Cards: AE, DC, MC, V. *Rooms:* 8 (8).

SHERATON COMMANDER — $$$$
16 Garden St, Cambridge. (800) 535-5007 or
(617) 547-4800. FAX (617) 868-8322. W www.sheratoncommander.com
Chic, old-fashioned hotel opposite Cambridge Common. Rooms are decorated in traditional colonial style.
Cards: AE, DC, MC, V, D. *Rooms:* 175 (14).

CHARLES HOTEL — $$$$$
One Bennett St, Cambridge. (800) 882-1818 or (617) 864-1200.
FAX (617) 864-5715. W www.charleshotel.com
This contemporary luxury hotel has rooms appointed with Shaker-style furnishings and quilts. Home of the excellent modern-Mediterranean Rialto restaurant and the Regatta-bar jazz club.
Cards: AE, DC, MC, V, D. *Rooms:* 293 (44).

HOTEL COMMONWEALTH — $$$$$
650 Beacon St, Boston. (617) 262-9554 or (866) 784-4000.
FAX (617) 927-4446. W www.hotelcommonwealth.com
The exterior of this hotel may be French Second Empire, but the interior is designed for today's business traveler. Academic gatherings are often held here, too. Wireless broadband in every room.
Cards: AE, DC, MC, V, D. *Rooms:* 149 (1).

KENDALL HOTEL — $$$$$
350 Main St, Cambridge. (617) 577-1300. FAX (617) 577-1377.
W www.kendallhotel.com Located close to MIT and convenient for conferences in the Cambridge Center, this firehouse has only recently been transformed into a hotel. Rooms are decorated in firehouse memorabilia and antique furniture.
Cards: AE, MC, V, D. *Rooms:* 65.

MASSACHUSETTS

CONCORD: *Colonial Inn* — $$$
48 Monument Sq. (800) 370-9200 or (978) 369-9200. FAX (978) 371-1533.
@ colonial@concordscolonialinn.com W www.concordscolonialinn.com
This historic site was built in 1716 and has been operating as a hotel since 1889. Beautiful Colonial-style rooms.
Cards: AE, DC, MC, V, D. *Rooms:* 56 (7).

CONCORD: *North Bridge Inn* — $$$$
21 Monument St. (888) 530-0007 or (978) 371-0014. FAX (978) 371-6460.
W www.northbridgeinn.com
A charming bed-and-breakfast with six suites, each named after a New England author. The building was constructed in 1885 and has recently undergone extensive renovations.
Cards: AE, MC, V. *Rooms:* 6 (6).

EDGARTOWN: *The Daggett House* — $$$$
59 North Water St. (800) 946-3400 or (508) 627-4600. FAX (508) 627-4611.
W www.thedaggetthouse.com
Delightful inn, comprised of four historic buildings, featuring rooms decorated in a warm country style. The garden leads right down to the harbor, where chairs are set out for use by the guests.
Cards: AE, MC, V, D. *Rooms:* 31 (8).

HYANNIS: *Captain Gosnold Village* — $$
230 Gosnold St. (508) 775-9111. W www.captaingosnold.com
Close to beaches and Hyannis Harbor, this family-oriented resort has a range of accommodations in cottage buildings. No air-conditioning. Breakfast is not included. Nov–Mar.
Cards: MC, V. *Rooms:* 50.

LENOX: *The Mayflower Motor Inn* — $
474 Pittsfield Rd. (413) 443-4468
A standard motel that provides comfortable lodging. Breakfast is not included in the room rate.
Cards: AE, MC, V, D. *Rooms:* 21.

LENOX: *Cranwell Resort and Golf Club* — $$$$$
55 Lee Rd. (800) 272-6935 or (413) 637-1364. FAX (413) 637-4364.
@ info@cranwell.com W www.cranwell.com
This luxurious resort offers accommodations in a number of magnificent lodgings. Amenities include a spa and an 18-hole championship golf course.
Cards: AE, DC, MC, V, D. *Rooms:* 107 (25).

For key to symbols see back flap

		CREDIT CARDS	NUMBER OF ROOMS	RECOMMENDED RESTAURANT	CHILDREN'S FACILITIES	GARDEN OR TERRACE

Price categories for a standard double room per night, inclusive of breakfast, service charges, and any additional taxes:

$ under $100
$$ $100–$150
$$$ $150–$200
$$$$ $200–$250
$$$$$ over $250

CREDIT CARDS
Major credit cards accepted: *AE* American Express; *DC* Diners Club; *MC* MasterCard/Access; *V* VISA, *D* Discover Card.

NUMBER OF ROOMS
Number of rooms in the hotel (suites shown in parentheses).

RECOMMENDED RESTAURANT
Good restaurant within the hotel.

CHILDREN'S FACILITIES
Hotel has various facilities for young children.

GARDEN OR TERRACE
Hotel has a garden, courtyard, or terrace.

NANTUCKET: *The Nesbitt Inn* $ 21 Broad St. ☎ (508) 228-0156 or (508) 228-2446. FAX (508) 228-2446. Located right in town, this Victorian bed-and-breakfast is operated by the exceptionally friendly hosts, Mr. and Mrs. Noblit, and is decorated with antiques and Oriental carpets. No air conditioning. Shared bath. TV in common room. Open March 1 to mid-December.		MC V	12 (2)		●	■
NANTUCKET: *Union Street Inn* $$$$ 7 Union St. ☎ (800) 225-5116 or (508) 228-9222. FAX (508) 325-0848. @ unioninn@nantucket.net W www.unioninn.com The recently restored Union Street Inn exemplifies Nantucket architecture and is located in the historic district. The rooms are tastefully decorated; many have fireplaces. Closed January to end of March.		AE MC V	12 (1)			■
NORTH ADAMS: *Porches Inn* $$$ 231 River St. ☎ (413) 664-0400. FAX (413) 664-0401. W www.porches.com Converted to a hotel from mill-workers' (c. 1910) houses, Porches has been thoroughly modernized. Located next to Massachusetts Museum of Contemporary Art walking distance to downtown. Rooms here have modern bathrooms, high-speed internet access, and luxurious linens. Breakfast is hearty and delicious.		AE MC V D	4 (1)			■
OAK BLUFFS: *The Nashua House* $ 30 Kennebec Ave. ☎ (508) 693-0043. FAX (508) 693-6283. @ calebcaldwellmv@hotmail.com W www.nashuahouse.com A Victorian house, built around 1810 and located in the center of town. The affordable rooms are sunny and offer a nice view, but do not have TV or air-conditioning. All rooms have shared baths. Breakfast is not included.		AE MC V	16			
OAK BLUFFS: *The Island Inn* $$ Beach Rd. ☎ (800) 462-0269 or (508) 693-2002. FAX (508) 693-7911. @ innkeeper@islandinn.com W www.islandinn.com Located on extensive lawns, very near the beach. The resort has cottages, studios, and suites, most of which offer spectacular views. Breakfast is not included. Closed December to March.		AE DC MC V D	51 (27)		●	■
PLYMOUTH: *Beachside Bed & Breakfast at Ellisville Harbor House* $$ 159 Ellisville Rd. ☎ (888) 738-2337 or (508) 888-3692. FAX (508) 888-5978. W www.ellisville.com Full breakfasts are served either in the dining room or on the large sundeck. This historic site has a private beach. Swans, deer, and seals can be seen on the grounds in the various seasons.		MC V	3			■
PLYMOUTH: *Pilgrim Sands Motel* $$ 150 Warren Ave. ☎ (800) 729-SAND or (508) 747-0900. FAX (508) 746-8066. @ thebeach@pilgrimsands.com W www.pilgrimsands.com Located across the street from Plimoth Plantation, this motel has a private beach and large, modern rooms. Breakfast not included.		AE DC MC V D	64 (2)		●	■
PROVINCETOWN: *The Beaconlight Guesthouse* $$ 12 Winthrop St. ☎ (800) 696-9603. FAX (508) 487-9603. W www.beaconlightguesthouse.com A romantic B&B in a sprawling beach house (built around 1900) in a quiet but convenient location for downtown. No children.		AE MC V	10			■
ROWLEY: *Country Garden Inn and Motel* $$ 101 Main St, Rte 1A. ☎ (800) 287-7773 or (978) 948-7773. FAX (978) 948-7947. @ reserve@countrygardenmotel.com W www.countrygardenmotel.com Beautiful gardens, picnic areas and hammocks surround the various lodgings. There is a gazebo, heated pool and a spa. Breakfast not included.		AE DC MC V D	24 (10)			■

SALEM: *Hawthorne Hotel* $$$$ AE DC MC V D | 89 (6)
18 Washington Sq W. ((800) SAY-STAY or (978) 744-4080.
FAX (978) 745-9842. @ info@hawthornehotel.com W www.hawthornehotel.com
This upscale Federal-style hotel combines tasteful decoration with modern amenities. The Hawthorne is centrally located in downtown Salem and hosts annual Halloween festivities.

STURBRIDGE: *Comfort Inn and Suites* $$ AE DC MC V D | 77 (44)
215 Charlton Rd, Rte 20. ((800) 228-5150 or (508) 347-3306.
FAX (508) 347-3514.
@ info@sturbridgecomfortinn.com W www.sturbridgecomfortinn.com
Surrounded by immaculate grounds and beautiful landscaping, this Comfort Inn has an impressive array of amenities and is located less than 1 mile (1.6 km) from Old Sturbridge Village.

STURBRIDGE: *Publick House Historic Inn* $$ AE DC MC V D | 17
Route 31. ((800) 782-5425 or (508) 347-3313. FAX (508) 347-5073.
@ lodging@publickhouse.com W www.publickhouse.com
A delightful inn offering a great view of the countryside. It has a large backyard with a patio, swimming pool, and swings. Tea is served in the afternoon. No television. Also a motel on the property.

WEST DENNIS: *The Barnacle Motel* $$ AE DC MC V D | 36
219 Main St. ((508) 394-8472. W www.barnaclemotel.com
Clean comfortable accommodations for very reasonable rates. Breakfast is not included.

WILLIAMSTOWN: *The Williams Inn* $$$ AE DC MC V D | 125
On the Green. ((800) 828-0133 or (413) 458-9371. FAX (413) 458-2767.
W www.williamsinn.com
Situated on the campus of Williams College, this inn has elegant rooms and has added a new building with updated amenities.

RHODE ISLAND

BLOCK ISLAND: *Rose Farm Inn* $$ AE MC V D | 19
Roslyn Rd. ((401) 466-2034. FAX (401) 466-2053.
W www.blockisland.com/rosefarm
Set in a peaceful sea and country setting, this inn was a working farm until 1963. The 20 acres (8 ha) of farmland are now home to marsh hawks, ring-neck pheasants, and white-tail deer. Two rooms have a shared bath. Closed mid-October to mid-April. Children 12 and older welcomed. No television or air conditioning.

BLOCK ISLAND: *1661 Inn and Hotel Manisses* $$$ MC V | 26
Spring St. ((800) 626-4773 or (401) 466-2421. FAX (401) 466-3162.
W www.blockislandresorts.com
This historic inn, animal farm, and Victorian hotel is a perfect base from which to explore Block Island. No air-conditioning. Some rooms have no television, and some have shared bathrooms.
mid-Oct–Mar.

BRISTOL: *King Philip Inn* $ MC V D | 33
400 Metacom Ave. ((800) 253-7610 or (401) 253-7600. FAX (401) 253-1857.
Located on Route 136 in Bristol, the King Philip Inn is minutes away from Newport beaches and naval facilities, Providence nightspots, museums and historic homes, Battleship Cove in Massachusetts, and Roger Williams University.

CHARLESTOWN: *General Stanton Inn* $$ AE MC V | 16
4115A Old Post Rd, Rte 1A. ((401) 364-8888. FAX (401) 364-3333.
W www.generalstantoninn.com
One of the oldest continuously run inns in North America, the General Stanton still has some of the old atmosphere, with its low ceilings, fireplaces, brick ovens and hand-hewn timbers. The weekend flea market is one of South County's best.

NEWPORT: *The Black Duck Inn* $$ AE MC V | 8
29 Pelham St. ((800) 206-5212 or (401) 841-5548. FAX (401) 846-4873.
W www.blackduckinn.com
Situated in the heart of downtown Newport. Each room is distinctly decorated in the romantic Laura Ashley tradition. Two rooms have a joint washroom for families or two couples traveling together.

For key to symbols see back flap

Price categories for a standard double room per night, inclusive of breakfast, service charges, and any additional taxes:

$ under $100
$$ $100–$150
$$$ $150–$200
$$$$ $200–$250
$$$$$ over $250

CREDIT CARDS
Major credit cards accepted: *AE* American Express; *DC* Diners Club; *MC* MasterCard/Access; *V* VISA, *D* Discover Card.

NUMBER OF ROOMS
Number of rooms in the hotel (suites shown in parentheses).

RECOMMENDED RESTAURANT
Good restaurant within the hotel.

CHILDREN'S FACILITIES
Hotel has various facilities for young children.

GARDEN OR TERRACE
Hotel has a garden, courtyard, or terrace.

Hotel	Credit Cards	Number of Rooms	Recommended Restaurant	Children's Facilities	Garden or Terrace
NEWPORT: *Beech Tree Inn* $$$ 34 Rhode Island Ave. ☎ *(800) 748-6565 or (401) 847-9794.* [FAX] *(401) 847-6824.* [W] *www.beechtreeinn.com* Victorian home built in 1887. Many rooms have fireplaces and Jacuzzis. Noted for "the biggest breakfast in Newport," with a variety of eggs, pancakes, five juices, and more. Older children welcome. 🚭 📺 🏋 [P]	*AE MC V D*	*8 (2)*			■
NEWPORT: *Best Western Mainstay Inn* $$$ 151 Admiral Kalbfus Rd. ☎ *(401) 849-9880.* [FAX] *(401) 849-4391.* @ *themainstayinn@aol.com* [W] *www.bestwestern.com* Located near all the main attractions in Newport, including the historic harbor, the Newport Mansions, and the beaches. Just across the street from the Jai Alai Fronton/Casino. 🚭 📺 🍸 🏊 🏋 [P] ♿	*AE DC MC V D*	*165 (5)*		●	
NEWPORT: *Castle Hill Inn and Resort* $$$$$ 590 Ocean Dr. ☎ *(888) 466-1355 or (401) 849-3800.* [FAX] *(401) 849-3838.* [W] *www.castlehillinn.com* This resort with a private beach includes several houses. The restaurant has repeatedly won the Wine Spectator Award of Excellence. Limited availability for children under 12. 🚭 📺 🍸 [P] ♿	*AE DC MC V D*	*25 (2)*	■		■
PROVIDENCE: *C.C. Ledbetter Bed and Breakfast* $ 326 Benefit St. ☎ *(401) 351-4699.* [FAX] *(401) 351-4699.* Located opposite John Brown House, a block from Brown University. Charming rooms with handmade quilts. Breakfast is included in the room rate. 🚭 [P]	*MC V*	*5 (1)*			■
PROVIDENCE: *Courtyard by Marriot* $$$ 32 Exchange Terrace. ☎ *(888) 887-2955 or (401) 272-1191.* [FAX] *(401) 272-1416.* [W] *www.courtyard.com* In the heart of downtown, adjacent to Waterplace Park, this low-rise hotel offers a convenient location to all points of interest. There are good views from all rooms, covered parking, and complimentary daily newspapers. 🚭 📺 ⇅ 🍸 🏊 💼 🏋 [P] ♿	*AE DC MC V D*	*216*	■	●	
PROVIDENCE: *The Westin Providence* $$$$$ One West Exchange St. ☎ *(800) WESTIN1 or (401) 598-8000.* [FAX] *(401) 598-8200.* [W] *www.westinprovidence.com* Four-time Pinnacle Award winner. The Agora restaurant was named Best in Hotel Dining by the Food Network in 2000. Connected to Providence Place Mall and the Rhode Island Convention Center. 🚭 📺 ⇅ 🍸 🏊 💼 🏋 [P] ♿	*AE DC MC V D*	*364 (19)*	■	●	
WARWICK: *Master Hosts Inn* $ 2138 Post Rd. ☎ *(877) 634-1780 or (401) 737-7400.* [FAX] *(401) 739-6483.* [W] *www.masterhosts.com* Located across from T.F. Green Airport, but away from the noise. Eight different types of rooms, from economy class singles to executive suites. Five minutes from Providence and 20 minutes from Newport. 🚭 📺 ⇅ [P] ♿	*AE DC MC V D*	*103 (13)*		●	
WESTERLY: *Sand Dollar Inn* $ 171 Post Rd. ☎ *(800) 910-SAND or (401) 322-2000.* [FAX] *(401) 322-1590.* [W] *www.visitri.com/sanddollarinn* Two miles from the coast, the inn is comprised of three buildings, including a cottage for four. The grounds contain many species of flowers and ornamental plantings. Closed from January to March. 🚭 📺 [P] ♿	*AE MC V D*	*33*		●	
WESTERLY: *Andrea Hotel* $$ 89 Atlantic Ave. ☎ *(401) 348-8788.* [FAX] *(401) 596-1790.* [W] *www.andreahotel.com* A local landmark for more than 50 years, the hotel is located directly on a 300-foot private stretch of Misquamicut Beach. Nightly entertainment is a magnet for area locals, and there is a game room for youngsters. The restaurant is also well known. During winter, it is open weekends only. 📺 🍸 [P] ♿		*25*	■	●	■

WESTERLY: *The Villa* $$$ AE MC V D — 7
190 Shore Rd. **[** (800) 722-9240 or (401) 596-1054. **FAX** (401) 596-6268.
W *www.thevillaatwesterly.com*
A romantic hideaway of flower gardens, Italian porticos, and private terraces. Features an outdoor Jacuzzi and a Mediterranean designer pool. Each room has its own decorative theme. Near Newport and the ferry to Block Island. No children. ■ ■ ■ **P**

WOONSOCKET: *Pillsbury House B&B* $$ AE MC V D — 4 (1)
341 Prospect St. **[** (800) 205-4112 or (401) 766-7983. **FAX** (401) 762-0442.
@ *rogerwnri@prodigy.net* **W** *www.pillsburyhouse.com*
Built in 1875 on historic Prospect Street in Woonsocket's fashionable north end. Guests share a kitchenette with a refrigerator and microwave. Children over 12. TV in sitting room only. ■ ■ **P**

CONNECTICUT

BROOKLYN: *Friendship Valley B&B Inn* $$ AE MC V — 5 (1)
60 Pomfret Rd, Rte 169. **[** (860) 779-9696. **FAX** (860) 779-9844.
@ *friendshipvalley@snet.net* **W** *www.friendshipvalleyinn.com*
A quintessential New England inn with history. Each room is named after one of the previous families who owned the house, some of them prominent locally or nationally. No air-conditioning. Television in common room only. Children seven and older welcome. ■ ■ **P** ■

COVENTRY: *Special Joys B&B* $ MC V D — 3
41 North River Rd. **[** (800) 750-3979 or (860) 742-6359. **FAX** (860) 742-9343.
The owners' special devotion to antique toys is reflected throughout the premises, conservatory, and gardens. There is an antique doll and toy shop and museum on the premises, along with flower gardens and a solarium-lit dining area. Shared bath in some rooms. Children over 6. ■ ■ ■ **P**

COVENTRY: *Bird-in-Hand B&B* $$ AE MC V — 4
2011 Main St. **[** (860) 742-0032. **FAX** (860) 742-1293.
@ *info@thebirdinhand.com* **W** *www.thebirdinhand.com*
A historic building operating as an inn since 1800. A secret closet in one of the rooms is believed to have hidden slaves traveling on the Underground Railroad. Television in common room. Children over 10. ■ ■ ■ **P**

EAST HADDAM: *Bishopsgate Inn* $$ DC MC V — 6 (1)
Route 82. **[** (860) 873-1677. **FAX** (860) 873-3898.
@ *ctkagel@bishopsgate.com* **W** *www.bishopsgate.com*
Built in 1818, each floor has its own sitting area. Fireplace in four rooms. The suite has a sauna. TV in common rooms only. Ample breakfast. ■ **P** ■

GREENWICH: *The Cos Cob Inn* $$$ AE DC MC V — 14 (5)
50 River Rd. **[** (877) 549-4063 or (203) 661-5845. **FAX** (203) 661-2054.
@ *innkeeper@coscobinn.com* **W** *www.coscobinn.com*
A federal-style inn built in the 1800s and located in historic Greenwich. Many of the elegant rooms have a marina view. Some suites have a Jacuzzi. Children over 10. ■ ■ ■ **P**

GROTON: *The Clarion Inn* $ AE DC MC V D — 69
156 King's Hwy. **[** (800) 252-7466 or (860) 446-0660. **FAX** (860) 445-4082.
W *www.clarionhotel.com*
Located close to the USS *Nautilus* Memorial, Mohegan Sun Casino, Foxwoods Casino, Mystic, and the beaches. ■ ■ ■ ■ ■ ■ **P** ■

HARTFORD: *Red Roof Inn* $ AE DC MC V D — 115
100 Weston St. **[** (800) RED-ROOF or (860) 724-0222. **FAX** (860) 724-0433.
W *www.redroof.com*
Hacienda design, 2 miles (3 km) from downtown. Movies and video games available in all rooms. Children under 18 stay free. Breakfast not included. ■ ■ ■ **P** ■

HARTFORD: *Crowne Plaza Hartford Downtown* $$$ AE DC MC V D — 350 (4)
50 Morgan St. **[** (860) 549-2400. **FAX** (860) 549-7844.
@ *cphartford@bristolhotels.com* **W** *www.sixcontinentshotels.com/crowneplaza*
A full-service hotel with simple elegance and luxury touches. There is a free shuttle within 3-mile (5-km) radius of the hotel. Walking distance to all the major attractions. ■ ■ ■ ■ ■ ■ ■ **P** ■

For key to symbols see back flap

Price categories for a standard double room per night, inclusive of breakfast, service charges, and any additional taxes:

$ under $100
$$ $100–$150
$$$ $150–$200
$$$$ $200–$250
$$$$$ over $250

CREDIT CARDS
Major credit cards accepted: *AE* American Express; *DC* Diners Club; *MC* MasterCard/Access; *V* Visa, *D* Discover Card.

NUMBER OF ROOMS
Number of rooms in the hotel (suites shown in parentheses).

RECOMMENDED RESTAURANT
Good restaurant within the hotel.

CHILDREN'S FACILITIES
Hotel has various facilities for young children.

GARDEN OR TERRACE
Hotel has a garden, courtyard, or terrace.

	CREDIT CARDS	NUMBER OF ROOMS	RECOMMENDED RESTAURANT	CHILDREN'S FACILITIES	GARDEN OR TERRACE
HARTFORD: *Goodwin Hotel* $$$ One Haynes St. (888) 212-8380 or (860) 246-7500. FAX (860) 247-4576. W www.goodwinhotel.com The turn-of-the-century Goodwin serves guests with poise and style, but without pretension. The restaurant has been voted Best Hotel Dining by Connecticut Magazine for 10 years running.	AE DC MC V D	124 (11)	■	●	
KENT: *Constitution Oak Farm* $ 36 Beardsley Rd. (860) 354-6495. Rustic environment on a 100-acre (40-ha) farm built in the 1830s. Rooms feature period furnishings. Two rooms have private baths. Television in one room. One mile from Lake Waramaug.		4			■
LEDYARD: *Stonecroft Country Inn* $$$ 515 Pumpkin Hill Rd. (860) 572-0771. FAX (860) 572-9161. @ stoncrft@cris.com W www.stonecroft.com A former sea captain's estate, the 1807 inn is listed on the National Register of Historic Places. Located in two buildings, some rooms have whirlpools or fireplaces. Some rooms have television. Older children only.	AE MC V D	10 (2)	■		■
LITCHFIELD: *Litchfield Inn* $$$ 432 Bantam Rd. (800) 499-3444 or (860) 567-4503. FAX (860) 567-5358. @ litchfieldinn@compuserve.com W www.litchfieldinnct.com A quaint country inn located just west of Litchfield. Features a gigantic chandelier, delicately carved main staircase, and four working fireplaces. Eight luxurious theme rooms.	AE DC MC V	32	■	●	■
MASHANTUCKET: *Foxwoods Resort Casino* $$$$ Rte 2. (800) 369-9663 or (860) 312-3000. W www.foxwoods.com Five casinos, 24 restaurants, and three hotels. The Great Cedars Hotel and the Grand Pequot Tower are above the casino. The Two Trees Inn, smaller and less expensive, is located half a mile away from the casino; shuttle bus service is provided.	AE DC MC V D	1392	■	●	■
MYSTIC: *Seaport Motor Inn* $$ Coogan Blvd. (877) 523-0993 or (860) 536-2621. FAX (860) 536-4493. Overlooking Olde Mistick Village and the Mystic Aquarium. Intimate dining steps away at Jamm's Restaurant and adjoining Captain's Lounge. Close to all the major attractions, including beaches and USS *Nautilus*.	AE MC V D	118		●	
MYSTIC: *Coastline Yacht Club* $$$ 44 Water St., Fort Rachel Marina. (800) 749-7245 or (860) 536-2689. FAX (860) 572-9161. An out-of-the-ordinary lodging alternative. The Yacht Club makes vessels available as floating B&Bs when the boats are in dock. Special deals are available for larger parties. Open mid-May to mid-October.		1 (1)			
MYSTIC: *Steamboat Inn* $$$$ 73 Steamboat Wharf. (860) 536-8300. FAX (860) 536-9528 @ sbwharf@aol.com W www.visitmystic.com/steamboat Spacious rooms are named after famous Mystic ships from the schooner days. All rooms have whirlpool baths and antique furnishings. Magnificent views of the river and the dock.	AE MC V D	10 (4)		●	
NEW CANAAN: *Village Inn of New Canaan* $$ 122 Park St. (800) 370-2224 or (203) 966-8413. FAX (203) 966-8413. @ frontdesk@villageinnnc.com W www.villageinnnc.com The 18th-century inn combines great atmosphere with up-to-date comfort. Adjoining rooms and family apartments with kitchen are available. Individual voice mail for each guest.	AE DC MC V D	32		●	■

NEW LONDON: *Lighthouse Inn* $$
6 Guthrie Place. **(** (888) 443-8411 or (860) 443-8411. **FAX** (860) 437-7027.
W www.lighthouseinn-ct.com
The former home of steel magnate Charles S. Guthrie, this 1902
Mediterranean-style mansion has a private beach, a fine restaurant,
beautiful views of Long Island Sound, and is located close to major
attractions in the area. ⚡ 🏋 📶 🍸 🔔 **P**

Credit cards: AE MC V D — Rooms: 53 (5)

SIMSBURY: *Iron Horse Inn* $
969 Hopmeadow St. **(** (800) 245-9938 or (860) 658-2216. **FAX** (860) 651-0822.
W www.ironhorseofsimsbury.com
A small inn located in the heart of Simsbury, close to a scenic walking
path leading behind the old estates. Each room has a voice mailbox
and most rooms have a private balcony. Ideal for traveling families.
Breakfast not included. ⚡ 🏋 ⛲ 🔔 **P**

Credit cards: AE MC V — Rooms: 27 (1)

STONINGTON: *The Inn at Stonington* $$$
60 Water St. **(** (860) 535-2000. **FAX** (860) 535-8193.
W www.innatstonington.com   Located on the waterfront, this clapboard inn
is close to the village's mini beach and shops. Some rooms have a harbor
view, and there is a private boat dock, too. ⚡ **P** ♿

Credit cards: AE MC V — Rooms: 18

WINDSOR: *Residence Inn by Marriott* $$$
100 Dunfey Lane. **(** (800) 331-3131 or (860) 688-7474. **FAX** (860) 683-8457.
Complimentary beverages and light meal Monday through Thursday. All
rooms have kitchens, movies, coffeemakers, microwaves, and refrigerators.
VCRs are available for rent. Fifteen minutes from downtown Hartford.
⚡ 🏋 ⛲ 🔔 **P** ♿

Credit cards: AE DC MC V D — Rooms: 96 (96)

VERMONT

ARLINGTON: *Inn on Covered Bridge Green* $$$$
3587 River Rd. **(** (800) 726-9489 or (802) 375-9489. **FAX** (802)-375-1208.
@ cbg@sover.net **W** www.coveredbridgegreen.com
In this 1792 farmhouse, the former home of Norman Rockwell, each
room has its own bath and fireplace. TV/VCR available. Rockwell's
former studio and a barn have been turned into fully equipped
cottages. Walking trails. Mountain biking and canoe rides can be
arranged. ⚡ 🏋 🔔 **P** ♿

Credit cards: MC V — Rooms: 9 (1)

ARLINGTON: *Arlington's West Mountain Inn* $$$$$
144 West Mountain Inn Rd. **(** (802) 375-6516 **FAX** (802) 375-6553
@ info@westmountaininn.com **W** www.westmountaininn.com
Situated on 150 acres (60 ha) of woodland, complete with skiing and
hiking trails, a bird sanctuary, and even llamas, the seven-gabled West
Mountain Inn is for those seeking outdoor activities and relaxation.
Inside, expect hearty country cuisine and charming decor. Dinner
included. TV in common room only. ⚡ 🏋 🔔 **P** ♿

Credit cards: AE MC V D — Rooms: 22 (6)

BRATTLEBORO: *The Inn of Brattleboro* $
959 Putney Rd. **(** (800) 329-7466 or (802) 254-4583 **FAX** (802) 254-4585
A modern and comfortable hotel. Good value with some extra amenities.
Breakfast is included in the price.
⚡ 🏋 ⛲ 📺 🔔 **P**

Credit cards: AE DC MC V D — Rooms: 46 (1)

BURLINGTON: *Radisson Hotel* $$$$
60 Battery St. **(** (800) 329-7466 or (802) 658-6500. **FAX** (802) 658-4659.
W www.radisson.com
The Radisson is Burlington's most upscale hotel and is right in the heart of the
downtown core. The best rooms have breathtaking views of Lake Champlain
with the Adirondacks rising behind. ⚡ 🏋 📶 🍸 ⛲ 📺 🔔 **P** ♿

Credit cards: AE DC MC V D — Rooms: 256 (8)

CHITTENDEN: *Mountain Top Inn* $$$$
195 Mountain Top Rd. **(** (800) 445-2100 or (802) 483-2311. **FAX** (802) 483-6373.
@ info@mountaintopinn.com **W** www.mountaintopinn.com
Intimate country inn with 35 rooms plus 10 separate cottages and chalets.
Private beach. Closed between Columbus Day and Christmas, and from
mid-March to Memorial Day. TVs in common rooms. 🏋 🍸 ⛲ 🔔 **P** ♿

Credit cards: AE MC V — Rooms: 45 (10)

COLCHESTER: *Fairfield Inn* $
84 South Park Dr. **(** (800) 228-2800 or 802-655-1400. **FAX** (802) 338-9158.
@ gmbvt@lodgian.com **W** www.fairfieldinn.com
Good value inn, especially since it is located close to downtown
Burlington. ⚡ 🏋 📶 ⛲ **P** ♿

Credit cards: AE DC MC V D — Rooms: 117

For key to symbols see back flap

Price categories for a standard double room per night, inclusive of breakfast, service charges, and any additional taxes:

$ under $100
$$ $100–$150
$$$ $150–$200
$$$$ $200–$250
$$$$$ over $250

CREDIT CARDS
Major credit cards accepted: *AE* American Express; *DC* Diners Club; *MC* MasterCard/Access; *V* Visa, *D* Discover Card.

NUMBER OF ROOMS
Number of rooms in the hotel (suites shown in parentheses).

RECOMMENDED RESTAURANT
Good restaurant within the hotel.

CHILDREN'S FACILITIES
Hotel has various facilities for young children.

GARDEN OR TERRACE
Hotel has a garden, courtyard, or terrace.

	CREDIT CARDS	NUMBER OF ROOMS	RECOMMENDED RESTAURANT	CHILDREN'S FACILITIES	GARDEN OR TERRACE
CRAFTSBURY COMMON: *The Inn on the Common* $$$$$ 1162 North Craftsbury Rd. (800) 521-2233 or (802) 586-9619. FAX (802) 586-2249. @ info@innonthecommon.com W www.innonthecommon.com Three restored Federal homes nestled in an idyllic village setting, Features elegantly decorated rooms, beautiful views, and outstanding cuisine as well as excellent cross-country skiing. Dinner included. TV in sitting room. Rooms do not have air-conditioning.	AE MC V	16 (1)	■	●	■
GRAFTON: *The Old Tavern at Grafton* $$$ 92 Main St. (800) 843-1801 or (802) 843-2231. FAX (802) 843-2245. @ info@old-tavern.com W www.old-tavern.com Along with 11 rooms in the main building, the Old Tavern rents out a number of charming guest houses around town. The Old Tavern is a place of peace and quiet—there are no televisions or telephones in the rooms. Only the executive suite is air-conditioned. Closed mid-March to end of April.	AE MC V	47 (8)	■		■
KILLINGTON: *Mountain Meadows Lodge* $$ 285 Thundering Brook Rd. (800) 370-4567 or (802) 775-1010. @ havefun@mtnmeadowslodge.com W www.mtmeadowslodge.com Vermont's only mountain lodge set on both a lake and the famous Appalachian Trail, the lodge is perfect for outdoor types. It features excellent family services, including baby-sitting (with advance notice). Closed from April to mid-May.	AE MC V	20 (1)	■	●	■
MANCHESTER: *The Equinox Resort* $$$$$ 3567 Main St. (802) 362-4747. FAX (802) 362-1595. @ reservations@equinoxresort.com W www.equinoxresort.com This historic 18th-century resort has stunning public spaces and spacious, country-style rooms. Guests can also take advantage of the resort's activities including golf, falconry, fishing, and off-road driving (separate charges apply for most activities).	AE DC MC V D	172 (17)	■	●	■
MIDDLEBURY: *The Middlebury Inn* $$$ 14 Court House Sq. (800) 842-4666 or (802) 388-4961. FAX (802) 388-4563. @ midinnvt@sover.net W www.middleburyinn.com The town's main hostelery since 1827, this historic inn offers well-equipped rooms furnished with reproduction antiques, all with private baths, some with whirlpool tubs. Two-room suites with shared bath are geared to families.	AE DC MC V D	75 (4)	■	●	
MONTPELIER: *Econo Lodge* $ 101 North Field St. (802) 223-5258. FAX (802) 223-0716. W www.econolodge.com Comfortable, clean, and basic, the EconoLodge is located less than a mile from downtown Montpelier.	AE DC MC V D	54		●	
MONTPELIER: *The Inn at Montpelier* $$ 147 Main St. (802) 223-2727. FAX (802) 223-0722. @ mail2inn@aol.com. W www.innatmontpelier.com. These two beautifully renovated adjacent Federal-style homes are the capital city's most stately lodgings. A large veranda wraps around the brick Lamp Langdon house. If it's winter, ask for one of the six rooms with fireplaces.	AE DC MC V D	19		●	■
NORTH HERO: *North Hero House Inn & Restaurant* $$$ Rte 2. (888) 525-3644 or (802) 372-4732. FAX (802) 372-3218. @ nhhlake@aol.com W www.northherohouse.com Three of this inn's four buildings are on beautiful Lake Champlain. The main house, complete with library and pub, sits just across the road. Private beach. Some rooms have air conditioning.	AE MC V	26 (3)	■	●	■

RICHMOND: *The Richmond Victorian Inn* $

191 East Main St. ☎ (888) 242-3362 or (802) 434-4410. [FAX] (802) 434-4411.
@ innkeeper@richmondvictorianinn.com [W] www.richmondvictorianinn.com
Located in the foothills of the Green Mountains, this inexpensive inn's six guest rooms are furnished in a country Victorian style with antiques. No televisions or air-conditioning in rooms. Children over 12. 🚭 👪 [P]

Cards	Rooms			
AE MC V D	6 (1)			■

ST. JOHNSBURY: *Comfort Inn and Suites* $$$

703 US Rte 5 S. ☎ (800) 228-5150 or (802) 748-1500. [FAX] (802) 748-1243.
@ vermonttajmahal@aol.com [W] www.vtcomfortinnsuites.com
A deluxe hotel with a full range of services and elegant interior decor. All rooms have separate sitting area with extra amenities such as in-room iron, coffeemaker, hair dryer, and movies. 🚭 👪 ⇅ 🏊 🏋 [P] ♿

Cards	Rooms			
AE DC MC V D	107 (11)		●	

SHELBURNE: *Inn at Shelburne Farms* $$$

1611 Harbor Rd. ☎ (802) 985-8498. [FAX] (802) 985-8123. [W] www.shelburnefarms.org
Built in 1897 on a bluff overlooking Lake Champlain, the inn is situated on a 1,400-acre (400-ha) property, landscaped by Frederick Law Olmsted. Guests can enjoy the private beach, views of the lake, and the sumptuous bedrooms, 17 of which have private baths. No televisions or air-conditioning. Closed mid-October to mid-May. 🚭 🍸 🍴 [P]

Cards	Rooms			
AE DC MC V D	24	■	●	■

STOWE: *Wood Chip Inn* $$

Mountain Rd. ☎ (800) 676-9181 or (802) 253-9080. [FAX] (802) 253-7873.
@ wdchipinn@aol.com [W] www.gostowe.com/members/woodchip
Charming and economical, the Wood Chip Inn offers homemade breads and soups in the fall and winter, and afternoon refreshments in the summer. Not all rooms have air-conditioning and television; two have shared baths. 🚭 👪 [P] ♿

Cards	Rooms			
AE MC V	9			■

STOWE: *Trapp Family Lodge* $$$$$

700 Trapp Hill Rd. ☎ (800) 826-7000 or (802) 253-8511. [FAX] (802) 253-5740.
@ info@trappfamily.com [W] www.trappfamily.com
World-famous 116-room resort on 2,700-acre (1.092-ha) property. Along with large Austrian-style main lodge, the resort features 100 guest houses, nightly entertainment, a range of recreational activities, and exquisite cuisine. Some rooms air-conditioned. 🚭 👪 🍸 🏊 🏋 🍴 [P] ♿

Cards	Rooms			
AE DC MC V D	116 (18)	■	●	■

WATERBURY: *Holiday Inn & Spa* $$$

45 Blush Hill Rd. ☎ (800) 621-7822 or (802) 244-7822. [FAX] (802) 244-6395.
@ holidays@together.net [W] www.holiday-inn.com/waterburyvt
Situated on a plateau in the heart of the Green Mountains central to Burlington, Montpelier, and Stowe, this is the perfect launching point for day trips around north and central Vermont. 🚭 👪 🍸 🏊 🏋 🍴 [P] ♿

Cards	Rooms			
AE DC MC V D	79		●	■

NEW HAMPSHIRE

ALTON BAY: *Bay Side Inn on Lake Winnipesaukee* $

Rte 11D. ☎ (603) 875-5005. @ info@baysideinn.com [W] www.bayside-inn.com
Open May to October, this lovely inn on Lake Winnipesaukee offers complimentary sailboats, a lakeside sundeck, and a breathtaking view of the White Mountains. Efficiencies available. No air-conditioning. 🚭 👪 🍴 [P] ♿

Cards	Rooms			
MC V	18		●	■

BRETTON WOODS: *The Mount Washington Hotel & Resort* $$$$$

Rte 302. ☎ (800) 258-0330 or (603) 278-1000. [FAX] (603) 278-8838.
@ hotelinfo@mtwashington.com [W] www.mtwashington.com
Since 1902, this elegant resort has offered high quality service in a beautiful natural setting. Dinner at any of the five restaurants is included, and the cool mountain air keeps the rooms comfortable during the summer season. Air conditioning in Tower Suites only. 🚭 👪 ⇅ 🍸 🏊 🏋 🍴 [P] ♿

Cards	Rooms			
AE MC V D	191 (6)	■	●	■

CONCORD: *The Centennial Inn* $$$

96 Pleasant St. ☎ (800) 360-4839 or (603) 225-7102. [FAX] (603) 225-5031.
@ centennialinn@totalnetnh.net [W] www.someplacesdifferent.com
Housed in a restored 1876 Victorian mansion, this centrally located inn provides handsomely furnished rooms and suites for the business and pleasure traveler. 🚭 👪 ⇅ 🍸 🍴 [P] ♿

Cards	Rooms			
AE DC MC V D	32 (5)	■	●	

ENFIELD: *Shaker Inn* $$

447 Rte 4A. ☎ (888) 707-4257 or (603) 632-7810. [W] www.theshakerinn.com
Built in the mid-19th century as the Great Stone Dwelling of the Shaker religious community, the inn retains the grace and minimalist style of Shaker workmanship, with added modern comforts. The excellent restaurant uses farm-fresh ingredients. Breakfast is included, dinner is extra. 🚭 👪 [P]

Cards	Rooms			
AE MC V D	24	■		■

For key to symbols see back flap

Price categories for a standard double room per night, inclusive of breakfast, service charges, and any additional taxes:

$ under $100
$$ $100–$150
$$$ $150–$200
$$$$ $200–$250
$$$$$ over $250

CREDIT CARDS
Major credit cards accepted: *AE* American Express; *DC* Diners Club; *MC* MasterCard/Access; *V* Visa, *D* Discover Card.

NUMBER OF ROOMS
Number of rooms in the hotel (suites shown in parentheses).

RECOMMENDED RESTAURANT
Good restaurant within the hotel.

CHILDREN'S FACILITIES
Hotel has various facilities for young children.

GARDEN OR TERRACE
Hotel has a garden, courtyard, or terrace.

	CREDIT CARDS	NUMBER OF ROOMS	RECOMMENDED RESTAURANT	CHILDREN'S FACILITIES	GARDEN OR TERRACE
EXETER: *The Inn and Conference Center of Exeter* $$$ 90 Front St. (*(800) 782-8444* or *(603) 772-5901*. FAX *(603) 778-8757*. @ *info@innofexeter.com* W *www.someplacesdifferent.com* Georgian style inn with good restaurant. Rooms have four-poster beds and antique furnishings.	AE DC MC V D	46 (3)	■	●	■
FRANCONIA: *Lovett's Inn* $$ 1474 Profile Rd. (*(800) 356-3802* or *(603) 823-7761*. FAX *(603) 823-8802*. W *www.lovettssinn.com* For 70 years the distinctive hospitality of this former country estate has attracted such guests as movie star Bette Davis and members of the Kennedy clan. Some rooms have television and most have air-conditioning. Closed April.	AE MC V D	21 (3)	■	●	■
FRANCONIA: *The Franconia Inn* $$$ 1300 Easton Rd. (*(800) 473-5299* or *(603) 823-5542*. FAX *(603) 823-8078*. @ *info@franconiainn.com* W *www.franconiainn.com* Cozy turn-of-the-century inn, surrounded by stunning scenery. This place has enough sports and activities to keep outdoor enthusiasts satisfied year round. No air-conditioning. Television in common room. Closed April to mid-May.	AE MC V	34 (2)	■	●	■
HAMPTON: *Ashworth by the Sea* $$$ 295 Ocean Blvd. (*(800) 345-6736* or *(603) 926-6762*. FAX *(603) 926-2002*. W *www.ashworthhotel.com* A year-round beachfront hotel with an air of old-fashioned elegance. Spacious rooms, most with ocean views.	AE DC MC V D	105 (1)	■	●	■
HANOVER: *Hanover Inn* $$$$$ Wheelock & Main. (*(800) 443-7024* or *(603) 643-4300*. FAX *(603) 643-4433*. W *www.hanoverinn.com* Attentive service and excellent dining mark this elegant inn, which has been operating for more than 200 years. All guest rooms are decorated in Colonial-style.	AE DC MC V D	92 (21)	■	●	
KEENE: *Carriage Barn Bed and Breakfast* $ 358 Main St. (*(603) 357-3812*. @ *carriagebarn@webryders.net* W *www.carriagebarn.com* Cheerfully decorated with local antiques, this home offers a relaxed, peaceful environment in the heart of town. Children over 5. No television.	AE MC V D	4		●	■
MANCHESTER: *The Highlander Inn* $$ 2 Highlander Way. (*(800) 548-9248* or *(603) 625-6426*. FAX *(603) 625-6466*. W *www.highlanderinn.com* A popular resort for Bostonians since the turn of the century. Its proximity to the airport is a great convenience for both business and pleasure travelers.	AE DC MC V D	88 (10)	■	●	■
MEREDITH: *Meredith Inn B & B* $$ 2 Waukewan St. (*(603) 279-0000*. FAX *(603) 279-4017*. @ *inn1897@meredithinn.com* W *www.meredithinn.com* A restored Victorian home refurbished with all the modern amenities. Convenient to Lake Winnipesaukee activities; walking distance to the beach on Lake Waukewan. Most rooms have air conditioning.	MC V D	8			
NEW LONDON: *The New London Inn* $$ 140 Main St. (*(800) 526-2791* or *(603) 526-2791*. FAX *(603) 526-2749*. @ *nlinn@tds.net* W *www.newlondoninn.net* Federal-style 1792 inn furnished with European and American antiques. It has a library, a bar area, and dining room overlooking the common. Some rooms have air conditioning and television.	AE MC V	23 (2)	■	●	■

NORTH CONWAY: *Junge's Motel* $ 1858 White Mountain Hwy. ☎ *(603) 356-2886.* [W] *www.jungesmotel.com* Affordable accommodations offering the outdoor enthusiast year-round access to sports and activities. Breakfast not included. 🚭 👪 🏊 [P]	AE DC MC V D	28 (2)		●	■
PORTSMOUTH: *The Inn at Christian Shore* $$ 335 Maplewood Ave. ☎ *(603) 431-6770.* [FAX] *(603) 431-7743.* [W] *www.portsmouthnh.com/christianshore* A well-preserved late 19th-century home furnished with a mix of antiques, African art, and contemporary paintings. The gourmet breakfasts offer vast choice. No children. 🚭 [P]	MC V	5			■
PORTSMOUTH: *Sheraton Harborside Portsmouth* $$$ 250 Market St. ☎ *(603) 431-2300.* [FAX] *(603) 433-5649.* [@] *info@sheratonportsmouth.com* [W] *www.sheratonportsmouth.com* A modern hotel ideally located in the historic waterfront district. Rates vary according to level of occupancy. 🚭 👪 ⇅ 🍸 🏊 🏋 🍴 [P] ♿	AE DC MC V D	200 (19)	■	●	
ROCHESTER: *The Governor's Inn* $ 78 Wakefield St. ☎ *(603) 332-0107.* [FAX] *(603) 335-1984.* [W] *www.governorsinn.com* Two 1920s Georgian Colonial-style homes, now an inn and restaurant. Meals are served in the courtyard in the summer months. 🚭 👪 🍸 🍴 [P] ♿	AE MC V D	22 (2)	■		■
SUNAPEE: *The Inn at Sunapee* $ 125 Burkehaven Hill Rd. ☎ *(800) 327-2466 or (603) 763-4444.* [FAX] *(603) 763-9456.* [@] *stay@innatsunapee.com* [W] *www.innatsunapee.com* An 1875 dairy farm overlooking beautiful Mount Sunapee. Country style hospitality with a touch of Asia in the food and decor. Television in common room; no air-conditioning. 🚭 🍸 🏊 [P]	AE MC V D	16 (5)		●	■
TROY: *The Inn at East Hill Farm* $ 460 Monadnock St. ☎ *(800) 242-6495 or (603) 242-6495.* [FAX] *(603) 242-7709.* [@] *info@east-hill-farm.com* [W] *www.east-hill-farm.com* Set on 150 acres (60 ha), this year-round resort has farm activities for children and pleasing amenities for adults. Rates quoted are per person; weekly rates are much lower. All meals are included. Some rooms have television and air-conditioning. 🚭 👪 🏊 [P] ♿	MC V D	30 (30)		●	■
WEIRS BEACH: *Lake Winnipesaukee Motel* $ 350 Daniel Webster Hwy. ☎ *(603) 366-5502.* [FAX] *(603) 366-2388.* [W] *www.lakewinnipesaukeemotel.com* This small motel takes pride in its warm hospitality, peaceful surroundings, and 45 years of experience. A private, two-bedroom house is also available for larger groups. Open February to October. 🚭 👪 🏊 [P] ♿	AE MC V D	16 (2)		●	■
WOLFEBORO: *The Wolfeboro Inn* $$$ 90 N. Main St. ☎ *(800) 451-2389 or (603) 569-3016.* [FAX] *(603) 569-5375.* [W] *www.wolfeboroinn.com* Historic inn on the waterfront of America's oldest summer resort, offering tastefully decorated rooms, fine dining, a private beach, and a solid reputation for comfort and service. 🚭 👪 🍸 🍴 [P] ♿	AE MC V D	44 (3)	■	●	■
MAINE					
BANGOR: *Fairfield Inn* $ 300 Odlin Rd. ☎ *(800) 228-2800 or (207) 990-0001.* [FAX] *(207) 990-0917.* [W] *www.marriott.com* A modern, fully equipped hotel, conveniently located less than 1 mile (1.6 km) from downtown Bangor. Continental breakfast, juice, and coffee available 24 hours a day. 🚭 👪 ⇅ 🏊 🏋 [P] ♿	AE DC MC V D	153		●	
BAR HARBOR: *Atlantic Eyrie Lodge* $$ Highbrook Rd. ☎ *(207) 288-9786.* Located at the edge of town, this motel is a good base for Bar Harbor, a ten minute walk away. Rooms are modern and spacious and some have kitchens. Tennis and gym facilities can be used at a nearby luxury hotel. 🚭 👪 ⇅ [P] ♿	AE MC V D	58		●	■
BAR HARBOR: *Mira Monte Inn and Suites* $$$ 69 Mount Desert St. ☎ *(800) 553-5109 or (207) 288-4263.* [FAX] *(207) 288-3115.* [W] *www.miramonte.com* Constructed in 1864, this is one of only two B&Bs in town owned by Bar Harbor natives. It features two formal gardens. All rooms have air-conditioning, private bath, fireplace and/or balcony. Open May to October. 🚭 🍴 [P] ♿	AE DC MC V D	16 (3)			■

For key to symbols see back flap

Price categories for a standard double room per night, inclusive of breakfast, service charges, and any additional taxes:

$ under $100
$$ $100–$150
$$$ $150–$200
$$$$ $200–$250
$$$$$ over $250

Credit Cards
Major credit cards accepted: *AE* American Express; *DC* Diners Club; *MC* MasterCard/Access; *V* VISA, *D* Discover Card.

Number of Rooms
Number of rooms in the hotel (suites shown in parentheses).

Recommended Restaurant
Good restaurant within the hotel.

Children's Facilities
Hotel has various facilities for young children.

Garden or Terrace
Hotel has a garden, courtyard, or terrace.

	Credit Cards	Number of Rooms	Recommended Restaurant	Children's Facilities	Garden or Terrace
Bethel: *Bethel Inn and Country Club* $$$$$ On the Common. ☎ *(800) 654-0125 or (207) 824-2175.* [FAX] *(207) 824-2233.* @ *info@bethelinn.com* [W] *www.bethelinn.com* A premier Maine resort, the property has its own championship golf course and a tennis court. Price includes free golf and dinner, except for town-house guests. Air conditioning in some rooms. 🚭 📺 ⇅ 🍸 ≋ 🏋 🍴 [P] ♿	*AE DC MC V D*	*140 (12)*	■	●	■
Cape Elizabeth: *Inn by the Sea* $$$$$ 40 Bowery Beach Rd. ☎ *(800) 888-4287 or (207) 799-3134.* [FAX] *(207) 799-4779.* @ *info@innbythesea.com* [W] *www.innbythesea.com* Every room in this luxurious inn is a suite, each with an ocean view from the porch or deck. Minutes away from Portland, the inn has a gourmet restaurant, pool, and tennis courts. Dogs welcome. 🚭 📺 ≋ [P] ♿	*AE MC V D*	*43 (43)*	■	●	■
Caribou: *Caribou Inn and Convention Center* $ 19 Main St. ☎ *(800) 235-0466 or (207) 498-3733.* [FAX] *(207) 498-3149.* @ *cicc3733@aol.com* [W] *www.caribouinn.com* With low rates and wide range of facilities and in-room amenities, this inn offers great value. The Greenhouse Restaurant is known for the best and least expensive breakfasts in the area. 🚭 📺 🍸 ≋ 🏋 🍴 [P] ♿	*AE DC MC V D*	*73 (3)*	■	●	■
Carrabassett Valley: *Sugarloaf/USA Resort* $$$$$ Rte 27. ☎ *(800) THE-LOAF or (207) 237-2000.* [FAX] *(207) 237-2718.* @ *info@sugarloaf.com* [W] *www.sugarloaf.com* One of New England's most renowned ski resorts. Guests may use health club and, for an extra charge, take ski or snowboard lessons. Golf course ranks as one of America's most picturesque. More than 200 one- to five-bedroom condo units also available. 🚭 📺 ⇅ 🍸 ≋ 🏋 🍴 [P] ♿	*AE MC V D*	*119 (21)*	■	●	■
East Machias: *Riverside Inn and Restaurant* $$ Rte 1. ☎ *(207) 255-4134.* [FAX] *(207) 235-0577.* @ *riversideinn@maineline.net* [W] *www.riversideinn-maine.com* Situated on the East Machias River, this serene getaway features rooms individually decorated with antiques. The terraced perennial garden is a great place for evening strolls. No air conditioning. Children over 12. 🚭 📺 [P]	*AE MC V*	*4 (2)*	■		■
Fryeburg: *Oxford House Inn* $$ 105 Main St. ☎ *(800) 261-7206 or (207) 935-3442.* [FAX] *(207) 935-7046.* @ *innkeeper@oxfordhouseinn.com* [W] *www.oxfordhouseinn.com* A charming bed-and-breakfast located in the activity-filled White Mountains and Western Lakes region of Maine. The inn has a gourmet restaurant and four beautifully decorated rooms. 🚭 📺 🍸 🍴 [P]	*AE DC MC V D*	*4*	■		■
Greenville: *Big Squaw Mountain Resort* $ Rte 15. ☎ *(800) 754-6246 or (207) 695-1000.* [FAX] *(207) 695-4384.* Cheap accommodation for skiers and outdoor enthusiasts visiting Big Moose Mountain. Dorm-style and private rooms have been renovated and accommodate up to eight people. Tennis courts. No air conditioning. 🚭 📺 🍸 🍴 [P] ♿	*AE MC V D*	*52*		●	
Greenville: *Greenville Inn* $$$ Norris St. ☎ *(888) 695-6000 or (207) 695-2206.* [FAX] *(207) 695-0335.* @ *gvlinn@moosehead.net* [W] *www.greenvilleinn.com* Along with the four rooms in the main building, this beautifully appointed Victorian inn has six cottages, all with porches or decks. Televisions in some rooms. No air-conditioning. Children over 7. 🚭 📺 🍸	*MC V D*	*12 (2)*	■		■
Kennebunkport: *Captain Jefferd's Inn* $$$ 5 Pearl St. ☎ *(800) 839-6844 or (207) 967-2311.* [W] *www.captainjefferdsinn.com* This sea captain's mansion, built in 1804, retains its antique charm and has beautifully landscaped gardens. There is also a wood-burning fireplace in the living room and some rooms have gas fireplaces. It's conveniently located, just one block from old Town Green. 🚭 📺 ≋ [P]	*AE MC V*	*14*		●	■

KENNEBUNKPORT: *The Colony Hotel* $$$$$ | AE MC V | 123
140 Ocean Ave. (800) 552-2363 or (207) 967-3331. FAX (207) 967-8738.
@ reservations@thecolonyhotel.com W www.thecolonyhotel.com
A short walk from Kennebunkport, the majestic Colony Hotel is perched overlooking the ocean. This environmentally responsible resort offers a heated saltwater pool, private beach, and extensive gardens. Closed from mid-October to mid-May. No air conditioning. Television in common room and bar only.

MILLINOCKET: *Best Western Heritage Motor Inn* $ | AE DC MC V D | 49
935 Central St. (800) 528-1234 or (207) 723-9777. FAX (207) 723-9777.
W www.bestwestern.com
Air-conditioned rooms at a reasonable cost. The property connects to most cross-country and snowmobile trails heading to northern Maine. A swimming pond is steps away.

NEW HARBOR: *Hotel Pemaquid* $ | 28 (5)
3098 Bristol Rd. (207) 677-2312. W www.hotelpemaquid.com
A classic Maine inn, decorated with antiques, this former farmhouse first welcomed guests in 1888. A short walk from the coast and near the Pemaquid Point lighthouse. Some rooms have shared bath. Breakfast not served. No air conditioning. Closed mid-Oct to mid-May.

NEWRY: *Sunday River Inn* $ | AE MC V D | 20
23 Skiway Rd. (207) 824-2410. FAX (207) 824-3181. @ info@sundayriverinn.com
W www.sundayriverinn.com Family-oriented inn located .5 miles (.8 km) from Sunday River ski hill. Cross-country ski center and skating and sliding areas located at the inn. Private and dorm-style rooms are available, and some rooms share baths. No air conditioning. Television in common room only. Closed from April to the end of November.

OGUNQUIT: *The Cliff House* $$$$ | AE MC V D | 194 (2)
Shore Rd. (207) 361-1000. FAX (207) 361-2122.
@ info@cliffhousemaine.com W www.cliffhousemaine.com
Oceanside resort built in 1872 with full floor devoted to recreation. All rooms are air-conditioned and have balconies. It also has a spa. Cliff House Trolley takes guests to spots of interest in the area in July and August. Closed from mid-December to March.

PORTLAND: *Inn at St. John* $$ | DC MC V D | 40
939 Congress. (800) 636-9127 or (207) 773-6481. FAX (207) 756-7629.
@ theinn@maine.rr.com W www.innatstjohn.com
Century-old inn just minutes from Portland's Old Port, Waterfront, and Arts districts. Rooms are tastefully decorated and all are air-conditioned, but some rooms share baths. Pets are welcomed.

PORTLAND: *Portland Regency Hotel* $$$$ | AE DC MC V D | 95 (8)
20 Milk St. (800) 727-3436 or (207) 774-4200. FAX (207) 775-2150.
@ public@the regency.com W www.theregency.com
Situated in the heart of the Old Port district, this is Portland's premiere full-service hotel. The fitness center is free for guests.

RANGELEY: *North Country Inn Bed and Breakfast* $ | AE MC V | 4
Main St. (800) 295-4968 or (207) 864-2440.
@ info@northcountrybb.com W www.northcountrybb.com
This 19th century Colonial bed and breakfast has a huge porch that looks out onto Rangeley Lake and surrounding mountains. No air conditioning. Children over six are welcome.

RANGELEY: *Rangeley Inn* $ | AE MC V D | 50 (1)
51 Main. (800) 666-3687 or (207) 864-3341. FAX (207) 864-3634.
@ rangeinn@rangeley.org W www.rangeleyinn.com
Rooms available in either the Main Inn or the Motor Lodge (prices nearly the same) as well as two lakeside cabins. Located two blocks from public beach. Jacuzzis in some rooms in Main Inn.

ROCKWOOD: *The Birches Resort* $ | AE MC V D | 50
Birches Rd. (800) 825-9453 or (207) 534-7305. FAX (207) 534-8835.
@ wwld@aol.com W www.birches.com
The Birches offers accommodation in cabins (15), lodge rooms (4), and private rental homes (6). The 11,000-acre (4,450-ha) resort is launching point and host for wilderness expeditions. Meal plans are offered. Also has outdoor Jacuzzi and sauna. Television in common room. No air conditioning.

For key to symbols see back flap

WHERE TO EAT

To MANY OUTSIDERS, New England is synonymous with simple, hearty, somewhat boring fare. While it is true that a traditional meal of the past often consisted of cod or boiled beef and cabbage served with potatoes, the regional menu is substantially more varied and tempting. Local cheeses and produce from rural areas complement the exquisite seafood, often caught fresh the same day, that is found up and down the coast. In recent years, the New England dining experience has been expanded to include a host of ethnic flavors,

Fanciful Maine eatery sign

thanks to a steady stream of immigrants into the large urban areas. Boston (Massachusetts), Portland (Maine), and Providence (Rhode Island) are the region's top dining destinations. Boston's restaurant scene is particularly vibrant. The city's top restaurants serve a medley of styles, such as French and Italian, often using other Mediterranean and Asian accents. Boston was once called "Bean Town" because of the popularity of its baked beans; now it has good Indian, Southeast Asian, Latin American, and Caribbean restaurants.

EATING THROUGH THE DAY

MOST RESTAURANTS usually serve breakfast from 6 or 7am until 11am or noon. Some establishments will serve you breakfast at any hour of the day. The choice is varied, with some spots offering little more than a bagel and a coffee and others whipping up portions of eggs, bacon, and sausages hefty enough to keep you going almost all day.

Lunch can run anytime from 11:30am until 3pm, and is equally varied. In busy Boston, businesspeople can be seen gulping down a sandwich at the counter of a local deli or sitting down to enjoy a

Relaxed ambience of a typical beachfront seafood eatery

An Italian atmosphere at Boston's Caffè Vittoria

sumptuous meal at one of the city's many fine restaurants. In many places, the lunch menu is the same as it is for dinner, with smaller portions and significantly lower prices.

Traditionally New Englanders serve up large dinners. You can usually sit down between 6 and 10pm. Some restaurants, notably those in Boston's Chinatown and Kenmore Square, stay open late, supported mostly by the hungry crowds heading home from the dance clubs and bars.

It is not uncommon for restaurants to be closed on Mondays or during select hours between lunch and dinner. Some of the finer establishments may serve dinner exclusively. As always, you should check in advance.

PAYING AND TIPPING

WAITERS ARE generally paid fairly low wages, meaning they earn the bulk of their income through tips. This means that all restaurants with table service expect some sort of gratuity at the end of the meal. Each state charges a different meal tax, but it is standard practice to leave between 15 and 20 percent of the pre-tax bill as the tip. If the service is good or bad, adjust the tip rate accordingly. If you are paying by credit card, you may include the tip in the charged amount on the space provided on the receipt. Some fast-food restaurants have optional tip-jars next to the cashier.

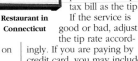

Restaurant in Connecticut

Rustic charm of the Grist Mill Restaurant in Killington, Vermont

ALCOHOL AND SMOKING

IN OTHER PARTS of New England, Boston has passed legislation banning smoking in all bars and restaurants, but almost all restaurants have designated smoking and non-smoking sections, though many ban smoking altogether. Bars, on the other hand, often allow smoking.

Twenty-one is the legal drinking age, so underage travelers should be aware that they will be denied access to most bars. They will also not be allowed to order wine with dinner in restaurants. The majority of places are very strict about this and will often require you to show photo ID before you are served. Passports are generally the best form of identification, as many people are unfamiliar with driver's licenses from abroad.

DRESS CODES

NEW ENGLAND is a relaxed place where, for the most part, people dress on the casual side when they are dining out. This is especially true along the coast, where the casual beach atmosphere carries over into restaurants. There, shorts and T-shirts are commonplace. However, some establishments do have very strict dress codes, For the top dining rooms, a jacket and tie are required for gentlemen and the equivalent is expected for women. Formal evening wear is uncommon, but in some of the finest restaurants it is not out of place.

TRADITIONAL NEW ENGLAND FOOD

COASTAL NEW ENGLAND is all about seafood, pure and simple. Of the many types of fish served up fresh from the fisherman's net, swordfish, bluefish, tuna, and striped bass are among diners' favorites. Shellfish are also plentiful. You will find just about every method under

Outdoor dining in the summer in Portsmouth, New Hampshire

the sun for preparing mussels, clams, and oysters – and all of them delicious. On chilly autumn days, nothing is quite as fortifying as a bowl of thick clam chowder.

Lobster, however, is the quintessential meal in maritime New England. Although they are found off Rhode Island and Massachusetts, the lobsters from Maine are most coveted. Eating a lobster can be a messy undertaking, which is why all seafood restaurants stock plastic bibs and a large supply of napkins for their customers. The more rudimentary eateries, tiny little shacks dotting the coastline and serving fresh seafood on paper plates, may not be as well equipped, which is why it is always a good idea to carry a roll of paper towels in your car.

Not all New England delicacies are pulled from the sea, however. Vermont is the dairy capital of the region, producing high-quality yogurt and cheese, especially cheddars.

Throughout the spring, summer, and fall, area restaurants and markets take advantage of the fresh produce being harvested locally. Delicate fiddleheads make a brief appearance on menus during the spring – though the uninitiated should eat them sparingly – as do fresh strawberries in the early summer. The region, particularly Maine, is also known for its delicious blueberries that are used in any number of pies, muffins, and pancakes. In the late summer, visitors can indulge in sweet New England corn.

NEW ENGLAND'S MAPLE SYRUP

During the spring thaw in late March and early April, New England farmers hammer spigots into the trunks of their sugar maple trees in order to collect the trees' clear, slightly sweet sap in buckets. Traditionally sap is then poured into vats back at the "sugarhouse" and boiled for hours. When most of the excess water has been evaporated, an amber-colored syrup is left – a highly concentrated, thoroughly delicious product that is distinctly New England. The finest quality syrup goes best on pancakes and waffles and over ice cream.

What to Eat in New England

Ice cream

NEW ENGLAND'S CUISINE reflects the many cultures that have settled since the 17th century, when English pilgrims first adapted their tastes to include local ingredients. Ethnic foods are common; the Irish brought corned beef and potatoes, the Italians pasta, and all adopted native ingredients. Many traditional dishes depended on foods that kept well – both beans and cod, for instance, lasted well through winter. Today it is not surprising to find elegant dining rooms, strongly influenced by tradition, serving variations on classical dishes.

Wild Blueberry Pancakes
Served in a stack with butter and maple syrup. Tiny wild blueberries from Maine are mixed in with the batter.

Deep Filled Sandwich
Huge, deep filled sandwiches are a Boston specialty. The choice of breads and fillings is almost endless.

Boston Baked Beans
White beans slow-baked with salt pork and molasses are served with codfish cakes, brown bread, and beets.

Mustard seasoning

Beets

Small whole onions

Beef

Cabbage

Pickles

Carrots

Boiled potatoes

New England Boiled Dinner
Originally an Irish dish, this home-style favorite consists of a large piece of beef, which is slow-boiled with cabbage, potatoes, carrots, and onions. It is served with mustard seasoning and pickled beets and cucumbers on the side.

Chicken Pot Pie
Served as individual pies or by the wedge, the filling contains chunks of chicken and vegetables in a creamy sauce.

Calamari Italian Style
Whole baked squid stuffed with bread crumbs, herbs, and garlic are served in a rich tomato and herb sauce.

Sushi
Seasoned rice topped with thin-sliced raw fish such as tuna, yellowfin, and salmon, form nigiri sushi. Maki sushi is rolled in seaweed to enclose the fish and rice. Both types come with horseradish and pickled ginger.

Italian salami

SAUSAGES

Cured hard sausages, such as Italian salami, are eaten cold and are often found in sandwiches. Semi-cured and fresh sausages, including German *wurst* and Irish bangers, are served hot. Polish *kielbasa* can be chopped into omelets, while *linguica* is found in Portuguese soup.

Semi-cured Polish *kielbasa*

Semi-cured Portuguese *linguica*

German *wurst*

Irish banger

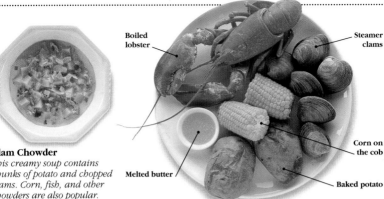

Boiled lobster

Steamer clams

Corn on the cob

Melted butter

Baked potato

Clam Chowder
This creamy soup contains chunks of potato and chopped clams. Corn, fish, and other chowders are also popular.

Clambakes
A boiled lobster and clams steamed with seaweed are served with fresh corn on the cob and baked potatoes. The lobster and clams are dipped into melted butter and eaten, usually, with the fingers.

Pretzel

Cookies

Muffin

Bagels

Wilted Spinach Salad
This side dish consists mainly of wilted spinach with crisp fried bacon crumbled on top. A light dressing may be added.

Baked Goods
Bagels and muffins are common breakfast foods. Cookies tend to be large, chewy, and hearty, with flavors such as oatmeal and chocolate chip. Large soft pretzels are a ballpark treat.

Squash
Summer squashes come in two varieties – green zucchini and yellow squash. They are a common side dish in late summer.

Indian Pudding
Served with ice cream or cream, this slow-baked soft pudding is made of cornmeal, sugar, molasses, spices, and milk.

Pumpkin Pie
This pumpkin, milk, egg, and spice custard pie is often eaten at Thanksgiving and typically served with whipped cream.

DRINKS

As well as simple brewed cups of American-style coffee, espresso, cappuccino, and latte have become New England favorites; decaffeinated coffee is also widely available. A host of microbreweries that brew beer to sell only in their restaurants have sprung up in the area. Samuel Adams, on the other hand, is on tap everywhere. Sakonnet Vineyards produces New England wines found in some restaurants. Fruit juices and frappés, a blend of ice cream and milk, are a refreshing alternative to alcoholic drinks.

Cranberry juice

Fruit frappé

A selection of microbrewery beers

Samuel Adams beer

Sakonnet wine

Choosing a Restaurant

RESTAURANTS HAVE been selected across a wide range of price categories for their value, good food, atmosphere, and location. The chart below highlights some of the factors that may influence your choice of where to eat. Restaurants are listed by area, and within these by price. Opening times are indicated by a "B" for breakfast, "L" for lunch, and "D" for dinner.

	CREDIT CARDS	OUTDOOR TABLES	VEGETARIAN	GOOD WINE	LATE OPENING

BOSTON

BEACON HILL AND THE THEATER DISTRICT

PARAMOUNT DELI-RESTAURANT $$
44 Charles St. **Map 1** B4. **(** (617) 720-1152.
Imagine a diner-turned-gourmet, and you have the Paramount. The urban "home cooking" from their open kitchen includes chicken *picatta* and *farfalle* with sun-dried tomatoes, feta, and garlic. B, L, D. 🚹 🕭

| AE MC V | | ■ | ● | |

FIGS $$$
42 Charles St. **Map 1** B4. **(** (617) 742-3447.
A side project of famed chef Todd English. The Mediterranean influence shows in the huge array of pizza, pasta, and appetizers. L (Sat, Sun), D. 🚹 🕭

| AE DC MC V | | ■ | ● | |

PANIFICO $$$
144 Charles St. **Map 1** B3. **(** (617) 227-4340.
Bakery and restaurant that serves a variety of unusual and delicious sandwiches, pizza, salads, and pastries. They also offer a few larger entrées, which are served through until dinner. B, L, D, Brunch Sun. 🚹 🕭

| AE MC V | | ■ | | |

CHINA PEARL $$$$
9 Tyler St. **Map 4** F2. **(** (617) 426-4338.
Boston's best dim sum, including seasonal favorites such as steamed dumplings and sesame balls. The atmosphere is noisy and exuberant. Reservations required. B, L, D, Brunch Sun. 🚹 🕭

| AE MC V D | | ■ | | |

EAST OCEAN CITY $$$$
25-29 Beach St. **Map 4** F2. **(** (617) 542-2504.
Tanks full of fish destined for diners' plates welcome visitors here. The menu includes seafood and more, in portions meant to be shared. L, D. 🚹 🕭

| AE MC V | | ■ | ● | ■ |

IMPERIAL SEAFOOD RESTAURANT $$$$
70 Beach St. **Map 4** F2. **(** (617) 426-8439.
Friendly Cantonese restaurant serving tasty seafood, vegetable, and meat dishes, as well as dim sum, selected from a roving trolley. L, D. 🚹

| AE MC V | | ■ | | |

JACOB WIRTH COMPANY RESTAURANT $$$$
31-37 Stuart St. **Map 4** E2. **(** (617) 338-8586.
Built by German Jacob Wirth, the 19th-century decor is unaltered. Delicious *wursts* and *schnitzel*. Great selection of beer. L, D. 🎵 🅿 🍸 🍴 🚹 🕭

| AE DC MC V D | ● | | ● | |

LEGAL SEAFOODS $$$$
26 Park Square. **Map 4** E2. **(** (617) 426-4444.
Legal has many locations throughout the city, all serving the freshest and best prepared seafood available. Try their raw bar for oysters, then one of their superb entrées. L, D. 🅿 🍸 🚹 🕭

| AE DC MC V D | | ■ | ● | ■ |

75 CHESTNUT $$$$
75 Chestnut St. **Map 1** B4. **(** (617) 227-2175.
The dark wood interior suggests an age-old private club; the menu, though, is anything but traditional. The seasonal menu includes seafood, meat and game. D, Brunch Sun (mid-Sep to end May). 🅿 🍴 🍸 🚹 🕭

| AE DC MC V D | | | ● | |

TEATRO $$$$
177 Tremont St. **Map 4** E2. **(** (617) 778-6841.
Relaxed but chic setting and perfect for pre-or post-theater dining. Fork-tender veal and charcoal-broiled game hen are house specialties. D. 🍸 🕭

| AE DC MC V | | | | ■ |

LOCKE-OBER $$$$$
3 Winter Place. **Map 1** C4. **(** (617) 542-1340.
New owners have rejuvenated one of America's most legendary restaurants, founded in 1875. Inventive twists enliven European and American classic dishes. Reservations essential. L, D. 🅿 🍸 🍴 🕭 🌑 Sat L, Sun.

| AE DC MC V | | | ● | |

Price categories include a three-course meal for one, half a bottle of house wine and all unavoidable extra charges such as sales tax and service.

$ under $20
$$ $20–30
$$$ $30–45
$$$$ $45–60
$$$$$ over $60

CREDIT CARDS
Major credit cards accepted: *AE* American Express; *MC* Master Card/Access; *DC* Diners Club; *V* VISA; *D* Discover Card.

OUTDOOR TABLES
Garden, courtyard, or terrace with outside tables.

VEGETARIAN
A good selection of vegetarian dishes available.

GOOD WINE
Extensive list of good wines, both local and international.

LATE OPENING
Full menu or light meals served after 11pm.

	CREDIT CARDS	OUTDOOR TABLES	VEGETARIAN	GOOD WINE	LATE OPENING
NO. 9 PARK $$$$$ 9 Park St. **Map** 1 C4. ☏ *(617) 742-9991.* The jazz-influenced retro decor in this restaurant puts diners in a light-hearted mood to enjoy the carefully considered and well-executed modern American menu. L (Mon–Fri), D. 🅿 🍸 🍽 🔥 ♿ ● Sun.	AE DC MC V D		■	●	
THE HUNGRY I $$$$$ 71 Charles St. **Map** 1 B4. ☏ *(617) 227-3524.* Chef-owner Peter Ballarin has given this beloved institution a sophisticated facelift. The inventive food has French influences and features fish and game. The enclosed terrace is a romantic oasis. L (Thu–Fri), D, Brunch Sun. 🍸 🍽 ● Mon, Aug.	AE DC MC V	●		●	
OLD BOSTON AND THE FINANCIAL DISTRICT					
DURGIN-PARK $$$ 340 North Market St. (Faneuil Hall Marketplace). **Map** 2 D3. ☏ *(617) 227-2038.* A Boston institution, serving all the New England standards that no one else seems to cook any more – Indian pudding, baked beans, and baked scrod, dished up by a sharp-tongued staff. L, D. 🎵 🍸 🔥 ♿	AE DC MC V D	●	■		
THE VAULT $$$$ 105 Water St. **Map** 2 D4. ☏ *(617) 292-9966.* This upscale restaurant in the business district features an American chop-house menu. Dishes include veal chop on gnocchi and grilled swordfish with lemon butter. L, D. 🎵 🍸 ● Sun.	AE DC MC V D			●	■
UNION OYSTER HOUSE $$$$ 41 Union St. **Map** 2 D3. ☏ *(617) 227-2750.* Boston's oldest restaurant, the Union Oyster House has managed to keep up with the times and features a respected updated menu of traditional New England seafood and more. Oyster bar is the best part. L, D. 🅿 🍸 🔥	AE DC MC V D			●	
JULIEN $$$$$ 250 Franklin St. (Hotel Meridien). **Map** 2 D4. ☏ *(617) 451-1900.* Unadulterated French haute cuisine, exquisitely prepared. Julien has the comfort and grace of a classic dining room that is confident of its quality. Reservations are recommended. D. 🎵 🅿 🍸 🍽 ♿ ● Sun.	AE DC MC V				
MAISON ROBERT $$$$$ 45 School St. **Map** 2 D4. ☏ *(617) 227-3370.* This is the beloved home of French cuisine in Boston, unfussy yet *au courant*. The café serves bistro fare for many budgets; the dining room is more expensive. L (Mon–Fri), D. 🅿 🍸 🍽 🔥 ♿ ● Sun.	AE DC MC V	●	■		
NORTH END AND THE WATERFRONT					
ERNESTO'S PIZZERIA $ 69 Salem St. **Map** 2 D4. ☏ *(617) 523-1373.* Absolutely nothing fancy here, just a few tables, sawdust on the floor, and an excellent variety of fresh pizza. Perfect for lunch in a rush. L, D. 🔥 ♿			■		
RUDI'S $ 30 Rowes Wharf (Boston Harbor Hotel). **Map** 2 E4. ☏ *(617) 330-7656.* Large delicatessen, where patrons order portions from the serving counter and seat themselves at café tables. Rudi's also sells beautiful pastries and gourmet food gifts to take home. B, L, D. 🔥 ♿	AE MC V D	●	■		
BARKING CRAB $$$ 88 Sleeper St. **Map** 2 E5. ☏ *(617) 426-2722.* Boston's classic shoreside seafood joint, facing the city from across channel in the harbor. L, D, Brunch Sun (winter only). 🎵 🅿 🍸 🔥 ♿	AE DC MC V	●	■	●	

For key to symbols see back flap

	CREDIT CARDS	OUTDOOR TABLES	VEGETARIAN	GOOD WINE	LATE OPENING

Price categories include a three-course meal for one, half a bottle of house wine and all unavoidable extra charges such as sales tax and service.

$ under $20
$$ $20–30
$$$ $30–45
$$$$ $45–60
$$$$$ over $60

CREDIT CARDS
Major credit cards accepted: *AE* American Express; *MC* Master Card/Access; *DC* Diners Club; *V* Visa; *D* Discover Card.

OUTDOOR TABLES
Garden, courtyard, or terrace with outside tables.

VEGETARIAN
A good selection of vegetarian dishes available.

GOOD WINE
Extensive list of good wines, both native and international.

LATE OPENING
Full menu or light meals served after 11pm.

LA FAMIGLIA GIORGIO'S $$$
112 Salem St. **Map** 2 D2. (*617) 367-6711.*
Huge portions of well-prepared pasta are the order of the day here, and La Famiglia is always ready to help you choose. Good value – you will leave full and happy. L, D.

AE DC MC V D — Vegetarian ■

MONICA'S $$$
143 Richmond St. **Map** 2 E3. (*617) 227-0311.*
An attractive restaurant in the North End, serving innovative Northern Italian cuisine. Homemade pastas, breads and deserts. Good salads. D.

AE MC V — Vegetarian ■ Good Wine ●

POMODORO $$$
319 Hanover St. **Map** 2 E2. (*617) 367-4348.*
Crowded, raucous, and aromatic, the small storefront housing Pomodoro brims with patrons at all hours. The menu has real Italian dishes that are always well prepared. Try the salmon with tomato risotto. L, D.

Vegetarian ■

ANTICO FORNO $$$$
93 Salem St. **Map** 2 D2. (*617) 723-6733.*
The menu features meals cooked in the large brick oven in the rear of the dining room. Pizza is excellent, as are the roasted meats. L, D.

AE MC V — Vegetarian ■ Good Wine ●

RABIA'S $$$$
73 Salem St. **Map** 2 D2. (*617) 227-6637.*
Romantic Italian restaurant, with helpful staff who combine with a talented chef to create a relaxed and convivial evening. L (Mon–Fri), D.

AE DC MC V D — Vegetarian ■ Good Wine ● Late Opening ■

TAVERNA TOSCANA $$$$
63 Salem St. **Map** 2 D2. (*617) 742-5233.*
Frescoes and subtle, golden-hued walls create a comfortable setting in this intimate Italian restaurant. Good choice of seasonally inspired entrées. L (Fri–Sun), D.

AE MC V D — Vegetarian ■

TERRAMIA $$$$
98 Salem St. **Map** 2 D2. (*617) 523-3112.*
Boisterous and mixed clientele line up nightly to dine on the trademark *gnocchi*, prepared daily, as well as on the sublime lobster fritters. Casual, friendly service and setting. D.

AE DC MC V D — Vegetarian ■ Good Wine ●

THE CHART HOUSE $$$$
60 Long Wharf. **Map** 2 E3. (*617) 227-1576.*
A steak and seafood dining room frequented by tourists wandering the waterfront. Decor is quaintly old-fashioned, with ships' wheels and other nautical paraphernalia. Only snacks are served outside. D.

AE DC MC V D — Outdoor Tables ● Vegetarian ■

TRATTORIA A SCALINATELLA $$$$
253 Hanover St. **Map** 2 E2. (*617) 742-8240.*
A refreshingly original take on the age-old Italian trattoria. Diners may choose to eschew the menu in favor of host and owner Paolo's re-commended progression of courses, chosen to suit your tastes. D.

AE MC V — Good Wine ●

ROWES WHARF RESTAURANT $$$$$
70 Rowes Wharf (Boston Harbor Hotel). **Map** 2 E4. (*617) 439-3995.*
Elegant dining room overlooking the Boston Harbor. Serves excellent seafood and meats, each paired to an outstanding wine. Reservations recommended. L, D, Brunch Sat–Sun.

AE DC MC V D — Vegetarian ■ Good Wine ●

BACK BAY AND SOUTH END

THE OTHER SIDE COSMIC CAFE $
407 Newbury St. **Map** 3 A3. (*617) 536-9477.*
Avant-garde juice bar (no alcohol) and sandwich restaurant with cheerful staff. Hip artsy crowd makes anyone feel at home. L, D.

Outdoor Tables ● Vegetarian ■ Late Opening ■

MEN TEI NOODLE HOUSE $ $
66 Hereford St. **Map 3 A2.** (617) 425-0066.
Osaka-style *udon* noodles and an array of snack foods and entrées that
any budget can afford. They don't serve alcohol. L, D.

PARISH CAFÉ $ $
361 Boylston St. **Map 3 C2.** (617) 247-4777.
Pub food rises to new heights. The meatloaf and fishcakes are good but specialties are designer sandwiches, such as lobster on pepper brioche. L.
AE DC MC V D

THE POUR HOUSE $ $
907-909 Boylston St. **Map 3 B3.** (617) 236-1767.
Casual and popular, with simple, well-cooked food. Burgers, fries, and
beer are the things to have here. B, L, D.
MC V D

STEVE'S $ $
316 Newbury St. **Map 3 A3.** (617) 267-1817.
This casual Greek restaurant is a bargain among its glamorous neighbors.
All the classics, and retsina to wash them down. B, L, D.
DC MC V D

CIAO BELLA $ $ $
240 Newbury St. **Map 3 A2.** (617) 536-2626.
This restaurant serves good quality southern Italian dishes. The main
feature, however, is the outside seating, which attracts a lively crowd,
including sports figures and celebrities. L, D.
AE MC V

FIREFLY AMERICAN BISTRO $ $ $
130 Dartmouth St. **Map 3 C3.** (617) 262-4393.
Cozy, intimate and warm neighborhood bistro serving reasonable-priced
creative American fare with a French twist. L, D, Brunch Sun. D Sun.
DC AE MC V

CHARLEY'S EATING AND DRINKING SALOON $ $ $ $
284 Newbury St. **Map 3 B2.** (617) 266-3000.
Typical American food, well prepared, is what Charley's does best. Large
outdoor seating area is cool and shady in the afternoon. The bar is busy
from after work onward. L, D, Brunch Sun.
AE DC MC V

GYUHAMA OF JAPAN $ $ $ $
827 Boylston St. **Map 3 B3.** (617) 437-0188.
One of the best sushi bars in Boston, with both tables and chairs and tatami
rooms. Drop by late-night for the surreal Rock-n-Roll Sushi, when waitresses
change from kimonos to dancing gear, with the appropriate music to
match. L, D.
AE DC MC V D

METROPOLIS CAFÉ $ $ $ $
584 Tremont St. **Map 4 D4.** (617) 247-2931.
A very pleasant environment in which to dine. The Sunday brunch
is festive, and dinner unassuming and tasty. Modern American cuisine
with Mediterranean influences. D, Brunch Sat & Sun.
AE MC V

SONSIE $ $ $ $
327 Newbury St. **Map 3 A3.** (617) 351-2500.
If you are a supermodel or actor, this is the hip place to go. The open-front
dining room is good for people-watching while you sip a cocktail and nibble
on gourmet pizza or roasted mussels. B, L, D, Brunch Sun.
AE DC MC V D

STEPHANIE'S ON NEWBURY $ $ $ $
190 Newbury St. **Map 3 B2.** (617) 236-0990.
A large patio offers good people-watching potential, the favorite
pastime on Newbury Street. Menu mainly has lighter fare, such
as salads, inventive sandwiches, and good pizzas. L, D.
AE DC MC V D

TAPEO $ $ $ $
266 Newbury St. **Map 3 B2.** (617) 267-4799.
A wonderfully earthy tapas bar right in the middle of pretentious Newbury
Street. Regulars are devoted to the sangria and the tiny dishes, though
there is a menu of full entrées and wines if you prefer. L (Sat, Sun), D.
AE DC MC V

THE JEWEL OF NEWBURY $ $ $ $
254 Newbury St. **Map 3 B2.** (617) 536-5523.
An elegant, friendly, and charming restaurant serving beautiful French
and North African cuisine, especially the couscous and tagine. L, D.
Mon (Nov–end Mar).
AE DC MC V D

For key to symbols see back flap

Price categories include a three-course meal for one, half a bottle of house wine and all unavoidable extra charges such as sales tax and service.

$ under $20
$$ $20–30
$$$ $30–45
$$$$ $45–60
$$$$$ over $60

CREDIT CARDS
Major credit cards accepted: *AE* American Express; *MC* Master Card/Access; *DC* Diners Club; *V* VISA; *D* Discover Card.

OUTDOOR TABLES
Garden, courtyard, or terrace with outside tables.

VEGETARIAN
A good selection of vegetarian dishes available.

GOOD WINE
Extensive list of good wines, both native and international.

LATE OPENING
Full menu or light meals served after 11pm.

	CREDIT CARDS	OUTDOOR TABLES	VEGETARIAN	GOOD WINE	LATE OPENING
AMBROSIA ON HUNTINGTON $$$$$ 116 Huntington Ave. **Map** 3 B3. (617) 247-2400. The warm-toned decor and high ceilings lend a spacious feel that is rare in urban restaurants. The chef uses classic French methods fused with Asian flavors; sorbets are his signature dish. L (Mon–Fri), D. ▣ ▮ ♿	AE DC MC V D		■	●	
AUJOURD'HUI $$$$$ 200 Boylston St. (Four Seasons Hotel). **Map** 4 D2. (617) 451-1392. One of Boston's best dining experiences, the contemporary cuisine is complemented by a lovely ambience and a view of the Public Garden. B, L (except Sat & Sun), D, Brunch Sun. ▣ ▮ ▮ ⚐ ♿	AE DC MC V D		■	●	
AZURE $$$$$ 61 Exeter St (Lenox Hotel). **Map** 3 B2. (617) 933-4800. Chef-owner Robert Fathman offers elegant and inventive variations on seafood, ranging from lobster soup with a corn pudding timbale, or a confit of sea bass served with daube of beef. B, D (Mon–Sat). ▣ ▮ ♿	AE DC MC V D		■	●	
CLIO $$$$$ 370A Commonwealth Ave. (Eliot Hotel). **Map** 3 A2. (617) 536-7200. Both the wonderful food and the Parisian dining-club ambiance account for the popularity of this French-inspired modern American restaurant. *Foie gras*, caramelized swordfish, and sweet butter-basted Maine lobster are highlights. Reservations suggested. B, D, Brunch Sun. ▣ ▮ ▮ ⚐ ♿	AE DC MC V		■	●	
HAMERSLEY'S BISTRO $$$$$ 553 Tremont St. **Map** 4 D4. (617) 423-2700. Top chef Gordon Hamersley wins consistent rave reviews for his convivial French provincial cuisine, including a stunning lemon-garlic roast chicken. D. ▮	AE MC V	●	■	●	
L'ESPALIER $$$$$ 30 Gloucester St. **Map** 3 B2. (617) 262-3023. In the absolute top tier of Boston restaurants, with impeccably classic decor, excellent service, and New England-influenced European cuisine. Prix-fixe menu. Reservations required. D. ▣ ▮ ⚐ ● Sun.	AE DC MC V D		■	●	
MISTRAL $$$$$ 223 Columbus Ave. **Map** 3 C3. (617) 867-9300. This restaurant serves French food with a Mediterranean influence. The cellar is as thoughtfully assembled as the menu, and the fashionable wine bar is always busy. Reservations recommended. D. ▣ ▮ ▮ ♿	AE DC MC V D		■	●	■
TREMONT 647 $$$$$ 647 Tremont St. **Map** 3 C4. (617) 266-4600. Pushing the boundaries of new and old American food alike, this youthful and unpretentious restaurant enjoys innovation, and succeeds. Try the sea bass on jasmine rice or the spice-rubbed steak. At Sundays' Pajama Brunch patrons are encouraged to dress in pajamas. D, Brunch Sun. ▣ ▮ ⚐ ♿	AE DC MC V	●	■	●	
FARTHER AFIELD					
CAMPO DE FIORI $ Holyoke Center Arcade, 1350 Massachusetts Ave., Cambridge. (617) 354-3805. This Italian gourmet bakery and café serves Roman flatbread made into the most subtly delicious sandwiches, very thin pizzas, fresh pastas and stews. Excellent lunch stop, great value. L. ▣ ♿ ● Sun.	AE MC V D		■		
MR. BARTLEY'S BURGER COTTAGE $ 1246 Massachusetts Ave., Cambridge. (617) 354-6559. A glorious profusion and variety of hamburgers and great sweet potato fries in a chaotic atmosphere. L, D. ⚐ ● Sun.		●	■		

One Arrow St. Crêpes ($)

1 Arrow St., Cambridge. 📞 *(617) 661-2737.*
Nestled off Massachusetts Avenue and serving sweet and savory crêpes.
Sip homemade lemonade and try a spiced pear, blue cheese, arugula, and
walnut crêpe, or stick with something simple. No alcohol. L, D. ● Mon.

Credit cards: MC, V

Pinocchio's ($)

74 Winthrop St., Cambridge. 📞 *(617) 876-4897.*
Excellent value and terrific pizza – Sicilian style pizza rectangles come
heaped with toppings and are an unbeatable fast meal, night or day. L, D.

Credit cards: MC, V

Stars on Boston ($)($)

393 Huntington Ave. 📞 *(617) 536-3232.*
Bright and cheerful with a clean and modern design. The menu features
classic American comfort food from the obligatory meatloaf and gravy to
burgers and lasagne. L, D, Brunch Sun.

Credit cards: AE, DC, MC, V, D

House of Blues ($)($)($)

96 Winthrop St., Cambridge. 📞 *(617) 491-2583.*
Music hall and restaurant devoted to bringing the beauty of Southern music
and food to the rest of the country. Succulent barbecue fare and moist
cornbread, adapted to Northern tastes. L, D, Brunch Sun. 🎵 🍷 🧒 ♿

Credit cards: AE, DC, MC, V, D

John Harvard's Brew House ($)($)($)

33 Dunster St., Cambridge. 📞 *(617) 868-3585.*
Features their excellent microbrewed beer on tap. Publike decor and a
menu of inspired American staples, such as all-white-meat chicken pot
pie. Try the beer sampler if indecisive. L, D. 🍷 🧒 ♿

Credit cards: AE, DC, MC, V, D

Les Zygomates ($)($)($)

129 South St., Boston. Map 4 F2. 📞 *(617) 542-5108.*
Wine is the *raison d'être* here, with delicious bistro fare, such as rabbit
pâté and venison *vol-au-vents*. L, D. 🎵 P 🍷 🧒 ● Sun.

Credit cards: AE, DC, MC, V, D

Pho Pasteur ($)($)($)

35 Dunster St., Cambridge. 📞 *(617) 864-4100.*
Pho is a Vietnamese soup, prepared with sublime complexity at this stylish
restaurant in Harvard Square. While other dishes are excellent, the grilled
pork *pho*, with mint and a delicate sauce, is definitive. L, D. 🍷 🧒

Credit cards: AE, MC, V

R. Wesley's ($)($)($)

31 Cambridge St., Charlestown. 📞 *(617) 242-7202.*
Worth going out of the way for: unusual beer and wine selections, and
the chef produces inventive fare (ostrich steak a specialty). ● Sun.

Credit cards: AE, MC, V

Chez Henri ($)($)($)($)

1 Shepard St., Cambridge. 📞 *(617) 354-8980.*
The offspring of French bistro and Cuban café, the relaxed and
romantic Chez Henri mixes classical methods with fresh Caribbean
and local ingredients. Try the nightly fixed-price menu. D. 🍷 🧒 ♿

Credit cards: AE, DC, MC, V

News ($)($)($)($)

150 Kneeland St., Boston. Map 2 D5. 📞 *(617) 426-6397.*
Open for lunch and dinner the real scene here is late, late-night dining
on sushi, bar munchies, steaks, and fish washed down with martinis. The
American breakfast menu is served at all hours. L, D. 🍷 🧒 ♿

Credit cards: AE, DC, MC, V, D

Olives ($)($)($)($)

10 City Square, Charlestown. 📞 *(617) 242-1999.*
Mediterranean-influenced cuisine by local celebrity chef Todd English,
served in a bistro-like setting. Perpetually crowded, they do not accept
reservations. Dress well to minimize your wait. D. P 🍷 🧒 ♿ ● Sun.

Credit cards: AE, DC, MC, V

Harvest ($)($)($)($)($)

44 Brattle St., Cambridge. 📞 *(617) 868-2255.*
MA favored haunt of university professors, and one of the finest restaurants
in Harvard Square. Modern American cuisine bursting with fresh flavors and
local produce. Reservations suggested. L, D, Brunch Sun. P 🍷 🧒 ♿

Credit cards: AE, DC, MC, V, D

Rialto ($)($)($)($)($)

1 Bennett St. (Charles Hotel), Cambridge. 📞 *(617) 661-5050.*
Rarely do the top restaurants create an atmosphere so down to earth.
The menu of seasonal dishes may include tender roast duckling, poached
shrimp in spiced oil, or Tuscan style sirloin steak. D 🍷 🍷 🧒 ♿

Credit cards: AE, DC, MC, V

For key to symbols see back flap

Price categories include a three-course meal for one, half a bottle of house wine and all unavoidable extra charges such as sales tax and service. **$** under \$20 **$$** \$20–30 **$$$** \$30–45 **$$$$** \$45–60 **$$$$$** over \$60	**CREDIT CARDS** Major credit cards accepted: *AE* American Express; *MC* Master Card/Access; *DC* Diners Club; *V* VISA; *D* Discover Card. **OUTDOOR TABLES** Garden, courtyard, or terrace with outside tables. **VEGETARIAN** A good selection of vegetarian dishes available. **GOOD WINE** Extensive list of good wines, both native and international. **LATE OPENING** Full menu or light meals served after 11pm.	**CREDIT CARDS**	**OUTDOOR TABLES**	**VEGETARIAN**	**GOOD WINE**	**LATE OPENING**

MASSACHUSETTS

AMHERST: *Judie's* **$$$** 51 N. Pleasant St. 〖 *(413) 253-3491.* Giant popovers are a signature here, along with eclectic food served in a sunny greenhouse or quieter back room. As well as full dinner, this is a good place for afternoon tea. L, D. 🍸 ♿ & ● Mon, Thanksgiving & Dec 25.	AE MC V D		■		
CAPE COD: *Jack's Outback* **$** 161 Main St., Yarmouth Port. 〖 *(508) 362-6690.* "Good food, lousy service" is the motto in this "cutesy" place with better food than Mom used to make. Breakfasts are models of Americana. B, L, Brunch Sun. 🅿 ♿ &					
CAPE COD: *Oystermen's Grill and Fish Market* **$$$** 975 Rte 6, Wellfleet. 〖 *(508) 349-3825.* Specialties include clams (owners dig them daily) and local fish – all grilled or steamed to order. Don't miss the sesame-seared tuna. L, D. 🅿 ♿ & ● mid-Oct–Apr.	AE MC V		■		
CAPE COD: *Scargo Cafe* **$$$** 799 Rte 6A, Dennis. 〖 *(508) 385-8200.* Welcoming ambience is matched by creative cuisine and excellent service. Handy location across from the Cape Playhouse. L, D. 🅿 🍸 ♿ &	AE MC V D		■		■
CAPE COD: *Belfry Inne & Bistro* **$$$$** 6-8 Jarves St., Sandwich. 〖 *(508) 888-8550.* Inside an old de-sanctified church is some of the best so-called "fusion" food on the Cape, a feast for eye and palate. D. 🎵 🅿 🍸 🍸 ♿ & ● Sun & Mon; Thu–Sat Nov–Apr.	AE MC V	●	■	●	
CAPE COD: *Regatta of Cotuit at the Crocker House* **$$$$** 4631 Falmouth Rd. 〖 *(508) 428-5715.* Contemporary American cuisine with French and Asian accents in this romantic Federal-style mansion, originally and old stage coach inn. D. 🎵 🅿 🍸 🍸 ♿ & ● Mon–Tue in winter.	AE MC V		■	●	
CAPE COD: *Chillingsworth* **$$$$$** 2449 Main St. (Rte. 6A), Brewster. 〖 *(508) 896-3640.* The epitome of fine dining served in a 300-year-old house. The place has charm, seamless service, and an elegant French prix fixe menu. Casual fare available in the Bistro. L, D, Brunch Sun. 🅿 🍸 🍸 ♿ & ● Mon; Dec—mid-May.	AE DC MC V	●	■	●	
CONCORD: *Aigo Bistro* **$$$$** 84 Thoreau St. 〖 *(978) 371-1333.* Exotic food (Mediterranean and Provencal cuisine) and fine service are "givens" in this sophisticated bistro upstairs in Concord depot. D. 🅿 🍸 & ● Sun, Mon.	AE DC MC V		■	●	
DEERFIELD: *Deerfield Inn* **$$$** 81 Old Main St. 〖 *(413) 774-5587.* The inn's Colonial decor suits the traditional menu of seafood, duck, beef and tenderloin lamb. B, L, D. 🅿 🍸 🍸 ♿ & ● Dec 25.	AE DC MC V	●	■	●	
ESSEX: *Woodman's of Essex* **$$** Rte 133. 〖 *(978) 768-6057.* This old summer favorite with families is known for clam *everything*, including clam bakes, and huge portions. L, D. 🅿 ♿ &		●			
GLOUCESTER: *McT's Lobster House and Tavern* **$$** 25 Rogers St. 〖 *(978) 282-0950.* Located on the waterfront this restaurant offers fish and lobster done simply and perfectly in a sailors' tavern atmosphere. L, D. 🍸 & ● Mon.	AE MC V D	●			■

LENOX: *Bistro Zinc* $$$$ AE MC V
56 Church St. ((413) 637-8800.
Strengths of this sophisticated cafe are wood-fired pizzas, stuffed quail, pan-seared tuna, other contemporary dishes. L, D. 🅿 🍸 🚻 ♿

LENOX: *Blantyre* $$$$$ AE MC V
16 Blantyre Rd. ((413) 637-3556.
This formal Scottish manor offers prix fixe special-occasion dining at its most elegant. Country-house cuisine menu features seafood and game, such as saddle of rabbit with Oregon truffles. Exceptional wine list. L (Jul–Aug), D. 🅿 🍸 ♿ ● Mon., also Nov-Apr.

MARTHA'S VINEYARD: *Black Dog Tavern* $$$ AE MC V D
Beach St. Extension, Vineyard Haven. ((508) 693-9223.
With crowded rustic quarters facing the harbor, this place is a hit for its littleneck clams, grilled bluefish sandwiches, and other fresh seafood. B, L, D (Mon–Sat); B, D Sun. 🚻 ♿

MARTHA'S VINEYARD: *Sweet Life Cafe* $$$ AE MC V D
63 Upper Circuit Ave., Oak Bluffs. ((508) 696-0200.
Three dining rooms in an old Victorian house and garden set the stage for unusual New American menu. D. 🍸 ♿ to garden only ● Wed; Dec–May.

NANTUCKET: *Atlantic Cafe* $$ AE DC MC V D
15 S.Water St. ((508) 228-0570.
Rowboats hung from the ceiling convey the nautical theme. As you might expect, seafood and snacks are the specialties. L, D. 🍸 🚻 ♿ ● Mon Nov–Mar; mid-Dec–mid-Jan.

NANTUCKET: *Chanticleer* $$$$$ AE DC MC V
9 New St., Sconset. ((508) 257-6231.
In a country cottage with garden setting, this premier French restaurant has a special way with local seafood. L, D. 🅿 🍸 🍸 ♿ ● Mon, also late Oct-mid-May.

NANTUCKET: *21 Federal* $$$$$ AE MC V
21 Federal St. ((508) 228-2121.
Four stylish minimalist dining rooms in an old house feature elegant New American fare. There's also a lighter, less expensive bistro menu. D. 🍸 🍸 ♿ ● Sun; mid-Dec–mid-Apr.

NORTHAMPTON: *Northampton Brewery* $$ AE MC V D
11 Brewster Court. ((413) 584-9903.
A popular college hangout for its snacks, sandwiches, casual meals and the well-sampled house-brewed microbeers. L, D. 🍸 🚻 ♿

NORTHAMPTON: *Eastside Grill* $$$ AE DC MC V D
19 Strong Ave. ((413) 586-3347.
Unprepossessing exterior, but loyal fans love fresh fish and seafood, the Cajun specialties – especially the fabulous New Orleans bread pudding. D. 🅿 🍸 🚻 ♿

PLYMOUTH: *Lobster Hut* $$ MC V
25 Town Wharf. ((508) 746-2270.
Fried clams, fish & chips, clam chowder, huge portions, all are notable at this self-serve waterfront spot. L, D. 🅿 🚻 ♿ ● Jan.

PLYMOUTH: *East Bay Grill* $$$ AE MC V D
173 Water St. ((508) 746-9751.
Traditional American fare is offered at this restaurant on historic Plymouth Harbor. Diners can expect a relaxed environment with waterfront views and attentive service. L, D, Brunch Sun. 🎵 🅿 🍸 🚻 ♿

ROCKPORT: *Lobster Pool Restaurant* $$ AE MC V D
329 Granite St (Rte. 127). ((978) 546-7808
This restaurant is known for its good prices and spectacular sunset views. Lobster is served in various forms (with lobster rolls being the speciality) along with fried and grilled seafoods. L, D. 🅿 🚻 ♿ ● end Oct–mid-Apr

SALEM: *Red Raven's Restaurant* $$$
75 Congress St. ((978) 745-8558.
This restaurant is tops for creative flair, both in its funky decor and original dishes, including some intriguing vegetable specials. D. 🅿 🍸 ● Sun & Mon.

For key to symbols see back flap

Price categories include a three-course meal for one, half a bottle of house wine and all unavoidable extra charges such as sales tax and service.

$ under $20
$$ $20–30
$$$ $30–45
$$$$ $45–60
$$$$$ over $60

CREDIT CARDS
Major credit cards accepted: *AE* American Express; *MC* Master Card/Access; *DC* Diners Club; *V* VISA; *D* Discover Card.

OUTDOOR TABLES
Garden, courtyard, or terrace with outside tables.

VEGETARIAN
A good selection of vegetarian dishes available.

GOOD WINE
Extensive list of good wines, both native and international.

LATE OPENING
Full menu or light meals served after 11pm.

	CREDIT CARDS	OUTDOOR TABLES	VEGETARIAN	GOOD WINE	LATE OPENING
SALEM: *Lyceum Bar & Grill* $$$$ 43 Church St. *(978) 745-7665.* In this historic building, where Alexander Graham Bell gave the first phone demo in 1877, you'll find a good assortment of New American and grilled dishes. L (except Sat), D, Brunch Sun.	AE MC V D	■			
SPRINGFIELD: *Hofbrauhaus* $$$ 1105 Main St. *(413) 737-4905.* Longtime favorite for its Bavarian coziness, German specialties, and seafood. L (Fri.only), D, Brunch Sun (Nov–May).	AE DC MC V D	■		●	
STOCKBRIDGE: *Truc Orient Express* $$ 1 Harris St. *(413) 232-4204.* Oriental decor and Vietnamese specialties are a natural here and make a nice change when you've had enough lobster and seafood. L (Jul–Aug only), D. Tue. Nov-Apr.	AE MC V	●	■	●	
STURBRIDGE: *Publick House* $$$ 295 Main St. *(508) 347-3313.* In the Sturbridge spirit, this atmospheric 1771 Colonial house with open hearths features Americana, such as lobster pie and prime rib. B, L, D.	AE DC MC V D	■			
SUDBURY: *Longfellow's Wayside Inn* $$$ 72 Wayside Inn Rd. *(978) 443-1776.* Historic surroundings make this a favorite for simple fare: prime rib, fresh seafood, and the like. L, D.	AE DC MC V D	■		●	
WALTHAM: *The Watch City Brewery* $$ 256 Moody St. *(781) 647-4000.* Once an old bank, this is a fun place for microbrewery beer aficionados, with pleasing ambience, snacks, meals. L (Mon–Sat), D.	AE MC V				
WALTHAM: *The Tuscan Grill* $$$$ 361 Moody St. *(781) 891-5486.* This stylish trattoria features some of the best northern Italian fare in the area, with open kitchen, wood-grilled specialties. D. Sun.	MC V D			●	
WELLESLEY: *Blue Ginger* $$$$$ 583 Washington St. *(781) 283-5790.* Foodies consider this East-West bistro unique in the this part of the state for its blend of Asian cuisines, extensive wine list, and blue-accented minimalist decor. It is worth a detour. Reservations required. L (Mon–Fri), D. Sun.	AE MC V	■		●	
WILLIAMSTOWN: *The Orchards* $$$$ 222 Adams Rd. *(413) 458-9611.* Continental food with contemporary touches is served in a romantic setting. Desserts are special. Reservations required. B, L, D.	AE DC MC V	●		●	

RHODE ISLAND

	CREDIT CARDS	OUTDOOR TABLES	VEGETARIAN	GOOD WINE	LATE OPENING
BLOCK ISLAND: *Eli's* $$ Chapel St. *(401) 466-5230.* A deceptively simple restaurant, Eli's features very good world cuisine served in ordinary surroundings of knotty pine walls and tables. Pesto-baked ziti in cream sauce is one of many delights. D. seasonally.	MC V		■	●	
BLOCK ISLAND: *Finn's Seafood Restaurant* $$ Water St. *(401) 466-2473.* The upstairs deck looks over the harbor. Lobster, steamed mussels, clam rolls, broiled swordfish are all tasty. L, D. mid-Oct–mid-May.	MC V	●			

BLOCK ISLAND: *Atlantic Inn* $$$$
High St. 🛈 *(401) 466-5883.*
A formal favorite of urbane locals for the spectacular ocean views and prix fixe menu with numerous sophisticated choices, such as grilled monkfish with truffled littleneck risotto. Reservations required.
D. 🅿 🍷 🍴 ♿ ● mid-Sep–Apr.

MC V D

BLOCK ISLAND: *Gazebo* $$$$$
Hotel Manisses, Spring St. 🛈 *(401) 466-2421.*
New American dishes with a seaward lilt. Grilled local swordfish and striped bass are beautifully done. The Gatsby Room has a more casual, less expensive menu and is also good. D. 🅿 🍷 ● Nov–Apr.

MC V

BRISTOL: *Lobster Pot Inc.* $$$
119-121 Hope St. 🛈 *(401) 253-9100.*
Unsurpassed ocean views in this casual waterfront spot, known for its fresh seafood. L (Mon–Sat), D. 🎵 🍷 🍴 ● Mon.

AE MC V

CHARLESTOWN: *Wilcox Tavern* $$$
5153 Post Rd., Rte 1. 🛈 *(401) 322-1829.*
Fresh seafood, roast beef, and steaks are specialties in this attractive vintage 1730 house. D. 🎵 🅿 🍷 🍴 ♿ ● Mon.

AE MC V

GALILEE: *George's of Galilee* $$$
250 Sand Hill Cove Rd. 🛈 *(401) 783-2306.*
A bustling, wildly busy waterfront landmark, famous in the area for its seafood platters, chowder, and clam cakes. L, D. 🎵 🍷 🍴 ♿ ● Dec.

MC V D

MIDDLETOWN: *Sea Shai* $$$
747 Aquidneck Ave. 🛈 *(401) 849-5180.*
Sushi is ocean-fresh at this, the state's only Korean restaurant. The menu carries Korean grilled BBQ meats and seafood and such Japanese specialties as shabu-shabu, sukiyaki, and tempura. L, D. 🍷 🍴 ♿ .

AE DC MC V D

MIDDLETOWN: *The Glass Onion* $$$$
909 E. Main Rd., Rte 138. 🛈 *(401) 848-5153.*
Located in the same building as Newport Vineyards, this perky place with its diverse menu also serves a popular Sunday brunch. L, D. 🅿 🍷 🍴 ♿

AE MC V D

NARRAGANSETT: *Coast Guard House* $$$$
40 Ocean Rd. 🛈 *(401) 789-0700.*
This renovated 1888 Coast Guard station has ocean views, good swordfish, and prime rib and is known especially for its Sunday brunch.
L, D. 🎵 🅿 🍷 🍴 ♿ ● Jan.

AE DC MC V D

NEWPORT: *The Black Pearl* $$$
Bannister's Wharf. 🛈 *(401) 846-5264.*
Justifiably famous for its clam chowder, this landmark blends classic French fare in the sedate Commodore Room with casual dining in the tavern and bar. Try the apple-raisin bread pudding. L, D. 🍷 ♿ ● mid-Jan–mid-Feb.

AE MC V

NEWPORT: *La Petite Auberge* $$$$
19 Charles St. 🛈 *(401) 849-6669.*
In five cozy rooms of a 1714 house, this charmer offers authentic French fare, such as snails with cepes, oysters thermidore, and lobster with truffles, all impeccably prepared and served. D. 🅿 🍷 🍴

AE MC V D

NEWPORT: *Le Bistro* $$$$
19 Bowen's Wharf. 🛈 *(401) 849-7778.*
Intimate, French, and romantic, with water views, this gem is known for its seafood prepared with Gallic flair. L, D, Brunch Sun. 🅿 🍷 🍴

AE DC MC V D

NEWPORT: *Sardella's* $$$$
30 Memorial Boulevard West. 🛈 *(401) 849-6312.*
Located between downtown Thames Street and historic Bellevue Avenue, this Italian restaurant is very popular with the locals. Their veal dishes are the most popular, try the sautéed Veal medallions. D 🅿 🍷

AE DC MC V

NEWPORT: *White Horse Tavern* $$$$
26 Marlborough St. 🛈 *(401) 849-3600.*
The oldest operating tavern in America, with low-beamed ceilings, hearth fires, colonial bric-a-brac, and candlelit dining rooms. Good American food with modern touches. L (except Mon & Tue), D, Brunch Sun.
🅿 🍷 🍴

AE DC MC V D

For key to symbols see back flap

<table>
<tr><td colspan="2">

Price categories include a three-course meal for one, half a bottle of house wine and all unavoidable extra charges such as sales tax and service.
Ⓢ under $20
ⓈⓈ $20–30
ⓈⓈⓈ $30–45
ⓈⓈⓈⓈ $45–60
ⓈⓈⓈⓈⓈ over $60

</td><td colspan="5">

CREDIT CARDS
Major credit cards accepted: *AE* American Express; *MC* Master Card/Access; *DC* Diners Club; *V* Visa; *D* Discover Card.
OUTDOOR TABLES
Garden, courtyard, or terrace with outside tables.
VEGETARIAN
A good selection of vegetarian dishes available.
GOOD WINE
Extensive list of good wines, both native and international.
LATE OPENING
Full menu or light meals served after 11pm.

</td></tr>
</table>

	CREDIT CARDS	OUTDOOR TABLES	VEGETARIAN	GOOD WINE	LATE OPENING
NORTH KINGSTOWN: *Red Rooster Tavern* ⓈⓈⓈ 7385 Post Rd., North Kingstown. 🄲 *(401) 295-8804.* Long a popular magnet, this traditional New England tavern specializes in seafood and Continental dishes. It has an exceptional wine list. D. 🎵 🅿 🆈 🆈 🛠 🦽 ⬤ Mon.	AE DC MC V D		■	●	
PORTSMOUTH: *Seafare Inn* ⓈⓈⓈⓈ 3352 E.Main Rd. 🄲 *(401) 683-0577.* A rejuvenated Victorian mansion plays host to a menu that is strong on seafood and regional specialties. Everything is well presented. D. 🅿 🆈 🛠 🦽 ⬤ Sun & Mon.	AE MC V			●	
PROVIDENCE: *Viva!* Ⓢ 234 Thayer St. 🄲 *(401) 331-6200.* Located in a vintage building with big storefront windows on College Hill, Viva! offers a casual setting for lunch or dinner. The restaurant is quieter than the café, where you can choose from tapas, soups, seafood, and steaks. L, D. 🅿 🆈 🦽	AE DC MC V		■	●	■
PROVIDENCE: *Al Forno* ⓈⓈⓈⓈ 577 S.Main St. 🄲 *(401) 273-9760.* Wood-fire grilled meats, pizzas from stone floor pizza ovens, and baked pasta dishes are signatures of this popular, informal, no-reservations-taken place. The chef-owners keep inventing new and fabulous dishes, using fresh local ingredients. D. 🅿 🆈 🦽 ⬤ Sun & Mon.	AE DC MC V	●	■	●	
PROVIDENCE: *Capriccio* ⓈⓈⓈⓈ 2 Pine St. 🄲 *(401) 421-1320.* Old-time Italian restaurant with a dark grotto-like dining room. It has livened up its menu and features light modern Italian dishes, the likes of grilled octopus and pastas with mascarpone cheese and sun-dried tomatoes. Impressive wine list. L, D. 🎵 🅿 🆈 🛠	AE DC MC V D		■	●	■
PROVIDENCE: *New Rivers* ⓈⓈⓈⓈ 7 Steeple St. 🄲 *(401) 751-0350.* Some of the best New American food can be found in this intimate town house. Look for dishes such as five-spice chicken, grilled pork tenderloin, and sweet local scallops. D. 🅿 🆈 🛠 ⬤ Sun.	AE MC V			●	
PROVIDENCE: *Pot au Feu* ⓈⓈⓈⓈ 44 Custom House St. 🄲 *(401) 273-8953.* Elegant, formal dining in top level Salon; brick-walled Bistro is at lower level. Both serve consistently excellent classic and regional French food. L (Mon–Fri), D (Bistro Mon–Sat; Dining room Thu–Sat). 🅿 🆈 🛠 ⬤ Sun June–Aug and most major holidays.	AE DC MC V			●	
WAKEFIELD: *Larchwood Inn* ⓈⓈ 521 Main St. 🄲 *(401) 783-5454.* Traditional old inn in pretty setting is still going strong, with standbys such as prime rib, seafood dishes. B, L, D. 🎵 🅿 🆈 🆈 🛠 🦽	AE DC MC V D	●		●	
WARWICK: *Legal Sea Foods* ⓈⓈⓈ 2099 Post Rd. 🄲 *(401) 732-3663.* A welcome outpost of the famous Boston chain, with similar nautical theme and freshest of fresh seafood, prepared a variety of ways. There's a sizeable raw bar. L, D. 🅿 🆈 🛠 🦽	AE DC MC V D	●	■	●	
WATCH HILL: *Olympia Tea Room* ⓈⓈⓈ 74 Bay St. 🄲 *(401) 348-8211.* This octogenarian has had a facelift in recent years, and now features an eclectic menu that roams the globe, with American regional dishes, Spanish, Asian, and others. B, L, D. 🆈 🦽 ⬤ Jan–Mar.	AE MC V	●	■	●	

WESTERLY: *Up River Cafe* $$$ 37 Main St., Westerly. ☎ *(401) 348-9700.* For serious diners, this charming place is worth a detour for creative food, presented artistically. The American bistro menu changes seasonally and always includes a daily fish special based on the fresh catch of the day. L, D. ♫ [P] 🍸 🚸 ♿	*AE MC V*		■	●	
CONNECTICUT					
BROOKLYN: *Golden Lamb Buttery* $$$$$ 499 Wolf Den Rd. ☎ *(860) 774-4423.* Prepare for a unique dining experience: lovely American food, hay ride, strolling musicians, in a restored barn on a working farm. Dinner prix fixe. Reservations are essential. L (Tue–Sat), D (Fri–Sat). ♫ [P] 👔 ♿		●	■	●	
CANAAN: *The Cannery* $$$$ 85 Main St. ☎ *(860) 824-7333.* Creative chef-owner and reliable food make this bistro a favorite spot with locals, featuring items such as ravioli with roasted eggplant, toasted walnuts, and caramelized onions. D. [P] 🍸 🚸 ♿ ● Nov–Apr: Tue & Wed.	*AE MC V*		■	●	
DARIEN: *Coromandel* $$$ 25-11 Old Kings Highway N. ☎ *(203) 662-1213.* This may be the state's best Indian restaurant, with South Indian specialties served amiably in limited, well-decorated space. L, D, Brunch Sun. [P] 🚸 ♿	*AE DC MC V*		■	●	
EAST HADDAM: *Gelston House River Grill* $$$$ 8 Main St. ☎ *(860) 873-1411.* Views of the river from this hilltop Victorian-Italianate house even outshine the tasty New American food. Close to Goodspeed Opera House. L, D, Brunch Sun. ♫ [P] 🍸 🚸 ♿ ● Mon & Tue.	*AE MC V*	●		●	
FARMINGTON: *Apricots* $$$$ 1593 Farmington Ave. ☎ *(860) 673-5405.* An airy two-story restored trolley barn overlooks river and sets the stage for creative New American cooking. L, D, Brunch Sun. ♫ [P] 🍸 🚸 ♿	*AE DC MC V D*	●	■	●	■
GREENWICH: *Penang Grill* $$ 55 Lewis St. ☎ *(203) 861-1988.* Young and old crowd into this cozy, Malayan-Chinese restaurant for the squid salad, sesame chicken, and other delights. L, D. 🍸 🚸	*AE MC V*		■		
GREENWICH: *Restaurant Jean-Louis* $$$$$ 61 Lewis St. ☎ *(203) 622-8450.* In this nationally acclaimed, chef-owned French restaurant, you may dine a la carte or on the menu dégustation. Either way, the food is memorable. L (Mon–Fri), D. [P] 🍸 👔 ● Sun.	*AE DC MC V D*		■	●	
GUILFORD: *Esteva* $$$ 25 Whitfield St. ☎ *(203) 458-1300.* The marble-topped bar and patio lend a continental feel to this American café with excellent meat and seafood dishes. The extensive wine list includes those from a nearby vineyard. L, D. [P] 🍸 ♿ ● Mon L.	*AE MC V*			●	
HARTFORD: *Shish Kebab House of Afghanistan* $$ 360 Franklin Ave. ☎ *(860) 296-0301.* Several small dining areas decorated with Afghan artifacts are a backdrop for well-seasoned Afghan specialties, a rarity in Connecticut. D. [P] 🍸 🚸 ♿ ● Sun.	*AE DC MC V D*		■	●	
HARTFORD: *Peppercorn's Grill* $$$ 357 Main St. ☎ *(860) 547-1714.* In this stylish, two-level dining room, look for creative northern Italian dishes, with a few Asian accents. L (Mon–Fri), D. [P] 🍸 👔 🚸 ♿ ● Sun.	*AE DC MC V*		■	●	■
HARTFORD: *Max Downtown* $$$$ City Place, 185 Asylum St. ☎ *(860) 522-2530.* Smart, modern, bustling, this favorite-with-locals downtown spot features excellent Modern American dishes. L (Mon–Fri), D. 🍸 🚸 ♿	*AE DC MC V D*		■	●	■
LEDYARD: *Stonecroft* $$$$ 515 Pumpkin Hill Rd. ☎ *(860) 572-0771.* Urbane fare, careful service, and high style dining room on six acres of beautiful land. Save room for the luscious desserts. D. ♫ [P] ♿ ● Tue, Thu.	*AE MC V D*	●		●	

For key to symbols see back flap

	CREDIT CARDS	OUTDOOR TABLES	VEGETARIAN	GOOD WINE	LATE OPENING
LITCHFIELD: *West Street Grill* **$$$** 43 West St. (860) 567-3885. The area's most popular gathering place for big-name New Yorkers who weekend in the vicinity offers pace-setting food in a comfortably casual setting. L, D 🅿 🚶 ● Mon & Tue in winter.	AE MC V	●	■	●	
MANCHESTER: *Cavey's* **$$$$** 45 E, Center St. (860) 643-2751. Schizophrenic place where one floor is casual Northern Italian fare, the other fancy formal French (jackets, pricier, and dinner only), with separate kitchens. Rest assured, both are terrific. L, D. 🎵 🅿 🍷 🚶 ♿ ● Sun & Mon.	AE MC V		■	●	
MYSTIC: *Mystic Pizza* **$** 56 W. Main St. (860) 536-3700. Immortalized by Julia Roberts' movie, this pizza-and-pasta parlor is a "must-stop" for most Mystic visitors. L, D. 🅿 🚶 ♿	DC MC V D		■		
NEW BRITAIN: *Fatherland* **$** 450 S. Main St. (860) 224-3345. This spic-and-span no-frills storefront piles on Cyclopean portions of hearty, home-style Polish cooking. L, D. 🅿 🚶 ♿	MC V D				
NEW HAVEN: *Frank Pepe Pizzeria* **$** 157 Wooster St. (203) 865-5762. Go early to avoid the lineups for white clam and other pizzas, long considered the state's best. No frills here is an understatement. L, D. 🅿 🚶 ● Tue.			■		
NEW HAVEN: *Bentara* **$$** 76 Orange St. (203) 562-2511. Authentic Malaysian food is served in spacious, high-ceilinged rooms decorated with Asian artifacts. Note the exceptional wine and beer lists. L, D. 🅿 🚶 ♿	AE DC MC V D		■	●	
NEW HAVEN: *Ibiza* **$$$** 39 High St. (203) 865-1933. Cheerful spot, well suited to eating Spanish style from an upscale full menu. L, D. 🍷 🚶 ♿ ● Mon.	AE MC V			●	
NEW HAVEN: *Union League Cafe* **$$$** 1032 Chapel St. (203) 562-4299. An historic building plays second fiddle to superb French food, impeccably prepared and served. L, D. 🅿 🍷 ♿ ● Sun	AE DC MC V			●	
NEW HAVEN: *Zinc* **$$$$** 964 Chapel St. (203) 624-0507. Stunning minimalist decor suits the vibrant food, a stylish blend of New American with Asian influences, producing unique results. L (Tue–Sat), D. 🍷 ♿	AE MC V		■	●	
NEW PRESTON: *The Birches Inn* **$$$$** 233 West Shore Rd. (860) 868-1735. Overlooking Lake Waramaug, the deck in warm weather is considered "the" place to enjoy grilled corn husk stuffed with seafood sausage and a selection of the chef-owner's surprising specialties. D. 🅿 🚶 ♿ ● Tue; Jan–Feb.	AE MC V	●	■	●	
NOANK: *Abbott's Lobster in The Rough* **$$$** 117 Pearl St. (860) 536-7719. Fresh lobsters, clam rolls, and other seafood at plain picnic-style tables facing harbor on Mystic River. L, D. 🅿 🚶 ♿ ● Oct–May.	AE MC V	●	■		

NORTH STONINGTON: *Randall's Ordinary* $$$
Rte. 2, 🌙 *(860) 599-4540.*
A landmark inn highlights 18th-century recipes, with dishes
cooked over an open hearth. A unique experience, prix fixe.
B, L, D. 🎵 🅿 🚹

AE MC V

NORWALK: *Meson Galicia* $$$
Wall St. 🌙 *(203) 866-8800.*
Elegant Spanish food is served in a setting resembling a country inn. A
well-chosen Spanish wine list and superlative service are signatures.
L, D. 🖐 ⬤ Mon.

AE DC MC V D

NORWALK: *Silvermine Tavern* $$$
194 Perry Ave. 🌙 *(203) 847-4558.*
Vintage New England inn overlooking river, features American classics
like chicken pot pie, with a popular Thurs. buffet and Sun. brunch.
L, D. 🎵 🅿 🍸 🍴 🚹 🖐 ⬤ Closed Tue.

AE DC MC V

NORWALK: *The Restaurant at Rowayton Seafood* $$$$
89 Rowayton Ave. 🌙 *(203) 866-4488.*
Crowded quarters facing a marina don't deter enjoyment of
fresh clams, oysters, and other seafood. L, D, Brunch Sun.
🅿 🍸 🚹 🖐

AE MC V D

OLD LYME: *The Bee & Thistle Inn* $$$$
100 Lyme St. 🌙 *(860) 434-1667.*
Old-time setting belies the sophisticated New American menu with many
extra touches. B, L, D, Brunch Sun. 🎵 🅿 🍸 🍴 ⬤ Tue.

AE DC MC V D

OLD SAYBROOK: *Al Forno* $$$
1654 Boston Post Rd. 🌙 *(860) 399-4166.*
This popular Italian restaurant and pizzeria features a huge
brick oven and a chianti wine list. Lively and usually crowded.
L, D. 🅿 🖐

AE DC MC V

OLD SAYBROOK: *Terra Mar Grille* $$$$
Saybrook Point Inn, 2 Bridge St. 🌙 *(860) 388-1111.*
Serene marina views compete with a menu of American and Northern
Italian dishes. Wild game is a specialty. B, L, D, Brunch Sun.
🅿 🍸 🍴 🚹 🖐

AE DC MC V D

PLAINVILLE (FARMINGTON): *Confetti* $$
393 Farmington Ave. 🌙 *(860) 793-8809.*
In an area where good restaurants are hard to find, this is
an oasis of hearty well-prepared American-Italian dishes,
good seafood. L, D, Brunch Sun (except Jul & Aug).
🅿 🍸 🚹

AE MC V

RIDGEFIELD: *Gail's Station House* $$
378 Main St. 🌙 *(203) 438-9775.*
Yeoman portions of well-prepared, eclectic American food
make this funky old storefront a popular local hangout.
Desserts are really special. B, L, D, Brunch Sun.
🅿 🚹

AE MC V D

SIMSBURY: *Metro Bis* $$$
928 Hopmeadow St. 🌙 *(860) 651-1908.*
Lively bistro setting offers inspired Asian-accented American food.
L, D. 🅿 🚹 🖐 ⬤ Sun.

AE MC V

SOUTH NORWALK: *Ocean Drive* $$$
128 Washington St. 🌙 *(203) 855-1665.*
A cool South Beach Miami look combines with inventive seafood dishes
in this "happening" new scene. D. 🎵 🍸 🚹 🖐

AE DC MC V

STAMFORD: *Bank Street Brewery* $$$
65 Bank St. 🌙 *(203) 325-2739.*
Favorite after-work hangout for the young, in handsomely restored old
bank, now a bustling brew pub. L, D. 🎵 🅿 🍸 🚹 🖐

AE MC V D

STONINGTON: *Boom* $$$
194 Water St. 🌙 *(860) 535-2588.*
Innovative American cuisine overlooking the docks at Dodson Boatyard,
on historic Stonington harbor. L, D. 🅿 🍸 🚹 🖐 ⬤ Mon; Mar.

AE DC MC V

For key to symbols see back flap

Price categories include a three-course meal for one, half a bottle of house wine and all unavoidable extra charges such as sales tax and service.

$ under $20
$$ $20–30
$$$ $30–45
$$$$ $45–60
$$$$$ over $60

CREDIT CARDS
Major credit cards accepted: *AE* American Express; *MC* Master Card/Access; *DC* Diners Club; *V* VISA; *D* Discover Card.

OUTDOOR TABLES
Garden, courtyard, or terrace with outside tables.

VEGETARIAN
A good selection of vegetarian dishes available.

GOOD WINE
Extensive list of good wines, both native and international.

LATE OPENING
Full menu or light meals served after 11pm.

	CREDIT CARDS	OUTDOOR TABLES	VEGETARIAN	GOOD WINE	LATE OPENING

VERMONT

BURLINGTON: *India House Restaurant* $$$
207 Colchester Ave. ☎ *(802) 862-7800.*
Specializing in traditional North Indian food, with both vegetarian and non-vegetarian choices. Authentic tandoori cooking. Good choice of beers. L, D. 🅿 ⚹ ♿

AE DC MC V D		▪	●	

BURLINGTON: *Leunig's Bistro* $$$$
115 Church St. ☎ *(802) 863-3759.*
Located in a 1920s Art Deco building in the middle of downtown, this award-winning Mediterranean grill and bistro serves fresh pasta, grilled fish and meat, and substantial vegetarian dishes. B, L, D, Brunch Sat & Sun. 🍽 ♿

AE DC MC V D	●	▪	●	

BURLINGTON: *New England Culinary Institute at NECI Commons* $$$$
25 Church St. ☎ *(802) 862-6324.*
On the Church Street Marketplace, run by the students of the Culinary Institute. High-quality eclectic American food with some French touches and emphasis on fresh, local ingredients. Reservations recommended. L, D, Brunch Sun. 🍽 ⚹ ♿

AE DC MC V D	●	▪	●	

BURLINGTON: *Trattoria Delia* $$$$
152 St. Paul St. ☎ *(802) 864-5253.*
Family-run Old-World style restaurant. Good regional Italian specialties in a rustic setting: stone walls, exposed beams, and fireplace. Homemade pasta and a fine selection of Italian wines. Award of excellence from *Wine Spectator.* Reservations recommended. D. 🍽 🍽 ⚹ ♿

DC MC V		▪	●	

CRAFTSBURY: *Inn on the Common* $$$$
1165 North Craftsbury Rd. ☎ *(800) 521-2233 or (802) 586-9619.*
Famous restaurant in a charming Federal inn in ski country. Cuisine is contemporary American. The prix fixe menu changes daily and includes such dishes as baked cherry planked salmon and sauteed breast of duck. Award-winning wine cellar. Reservations required. D. 🅿 🍽 🍽

AE MC V	●	▪	●	

GRAFTON: *Old Tavern at Grafton* $$$$
92 Main St. ☎ *(800) 843-1801 or (802) 843-2231.*
Housed in an inn built in 1801. Classic gourmet cooking with seasonal and cross-cultural influences. Only the freshest produce is used, including herbs from the inn's garden, and local meat and dairy products. Reservations required. B, L, D. 🎵 🅿 🍽 🍽 ⚹ ♿ ⬤ mid-Mar–May

AE MC V D		▪	●	

KILLINGTON: *The Grist Mill Restaurant* $$$
Killington Rd. ☎ *(802) 422-3970.*
Designed to look like an old mill, this award-winning building has a dining room and separate entertainment lounge. The menu offers a wide range of reasonably priced New England-style food. Smoking is allowed in the lounge, which features live music and a signature cocktail called the "Goombay Smash". L, D, Brunch Sun. 🎵 🅿 🍽 ⚹ ♿

AE MC V	●	▪	●	▪

LOWER WATERFORD: *The Rabbit Hill Inn* $$$$
48 Lower Waterford Rd. ☎ *(800) 762-8669 or (802) 748-5168.*
New American cuisine served in a tranquil 1795 country inn near St. Johnsbury. Prix fixe five-course meal, with local specialties. Reservations required; children 13 and over. D. 🎵 🅿 🍽 🍽 ♿

AE MC V		▪	●	

MANCHESTER CENTER: *Up For Breakfast* $
4935 Main St. ☎ *(802) 362-4204.*
Delicious, nutritious breakfasts, with many varieties of eggs, pancakes, French toast, waffles, fruit plates, and tofu "eggs vegetarian." Choice of coffees, including a maple latte, fresh-squeezed orange or grapefruit juice or a champagne-and-OJ mimosa. Full champagne menu. B. ⚹

MC V		▪		

MARLBORO: *The Skyline Restaurant* $
Rte 9. 📞 *(802) 464-5535.*
High up on Hogback Mountain, between Wilmington and Brattleboro,
this establishment offers its diners a splendid 100-mile view and American
cooking, including steak, chicken, seafood, and pasta. Extensive breakfast
and lunch menu. Accessible by snowmobile in the winter.
B, L, D. 🅿 🍴 ♿ ⬤ seasonally Nov.

MC
V

NORTH HERO: *North Hero House Inn and Restaurant* $$$
3643 US Rte 2. 📞 *(888) 525-3644 or (802) 372-4732.*
An 1891 inn located in the picturesque Champlain Islands. Chefs serve up
a wide range of American food, from herb-roasted chicken with sauteed
apples, raisins, cranberries, and maple syrup to rainbow trout stuffed with
crabmeat. Lobster buffet Friday nights in summer. A glassed- or screened-
in porch overlooks the lake. B, D, Brunch Sun. 🎵 🅿 🍷 👶 ♿

AE
MC
V

SHELBURNE: *Sirloin Saloon* $$$
2545 Shelburne Rd. 📞 *(802) 985-2200.*
This restaurant is famous for its aged, hand-cut steaks and prime rib, as
well as Maine lobster and fresh fish. Outstanding salad bar with fresh
produce from local farms; some organic products. Children's menu is an
excellent value. Warm, western-style decor and friendly service.
Reservations recommended. D. 🅿 🍷 👶 ♿

AE
DC
MC
V
D

SHELBURNE: *Restaurant at the Inn at Shelburne Farms* $$$$$
1611 Harbor Rd. 📞 *(802) 985-8498.*
Creative regional cuisine in an historic mansion overlooking
Lake Champlain. Some produce comes straight from their market
garden; the farms produce cheese and bread for the restaurant as well.
Free-range chicken, lamb, beef, fish and seafood, with menu changing
a few times per season. Reservations required.
B, D, Brunch Sun. 🅿 🍷 🍴 👶 ⬤ mid-Oct–mid-May

AE
DC
MC
V
D

STOWE: *Maxwell's at Top Notch* $$$$$
4000 Mountain Rd. 📞 *(800) 451-8686 or (802) 253-8585.*
The fine dining option at the Top Notch at Stowe Resort and Spa, Maxwell's
serves gourmet American cuisine with many health-conscious options,
specializing in game and prime aged meats. This is an elegant room with
beautiful views from large windows. It has received the Award of
Excellence from *Wine Spectator.* B, D. 🎵 🅿 🍷 🍴 👶 ♿

AE
DC
MC
V
D

STRATTON: *Stone Chimney Grill* $$$$
61 Middle Ridge Rd. 📞 *(802) 297-2500.*
In the Stratton Mountain Inn, a short walk from the base of the ski
hill and the Village Square. Cuisine in a dining room with
a fireplace and scenic views. Menu includes grilled steaks and seafood
with daily specials. B, D. 🅿 🍷 🍴 👶 ♿ ⬤ Apr–end Jun.

AE
MC
V

NEW HAMPSHIRE

CENTER SANDWICH: *Corner House Inn* $$$
22 Main St. 📞 *(603) 284-6219.*
Local residents have been dining at this country inn for more than a
century. Traditional American country cuisine served in four cozy rooms.
L (Jun–Oct), D, Brunch Sun. 🎵 🅿 🍷 🎵 👶 ♿ ⬤ Mon, Nov–May.

AE
MC
V
D

CONCORD: *Cat'n Fiddle* $$$
118 Manchester St. 📞 *(603) 228-8911.*
This 26-year-old family business is a Concord institution. The traditional
American fare includes prime rib, steak, seafood, a huge salad bar, and
shish kebabs. Casual setting. Reservations on weekends. L, D. 🅿 🍷 👶 ♿

AE
MC
V
D

DANBURY: *The Inn at Danbury* $$$$
67 Rt.104. 📞 *(603)-768-3318.*
As well as being a guest house, the Inn at Danbury also serves excellent
traditonal New England and European cuisine, in their very popular
restaurant. Children menu available. Sunday Brunch, D (Wed-Sat). 🅿 🍷

MC
V
D

DURHAM: *The Three Chimneys Inn* $$$$
17 Newmarket Road. 📞 *(603) 868-7800.*
Fine American and European cuisine such as New England bouillabaise
and duck confit, in a beautiful colonial mansion dining room. Vegetarian
dishes upon request. L (Tue-Sat), D. 🅿 🍷 🍴 👶 ♿

AE
DC
MC
V
D

For key to symbols see back flap

Price categories include a three-course meal for one, half a bottle of house wine and all unavoidable extra charges such as sales tax and service.
$ under $20
$$ $20–30
$$$ $30–45
$$$$ $45–60
$$$$$ over $60

Credit Cards
Major credit cards accepted: *AE* American Express; *MC* Master Card/Access; *DC* Diners Club; *V* Visa; *D* Discover Card.

Outdoor Tables
Garden, courtyard, or terrace with outside tables.

Vegetarian
A good selection of vegetarian dishes available.

Good Wine
Extensive list of good wines, both native and international.

Late Opening
Full menu or light meals served after 11pm.

	Credit Cards	Outdoor Tables	Vegetarian	Good Wine	Late Opening
Exeter: *The Terrace Restaurant at The Exeter Inn* $$$$ 90 Front St. ☎ *(603) 772-5901.* A deliciously elegant dining experience in an equally elegant inn. Award-winning chef serves up such dishes as grilled rock cornish hen, pecan salmon, and touredos of beef. B, L, D,Brunch Sun. [P] 🍸 👔 🧒 ♿	*AE MC V D*	●	■	●	
Hanover: *The Daniel Webster Room* $$$$ Main St. ☎ *(603) 643-4300.* The Hanover Inn's Edwardian style dining room specializes in contemporary American seafood, meat, and vegetable dishes. Recipient of a *Wine Spectator* Award. B, L, D, Brunch Sun. [P] 🍸 👔 🧒 ♿ ⬤ Sun & Mon dinner, Sat lunch	*AE DC MC V D*	●		●	
Keene: *Elm City Brewing Company* $$$$ 222 West St. ☎ *(603) 355-3335.* This renovated 19th-century woolen mill turned restaurant/brewery offers freshly prepared creative American cuisine and eight homemade beers on tap in a lively atmosphere. L, D. [P] 🍸 🧒 ♿	*MC V D*	●	■		■
Lebanon: *Three Tomatoes Trattoria* $$$ 1 Court St. ☎ *(603) 448-1711.* A popular spot for authentic Italian food in a friendly relaxed environment across from the Lebanon Green. L (Mon–Fri), D. [P] 🧒 ♿	*AE MC V*	●	■	●	
Meredith: *Hart's Turkey Farm Restaurant* $$$ Rte 3 & Jct. 104 ☎ *(603) 279-6212.* The country-style turkey dinner remains a staple of this family business. A huge selection of non-turkey dishes are also available, such as prime rib and a full line of seafood. L, D. [P] 🍸 🧒 ♿ ⬤ Dec 25	*AE DC MC V D*		■		
Portsmouth: *Chestnuts at the Nest* $$ 3548 Lafayette Road. ☎ *(603) 436-2481.* Located on the grounds of The Wren's Nest Village Inn. This fine dining pub-restaurant serves a selection of game and fish cuisine. Try their duck duo (duck breast and leg confit) served with black current demi-glase. D. [P] 🍸	*MC V*		■		●
Portsmouth: *Cafe Mirabelle* $$$$ 64 Bridge St. ☎ *(603) 430-9301.* Creatively original country-style French cuisine prepared by a classically trained chef in an elegant yet casual environment. Reservations required. D. [P] 🧒 ⬤ Mon & Tue.	*MC V*		■		
Portsmouth: *The Blue Mermaid World Grill* $$$$ 409 The Hill ☎ *(603) 427-2583.* A wonderful selection of internationally flavored dishes that include spiced pork, marinated lamb, and a great choice of seafoods prepared on a wood burning grill. Beverage list has 12 different Margaritas, tropical coolers, martinis, and a good wine list. L, D, Brunch Sun. ♬ [P] 🍸 🧒	*AE DC MC V D*	●	■	●	
Portsmouth: *The Oar House* $$$$ 55 Ceres St. ☎ *(603) 436-4025.* A museum restaurant in a restored 1803 waterfront warehouse. Both the decor and mainly seafood menu reflect Portsmouth's maritime heritage. Reservations are recommended. L, D, Brunch Sun. [P] 🍸 🧒 ♿	*AE DC MC V D*	●	■	●	
Sugar Hill: *Sunset Hill House – A Grand Inn* $$$$ 231 Sunset Hill Road. ☎ *(800) 786-4455 or (603) 823-5522.* Combine a talented chef with the phenomenal effect of sunset on the White Mountains to the east and the result is a memorable dining experience. Reservations required. B (guests only), D (summer: Tue–Sun; mid-Oct–May: Thu–Sun). [P] 🍸 👔 🧒 ♿ ⬤ Mon	*AE MC V D*	●	■	●	

MAINE

BAR HARBOR: *George's Restaurant* $$$$
7 Stephens Lane. ((207) 288-4505.
Mediterranean-based cuisine with an eclectic twist is the best way to describe this culinary adventure. There is a fixed price, three-course meal. D. ♫ P ⚡ ● Nov–May.

AE DC MC V D

BETHEL: *Bethel Inn and Country Club* $$$$
Broad St. ((207) 824-2175. New England gourmet cuisine in lovely surroundings. A glassed-in veranda allows for year-round views. B, D. ♫ P Y ⚡ ⚡ & ● mid-Oct–mid-Dec and mid-Mar–mid-May.

AE MC V D

CARIBOU: *Greenhouse Restaurant* $$
19 Main St. ((207) 498-3733.
Located in the Caribou Inn and Convention Center, this restaurant offers good home cooking at reasonable prices. Known for its inexpensive breakfast menu and the for the full turkey dinners served every Sunday. B, L, D. P Y ⚡ &

AE DC MC V D

EUSTIS: *The Porter House Restaurant* $$$
Rte 27. ((207) 246-7932.
The Porter House features a high quality of food at quite reasonable prices. The restaurant is a converted 1908 farmhouse with several dining rooms. D. P Y ⚡ & ● Mon and Tue.

MC V

GREENVILLE: *The Greenville Inn* $$$$
Norris St. ((888) 695-6000 or (207) 695-2206.
Housed in an 1895 Victorian mansion, the Greenville is a gourmet restaurant hidden away in remote Northern Maine. The chef will cater to vegetarian and other special requests, serving rack of lamb, venison, fresh fish and roast duckling. D. P Y ● Sun; Nov 1–Apr 30.

MC V D

KENNEBUNKPORT: *The Clam Shack* $
2 Western St. ((207) 967-3321.
This take-out stand is the quintessential seaside experience. The menu consists of some of the best fast food seafood you'll find, including fried and steamed clams, scallops, and a truly remarkable lobster roll. Known for its fresh-cut onion rings. L, D. P ⚡ & ● mid-Oct–mid-May.

OGUNQUIT: *Barnacle Billy's* $$$
Perkins Cove Rd. ((207) 646-5575.
This is a classic, bare-bones Maine lobster house. A casual atmosphere and seaside surroundings set the tone for this spot. The more full-service Barnacle Billy's Etc. is right next door. L, D. P Y ⚡ & ● Nov–Apr.

AE MC V

OGUNQUIT: *Arrows Restaurant* $$$$$
Berwick Rd. ((207) 361-1100. Considered one of the best restaurants in New England, the Arrows has won many awards. The menu consists of innovative American cuisine, with fresh produce taken from the vegetable garden on the grounds. Reservations required and dressy attire is strongly advised. D. P Y ⚡ & ● mid-Dec–mid-Apr. Call for details.

MC V

PORTLAND: *Back Bay Grill* $$$$
65 Portland St. ((207) 772-8833.
The Back Bay Grill has a seasonal menu and offers elegant food in a modern setting. A *Wine Spectator* Award of Excellence winner, this restaurant has an enormous selection of wine and also is known for superb desserts. D. & ● Sun.

AE DC MC V D

PORTLAND: *Katahdin* $$$$
106 High St. ((207) 774-1740.
The Katahdin features an eclectic but laid back setting matched by a wide variety of high quality fusion dishes. They don't take reservations, so be sure to get there early. D. Y ⚡ & ● Sun, Mon.

MC V

RANGELEY: *People's Choice Restaurant* $$$
Main St. ((207) 864-5220.
Family dining in a casual environment. On Saturdays, the lounge offers live music and a rockin' dance floor. B, L, D. ♫ P Y ⚡ &

AE MC V D

RANGELEY: *People's Choice Restaurant* $$$
Main St. ((207) 864-5220.
Family dining in a casual environment. On Saturdays, the lounge offers live music and a rockin' dance floor. B, L, D. ♫ P Y ⚡ &

AE MC V D

For key to symbols see back flap

SHOPPING IN NEW ENGLAND

Outlet banner in Kittery

WHILE MOST PEOPLE seldom equate New England with shopping sprees, the region certainly offers a wide and ever-growing variety of high-quality stores and merchandise. Tourists looking for gifts with a regional flavor should sample the maple syrup and maple sugar candy, especially plentiful in the northern states of Vermont, New Hampshire, and Maine. Many coastal souvenir shops carry beautiful replicas of whalebone scrimshaw carvings. Regional arts and crafts can be found everywhere, particularly in places such as Provincetown, Massachusetts. In Boston shoppers have a choice of shops, from out-of-the-way second-hand bookstores to trendy fashion boutiques. Of course, some of New England's most well-known shopping experiences happen at the factory outlet stores in Freeport and Kittery, Maine, and North Conway, New Hampshire, where brand name clothing can be found at a discount. These pages offer information for people seeking serious shopping while in New England.

OPENING HOURS

MOST STORES' HOURS are from 9 or 10am to 6pm Monday through Saturday and from 12pm to 5 or 6pm on Sunday. Many retail stores stay open until 9pm on Thursday night and the major department stores often stay open until 9 or 10pm during the week. It is always good to keep in mind that the larger malls, department stores, and factory outlet shops are usually busiest Saturdays, lunch hours, and evenings. Weekday mornings are the best times to shop.

SALES

THERE ARE TWO major sale seasons in New England, particularly in the major urban centers such as Boston. In July many summer clothes are offered at reduced prices in order to make room for the fall fashions. In January clothing and merchandise are cleared after the holidays. In general, the best bargains – and the most frenzied shopping – can be found in the two weeks immediately following Christmas Day.

PAYMENT AND TAXES

MAJOR CREDIT CARDS are accepted at most stores, and many are equipped to handle direct payment transactions with your bank card. Traveler's checks with the proper ID are also accepted at

Large glass atrium of busy Prudential Center shopping mall

many stores in the larger urban areas. In general, the prices on tags in New England stores do not include sales tax. This tax varies from state to state *(see p367)*, ranging from 5 to 7 percent in all states except New Hampshire, which charges no sales tax on retail goods. It is always prudent to keep your bill or credit card receipt as proof of purchase should your merchandise be defective. Most stores will offer a full refund or replace the item.

SHOPPING MALLS

SHOPPING MALLS – clusters of shops, restaurants, and cinemas all within one large complex – have become top destinations for shoppers, offering variety, dining, and entertainment. The practical beauty of malls is that they gather under one expansive roof a wide range of retail stores, from the major department stores to smaller specialty shops. New England's long, cold winters make malls a popular place for residents. Most malls also offer free parking, and even out-of-town shopping centers are located on public bus lines.

Boston has its share of popular malls. **Copley Place** has more than 100 shops and restaurants, and an 11-screen cinema complex, all centered

New England T-shirts, popular and ubiquitous

Filene's, a Boston shopping mecca for more than a century

around a dazzling 60-ft (18-m) atrium and waterfall. The **Shops at Prudential Center** include two department stores, a huge food court, and many smaller specialty shops. The upscale **Heritage on the Garden** overlooks Boston's Public Garden and features the boutiques of top designers, fine jewelers, and stores selling other luxury goods. Across the Charles River, **Cambridgeside Galleria** has over 100 shops and a waterfront food court.

Travelers looking for a shopping experience of a different kind should visit **Olde Mistick Village** in Mystic, Connecticut. Designed to look like a village from the 1700s, this 26-building complex houses a variety of restaurants and stores selling everything from handmade arts and crafts to fine imported wine.

DEPARTMENT STORES

THE LARGE DEPARTMENT stores are shopping complexes in their own right, offering a host of goods and services, from free gift-wrapping by assistants who will help customers with their shopping.

In general, the major chains are found throughout the US, with each having a particular reputation. For example, Bloomingdale's is known for the latest fashions. Popular discount chains such as K-Mart and Wal-Mart are the places to go for no-frills shopping for just about everything. Sears and Target also deal in general merchandise. These stores are found throughout New England.

There are five major department stores in Boston, each offering a large and varied selection of clothing, accessories, cosmetics, and gifts. They also have restaurants and beauty salons, and provide a variety of personal shopping services. For those wanting to shop at several stores, **Concierge of Boston** provides a shopping service.

At Boston's **Downtown Crossing** *(see p70)*, a bustling shopping district between Boston Common and the Financial District, generations of Bostonians have shopped at **Filene's**, a store that was founded in 1881. Featuring apparel from some of the best known American designers, as well as brand labels for women, men, and children, Filene's offers six floors of high-quality merchandise. It is famous for its bargain basement, now owned and operated separately. The store reduces basement items by 25 percent after 14 days, 50 percent after 21 days, and 75 percent after 28 days. After 35 days the clothes go to charity. Across the street, **Macy's**, the legendary New York emporium, offers an equally impressive array of fashions, cosmetics, and furnishings.

The Prudential Tower houses a complex of shops, including **Lord and Taylor**. The store is well known for its classic American designer labels, juniors and children's department, and men's wear, but it also carries crystal, china, and gifts. Next door, **Saks**

Fifth Avenue caters to a more upscale clientele.

However, for the ultimate high-fashion, high-profile shopping experience, visitors should stop by **Neiman Marcus**, which specializes in haute couture, precious jewelry, furs, and gifts. The store is famous for its Christmas catalog, with presents that have included authentic Egyptian mummies and vintage airplanes.

DISCOUNT AND OUTLET STORES

DEDICATED BARGAIN hunters will want to pay a visit to some of New England's famed outlet centers, where many top designers and major brand manufacturers offer late-season and over-stocked clothing and goods at big discounts. Generally sold at 20 to 30 percent less than regular retail prices, some items can be found reduced by as much as 75 percent.

In Wrentham, Massachusetts, 33 miles (53 km) southwest of Boston, are the **Wrentham Village Premium Outlets**. The stores here sell designer clothing, housewares, and accessories from many leading manufacturers.

Kittery *(see p278)*, Maine, is an even larger outlet destination, with more than 125 shops selling everything from footwear and designer clothes to sports equipment, perfume, books, china, glass, and gifts. There are also numerous restaurants. Also in Maine, **Freeport** *(see p284)* is home to a wide range of outlet stores as well as the outdoor equipment specialist **L.L. Bean**.

L.L. Bean Inc., purveyor of outdoor equipment and clothing

ANTIQUING

NEW ENGLAND IS an antique hunter's dream, with a great multitude of stores offering a wide array of furniture, accessories, and collectibles. From the sprawling antique markets, collectives, and fairs to the smaller specialty shops, there are abundant opportunities to indulge a passion for the past.

Included among the prime antiquing areas in Massachusetts is the Charles Street section of Boston's Beacon Hill (see p62). One of the larger stores is **Antiques at 80 Charles**, which has two floors of merchandise ranging from silver tea sets to jewelry, paintings, clocks, and collectibles. Collectors of fine Asian antiques should not bypass **Alberts-Langdon, Inc.** and **Judith Dowling Japanese Art**.

Boston visitors will also find several antique markets and dealers' collectives, such as the **Boston Antique Cooperative I and II**, which carries everything from antique quilts to candlesticks.

Antique carved whalebone, called scrimshaw

The Berkshires region (see pp166–7) is known for its antiquing, particularly in the town of Sheffield. Shops such as **Antiques Center of Sheffield** and **Darr Antiques** cover a broad range of Americana. Perhaps the state's most famous antiquing event is the **Brimfield Antique Show** (see p161), which is held three times a year in Brimfield. On the coast, scenic Route 6 through Cape Cod (see pp156–9) is peppered with antique shops, especially in the charming towns of Brewster and Dennis.

Connecticut's Litchfield Hills area is another antiques hotbed. The town of Woodbury has dozens of high-quality shops lining its Main Street, including **Wayne Pratt Antiques**, with its collection of impeccable 18th-century furniture. For antiques in Rhode Island, go to Spring Street and lower Thames Street in Newport.

In Maine, Route 1 between Kittery and Scarborough is loaded with shops that carry an eclectic selection of antiques and collectibles. New Hampshire's antiquing areas include Route 4 east of Concord, Route 101A in Milford, and Route 119 in Fitzwilliam. In Vermont, a large selection of antique shops can be found within the "Southern Circle" bounded by Route 9, Route 7A, and Route 30.

BOSTON FASHION

A STATELY INTERNATIONAL city, Boston has many stores featuring fine clothes from Italy, France, England, and Japan, along with fashions from top American designers. Many offer quality clothing for both men and women. **Louis Boston** has long been known as the city's most exclusive men's outfitter. It now also features similarly beautiful clothing for women. Nearby on Newbury Street, **Giorgio Armani** and **Gianni Versace** carry extravagantly stylish and outrageously expensive clothing and accessories. **Alan Bilzerian** attracts celebrities looking for his label and the latest in fashion apparel from Europe and Japan.

Still on Newbury Street, women will find a wide range of stores catering to their every taste, be it the haute mode of **Chanel** in Boston's Ritz-Carlton Hotel or the colorful prints and youthful designs of the Dutch boutique **Oilily**. The street is filled with sumptuous, high-fashion boutiques, including **SASO** and **Max Mara**, Italy's most luxurious ready-to-wear manufacturer.

Men seeking the perfect Boston look need go no farther than **Brooks Brothers**, longtime purveyors of traditional, high-quality men's and boys' wear. America's foremost fashion house, **Polo/Ralph Lauren** offers top-quality and highly priced sports and formal attire.

Elsewhere **Abercrombie and Fitch** is favored by teenagers and college students, as is the original **Levi's Store**.

Well-made and distinctive gifts from shop in Sabbathday Lake Shaker Community, Maine

Arts and crafts, a regional specialty

DIRECTORY

SHOPPING MALLS

Copley Place
100 Huntington Ave,
Boston, MA.
(617) 369-5000.

Heritage on the Garden
300 Boylston St, Boston, MA.
(617) 426-9500;
(800) 746-7778.

Shops at Prudential Center
800 Boylston St,
Boston, MA.
(617) 236-2366 or
(800) 746-7778.

DEPARTMENT STORES

Concierge of Boston
165 Newbury St,
Boston, MA.
(617) 266-6611.
www.concierge.org

Filene's
426 Washington St,
Boston, MA.
(617) 357-2100.

Lord and Taylor
760 Boylston
Boston, MA.
(617) 262-6000.

Macy's
450 Washington St,
Boston, MA.
(617) 357-3000.

Neiman Marcus
5 Copley Place,
Boston, MA.
(617) 536-3660.

Saks Fifth Avenue
Prudential Center,
Boston, MA.
(617) 262-8500.

DISCOUNT AND OUTLET STORES

Kittery Outlets
Kittery, ME.
(888) KITTERY.

North Conway Factory Outlets
North Conway, NH.
(888) 667-9636 or
(800) 407-4078.

L.L. Bean
Freeport, ME.
(207) 865-4761.
www.LLBean.com

Westbrook Factory Stores
Westbrook, CT.
(888) SHOP-333.

Vermont Factory Outlets
Manchester, VT.
(802) 362-3736.

Wrentham Village Premium Outlets
Wrentham, MA.
(508) 384-0600.

ANTIQUES

Alberts-Langdon, Inc.
126 Charles St,
Boston, MA.
(617) 523-5924.

Antiques at 80 Charles
80 Charles St,
Boston, MA.
(617) 742-8006.

Antiques Center of Sheffield
33 S Main St,
Sheffield, MA.
(413) 229-3400.

Boston Antique Cooperative I and II
119 Charles St,
Boston, MA.
(617) 227-9811.

Darr Antiques
28 S Main St,
Sheffield, MA.
(413) 229-7773.

Judith Dowling Japanese Art
133 Charles St,
Boston, MA.
(617) 523-5211

Wayne Pratt Antiques
346 Main St, South,
Woodbury, CT.
(203) 263-5676.

New Hampshire Antique Dealers' Association
www.NHADA.org

Vermont Antique Dealers' Association
(802) 484-7799.
www.vermontada.com

BOSTON FASHION

Abercrombie and Fitch
1 Faneuil Hall Marketplace,
Boston, MA.
(617) 742-6838.

Alan Bilzerian
34 Newbury St,
Boston, MA.
(617) 536-1001.

Brooks Brothers
46 Newbury St,
Boston, MA.
(617) 267-2600.

Chanel
5 Newbury St,
Boston, MA.
(617) 859-0055.

Gianni Versace
12 Newbury St,
Boston, MA.
(617) 536-8300.

Giorgio Armani
22 Newbury St,
Boston, MA.
(617) 267-3200.

Levi's Store
Prudential Center,
Boston, MA.
(617) 375-9010.

Louis Boston
234 Berkley St,
Boston, MA.
(617) 262-6100.

Max Mara
69 Newbury St,
Boston, MA.
(617) 267-9775.

Oilily
31 Newbury St,
Boston, MA.
(617) 247-9299.

Polo/Ralph Lauren
100 Huntington Ave,
Boston, MA.
(617) 266-4121.

SASO
337 Newbury St,
Boston, MA.
(617) 437-0906.

ENTERTAINMENT IN NEW ENGLAND

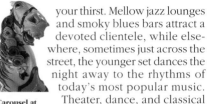

EW ENGLAND is a traveler's dream because it offers a wide range of entertainment opportunities. The sports-minded can take advantage of the region's plethora of outdoor activities *(see pp356–63)*. Those looking for a less strenuous afternoon or evening will never be at a loss. Free concerts and festivals abound throughout the New England summer, and there is no shortage of bars and nightclubs in which to slake, or build,

Carousel at Bushnell Park

your thirst. Mellow jazz lounges and smoky blues bars attract a devoted clientele, while elsewhere, sometimes just across the street, the younger set dances the night away to the rhythms of today's most popular music. Theater, dance, and classical music have long been the mainstays of the region's cultural identity, although pro sports may attract more fervent fans. Family activities and events fill out the range of possibilities.

A waltz evening at the Fairmont Copley Plaza Boston

PRACTICAL INFORMATION

THE BEST SOURCES for listings of films, concerts, theater and dance performances, and exhibitions in New England are the Thursday and Friday editions of local newspapers, such as the *Providence Journal,* in Providence, Rhode Island, and the *Newport Daily News* in Newport, Rhode Island. In Boston check the Thursday "Calendar" of the *Boston Globe* and the entertainment weekly *The Boston Phoenix.* Even more up-to-the-minute listings can be found on the Internet at Ticketmaster's boston.city search.com the *Boston Globe*

site www.boston.com, and the *Boston Phoenix* site www.bostonphoenix.com.

BOOKING TICKETS

TICKETS TO SOME of New England's most popular shows, especially some of Boston's popular musicals and theater productions, can be hard to come by, sometimes selling out months in advance. Your best bet is to book early, even for extended events such as the Boston Symphony Orchestra's summer-long Tanglewood concert series *(see p167)*.

Two advance ticket agencies dominate New England for concerts, plays, and sports events: **Ticketmaster** and **NEXT Ticketing**. However, tickets for many of Boston's

Keith Lockhart, conductor of the well loved Boston Pops

concerts and sporting events can also be booked online at CitySearch by using your credit card. Half-price tickets to most non-commercial and some commercial productions in the Boston area are available beginning at 11am on the day of the performance at **BosTix** booths. However, purchases must be made in person and only with cash.

OPEN-AIR FREE ENTERTAINMENT

THE WONDERFUL thing about New England is that there are so many free events to keep you entertained throughout the spring, summer, and fall. Revolutionary War reenactments, Native American celebrations, numerous regattas along the coast, and a host of free concerts offer something for everyone. Local newspapers are usually the best source of free show listings.

Boston's Harvard Square has been famous for four decades for its nightly and weekend scene of street performers. Many recording stars paid their dues on Brattle Street and Massachusetts Avenue, and many more flock there in the hope of being discovered – or at least picking up the cost of dinner by passing the hat. The best free outdoor summer entertainment in Boston is found at the Hatch Memorial Shell on the Charles River Esplanade. The Boston Pops

Independence Day fireworks display over Boston Harbor

performs there frequently during the week of July 4, culminating in a huge Independence Day concert complete with booming cannons and a stunning fireworks display. During July and August, the venue resonates with classical music on Wednesday nights, jazz on Sunday afternoons, and pop and rock on select Saturday evenings. On Friday evenings from late June through the Friday before Labor Day, the Hatch Memorial Shell shows big-screen family films.

College towns in New England, such as Burlington in Vermont, Hanover in New Hampshire, and New Haven in Connecticut, also host a wide variety of concerts and events. Many of them have no admission charge.

POPULAR MUSIC

A NUMBER OF LARGER CITIES, such as Worcester, Massachusetts, Providence and Newport, Rhode Island, Hartford and New Haven, Connecticut, and Burlington, Vermont, have vibrant music scenes. Bands and musicians can be found year-round playing everywhere from small clubs to large concert venues. The smaller concerts, especially if they are free, often fill up quickly, so it is wise to arrive a little early.

As you might expect, Boston's cosmopolitan spirit

and lively nightlife lend themselves to a wide range of musical influences, be it pop, punk, or smoky blues. One of Boston's leading venues for name rock bands and up-and-coming groups is **Avalon Ballroom**. The musicians at this Lansdowne Street club play early in order to clear the house out for a stylish late-night dance crowd. The two stages of the **Middle East** in Cambridge's Central Square lead the alternative rock scene, featuring both local bands and touring newcomers. Larger rock venues are the **Orpheum Theatre** and the stadium seating of the **FleetCenter**, which is otherwise occupied by hockey and basketball games.

Elsewhere Providence, Rhode Island, is home to **Lupo's Heartbreak Hotel**, a legendary spot for acts ranging from rock to R&B. In New Haven, Connecticut, **Toad's Place** is one of the city's hottest nightclubs and an intimate setting for pop, country, and folk concerts.

Boston has been particularly hospitable to jazz since the 1920s. The **Berklee Performance Center** in Back Bay is Boston's premier large concert venue for jazz. More intimate settings include **Scullers Jazz Club**

overlooking the Charles River in Brighton and the upscale martini-Scotch-cigar scene of the **Oak Bar** at the Fairmont Copley Plaza Boston.

The musical parent of jazz, blues is also alive and well in Boston. The charter room of the **House of Blues** chain at Harvard in Cambridge has a Hollywood ambience, but the music is genuine and the Sunday gospel-music brunch is legendary. The **Cantab Lounge** in Cambridge's Central Square is a blues-lover's gem with Wednesday and Sunday jams. Musician-owner "Little" Joe Cook occasionally performs his 1950s R&B to enthusiastic audiences. The Cantab also runs Wednesday night poetry slams in a downstairs room.

Of course, Boston does not have a lock on blues and jazz. Newport, Rhode Island, has a number of famous spots, including **The Red Parrot**, a two-floor jazz bar, and the **Newport Blues Café**, a popular R&B club.

Boston's musical pastiche is rounded out by a host of top-rate folk and world music clubs. Harvard Square's **Club Passim** is a folk music legend. The club was the late-1950s and early-1960s hangout for the likes of Joan Baez and Van Morrison, and is still one of North America's key clubs in the touring life of singer-songwriters. To catch some local Caribbean tunes and dancing, the best bet is a weekend night at **Rhythm & Spice Caribbean Grill** in Cambridge's Central Square.

The Puerto Rico Festival at Salem, Massachusetts

An evening at the Axis, a dance club in Boston, Massachusetts

BARS AND NIGHTCLUBS

VIRTUALLY EVERY fair-sized city or town you come upon in New England has some type of bar or club. Often there is live entertainment on tap, be it music or stand-up comedy. This usually means having to pay some sort of cover change.

Boston has a club for just about every dance scene, though little happens before 11pm. **Axis** is one of the edgier Lansdowne Street choices, with several nights of trance, techno, and house music, and gay male night on Sundays. At the other end of the spectrum, **The Big Easy** in the Theater District spins popular music for urban professionals. Located in the rear of a stylish restaurant, **Pravda 116** plays House and Techno music, and also has a Latin night.

Boston bars come in all shapes and sizes. Located in the basement of the Wilbur Theatre, the extravagantly decorated **Aria** is one of the chic places to be seen. Far more earnest, the venerable **Jacob Wirth Co. Restaurant** is the place to be on Friday if you enjoy piano bar singalongs. Over the years, **Jillian's of Boston** has had a personality transplant, going from the city's best pool hall to a three-level entertainment complex complete with dart boards, video games, and 50 pool tables.

GAY CLUBS AND BARS

NEW ENGLAND HAS some areas that cater to gays and lesbians. Boston's gay scene comes into sharpest focus in the South End and Bay Village. You should consult the weekly *Bay Windows* newspaper for entertainment listings. The perpetually packed **Fritz Lounge** attached to the Chandler Inn is a stalwart bar of the South End. Boston's longest-running gay bar, **Jacques**, features rock acts Friday through Monday and female-impersonator acts the rest of the week.

In Massachusetts, Cape Cod's Provincetown is the real center of the region's gay scene, particularly in the summer. Bars such as **Pied Bar** and **Atlantic House** cater almost exclusively to either an all-male or all-female crowd.

In the summer, a gay and lesbian crowd gathers at the **Crown & Anchor** for the daily afternoon tea dance and nightly disco.

SPECTATOR SPORTS

NEW ENGLANDERS love their sports, as can be seen in the wide array of professional and semi-professional teams found throughout the region. Boston alone has three pro teams. The **Boston Red Sox** is one of the most storied teams in Major League Baseball. Baseball's regular season lasts from early April until early October, and the "Bosox" play their home games in Fenway Park.

The **Boston Bruins** hockey team has five Stanley Cup titles to its credit. During the regular season, running from September to April, the Bruins play in the FleetCenter. Tickets for their games are hard to come by, especially when their long-time rivals, the Montreal Canadiens, skate into town. The most successful Boston sports franchise is undoubtedly the **Boston Celtics**, a team that has won a remarkable 16 National Basketball Association (NBA) championships. Their regular season extends from October through April, often playing to sold-out crowds at the 19,600-seat FleetCenter.

New England Patriots helmet

The region's only major sports team that does not call Boston home is the **New England Patriots**. The "Pats" play their National Football League (NFL) opponents in the Gillette Stadium, an hour's drive south of downtown Boston. Most NFL games are played on Sunday during the autumn and early winter, although they also play some Monday night games.

Washington Capitals' Andrei Nikolishin taking a shot at Boston Bruins' goaltender Byron Dafoe

DIRECTORY

BOOKING TICKETS

BosTix
Copley Sq & Faneuil Hall
Marketplace, Boston, MA.
📞 (617) 482-2849.
🌐 www.bostix.com

NEXT Ticketing
📞 (617) 423-NEXT.
🌐 www.nextticketing.com

Ticketmaster
📞 (617) 931-2000 (Boston).
📞 (413) 733-2500 (Western MA).
📞 (207) 775-3331 (ME).
📞 (603) 868-7300 (NH).
📞 (401) 331-2211 (RI).
📞 (802) 862-5300 (VT).
🌐 www.ticketmaster.com

POPULAR MUSIC

Avalon Ballroom
15 Lansdowne St,
Boston, MA.
📞 (617) 262-2424.

Berklee Performance Center
Berklee College of Music,
136 Massachusetts Ave,
Boston, MA.
📞 (617) 266-7455.

Cantab Lounge
738 Massachusetts Ave (Central Sq),
Cambridge, MA.
📞 (617) 354-2685.

Club Passim
47 Palmer St (Harvard Sq),
Cambridge, MA.
📞 (617) 492-7679.

FleetCenter
1 Fleet Center,
Boston, MA.
📞 (617) 624-1000.
🌐 www.fleetcenter.com

House of Blues
96 Winthrop St (Harvard Sq),
Cambridge, MA.
📞 (617) 497-2229.

Lupo's Heartbreak Hotel
239 Westminster St,
Providence, RI.
📞 (401) 272-5876.

Middle East
472/480 Massachusetts Ave
(Central Sq),
Cambridge, MA.
📞 (617) 492-9181.

Newport Blues Café
286 Thames St,
Newport, RI.
📞 (401) 841-5510.

Oak Bar
Fairmont Copley Plaza Boston,
138 St James Ave,
Boston, MA.
📞 (617) 267-5300.

Orpheum Theatre
One Hamilton Place,
Boston, MA.
📞 (617) 679-0810.

The Red Parrot
348 Thames St,
Newport, RI.
📞 (401) 847-3800.

Rhythm & Spice Caribbean Grill
315 Massachusetts Ave (Central Sq),
Cambridge, MA.
📞 (617) 497-0977.

BARS AND NIGHTCLUBS

Aria
246 Tremont St,
Boston, MA.
📞 (617) 338-7080.

Axis
13 Lansdowne St,
Boston, MA.
📞 (617) 262-2437.

The Big Easy
One Boylston Place,
Boston, MA.
📞 (617) 351-7000.

Jacob Wirth Co. Restaurant
31 Stuart St,
Boston, MA.
📞 (617) 338-8586.

Jillian's of Boston
145 Ipswich St,
Boston, MA.
📞 (617) 437-0300.

Pravda 116
116 Boylston St,
Boston, MA.
📞 (617) 482-7799.

Scullers Jazz Club
400 Soldiers Field Rd,
Brighton, MA.
📞 (617) 562-4111.

Toad's Place
300 York St,
New Haven, CT.
📞 (203) 624-8623.

GAY CLUBS AND BARS

Atlantic House
4-6 Masonic Pl,
Provincetown, MA.
📞 (508) 487-3821.

Crown & Anchor
247 Commercial St,
Provincetown, MA.
📞 (508) 487-1430.

Fritz Lounge
26 Chandler St,
Boston, MA.
📞 (617) 482-4428.

Jacques
79 Broadway,
Boston, MA.
📞 (617) 426-8902.

Pied Bar
193A Commercial St,
Provincetown, MA.
📞 (508) 487-1527.

SPECTATOR SPORTS

Boston Bruins Hockey
FleetCenter,
Boston, MA.
📞 (617) 931-2000
(Ticketmaster).
🌐 www.bostonbruins.com

Boston Celtics Basketball
FleetCenter,
Boston, MA.
📞 (617) 931-2000
(Ticketmaster).
🌐 www.celtics.com

Boston Red Sox Baseball
Fenway Park,
Boston, MA
📞 (617) 267-8661
🌐 www.redsox.com

New England Patriots Football
Gillette Stadium,
Rte 1,Foxboro, MA.
📞 (617) 931-2000
(Ticketmaster).
🌐 www.patriots.com

The Arts in New England

CULTURAL ACTIVITIES are a hallmark of New England. The larger towns and cities (especially Newport and Providence, Rhode Island, and New Haven, Connecticut) all have good symphony orchestras, dance companies, and playhouses. The hub of New England performing arts is Boston, with its world-famous symphony orchestra and bustling theater district.

CLASSICAL MUSIC AND OPERA

WHEN IT COMES to classical music, New Englanders are of one mind. The **Boston Symphony Orchestra** (BSO) and its popular music doppelganger, the Boston Pops, are cherished institutions with a long history of being led by some of America's finest conductors. The BSO performs a full schedule of concerts at Symphony Hall from October through April. The Pops moves in for May and June. In the summer, the BSO takes up residence at the **Tanglewood** (see p167) estate in Lenox.

Boston's oldest musical organization is the Handel & Haydn Society (H&H), founded in 1815. As the first producer of such landmark works as Handel's *Messiah* (performed annually since 1818), Bach's *B-Minor Mass* and *St. Matthew Passion*, and Verdi's *Requiem*, H&H is one of the country's musical treasures. The organization gives regular performances at Symphony Hall, Jordan Hall, and Old South Church in Copley Square.

Classical music is ubiquitous in Boston. Emmanuel Music, for example, performs the entire Bach cantata cycle at services at Emmanuel Church on Newbury Street. The Isabella Stewart Gardner Museum (see p105) hosts a series of chamber music concerts, continuing a 19th-century tradition of professional chamber concerts in the homes of the social elite.

Boston once had a proud opera tradition, and retains a dormant major company and a grand opera house that was recently restored. **Boston Lyric Opera** has jumped into the breach, performing small-cast and light opera at a number of places. In Great Barrington, Massachusetts, the **Berkshire Opera Company** produces three operas every July and August.

DANCE

THE REGION'S BEST dance is found in Boston. The city's largest and most popular resident company, the **Boston Ballet** performs a five-ballet season of classics and new choreography at the **Shubert Theatre** and **Wang Center for the Performing Arts**. The annual Nutcracker performances during the Christmas season are a Boston tradition. The more modest **José Mateo's Ballet Theatre** has built a strong body of repertory and choreography. The company performs in the Neo-Gothic old Cambridge Baptist church, which is located near Harvard Square. Modern dance in Boston is represented by many small companies, collectives, and independent choreographers who often perform in the **Dance Complex** and **Green Street Studios** in Cambridge. Touring companies often perform at the major performing arts venue **Cutler Majestic Theatre**.

From late June to late August, **The School at Jacob's Pillow** in Becket, Massachusetts, hosts the famous Jacob's Pillow Dance Festival. This brilliant celebration attracts some of the world's top performers and highlights all styles of dance.

THEATER

THEATER IS ALIVE and well on stages throughout New England's six states. The epicenter of this dynamic world is, of course, Boston. The city's Theater District (see pp70–71) remains the most architecturally eminent group of early theaters in the US. Moreover, the active houses were largely restored to their original grandeur during the 1990s. Commercial theaters such as the Wilbur, Colonial, and Shubert and the Wang Center generally program road shows of Broadway productions.

The most avant-garde contemporary theater in Boston is found at the **American Repertory Theatre** (ART). ART often premiers new plays, but is best known for often-radical interpretations of traditional and modern classics. By contrast, the **Huntington Theatre** is widely praised for its traditional interpretations.

Several smaller companies, including **Lyric Stage**, devote their energies to showcasing local actors and directors and often premiere the work of Boston-area playwrights. Many of the most adventurous companies perform on one of the three stages at the **Boston Center for the Arts**.

On Cape Cod, the **Wellfleet Harbor Actors Theatre** is the most provocative. The **Provincetown Repertory Theatre** maintains the town's reputation for adventurous work and the **Cape Playhouse** in Dennis is popular for summer theater.

Shakespeare & Company stages productions in its new home in Lenox, Massachusetts, where it is constructing an exact replica of the Elizabethan London playhouse The Rose of the late 1580s.

In Connecticut, at New Haven, the **Long Wharf Theatre** and **Yale Repertory Theatre** run acclaimed programs from October to May. Providence, Rhode Island, is home to another company with a deservedly sterling reputation, the **Trinity Repertory Company**, which has an entertaining and interesting mix of programs.

DIRECTORY

STATE ARTS COUNCILS

Connecticut
CT Commission on the Arts
(860) 566-4770.
W www.ctarts.org

Maine
Maine Performing Arts Network
(207) 942-7589.
W www.maineperforming arts.org
W www.mainemusic.org

Massachusetts
Massachusetts Cultural Council
(617) 727-3668.
W www.massculturalcouncil.org

New Hampshire
NH State Council on the Arts
(603) 271-2789.
W www.state.nh.us/nharts/

Rhode Island
RI State Council on the Arts
(401) 222-3880.
W www.risca.state.ri.us

Vermont
Vermont Council on the Arts
(802) 828-3291.
W www.vermontartscouncil.org

CLASSICAL MUSIC AND OPERA

Berkshire Opera Company
40 Railroad St,
Great Barrington, MA.
(413) 644-9988.
W www.berkshireopera.org

Boston Lyric Opera
Various venues,
Boston, MA.
(617) 542-4912.
W www.blo.org

Boston Symphony Orchestra
Symphony Hall,
301 Massachusetts Ave,
Boston, MA.
(617) 266-1492 or 266-1200.
W www.bso.org

Tanglewood Music Festival
297 West St,
Lenox, MA.
(413) 637-5165) (estate).
(617) 266-1492 (for listings).
W www.bso.org

DANCE

Boston Ballet
Various venues,
Boston, MA.
(617) 695-6950.
W www.bostonballet.org

Dance Complex
536 Massachusetts Ave,
Cambridge, MA.
(617) 547-9363.
W www.dancecomplex.org

Cutler Majestic Theatre
219 Tremont St,
Boston, MA.
(617) 824-8000.
W www.maj.org

Green Street Studios
185 Green St,
Cambridge, MA.
(617) 864-3191.
W www.greenstreetstudios.com

José Mateo's Ballet Theatre
1151 Massachusetts Ave,
Cambridge, MA.
(617) 354-7467.
W www.btb.org

The School at Jacob's Pillow
358 George Carter Rd,
Becket, MA.
(413) 637-1322.
W www.jacobspillow.org

Shubert Theatre
265 Tremont St,
Boston, MA.
(617) 482-9393.

Wang Center for the Performing Arts
270 Tremont St,
Boston, MA.
(617) 484-9393.
W www.wangcenter.org

THEATER

American Repertory Theatre
Loeb Drama Center,
64 Brattle St,
Cambridge, MA.
(617) 547-8300.
W www.amrep.org

Boston Center for the Arts
539 Tremont Ave,
Boston, MA.
(617) 426-2787.
W www.bcaonline.org

Cape Playhouse
Dennis, MA.
(508) 385-3911.
W www.capeplayhouse.com

Colonial Theatre
106 Boylston St,
Boston, MA.
(617) 426-9366.

Huntington Theatre
264 Huntington Ave,
Boston, MA.
(617) 266-0800.
W www.bu.edu/huntington

Long Wharf Theatre
222 Sargent Drive,
New Haven, CT.
(203) 787-4282.
W www.longwharf.org

Lyric Stage
140 Claredon St,
Boston, MA.
(617) 437-7172.
W www.lyricstage.com

Provincetown Repertory Theatre
Provincetown, MA.
(508) 487-0600.

Shakespeare & Company
70 Kemble St, Lenox, MA.
(413) 637-3353.
W www.shakespeare.org

Trinity Repertory Company
201 Washington St, Providence, RI.
(401) 521-1100 or
(401) 351-4242.
W www.trinityrep.com

Wellfleet Harbor Actors Theatre
Wellfleet, MA.
(508) 349-6835.
W www.WHAT.org

Wilbur Theatre
246 Tremont St,
Boston, MA.
(617) 423-4008.

Yale Repertory Theatre
1120 Chapel St,
New Haven, CT.
(203) 432-1234.
W www.yalerep.org

Outdoor Activities

SQUEEZED WITHIN NEW ENGLAND's relatively compact borders there is a wealth of outdoor activities. Mountain ranges, forests, rivers, and miles of coastline have been preserved as natural playgrounds for outdoor enthusiasts ranging from people just looking for a quiet afternoon in the sun to serious backcountry trekkers. While the majority of unspoiled wilderness is found in northern New England, the much more densely populated south has plenty of adventures in store for visitors as well.

Boston's Swan Boats awaiting those looking for gentle cruises

Camping in White Mountain National Forest, New Hampshire

CAMPING

ALWAYS A POPULAR activity in New England, camping can also save you money on accommodations – depending on how much you are willing to rough it. While there are designated primitive camping areas in the backcountry of selected national forests, the more established campgrounds make up the majority of sites. Standard campgrounds, usually found in state and national forests, are equipped with facilities such as toilets, garbage disposal, and often facilities for hot showers. The tent sites at such places are usually spaced well apart and cost between $12 and $20 a night. For the

hardcore camper, primitive campsites found in national forests offer only the bare minimum: rudimentary cooking areas, pit toilets, and cold running water. These sites are perfect for the frugal outdoor enthusiast, usually costing around $10 a night.

On the opposite end of the spectrum, private campgrounds are models of luxury. Most cater to large recreational vehicles (RVs) and motor homes, with running water and electrical hookups. Hot showers and sewage hookups are often provided as well. Many upscale campgrounds have a host of recreational facilities that range from swimming to miniature golf courses. These sites are somewhat more expensive, costing $20 to $40 dollars or so a night.

Government-run campgrounds usually follow the summer season from the end of May through to early October. For the most part, private campgrounds have a much longer season, with some staying open year-round. Regardless of the type of camping that will be

done, it is always a good idea to reserve a campsite early, especially during the busy summer months. Contact the **National Park Service** or the **National Recreation Reservation Service** for campground information and reservations. Always remember to notify someone of your itinerary and your approximate time of arrival at your destination should you decide to camp or hike by yourself.

HIKING

HIKING TRAILS crisscross almost all of New England, with the two most popular being the New England section of the Appalachian Trail *(see pp22–3)* and Vermont's 265-mile (426-km) Long Trail. Both trails can be quite challenging in spots, with extremely steep mountain climbs to stunning vistas. Maine's Baxter State Park *(see p298)* and New Hampshire's White Mountain National Forest *(see p265)* are both well known for their extensive networks of demanding trails. Not all nature walks need be difficult, however. Acadia National Park *(see pp288–9)* in Maine has an excellent system

Friendly welcome sign typical of campsites in New England

DIRECTORY

CANOEING AND RAFTING

Maine Island Trail Association
PO Box C, Rockland, ME 04841.
📞 *(207) 596-6456.*
🌐 *www.mita.org*

Raft Maine
PO Box 3, Bethel, ME 04217.
📞 *(207) 824-3694 or (800) 723-8633.*
🌐 *www.raftmaine.com*

HIKING AND BIKING

Appalachian Trail Conference
799 Washington St, PO Box 807, Harpers Ferry, WV 25425-0807.
📞 *(304) 535-6331.*
🌐 *www.appalachiantrail.org*

Green Mountain Club
4711 Waterbury-Stowe Rd, Waterbury Center, VT 05677.
📞 *(802) 244-7037.*
🌐 *www.greenmountainclub.org*

New England Hiking Holidays
PO Box 1648,
North Conway, NH 03860.
📞 *(603) 356-9696 or (800) 869-0949.*
🌐 *www.nehikingholidays.com*

Rails-to-Trails Conservancy
1100 17th St NW, 10th Floor, Washington, DC 20036.
📞 *(202) 331-9696.*
🌐 *www.railtrails.org*

Vermont Bicycle Touring
PO Box 711, Bristol, VT 05443.
📞 *(802) 453-4811 or (800) 245-3868.* 🌐 *www.vbt.com*

TECHNICAL OR ROCK CLIMBING

Acadia Mountain Guides Climbing School
36 Main St, Orono, ME 04473 or 198 Main St, Bar Harbor, ME 04609 (summer only).
📞 *(207) 866-7562 or (888) 232-9559.* 🌐 *www.acadiamountainguides.com*

Climb New Hampshire
🌐 *www.climbnh.com*

New England Climbing
🌐 *www.neclimbs.com*

Rhinoceros Mountain Guides
10 Mountain View Rd, Campton, NH 03223.
📞 *(603) 726-3030.*
🌐 *www.navbuoy.com/rhino/*

---

of easier hiking trails that lead past some of the most breathtaking coastal scenery. The **Rails-to-Trails Conservancy** provides information and maps on the almost 500 miles (800 km) of abandoned railroad tracks that have been converted into paths for cyclists and pedestrians alike. These paths stretch across a vast portion of New England. Companies such as **New England Hiking Holidays** organize excursions that last from two to five days.

Easy biking amid New England wildflowers

Hiking at Center Sandwich, New Hampshire

BIKING

IN ADDITION TO the more formal bike paths, the region possesses hundreds of miles of quiet back roads that are a cyclist's paradise. The pastoral scenery is beautiful, but the distances between towns are rarely so great that you will feel isolated. Cape Cod *(see pp154–59)* is famous for its wonderful bike paths, as is Nantucket *(see p153)* with its network of easy trails leading to pristine beaches. Many people believe that the best way to see Martha's Vineyard *(see pp152–3)*, Block Island *(see pp192–3)*, and the Litchfield Hills *(see pp208–209)* is by bike. Outfitters such as **Vermont Bicycle Touring** can help

organize bike tours for some of New England's most scenic regions, supplying everything from bicycles and protective gear to maps and accommodations.

Mountain bikers also have plenty to choose from. Some ski areas let bikers use their lifts and slopes in the summer, and many of the region's forests are open to biking. Acadia National Park, Mount Desert Island *(see pp288–9)*, and the White *(see p265)* and Green *(see p244)* mountains all have excellent facilities. To avoid damaging the surrounding environment, mountain bikers should stick to the marked trails. Cyclists should wear helmets and other protective gear.

FISHING

I F YOU LIKE TO FISH, you will love New England. Deepsea fishing is best at Point Judith in Rhode Island, where you can rent boats through the **Rhode Island Party and Charterboat Association**. Farther up the coast at Cape Cod, surfcasters test the waters for striped bass and bluefish, which are most plentiful between July and October. Brook trout, walleye, and bass are plentiful in the inland streams and lakes, especially in Maine. Contact the **Maine Sporting Camp Association** for information regarding the state's top fishing camps and lodges. Fly-fishermen seeking to hone their skills can do so in one of the highly regarded programs run by **Orvis** in Manchester, Vermont. Freshwater fishing licenses are mandatory throughout New England and can be obtained at fishing supply stores.

Turbulent rapids in one of New England's mountain rivers

CANOEING, KAYAKING, AND WHITE-WATER RAFTING

M AINE IS THE premier destination for paddlers, beginning with sea kayakers who flock here each summer to ply the waters along the 3,500-mile (5,630-km) coast. One of the state's most popular excursions is the 325-mile (525-km) Maine Island Trail, which goes from Portland to Machias.

Maine's latticework of rivers is ideal for canoeing, with its most famous trek being down the challenging Allagash Wilderness Waterway *(see*

Large striped bass, trophy from Woods Hole, Massachusetts

p299). New Hampshire's Androscoggin River is another demanding waterway best tested by experienced paddlers. Canoeists looking for a more leisurely ride can skim across the calm waters of northern New England's lakes and ponds.

White-water rafting is the paddler's roller-coaster ride and, once again, Maine is the region's best theme park. The state's three major rivers, the Penobscot, Kennebec, and Dead, offer gut-wrenching tests of rafters' skills. **Raft Maine** will put you in touch with the proper outfitter. New Hampshire's Saco River is another favorite among the white-water set.

BOATING

N EW ENGLAND'S reputation as one of the world's great cruising areas is well deserved. The thousands of miles of shoreline are dotted with hundreds of anchorages. Penobscot Bay, Maine, and Newport, Rhode Island, are both considered sailing meccas. For those who want something a little calmer than the Atlantic Ocean, New England has countless lakes, large and small, including popular cruising destinations such as Sebago Lake, Lake Champlain, and Lake Winnipesaukee. Boat rentals are available at many seaside and lakeside resorts in New

England. A few outlets will rent a large sailboat for a day or night. These so-called "bareboat charters" are only for experienced sailors, particularly in Maine, where water and weather conditions can be treacherous. **Hinckley Yacht Charters** in Southwest Harbor, Maine, is one of New England's larger companies, with 25 crafts available. This company will also provide fully crewed yacht charters.

Top-notch windsurfing sites and rentals are also available at many locations up and down the coast.

CRUISES

W HALE-WATCHING cruises have become one of the region's most popular activities, with more and more coastal towns trying to cash in. Not quite an exact science, a successful whale-watching trip relies both on the experience of the ship's captain and on the guidance offered by high-tech sounding gear to find these majestic mammals. Most companies will offer a rain check if no whales are sighted.

Plan whale-watching trips carefully. Choose a calm day. Choppy water causes most people to become seasick. If you fear you will get sick, buy some ginger capsules at a health food store and take the recommended dose just before boarding.

Sightseeing and nature cruises are also available throughout New England. For a different view of the city, **Boston Harbor Cruises**

Group rafting run on the Cold River at Charlemont, Massachusetts

DIRECTORY

BIRD-WATCHING

**United States
Fish and
Wildlife Service**
Regional Office,
300 Westgate Center Dr,
Hadley, MA 01035-9589.
((413) 253-8200.
w http://northeast.fws.gov/

**Connecticut
Audubon
Society**
2325 Burr St,
Fairfield, CT 06430.
((203) 259-6305 or
(800) 996-8747.
w www.ctaudubon.org

**Maine Audubon
Society**
20 Gilsland Farm Rd,
Falmouth, ME 04105.
((207) 781-2330.
w www.maineaudubon.org

**Massachusetts
Audubon Society**
208 S Great Rd, Lincoln, MA
01773. ((781) 259-9500 or
(800) 283-8266.
w www.massaudubon.org

**Audubon Society of New
Hampshire**
3 Silk Farm Rd,
Concord, NH 03301.
((603) 224-9909.
w www.nhaudubon.org

**Audubon Society of
Rhode Island**
12 Sanderson Rd,
Smithfield, RI 02917-2600.
((401) 949-5454.
w www.asri.org

Audubon Vermont
255 Sherman Hollow Rd,
Huntington, VT 05462.
((802) 434-3068.
w www.audubon.org/chapter/vt/

BOATING

**Hinckley Yacht
Charters**
Great Harbor Marina,
PO Box 950,
Southwest Harbor, ME 04679.
((800) HYC-SAIL or
(207) 244-5008.
w www.hinckleycharters.com

CAMPING

**National Park Service
Northeast Region**
Custom House, 200 Chestnut St,
Philadelphia, PA 19106.
((800) 365-2267 or
(215) 597-7013. w www.nps.gov

**National Recreation
Reservation Service**
40 South St,
Balliston Spa, NY 12020.
((518) 885-3639 or (877) 444-
6777. w www.reserveusa.com

**Connecticut Campground
Owners Association**
14 Rumford St,
West Hartford, CT 06107.
((860) 521-4704.
w www.campconn.com

**Maine Campground
Owners Association**
655 Main St,
Lewiston, ME 04240.
((207) 782-5874.
w www.campmaine.com

**New Hampshire
Campground Owners
Association**
PO Box 320,
Twin Mountain, NH 03595.
((800) 822-6764.
w www.ucampnh.com

**Bureau of Outdoor
Recreation, State Parks
Division**
79 Elm St, Hartford, CT 06106.
((860) 424-3200.
w www.dep.state.ct.us/rec/

**Maine Bureau of
Parks and Lands**
286 Water St,
Augusta, ME 04333.
((207) 287-3821.
w www.state.me.us/doc/parks

**Massachusetts Division
of Forests and Parks**
251 Causeway St, Suite 600,
Boston, MA 02114.
((617) 626-1250.
w www.state.ma.us/dem/
forparks

**New Hampshire Division
of Parks and Recreation**
PO Box 1856,
Concord, NH 03302.
((603) 271-3556.
w www.nhparks.state.nh.us

**Rhode Island Department
of Parks and Recreation**
2321 Hartford Ave,
Johnston,
RI 02919-1719.
((401) 222-2632.
w www.riparks.com

**Vermont Department
of Forests, Parks
and Recreation**
103 S Main St,
Waterbury, VT 05671.
((802) 241-3655.
w www.vtstateparks.com

CRUISES

**Bar Harbor Whale
Watch Company**
1 West St,
Bar Harbor, ME, 04609.
((800) WHALES-4 or
(207) 288-2386.
w www.whalesrus.com

Boston Harbor Cruises
One Long Wharf,
Boston, MA 02110.
((617) 227-4320.
w www.bostonharborcruises.com

FISHING AND
HUNTING

**Maine Sporting
Camp Association**
PO Box 119, Millinocket, ME 04462.
((207) 723-6622.
w www.mainesportingcamps.com

**Rhode Island Party and
Charterboat Association**
PO Box 3198,
Narragansett, RI 02882.
((401) 737-5812.
w www.rifishing.com

Orvis
Rte 7A, Manchester, VT 05254.
((802) 362-3622 or
(888) 235-9763.
w www.orvis.com

HANG GLIDING
AND PARAGLIDING

**Vermont Hang Gliding
Association**
w www.vhga.org

Morningside Flight Park
357 Morningside Lane,
Charlestown, NH 03603.
((603) 542-4416.
w www.flymorningside.com

Boats at pier in Edgartown Harbor, Martha's Vineyard

offers sunset tours throughout the summer. River cruises are available on several New England waterways, including both the Charles and the Connecticut rivers in Massachusetts and Connecticut's Mystic River.

Windjammer cruises are also popular at many coastal towns in Massachusetts, Rhode Island, and Maine.

BIRD-WATCHING

Wᴵᵀᴴ ɪᴛꜱ ᴅɪᴠᴇʀꜱᴇ habitats, ranging from mountains to coastal marshes and sand flats to conifer and mixed hardwood forests, New England offers some of the most interesting birding in the United States.

Massachusetts, home to the first Audubon Society in America, is famous for several areas, most notably the north-east coast at Newburyport, Cape Cod, and around the Berkshires. At Machias Seal Island, Maine, birders have a good opportunity to sight nesting colonies of Atlantic puffins. Special boat excursions to the island are offered by local charters.

National parks along with national wildlife refuges and protection areas are often the best places to bird since they are protected and unspoiled. **The US Fish and Wildlife Service** can provide

information on the location of refuges and the birding opportunities at each. Every state's **Audubon Society** will provide information on birding in the state as well as on Audubon field trips to various hotspots.

GOLF

Nᴇᴡ ᴇɴɢʟᴀɴᴅ has more than its share of outstanding golf courses – in all price ranges and at all levels of difficulty.

Dedicated golf vacationers have a choice between some stunning coastal and mountain resorts. Of the former, Samoset Resort, located in Rockport, Maine, stands out above all the rest.

With ocean views on 14 holes, Samoset has been called the most visually appealing course in New England. Two other terrific coastal links, the Seaside course at New Seabury and the Ocean Edge Resort and Golf Club, are located on Cape Cod. For a full-fledged mountain golf holiday, consider the Equinox resort in Manchester, Vermont.

It features a championship 1927 Walter J. Travis design surrounded by the Green Mountains. Some famous ski destinations offer great golf as well. In western Maine, Sugarloaf/USA Golf Club presents a memorable Robert Trent Jones, Jr. layout that *Golf Digest* has ranked among the top ten for both memorability and aesthetics. Mount Snow is ranked as one of Vermont's top five courses. Both courses also offer summer golf schools, as does Quechee in Vermont. Other worthwhile mountain courses include The Balsams in north-

Signature of New England: a beautiful golf course

eastern New Hampshire and Cranwell Resort and Golf Club in the Berkshires.

TECHNICAL OR ROCK CLIMBING

W ITH NEW ENGLAND'S Green Mountains and White Mountains, it's little surprise that this part of the country offers some great climbing.

In Maine the vast majority of cliff climbing falls along its rugged south coast, with high-quality routes in a setting that is truly stunning. Acadia National Park is the most popular destination. Alpine climbers will also find a worthy test in Maine. Mount Katahdin, the state's highest peak, has some of the longest routes in New England.

New England's best climbing, however, is found in New Hampshire, where Cannon Cliff, Cathedral Ledge, and Whitehorse Ledge make up a triumvirate of diverse, challenging peaks. New Hampshire also offers bouldering and sport climbing at several sites, the best of which is Rumney in the center part of the state.

Connecticut and Rhode Island are not especially famed for their climbing, but both offer several quite good bouldering sites, most notably at Lincoln Woods, Rhode Island.

Climbing in Massachusetts is varied, with the central area of the state offering longer scenic routes and Boston providing some of the country's best urban cragging.

Vermont has few developed sites, though the treacherous sport of ice climbing is practiced at Smuggler's Notch and Lake Willoughby.

HUNTING

W ITH ITS WIDE range of game spread across its diverse woodlands, New England offers something for every hunter. The hunting seasons are concentrated in the late summer and fall, with limited exceptions. Hunters in

Climber in bold ascent of New Hampshire's White Mountains

Ruffed grouse

all six states require licenses. In most cases, the fees are significantly higher for out-of-state hunters. Guns must be kept unloaded during transport in all states, and in some of them, a secure transport case is mandatory. There are also regulations that govern transport of game out-of-state. For specific information on regulations in each state, contact the government department responsible for wildlife management in that state.

HANG GLIDING AND PARAGLIDING

G OOD HANG gliding and paragliding sites abound in New England. That's no surprise, considering the large number of accessible places throughout the Green Mountains and the White Mountains. The best place to start is Morningside Flight Park in Charlestown, New Hampshire. It is the only full-time flight school and flying center in New England, and it has a 450-ft (137-m) summit launch site on the premises. Not far away in Vermont, Mount Ascutney is known as the premier cross-country hang-gliding site in New England, with flights having reached the Atlantic coast.

Southern New England is not without its advantages, however. Two of the best sand cliff launches are located in Cape Cod, Massachusetts, and Block Island, Rhode Island. Training is essential before attempting these sports. It is important to check local regulations before making any flight. You will find that many sites require memberships or have strict guidelines about landing areas. At state sites in Vermont, gliders must sign a waiver before making any flight. Contact the state association or a local club before making any jump.

Daring way to view the Berkshires at North Adams, Massachusetts.

Winter Activities

Snowmobile

FAR FROM LAMENTING the end of the stunning fall foliage season, New Englanders instead begin readying themselves for winter activities. Skis and snowboards are pulled out and dusted off, snowmobiles are tuned up, and skates are sharpened in anticipation of cold weather and the slate of outdoor fun it brings. In New England top-notch ski hills and cross-country ski and snowmobiling trails are never far away. This is especially true in the region's northernmost reaches, where the annual blanket of snow is thickest and, for outdoor enthusiasts, most inviting.

Sleigh ride through Hancock Shaker Village in Pittsfield, Massachusetts

SKIING

PEOPLE HAVE been downhill skiing on New England's rounded peaks for more than a century. While the region does not have the elevation of the Rockies, it does offer many large hills, some with a vertical rise of more than 2,000 ft (610 m). The best skiing and snowboarding is concentrated in the three northern states. Vermont has the most high-quality peaks, with **Killington** offering the most trails at 200. But it is **Stowe** that can claim the title of New England's ski capital. A world-famous resort set in the quaint village of the same name, Stowe has the state's highest peak and offers excellent trails for skiers of all levels. For the experienced skier, **Mad River Glen** near Waitsfield provides a stern test in one of the most pristine settings in the world. It also forbids snowboarding.

The White Mountains in New Hampshire have a plethora of good ski hills; downhill, alpine, and cross-country trails are arguably the best in the Northeast. In Maine, **Sugarloaf/USA** and **Sunday River** are considered to be the best hills in the state.

Downhill ski trails in New England are accurately rated following a standard code: Easier = green circle; More Difficult = blue square; Most Difficult = black diamond; and Expert = double diamond. Rental equipment is available at all resorts, as are skiing and snowboarding lessons for all levels. Where price is concerned, in general, the larger, more famous resorts charge more for lift tickets. If you have time, look for off-site sellers. They typically offer reduced prices. Also ask about package deals and senior or child discounts.

Cross-country ski trails are also plentiful in New England. Towns such as Craftsbury Common, Vermont, and **Jackson, New Hampshire** have miles of groomed trails. State parks also often provide good trails. These are good areas for other winter activities such as sliding and snowshoeing. **Catamount Trail**, set aside for skiers and snowshoers, runs 300 miles (482 km) down the length of Vermont. Many renowned downhill resorts also offer cross-country trails. The trails at the **Trapp Family Lodge Ski Center** in Stowe are considered among the best in New England.

Low in the turn at Vermont's majestic Stowe resort

SNOWMOBILING

S NOWMOBILING is extremely popular all across New England, but Maine is truly the mecca for this activity. The state is interconnected by 12,500 miles (20,000 km) of trails and has more than 85,000 registered snow-mobiles using them. Resorts such as **Northern Outdoors** in The Forks and the **New England Outdoor Center** in Millinocket will rent snow-mobiles and accommodations, and supply guides for excursions. Most agencies require that renters have a valid driver's license.

SKATING

I N WINTER, New England has plenty of frozen lakes and rivers for skating. Always check with local authorities to be sure the ice is safe.

Winter also brings droves of bundled-up skaters to the Boston Commons Frog Pond in Boston. Rentals are available in the warm-up shed or alternatively at the **Beacon Hall Skate Shop**. The **Metropolitan District Commission** also runs 23 indoor rinks in Boston, Cambridge, and the surrounding communities.

Freestyle skiing, common at New England ski resorts

SURVIVAL
GUIDE

PRACTICAL INFORMATION

NEW ENGLAND OFFERS a wide variety of recreational activities within a relatively small area. Vacationers can hike the White Mountains of New Hampshire in the morning, swim at Maine's Ogunquit Beach in the afternoon, and take in the Boston Symphony Orchestra at night. Because tourism is such an important part of the regional economy, visitors will find numerous agencies and facilities geared toward making their stay an enjoyable one. Accommodations and restaurants (see

Acadia welcome sign

pp302–345) come in all price ranges, allowing you to sleep and eat in comfort while staying on budget. For people without cars, transportation is readily available in Boston and throughout the six states (see pp375–9). The following pages offer some practical advice for people traveling in the New England states. Personal Security and Health (see pp370–71) outlines some general guidelines, while Banking/Currency and Communications (see pp372–3) answers some basic financial and media queries.

WHEN TO GO

NEW ENGLAND IS a four-season vacation destination but is particularly popular in the summer and fall. Generally speaking, the peak tourist period is from mid-June, when schools let out, through October. During this time accommodations and restaurant reservations can be hard to come by, especially in the busy resort towns along the coast. There is another rush during fall-foliage season (see pp20–21), which lasts from sometime in mid-September to late October. During this month-long stretch the hotels and B&Bs farther inland near the woods are booked solid. The length of the ski season depends entirely on the weather. It is not unheard of for New England winters to run from late November right

Enough signs to keep visitors busy in Center Sandwich, New Hampshire

through March, during which time New Hampshire and Vermont, which possess the bulk of New England's ski centers (see pp362–3), are busiest. If you are planning a backwoods vacation, it is prudent to avoid wooded areas in April and May, when the ground can be extremely muddy and swarms of hungry black flies fill the air. Don't be fooled by their small size; they have a big bite.

ENTRY REQUIREMENTS

ALL TRAVELERS to New England and the rest of the US should have a passport valid for six months longer than their intended period of stay. Those holding citizenship in the UK, most western European countries, Australia, New Zealand, and Japan require a passport, but do not need a visa if their stay is less than 90 days and

they hold a return ticket. Canadian residents require only proof of residence with a photo ID. Citizens of all other countries require a valid passport and a tourist visa, which can be obtained at a US consulate or embassy for a charge of around $45. Always make sure to have your passport with you in a secure place, such as a money belt.

CUSTOMS ALLOWANCES

VISITORS OVER THE age of 21 are permitted to enter the US with two pints (1 l) of alcohol, 200 cigarettes, 50 cigars or four lbs (2 kg) of smoking tobaccos, and gifts worth up to $100. Prohibited items include meat products, cheese, and all fresh fruit. Travelers entering the country with more than $10,000 in cash or in traveler's checks must declare the money to customs officials upon entry.

Snowboarding, popular with the young, daring, and fit

TAXES IN NEW ENGLAND

State	Lodging	Meal	Sales
Connecticut	12%	6%	6%
Maine	7%	7%	5%
Massachusetts	12.5%	5%	5%
New Hampshire	8%	8%	–
Rhode Island	13%	7%	7%
Vermont	9%	9%	5%

TOURIST INFORMATION

STATE TOURISM offices are excellent sources of information and are happy to send road maps, brochures, and listings of accommodations, seasonal events, and attractions free of charge. Some offices also carry discount vouchers for lodging, restaurants, and admission fees. Tourist information booths or welcome centers are equipped with toilets and rest areas are usually found upon entering states on major highways. Many towns maintain a visitors' bureau that dispenses information on local activities, lodgings, and restaurants.

OPENING HOURS

OFFICES ARE generally open from 9am to 5pm Monday to Friday and do not close for lunch. Most stores keep hours from 9 or 10am to 6pm Monday to Saturday, although they often stay open until 9 or 10pm on Thursday and Friday. More and more stores are opening on Sunday. Most New England banks are open from 9am to 3 or 4pm Monday to Friday. Many banks are open on Saturday mornings from 9am to noon or 1pm. The larger museums are usually open 10am to 5pm Tuesday through Sunday, but

Making the most of summer weather at outdoor cafés

check with the hours listed in this guide. Smaller museums may have seasonal hours and often shut down during the winter. An increasing number of gas stations and convenience stores now stay open 24 hours a day.

ALCOHOL AND CIGARETTES

THE LEGAL drinking age throughout New England is 21, and most young people will be asked to produce a photo ID as proof of age in order to buy alcohol or enter a bar. Your passport is usually your best bet. Drinking in public spaces is against the law, and the

penalties for driving under the influence of alcohol are severe, including the loss of your driver's license.

Cigarettes can be sold only to people 18 years of age or older. It is against the law to smoke in public buildings, such as hospitals, and on public conveyances, including subways and buses. Some restaurants still permit smoking in designated sections, although more and more are completely "smoke-free."

ELECTRICITY

ELECTRICITY FLOWS at the standard US110-120 volts AC (alternating current). Foreign-made electrical appliances may require a US-style plug adapter and a voltage converter.

TAXES

TAXES VARY ON a state-by-state basis. There is no federal sales tax, but all New England states, with the exception of New Hampshire, levy their own sales tax. All states charge taxes on hotel rooms and restaurant meals and some cities have additional taxes. Many accommodations tack on additional surcharges such as housekeeping and parking fees to bills that can increase the total by up to 15 percent. To avoid unpleasant surprises at the end of a stay, visitors should inquire about extra service charges before they check in.

TIPPING

ALTHOUGH THERE are no set guidelines for tipping, a gratuity is usually given for most services. Travelers should give waiters 15 to 20 percent of the bill, bartenders 50¢ to $1 per drink, barbers 15 percent of the bill, and taxi drivers between 12 and 18 percent of the fare. Porters usually get $1 per piece of luggage and hotel maids $1 per night of stay. Tipping is not usually required at fast-food restaurants, although there is sometimes a jar by the cash register for tips that will be shared by employees.

Mopeds, a popular form of transportation for visitors on the go

HOLIDAYS

WHILE EACH STATE may have its own set of holidays, some major public holidays are celebrated throughout the US. Visitors should keep in mind that on these days schools, banks, and government offices are closed. Museums and transportation services operate on limited schedules, but many retail stores and restaurants maintain regular business hours.

New Year's Day
Jan 1.
Martin Luther King, Jr. Day
3rd Mon in Jan.
President's Day
3rd Mon in Feb.
Memorial Day
Last Mon in May.
Independence Day
Jul 4.
Labor Day
1st Mon in Sep.
Columbus Day
2nd Mon in Oct.
Veterans' Day
Nov 11.
Thanksgiving
4th Thu in Nov.
Christmas Day
Dec 25.

Patriotic decorations for Independence Day

Youngsters taking a break from sightseeing on a New England wharf

TRAVELING WITH CHILDREN

NEW ENGLAND is a fairly child-friendly place. Many museums, zoos, and aquariums offer hands-on and interactive exhibits that encourage younger participants. The multitude of state parks and forests and public beaches give children lots of space to burn excess energy.

Many establishments and services cater to families by having children's menus and reduced admission rates. Most hotels and motels will charge $10 to $20 per cot so that children can stay in the same room as their parents. The same is generally not true for inns and bed and breakfasts (B&Bs), some of which will not take children under a certain age.

STUDENT TRAVELERS

STUDENTS FROM abroad should buy an **International Student Identification Card** (ISIC) before traveling to New England. Numerous discounts are available to cardholders at such places as hostels, museums, and theaters. This is especially true in Boston. The **Student Advantage Card** is a similar card and is available to all American university students. It is advisable for young travelers to carry their passports or driver's license for entry into bars or to buy alcohol in restaurants.

SENIOR CITIZENS

SENIORS ARE ELIGIBLE for a myriad of discounts ranging from car rentals and lodgings to national parks and museums. Depending on the place, the minimum qualifying age for seniors can be as low as 50. Visitors should contact the **American**

Easy bird-watching at Claremont Hotel, Southwest Harbor, Maine

Association of Retired Persons (AARP) for more information. Also, travelers should try the Boston-based, international senior travel organization **Elderhostel**. The organization offers discount lodgings, educational programs, and field trips throughout New England and the US for travelers over the age of 55.

DISABLED TRAVELERS

WHILE US FEDERAL LAW requires that businesses are accessible to the disabled, some historic buildings have limited access for wheelchairs. Most hotels and restaurants are equipped for people with special needs, and more and more small inns are retrofitting some of their rooms. Many outdoor recreation areas, including all national parks, now provide rest rooms and facilities for the disabled, including tour buses and wheelchair-friendly trails. The best advice for disabled travelers is to call ahead or to contact organizations such as the **Society for the Advancement of Travel for the Handicapped** or Mobility International. Both groups provide information and comprehensive guides on the issues of accessibility for the disabled.

Celebration of the first same-sex civil union in Vermont

GAY AND LESBIAN TRAVELERS

NEW ENGLAND has a number of vibrant gay communities. Most notable is Provincetown *(see pp156–7)* on northernmost Cape Cod. Other gay enclaves include Ogunquit *(see pp278–9)*, Maine, and Boston's South End. *Bay Windows*, New England's largest gay and lesbian weekly, includes arts and cultural listings for all six states, as well as local and regional news. Vermont, which became the first state in the US to legally acknowledge same-sex civil unions, has a well regarded monthly news-letter called *Out in the Mountains*.

DIRECTORY

TOURIST INFORMATION

Connecticut Office of Tourism
505 Hudson St,
Hartford, CT 06105.
(860) 270-8080 or (800) 282-6863.
www.ctbound.org

Greater Boston Convention and Visitors Bureau
2 Copley Place, Suite 105,
Boston, MA 02116.
(888) SEE BOSTON or (617) 536-4100.
www.bostonusa.com

Maine Office of Tourism
59 State House Station,
Augusta, ME 04333-0059.
(207) 287-5711 or (888) 624-6345.
www.visitmaine.com

Massachusetts Office of Travel & Tourism
10 Park Plaza, Suite 4510,
Boston, MA 02116.
(617) 973-8500 or (800) 227-6277.
www.massvacation.com

New Hampshire Division of Travel & Tourism Development
172 Pembroke Rd, PO Box 1856,
Concord, NH 03302.
(603) 271-2665 or (800) FUN-IN-NH.
www.visitnh.gov

Rhode Island Tourism Division
1 West Exchange St,
Providence, RI 02903.
(401) 222-2601 or (800) 556-2484.
www.visitrhodeisland.com

Vermont Department of Tourism and Marketing
6 Baldwin St, Drawer 33,
Montpelier, VT 05633-1301.
(802) 828-3237 or (800) VERMONT.
www.1-800-vermont.com

STUDENTS

International Student Identity Card (ISIC)
6 Hamilton Place,
4th floor, ID Dept,
Boston, MA 02108.
(800) 2COUNCIL.
www.counciltravel.com

Student Advantage Card
280 Summer St,
Boston, MA 02210.
(617) 912-2011 or (800) 333-2920.
www.studentadvantage.com

SENIOR CITIZENS

American Association of Retired Persons (AARP)
601 E St NW,
Washington, DC 20049.
(800) 424-3410.
www.aarp.org

Elderhostel
11 Ave de Lafayette, Boston,
MA 02111. *(617) 426-7788 or (877) 426-8056.*
www.elderhostel.org

GAY AND LESBIAN

Bay Windows
631 Tremont St,
Boston, MA 02118.
(617) 266-6670.
www.baywindows.com

Out in the Mountains
PO Box 1078,
Richmond VT 05477.
(802) 434-6486.
www.mountainpridemedia.org

DISABLED VISITORS

Society for Accessible Travel and Hospitality
347 Fifth Ave, Suite 610,
New York City,
NY 10016.
(212) 447-7284.
www.sath.org

USEFUL WEBSITES

NewEngland.com
www.newengland.com

Visit New England.com
www.visitnewengland.com

Boston Globe Online
www.boston.com

Boston Citysearch
boston.citysearch.com

Personal Security and Health

Park Ranger

NEW ENGLAND'S COMPARATIVELY low crime rate makes it a safe vacation destination. Even its largest metropolitan area, Boston, has seen crime on a steady decrease since the early 1990s. Nonetheless, it is always a good idea for travelers to take a few simple precautions to make sure that their trip is a safe one. This same rule of thumb applies to the wilderness areas. Almost free of crime, these areas possess a number of natural hazards that can be minimized.

Motorized police patrol on Surfside Beach, Nantucket, Massachusetts

LAW ENFORCEMENT

THREE AGENCIES share law enforcement duties: city police, sheriffs (who patrol county areas), and the state Highway Patrol, which deals with traffic accidents and offenses outside city boundaries. New England law enforcement officials are friendly and helpful.

EMERGENCIES

SHOULD YOU require emergency medical, police, or fire services, call 911. The call is free from public phones. Emergency phone boxes are located along major highways. **The Travelers' Aid Society** specializes in providing assistance for those travelers who find themselves stranded.

LEGAL ASSISTANCE

TRAVELERS FROM outside the US who are in need of legal assistance should immediately contact their nearest consulate or their embassy in Washington, D.C. Should you be arrested you have the right to remain silent and are given the right to make one phone call. The police will provide you with the embassy and consulate telephone numbers upon request.

GUIDELINES ON SAFETY

AS WITH ALL large urban centers, New England's major cities, including Boston, Burlington, Worcester, Springfield, New Haven, Hartford, Providence, and Portland, have pockets of crime. Generally speaking, the main tourist areas are safe as most of the problems occur in neighborhoods not usually frequented by travelers. While the numbers of street people or "panhandlers" in cities is on the rise, they are almost always harmless.

It is a good policy to avoid wandering into city neighborhoods that are off the beaten track. Pickpockets are sometimes at work in the busy centers and will target anyone who looks like a tourist. Your best defense is common sense. Avoid wearing expensive jewelry and carry cameras and camcorders securely. As well, you should carry only small amounts of cash. Credit cards and traveler's checks are the most secure options. Money belts or pouches worn under clothing provide maximum security against pickpockets, especially in crowded areas such as buses and malls. While theft in hotels is not common, it is prudent to store valuables in the safe when you are out.

Always lock your car when you leave it and store bags and valuables in the trunk. Valuables left in the open in unattended cars are easy targets for smash-and-grab thieves. In major urban areas it is best to avoid walking through parks or strange neighborhoods at night. Always use automatic teller machines (ATM) on busier, well-lit streets.

Before you leave home, make a photocopy of important documents, including your passport and visa, and keep them with you, but separate from the originals. Also make a note of the numbers of your traveler's checks and credit cards, in the event they are stolen.

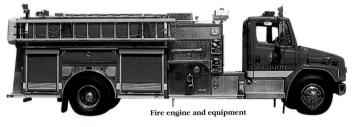

Fire engine and equipment

Lost and Stolen Property

Although the chances of retrieving lost or stolen property are very slim, report all missing items to the police and make sure you get a copy of the police report for your insurance claim. In the event of a loss or a theft, it is useful to have a record of your valuables' serial numbers and receipts as proof of possession. If you have misplaced something, retracing your steps can also help: try to remember the taxi companies and bus or train routes you were using when the item went missing. Most taxi and transport companies have Lost and Found departments which can be reached by phoning the general access phone number.

Passport

A stolen passport should be reported immediately to your country's embassy or consulate. Most credit card companies have toll-free numbers to report a lost or stolen card, as do Thomas Cook and American Express for lost traveler's checks (see right), which can often be replaced within a few hours.

Travel Insurance

The US does not have a national health program and, as a result, emergency medical and dental care, though excellent, can be very expensive. Medical travel insurance is highly recommended in order to defer some costs related to an unscheduled stop in a US hospital. Even with medical coverage you may have to pay for services

Passports, easily stolen from careless visitors

when you receive them, then claim reimbursement from your insurance company later. Make sure the insurance policy you choose covers trip cancellation and baggage or document loss, emergency medical care, and accidental death.

Outdoor safety

New England offers a wide variety of outdoor recreational activities, some of which entail certain risks. Helmets and other protective items are essential, and often mandatory, for such activities as white-water rafting and mountain biking, as are life jackets for all types of boating. Hikers should always stay on marked trails; those who are hiking or camping alone should notify someone of their destination and estimated time of arrival. Campers should never feed animals and should suspend food from a tree branch to avoid visits from bears. If you see a bear in the distance, yell and wave your arms so as not to surprise it, then back away. If the bear is close, don't look it in the eyes. Back away slowly, while talking softly. Do not run.

Hiking trail marker

Campfires should be carefully extinguished with water. Mountain hikers and rock climbers should always be prepared for sudden changes in the weather. Ocean swimmers are advised to use beaches with lifeguards and should ask about undertows. Wear a hat and apply sun block in summer. Hikers would be smart to wear bright-colored clothes and avoid forests and fields during hunting season. To avoid any risk of catching Lyme Disease from tics, always cover up well when walking through woods and fields.

Ambulance

Banking/Currency and Communications

Because many New England banks outside of Boston do not exchange foreign currency, travelers from abroad should plan to use their credit cards, US-dollar traveler's checks, or, most conveniently, Automatic Teller Machine (cash machine) cards. Never carry all your money and credit cards with you at the same time, and keep in mind that most banks and foreign currency exchanges are closed on Sundays.

A dollar bill ($1), a quarter (25¢), pennies (1¢), and a nickel (5¢)

BANKING

Most New England banks are open from 9am to 3 or 4pm Monday to Friday. Many banks are open on Saturday mornings from 9am to noon or 1pm. All banks are closed on Sunday and public holidays.

Traveler's checks can usually be cashed at banks with a recognized photo ID, such as a passport. Main branches of national banks are located in the large urban areas and will exchange foreign currency for a small fee. It is always a good idea to ask about hidden service charges or commissions before you make a transaction. In general, you will get the best rates at big city banks or private exchange bureaus in larger centers.

The most commonly accepted credit cards in New England

AUTOMATIC TELLER MACHINES

Automatic teller machines (ATMs) are found throughout New England, even in tiny country villages. Look for them in bank foyers or just outside the entrances. ATMs are also found in airports, train stations, shopping malls, supermarkets, large gas stations, and along streets of most major cities. Widely found bank-card networks include Cirrus, Plus, NYCE, and Interlink. The machines also will dispense money to credit cards such as VISA or MasterCard. Before leaving home, ask your bank if your card can be used in New England. Bank cards can also be used to pay at many hotels, restaurants, retail stores, and gas stations.

CREDIT CARDS

The most commonly accepted credit cards in New England are MasterCard, VISA, and American Express, although Diner's Club and the Discover Card are gaining popularity. Credit cards can be used at restaurants, shops, and hotels, as well as to reserve tickets over the phone or to book a rental car. The biggest benefit of credit cards is that they offer you much more security than having to carry around large sums of cash, and they can be very useful in emergency situations.

TRAVELER'S CHECKS

The major advantage offered by traveler's checks is that, unlike cash, they can be refunded if they are lost or stolen. American Express and Thomas Cook traveler's checks are accepted in many US shops, restaurants, and hotels, especially in the major tourist centers. It is often easier to pay directly with US-dollar traveler's checks than cashing them in advance, and you will get your change in cash.

Banks and exchange bureaus will exchange your US-dollar traveler's checks directly into cash. Traveler's checks in foreign currency can be cashed at a bank or with a cashier at some major hotels. Exchange rates and commission charges are always posted and sometimes a little shopping around will save you some money. Personal checks drawn on overseas banks are rarely accepted in the US.

FOREIGN EXCHANGE

Once you are outside the major cities, you may find it difficult to exchange your foreign currency. Most foreign exchange offices are open from 9am to 5pm weekdays. Among the best-known agencies are **American**

Imaginative country mailboxes near Grafton, Vermont

Express Travel Agency and **Thomas Cook Currency Services**. For the best rates, avoid exchanging your money at airports or train or bus stations. Banks will usually give you the most favorable rates.

TELEPHONES

WHILE ALL New England pay phones accept coins (5¢, 10¢, and 25¢), more and more are being retooled to take phone and credit cards as well, especially in the major urban areas. Local calls cost between 25¢ and 35¢ for three minutes from pay phones, while long-distance rates vary and include both a fixed call charge and a per-minute charge. The easiest way to find out the ever-changing rates is to dial **0** and ask the operator. Do not get the operator to put the call through, however, as calling direct is substantially cheaper. Of course, dialing direct from your hotel room can carry hefty surcharges, meaning it is usually cheaper to place the call yourself using the pay phone in the lobby. Generally speaking, the least expensive times to make long-distance calls are between 11pm and 8am on weekdays and on weekends (except 5pm to 11pm on Sunday). During these periods, you can benefit from a discount of up to 60 percent.

All numbers with a **1-800**, **1-888**, or **1-877** prefix are free of charge, as is directory

assistance from a pay phone (dial **411** for local, **00** for international), and emergency services (**911**). Operator assistance (**0** for local, **01** for international) has a charge.

Mobile phones can be rented in many New England centers. Visitors from abroad who wish to bring their mobile phones with them should check with their providers before leaving home. Some plans do have international plans that cover the US, but it may be easier to rent a mobile phone once you are in the US.

POSTAL SERVICE

POST OFFICES ARE open weekdays from 9am to 5pm, with some branches offering service on Saturday. All are closed on Sunday and federal holidays. Letters and small parcels (less than 16 ounces) with the proper postage can be placed in any blue mailbox. Domestic mail takes one to five days for delivery – longer if you forget the zip code. You can speed up delivery by several days by paying for **Priority Mail** or **Express Mail**'s next-day delivery for domestic mail. It is faster to send overseas mail via airmail.

Public pay phone

COMMUNICATIONS AND MEDIA

THE MOST POPULAR US newspaper in terms of circulation is the *Wall Street*

Journal, followed by *USA Today*, *The New York Times*, and the *Los Angeles Times*. They can be found in virtually all major cities. The *Boston Globe* is the most well-respected and widely read newspaper coming out of New England. The *Boston Herald* is a popular tabloid-style daily. The region has many fine local newspapers.

Reality shows, soaps, sitcoms, and talk shows dominate the US television airwaves. Cable channels offer 24-hour access to sports, movies, music videos, and news. Public station PBS offers a more highbrow diet of documentaries, concerts, and classic films. Hotels usually have access to the major networks such as CBS, NBC, and ABC, as well as the more popular cable channels such as ESPN (specializing in sports) and CNN (the top news station).

In general, radio stations follow a specific programming format. Those stations on FM frequencies tend to stick to a particular type of music, be it rock, jazz, Top 40, or country western. AM stations are usually geared toward talk-radio shows in which listeners call in to discuss the issues of the day.

Surfing the Internet is fairly easy. Many New England libraries are plugged into the Internet and have terminals, although you may have to pay at some locations. Cyber cafés have declined in popularity, even in the larger cities. More and more hotels also offer Internet access.

Some of New England's many fine local newspapers

Getting to New England

WHILE THE MOST COMMON WAYS to get to New England are by plane or by car, train and bus services also provide decent access to many regions, particularly the southern New England states. Many people like to begin their vacation in Boston because the city's Logan International Airport handles international flights. Boston is also the hub for rail and bus services coming in from all over the US and parts of Canada.

Bird's-eye view of Camden Harbor in Maine

ARRIVING BY AIR

BOSTON'S **LOGAN International Airport** (BOS) is the region's busiest, although some domestic and international carriers use **Worcester Airport** (ORH) in Worcester, Massachusetts, **T.F. Green Airport** (PVD) in Warwick, Rhode Island, which serves Providence, and **Bradley International Airport** (BDL) in Windsor Locks, Connecticut, which serves Hartford. A few major commercial airlines also fly into Bangor (BGR) and Portland (PWM), Maine; Manchester (MHT), New Hampshire; and Burlington (BTV), Vermont. Other gateways to New England include Montreal, Quebec, and, of course, New York City's three major airports.

Smaller domestic airlines cover specific geographical regions while also offering a few national flights. Although they have fewer flights than the major carriers, they often have substantially reduced fares. A number of regional commuter airlines shuttle passengers around New England, with small, single-prop planes flying to such destinations as Cape Cod and the various islands off the coast.

International travelers will be given a customs and immigration form during their flight and will be required to hand in the completed form to customs officials in the airport. At the immigration area there are two lines, one for US citizens and another for non-US citizens. If you are entering the country via New York's busy JFK, be forewarned that the immigration lines are often long and the process can be a time-consuming ordeal.

AIRFARES

IT IS ALWAYS BEST to plan your vacation early and to shop around for the best airfares; a little research can go a long way in terms of securing a substantial discount. For inexpensive consolidated tickets, contact **Intrepid Traveler** online or **IAATC** online. **CheapAirfare.com** gives you instant access to the best published prices on the web. Keep in mind that even with the small fees they may charge, travel agents are often your best allies in your search for savings.

The busiest times of year for travel to New England are June through September, as well as the major holidays of Christmas, Easter, Labor Day, and most especially Thanksgiving. Book flights during these periods well in advance. In general, you will get the lowest airfares if you plan to travel during non-peak periods of the year – for instance, prices drop substantially following Labor Day. It is almost always cheaper to fly in and out of New England on weekdays rather than on weekends.

Passenger jet in flight

AIRPORT	INFORMATION	DISTANCE FROM CITY
Logan International (Boston, MA)	(617) 561-1800	3 miles (4.8 km) from Downtown Boston
Worcester Airport (Worcester, MA)	(508) 799-1741	5 miles (8 km) from Downtown Worcester
T.F. Green Airport (Warwick, RI)	(401) 737-8222	10 miles (16 km) from Downtown Providence
Bradley Intl. (Windsor Locks, CT)	(860) 292-2000	12 miles (19 km) from Downtown Hartford

ARRIVING BY TRAIN

THE MAJOR AMERICAN RAILROAD is **Amtrak**. One of Amtrak's busiest routes services southern and central New England up to Boston. Amtrak recently unveiled its high-speed *Acela Regional* train service between New York and Boston, which has cut 90-minutes off regular travel time of about 6 hours. While it is available at a premium price, it is still less expensive than most airfares and has the added convenience of taking you from downtown to downtown without the added expense of taxis or shuttle buses. In November 2001, a rail service between Boston and Portland, Maine was inaugurated. During the summer, there is a stop at Old Orchard Beach in Maine.

Train station in North Conway, New Hampshire

Wheeled luggage

ARRIVING BY CAR

GETTING TO New England by car is relatively easy, and you have several options. Beginning in Florida, I-95, also known as Route 128 in the Boston area, is one of the most popular drives for travelers coming from the South. This major interstate highway sticks close to the coast as it passes through Connecticut and Providence, Rhode Island, en route to the outskirts of Boston. Circumventing the city, the highway continues up through New Hampshire and Maine before crossing the border into Canada. Drivers should note that truck traffic along I-95 can be particularly heavy, especially when approaching Boston.

The two major gateways into New England from the north are I-89 and I-91. The latter crosses from Canada into Vermont at Derby Line and then follows a relatively straight line south along the Vermont/New Hampshire border, through both central Massachusetts and Connecticut all the way down to New Haven. I-89 starts in Vermont's northwest-ernmost corner and then from Burlington cuts diagonally to Concord, New Hampshire where it links up with I-93 into Boston. The major western points of entry into New England are I-84 and I-90 from New York state.

ARRIVING BY BUS

AS IT STANDS, you can get just about anywhere in New England via bus, so long as you are not in a hurry. Many of the bus companies serve particular sections of New England. **Concord Trailways** has routes in Maine and New Hampshire, and **Vermont Transit** serves Vermont, Maine, and New Hampshire. **Bonanza** is the main Connecticut bus line, while **Peter Pan** has stops in Connecticut and western Massachusetts. Other parts of Massachusetts, most notably Cape Cod and the South Shore, are served by **Plymouth & Brockton**. **Greyhound Lines** is a nationwide carrier and has stops throughout New England. Greyhound works in conjunction with Bonanza, Vermont Transit, and Peter Pan lines. Most major bus lines offer discount rates for students and seniors (with proper ID), and offer unlimited travel during a set period.

A Greyhound bus

Driving in New England

Important road sign

W HILE FLYING IS THE FASTEST and most efficient way to get to New England, driving is by far the best way to explore the region. In fact, much of New England's charm is found along scenic jaunts down the coast and driving tours during fall-foliage season. It is important to remember that large areas of the region are essentially wild, so you should always be prepared for any eventuality, such as a breakdown. This is doubly true in the winter, when sudden blizzards and white-outs caused by blowing snow can leave motorists stranded. Boston's public transit system makes it possible to do without a car (see pp376–7), but once outside the city you will need a vehicle to do your best exploring.

A rented convertible, perfect for exploring in good weather

CAR RENTAL

T HE MAJOR CAR rental chains have outlets in most of New England's major cities and larger airports. These national chains include **Avis**, **Budget**, **Enterprise**, **Hertz**, **National**, **Rent-A-Wreck**, and **Thrifty**. While their rates are somewhat higher than smaller local companies, they usually offer extremely efficient service.

In order to rent a car, you must be 21 and possess a valid driver's license. People under 25 will sometimes have to pay a surcharge. A major credit card is usually required as well, unless you are prepared to put down a hefty cash deposit. Credit cards sometimes provide coverage against damage or theft of the vehicle, but it is wise to check what the terms are with your credit card company. Regardless, make sure that your car

rental agreement includes Collision Damage Waiver (CDW) – also known as Loss Damage Waiver (LDW) – or else you will be liable for any damage to the car, even if it was not your fault. This supplemental insurance can cost between $10 and $20 extra a day.

Sightseeing by car, stopping where and when you want

Country roads beckoning drivers to leave the crowds behind

SPEED LIMITS

I T IS IMPORTANT to pay attention to the signs, as speed limits can vary from one place to the next depending on your proximity to a town or city. In general, the maximum speed on an interstate highway varies from 55 to 65 mph (88–105 km/h). On smaller highways, it can range between 30 and 55 mph (50–88 km/h). Cities and towns set speed limits between 20 and 35 mph (32–56 km/h), drastically lower around hospitals and schools. Police often pick strategic points along highways – often right after a sign for lower speed – to set up their radar equipment in order to catch drivers who are going too fast. Do not try to pay tickets or fines directly to the police officer who pulled you over; this can be interpreted as attempted bribery and can land you deeper in hot water.

DRIVING TOURS

T HERE ARE A number of books on the market listing the best driving tours of the region. Some publications, such as **Yankee** magazine, include a complete itinerary of recommended routes, historic stops, and the best places to eat and stay. Tours vary from a single day to an entire week and take in everything from dramatic coastal scenery to tiny fishing villages to mountainous terrain and country towns.

expensive than those in other US cities, except New York. Taxis to Logan Airport are required to charge an airport use fee ($2); those coming from the airport charge for the harbor tunnel toll ($3). Additional surcharges may apply late at night. A full schedule of fares should be posted inside the vehicle.

Boston parkland, ideal for walking

The driver's photograph and permit and the taxi's permit number will also be posted inside all legitimate taxicabs, along with directions for reporting complaints.

WALKING IN BOSTON

Boston is considered North America's premier walking city, partly because it is so compact and partly because virtually all streets are flanked by sidewalks. It is nonetheless essential to wear comfortable walking shoes with adequate cushioning and good support.

Because Boston is principally a city of neighborhoods, it is often best to use public transportation to get to a particular neighborhood, and then walk around to soak up the atmosphere. Walking also allows you to see parts of the city that are impractical to explore by car because streets are too narrow; for example, Beacon Hill, parts of the North End, and Harvard Square.

DIRECTORY

SUBWAY AND BUSES

MBTA
(Route and schedule information)
10 Park Plaza.
☎ (617) 222-3200.
ⓦ www.mbta.com

TAXIS

Boston Cab Dispatch, Inc.
☎ (617) 262-2227.

Checker Cab Co.
(Cambridge)
☎ (617) 497-9000.

New Town Taxi
☎ (617) 536-5000.

Yellow Cab
(Cambridge)
☎ (617) 547-3000.

THE BOSTON "Ⓣ"

KEY

▬ Red line

▬ Green line (including green lines B, C, D, & E)

▬ Orange line

▬ Blue line

◯ Terminal station

●—● Interchange with other lines

MBTA website: www.mbta.com
© MBTA 2000

Driving in New England

Important road sign

W HILE FLYING IS THE FASTEST and most efficient way to get to New England, driving is by far the best way to explore the region. In fact, much of New England's charm is found along scenic jaunts down the coast and driving tours during fall-foliage season. It is important to remember that large areas of the region are essentially wild, so you should always be prepared for any eventuality, such as a breakdown. This is doubly true in the winter, when sudden blizzards and white-outs caused by blowing snow can leave motorists stranded. Boston's public transit system makes it possible to do without a car *(see pp376–7)*, but once outside the city you will need a vehicle to do your best exploring.

Country roads beckoning drivers to leave the crowds behind

A rented convertible, perfect for exploring in good weather

CAR RENTAL

T HE MAJOR CAR rental chains have outlets in most of New England's major cities and larger airports. These national chains include **Avis**, **Budget**, **Enterprise**, **Hertz**, **National**, **Rent-A-Wreck**, and **Thrifty**. While their rates are somewhat higher than smaller local companies, they usually offer extremely efficient service.

In order to rent a car, you must be 21 and possess a valid driver's license. People under 25 will sometimes have to pay a surcharge. A major credit card is usually required as well, unless you are prepared to put down a hefty cash deposit. Credit cards sometimes provide coverage against damage or theft of the vehicle, but it is wise to check what the terms are with your credit card company. Regardless, make sure that your car

rental agreement includes Collision Damage Waiver (CDW) – also known as Loss Damage Waiver (LDW) – or else you will be liable for any damage to the car, even if it was not your fault. This supplemental insurance can cost between $10 and $20 extra a day.

Sightseeing by car, stopping where and when you want

SPEED LIMITS

I T IS IMPORTANT to pay attention to the signs, as speed limits can vary from one place to the next depending on your proximity to a town or city. In general, the maximum speed on an interstate highway varies from 55 to 65 mph (88–105 km/h). On smaller highways, it can range between 30 and 55 mph (50–88 km/h). Cities and towns set speed limits between 20 and 35 mph (32–56 km/h), drastically lower around hospitals and schools. Police often pick strategic points along highways – often right after a sign for lower speed – to set up their radar equipment in order to catch drivers who are going too fast. Do not try to pay tickets or fines directly to the police officer who pulled you over; this can be interpreted as attempted bribery and can land you deeper in hot water.

DRIVING TOURS

T HERE ARE A number of books on the market listing the best driving tours of the region. Some publications, such as **Yankee** magazine, include a complete itinerary of recommended routes, historic stops, and the best places to eat and stay. Tours vary from a single day to an entire week and take in everything from dramatic coastal scenery to tiny fishing villages to mountainous terrain and country towns.

ARRIVING BY TRAIN

THE MAJOR AMERICAN RAILROAD is **Amtrak**. One of Amtrak's busiest routes services southern and central New England up to Boston. Amtrak recently unveiled its high-speed *Acela Regional* train service between New York and Boston, which has cut 90-minutes off regular travel time of about 6 hours. While it is available at a premium price, it is still less expensive than most airfares and has the added convenience of taking you from downtown to downtown without the added expense of taxis or shuttle buses. In November 2001, a rail service between Boston and Portland, Maine was inaugurated. During the summer, there is a stop at Old Orchard Beach in Maine.

Wheeled luggage

ARRIVING BY CAR

GETTING TO New England by car is relatively easy, and you have several options. Beginning in Florida, I-95, also known as Route 128 in the Boston area, is one of the most popular drives for travelers coming from the South. This major interstate highway sticks close to the coast as it passes through Connecticut and Providence, Rhode Island, en route to the outskirts of Boston. Circumventing the city, the highway continues up through New Hampshire and Maine before crossing the border into Canada. Drivers should note that truck traffic along I-95 can be particularly heavy, especially when approaching Boston.

The two major gateways into New England from the

Train station in North Conway, New Hampshire

north are I-89 and I-91. The latter crosses from Canada into Vermont at Derby Line and then follows a relatively straight line south along the Vermont/New Hampshire border, through both central Massachusetts and Connecticut all the way down to New Haven. I-89 starts in Vermont's northwest-ernmost corner and then from Burlington cuts diagonally to Concord, New Hampshire where it links up with I-93 into Boston. The major western points of entry into New England are I-84 and I-90 from New York state.

ARRIVING BY BUS

AS IT STANDS, you can get just about anywhere in New England via bus, so long as you are not in a hurry. Many of the bus companies serve particular sections of New England. **Concord Trailways** has routes in Maine and New Hampshire, and **Vermont Transit** serves Vermont, Maine, and New Hampshire. **Bonanza** is the main Connecticut bus line, while **Peter Pan** has stops in Connecticut and western Massachusetts. Other parts of Massachusetts, most notably Cape Cod and the South Shore, are served by **Plymouth & Brockton**. **Greyhound Lines** is a nationwide carrier and has stops throughout New

England. Greyhound works in conjunction with Bonanza, Vermont Transit, and Peter Pan lines. Most major bus lines offer discount rates for students and seniors (with proper ID), and offer unlimited travel during a set period.

DIRECTORY

AIRFARES

IAATC
(International Association of Air Travel Couriers), PO Box 847, Scotts Bluff, NB, 69363.
📞 *(308) 632-3273.*
🌐 www.courier.org

Intrepid Traveler
PO Box 531, Branford, CT 06405.
📞 *(203) 448-5341.*
🌐 www.intrepidtraveler.com

TRAIN

Amtrak
📞 *(800) 872-7245.*
🌐 www.amtrak.com

BUS LINES

Concord Trailways
📞 *(617) 426-8080 or (800) 639-3317.*

Vermont Transit
📞 *(800) 451-3292 or (802) 864-6811.*

Bonanza
📞 *(617) 720-4110 or (800) 556-3815.*

Peter Pan
📞 *(413) 781-2900 or (800) 343-9999.*

Plymouth & Brockton
📞 *(508) 746-0378.*

Greyhound Lines
📞 *(617) 526-1800 or (800) 231-2222.* 🌐 www.greyhound.com

A Greyhound bus

Getting Around Boston

Pᴜʙʟɪᴄ ᴛʀᴀɴsᴘᴏʀᴛᴀᴛɪᴏɴ in Boston and Cambridge is very good. In fact it is considerably easier to get around by public transportation than by driving, with the added benefit of not having to find a parking space. All major attractions in the city are accessible on the subway, by bus, or by taxi. The central sections of the city are also extremely easy to navigate on foot.

MBTA commuter bus, with distinctive yellow paint

Fɪɴᴅɪɴɢ ʏᴏᴜʀ ᴡᴀʏ ɪɴ Bᴏsᴛᴏɴ

Tʜᴇ ᴍᴏʀᴇ ᴘʟᴀɴɴɪɴɢ you do before your trip, the easier it will be to locate sights and find your way around the city. The **Greater Boston Convention and Visitors Bureau** (see p369) will be a helpful contact point, and your hotel is also likely to be able to offer advice. To find out about any upcoming cultural events, check websites for **Boston Citysearch** and the **Boston Globe** (see p369).

Most of Boston is laid out "organically" rather than in the sort of strict grid found in most American cities. When trying to orient yourself, it helps to think of Boston as enclaves – of neighborhoods around a few central squares. In general, uphill from Boston Common is Beacon Hill, downhill is Downtown. Back Bay begins west of Arlington Street. The North End sticks out from the north side of Boston, while the Waterfront is literally that, where Boston meets the sea.

Visitor's Passport, valid on all MBTA services

MBTA Sᴜʙᴡᴀʏ ᴀɴᴅ Tʀᴏʟʟᴇʏ Bᴜsᴇs

Bᴏsᴛᴏɴ's subway system is the oldest in North America, but it has been vastly expanded and modernized since the first cars rolled between Park Street and Boylston Street on September 1, 1897. The street trolley system is even older, having begun in 1846 with trolleys drawn along tracks by horses. The system was electrified in 1889. The combined subway and trolley lines (most lines move above ground when they leave the city center) are generally known as the "T." The T operates 5am to 12:45am Monday through Saturday and 6am to 12:45am Sunday. Weekday service is every 3 to 15 minutes, on weekends less frequently. There are four lines. The Red line runs from south of the city to Cambridge. The Green line runs from the Museum of Science westward into the suburbs. The Blue line begins near Government Center and goes to Logan Airport, then on to Revere. The Orange line connects the northern suburbs to southwest Boston. Maps of the system are available at the Downtown Crossing MBTA station.

Admission to subway stations is via turnstiles into which you insert a $1 T token or swipe an electro-magnetic pass card. Visitor's Passport passes for unlimited travel for one, three, or seven days ($6/$11/$22) can be purchased at Downtown Crossing, South Station, Back Bay, Government Center, and North Station subway stops.

MBTA Bᴜsᴇs

Tʜᴇ ʙᴜs sʏsᴛᴇᴍ complements the subway system and in effect enlarges the entire transit network to cover more than 1,000 miles (1,600 km). However, buses are often crowded and schedules can be hard to obtain. Two useful routes for sightseeing are Charlestown-Haymarket, (from Haymarket, near Quincy Market, to Bunker Hill) and Harvard-Dudley (from Harvard Square via Massachusetts Avenue through Back Bay and the South End to Dudley Square in Roxbury.) Exact change (75 cents) or a pass is required for the fare.

Tᴀxɪs

Fɪɴᴅɪɴɢ ᴀ ᴛᴀxɪ in Boston and Cambridge is rarely difficult except when it is raining. Taxis can be found at stands in tourist areas and can be hailed on the street. Taxis may pick up fares only in the city for which they are licensed – Cambridge taxis only in Cambridge, Boston taxis only in Boston. If you need to be somewhere on time, it is advisable to call a taxi company and arrange a definite pickup time and place.

Rates are calculated by both mileage and time, beginning with a $1.10 "pick-up" fee when the meter starts running. In general, the taxis in Boston and Cambridge are more

Boston taxis waiting for fares at one of the city's many taxi stands

Of course, the favorite season for drivers is in the fall, when the rural roads are flanked by the brilliant colors of leaves *(see pp20–21)*.

State tourism offices *(see p369)* can give you the contact information for organizations that plan foliage tours. Each state also has a hotline number that gives frequently updated foliage reports. Remember, though, that traffic on New England's roads peaks in the fall.

SAFETY TIPS

If you are planning on spending a lot of time in your car, you should follow these simple procedures to ensure your safety and that of your passengers. The **National Highway Traffic Safety Administration** offers news on everything from school bus safety to road rage and operates an Auto Safety Hotline.

- Passengers should wear their seat belts at all times. Infants and young children should be secured in a car seat in the back seat. Follow child seat instruction manuals precisely. A rear-facing child seat should NEVER be placed in the front seat of a vehicle equipped with an air bag.

- Never leave children unattended in your car.

- Clean your windshield and adjust your mirrors for optimum visibility.

- Check your oil, radiator reservoir, brake fluids, and your fan belt before setting off on a long drive.

- Make sure all your lights and turn signals are working properly.

- Check your tires for undue tread wear and make sure that the air pressure is correct. Also see that your spare tire is roadworthy.

- Be sure that you have a working jack and road flares or reflective triangles in the trunk. Pack extra windshield wipers, and in winter stock salt, a snow brush and an ice scraper, and small shovel.

- Also keep a small medical kit in your trunk, along with a blanket and an emergency flashlight. In winter, make sure you have extra gloves, boots, and warm clothes.

- If you do get stuck in winter in an out-of-the-way place, stay inside your car. Keep the motor running for warmth, but open your window slightly to guard against carbon monoxide buildup. Make sure your exhaust pipe is clear of snow.

- Check road conditions on the radio, especially in winter. Heavy snowfalls can leave many areas impassable. Individual state transportation departments often have hotlines dispensing up-to-date information on road conditions and closures.

- Be wary of deer and moose that may run onto the road. Hitting a moose poses more of a threat to you than it does to the animal.

Sign on a Vermont highway warning drivers to watch for moose

DIRECTORY

CAR RENTALS

Avis
[(800) 831-2847.

Budget
[(800) 527-7000.

Enterprise
[(800) 736-8222.

Hertz
[(800) 654-3131.

National
[(800) 227-7368.

Rent-A-Wreck
[(800) 296-6768.

Thrifty
[(800) 847-4389.

DRIVING TOURS

Yankee magazine
W www.newengland.com

FOLIAGE HOTLINES

Connecticut
[(800) 252-6863.

Maine
[(800) 533-9595.

Massachusetts
[(800) 227-6277.

New Hampshire
[(800) 258-3608.

Rhode Island
[(800) 556-2484.

Vermont
[(800) 828-3239.

HIGHWAY MANAGEMENT

National Highway Traffic Safety Administration
55 Broadway-Kendall Sq,
Cambridge, MA 02142
[(617) 494-3427.
W www.NHTSA.gov

Acknowledgments

DORLING KINDERSLEY would like to thank the following people whose contributions and assistance have made the preparation of this book possible.

MAIN CONTRIBUTORS

Eleanor Berman is an award-winning travel writer and author of 11 travel guides, including *Away for the Weekend: New England* and *Recommended Bed and Breakfasts: New England*. She was the principal contributor to the *Eyewitness Guide to New York*.

Patricia Brooks, a longtime freelance travel and food writer, has lived in Connecticut since 1956. She has authored or co-authored 16 books and writes frequently for national US magazines. Since 1977 she has been the food critic for *The New York Times*' Connecticut Weekly section and writes its weekly Dining Out column of restaurant reviews.

Helga Loverseed's work has taken her to 165 destinations in her 23 years as a travel journalist and photographer. She has won awards both for her photography and her writing, has contributed to six travel guides, and is a travel columnist for several leading newspapers and magazines.

Pierre Home-Douglas has worked as a travel writer and book editor since the late 1980s. His articles on subjects ranging from bicycling through Vermont to sailing up the Nile have appeared in many newspapers and magazines. He has also written for *Great Railway Journeys of the World* and *Explore America*.

FOR DORLING KINDERSLEY

Senior Publishing Manager Louise Bostock Lang
Publishing Managers Kate Poole, Helen Townsend, Jane Ewart
Project Editor Marcus Hardy
Art Editor Nicola Rodway
Editor Simon Hall
Designers Elly King, Nikala Sim
Map Co-ordinators Dave Pugh, Casper Morris
DTP Maite Lantaron, Jason Little, Conrad van Dyk
Picture Researcher Brigitte Arora
Production Michelle Thomas, Marie Ingledew
Design & Editorial Assistance Sam Borland, Katherine Mesquita, Lynne Robinson
U.S Editor Mary Sutherland
Researcher Timothy Kennard

Revisions Brigitte Arora, Tessa Bindloss, Sherry Collins, Esther Labi, Ellen Root, Ros Walford
Contributors Tom Bross, Brett Cook, Patricia Harris, Carolyn Heller, David Lyon, Juliette Rogers, Kem Sawyer
Photographers Demetrio Carrasco, Linda Whitwam (Additional photography: Peter Anderson, Clive Streeter)
Illustrators Stephen Conlin, Gary Cross, Richard Draper, Chris Orr & Associates, Robbie Polley, John Woodcock
Maps Ben Bowles, Rob Clynes, Sam Johnston, James Macdonald (Colourmap Scanning Ltd)

THANKS TO

Philippe Arnoldi, Danny-Pierre Auger, Rosemary Barron, Lorraine Doré, Joey Fraser, Dominique Gagné, Pascale Hueber, Solange Laberge, Rob Lutes, Edward Renaud, Odette Sévigny.

SPECIAL ASSISTANCE

Sam Ankerson, Shelburne Museum; Amy Bassett, New Hampshire Parks and Recreation Division; Janel Blood, Concord Chamber of Commerce; Don Boccaccio, The Quality Group; Nancy E. Boone, State of Vermont Division for Historic Preservation; Becky Bovill, R.I. Tourism Division; David Bush, Karen Miller, The Mark Twain House; Andrea Carneiro, Melissa Fanny, Preservation Society of Newport County; Heidi Clarke, South County Tourism Council; Katherine Fox, Destination Salem; Margaret Joyce, New Hampshire Office of Travel and Tourism Development; Lauren Kedski, Providence Warwick Convention and Visitors Bureau; Valerie Kidney, New Brunswick Tourism; Sharon Kotok, Strawbery Banke; Linda Levin, Connecticut Dept. of Environmental Protection-Parks Division; Pierre L'Heureux, Dawson College; Renny Loisel, Greater New Haven Convention & Visitors Bureau; Amanda C. Lowe, Massachusetts Office of Travel & Tourism; Caroline Marshall, Greater Portsmouth Chamber of Commerce; Brenda Milkofsky, Wethersfield Historical Society; Wanda Moran, NPS-Acadia National Park; Mike Morand, New Haven and State Affairs Department of Yale University; Sue Moynahan, Marianne McCaffery - NPS - Cape Cod National Seashore; Dr. Virginia Nixon, Liberal Arts College, Concordia University; Amy O'Brien, Greater Boston Convention and Visitors Bureau; Michele Pecoraro, Plimoth Plantation; Greg Gerdel, Vermont Department of Tourism and Marketing; Janice Putnam, Susanna Bonta, Old Sturbridge Village; Jessica Roy, Maine Office of Tourism; Janet L. Serra, Litchfield Hills Visitors Bureau; Tim Shea, Burlington Chamber of Commerce; Sherry Smardon, Greater Hartford Tourism District; Evan Smith, Jan Hagerstrom, Newport County Convention and Visitors Bureau; James R. Spencer, Connecticut Department of Transportation; Amy Strack, Massachusetts Office of Travel and Tourism; Paulette Weaver, Lakes Region Association; Katrina White, North of Boston Convention and Visitors Bureau; Leah Wiedmann, Portland Convention and Visitors Bureau; Tricia Wood, Sarah Fisher, Mystic Seaport Museum; Mary Woods, The Coastal Fairfield County Convention & Visitor Bureau; Janie Young, Canterbury Shaker Village.

PHOTOGRAPHY PERMISSIONS

DORLING KINDERSLEY would like to thank all those who gave assistance and permission to photograph at their churches, museums, hotels, restaurants, shops, galleries, and other sights too numerous to list individually.

PICTURE CREDITS

t = top; tl = top left; tlc = top left centre; tc = top centre; tr = top right; cla = centre left above; ca = centre above; cra = centre right above; cl = centre left; c = centre; cr = centre right; clb = centre left below; cb = centre below; crb = centre right below; bl = bottom left; b = bottom; bc = bottom centre; bcl = bottom centre left; br = bottom right; d = detail.

Every effort has been made to trace the copyright holders and we apologize in advance for any unintentional omissions. We would be pleased to insert the appropriate acknowledgments in any subsequent edition of this publication.

AROOSTOOK STATE PARK/Bruce Farnham: 299tl; DAVID J. BOOKER: 82; BOSTON POPS ORCHESTRA: Michael Lutch 350bc.

ROBERT CHARTIER: 372bl; BRUCE COLEMAN INC., NEW YORK: Mark Newman 4bl; Gene Ahrens 1, 226, 300/301; John M. Burnley 249; Jeff Foott 268/269; Carolyn Schaefer 364/365; CORBIS: John L. Amos 29c; Archivo Iconografico S.A.: 35 tr; Bettmann: 29tl, 28cl, 28c, 28br, 30c, 30br, 37t, 38t, 42bl, 43cl, 44cr, 44br, 45bc, 47bl, 48 bl, 48br, 71br, 120b, 128/129, 142b, 253t; Burstein Collection: 39br; Steve Jay Crise 41br, 47bl; Edifice, Philippa Lewis 56c; Kevin Fleming 28tr, 352tl, 368cr; George Hall 374b; Historical Picture Archive: 36; Anne Hodalio 29 br; Robert Holmes 31t, 102; Hulton-Deutsch Collection: 29bl, 47t, 48tr, 267c; Todd Gipstein 30tr, 47br; Farrell Grehan 30bl; Kelly-Mooney Photography: 32bc; Lake County Museum: 38b; Magma: 25t, 28bl, 29cl, 37b, 45tl, 46cr, 47c; John-Marshall Mantel 31br; Francis G. Mayer 40-41c; Gail Mooney 347tl; David Muench 40tr, 273cb; Greg Nikas 351tl; Reuters Newsmedia Inc.: 29cr, 120t, 352b, 352b, 369; Bill Ross 371t; Bob Rowan/Progressive Image: 28cb;

Phil Shermeister 34t, 378; Joseph Sohm 40bl, 43bc; Paul A. Souders 41cr; Ted Spiegel 35br, 350cl; Peter Turnley 29tr; CONNECTICUT STATE PARKS DIVISION: 219tl, 219br.

JACQUES DE TONNACOURT: 181cr.

MARY EVANS PICTURE LIBRARY: 8/9, 9c, 31c, 38c, 39t, 39cl, 39bc, 40tl, 41t, 42tl, 42c, 43tc, 43cr, 44t, 44cl, 45cr, 46t, 47tr, 48c, 129c, 301c, 365c.

FOXWOODS RESORT CASINO: 302c.

GRANGER COLLECTION, NEW YORK: 51 (inset); 81b.

HARVARD UNIVERSITY ART MUSEUMS: © President and Fellows of Harvard College, courtesy of Fogg Art Museum, Alpheus Hyatt Purchasing and Friends of the Fogg Art Museum Funds *Kneeling Angel* Gian Lorenzo Bernini, c.1674-1675 – 114cr; courtesy of the Busch-Reisinger Museum, Gift of Sibyl Moholy-Nagy, © DACS, London 2000 *Light-Space Modulator*, Laszlo Moholy-Nagy, 1930 – 114b; courtesy of Fogg Art Museum, The Hervey E. Wetzel Bequest Fund *Christ on the Cross between the Virgin and Cardinal Torquemada and St. John the Evangelist* Fra Angelico, c.1446 – 115b; courtesy Fogg Art Museum, Bequest: Collection of Maurice Wertheim *Skating*, Edouard Manet, 1877 - 115cl; HISTORIC DEERFIELD, INC./Amanda Merullo: 163b; DAVE G. HOUSER: 130tr, 178/179; HULTON GETTY COLLECTION: 76b.

PHILIP C. JACKSON: 131br, 169, 171b, 180cl, 182tr, 182tl, 182c, 183tl, 184tl, 184tr, 184cr, 184br, 185tl, 185c, 185br, 186tr, 187tr, 187cr.

KILLINGTON, VERMONT: 366bl; JAMES LEMASS: 70br, 72, 95crb.

MAINE OFFICE OF TOURISM: 21bl, 23tr, 303br; Gary Pearl 23c, 131tr, 295b, 303br; THE MARK TWAIN HOUSE: 130bl, 200bl, 201tl.; MASSACHUSETTS OFFICE OF TRAVEL AND TOURISM/Kindra Clineff: 20tr, 32t, 303bl, 356tr, 357cr, 358br, 360b, 361b, 362c; MUSEUM OF FINE ARTS, BOSTON: HU-MFA Expedition *Shawabtis of Taharka* 52b, 106t; Bequest of Mrs. Beatrice Constance (Turner) Maynard in Memory of Winthrop Sargent *Revere Silver Teapot* 106ca; Egypt Exploration Fund *Inner Coffin of Nes-mut-aat-neru* 106cb; Picture Fund *Dance at Bougival* Pierre-Auguste Renoir, 1883 – 107t; Ruth and Carl J. Shapiro Colonnade and Vault *John Singer Sargent Murals* 107c; Francis Bartlett Donation of 1900 *Head of Aphrodite*, Greek Late Classical or Early Hellenistic period –107b; George Nixon Black Fund *Ewer and basin* 108t; M. and M. Karolik Collection of American Paintings, 1815 – 1865, by exchange, *Boston Harbor* Fitz Hugh Lane

108c; Bequest of John T. Spaulding *La Berceuse* Vincent van Gogh, 1889 – 108b; Maria Antoinette Evans Fund *Babylonia: Nebuchadnezzar II* 109t; Gift by Contribution *Horse, early 8th century, China* 109c; Richard Norton Memorial Fund *Fragment of fresco from villa at Contrada Bottaro* 109b; MUSEUM OF NEW HAMPSHIRE HISTORY/Bill Finney: 259t.
NANTUCKET ISLAND CHAMBER OF COMMERCE/Michael Glavin: 32cl. NEW ENGLAND AQUARIUM: Bob Kramer 78t/b, 79t. DAVID NOBLE: 50–51

OLD STURBRIDGE VILLAGE/Thomas Neill: 130cl; OMNI PARKER HOUSE: 74clb.

LAURENCE PARENT PHOTOGRAPHY, INC: 2/3, 146/147, 274; PEABODY MUSEUM OF ARCHAEOLOGY AND ETHNOLOGY/ HARVARD UNIVERSITY: © President and Fellows of Harvard College 1976. All Rights Reserved. Photos Hillel Burger 116c/b. PHOTO RESEARCHERS INC.: WORLDSAT INTERNATIONAL INC. 12br; THE PRESERVATION SOCIETY OF NEWPORT COUNTY: 186c, 186b, 187tl, 187b; PROVIDENCE WARWICK CONVENTION & VISITOR'S BUREAU: 367t.

ROCKLAND-THOMASTON AREA CHAMBER OF COMMERCE/Richard V. Procopio: 33tr.

SEAPORT HOTEL/Peter Vanderwalker: 304b; SPRINGFIELD SCIENCE MUSEUM, SPRINGFIELD, MA./DINOSAUR HALL: 162tr; STATE OF NEW HAMPSHIRE DIVISION OF TRAVEL AND TOURISM DEVELOPMENT: 362tl; David Brownell 254tr, 356cl; Nancy G. Horton 325c; Craig Alness 357bl; Jeffery E. Blackman 358cl, 361t; STOWE MOUNTAIN RESORT/Chuck Waskuch: 362b; Don Landwehrle 363tr.

TOPHAM PICTUREPOINT: 53tr.
THE UNION-NEWS AND SUNDAY REPUBLICAN/David Molnar: 161br; USFWS PHOTO: 19tr.

VERMONT DEPARTMENT OF TRAVEL AND TOURISM: 49cr, 237b. YALE CENTER FOR BRITISH ART/Richard Caspole: 223t; YALE UNIVERSITY OFFICE OF PUBLIC AFFAIRS: 222t.

FRONT ENDPAPER: All commissioned photography with the exception of BRUCE COLEMAN INC: Gene Ahrens tl; LAURENCE PARENT PHOTOGRAPHY, INC: tr.

JACKET
Front – DK PICTURE LIBRARY bl; David Lyons br, bc; MASTERFILE UK: Roy Ooms main image. Back – DK PICTURE LIBRARY: Alan Briere b; ROBERT HARDING PICTURE LIBRARY: R. Rainford t. Spine – MASTERFILE UK: Roy Ooms.

All other images © Dorling Kindersley.
See **www.dkimages.com** for further information.

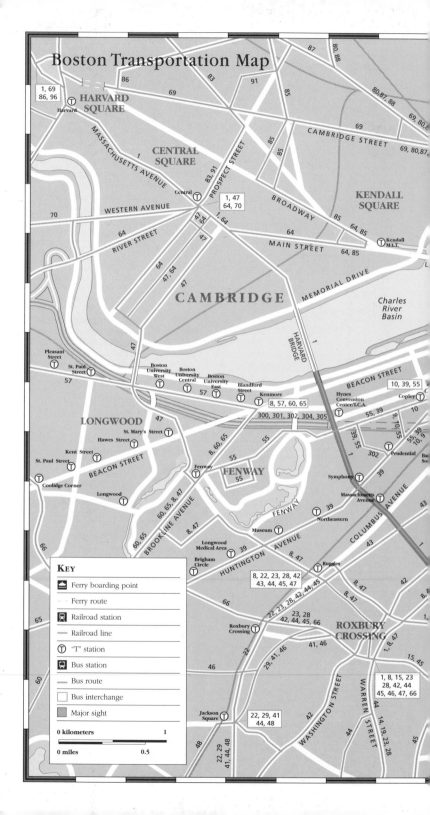